A Guide to the Latin American Art Song Repertoire

INDIANA REPERTOIRE GUIDES

A GUIDE TO THE
Latin American
ART SONG REPERTOIRE

*An Annotated Catalog of
Twentieth-Century Art Songs for Voice and Piano*

Edited by

Maya Hoover

WITH CONTRIBUTIONS BY

Stela M. Brandão, Ellie Anne Duque, Jean-Ronald LaFond,
José-Luis Maúrtua, Allison L. Weiss, and Kathleen L. Wilson

INDIANA UNIVERSITY PRESS

Bloomington & Indianapolis

This book is a publication of

Indiana University Press
601 North Morton Street
Bloomington, IN 47404-3797 USA

www.iupress.indiana.edu

Telephone orders 800-842-6796
Fax orders 812-855-7931
Orders by e-mail iuporder@indiana.edu

© 2010 by Indiana University Press
All rights reserved

No part of this book may be reproduced or utilized in any form or by any means, electronic or mechanical, including photocopying and recording, or by any information storage and retrieval system, without permission in writing from the publisher. The Association of American University Presses' Resolution on Permissions constitutes the only exception to this prohibition.

⊚ The paper used in this publication meets the minimum requirements of the American National Standard for Information Sciences—Permanence of Paper for Printed Library Materials, ANSI Z39.48-1992.

Library of Congress Cataloging-in-Publication Data

A guide to the Latin American art song repertoire : an annotated catalog of twentieth-century art songs for voice and piano / edited by Maya Hoover ; with contributions by Stela M. Brandão, ... [et al.].
    p. cm. — (Indiana repertoire guides)
  Includes bibliographical references and index.
  ISBN 978-0-253-35382-5 (cloth : alk. paper)
  — ISBN 978-0-253-22138-4 (pbk. : alk. paper)
  1. Songs—Latin America—20th century—Bibliography. I. Hoover, Maya Frieman. II. Brandão, Stela M.
  ML128.S3H85 2009
  016.78242168098—dc22
                                    2009032870

1 2 3 4 5   15 14 13 12 11 10

To Barett

Contents

- *Preface · ix*
- *Acknowledgments · xi*
- *Introduction · xiii*

1. Argentina · *Allison L. Weiss* · 1
2. Bolivia · 56
3. Brazil · *Stela M. Brandão* · 59
4. Chile · 128
5. Colombia · *Ellie Anne Duque* · 134
6. Costa Rica · 140
7. Cuba · 148
8. Dominican Republic · 155
9. Ecuador · 157
10. El Salvador · 159
11. Guatemala · 162
12. Haiti · *Jean-Ronald LaFond* · 166
13. Honduras · 174
14. Jamaica · 175
15. Mexico · 177
16. Nicaragua · 188

17 Panama · *190*

18 Paraguay · *192*

19 Peru · *José-Luis Maúrtua* · *194*

20 Puerto Rico · *198*

21 Uruguay · *202*

22 Venezuela · *Kathleen L. Wilson* · *207*

- *Appendix A: List of Countries and Regions in Latin America* · *213*
- *Appendix B: Statistics by Geographic Region* · *214*
- *Appendix C: List of Publishers* · *224*
- *Appendix D: List of Suggested Repertoire* · *235*
- *Notes* · *239*
- *Bibliography* · *253*
- *List of Contributors* · *267*
- *Index of General Subjects and Song Composers* · *269*
- *Index of Poets and Text Sources* · *275*
- *Index of Song and Song Cycle Titles* · *290*
- *Index of Tessituras and Voice Types* · *340*

Preface

As I sat down to gather my thoughts before embarking on this voluminous publication, I asked myself what I as a singer would want to get out of such a source. I came up with the following: to become aware of new Latin American song repertoire, to be able to find it, and then to be able to understand it. Often overwhelmed by tomes of information on Latin American culture and politics, I wanted to give singers a summary source—a take-off point. While there is no substitute for in-depth musicological, sociological, and political research, there is a need for direction in this quest. How does one study the history surrounding a Bolivian art song from the mid-twentieth century? Which historical sources should one consider? Upon which political events should one focus? And, just as pertinent, where does one begin looking to understand the complicated ethnomusicological background of the country? This book is intended to begin fulfilling that need.

This volume is also intended to serve as a research guide by singers and for singers. It will help singers and teachers find out who is writing Latin American art song, what is being written, where the music can be located, and how to get it. Composers and their works are listed according to their country of origin, and singers or teachers may use the descriptive annotations (language, poet) or pedagogical annotations (range, tessitura) given with each song to decide whether or not repertoire is appropriate for consideration for their voices or programming needs.

This is not meant to be a definitive work, as such a volume would take decades to complete, but rather a representative one. It is not intended to be a musicological work, but it does aim to serve as a guide for more in-depth study.

PREFACE

There are basically three types of song repertoire included in this catalog, ranging from easily accessible to more challenging to obtain, depending on the desired level of research. These three types are as follows:

1. Music that is readily available for purchase or study within the United States. This category includes music that is immediately available for purchase from popular classical music sources such as T.I.S. MusicGroup, Hal Leonard, Amazon.com, and other online music sources such as Classical Vocal Repertoire, alma.usa.com, Sheet Music Plus, and so on, as well as music that is available for study or research at various U.S. libraries. This includes the Latin American Music Center (LAMC) at Indiana University, which houses many of the scores in this catalog that are issued by Latin American and European publishers. The LAMC is a good place to go to examine repertoire in person before contacting international publishing houses to acquire the scores. To determine whether or not a song is available in the United States from a source other than the LAMC, readers should check the WorldCat or Library of Congress online databases.
2. Music that is accessible through libraries or collections in Latin America. These might include holdings at one of the national university libraries, or collections that may be accessed via an international database, such as the online catalog maintained by the Federal University of Minas Gerais (Universidade Federal de Minas Gerais) in Brazil.
3. Music that is available directly from composers or other new music sources. For these acquisitions, it is most useful to contact research centers such as the LAMC, the Latin American Art Song Alliance (LAASA), or other new music resources such as The Living Composers Project website for help.

Indeed, there is still a lot of work to do. There are conservatories and libraries to visit, collections to uncover, composers to discover, and songs to bring to the surface. However, it is our hope that this guide will serve as a good starting point, and that it will inspire the incorporation of Latin American art song into the repertoire and recital programs of singers throughout the United States and beyond.

Acknowledgments

Any book like this one is the product of many minds coming together for one purpose. In this case, it was the invaluable contributions of Stela M. Brandão, Ellie Anne Duque, Jean-Ronald LaFond, José-Luis Maúrtua, Allison L. Weiss, and Kathleen L. Wilson that helped to make this guide what it is. Without them this book would not exist, and I am grateful for their dedication, hard work, and especially for their support and friendship. Many people also donated repertoire from their personal collections in support of this project, and I would like to give special thanks to Kim Carballo and Emilio Jimenez-Pons for access to their collections. I am also grateful for the invaluable input of Leonora Saavedra, for her help with Mexican music.

I would like to thank Luiz Fernando Lopes, Carmen Téllez, and the Latin American Music Center at Indiana University for not only assisting me in my research, but also for helping to facilitate the study of Latin American music in the United States. The Center and its staff are an unrivaled resource for Latin American music in higher education. I am especially grateful to Professor Lopes for his work on the "Sample Repertoire" song lists originally generated and published for the Fifth Annual Competition in the Performance of Music from Spain and Latin America (2002).

The book's collaborators and I are grateful to Professors Guida Borghoff and Luciana Monteiro de Castro of the Federal University of Minas Gerais in Brazil for their exceptional catalog of Brazilian art song, the *Guia canções brasileiras*.

On a personal note, I want to thank my students and colleagues for their infinite patience and understanding, especially during the final hours of manuscript preparation.

I would like to thank my mentors—my voice teachers past and present, especially Patricia Havranek for her endless patience and kindness, Mary Burgess, Laura Brooks Rice, and Virginia Zeani. I owe special gratitude to Estelle Jorgensen, who is an endless fount of inspiration and who guided the initial stages of this project, encouraging me to push it farther than I could have ever imagined.

Coming from a family of teachers, I am lucky to have had the commiseration of my parents, authors and professors themselves, and no strangers to spending entire days considering punctuation, during this process. In addition to love and support, they have provided research help, editing advice, and grammar consultations free of charge.

This project would have never been started were it not for those first few Figueroa songs handed to me by my longtime partner and close friend, pianist José Meléndez. I thank him for first teaching me about this incredible repertoire and for playing it with so many beautiful colors. He is the soul of many of these songs for me.

Finally, I want to thank my all-in-one research assistant, best friend, partner, and personal chef, my husband Barett Hoover, who has participated in this project on more levels than I can name here. I would have never survived without him.

Introduction

This volume will serve as a reference for performers and teachers of vocal music. Its main purpose is to introduce readers to the vast array of art song literature and composers from Latin America, and to give brief information about each song included in the catalog, such as song title, title of cycle (if any), year of composition or publication, poet, language, range, and tessitura. The book will also serve as a location guide, giving publication information or library housing information, so that works can be obtained for purchase or study.

THE CHALLENGE

The challenge for musicians who want to explore Latin American art song is that no source such as this one exists at present. Teachers and performers who wish to delve into this wealth of performance literature do not know where to turn, and end up abandoning this repertoire for other songs that are readily available and already in the public eye. This volume will provide the guidance needed to identify and locate Latin American songs.

As the following review of literature shows, English-language reference works on Latin American music are limited, and many of those that do exist are outdated. An English-language work on Latin American art song will provide a useful means for English speakers and non-native speakers of Spanish to explore this vast repertoire. There is also currently no catalog of Latin American music exclusively devoted to the genre of art song. Such a catalog will provide guidance and be greatly useful to performers and teachers alike.

INTRODUCTION

EXISTING LITERATURE

Information on art music has seen an enormous change in medium over the last few years. As we have ushered in a new millennium, so have we begun to explore new ways to research music and share ideas about it. Library holdings and new publications of books, scores, and recordings have become more accessible via the internet, and although not every country and region of Latin America is as technologically connected as the United States is, it seems that the world of Latin American art music is beginning to join this larger network and make its way through the intricate wirings of the worldwide web.[1] Although this literature review will discuss works published in traditional, non-electronic format, the importance of the internet should be noted, and websites crucial to the development and research of Latin American music will be identified later in the volume. Readers should also take note of the comment in the preface which suggests that any search for Latin American music begin with WorldCat or the Library of Congress.[2]

On the subject of Latin American music, there exist two main types of literature: discussions involving stylistic elements of Latin American music, and lists of Latin American repertoire. Research exists in all major forms: books, articles, dissertations and theses, and internet discussions. The following literature review highlights some of the major sources.[3]

Nicholas Slonimsky's *Music of Latin America* is an excellent secondary source on the stylistic elements of Latin American Music.[4] Originally published in 1945, it was reprinted in 1972 with no major changes. Probably the most commonly used reference is Gerard Béhague's book *Music in Latin America: An Introduction* (1979).[5] Although now outdated, it is still valuable for its detailed information covering roughly thirteen countries or regions of Latin America, and continues to be used as the main source of information for many current articles on Latin American music. The book is arranged according to musical trends and the stylistic evolution of Latin American music in general. In his introduction, Béhague states that he chose to sacrifice a comprehensive look at Latin American music in favor of examining fewer countries and works more closely. The book is not meant as an exclusive discussion of song; however, there are a handful of song examples throughout. The most valuable feature of Béhague's book is the bibliographic section at the end of each chapter, although many of the recommended readings are in Spanish-language sources.

For a broader look at Latin American music, consult the series *Music in Latin America and the Caribbean: An Encyclopedic History*, edited by Malena Kuss. These volumes present an ethnographic look at Latin American music from its indigenous roots to contemporary society and urban trends.[6]

Another important recent publication is the second edition of *Latin American Classical Composers: A Biographical Dictionary*, compiled and edited by Miguel Ficher, Martha Furman Schleifer, and John M. Furman.[7] This biographical dictionary is essential to the library of any Latin Americanist.[8]

With regard to catalogs, lists, and bibliographies, there are two main sources in the United States: The Pan American Union in Washington, D.C., and the Latin American Music Center at Indiana University. The Pan American Union published several lists of existing Latin American music in the 1930s and 1940s. The first edition was published under the title *List of Latin American Music*.[9] In the second edition, the title was changed to *Music in Latin America*, and a revision of this edition was retitled *A Guide to the Music of Latin America*.[10] Gilbert Chase, the editor of the revised edition, was revered as one of the leading scholars on music from Spain and Latin America. A stylistic companion to these lists, published as *Music of Latin America*, discusses some specific elements of form and folk tradition by country and also lists composers from each country.[11]

The Pan American Union also produced *Composers of the Americas*, a good biographical reference work for Latin American composers.[12] Published in nineteen volumes and spanning the same time period as does Béhague's book, *Composers of the Americas* also contains useful bibliographic information for specific Latin American composers.

The most recent comprehensive list of available Latin American music was published by the Latin American Music Center (LAMC) of Indiana University in 1995.[13] Although a more recent source, it is only a list of the LAMC's holdings and not exclusively devoted to song repertoire. Smaller lists are also available, such as Kerlinda Dagláns and

Luis E. Pabón Roca's *Catálogo de música clásica contemporánea de Puerto Rico*.[14] This catalog is similarly not limited to song literature. Also of importance are the lists of sample repertoire compiled for the Fifth Annual Competition in the Performance of Music from Spain and Latin America.[15] These lists comprise repertoire held by the LAMC.

There are a few useful books and articles which target specific areas of Latin American art song, such as Enrique Alberto Arias's article on Argentine song, published in 1985.[16] Although outdated, it is still a good source on Argentine literature. Another helpful essay is Gilbert Chase's chapter in *A History of Song*, in which he addresses Latin American song before 1960.[17] Again, the chapter is informative and extremely useful, but does not include more recent composers and works. Additional works, such as Jonathan Kulp's "Carlos Guastavino: The Intersection of Música culta and Música popular in Argentine Song," John L. Walker's "The Younger Generation of Ecuadorian Composers," and Marie Elizabeth Labonville's *Juan Bautista Plaza and Musical Nationalism in Venezuela*, target specific composers or groups of composers.[18]

There are quite a few serial publications that focus on Latin American music in general, but many of these potentially useful sources are in Spanish. For example, the annual serial publication *Revista Argentina de musicología* is a current source, but not accessible to non-Spanish speakers. *Revista musical puertorriqueña*, *Revista musical de Venezuela*, and *Revista musical chilena* are other examples of Spanish-language serials that may be useful but are inaccessible to many performers and teachers whose command of Spanish is limited.[19] One of the best sources for articles on Latin American music is the *Latin American Music Review/Revista de música latinoamericana*, published by the University of Texas Press.[20] A multi-lingual journal, its articles are not exclusively in English, but it is one of the most important sources for current scholarship in Latin American musicology.

Other general articles on Latin American music that may be helpful are Gerard Béhague's "Boundaries and Borders in the Study of Music in Latin America: A Conceptual Remapping," and "Ethnomusicology and the Study of Africanisms in the Music of Latin America: Brazil" by Kazadi wa Mukuna.[21] Examples of excellent articles in Spanish or Portuguese include Vanda Lima Bellard Freire's "Panorama da musico latino-americana" and Benjamin Chamorro Yepez's "El camino de las sombras: La música de los Guahibo," an article on folk traditions.[22]

Some of the most current and specific information for the music of Latin America can be found in theses and dissertations. There are a handful of dissertations that are specific to the area of Latin American art song, many of which discuss the works of particular composers. Some are available for order from UMI, and almost all are available in some format for interlibrary loan.[23] Dissertations on specific composers include "The Published Art Songs of Juan Bautista Plaza" (Venezuela), by Harry M. Switzer; "João de Souza Lima: A Performer's Guide to the Songs for Voice and Piano" (Brazil), by Adriana Giarola; and "The Solo Songs for Voice and Piano of Carlos Chavez" (Mexico), by Robert Gerald Magee.[24]

Three dissertations on the songs of Carlos Guastavino are of particular interest: "Carlos Guastavino: An Annotated Bibliography of His Solo Vocal Works," by Deborah Rae Wagner; "Carlos Guastavino: A Study of His Songs and Musical Aesthetics," by Jonathan Lance Kulp; and "Carlos Guastavino's Song Cycles 'Las nubes' and 'Cuatro sonetos de Quevedo': The Relationship of Text and Music" by Roxane Marie LaCombe.[25]

The work that comes closest to this volume is Hugh F. Cardon's dissertation, "A Survey of Twentieth-Century Mexican Art Song."[26] While Cardon's study focuses on the songs of only one country, it is as close to a comprehensive guide to any area of Latin American song as any that exists. Although written in 1970, it remains a pioneering study in this area of research.

The introduction to Patricia Caicedo's *The Latin American Art Song: A Critical Anthology and Interpretive Guide for Singers* gives an excellent overview of the history of Latin American art song in general. It also contains notes on interpretation as well as on Latin American Spanish and Brazilian Portuguese diction.[27]

ORGANIZATION

Each chapter of this book focuses on a single country. A brief introduction to the region opens each chapter, followed by an annotated catalog of compositions organized alphabetically by composer. Each chapter concludes with notes on publishers and collections. Each song in the catalog has its own entry, which includes the collection or cycle title (if applicable), the individual song title(s), and location information (publisher, library, collection, or other source). Song entries also include the range and tessitura, and notes such as dedications or other indications from the composer.[28]

Each song has a catalog number which follows a system of designation by country chapter. Songs within a song cycle are further designated by letters.

Composer and Text Information

Composers are alphabetized by last name, with birth and death dates listed immediately following the name. For living composers and those for whom only a birth date has been found, the year is listed with a dash (e.g., 1945–). Poets are listed by first name followed by last name.

Song Information

When available, the year of the song's composition is listed. If only a copyright or publication date could be found, that is indicated by a copyright symbol or the letter "p" before the year: ©1978 or p1988. In the case of songs without published titles, the first phrase of the song text appears in brackets.

Range and Tessitura

Pitch ranges are indicated according to the system used in most current U.S. theory and harmony texts, where C_4 equals middle C, and C_4–C_5 designates the octave above. Tessitura is defined in the following manner: Low tessitura, G_3–G_4; Medium, C_4–C_5; and High, G_4–G_5 and above. Medium-High tessitura indicates a song that frequently traverses or lingers in the passaggio (approximately $E\flat_5$–$F\sharp_5$ for treble clef and C_4–F_4 for bass clef). Tessitura may be defined as the range in which the majority of the piece lies, and should not be confused with the vocal range of the piece. Indicating tessitura will give pedagogical guidance with regard to vocal line difficulty in dealing with vocal registers. Please note that occasionally there is a designation for tessitura followed by a specific voice type. The tessitura is always abbreviated, so that a song with a medium tessitura for medium voice is designated as follows: Med, Medium; or Med, Mezzo.

Publication and Holding Information

Publishers' names are abbreviated according to the key outlined at the end of each chapter as well as in appendix C. Publication information may include a U.S., European, or Latin American publishing company, or a source such as a journal in which the song is published. When available, publishing catalog numbers are also included. For example, publication numbers for Ricordi Americana in Buenos Aires appear as follows: RA BA3576. A year appearing directly after the publisher (e.g., EM 1943) indicates the year of publication.

If a song is part of a collection held at a library or other institution, the collection is indicated. Due to the varied nature of publications, libraries, and collections throughout the world, layout details regarding this information may vary by region. Holding information may also identify personal collections or online sources, especially in the case of living performers. LAMC holdings are designated by a plus sign: +. Another abbreviation used throughout the catalog is m (manuscript). Some entries may also include items such as dedications, performance indications, additional text information, and other available arrangements.

Chapter Variations

Some chapters vary regarding the kind of information included following the catalog section. The chapters on Argentina and Brazil, for example, contain information on sources for further study and additional bibliographic information. An additional titles section may also be present in some chapters. Publishers for these titles (when known) are noted in brackets immediately following the titles.

The catalog entries follow this format:

Composer's last name, first name, birth and death dates (when known) in boldface type	**Aguirre, Julián, 1868–1924**
Catalog number, followed by the name of the song	1.1, *Canciones argentinas*
Songs within the song cycle are listed immediately below, each with its own catalog number	1.1a, Caminito, —, Leopoldo Lugones, D4–G5, Med-high, Leopoldo Lugones, Gurina, UCA
Each song is followed by information delimited by commas; the information in the entries follows the same order throughout: catalog no., song name, date (see "Song Information," above), text author (poet), pitch range, tessitura, additional notes about the song, publisher, collection (see example at right)	1.1b, El nido ausente, op. 50, 1898, Leopoldo Lugones, E4–G5, Med-high, Juana Gonzalez de Lugones, Gurina, UCA
When no information is available, such as date of composition or publication, an em dash (—) denotes that fact.	(as in 1.1a, above)
Additional source information is available for a few songs, and is added at the end of those entries.	(see p. 4)

GUIDELINES FOR INCLUSION

Boundary lines between so-called folk, art, and popular songs can be rather blurry. Estelle Jorgensen points out that musics from all kinds of traditions draw on and influence each other in a symbiotic manner, making it hard to distinguish a "pure" style or genre.[29] In this guide, a song's eligibility for inclusion is determined by the following characteristics: 1. It has a written-out accompaniment, not symbols or signs indicating the harmonies; 2. It is intended to be sung and played by classically trained musicians; and 3. It is intended to be included in the "art song" genre by the composer. This last characteristic may be evidenced by the song's inclusion in a set of songs or collection of songs intended to be sung by classically trained singers.

Delimitations

To produce a definitive catalog of songs from all Latin American countries and regions would be beyond the scope of this study.[30] Rather, our focus has been on obtaining a representative selection of literature that includes songs and composers from each major region of Latin America.[31]

This guide does not include folk songs unless they exist in composed arrangements, according to the guidelines outlined above. It cannot include popular songs that are intended to be sung in a popular or untrained singing style, as these songs are considered a different genre from classical art song, although there may be songs that are popular in style that can be included according to the guidelines above. The selected songs fall within the classical tradition.[32]

The catalog does not include songs that are a part of larger works, such as oratorios, operas, *zarzuelas*,[33] or other large-scale chamber works, unless they are voice and piano reductions by the same composer and intended for smaller performance venues. Limiting the study to works intended for voice and piano allows this volume to remain focused on repertoire appropriate for the recital arena, as opposed to the larger concert hall or the dramatic stage. Works with accompanying instruments other than piano may be included if they are part of a set, cycle, or collection that also uses piano. For example, all four songs in Andres Sás's *Cuatro melodías* are included in the catalog, although the first three songs are written for voice and piano and the fourth for voice and flute.[34]

A Guide to the Latin American Art Song Repertoire

Argentina

Allison L. Weiss

With the goal of catapulting their young nation to cultural and economic prominence, the urban elite of nineteenth-century Argentina openly encouraged the study of Western literature, art, and music at home and abroad. No different than their predecessors of the colonial period, they kept current with art music and composition as it was being performed and taught in Europe, particularly in France, Spain, and Italy. Amancio Alcorta (1805–1862), a politician, and Juan Pedro Esnaola (1808–1878), a professional musician, were two of the first Argentines to create, publish, and perform songs for upper-class audiences in salon and concert settings.[1]

Toward the end of the nineteenth century, composers began looking to the French *mélodie* as a suitable starting place for their own treatment of the genre, and many wrote their first art songs while studying in Paris. Francisco Hargreaves (1849–1900), Eduardo García Mansilla (1871–1930), and Hermann Bemberg (1859–1931) based almost the entirety of their output on poems by Paul Verlaine, Paul Mariéton, Alfred de Musset, or other French poets. Soon thereafter, Argentine composers began creating songs based on the traditional texts and music found within their own nation's borders. By 1910, it was the objective of several prominent composers and teachers to create a national school of composition and a system of musical education comparable in quality to those then found in Europe.

Julián Aguirre (1868–1924) and Carlos López Buchardo (1881–1948), two of the pioneers of song composition in Argentina, also began by writing their songs in French but then transitioned to writing songs of a more national flavor in their native Spanish tongue. Both are good examples of the "composer-professor," working at a number of conservatories in and around Buenos Aires and dividing their time between creative, pedagogical, and administrative tasks. In contrast, Carlos Guastavino (1912–2000), a chemist by training who lived in the provincial city of Santa Fe, seemed less concerned with existing European song models. Instead, he focused on combining original, folk-inspired vocal lines and subtle piano accompaniments into a style very much his own. His numerous songs, along with those of Alberto Ginastera (1916–1983), are perhaps the most well-known of the Argentine repertoire today.

Of the nationalist composers, José André (1881–1944), Felipe Boero (1884–1958), Pascual De Rogatis (1880–1980), Emilio Dublanc (1911–1990), Constantino Gaito (1878–1945), Luis Gianneo (1897–1968), Gilardo Gilardi (1889–1963), Ángel Lasala (1914–2000), Athos Palma (1891–1952), Julio Perceval (1903–1963), Luis Sammartino (1888–1973), Floro Ugarte (1884–1975), and Alberto Williams (1862–1952) stand out as some of the most influential and dedicated to the genre. Other composers writing later in the century promoted more experimental styles, often declamatory or dramatic in nature. These include Roberto Caamaño (1923–1993), Pompeyo Camps (1924–1999), Jacobo Ficher (1896–1978), Juan Francisco Giacobbe (1907–1990), Juan Carlos Paz (1897–1972), Alejandro Pinto (1922–1991), and Alicia Terzián (1934–). Today, living composers like Jorge César Armesto (1933–), Lucio Bruno-Videla (1968–), Irma Urteaga (1929–) and many others residing outside of Argentina continue to write and perform art songs, though their output is generally less nationalistic.

Given the inclination toward nationalism during the early to mid-twentieth century, it comes as no surprise that certain Argentine poets tended to be especially attractive to Argentine composers. León Benarós, Alfredo R. Bufano, Miguel A. Camino, Gustavo Caraballo, Arturo Vázquez, Agustín Dentone, Juan Bautista Grosso, Jorge Luis Borges, Rafael Jijena Sánchez, Hamlet Lima Quintana, Francisco Luis Bernárdez, Leopoldo Lugones, Silvina Ocampo, Ida Réboli, and Conrado Nalé Roxlo were especially popular choices. Composers also turned to other poets from Latin America, including Gabriela Mistral (Chile),

Pablo Neruda (Chile), Fernán Silva Váldez (Uruguay), Amado Nervo (Mexico), Rubén Darío (Nicaragua), as well as to writers from Spain, including Federico García Lorca, Miguel Hernández, Rafael Alberti, Francisco de Quevedo Villegas, and Gustavo Adolfo Bécquer.

There are a number of composers who were born in Europe but whose training and careers transpired almost completely in Argentina, and who eventually became Argentine citizens. Composers who fall into this category include Julián Bautista (Spain), Montserrat Campmany (Spain), Pascual De Rogatis (Italy), Jacobo Ficher (Russia), Andrés Gaos (Spain), Arturo Luzzatti (Italy), Jaime Pahissa (Spain), Julio Perceval (Belgium), Alejandro Pinto (Poland), Pascual Quaratino (Italy), and César Stiatessi (France). The diverse backgrounds of these composers are reflected in their treatments of Catalán, English, French, Galician, German, and Italian texts.

The following catalog also features songs written by Argentine women composers, whose access to Western music education and piano pedagogy during the first part of the twentieth century perhaps surpassed that of any other Latin American country. Singers who have a desire to promote women composers are especially encouraged to seek out songs by Suzanne Baron Supervielle (1910–2004), Ana Schneider de Cabrera (1897–1970), Elsa Calcagno (1910–1978), Montserrat Campmany (1901–1995), Ana Carrique (1886–1979), Lia Cimaglia Espinosa (1906–1998), Ana Serrano Redonnet (1910–1993), Yvette Souviron (1914–), Lita Spena (1904–1989), and Celia Torrá (1884–1962).

In reality, the largest obstacle to singers and pianists interested in this repertoire is one of access and commercial distribution. This catalog represents the sincere belief that such challenges will eventually be overcome in the wake of increased public and scholarly interest. For this reason, a special effort was made to document exactly where in Argentina (or in the United States, when applicable) each song could be most easily located. It is hoped that performers and scholars will take what is offered here and proceed to develop a more comprehensive catalog and analysis of each composer's songs.

Aguirre, Julián, 1868–1924

1.1, *Canciones argentinas*
1.1a, Caminito, —, Leopoldo Lugones, D4–G5, Med-high, Leopoldo Lugones, Gurina, UCA
1.1b, El nido ausente, op. 50, 1898, Leopoldo Lugones, E4–G5, Med-high, Juana Gonzalez de Lugones, Gurina, UCA
1.1c, Las mañanitas, op. 43, —, Tomás Allende Yragorri, C#4–Eb5, Med-high, Dolly Mills de Mastroggiani, Gurina, UCA
1.1d, Rosas orientales, op. 51, 1898, Leopoldo Lugones, D#4–G#5, Med-high, Ninón Vallin, EAM, UCA
1.1e, Serenata campera, op. 42, 1904–1905, Leopoldo Lugones, Bb3–F#5, Med-high, Ana G. de la Guardia, EAM, UCA
1.2, Cueca, op. 61, 1914, Leopoldo Lugones, Eb4–Gb5, High, José Ojeda, Gaudiosi, UCA

1.3, *Dos canciones de cuna, op. 57*
1.3a, Evocaciones indias, 1923, Julián Aguirre, C4–F5, Med-high, Luisa Fanlo, GRic, CNMA
1.3b, Ea, 1923, Julián Aguirre, D4–F5, Med-high, Luisa Fanlo, GRic, CNMA
1.3c, El zorzal (Canto tucumano), op. 54, 1939, Julián Aguirre, D4–D5, Med, Mario Bravo, RA BA7676, UCA

1.4, *Jardins . . .*
1.4a, Chi mi ridona, 1914, Johann Wolfgang von Goethe, E4–G5, High, Felia Litvinne, Gurina 74, UCA
1.4b, Llorando yo en el bosque, 1914, Heinrich Heine, C#4–Gb5, Med-high, Cárlos Farelli, Gurina 74, UCA
1.4c, Berceuse, 1914, Robert Burns, C4–G5, Med-high, Edoardo Mascheroni, Gurina 74, UCA
1.4d, La rose, 1914, Hans Christian Andersen, Eb4–Ab5, High, Emilia Strömberg, Gurina 74, UCA
1.4e, Ton image, 1914, Joseph Freiherr von Eichendorff, Eb4–Gb5, High, Joseph Freiherr von Eichendorff, Gurina 74, UCA
1.4f, Le ciel est transi, 1914, Jean Richepin, B3–G5, High, Jean Richepin, Gurina 74, UCA
1.4g, La lune, 1914, Paul Verlaine, C4–F5, Med-high, Paul Verlaine, Gurina 74, UCA

1.5, Lied, op. 60, 1924, Conrado Nalé Roxlo, F4–F#5, High, —, Diario "La Razón", INM
1.6, Vidalita, op. 36, 1932, Edmundo Montagne, G4–G5, Med-high, Edmundo Montagne, RA BA6707, UCA

Additional titles: Canciones escolares argentinas; Chansons pour elle; Fábulas I; Fábulas II [UCA]. Huella [INM]. J'ai vu ton sourire et tes larmes; L'éventail [*Diccionario de la música española e hispanoamericana*].

Albano, Enrique, 1910–1992

1.7, Décima, 1956, María Raquel Adler, F#4–G5, Med-high, Nina Carini, CLSRL, IU
1.8, Tonada, —, Rodolfo Álvarez, E4–G5, Med-high, Brígida Frías de López Buchardo, J. Feliú, IU
1.9, Yo bajé del monte (Tonada), 1962, María Raquel Adler, D4–F#5, Med-high, Miguel Ángel Giella, Aída E. Lammers de Giella, CLSRL, UCA

Additional titles: Misa Argentina a los ámbitos todos de la patria [SADAIC]. Vidala; Virgencita del Carmen [CNMA].

André, José, 1881–1944

1.10, Al pampero (Décima), —, —, D4–D#5, Med, —, Breyer, UCA

1.11, *Canciones infantiles*
1.11a, Los Reyes Magos, 1923, —, D4–Eb5, Med, —, Gurina 142, CNMA
1.11b, Gallinita blanca, 1923, —, D4–E5, Med, —, Gurina 142, CNMA
1.11c, Al maestro que se fué, 1923, —, E4–D5, Med, —, Gurina 142, CNMA

1.11d, Abuelita, 1923, —, D4–D♭5, Med, —, Gurina 142, CNMA

1.11e, Canción del árbol, 1923, —, E4–E5, Med, —, Gurina 142, CNMA

1.12, Décima de Pavón, —, Rafael Obligado, D4–E♭5, Med, —, Breyer, UCA

1.13, *Elogio de las rosas*

1.13a, La rosa de la aurora, 1928, Leopoldo Lugones, E4–F♯5, Med-high, Jane Bathori; text in Spanish and French; French version by Henri Collet (p1931), ES 8228, UCA

1.13b, Las rosas de la tarde, 1928, Leopoldo Lugones, E4–F5, Med-high, Jane Bathori; text in Spanish and French; French version by Henri Collet (p1931), ES 8228, UCA

1.13c, La rosa y el colibrí, 1928, Leopoldo Lugones, D4–B♭4, High, Jane Bathori; text in Spanish and French; French version by Henri Collet (p1931), ES 8228, UCA

1.13d, La rosa del ensueño, 1928, Leopoldo Lugones, D4–F5, Med-high, Jane Bathori; text in Spanish and French; French version by Henri Collet (p1931), ES 8228, UCA

1.13e, El alma de la rosa, 1928, Leopoldo Lugones, E♭4–G5, High, Jane Bathori; text in Spanish and French; French version by Henri Collet (p1931), ES 8228, UCA

1.14, Hueya, —, —, C4–D5, Med-high, —, Breyer, UCA

1.15, *Las canciones de Natacha*

1.15a, 1. Se enojó la luna, se enojó el lucero, 1928, Juan Ibarbourou, D4–D5, Med, María Augusta Palma (Chichita), Gurina 143, UCA

1.15b, 2. La loba, la loba le compró al lobito, 1928, Juan Ibarbourou, D♯4–D♯5, Med, María Augusta Palma (Chichita), Gurina 143, UCA

1.15c, 3. Por los campos verdes de Jerusalém, 1928, Juan Ibarbourou, C♯4–D5, Med, María Augusta Palma (Chichita), Gurina 143, UCA

1.15d, 4. Señor jardinero; déme usted a mí, 1928, Juan Ibarbourou, C♯4–E5, Med, María Augusta Palma (Chichita), Gurina 143, UCA

1.15e, 5. La señora Luna le pidió al naranjo, 1928, Juan Ibarbourou, E4–D♯5, Med, María Augusta Palma (Chichita), Gurina 143, UCA

1.15f, 6. El sueño hoy no quiere venir por acá, 1928, Juan Ibarbourou, D4–E5, Med, María Augusta Palma (Chichita), Gurina 143, UCA

1.16, *Mélodies et chansons*

1.16a, 1. Un grand sommeil noir, 1928, Paul Verlaine, D♯4–F5, Med, —, ES 7540, CNMA

1.16b, 2. Chanson d'automne, 1928, Paul Verlaine, D4–F5, Med-high, —, ES 7540, CNMA

1.16c, 3. Chanson de Barberine, 1928, Alfred de Musset, E♭4–F♯5, Med-high, —, ES 7540, CNMA

1.16d, 4. A Saint Blaise a la Zuecca, 1928, Alfred de Musset, E4–A4, High, —, ES 7540, CNMA

1.16e, 5. Lorsque la coquette Espérance, 1928, Alfred de Musset, D4–G5, Med-high, —, ES 7540, CNMA

1.16f, 6. Chanson au bord de l'eau, 1928, Tristan Klingsor, C4–E5, Med-high, —, ES 7540, CNMA

1.16g, 7. Chanson de bergère, 1928, Tristan Klingsor, D4–G5, Med-high, —, ES 7540, CNMA

1.16h, 8. Chanson du chat qui dort, 1928, Tristan Klingsor, D♭4–F♯5, Med-high, —, ES 7540, CNMA

1.16i, 9. Il était jadis un berger, 1928, Paul Bru, D4–E5, Med-high, —, ES 7540, CNMA

1.16j, 10. Il était une fois, 1928, Jean Ajalbert, F4–F5, Med-high, —, ES 7540, CNMA

1.16k, 11. Le Ruisseau, 1928, Jean Ajalbert, F4–F5, Med-high, Mademoiselle María Magdalena de Ezcurra, ES 7540, CNMA

1.16l, 12. Là-bas, 1928, Jacques Madeleine, E♭4–F5, Med-high, —, ES 7540, CNMA

1.17, *Mensajes líricos*
1.17a, 1. La tapera, 1920, Carlos Ortiz, C4–F5, Med-high, María de Pini de Chrestia, —, SADAIC
1.17b, 2. La tarde, 1920, Carlos Ortiz, C4–A5, Med-high, María de Pini de Chrestia, —, SADAIC
1.17c, 3. Flor de cardo, 1920, Carlos Ortiz, D4–G♭5, Med-high, María de Pini de Chrestia, —, SADAIC

Additional titles: Cette petite brunette; *Deux poèmes de Paul Verlaine*; Fleurissant les roses; Le lac; María; Mi alma; Mirondón; Navidad; *Rondas populares argentinas*; Serenidad; Simple paisaje; *Tres poemas*; *Trois chansons d'Alfred de Musset*; *Trois chansons de Valet de Cœur* [*Diccionario de la música española e hispanoamericana*].

Aretz, Isabel, 1913–2005

1.18, *Cinco fulias sobre melodias folklóricas venezolanas*
1.18a, Yo pensé enamorarte, 1966, D4–G5, Med-high, Morella Muñoz, RA, UCA
1.18b, Qué bonito está el altar, 1966, E4–D5, Med, Morella Muñoz, RA, UCA
1.18c, Por debajo corre el agua, 1966, G3–G5, Med-high, Morella Muñoz, RA, UCA
1.18d, Mañana me voy, 1966, D4–E♭5, Med, Morella Muñoz, RA, UCA
1.18e, Francisca'e Paula Chirimoya, 1966, D♭4–G♭5, Med-high, Morella Muñoz, RA, UCA

Additional titles: La Imilla; Poema angaité, *Tres cantos indios* [*Enciclopedia de la música argentina*].

Armesto, Jorge César, 1933–

1.19, *Canciones con árboles (Cuaderno 1)*
1.19a, I. Algarrobo, 1996, Leonardo Martínez, B♭3–G♭4, High, Written in bass clef, IU
1.19b, II. Espinillo, 1996, Leonardo Martínez, D3–B3, Med, Written in bass clef, IU
1.19c, III. Lapacho, 1996, Leonardo Martínez, B♭2–E4, Med-high, Written in bass clef, IU
1.19d, IV. Tarco, 1996, Leonardo Martínez, E3–F4, High, Written in bass clef, IU
1.19e, V. Mistol, 1996, Leonardo Martínez, B2–E4, Med-high, Written in bass clef, IU
1.19f, VI. Laurel, 1996, Leonardo Martínez, B2–F♯4, Med-high, Written in bass clef, IU

1.20, *Canciones con árboles (Cuaderno 2)*
1.20a, VII. Yuchán (Palo borracho), 1996, Leonardo Martínez, A♯2–F♯4, High, Written in bass clef, IU
1.20b, VIII. Pacará, 1996, Leonardo Martínez, B2–F4, High, Written in bass clef, IU
1.20c, IX. Chañar, 1996, Leonardo Martínez, A2–G4, Med-high, Written in bass clef, IU
1.20d, X. Quebracho, 1996, Leonardo Martínez, C3–E4, Med-high, Written in bass clef, IU
1.20e, XI. Molle, 1996, Leonardo Martínez, B♭2–F4, Med-high, Written in bass clef, IU
1.20f, XII. Brea, 1996, Leonardo Martínez, D3–F♯4, Med-high, Written in bass clef, IU

1.21, *Canciones de la infancia*
1.21a, I. Tardes, 1994, Leonardo Martínez, C4–A4, Med-high, —, IU
1.21b, II. Ahora sé, 1994, Leonardo Martínez, C♯4–G5, Med, —, IU
1.21c, III. De la infancia queda todo, 1994, Leonardo Martínez, C♭4–G5, High, —, IU
1.21d, IV. Recuerdo, 1994, Leonardo Martínez, C4–A4, Med-high, —, IU
1.21e, V. Entonces, 1994, Leonardo Martínez, D4–G5, Med-high, —, IU
1.21f, VI. En la arboleda, 1994, Leonardo Martínez, B♭3–B5, Med-high, —, IU
1.21g, VII. El ruido de las grandes crecien-

tes, 1994, Leonardo Martínez, C4–C6, High, —, IU

Baron Supervielle, Suzanne, 1910–2004
1.22, *Cuatro canciones de Federico García Lorca*
1.22a, Canción de las siete doncellas (Teoría del arco iris), 1940, Federico García Lorca, E4–F5, Med-high, GRic, UCA
1.22b, Canción china en Europa, 1940, Federico García Lorca, C4–E5, Med, GRic, UCA
1.22c, Cancioncilla sevillana, 1940, Federico García Lorca, (A3)C4–G5, Med-high, GRic, UCA
1.22d, Paisaje, 1940, Federico García Lorca, C♭4–E♭5, Med, GRic, UCA

1.23, *Mélodies*
1.23a, A la santé, 1934, Guillaume Apollinaire, B3–F♯5, Med-high, ES 8606, UCA
1.23b, Chanson à boire, 1934, Raoul Ponchon, D4–A5, Med-high, ES 8606, UCA
1.23c, Le papillon, 1934, Jules Renard, D♯4–F♯5, Med-high, ES 8606, UCA
1.23d, L'oiseau, 1934, Marie Laurencin, E♭4–G5, Med-high, ES 8606, UCA
1.23e, Le lac endormi, 1934, Jules Supervielle, C♯4–E5, Med-high, ES 8606, UCA
1.23f, Elle s'avance, elle s'éloigne ..., 1934, Jules Supervielle, C4–G5, Med-high, ES 8606, UCA
1.23g, Pour endormir la belle au bois, 1934, Jules Supervielle, D4–A4, Med-high, ES 8606, UCA
1.23h, Les grenades, 1934, Paul Valéry, B3–G5, Med-high, ES 8606, CA
1.23i, Le sylphe, 1934, Paul Valéry, D4–G5, Med-high, ES 8606, UCA

1.24, *Nueve canciones de Federico García Lorca*
1.24a, 1. Canción de jinete (1860) (Andaluzas), 1952, Federico García Lorca, C4–E5, Med, RA, UCA
1.24b, 2. Adelina de paseo, 1952, Federico García Lorca, A3–C5, Med, RA, UCA
1.24c, 3. Zarzamora con el tronco gris, 1952, Federico García Lorca, D4–D5, Med, RA, UCA
1.24d, 4. Mi niña se fue a la mar, 1952, Federico García Lorca, C4–G5, Med, RA, UCA
1.24e, 5. Tarde (¿Estaba mi Lucía con los pies en el arroyo?) (Andaluzas), 1952, Federico García Lorca, B3–E5, Med, RA, UCA
1.24f, 6. Canción de jinete, 1952, Federico García Lorca, B♭3–D5, Med, RA, UCA
1.24g, 7. Es verdad (Andaluzas), 1952, Federico García Lorca, A3–C5, Med, RA, UCA
1.24h, 8. Arbolé Arbolé ... (Andaluzas), 1952, Federico García Lorca, A3–F♯5, Med, RA, UCA
1.24i, 9. Galán, galancillo ..., 1952, Federico García Lorca, B3–E5, Med, RA, UCA

Additional titles: A Irene García; Amo el amor de los marineros; Caracola; Cuarto solo; *Cuatro canciones; Cuatro poemas;* Dans l'oubli de mon corps; *Dos melodías criollas; Dos poemas con música;* El ausente I; El lagarto está llorando; Espero los días que vendrán; Faire place; Fiesta; La belette; L'âme; La mer secrète; La pluie et les tyrans; La última inocencia; Le pont; L'escargot; Les poissons; Los delfines; Mélodies; Poema; Por un minuto de vida breve; Que voulez-vous que je fasse du monde; Quién alumbra; Sentido de su ausencia; Sombra de los días a venir; Soneto de evasión; Tiempo; Vértigo o contemplación de algo que termina; Visages [*Diccionario de la música española e hispanoamericana*].

Bautista, Julián, 1901–1961
1.25, *Tres cuidades*
1.25a, 1. Malagueña, Federico García Lorca, C♯4–F5, Med-high, ECCM, TC
1.25b, 2. Barrio de Córdoba (Tópico nocturno), Federico García Lorca, D4–D5, Med-high, ECCM, TC

1.25c, 3. Baile, Federico García Lorca, E4–F♯5, Med-high, ECCM, TC

Additional titles: Canciones sobre poesías de Bécquer [Enciclopedia de la música argentina]. Dos canciones [Diccionario de la música española e hispanoamericana]. La flûte de jade [CNMA].

Bemberg, Hermann, 1859–1931

1.26, *20 Mélodies*

1.26a, Aime-moi!..., 1896, Armand Ocampo, D4–A5, High, Text in French, RL 6154, CNMA

1.26b, Les anges pleurent, 1896, G. Audigier, D♭4–G5, Med-high, Text in French, RL 6154, CNMA

1.26c, Chant arabe, 1896, Fernand Danel, G4–G5, High, Text in French, RL 6154, CNMA

1.26d, Chant de l'aube, 1896, Armand Ocampo, C♯4–F♯5, Med, Text in French, RL 6154, CNMA

1.26e, Chant hindou, 1896, Armand Ocampo, F♯4–G5, High, Madame Conneau; text in French, RL 6154, CNMA

1.26f, Chant vénitien, 1896, —, D♭4–B♭5, Med-high, Text in French, RL 6154, CNMA

1.26g, L'enfant de Bohème, 1896, —, C4–G5, Med-high, Text in French, RL 6154, CNMA

1.26h, Est-ce toi?, 1896, A. Ribaux, F4–A♭5, Med-high, Text in French, RL 6154, CNMA

1.26i, L'étoile, 1896, Philippe Gille, D4–G5, Med, Text in French, RL 6154, CNMA

1.26j, La fée aux chansons, 1896, Armand Silvestre, D4–B5, High, Text in French, RL 6154, CNMA

1.26k, J'ai gardé dans mon cœur, 1896, Armand Ocampo, B3–F♯5, Med, Text in French, RL 6154, CNMA

1.26l, J'ai soif de ton âme, 1896, Paul Mariéton, E♭4–F5, Med, Text in French, RL 6154, CNMA

1.26m, Lied ancien, 1896, François Coppée, C4–F5, Med-high, Text in French, RL 6154, CNMA

1.26n, Madeleine, 1896, Phillippe Gille, E4–G5, Med-high, Text in French, RL 6154, CNMA

1.26o, Persévérance, 1896, François Coppée, E4–G5, Med-high, Text in French, RL 6154, CNMA

1.26p, Repose-toi, 1896, Armand Ocampo, C4–F5, Med, Text in French, RL 6154, CNMA

1.26q, Soupir, 1896, Sully Prudhomme, C4–G5, Med-high, Text in French, RL 6154, CNMA

1.26r, Souvenance, 1896, Paul Mariéton, D4–G5, Med-high, Text in French, RL 6154, CNMA

1.26s, Tu veux savoir, 1896, Armand Ocampo, D4–A5, Med-high, Text in French, RL 6154, CNMA

1.26t, Un ange est venu, 1896, Paul Mariéton, D4–G5, Med-high, Text in French, RL 6154, CNMA

1.27, Arioso, 1910, Casimir Delavigne, D4–A5, Med-high, Text in French and English; from Bemberg's cantata *La mort de Jeanne d'Arc* (1886) for soprano, chorus, and orchestra, University Society 718, CNMA

1.28, Il ne revient pas!, 1904, Ant. Roque, D♯4–F♯5, Med, Madame Cavalieri; text in French, GRic 109652, TC

1.29, La chanson des baisers, 1900, Hermann Bemberg, D4–A5, Med-high, Madame Melba; text in French, GRic 103147, TC

1.30, Nymphes et sylvains (Ninfe e silvani), —, Armand Ocampo, B♭3–A♭5, High, Madame Melba; text in French and Italian; Italian translation by Gustave Cenci, Grech 3034, TC

Additional titles: A toi! [INM]. Chanson créole; Complainte-placet de Faust-fils; Rosette [Diccionario de la música española e hispanoamericana]. La ballade du désespéré [Enciclopedia de la música argentina].

Boero, Felipe, 1884–1958

1.31, Canción de cuna, 1937, Fernando Fusoni, E♭4–F5, Med, —, Ortelli, ALW

1.32, Compañero viento, 1956, Agustín Dentone, C♯4–E5, Med-high, —, CLSRL, CNMA

1.33, Coplas para un bailecito, 1957, Agustín Dentone, E♭5–B♭5, High, —, CLSRL, CNMA

1.34, *Cuatro canciones en el estilo popular argentino*

1.34a, Si muero . . . , 1948, —, C♯4–F♯5, Med-high, —, CLSRL, UCA

1.34b, ¡Ay, mi amor!, 1948, —, D4–F5, Med-high, —, CLSRL, ALW

1.34c, La tapera, 1948, Fernando Fusoni, E♯4–F♯5, Med-high, Julio Lottermoser, CLSRL, ALW

1.34d, Serenata, 1948, —, E5–A♭5, High, —, CLSRL, CNMA

1.35, *De la sierra . . . (Cinco canciones argentinas)*

1.35a, I. Mensaje, 1920, Juan Carlos Dávalos, E4–F5, Med-high, —, CLSRL, UCA

1.35b, II. Serrana, 1920, César Carrizo, C♯4–F♯5, Med-high, String orchestra accompaniment available, CLSRL, UCA

1.35c, III. Ruego, 1920, Juan Carlos Dávalos, E4–E5, Med-high, —, CLSRL, UCA

1.35d, IV. Jujeña, 1920, E. N. González López, D♯4–G♯5, Med-high, Las acacias and Jujeña are both listed as fourth in this cycle, depending on the year of publication, CLSRL, UCA

1.35e, IV. Las acacias, 1920, Juan Carlos Dávalos, E4–A5, Med-high, Las acacias and Jujeña are both listed as fourth in this cycle, depending on the year of publication, CLSRL, UCA

1.35f, V. Silueta, 1920, Juan Carlos Dávalos, C♯4–F5, Med-high, —, CLSRL, UCA

1.36, El colibrí, 1930, Leopoldo Díaz, D♯4–B5, High, —, CLSRL, SADAIC

1.37, El día inútil, 1952, Mayorino Ferraría, C♯4–F♯5, Med-high, —, RA BA10655, UCA

1.38, El lago, 1933, Leopoldo Díaz, D♭4–F♯5, High, —, Ortelli, UCA

1.39, El mate amargo, 1952, Fernán Silva Valdez, C3–F4, High, —, RA BA10732, SADAIC

1.40, El quetzal, 1940, Leopoldo Díaz, B♭3–C5, Med, —, CLSRL, CLP

1.41, El rosal, 1949, Héctor Díaz Leguizamón, C4–C5, Med, —, CLSRL, ALW

1.42, El yaraví, —, Leopoldo Díaz, C♯4–F♯5, Med-high, —, RA, CLP

1.43, Flores de cardón, 1936, Ismael Moya, F♯4–F♯5, Med-high, String orchestra accompaniment available, Ortelli, UCA

1.44, Funeral coya, 1953, Agustín Dentone, C4–F5, Med-high, —, RA BA11032, UCA

1.45, Invierno, 1956, Agustín Dentone, B3–E5, Med-high, —, RA BA11383, CNMA

1.46, La flor del aire, 1954, Leopoldo Díaz, D♭4–B♭5, Med-high, —, CLSRL, ALW

1.47, La pasionaria, 1942, Leopoldo Díaz, E4–F♯5, Med-high, String orchestra accompaniment available, RA BA8501, INM

1.48, La ruina y el viento, 1940, Leopoldo Díaz, E♭4–A♭5, High, String orchestra accompaniment available, RA BA7696, UCA

1.49, Las siete notas, —, Leopoldo Díaz, C4–E5, Med, —, CLSRL, UCA

1.50, Lluvia, 1956, Agustín Dentone, E4–G5, Med-high, —, CLSRL, CNMA

1.51, Lluvia en el campo, 1951, J. L. Fernández de la Puente, D4–G5, Med-high, —, CLSRL, UCA

1.52, Los reseros, 1950, Julián de Charras, A3–B4, Med, —, CLSRL, LBV

1.53, Ofrenda a Guido Spano, 1946, Leopoldo Díaz, B♭3–G♭5, High, —, CLSRL, ALW

1.54, Vidalita, 1949, Ricardo de Elías Tarnassi, E4–A♭5, High, String orchestra accompaniment available, RA BA7465, UCA

1.55, Vidita, 1937, E. González López, D♯4–G♯5, High, —, Ortelli, ALW

Additional titles: La flor del aire; La mére; Les ombres d'hellas; *Quatre poèmes* [UCA]. *Canciones infantiles;* Como tú . . . ; Leyenda; ¿Por qué?; Tonadilla (Romance) [CNMA]. Ariana y Dionysos; Raquela [LBV]. Ave María; Coplas para un bailecito; Incantesimo; La diligencia; Madrigal antiguo; Nid d'hiver; Oración a Ricardo Gutiérrez; Páginas breves; Poesías de Agustín Dentone; Puerto; Romance [ALW]. Evocaciones americanas [INM].

Bruno-Videla, Lucio, 1968–

1.56, *Tres canciones, op. 1*
1.56a, Fin del mundo, 1993–1995, Else Lasker Schüler, B3–A5, Med-high, m, LBV
1.56b, Remansos, 1993–1995, Federico García Lorca, B3–F#5, Med-high, m, LBV
1.56c, La canción mi vida, 1993–1995, Else Lasker Schüler, B♭3–B♭5, Med-high, m, LBV

Additional titles: Cuatro canciones en estilo popular, op.2; Dos canciones, op.11; Es el alba una sombra; Mar; Por los caminitos; Ronda de la vida; Soñe que tu me llevabas; *Tres momentos para canto y piano, op.6* [LBV].

Caamaño, Roberto, 1923–1993

1.57, *Dos cantares galaico-portugueses del siglos XIII, op. 18*
1.57a, I. Ay madre, nunca mal sentíu, 1958, Joyão Bólseyro, B3–E5, Low, Text in Galician-Portuguese, RA BA11624, UCA
1.57b, II. Filha, se grado edes, 1958, Lopo, D4–E5, Low, Text in Galician-Portuguese, RA BA11624, UCA

1.58, *Dos cantos gallegos, op. 3*
1.58a, I. A xusticia pol-a-man (La justicia por su mano), 1955, Rosalía de Castro, A3–G5, Low, Hina Spani; text in Galician, RA BA11174, UCA
1.58b, II. Vamos bebendo (Vamos bebiendo), 1955, Rosalía de Castro, A3–D5, Low, Hina Spani; text in Galician, RA BA11174, UCA

1.59, Lamento (en la tumba de Manuel de Falla), op. 13, 1953, —, B3–F5, Med, Hina Spani; Vocalise, RA BA10864, UCA

1.60, *Tres cantos de Navidad, op. 4*
1.60a, I. Alegráos pastores, 1954, Lope de Vega, C4–F#5, Med, Hina Spani; English version by Jorge C. Romero, Barry 2004, UCA
1.60b, II. ¿Dónde vais zagala?, 1954, Lope de Vega, D4–E5, Med, Hina Spani; English version by Jorge C. Romero, Barry 2004, UCA
1.60c, III. Temblando estaba del frío, 1954, Lope de Vega, A4–F5, Med, Hina Spani; English version by Jorge C. Romero, Barry 2004, UCA

1.61, *Tres sonetos de Francisco Luis Bernárdez, op. 17*
1.61a, Todo, 1954, Francisco Luis Bernárdez, A3–F#5, Med, Ángel Mattiello, m, UCA
1.61b, El vuelo, 1954, Francisco Luis Bernárdez, C4–F5, Med-high, Ángel Mattiello, m, UCA
1.61c, Esto, 1954, Francisco Luis Bernárdez, D4–F#5, Med-high, Ángel Mattiello, m, UCA

Additional titles: Baladas amarillas; Benedictus [UCA]. Poema [*Enciclopedia de la música argentina*].

Cabrera, Ana Schneider de, 1897–1970

1.62, Achalay, 1942, Rafael Jijena Sánchez, E3–C#5, Low, —, RA BA7442, UCA
1.63, Canción del regreso, 1940, Ana S. de Cabrera, B3–D5, Med, —, RA BA7443, UCA

1.64, *Danzas y canciones argentinas (1st Album): 6 Cantos*
1.64a, La campera (Estilo zamba), 1938, Francisco A. Riu, C#3–D5, Med, —, RA BA6078, UCA
1.64b, La belenista (Chacarera catamar-

queña), 1938, Segundo Barrios, C4–C5, Med, —, RA BA6078, UCA

1.64c, Adiós te digo (Vidala indígena), 1938, —, A3–C5, Med, Reminiscencia de la infancia, RA BA6078, UCA

1.64d, La moza que quiere un viejo (Tonada), 1938, Song taken from some folk singers in Famaillá, D#4–B4, Med, —, RA BA6078, UCA

1.64e, Por vos penando (Zamba), 1938, Hipólito Lobo, C#4–B4, Med, —, RA BA6078, UCA

1.64f, El palito (Danza), 1938, Hipolito Lobo, A4–F#5, High, —, RA BA6078, UCA

1.65, *Danzas y canciones argentinas (2nd Album): 5 Cantos*

1.65a, Ñuritay (Vidala), 1940, Ana S. de Cabrera, G3–D5, Med, —, RA BA7365, UCA

1.65b, Pa que me estás mirando (Gato al modo popular), 1940, Ricardo Velasco, B2–D4, Med, Baritone, RA BA7365, UCA

1.65c, Que si, que no (Bailecito al modo popular), 1940, Rafael Jijena Sánchez, B♭3–C5, Med, —, RA BA7365, UCA

1.65d, La chacarerita doble (Danza), 1940, Diego Novillo Quiroga, C#4–B4, Med, —, RA BA7365, UCA

1.65e, Mi corazón se ha perdido (Aire cuyano), 1940, Letrilla popular, B3–D5, Med, —, RA BA7365, UCA

1.66, Vida, vidita (Canción norteña), 1945, Rafael Jijena Sánchez, B♭3–B♭4, Med, —, CNC, CNMA

Additional titles: De mi pago; El casorio de la Juanita; No escondás [INM]. *Canciones y danzas argentinas; Cantos nativos y danzas del norte argentino;* Cuyanita linda; De ida y vuelta; El Pala Pala; Mozo jinetazo ahijuna; Viva vidita [*Diccionario de la música española e hispanoamericana*].

Calcagno, Elsa, 1910–1978

1.67, Casita de mis recuerdos (Lied para canto y piano), 1938, Elena Serry de Gonzales Bonorino, D4–G5, Med-high, Corina Henriquez de Lima, GRic, +

1.68, Chingolo ante las espumas, —, Arturo Vázquez, B3–E5, Med, —, CNC, CNMA

1.69, Elogio del poncho (Canción pampeana), 1967, Julia Bustos, C4–E5, Med, —, m, UCA

1.70, La parra quebrada, 1946, Juan Bautista Grosso, C4–F5, Med, Angelina Mayol, RA BA9637, +

1.71, Lo que yo quiero (Lied para canto y piano), 1949, Pedro B. Palacios, C4–A♭5, Med-high, Julia Usoz, Vieri Fidanzini, ESar, +

1.72, ¡Madrecita! (Canción de cuna infantil), 1959, Arturo Capdevila, D#4–C#5, Med, María Celia Pechieu, CLSRL, +

1.73, Madre vidalitay, 1953, Fernán Silva Valdés, C4–A4, High, —, RA, UCA

1.74, Pescadores, —, Arturo Vázquez, B3–E5, Med, —, —, CNMA

1.75, Poema del sembrador (Poem of the Sower), 1939, Constancio C. Vigil, A3–E5, Med, Constancio C. Vigil, Félix Real Torralba; translation into Spanish by Sra. de Barcia, GRic, +

1.76, Sueños negros, —, —, C4–A♭4, Med-high, Argentina Esther Duce, Yascha Galperia, CLSRL, +

1.77, *Tres poemas galegos*

1.77a, I. Amores cativos, 1963, Rosalía de Castro, C4–F5, Med-high, Text in Galician, m, UCA

1.77b, II. Sin niño, 1963, Rosalía de Castro, D4–F5, Med-high, Text in Galician, m, UCA

1.77c, III. Tionti mañan eu, 1963, Rosalía de Castro, E♭4–G♭5, Med-high, Text in Galician, m, UCA

1.78, Tu secreto (Lied en ritmo de tango estilizado), 1940, Evaristo Carriego, B3–E♭5, Med-high, —, Garrot, Tasso y Vita, UCA

Additional titles: Cariñito; Jugando con las vocales; La primavera; Numeritos [UCA]. Blancanieves; Canción de America; La canción del bosque; La casa de Sarmiento

[+]. A dos claveles; Alegrías del verano; Angelus; Angustia mística; Bajo el jazmín del país; Búsqueda; Cajita de música; Cantar para un atardecer en la sierra; Canto a Buenos Aires; Cantos de amor; Cuando de noche regreso; Despertar; *Dos cantos de Navidad*; Eclipse; El gato de mis pagos; El niño de Yapeyú; El niño maravillas y los niños; Flor del aire; Gaviota pico cruel; Gloria; La herida; La ovejita; La torta de cumpleaños; Las manitas del niñito; Las tres lágrimas; Me parece estar soñando; Muñequita preciosa; Noche de lluvia; Quiero para ti; Tu nombre; Umbrales del mar [SADAIC]. A mi patria; Dentro de tus llagas escóndeme; El pícaro pollito; La ronda; Mbucuruyá; Ronda para mi maestra; Ronda primaveral; *Seis cantos de amor; Tres poemas dramáticos* [*Diccionario de la música española e hispanoamericana*].

Campmany, Montserrat, 1901–1995

1.79, Azul, 1954, Agustín Dentone, F♯4–A♯5, High, Zulema Rosés Lacoigne, RA BA11051, TC

1.80, Bailecito Navideño, —, Agustín Dentone, C4–A5, High, —, m, IU

1.81, Canto de amor, 1944, Agustín Dentone, F4–F♯5, High, Conchita Badía, RA BA11044, UCA

1.82, Carita de cielo (Serenata serrana), 1971, Agustín Dentone, F4–E♭5, Med-high, French translation by Andrée Vibert, m, IU

1.83, Coplas a la acequia con luna, 1928, Alfredo R. Bufano, D4–A5, High, —, m, IU

1.84, Cumbre, 1974, Agustín Dentone, F4–A5, High, —, m, IU

1.85, El barrilete (Le cerf-volant), —, Jeronimo Zanné, D4–D5, Med, Elsa Herzfeld; French translation by Tristan Klingsor, —, AW

1.86, El pájaro y el gato (L'oiseau et le chat), —, Jeronimo Zanné, C♯4–C♯5, Med, Lola Vidal de Costantini; French translation by Tristan Klingsor, —, AW

1.87, Filant, —, J. Martí y Folguera, E♭4–A5, High, Elisa Ramoneda Juliá; text in French, SNM 29, CNMA

1.88, Juierio, 1932, Rafael Jijena Sánchez, E♭4–A♭5, Med-high, —, CNC, CNMA

1.89, L'absence, 1921, Théophile Gautier, E♭4–G♭5, High, Text in French, m, AW

1.90, Las calesitas (Les chevaux de bois), —, Jeronimo Zanné, C4–D5, Med, Avlina Ibáñez; French translation by Tristan Klingsor, —, AW

1.91, Madrigal, —, Gutierre de Cetina, F4–A5, High, —, m, IU

1.92, Momento (Lied), —, Margarita Abella Caprile, E4–F5, High, Margarita Abella Caprile, —, UCA

1.93, Petit rondell, —, Gerori Zanné, F♯4–F5, High, Paguita Ll. de Masllorens; text in Catalan, SNM 28, UCA

1.94, *Poema otoñal*

1.94a, Parte I., 1922, Rubén Darío, C♯4–F♯5, Med-high, —, CLSRL, IU

1.94g, Parte VII., 1922, Rubén Darío, E4–G♯5, Med-high, —, CLSRL, IU

1.94h, Parte VIII., 1922, Rubén Darío, B3–D♭5, Med, —, CLSRL, IU

1.95, Primaveral, 1921, Rubén Darío, C♯4–G5, Med-high, —, m, AW

1.96, Tonada, —, Alfredo R. Bufano, E4–G5, High, Enriqueta Basavilbaso de Catelín, SNM, IU

1.97, Un asra, —, Heinrich Heine, D♯4–F♯5, High, —, SNM 27, UCA

Additional titles: El pollito piu; Firulete [ANA]. 25 de Mayo; La casita de Tucumán [TC]. Canto amargo; El gorrión más chiquitito; El reloj de circo; En el verde prado; Los puñalitos; Ronda de abejas; Tres canciones escolares [*Diccionario de la música española e hispanoamericana*].

Camps, Pompeyo, 1924–1999

1.98, *Cuatro sonetos de amor, op. 97*

1.98a, 1. Que vos me permitáis, —, Francisco de Quevedo Villegas, E4–G5, Med-high,

String orchestra accompaniment available, m, IU

1.98b, 2. Dióme el cielo dolor, —, Francisco de Quevedo Villegas, D♯4–A5, Med-high, String orchestra accompaniment available, m, IU

1.98c, 3. Colora abril el campo, —, Francisco de Quevedo Villegas, C♯4–G5, Med-high, String orchestra accompaniment available, m, IU

1.98d, 4. Cerrar podrá mis ojos, —, Francisco de Quevedo Villegas, D♯4–A♭5, Med-high, String orchestra accompaniment available, m, IU

1.99, *De puerta en puerta, op. 50*

1.99a, 1. De puerta en puerta, 1962, Javier Villafañe, E♭4–E♭5, Med, Mary, mi mujer, primera inteprete de estas canciones, m, UCA

1.99b, 2. La mano del hombre, 1962, Javier Villafañe, B♭3–E5, Med, Mary, mi mujer, primera inteprete de estas canciones, m, UCA

1.99c, 3. Caras, 1962, Javier Villafañe, B3–E5, Med, Mary, mi mujer, primera inteprete de estas canciones, m, UCA

1.99d, 4. Génesis, 1962, Javier Villafañe, C♭4–C♯5, Med, Mary, mi mujer, primera inteprete de estas canciones, m, UCA

1.99e, 5. El sueño, 1962, Javier Villafañe, A3–D5, Med, Mary, mi mujer, primera inteprete de estas canciones, m, UCA

1.100, *La saca, op. 56*

1.100a, 1. La muerte sube que sube, 1968, Luis Alberto Quesada, A3–F5, Med, —, EAM 146, UCA

1.100b, 2. De pronto, hay un dolor de cerrajos, 1968, Luis Alberto Quesada, C4–G♭5, Med-high, —, EAM 146, UCA

1.100c, 3. La muerte ya no es un toro, 1968, Luis Alberto Quesada, B♭3–G5, Med-high, —, EAM 146, UCA

Additional titles: Seis romances españoles; Tres poemas de Rafael Alberti [CMA]. Blues para una muchacha muerta for voice and four instruments; Canción; Canción del zagal; Canción de Nochebuena; Canciones clásicas españolas; Canciones populares; Cantares de la cordillera; Corazón de piedra; Desde que tengo tu amor; ¡Dios no ha de devolvértela porque llores!; Dirindín, dirindín; El huésped; El recuerdo; En un país extraño; La vida; Niña que pasa cantando; Niña que vas a la fuente; Será todo un canto; Sueño; *Tres canciones* for mezzo soprano, viola, and piano; Trovadorescas castellanas y catalanas; Villaguay [*Diccionario de la música española e hispanoamericana*]. *Sinfonía para un poeta* for baritone and orchestra [*Enciclopedia de la música argentina*].

Carrique, Ana, 1886–1979

1.101, Abrojo Pampa (Milonga), 1956, Agustín Dentone, B3–B4, Med, —, —, UCA, —

1.102, Borriquito Blanco (Canción de Navidad), 1949, Juan Bautista Grosso, C4–F5, Med-high, —, CLSRL, TC, —

1.103, Canción marinera, 1949, Alfredo R. Bufano, C4–E♭5, Med-high, Renée Tarce de Teucini, m, IU, —

1.104, Cantarcillo (de Canciones Gallegas), 1950, Alfredo R. Bufano, C4–G5, Med-high, —, m, IU, —

1.105, Capillita de Renca, —, Francisco Luis Bernárdez, E♭4–E♭5, Med-high, —, m, IU, —

1.106, Copla, 1930, Rafael Jijena Sánchez, D4–F5, Med, —, m, ZL, —

1.107, *Coplas puntanas*

1.107a, En San Luis no te enamores . . . , 1936, Alfredo R. Bufano, D4–E♭5, Med, —, m, IU, —

1.107b, A Patay huele la luna, 1936, Alfredo R. Bufano, F4–F5, Med-high, —, m, IU, —

1.107c, En vano me has de buscar, 1936, Alfredo R. Bufano, F♯4–C♯5, Med-high, —, m, IU, —

1.107d, Pajarito de la nieve, 1936, Alfredo R. Bufano, F4–E5, Med-high, —, m, IU, —

1.108, El charquito, —, Francisco Luis Bernárdez, F♯4–F♯5, High, —, m, IU, —

1.109, El payador, 1959, Agustín Dentone, B3–E5, Med-high, —, RA BA11824, ZL, —

1.110, Escondido (Estilización), 1939, Isabel Cascallares Gutiérrez, C♯4–F♯5, Med-high, —, ACA, ZL, —

1.111, Hijo'el pais (a la manera popular), 1956, Agustín Dentone, A4–D♭5, Med, —, CLSRL, UCA, —

1.112, Homenaje a Julián Aguirre, 1954, Mary Rega Molina, D4–E5, Med-high, —, m, IU, —

1.113, Idilio, 1930, Rafael Jijena Sánchez, D4–F5, Med-high, —, m, ZL, —

1.114, Miel y canela, 1956, Andrée Vibert, C4–D5, Med, French translation by Andrée Vibert, —, UCA, —

1.115, Pasto puna (Milonga), 1956, Agustín Dentone, B♭3–D5, Med, —, —, UCA, —

1.116, Presentimiento, —, Leopoldo Lugones, F♯4–G♭5, High, —, —, CLP, —

1.117, Selva apacible (Tonada), 1942, Juan de Navas, C♯4–E♭5, Med-high, —, —, IU, Published in *Joya de canciones españolas*

Additional titles: Cardón; Dos rondas escolares; Raíz de raza; Seis cantos y una profecía [UCA]. Ronda de noche buena [TC]. Homenaje a Julián Aguirre [ZL]. A la entrada de tu casa; A una tejedora; Baguala; Cajas carnavalescas; Caminito de la sierra; Canción; Canción de cuna; Canción del molinero; Canción serrana; Canta la lluvia; Cariñito volador; Carne y uña; Casamiento; Cerrazón; Coplas de la luna de madrugada; Coplas puntanas (2nd series); Dije al pájaro blanco; El ceibo se enamoró; El niño y la luna; El triunfo; En lo sombrío del monte; Himno al libro; La noche; Letras para cantar; Marcha de los gimnastas; Mariposa blanca; Mi gato; Nochebuena; Pájaros; Piquillín; Porque no se duerme; Porque sí; Puñadito de grajea; Siempre detrás de tus rejas; Son de Huankara; Tonada; Tu nombre; Vidala rústica; Vidita; Yaraví [*Diccionario de la música española e hispanoamericana*].

Casella, Enrique Mario, 1891–1948

1.118, Alma mía (Estilo), —, —, B♭3–G5, High, From "Guajiras" (Creación de la gentil artista Inés Berutti del Teatro de la Ópera), De Francisco de Paula, LBV

1.119, Balada triste y equívoca de primavera, 1920, J. R. Gimenez, E4–F♯5, Med-high, —, m, LBV

1.120, Caminito de la pena, 1939, Rubén F. de Olivera, D4–G♯5, Med-high, —, m, LBV

1.121, Canción de cuna, 1919, R. G. Gauna, C♭4–G5, Med-high, —, m, LBV

1.122, *Cuatro canciones*

1.122a, Por el caminito, 1943, J. Torres Botet, D4–A5, High, —, m, LBV

1.122b, La mañana está de fiesta, 1943, J. Torres Botet, B4–A5, High, —, m, LBV

1.122c, Como el bosque . . . , 1943, J. Torres Botet, C4–A5, High, —, m, LBV

1.122d, Nada alumbra, 1943, J. Torres Botet, C♯4–F♯5, High, —, m, LBV

1.123, *Cuatro coplas*

1.123a, Saca ejemplo del río, 1944, Alfredo R. Bufano, D4–G5, High, —, m, LBV

1.123b, Cuando en silencio me veas, 1944, Alfredo R. Bufano, F4–B♭5, High, —, m, LBV

1.123c, Cuando salgo con mi niño, 1944, Alfredo R. Bufano, E♭4–G♯5, High, —, m, LBV

1.123d, Mientras sean nuestras almas dulce hoguera, 1944, Alfredo R. Bufano, D4–F♯5, Med-high, —, m, LBV

1.124, Elle est si jolie, —, C. Hiolivichc, C4–F5, Med-high, Text in French, David Poggi, LBV

1.125, ¿Eres tú?, 1918, Rabindranath Tagore, C4–F5, —, Meda Quica, m, LBV

1.126, ¿Has venido a mi, llena de pena?, 1923, Rabindranath Tagore, A3–F♯5, Med-high, Also arranged for string quartet and voice, m, LBV

1.127, Ho sognato, 1915, L. Stechetti, A♭3–A♭5, Med-high, Angelita Piccinini; text in Italian, m, LBV

1.128, Huella, 1925, Gustavo Caravallo, D4–A5, High, —, m, LBV

1.129, Juierio, 1932, Rafael Jijena Sánchez, E♭4–A♭5, High, —, SNM, UCA

1.130, Madrigal amable, 1918, Belisario Roldán, E4–F♯5, Med-high, A Quica, m, LBV

1.131, Mor, 1931, Rafael Jijena Sánchez, F4–A5, High, —, m, LBV

1.132, Olvido, —, M. A. Daneri, C4–A5, High, —, m, LBV

1.133, Palomitay vidala, 1932, Rafael Jijena Sánchez, E♭4–F5, High, —, m, LBV

1.134, Romanza, 1921, L. Stechetti, E♭4–B♭4, High, Text in Italian, m, LBV

1.135, Si me está negado el amor, 1923, Rabindranath Tagore, B♭3–E5, Med-high, Also arranged for string quartet and voice, m, LBV

1.136, Trigueña mía, —, Enrique Mario Casella, D4–F5, Med-high, —, m, SADAIC

1.137, Vidalita Tucumana, 1927, María T. C. de Rivas Jordán, D♭4–F5, Med-high, —, m, LBV

1.138, Vos yeux ont des langueurs, 1916, A. Perrey, C♯4–G♭5, Med-high, Pour l'aimée; text in French, m, LBV

Additional titles: Achalay; Arrullo; *A Santa Teresita del Niño Jesús* for voice, violin, organ, and choir; *Brumas* for voice and chamber orchestra; Caminito de flores; Canción de la Vendimia; Canción serrana; Canta el pájaro en la rama; Cantares tucumanos; Cantos incaicos; Cuatro canciones calchaquíes; El girasol; El maíz; Esclava; Io tengo un ranchito; La nieve; Lejos de mi amor; Los árboles; No te vayas tú, amor mío; *Seis canciones* for voice and string quartet; Troncos y ramas; Vidala [LBV].

Castro, José María, 1892–1964

1.139, Balada del amor que no se dijo, 1949, Luis Cané, F4–G5, High, Juanita Ruth, EAM 50, UCA

1.140, *Cuatro canciones escolares*

1.140a, I. Otoño, 1942, José Mazzanti, C4–C5, Med, —, —, UCA

1.140b, II. Invierno, 1942, José Mazzanti, C4–C5, Med, —, —, UCA

1.140c, III. Primavera, 1942, José Mazzanti, D4–D5, Med, —, —, UCA

1.140d, IV. Verano, 1942, José Mazzanti, E♭4–C5, Med, —, —, UCA

1.141, El sueño (Il sogno), 1940, Rafael Alberto Arrieta, E4–D5, Med-high, Translated into Italian by Honorio Siccardi, RA BA7369, UCA

1.142, La luna se llama Lola, 1933, Francisco Vighi, C4–D5, Med, —, —, CNMA

1.143, Romance de morenita, 1942, Luis Cané, A4–F5, Med-high, —, Gordon 8631, UCA

1.144, Romances de la niña negra, 1949, Luis Cané, C♭4–G5, Med-high, —, EAM 52, UCA

1.145, *Tres líricas para canto y piano*

1.145a, I., 1939, Garcilaso de la Vega, G4–F♯5, High, Carlos Rodriguez, —, UCA

1.145b, II., 1939, Garcilaso de la Vega, E4–E5, Med-high, Luisita Ruth, —, UCA

1.145c, III., 1939, Garcilaso de la Vega, D4–E5, Med-high, Antonieta Silveira de Lednharson, —, UCA

1.146, Vente con nosotros, 1931, Amado Nervo, F4–E♭5, Med-high, —, —, UCA

1.147, Yo digo si y es que si, 1942, Luis Cané, D4–F5, Med-high, —, Gordon 8697, UCA

Additional titles: Canción de las alumnas [UCA]. *Cinco líricas* for tenor and chamber orchestra [CNMA]. Balada matinal; Canción sin sentido; Colores; Después del dulce lamantar de dos pastores; *Dos rimas*; El manatial; Lied; Romances y coplas; Solidaridad; *Tres villancicos para Gabriela en Nueva York* [*Diccionario de la música española e hispanoamericana*]. Canción de cuna; *Dos canciones*; Duérmete yá; El fin; El vado; La canción perdida; Lírica; Ojos claros, serenos; Rima; Rima de Bécquer; Serranilla; *Tres poemas* [CNC].

Castro, Juan José, 1895–1968

1.148, Canción de los caballitos blancos, 1949, —, E4–G5, Med-high, —, —, UCA

1.149, Cantares de amor, 1951, Juyas Bolseyro, G4–G5, High, Spanish translation by L. Bernárdez, —, UCA

1.150, Dichosa historia del amor pensado, 1949, —, E4–G♯5, Med-high, Catalan text, —, UCA

1.151, *Dos sonetos del toro*
1.151a, I. El toro sabe, 1946, Miguel Hernández, B♭2–E♭4, Med, —, m, UCA
1.151b, II. Como el toro..., 1946, Miguel Hernández, B2–D♭4, Med, —, m, UCA

1.152, El pino que fue monje, —, Vicente Barbieri, C4–G5, Med-high, —, —, UCA

1.153, El viento, 1916, M. Machado, F♯4–F♯5, Med-high, A mis hermanos Rodolfo y Luis, Correo Musical, UCA

1.154, Epitafio de una rosa, 1945, Silvina Ocampo, E♭4–G♭5, Med-high, —, m, UCA

1.155, Es verdad..., —, Federico García Lorca, E♭4–A♭4, High, —, m, UCA

1.156, La casada infiel, 1946, Federico García Lorca, E4–A♭5, Med-high, —, RA BA9338, UCA

1.157, Por las ramas del laurel, 1949, Federico García Lorca, D♭4–G♭5, Med-high, —, m, UCA

1.158, ¡Qué hermosa te dou dios!, —, Rosalía de Castro, A4–G5, High, Text in Catalan, m, UCA

1.159, Romance de la Luna, Luna, —, Federico García Lorca, D♭4–A5, High, —, m, UCA

1.160, Romance de la pena negra, 1985, Federico García Lorca, A♭3–E5, Med, —, EAC 11, UCA

1.161, *Tres canciones cordobesas*
1.161a, El arroyo, —, Francisco Luis Bernárdez, D♭4–F5, Med-high, —, CNC, CNMA

1.162, *Tres cantos negros*
1.162a, La guitarra de los negros, 1939, —, B♭3–G5, Med-high, —, m, UCA
1.162b, Canción de cuna para dormir a un negrito, 1939, —, E♭4–G♯5, Med-high, —, m, UCA
1.162c, Cachumba, caracatachún, 1939, —, C4–G5, Med-high, —, m, UCA

1.163, Verde que te quiero verde, 1936, Federico García Lorca, C4–F♯5, Med-high, —, m, UCA

Additional titles: Balada del poeta a caballo; Canción de mi llegada; *Dos canciones de Rilke; Dos canciones de Rosalía de Castro; Dos canciones de Vicente Barbieri; Dos líricas de Heine;* Mantan-tiru-liru-la; *Seis canciones de García Lorca; Seis poemas de Rabindranat Tagore; Tres canciones cordobesas* [*Diccionario de la música española e hispanoamericana*]. Ala de plata; Arbolé Arbolé; Chanson; Eau qui se presse; Eu levo una pena; Mi ciudad [CNC].

Cimaglia Espinosa, Lía, 1906–1998

1.164, Balada, —, Susana Calampelli, D4–F♯5, Med-high, Myrta Garbarini, m, IU

1.165, Botoncito (Canción de cuna), 1945, Gabriela Mistral, G4–F♯5, High, A mi madre, CLSRL, CNMA

1.166, Cantar, —, Juan O. Ponferrada, C♯4–F♯5, Med-high, Emila Zulfertz, m, IU

1.167, Copla, —, Juan O. Ponferrada, C♯4–F♯5, Med-high, Amalia Bazán, m, IU

1.168, Copla de la soledad, —, Juan O. Ponferrada, G4–G5, High, —, m, IU

1.169, La profecía, —, Jorge Obligado, F4–G♭5, Med-high, —, m, IU

1.170, Nocturno, 1979, Juan O. Ponferrada, G4–G5, High, Martha Millan, m, CMA

1.171, *Tres canciones argentinas*
1.171a, Vidita, —, Miguel A. Camino, D4–E5, Med, Julieta Telles de Menezes, CLSRL, UCA

1.171b, La razón de mi cariño, —, Fermín Estrella Gutiérrez, B3–F5, Med-high, Juan Carlos Pini, CLSRL, UCA

1.171c, La canción del chingolo, —, F. Silva Valdés, E4–G5, Med-high, Enriqueta Basavilbaso de Catelin, CLSRL, UCA

1.172, Vidala, —, Rafael Jijena Sánchez, E♭4–F5, Med-high, Noemi Souza, m, IU

Additional titles: Ronda de la niña rubia [UCA]. Dame la mano; Señora santana [IU]. Canciones de cuna y ronda; Chacarera; Changuito; En donde tejemos la ronda; La palma [INM]. Sueño; Sueño del atardecer [*Diccionario de la música española e hispanoamericana*].

De Rogatis, Pascual, 1880–1980

1.173, Álamo serrano, 1942, M. Lopez Palmero, C♯4–A5, Med-high, —, RA BA9160, INM

1.174, A ti única, 1918, Leopoldo Lugones, E♭4–G♭5, Med-high, Elena Rakowska de Serafín, SNM 6, UCA

1.175, *Cinco canciones argentinas*

1.175a, I. Vidala, 1930, Rafael de Diego, C♯4–F♯5, Med-high, Antonieta Silveyra de Lenhardsson, RA BA6093, UCA

1.175b, II. Canción de cuna, 1930, Gabino Coria Peñaloza, D♭4–F5, Med, Carlos Rodriguez, RA BA6093, UCA

1.175c, III. Chacarera, 1930, Gabino Coria Peñaloza, E4–F♯5, Med-high, Ninon Vallín, RA BA6093, UCA

1.175d, IV. La sombra (Yaraví), 1930, Miguel A. Camino, C4–G5, Med-high, Didah, RA BA6093, UCA

1.175e, V. Gato, 1930, Gabino Coria Peñaloza, D4–F5, Med-high, Armand Crabée, RA BA6093, UCA

1.176, Coplas, 1932, Miguel A. Camino, F4–F5, Med-high, —, SNM, INM

1.177, Fantasía (Romanza), 1904, Cimino, E4–G5, High, Julián Aguirre; text in Italian, SNM, CLP

1.178, Güeya, 1954, Agustín Dentone, D4–F♯5, Med-high, —, RA BA11064, UCA

1.179, Miel, 1956, Agustín Dentone, D4–E5, Med-high, —, RA BA11384, UCA

1.180, Odas de safo, op. 14, no. 2, 1904, María Magdalena de Ezcurra, E4–G5, High, —, The entire opus in manuscript form appears in the INM catalog, SADAIC

Additional titles: Concierto de las campanas; La campiña dormida; Marina; Miel; Nocturno, *Tres canciones escolares* [INM]. Nevermore; Canción americana [*Diccionario de la música española e hispanoamericana*]. Tres poemas [*Enciclopedia de la música argentina*].

D'Espósito, Arnaldo, 1907–1945

1.181, Canción de la primavera (de la comedia infantil "Pedro, Pedrito y Pedrin"), —, Eugenia de Oro, C4–F5, Med-high, —, RA BA9170, LBV

1.182, Canción del trovero Pedro Vidal (from ballet "Cuento de abril"), —, Arnaldo D'Esposito, D4–G5, Med-high, Héctor Iglesias Villoud, RA BA9137, CNMA

1.183, El gnomo silbado, —, Juan Bautista Grosso, B♭3–D♭5, Med, Martíal Sigher, RA BA8834, ZL

1.184, *Tres piezas*

1.184a, Copla, 1943, Héctor Iglesias Villoud, D4–G5, Med-high, Brígida Frías de López Buchardo, RA BA8784, UCA

1.184b, Lloraba la niña, 1943, Tristán Fernández, B3–G5, Med-high, Roberto Locatelli, RA BA8784, UCA

1.184c, El arroyuelo, 1943, Ernesto Marín, D4–G♭5, Med-high, Clara Oyuela, RA BA8784, UCA

Additional titles: Ave María (from the opera Lin Calel) [ZL]. Campanita [*Diccionario de la música española e hispanoamericana*]. Tres canciones infantiles [CNC].

Drangosch, Ernesto, 1882–1925

1.185, *Cuatro melodías, op. 26*
1.185a, I. Auf eine Tänzerin, 1920, Ludwig Uhland, E♭4–A♭5, High, —, m, LBV
1.185b, II. Contemplación, 1920, Friedrich Holderlin, D♯4–G♯5, Med-high, —, m, LBV
1.185c, III. En paz, 1920, Amado Nervo, D♯4–B♭5, High, —, CNC, UCA
1.185d, IV. Amemos, 1920, Amado Nervo, C♯4–F♯5, Med, —, CNC, UCA

1.186, *Dos poesías de Amado Nervo, op. 28*
1.186a, Ofertorio: Deus dedit, deus abstulit, —, Amado Nervo, C4–G♯5, High, Orchestral accompaniment available, m, LBV
1.186b, Un signo, —, Amado Nervo, F♯4–A5, High, Orchestral accompaniment available, m, LBV

1.187, *Dos melodías, op. 31*
1.187a, En la ribera, —, Rafael Alberto Arrieta, E♭4–G♯5, High, —, m, LBV
1.187b, Lied, —, Rafael Alberto Arrieta, F♯4–A♭5, High, —, m, LBV

1.188, *Drei Lieder—, Trois mélodies, op. 19*
1.188a, Si les étoiles pouvaient te dire, 1915, Enriqueta Sales, D4–B♭5, High, Enriqueta Basavilbaso de Catelin, Otto Beines, LBV
1.188b, Zwei Augen, 1915, Max Bewer, C4–G5, Med-high, —, Otto Beines, CNMA
1.188c, Ein geistlich' Abendlied, 1915, Gottfried Kinkel, D4–G5, High, —, Otto Beines, LBV

1.189, Plegaria, op. 24, 1916, Blanca Piñero, E♯4–A5, High, Tulia Piñero, Otto Beines, UCA

1.190, *Sechs Lieder, op. 4*
1.190a, Rechtfertigung, 1906, Ludwig Uhland, C♯4–G5, Med-high, Delia M. de Iturralde, Stahl/Schirmer, LBV
1.190b, In der Ferne, 1906, Ludwig Uhland, C♯4–G♯5, Med-high, Delia M. de Iturralde, Stahl/Schirmer, LBV
1.190c, Das Ständchen, 1906, Ludwig Uhland, C4–A♭5, Med-high, Delia M. de Iturralde, Stahl/Schirmer, LBV
1.190d, Ich wollte bei dir weilen, 1906, Ludwig Uhland, D4–F♯5, Med-high, Delia M. de Iturralde, Stahl/Schirmer, LBV
1.190e, Schäfers Sonntagslied, 1906, Heinrich Heine, C4–G5, Med-high, Delia M. de Iturralde, Stahl/Schirmer, LBV
1.190f, Lauf der Welt, 1906, Ludwig Uhland, C4–A5, High, Delia M. de Iturralde, Stahl/Schirmer, LBV

1.191, *Vier Lieder, op. 9*
1.191a, Entschluss, 1906, Ludwig Uhland, D♯4–G♯5, Med-high, Hugo Drangosch, R/E, LBV
1.191b, Abendgang, 1906, Mathilde Gräfin Sterbenburg, D4–A5, Med-high, Hugo Drangosch, R/E, LBV
1.191c, Ein Lied . . . , so schön, 1906, Friedrich Albert Meyer, C4–A♭5, Med-high, Hugo Drangosch, R/E, LBV
1.191d, Frühlingsfeier, 1906, August Heinrich Hoffmann von Failersleben, D♯4–A5, High, Hugo Drangosch, R/E, LBV

Additional titles: Canción de la Marina; El carnaval; Yo tuve un cariño (Tango) [LBV].

Dublanc, Emilio, 1911–1990

1.192, A todas las albas, —, Concha Méndez Cuesta, E♭4–F5, Med-high, —, m, IU
1.193, El ama y la chinita, —, Rafael Jijena Sánchez, F4–F5, High, Athos Palma, —, CNMA
1.194, El caballo de mar, —, José G. Huertas, D4–G5, Med-high, —, m, IU
1.195, El Chasque (Milonga), —, Agustín Dentone, D4–F5, Med-high, —, m, TC
1.196, Flores de almendro, —, Iverna Codina de Giannoni, D♭4–F♯5, Med-high, —, m, CLP
1.197, Milagro, 1954, Agustín Dentone, C4–E5, Med-high, Raquel Zipris, RA BA11016, UCA
1.198, Pajarillo del querer, 1959, Guislaine

Lahore, C4–E♭5, Med-high, Esperanza Lothringer, CLSRL, CNMA

1.199, Tarde en el río, —, Iverna Codina de Giannoni, D4–F5, Med-high, —, m, IU

1.200, *Tres canciones de soledad*

1.200a, Por eso, 1950, Hortensia Margarita Raffo, C♯4–E5, Med-high, Orchestration available [SADAIC], CLSRL, UCA

1.200b, Mi sueño, 1950, Hortensia Margarita Raffo, E4–E♭5, Med-high, Orchestration available [SADAIC], CLSRL, UCA

1.200c, ¿Por qué?, 1950, Hortensia Margarita Raffo, F♯4–D♯5, Med-high, Orchestration available [SADAIC], CLSRL, UCA

1.201, Trigo limpio, 1957, Agustín Dentone, E4–F5, Med, —, RA BA11478, UCA

Additional titles: Flor del cielo; Si no te canto [UCA]. El río es el mismo; Extraño; Pluma; Yaraví [CNMA]. Caprice [SADAIC]. *Cuatro canciones argentinas; Cuatro canciones, op. 16; Cuatro canciones, op. 51; Dos canciones de primavera;* Flor de Jarilla; *Ocho canciones; Seis canciones; Siete canciones; Tres canciones con texto en francés; Tres canciones, op. 7; Tres canciones, op. 23* [Diccionario de la música española e hispanoamericana].

Espoile, Raúl Hugo, 1889–1958

1.202, A una coqueta, —, Jacobo Peña, A♭3–G5, Med-high, María de Pini de Chrestia, —, CNMA, —

1.203, Ay, que el alma, —, León Benarós, D4–E5, Med, —, m, CLP, —

1.204, *Chacayaleras*

1.204a, Si quieres que yo te diga . . . , 1935, Miguel A. Camino, C4–F5, Med-high, Tito Schipa, RA BA6874, UCA, —

1.204b, Llankirái, 1935, Miguel A. Camino, C♯4–F♯5, Med-high, Ernani Braga, RA BA6874, UCA, —

1.204c, Chacayalera (Serranilla), 1935, Miguel A. Camino, D4–F♯5, Med-high, P. Humberto Allende, RA BA6874, UCA, —

1.204d, Yaraví, 1935, Miguel A. Camino, D4–F♯5, Med-high, Carlos López Buchardo, RA BA6874, UCA, —

1.204e, Huaynu, 1935, Miguel A. Camino, D4–G5, Med-high, Ricardo Rodriguez, RA BA6874, UCA, —

1.204f, La tabaquerita, 1935, Miguel A. Camino, F♯4–G5, High, Rafael Gonzales, RA BA6874, UCA, —

1.205, *Cinco canciones*

1.205a, I. Agua de fuente, 1935, Juan Manuel Jordán, B♭3–G♭5, High, —, Gaudiosi, SADAIC, —

1.205b, II. El benteveo, 1935, Juan Manuel Jordán, A4–G5, High, —, Gaudiosi, SADAIC, —

1.205c, III. El zorzal, 1935, Juan Manuel Jordán, D4–G5, Med-high, —, Gaudiosi, SADAIC, —

1.205d, IV. El abanico, 1935, Juan Manuel Jordán, C4–F5, Med-high, —, Gaudiosi, SADAIC, —

1.205e, V. La plegaria, 1935, Juan Manuel Jordán, C4–A♭5, Med-high, —, Gaudiosi, SADAIC, —

1.206, *Collares de perlas*

1.206a, I. Perlas blancas, —, Santiago M. Lugones, D4–G5, Med-high, —, RA BA6975, IU, —

1.206b, II. Perlas negras, —, Santiago M. Lugones, B3–F♯5, Med, —, RA BA6975, IU, —

1.207, El palito (Aire nacional), —, —, B3–C♯5, Med, Tomada a Pedro Lugones Carol; optional duet, RA BA6879, UCA, —

1.208, Florcita de aire, —, Miguel A. Camino, F4–G5, High, Monseñor Dioniso R. Napal, Gaudiosi, UCA, —

1.209, Huainito, 1924, Hilario Sáenz, C♯4–D5, Med, A la memoria de mi madre, RA, UCA, —

1.210, J'ai cueilli cette fleur . . . , —, Victor Hugo, C4–G5, Med-high, Madame Henriette Basavilbaso de Catelin; text in French, —, CNMA, —

1.211, La dernière feuille, —, Théophile

Gautier, C♯4–E5, Med, Text in French, SNM 32, CNMA, —

1.212, Les roses de saadi, —, Marceline Desbordes-Valmore, E4–E5, Med-high, Text in French, SNM 31, CNMA, —

1.213, Les séparés (Romance), —, Marceline Desbordes-Valmore, E4–G♯5, Med-high, Text in French, SNM 34, CNMA, —

1.214, Lied no. 14 de "Rimas y abrojos", —, Rubén Darío, C4–G5, Med-high, —, RA BA11542, CNMA, —

1.215, Madrigal, —, Jacobo Peña, A3–F5, Med-high, —, SNM, ZL, —

1.216, Madrigal amargo, —, Belisario Roldán, E♭4–G♭5, Med-high, —, SNM 30, AW, —

1.217, No faltes, —, Jacobo Peña, D♯4–G♯4, Med-high, María Rosa, —, CNMA, —

1.218, Pasacalle, —, José Marín, C4–A5, Med-high, —, —, IU, Published in *Joya de canciones españolas*

1.219, Rondel violet, —, Gilda Arabéhéty de González, C4–F5, Med-high, Text in French, SNM 33, CNMA, —

1.220, Silenciosamente (Yaraví), —, Amado Nervo, C4–G5, Med-high, —, RA, CNMA, —

1.221, Tu pie (Madrigal), —, Santiago M. Lugones, B3–G♯5, Med-high, —, RA BA6974, UCA, —

1.222, Zorzal, —, Arturo Vazquez Cey, F4–A♭5, High, —, —, IU, —

Additional titles: Caballito criollo [UCA]. El secreto; Patria en el mar; Tu caballera [CNMA]. Laudes de Cristo Rey; Romanza de Esther (La Ciudad Roja) [IU]. Canción de Orfeo; Una rima y dos miniaturas [*Diccionario de la música española e hispanoamericana*]. Canción de la vendimia; Canción dórica de Elena (Frenos); Duerme vida mía; Parole e fatti; Romanza de Enrique for tenor (La Ciudad Roja); Rondel [RA].

Ficher, Jacobo, 1896–1978

1.223, *Cuatro baladas del paraná, op. 79*
1.223a, I. Balada de Don Amarillo, 1969, Rafael Alberti, E4–G5, Med-high, Mirtha Garbarini, —, UCA

1.223b, II. Te voy a llevar conmigo, 1969, Rafael Alberti, E♭4–G5, Med-high, Mirtha Garbarini, RA BA12839, UCA

1.223c, III. Balada que trajo un barco, 1969, Rafael Alberti, D♯4–F♯5, Med-high, Mirtha Garbarini, RA BA12839, UCA

1.223d, IV. Balada de los mosquitos, 1969, Rafael Alberti, E4–G♯5, High, Mirtha Garbarini, RA BA12839, UCA

1.224, *Ocho poemas, op. 33*

1.224d, IV. Alta está mi ventana sobre el mundo, 1935, César Tiempo, C♯4–A5, Med-high, Italian translation by Honorio Siccardi, EAM, +

1.225, *Siete canciones de Amado Villar, op. 45*

1.225a, I. Marimorena, 1941, Amado Villar, E♭4–G♭5, Med-high, Jean Bathori; Italian translation by Honorio Siccardi, EAM, +

1.225b, II. Dolores y Consuelo, 1941, Amado Villar, D4–F♯5, Med, Frederick Fuller; Italian translation by Honorio Siccardi, EAM, +

1.225c, III. Polvo, caldén, espinillo, 1941, Amado Villar, D4–G5, Med-high, Onelia Talenton de Fonseca; Italian translation by Honorio Siccardi, EAM, +

1.225d, IV. Me dice palabras tiernas, 1941, Amado Villar, E4–F5, Med-high, Janet Fraser; Italian translation by Honorio Siccardi, EAM, +

1.225e, V. Azúcar, malvones, menta..., 1941, Amado Villar, E4–G5, Med-high, Gabriela Moner; Italian translation by Honorio Siccardi, EAM, +

1.225f, VI. Déjame dormir, amor..., 1941, Amado Villar, D4–G5, Med-high, Carmen Benedit de Scavino; Italian translation by Honorio Siccardi, EAM, +

1.225g, VII. Canción de tu dedo meñique, 1941, Amado Villar, D4–G5, Med-high, Concepción Badia; Italian translation by Honorio Siccardi, EAM, +

Additional titles: Cinco poemas; Cinco sonetos de amor; Dos canciones de Longfellow;

Dos piezas; Ocho poemas; Seis canciones del Paraná for voice and orchestra; *Siete cantos de amor; Tres canciones; Tres décimas de Manuel Felipe Rugeles; Tres poemas; Tres sonetos; Tres sonetos para contralto* [INM]. *El organillero* for baritone and orchestra; *Five Sonnets* for voice and orchestra [MF].

Gaito, Constantino, 1878–1945

1.226, Flor de ceibo, 1944, Ismael Moya, D4–D5, Med, —, RA BA8886, UCA

1.227, Flower of Hope (Fior di speranza), 1918, Carlo d'Ormeville, B♭3–F5, Med-high, Text in English and Italian, Bryant, CNMA

1.228, Meteoros, —, Y. C. Servetti Reeves, E♭4–G5, Med-high, —, m, UCA

1.229, Rimas de Becquer, —, Gustavo Adolfo Bécquer, E♭4–F♯4, High, —, Ortelli, UCA

Additional titles: Cielito [UCA]. Ave María; Lamento de María; Mística; Ollantai (from "La sangre de las guitarras") [INM]. Lacrime amare; Pensiero dominante; Serenata; Vals fantástico; Vecchia canzona [*Diccionario de la música española e hispanoamericana*].

Gaos, Andrés, 1874–1979

1.230, ¡Ay! ¡Mi amor! (Canción), 1920–1925, Andrés Gaos, C4–F5, Med-high, —, Arista, CNMA

1.231, Canción de primavera (Romanza), 1920, Juan de Dios Peza, D4–G5, Med-high, Bernardo Yriberri, Gurina, AG

1.232, En mai, 1905–1909, Heinrich Heine, C♯4–G♯5, Med-high, —, Gurina, AG

1.233, Fleur mourante, 1896–1909, —, C♯4–F♯5, Med-high, Text in French, m, AG

1.234, Fleurs d'amour (Romance), 1905–1909, Andrés Gaos, C♯4–G5, Med-high, Carlos López Buchardo; Text in French, Gurina, AG

1.235, La rose, 1896–1909, Hans Christian Andersen, D4–G5, Med-high, H. C. Anderson, *Revista musical*, AG

1.236, La silenciosa, 1920–1925, Tomás Allende Iragorri, C♯4–G5, Med-high, —, m, AG

1.237, Rosa de abril (Romanza), 1959, Rosalía de Castro, C4–F5, Med-high, —, m, AG

1.238, Solitude . . . (Romance), 1896–1909, Andrés Gaos, C4–A♯5, Med-high, —, —, AG

1.239, Vidalita, 1920–1925, Andrés Gaos, D4–G5, Med-high, —, Arista, UCA

Additional titles: Au point du jour; Couplet; Paix suprême; Sérénade [*Diccionario de la música española e hispanoamericana*]. Canto del gallo; El dadivoso; Pastoral; Premier printemps [AG].

García Mansilla, Eduardo, 1871–1930

1.240, El mágico jardín, —, Eduardo García Mansilla, C4–A5, High, A mi hija Danila Breyer; excerpt from composer's opera *La Angelical Manuelita*, —, LBV

1.241, En Madrid la bella (Bolero), —, Eduardo García Mansilla, F4–B♭4, High, A mi hija Danila Breyer; excerpt from composer's opera *La Angelical Manuelita*, —, LBV

1.242, Saphirs, 1903, Daniel García Mansilla, B♭3–D5, Med, Général Baron de Stackelberg, Choudens, UCA

Additional titles: Arietta antica; Au cimetière; C'est l'extase langoureuse; Chrysanthème; Clair de lune; Hymne à Apollon; Il pleure dans mon cœur . . . ; J'ai peur d'un baiser; Le loup et l'agneau; Le rat de ville et le rat des champs; Muguet; Narcisse; Seulette; Silence, silence!; Sous la ramée; Tu ne veux pas aimer . . . [LBV]. Agnus Dei; Ancor sento cantar; Andréas; Angelus; Aumône royale; Avec un bouquet; Ave María; Chanson hindou; Chanson slave; Cinéraires; Dans la forêt de Brocéliande; Dédicace; Donc ce sera par un clair jour d'été; Elegía; En chasse au son des cors!; Étant cygne; Guitare;

Hymne; Je t'ai beaucoup aimée; Jeune homme au cœur de vierge; L'abeille; La blanche basilique; La lettre du soldat à sa mère; L'averse; Le Crétien rouge; Le feu divin; Légende russe; Le son du cor s'afflige vers les bois; Les Béatitudes; Les roses; Les tours; Lettre à Marie; L'herbe est bien douce; L'heure; L'hirondelle et le poisson rouge; Maggio; Nenufars; Non vi affacciate; O carillon; O carillon, gai carillo; O douce Infante!; Oh, ferme, ferme ta paupière; O triste, triste était mon âme...; Oublieuse; Parisienne; Quand les roses seront flétries...; Quel problème... quand on aime!; Réveil des fleurs; Ricordatevi; Sais-tu, la brune fille?; Salutation angélique; Sanctus; Sérénade argentine; Sérénade triste; Ses yeux gris; Spleen en 1200; Ton amour; Un clair matin; Veux-tu, ma rieuse amie? [*Diccionario de la música española e hispanoamericana*].

García Morillo, Roberto, 1911–2003

1.243, *Cinco canciones de la cantata "El Tamarit"*

1.243a, 1. Del amor maravilloso (Gacela), 1957, Federico García Lorca, C4–B♭5, High, —, RA, UCA

1.243b, 2. De la muchacha dorada (Casida), 1957, Federico García Lorca, D4–G♯5, Med-high, —, RA, UCA

1.243c, 3. De la rosa (Casida), 1957, Federico García Lorca, F4–E5, Med-high, —, RA, UCA

1.243d, 4. Del amor con cien años (Gacela), 1957, Federico García Lorca, D♭4–B♭5, High, —, RA, UCA

1.243e, 5. De los ramos (Casida), 1957, Federico García Lorca, G4–G5, Med-high, —, RA, UCA

1.244, *Villancicos, op. 42*

1.244a, 1. La vaca dorada, 1975, Juan Oscar Ponferrada, D4–B♭5, High, Brígida Frías de López Buchardo, RA, UCA

1.244b, 2. Hoy es Nochebuena, 1975, Juan Oscar Ponferrada, D♭4–A♭5, Med-high, Brígida Frías de López Buchardo, RA, UCA

1.244c, 3. Don pastores de Belén, 1975, Juan Oscar Ponferrada, E4–B5, Med-high, Brígida Frías de López Buchardo, RA, UCA

1.244d, 4. Glosa, 1975, Juan Oscar Ponferrada, D♭4–B♭5, High, Brígida Frías de López Buchardo, RA, UCA

Additional titles: Cuatro canciones de la "Cantata Marín"; Cuatro líricas; Romances del Amor y de la Muerte for baritone and chamber orchestra [UCA]. *Cantata de Navidad* for soprano and orchestra; Cuarta cantata (Cantata de los caballeros) for soprano and orchestra; *Cuatro líricas de Antonio Machado*; *Dos sátiras*; *El Tamarit* for soprano, baritone, and orchestra [*Diccionario de la música española e hispanoamericana*].

García Robson, Magdalena, 1916–

1.245, *Coplas de soledad*

1.245a, I. A mi puerta has de golpear, 1940, Traditional poetry, E♭4–E♭5, Med-high, Manuel de Falla; orchestration available for string quintet; timpani, oboe, bassoon, and celeste, CNC, CNMA

1.245b, II. Candela fuí, 1940, Traditional poetry, C4–D5, Med, Manuel de Falla; orchestration available for string quintet; timpani, oboe, bassoon, and celeste, CNC, CNMA

Additional titles: Canciones criollas [CNMA]. Granito de trigo; La costurerita; Las manos del bebe; Los Molineritos; Poema de rosa y clavel [SADAIC]. *Dos canciones* [INM]. Balada de las flores; Bichito dos mil colores y Pedrito el caracol; Cantos del corazón; Coplas; Coplas de amores for soprano, viola, cello, and piano; *Dos elegías*; El jardín de los niños; Huella; La costurerita; Las Malvinas; Lieder; *Tres lieder* [*Diccionario de la música española e hispanoamericana*]. Canción de cuna; Copla festiva [*Enciclopedia de la música argentina*]. Alba con luna; Lied; Sueña el Alfafero [CNC].

Giacobbe, Juan Francisco, 1907–1990

1.246, *Canto chico (Seis canciones sobre temática infantil), Serie II, op. 18*
1.246a, Villancico del rey negro, 1944, Juan Francisco Giacobbe, G_4–D_5, Med, —, m, RD
1.246b, Villanela natalicia, 1944, Juan Francisco Giacobbe, C_4–D_5, Med, —, m, RD
1.246c, Muñeca, 1944, Mary Rega Molina, C_4–F_5, Med-high, —, m, RD
1.246d, Cunita (Arrorró), 1944, Mary Rega Molina, C_4–E_5, Med, —, m, RD
1.246e, Pianito, 1944, Mary Rega Molina, C_4–F_5, Med-high, —, m, RD
1.246f, Rondel, 1944, Mary Rega Molina, C_4–F_5, Med-high, —, m, RD

1.247, *Diez epigramas, op. 114*
1.247a, Epigrama 1, 1970, —, $E\flat_4$–$F\sharp_5$, Med-high, —, m, RD
1.247b, Epigrama 2, 1970, —, $F\sharp_4$–G_5, Med-high, —, m, RD
1.247c, Epigrama 3, 1970, —, C_4–G_5, Med-high, —, m, RD
1.247d, Epigrama 4, 1970, —, D_4–F_5, Med-high, —, m, RD
1.247e, Epigrama 5, 1970, —, D_4–$F\sharp_5$, Med, —, m, RD
1.247f, Epigrama 6, 1970, —, E_4–F_5, Med-high, —, m, RD
1.247g, Epigrama 7, 1970, —, D_4–$G\flat_5$, Med-high, —, m, RD
1.247h, Epigrama 8, 1970, —, F_4–E_5, Med-high, —, m, RD
1.247i, Epigrama 9, 1970, —, F_4–G_5, Med-high, —, m, RD
1.247j, Epigrama 10, 1970, —, $E\flat_4$–G_5, Med-high, —, m, RD

1.248, *Goces de la creación, op. 113*
1.248a, 1., 1978, Juan Francisco Giacobbe, $E\flat_4$–F_5, Med-high, —, m, RD
1.248b, 2., 1978, Juan Francisco Giacobbe, F_4–A_5, Med-high, —, m, RD
1.248c, 3., 1978, Juan Francisco Giacobbe, E_4–G_5, Med-high, —, m, RD
1.248d, 4., 1978, Juan Francisco Giacobbe, A_3–G_5, High, —, m, RD
1.248e, 5., 1978, Juan Francisco Giacobbe, $C\sharp_4$–$F\sharp_5$, Med-high, —, m, RD
1.248f, 6., 1978, Juan Francisco Giacobbe, D_4–G_5, Med-high, —, m, RD

1.249, *Las canciones felices*
1.249a, El puente, 1953, Amado Nervo, D_4–$E\flat_5$, Med-high, Germancito; from the album *Canciones para mis niños, op. 13*, JK, UCA
1.249b, Antonino, 1953, Amado Nervo, $B\flat_3$–$E\flat_5$, Med, Yin-Yin; From the album *Canciones para mis niños, op. 13*, JK, UCA
1.249c, Nenina, 1953, Mary Rega Molina, E_4–F_5, Med-high, Nenina; from the album *Canciones para mis niños, op. 13*, JK, UCA
1.249d, Nana, 1953, Mary Rega Molina, C_4–C_5, Med, Coralito; from the album *Canciones para mis niños, op. 13*, JK, UCA
1.249e, Luz, 1953, Mary Rega Molina, F_4–F_5, Med-high, María Cristina; from the album *Canciones para mis niños, op. 13*, JK, UCA
1.249f, El gato, 1953, Mary Rega Molina, B_3–C_5, Med, Horacio; from the album *Canciones para mis niños, op. 13*, JK, UCA

1.250, *Pajaritos criollos, op. 6*
1.250a, La viudita, 1945, Juan Francisco Giacobbe, E_4–A_5, High, Amalia María Raffo, RA BA9087, UCA
1.250b, La paloma torcaza, 1945, Juan Francisco Giacobbe, $B\flat_3$–$B\flat_5$, Med-high, Zena Possenti de Seta, RA BA9087, UCA
1.250c, El sirirí, 1945, Juan Francisco Giacobbe, $C\sharp_4$–A_5, High, Dr. Héctor de Cusatis, RA BA9087, UCA

1.251, *Tonadas de Navidad*
1.251a, En el portal de Belén, 1953, Traditional text, C_4–D_5, Med, Dora Castro; from the album *Canciones para mis niños, op. 13*, JK, UCA

1.251b, Canción de cuna de la virgen (A dos voces), 1953, Traditional text, E4–E5, Med, Mercedes Torres; from the album *Canciones para mis niños, op. 13*, JK, UCA

1.251c, Villancico y bailecito de Noche Buena, 1953, —, F4–F5, Med-high, Venancio Francia; from the album *Canciones para mis niños, op. 13*, JK, UCA

1.251d, Villancico de la adoración, 1953, Traditional text, E4–F5, Med-high, Flor de Nieve; From the album *Canciones para mis niños, op. 13*, JK, UCA

Additional titles: Canciones de Navidad; Prosas sentimentales, op. 42 [UCA]. Eros in me for voice and flute [SADAIC]. Calabria canta (Serie I); Calabria canta (Serie II); Cancioncillas de Navidad; Cantos a Jesús; Goces del Vía Crucis (Serie I); Presencias del Gallo; Prosas sentimentales, op. 27 [*Diccionario de la música española e hispanoamericana*]. Cancioncillas de Navidad; Cántigas del domingo; Cantos a Jesús; Dos cantatas para El infanto muerto, op. 16 for soprano and string quartet; Gl'indovenelli; Le stagioni nella ninna nanna [RD Catalog].

Gianneo, Luis, 1897–1968

1.252, Alba con luna, 1946, Alfredo R. Bufano, E4–G5, Med-high, Cecilia Benedit de Debenedetti, EAM 18, +

1.253, Canción del beso robado, 1939, Fernán Silva Valdés, A♭3–G♭5, High, —, —, UCA

1.254, La danza de las liebres, 1946, Conrado Nalé Roxlo, D4–G5, Med-high, Concepción Badia, EAM 16, +

1.255, Lied, 1946, Alfredo R. Bufano, D4–F♯5, Med-high, Pepita, EAM 17, UCA

1.256, *Pampeanas*

1.256a, I. El ombú, 1928, R. Chirre Danós, F♯4–G♯5, Med-high, Eduardo Fornarini, RA BA6198, UCA

1.256b, II. El sol, 1928, R. Chirre Danós, F♯4–A5, High, Enrique M. Casella, RA BA6198, UCA

1.256c, III. El zorzal, 1928, R. Chirre Danós, G4–G5, High, María Pini de Chrestia, RA BA6198, UCA

1.256d, IV. Llora el gaucho (Estilo), 1928, R. Chirre Danós, F4–G5, Med-high, Juan Solas, RA BA6198, UCA

1.257, *Seis coplas*

1.257a, 1., 1929, Traditional Argentine poetry, E4–E5, Med-high, —, GRic 10518, UCA

1.257b, 2., 1929, Traditional Argentine poetry, G4–G5, High, —, GRic 10518, UCA

1.257c, 3., 1929, Traditional Argentine poetry, A4–F♯5, High, —, GRic 10518, UCA

1.257d, 4., 1929, Traditional Argentine poetry, B3–E5, High, —, GRic 10518, UCA

1.257e, 5., 1929, Traditional Argentine poetry, F4–G♯5, Med-high, —, GRic 10518, UCA

1.257f, 6., 1929, Traditional Argentine poetry, A4–F♯5, High, —, GRic 10518, UCA

Additional titles: Canción del pececillo que quiso ser marinero [UCA]. Canción del estudiante; Canto a la zafra; El secreto; Esta iglesia no tiene; Fábulas argentinas; Himno a Tucumán; Nocturno; Poema de la Saeta for soprano and orchestra; Raggio d'amor; Seis coplas (Serie II); Transfiguración for baritone and orchestra [*Diccionario de la música española e hispanoamericana*].

Gil, José, 1886–1947

1.258, Canción de cuna (Canción escolar), —, Collection of traditional songs, B3–B4, Med, A mi sobrinita Elsa, —, SADAIC

1.259, La primavera viene (Melodía), 1927, Pedro Miguel Obligado, D4–A5, Med-high, Luis Ángel Cúneo, SNM, UCA

Additional titles: Canción patriótica del año 1810 [CNMA]. Madrigal; Paisaje [IU]. Madrigales de Miguel Ángel for voice, strings, and harp [LBV]. Canción del arado; Gli occhi miei vaghi; Morera de mi tierra; Patria grande [*Diccionario de la música española e hispanoamericana*].

Gilardi, Gilardo, 1889-1963

1.260, Boyerito lindo, —, Cecilia Borja, D4–E5, Med-high, —, Gaudiosi, UCA, —

1.261, Canción de cuna india, 1942, Ana Serrano Redonnet, E4–G5, Med-high, Brígida Frías de López Buchardo; orchestral accompaniment available, RA BA8605, UCA, —

1.262, Coplas para tus ojos, 2005, Gilardo Gilardi, D4–A♭5, Med-high, —, TR, LC, *The Latin American Art Song*, +

1.263, Danza irregular, 1963, Alfonsina Storni, D4–G5, Med-high, —, EAM 120, UCA, —

1.264, Dulce río Paraná, 1955, Hugo MacDougall, E4–F5, Med-high, —, EAM, UCA, —

1.265, La canción de los ojos amados, —, Leopoldo Lugones, E4–G5, Med-high, María de Pini de Chrestia, M. Calvello, UCA, —

1.266, Ñudo, 1955, Agustín Dentone, D4–E5, Med, —, ESar, CLP, —

1.267, *Trece Lieder*

1.267a, I. Lied del pájaro y la muerte, 1924, Leopoldo Lugones, F4–G5, High, Estilizaciones de canciones y danzas autóctonas, RA, UCA, —

1.267b, II. Lied de la estrella marina, 1924, Leopoldo Lugones, E4–F5, Med-high, Estilizaciones de canciones y danzas autóctonas, RA, UCA, —

1.267c, III. Lied del tesoro escondido, 1924, Leopoldo Lugones, F♯4–G5, Med-high, Estilizaciones de canciones y danzas autóctonas, RA, UCA, —

1.267d, IV. Lied del amor verdadero, 1924, Leopoldo Lugones, F♯4–E♭5, Med-high, Estilizaciones de canciones y danzas autóctonas, RA, UCA, —

1.267e, V. Lied de los ojos amados, 1924, Leopoldo Lugones, E4–G5, Med-high, Estilizaciones de canciones y danzas autóctonas, RA, UCA, —

1.267f, VI. Lied de las manos amigas, 1924, Leopoldo Lugones, F♯4–A5, High, Estilizaciones de canciones y danzas autóctonas, RA, UCA, —

1.267g, VII. Lied del viento y de la fuente, 1924, Leopoldo Lugones, D4–F♯5, Med-high, Estilizaciones de canciones y danzas autóctonas, RA, UCA, —

1.267h, VIII. Lied de la boca Florida (Chacarera), 1924, Leopoldo Lugones, E4–E5, Med-high, Estilizaciones de canciones y danzas autóctonas, RA, UCA, —

1.267i, IX. Lied de la gracia triunfante, 1924, Leopoldo Lugones, F4–F♯5, Med-high, Estilizaciones de canciones y danzas autóctonas, RA, UCA, —

1.267j, X. Lied de la ciencia de amar, 1924, Leopoldo Lugones, G4–G♭5, Med-high, Estilizaciones de canciones y danzas autóctonas, RA, UCA, —

1.267k, XI. Lied del misterio gentil, 1924, Leopoldo Lugones, D4–E5, Med-high, Estilizaciones de canciones y danzas autóctonas, RA, UCA, —

1.267l, XII. Lied de la eterna ventura, 1924, Leopoldo Lugones, E4–E5, Med-high, Estilizaciones de canciones y danzas autóctonas, RA, UCA, —

1.267m, XIII. Lied del secreto dichoso, 1924, Leopoldo Lugones, D♭4–F5, Med-high, Estilizaciones de canciones y danzas autóctonas, RA, UCA, —

1.268, *Tres coplas*

1.268a, I. Coplas para el amor que se fue, 1945, Antonio de la Torre, C4–E5, Med-high, Concepción Badia, —, EAM 10, +

1.268b, II. Coplas para la herida reciente, 1945, Antonio de la Torre, D4–F5, Med-high, Concepción Badia, —, EAM 10, +

1.268c, III. Coplas para tu boca, 1945, Antonio de la Torre, G4–G5, Med-high, Concepción Badia, —, EAM 10, +

1.269, Vidala santiagueña, 1937, —, B♭4–G5, High, —, RA BA7344, UCA, —

Additional titles: Coplas para tus ojos [TR]. Collita llamero [CNMA]. Zapateado for soprano and chamber orchestra [LBV].

Ausente; Canción de la acequia; Canción del rayo de luna; Canción del torpedista; Cantares de mi cantar; Coplas; Coplas del sol; *Seis canciones de amor* [INM]. Al brillar un relámpago nacemos; Amore; Arcano; *Canciones poemáticas*; Claror lunar; Estampa; Lamentación; Le rose sono sfiorite; Nenia; No te basta que pálido el semblante; O dolce sole; Ojos claros, serenos; Ombra; Primavera; Ricordati; Sconforto; Sombra; Stella cadente; *Tres canciones españolas*; Un entierro [*Diccionario de la música española e hispanoamericana*]. Dos canciones; Gajos de hiedra [*Enciclopedia de la música argentina*].

Ginastera, Alberto, 1916–1983

1.270, Canción del beso robado, —, Fernán Silva Valdés, E4–A4, Med, —, m, IU

1.271, *Cinco canciones populares argentinas*
1.271a, I. Chacarera, 1943, Collection of traditional songs, E4–G5, Med, —, RA BA8791, +
1.271b, II. Triste, 1943, Collection of traditional songs, E♭4–G5, Med-high, —, RA BA8791, +
1.271c, III. Zamba, 1943, Collection of traditional songs, F4–F5, Med-high, —, RA BA8791, +
1.271d, IV. Arrorró, 1943, Collection of traditional songs, G4–G5, Med-high, —, RA BA8791, +
1.271e, V. Gato, 1943, Collection of traditional songs, G4–G5, High, —, RA BA8791, +

1.272, *Dos canciones, op. 3*
1.272a, I. Canción al árbol del olvido, 1938, Fernán Silva Valdés, G4–G5, High, Brígida Frías de López Buchardo, RA BA8226, UCA
1.272b, II. Canción a la luna lunanca, 1938, Fernán Silva Valdés, E4–F♯5, Med-high, Brígida Frías de López Buchardo, RA BA10518, UCA

1.273, En la cuna blanca (Canción escolar), 1958, María Rosario Cipriota, E4–D5, Med, —, RA BA7965, UCA

1.274, *Las horas de una estancia, op. 11*
1.274a, I. El alba, 1945, Silvina Ocampo, E♭4–G5, Med, —, EAM 7, +
1.274b, II. La mañana, 1945, Silvina Ocampo, F4–G5, Med-high, —, EAM 7, +
1.274c, III. El mediodía, 1945, Silvina Ocampo, F♯4–G5, Med-high, —, EAM 7, +
1.274d, IV. La tarde, 1945, Silvina Ocampo, E♭4–A5, Med-high, —, EAM 7, +
1.274e, V. La noche, 1945, Silvina Ocampo, E4–A♭5, Med-high, —, EAM 7, +

Gómez Carrillo, Manuel, 1883–1968

1.275, Corazón mío no llores (Canción criolla), —, —, E♭4–G5, Med-high, —, m, LBV
1.276, El amor en los pañelos (Zamba para canto y piano), —, Ismael Moya, E4–D5, Med, Dora Vierci de Diaz Guerra; optional duet, RA BA7451, UCA
1.277, Huainito (Manchay Puito), —, —, F♯4–E5, Med-high, Optional duet, RA BA8783, UCA
1.278, La chileciteña (Zamba), —, Traditional poetry, D4–D5, Med, Tomada en Chilecito, La Rioja, a los Hnos. Martinez, RA BA9410, ZL
1.279, La ofrenda del trovado (Estilo), 1947, Manuel Ugarte, E4–F♯5, Med-high, —, RA BA9776, ZL
1.280, La telesita (Estilo), 1951, Gabino Coria Peñaloza, C4–G5, Med-high, Sara Solari Santillán de Puente; fragment of a lyric-choreographic work, RA BA10456, LBV
1.281, Mis ojos tienen la culpa (Canción al estilo nativo), 1945, —, D♯4–G5, High, María de Pini de Chrestia, RA BA9222, UCA
1.282, Nostalgia indígena (Canción serrana), 1961, Gabino Coria Peñaloza, D4–E5, Med-high, Lola Dabat, RA BA12044, UCA

1.283, Pobre mi negra (Vidala), —, Med, F♯4–E5, —, —, RA BA8807, ZL

1.284, Romanza gaucha, 1941, Ricardo Gutiérrez, E♭4–G5, High, —, RA, UCA

1.285, Siete de abril (Zamba), 1987, Leda Valladares, F♯4–E5, Med, —, RA BA10276, LBV

1.286, Vidala del regreso, 1945, Ricardo Rojas, G4–F5, Med-high, D. Absalón Rojas, RA BA9924, UCA

Additional titles: Bailecito cantado (Mucho te quiero); *Danzas y cantos regionales del Norte Argentino.* 2 vols. [UCA]. Trova (Quiero entonar a tu oído) [CNMA]. La ofrenda del trovador (Estilo) ¡Qué linda sois! (Vidala); [ZL]. La negrita (Zamba); Yerba buena (Zamba); Zamba de Vargas [INM]. A Sarmiento; Ave María; Canción y zapateado; Vidala del terruño [*Diccionario de la música española e hispanoamericana*].

Grisolía, Pascual, 1904–1983

1.287, Adiós, —, Félix Aldalur, E4–G5, Med-high, —, m, IU

1.288, Amor, 1946, Conrado Nalé Roxlo, G4–G5, High, —, m, SADAIC

1.289, Añoranza con un adiós, 1958, E. D. Marrone, C♯4–G5, Med-high, —, m, SADAIC

1.290, Antigüedad de cielo, 1959, E. D. Marrone, D4–G5, Med-high, —, m, SADAIC

1.291, Balada del jinete muerto, 1958, Conrado Nalé Roxlo, D♯4–A♭5, High, —, RA BA11712, TC

1.292, Canción del peligro, 1967, Félix Aldalur, D4–E5, Med-high, Ika Aldalur, m, SADAIC

1.293, Capricho de la rueda redonda, 1949, Conrado Nalé Roxlo, E4–F5, Med-high, —, RA, CLP

1.294, Los álamos bajo la luna, 1947, Aida Grisolia de Domingues García, D4–G5, Med-high, A Juanita, mi esposa, RA BA9805, CNMA

1.295, Nocturno, 1947, Conrado Nalé Roxlo, E4–E5, Med, Elda Sobrero Cantú, RA BA9804, CNMA

1.296, Silencio, 1946, Leopoldo Lugones, E4–E♭5, Med-high, —, m, SADAIC

1.297, Tiempo, —, E. D. Marrone, D4–G♯5, Med-high, —, m, SADAIC

Additional titles: Álamos bajo el rocío [UCA]. Canción de invierno; El gato; La muñeca; Será mejor así [SADAIC]. Angustia; El viaje; Inmovilidad; La mañana; Será mejor así; *Tres líricas;* Viento y olas [*Diccionario de la música española e hispanoamericana*].

Guastavino, Carlos, 1912–2000

1.298, *3 Canciones*

1.298a, Violetas, 1954, Luis Cernuda, F4–G5, Med-high, Donato Oscar Colacelli, RA BA10987, UCA, —

1.298b, Pájaro muerto, 1954, Luis Cernuda, C4–F5, Med-high, Francisco Javier Ocampo, RA BA10987, UCA, —

1.298c, Donde habite el olvido, 1954, Luis Cernuda, D4–D5, Med, Pedro A. Sáenz, RA BA10987, UCA, —

1.299, *3 Canciones sobre poesías de José Iglesias de la Casa*

1.299a, La palomita, 1952, José Iglesias de la Casa, D4–F5, Med-high, Ellabelle Davis, RA BA10544, UCA, —

1.299b, Cantilena, 1952, José Iglesias de la Casa, E4–E5, Med-high, Lyra Lorenzi, RA BA10544, UCA, —

1.299c, Dones sencillos, 1952, José Iglesias de la Casa, D4–G♭5, Med-high, Elena Arizmendi, RA BA10544, UCA, —

1.300, *4 Canciones argentinas*

1.300a, Desde que te conocí, 1950, —, F4–E♭5, Med-high, —, —, +, RA BA10217

1.300b, Viniendo de Chilecito..., 1950, —, A4–D5, Med-high, Isabelita Alonso, —, +, RA BA10217

1.300c, En los surcos del amor..., 1950, —, D4–E♭5, Med, Herbert Murill, Esq., —, +, RA BA10217

1.300d, Mi garganta..., 1950, —, D4–F5, Med, Juan José Castro, —, +, RA BA10217

1.301, *4 Canciones coloniales*

1.301a, Cuando acaba de llover..., 1966, León Benarós, C4–D5, Med, —, —, +, RA BA12578

1.301b, Prestame tu pañuelito..., 1966, León Benarós, C4–D5, Med, —, —, +, RA BA12578

1.301c, Ya me voy a retirar..., 1966, León Benarós, C4–E5, Med, —, —, +, RA BA12578

1.301d, Las puertas de la mañana..., 1966, León Benarós, C♯4–D5, Med, —, —, +, RA BA12578

1.302, *12 Canciones populares*

1.302a, Bonita rama de sauce, 1968, Arturo Vázquez, C♯4–E5, Med, —, LAGOS, CNMA, —

1.302b, El sampedrino (Canción pampeana), 1968, León Benarós, C♯4–D5, Med, —, LAGOS, +, —

1.302c, Los desencuentros (Canción del litoral), 1968, Guiche Aizenberg, D4–E5, Med-high, —, LAGOS, CNMA, —

1.302d, Quisiera ser por un rato... (Zamba), 1968, León Benarós, B3–E5, Med, —, LAGOS, CNMA, —

1.302e, Vidala del secadal (Vidala), 1968, León Benarós, D4–D5, Med, —, LAGOS, CNMA, —

1.302f, Pampamapa (Aire de huella), 1968, Hamlet Lima Quintana, C♯4–E5, Med, —, LAGOS, PEN, +, *The Art Song in Latin America*

1.302g, Abismo de sed (Zamba), 1968, Alma García, C4–E♭5, Med, —, LAGOS, CNMA, —

1.302h, Pampa sola (Canción del sur), 1968, Guiche Aizenberg, B3–D♯5, Med, —, LAGOS, +, —

1.302i, El forastero (Canción), 1968, Atahualpa Yupanqui, C4–C5, Med, —, LAGOS, +, —

1.302j, La Siempre Viva (Canción del litoral), 1968, Arturo Vázquez, C4–D5, Med, —, LAGOS, CNMA, —

1.302k, Hermano (Canción del sur), 1968, Hamlet Lima Quintana, D4–F5, Med-high, —, LAGOS, CNMA, —

1.302l, Mi viña de Chapanay (Cueca), 1968, León Benarós, D♯4–F♯5, Med-high, —, LAGOS, CNMA, —

1.303, *15 Canciones escolares*

1.303a, En mi escuela hay un naranjo, 1965, León Benarós, C4–C5, Med, Carmencita Copes, LAGOS, UCA, —

1.303b, Está lloviendo en mi escuela, 1965, León Benarós, D4–B4, Med, Carmencita Copes, LAGOS, UCA, —

1.303c, El pajarito del frío, 1965, León Benarós, D♯4–B4, Med, Carmencita Copes, LAGOS, UCA, —

1.303d, Belgrano nos dio bandera, 1965, León Benarós, B♭3–C5, Med, Carmencita Copes, LAGOS, UCA, —

1.303e, Química, 1965, León Benarós, D4–D5, Med, Carmencita Copes, LAGOS, UCA, —

1.303f, El viaje de papel, 1965, León Benarós, D♭4–C5, Med, Carmencita Copes, LAGOS, UCA, —

1.303g, Me gustan las matemáticas, 1965, León Benarós, C4–C5, Med, Carmencita Copes, LAGOS, UCA, —

1.303h, Buen día, señor invierno, 1965, León Benarós, B3–D5, Med, Carmencita Copes, LAGOS, UCA, —

1.303i, La música, 1965, León Benarós, C4–C5, Med, Carmencita Copes, LAGOS, UCA, —

1.303j, La última hoja, 1965, León Benarós, C4–C5, Med, Carmencita Copes, LAGOS, UCA, —

1.303k, ¡Quién fuera granaderito!, 1965, León Benarós, C♯4–D5, Med, Carmencita Copes, LAGOS, UCA, —

1.303l, Me gusta la mitología, 1965, León

Benarós, D♭4–C5, Med, Carmencita Copes, LAGOS, UCA, —

1.303m, Doña Paula Albarracín, 1965, León Benarós, D4–C5/B♭3–A4, Med, Carmencita Copes; optional duet, LAGOS, UCA, —

1.303n, Sarmiento fundaba escuelas, 1965, León Benarós, D4–C5, Med, Carmencita Copes, LAGOS, UCA, —

1.303o, Ya llegan las vacaciones, 1965, León Benarós, C4–D5, Med, Carmencita Copes, LAGOS, UCA, —

1.304, Adiós, quebrachito blanco, 1963, Atahualpa Yupanqui, B3–D5, Med, Rosa Elvira Carreño, LAGOS, —, +

1.305, Anhelo, 1942, Domingo Zerpa, C4–F5, Med-high, —, EAM 60, +, —

1.306, Arroyito serrano (Canción escolar), 1941, Carlos Guastavino, D4–D5, Med, Optional duet, RA BA8002, +, —

1.307, A un árbol (Canción pampeana), 1965, Luis Ricardo Furlán, C4–D5, Med, Enriqueta Legorreta, LAGOS, SLM, —

1.308, Ay, que el alma, 1965, León Benarós, C4–E♭5, Med, Guitar accompaniment available [RA BA12442], RA BA12428, CNMA, —

1.309, Campanas, 1941, Francisco Silva, B♭3–D♭5, Med, Lydia Kindermann, RA BA9866, UCA, —

1.310, Canción de Navidad, 1947, Francisco Silva, G3–E5, Low, Optional duet, RA BA9924, TC, —

1.311, Canción de Navidad (no. 2), 1955, Carlos Guastavino, D4–E5, Med, —, RA BA1955, INM, —

1.312, *Canciones del alba*

1.312a, Los llantos del alba, 1974, León Benarós, E♭4–C5, Med, Margot Arrillaga, LAGOS, TC, —

1.312b, El cerro estaba plateado, 1974, León Benarós, C♯4–F♯5, Med, Margot Arrillaga, LAGOS, TC, —

1.312c, El paso de las estrellas, 1974, León Benarós, D4–F5, Med, Margot Arrillaga, LAGOS, TC, —

1.312d, El albeador, 1974, León Benarós, D4–F5, Med, Margot Arrillaga, LAGOS, TC, —

1.313, Cita, 1957, Lorenzo Varela, B3–E5, Med, Rudolf Firkusny, RA BA9869, +, —

1.314, *Cuatro sonetos de Quevedo*

1.314a, Soneto I, 1970, Francisco de Quevedo y Vilegas, D4–E♭5, Med, Linda Rautenstrauch, LAGOS, CNMA, —

1.314b, Soneto II, 1970, Francisco de Quevedo y Vilegas, D4–E5, Med, Linda Rautenstrauch, LAGOS, CNMA, —

1.314c, Soneto III, 1970, Francisco de Quevedo y Vilegas, D♯4–E5, Med, Linda Rautenstrauch, LAGOS, CNMA, —

1.314d, Soneto IV, 1970, Francisco de Quevedo y Vilegas, C♯4–F♯5, Med-high, Linda Rautenstrauch, LAGOS, CNMA, —

1.315, Déjame esta voz, 1956, Luis Cernuda, B♭2–E♭4, Med-high, Gerard Souzay, RA BA11437, UCA, —

1.316, *Edad del asombro*

1.316a, Los asombros: El día, 1969, Hamlet Lima Quintana, C4–D5, Med, Alberto Balzanelli, LAGOS, TC, —

1.316b, Los asombros: La noche, 1969, Hamlet Lima Quintana, D4–C5, Med, Alberto Balzanelli, LAGOS, TC, —

1.316c, Los asombros: El sueño, 1969, Hamlet Lima Quintana, C♯4–C♯5, Med, Alberto Balzanelli, LAGOS, TC, —

1.316d, Los seres: El árbol, 1969, Hamlet Lima Quintana, C♯4–B4, Med, Alberto Balzanelli, LAGOS, TC, —

1.316e, Los seres: Los pájaros, 1969, Hamlet Lima Quintana, C♯4–D♯5, Med, Alberto Balzanelli, LAGOS, TC, —

1.316f, Los seres: El amigo, 1969, Hamlet Lima Quintana, C4–D5, Med, Alberto Balzanelli, LAGOS, TC, —

1.316g, La frontera: Era un día de lluvia, 1969, Hamlet Lima Quintana, C4–C5, Med, Alberto Balzanelli, LAGOS, TC, —

1.316h, La frontera: En el sueño de la calle, 1969, Hamlet Lima Quintana, C4–C5, Med, Alberto Balzanelli, LAGOS, TC, —

1.316i, La frontera: Detrás de la pared, 1969, Hamlet Lima Quintana, C#4–D5, Med, Alberto Balzanelli, LAGOS, TC, —

1.317, Elegía para un gorrión, 1965, Alma Garcia, C4–E5, Med, —, LAGOS, SLM, —

1.318, El labrador y el pobre, 1954, Anonymous, B3–E5, Med, Juan Andrés Salas, RA BA11091, TC, —

1.319, El prisionero, 1947, Anonymous, B3–E5, Low-med, —, EAM 19152, +, —

1.320, El único camino, 1964, Hamlet Lima Quintana, C#4–D5, Med, Susana Palas, LAGOS, SLM, —

1.321, El vaso, 1960, Gabriela Mistral, C#4–F#5, Med, Olga Linne, RA BA11994, +, —

1.322, En el pimpollo mas alto, 1965, León Benarós, C#4–E5, Med, —, RA BA11427, CNMA, —

1.323, Esta iglesia no tiene..., 1948, Pablo Neruda, F4–G5, Med-high, Hanna, RA BA10172, +, —

1.324, *Flores argentinas*

1.324a, Cortadera, plumerito..., 1970, León Benarós, C4–C5, Med, Mario Mercadante, LAGOS, UCA, —

1.324b, El clavel del aire blanco, 1970, León Benarós, C#4–D5, Med, Adela Olivier de Larrocha, LAGOS, UCA, —

1.324c, Campanilla, ¿adónde vas?, 1970, León Benarós, C4–C5, Med, Ethel Manghi, LAGOS, UCA, —

1.324d, El vinagrillo morado, 1970, León Benarós, D#4–C#5, Med, Leonor de la Hoz de Asté, LAGOS, UCA, —

1.324e, ¡Qué linda la madreselva!, 1970, León Benarós, C#4–C#5, Med, Berta Pane y Enrique Bramante Jáuregui, LAGOS, UCA, —

1.324f, Las flores del macachín, 1970, León Benarós, B3–B5, Med, Lilia Mariani de Balagué, LAGOS, UCA, —

1.324g, Las achiras coloradas, 1970, León Benarós, B3–C5, Med, Blanca Peralta Parodi, LAGOS, UCA, —

1.324h, Jazmín del país: ¡qué lindo...!, 1970, León Benarós, C4–D5, Med, María Teresa Branda Cárcano, LAGOS, UCA, —

1.324i, Aromito, flor de tusca..., 1970, León Benarós, C#4–C#5, Med, Graciela Patiño Andrade de Copes, LAGOS, UCA, —

1.324j, La flor de aguapé, 1970, León Benarós, C4–D♭5, Med, Carmen Vivérn y Rogelio Sciarrillo, LAGOS, UCA, —

1.324k, Ay, aljaba, flor de chilco..., 1970, León Benarós, C#4–C#5, Med, Norma Romano, LAGOS, UCA, —

1.324l, Ceibo, ceibo, zuiñandí, 1970, León Benarós, C#4–D5, Med, Francisco Vivérn de Bianchi, LAGOS, UCA, —

1.325, La primera pregunta (El adolescente muerto), 1956, Nina Cortese, F4–A♭5, Med-high, Juan Carlos Legarre, RA BA11446, +, —

1.326, La rosa y el sauce, 1942, Francisco Silva, C#4–F#5/D4–G5, Med, Med-high, —, RA BA9770, +, —

1.327, *Las nubes*

1.327a, Jardín antiguo, 1954, Luis Cernuda, F4–G♭5, Med-high, Juan Carlos Legarre, RA BA10971, UCA, —

1.327b, Deseo, 1954, Luis Cernuda, F4–G♭5, High, Juan Carlos Legarre, RA BA10971, UCA, —

1.327c, Alegría de la soledad, 1954, Luis Cernuda, E♭4–G♭5, High, Juan Carlos Legarre, RA BA10971, UCA, —

1.328, La tempranera, 1963, León Benarós, C4–D♭5, Med, Eduardo Falú, LAGOS, +, —

1.329, Los días perdidos (Soneto), 1962, Ana María Chouhy Aguirre, B3–E5, Med-high, Luis Borbolla, RA BA12204, UCA, —

1.330, *Los ríos de la mano*

1.330a, Plancha, 1973, José Pedroni, C4–E♭5, Med, —, LAGOS, CNMA, —

1.330b, Dedal, 1973, José Pedroni, D4–C#5, Med, —, LAGOS, CNMA, —

1.330c, Acerico, 1973, José Pedroni, E4–D5, Med, —, LAGOS, CNMA, —

1.330d, Escuadra, 1973, José Pedroni, D4–C#5, Med, —, LAGOS, CNMA, —

1.330e, Horquilla, 1973, José Pedroni, C4–C5, Med, —, LAGOS, CNMA, —

1.330f, Garlopin, 1973, José Pedroni, C4–C5, Med, —, LAGOS, CNMA, —

1.330g, Plomada, 1973, José Pedroni, C4–C5, Med, —, LAGOS, CNMA, —

1.330h, Tijera, 1973, José Pedroni, D4–C5, Med, —, LAGOS, CNMA, —

1.330i, Destornillador, 1973, José Pedroni, C4–A4, Low, —, LAGOS, CNMA, —

1.330j, Carretilla de Madera, 1973, José Pedroni, D4–D5, Med, —, LAGOS, CNMA, —

1.331, Milonga de dos hermanos, 1963, Jorge Luis Borges, D4–E♭5, Med, —, LAGOS, INM, —

1.332, Noches de Santa Fé, 1964, Guiche Aizenberg, B♭3–D♭5, Med, Arturo Molina, LAGOS, UCA, —

1.333, Ojos de tiempo (Zamba), 1963, Alma García, B3–E♭5, Med-high, Haydee Perez Bidart, LAGOS, TC, —

1.334, Paisaje, 1947, Francisco Silva, G♭4–G♭5, Med-high, Sergio Zouboff, RA BA9771, UCA, —

1.335, *Pájaros*

1.335a, Benteveo, 1974, León Benarós, D4–D5, Med, —, LAGOS, SLM, —

1.335b, Torcacita, 1974, León Benarós, C4–D5, Med, —, LAGOS, SLM, —

1.335c, Hornero, 1974, León Benarós, C4–C5, Low, —, LAGOS, SLM, —

1.335d, Tacuarita, 1974, León Benarós, D#4–D5, Med, —, LAGOS, SLM, —

1.335e, Alférez, 1974, León Benarós, C#4–C#5, Med, —, LAGOS, SLM, —

1.335f, Pirincho, 1974, León Benarós, C4–C5, Med, —, LAGOS, SLM, —

1.335g, Chingolo, 1974, León Benarós, C4–D5, Med, —, LAGOS, SLM, —

1.335h, Gorrión, 1974, León Benarós, D4–C#5, Med, —, LAGOS, SLM, —

1.335i, Terú-terú, 1974, León Benarós, B♭3–C5, Med, —, LAGOS, SLM, —

1.335j, Leñatero, 1974, León Benarós, D4–B4, Med, —, LAGOS, SLM, —

1.336, Piececitos, 1960, Gabriela Mistral, E4–G#5, High, Luis Borbolla, RA BA11953, UCA, —

1.337, Por los campos verdes, 1942, Juana de Ibarbourou, C4–G5, Med-high, Elizalde de Blaquier; English version by S. Borton, French version by G. de Elizalde Mercedes, RA BA9870, +, —

1.338, Pueblito, mi pueblo, 1942, Francisco Silva, E4–D#5, Med-high, Mamá and Paíto, RA BA8565, UCA, —

1.339, Riqueza, 1956, Gabriela Mistral, G4–G5, High, Carlos Stettenheimer, RA BA11438, CNMA, —

1.340, Romance de José Cubas, 1965, León Benarós, C4–E5, Med, —, RA BA12431, +, —

1.341, Romance de la Delfina, 1964, Guiche Aizenberg, B3–D5, Med, Celia Dolores Calcaterra, LAGOS, +, —

1.342, Se equivocó la paloma, 1941, Rafael Alberti, D4–E5, Med-high, María de Pini de Chrestia, RA BA8278, +, —

1.343, *Seis canciones de cuna*

1.343a, Hallazgo, 1961, Gabriela Mistral, A♭4–D5, Med, Juan Carlos Legarre, RA BA11970, UCA, —

1.343b, Apegado a mí, 1961, Gabriela Mistral, D4–F5, Med-high, Juan Carlos Legarre, RA BA11970, UCA, —

1.343c, Encantamiento, 1961, Gabriela Mistral, D4–C5, Med, Juan Carlos Legarre, RA BA11970, UCA, —

1.343d, Corderito, 1961, Gabriela Mistral, D4–E5, Med, Juan Carlos Legarre, RA BA11970, UCA, —

1.343e, Rocío, 1961, Gabriela Mistral, D#4–F5, Med, Juan Carlos Legarre, RA BA11970, UCA, —

1.343f, Meciendo, 1961, Gabriela Mistral,

E4–E5, Med, Juan Carlos Legarre, RA BA11970, UCA, —

1.344, Severa Villafañe, 1964, León Benarós, C4–E5, Med, Meny Bergel; guitar accompaniment available [RA BA12444], RA BA12330, TC, —

1.345, Siesta, 1953, Francisco Silva, D4–G5, Med-high, Nilda Hofmann, RA BA10913, CNMA, —

1.346, *Siete canciones*

1.346a, Jardín de amores, 1975, Rafael Alberti, B3–D5, Med, —, LAGOS, UCA, —

1.346b, ¡A volar!, 1975, Rafael Alberti, C4–F5, Med-high, —, LAGOS, UCA, —

1.346c, Nana del niño malo, 1975, Rafael Alberti, D4–E5, Med-high, —, LAGOS, UCA, —

1.346d, La novia, 1975, Rafael Alberti, C4–D5, Low, —, LAGOS, UCA, —

1.346e, Geografía física, 1975, Rafael Alberti, D4–D5, Med, —, LAGOS, UCA, —

1.346f, ¡Al puente de la golondrina!, 1975, Rafael Alberti, C4–E♭5, Med, —, LAGOS, UCA, —

1.346g, Elegía, 1975, Rafael Alberti, C4–E♭5, Med-high, —, LAGOS, UCA, —

1.347, Soneto a la armonía, 1962, Ana María Chouhy Aguirre, B♭3–C5, Med, Augusto Orfeo, RA BA12203, TC, —

1.348, Zamba del quiero, 1964, Inés Malinow, C4–D5, Med, Meny Bergel, RA BA12329, TC, —

Additional titles: La canción del estudiante [UCA]. Balada; Canción del litoral (El pitogüe); El río feliciano; En la mañana rubia; Familia; Gratitud; La difunta Correa; La nube; La rosa; Lejos de Santa Fé; Luna de los tristes; Manitas; Mi canto; Ombú; Pampa fértil; Paralelo; Pequeño mío; Primavera; Propósito; Yegua; Yo, maestro [INM]. La loba [*Diccionario de la música española e hispanoamericana*].

Hargreaves, Francisco, 1849–1900

1.349, Ave María, D♯4–A5, Med-high, Virgen de Lujan; text in Italian, LBV

1.350, Ricordi? (Romanza), C4–G5, Med-high, Adela Llambi de Woodgate; text in Italian, ALW

Additional titles: La tejedora de Ñanduty for piano and narrator; Llora, llora, Urutaú for piano and spoken voice [LBV]. ¡Ay de mí! [INM]. Al Paraguay; Canción nocturno; Il palpito; Romanza [*Diccionario de la música española e hispanoamericana*].

Iglesias Villoud, Héctor, 1913–1988

1.351, *Cantares de la tierra mía*

1.351a, Dicen que tu cariño . . . , 1953, Héctor Iglesias Villoud, F4–G5, Med-high, JK 16176, CNMA

1.351b, El castigo, 1953, Héctor Iglesias Villoud, F4–F5, Med-high, JK 16176, CNMA

1.351c, ¡Me miras mucho!, 1953, Héctor Iglesias Villoud, G♯4–E5, Med-high, JK 16176, CNMA

1.352, Triste, 1944, Héctor Iglesias Villoud, E♭4–G♭5, Med-high, CNC, CNMA

1.353, Una noche de luna, —, Héctor Iglesias Villoud, G4–F5, Med-high, —, LBV

Additional titles: Balada; Canción del valle; Cantando a trabajar; Cantares a la muerte; Chacarera; *Cinco epigramas dramáticos; Cinco poemas del ayer iluminado* for voice and string orchestra; Córdoba; Cuando canta mi hija; *Dos aires populares;* Estilo criollo; Guerrero del Inca; Lamento indio del Viernes Santo; Libres del Sur; Martín Fierro for voice and orchestra; Niños de mi patria; Norteña; Redención (Misterio lírico) for voice and orchestra; Río sereno; Silencio; *Tres Canciones;* Triste; Tu rostro junto al mar [LBV]. Canción [INM]. Coros para la tragedia Quilliscacha; Poema Serrano [*Diccionario de la música española e hispanoamericana*].

Inzaurraga, Alejandro, 1882–1956

1.354, Arrorró de la esposa, 1937–1943, Alejandro Inzaurraga, C♯4–D♯5, Medium, —, m, ZL, —

1.355, El arriero invisible, —, Alejandro Inzaurraga, D4–G♯5, Med-high, —, m, ZL, —

1.356, La dulce noche, —, Alejandro Inzaurraga, D4–F♯5, Med-high, —, m, ZL, —

1.357, La vaquera esquiva, 1932, Íñigo López de Mendoza, D4–E5, Med-high, —, SNM, SADAIC, —

1.358, Minue, —, Marqués de Santillana, B3–A♭5, High, —, —, IU, Published in *Joya de canciones españolas*

1.359, Pourquoi me fuir?..., —, Alphonse de Lamartine, E♭4–A♭5, High, —, m, ZL, —

1.360, ¡Toda una vida!, —, Alejandro Inzaurraga, D4–E♯5, Med-high, —, SNM 23, UCA, —

1.361, *Tres canciones*

1.361a, I. La flor en el alma, 1950, Alejandro Inzaurraga, F4–F5, Med-high, A tu santa memoria, hermana Elvira, CLSRL, UCA, —

1.361b, II. Cántame..., 1950, Alejandro Inzaurraga, D♯4–F♯5, Med-high, A tu santa memoria, hermana Elvira, CLSRL, UCA, —

1.361c, III. Y no me atreví..., 1950, Alejandro Inzaurraga, C♯4–F♯5, Med-high, A tu santa memoria, hermana Elvira, CLSRL, UCA, —

1.362, Voy caminito, 1949, —, D4–F5, Med-high, —, CLSRL, SADAIC, —

Additional titles: Al galope; Circo de aldea; Endecha; Idilio; Marisa; Scherzo [UCA]. Cuando venga el príncipe [AW]. El gato de tía [LBV]. El arriero insensible [ZL]. Matinal; Por sierras de Córdoba [INM]. El jilguero en la tapera; Todo o nada [*Diccionario de la música española e hispanoamericana*].

Jurafsky, Abraham, 1906–1993

1.363, *Coplas*

1.363a, Sin poder con esta lengua, 1942, Luis L. Franco, D4–G5, Med-high, Brígida Frías de López Buchardo, RA BA8506, CNMA

1.363b, En la punta del aquel cerro, 1942, Luis L. Franco, E4–G5, High, Brígida Frías de López Buchardo, RA BA8506, CNMA

1.363c, ¡Qué me has hecho, qué me has hecho!, 1942, Luis L. Franco, F4–A5, High, Brígida Frías de López Buchardo, RA BA8506, CNMA

1.364, *Cuatro canciones al estilo popular argentino*

1.364a, 1. Canción de la niña gaucha, 1954, Gustavo Caraballo, D4–A5, Med-high, Lita y Rafael González; chamber orchestra accompaniment available, RA BA11038, UCA

1.364b, 2. Nostalgia, 1954, Gustavo Caraballo, D4–G5, Med-high, Lita y Rafael González; chamber orchestra accompaniment available, RA BA11038, UCA

1.364c, 3. La tapera, 1954, Gustavo Caraballo, E♭4–G5, High, Lita y Rafael González; chamber orchestra accompaniment available, RA BA11038, UCA

1.364d, 4. Se casa el boyero, 1954, Gustavo Caraballo, F4–B♭5, High, Lita y Rafael González; chamber orchestra accompaniment available, RA BA11038, UCA

1.365, Dame la mano.... (Canción escolar), —, Gabriela Mistral, F4–E♭5, Med-high, Dora Augusta Palma (Dodyn), RA, UCA

1.366, *Tres canciones* (also titled *Canciones argentinas*)

1.366a, 1. Copla, 1934, Luis L. Franco, E4–F♯5, Med-high, Odette, RA BA8502, UCA

1.366b, 2. Vidala, 1934, Luis L. Franco, F4–D5, Med, Odette, RA BA8502, UCA

1.366c, 3. Vidalita, 1934, Luis L. Franco, E♭4–A♭5, Med-high, Odette, RA BA8502, UCA

1.367, *Tres melodías*

1.367a, 1. Poema para una muerta voz, 1954, Fermín Estrella Gutiérrez, D4–G5, Med-high, Ruzena Horakowa, RA BA10995, UCA

1.367b, 2. Tarde, 1954, Fermín Estrella Gutiérrez, C4–G5, Med-high, Ruzena Horakowa, RA BA10995, UCA

1.367c, 3. Romance de la muerte temprana, 1954, Fermín Estrella Gutiérrez, C4–A♭5, Med-high, Ruzena Horakowa, RA BA10995, —, UCA

Additional titles: El marinerito; Entre los sauces del río; Romancillo del gato con botas [CNMA]. El barrilete [ANA]. Caperucita; Chilindorina; *Cinco canciones infantiles;* Coplitas del corazón; El pino verde; El sapito glo, glo, glo; La casita; La estrellita bailarina; Luna de verano [CNC].

Lasala, Ángel, 1914–2000

1.368, *Baladas del querer*

1.368a, I. Cuando la luna..., 1941, Ángel E. Lasala, E♭4–F5, Med-high, —, ACA, UCA

1.368b, II. Amalhaya..., 1941, Cancionero popular, F♯4–F5, Med-high, —, ACA, UCA

1.368c, III. Silenciosamente..., 1941, Ángel E. Lasala, E4–E5, Med-high, —, ACA, UCA

1.369, *Canciones argentinas*

1.369a, Tropilla de estrellas, 1951, Fernán Silva Valdás, E4–F♯5, Med-high, Gotardo Stagnaro; optional duet, RA BA10405, UCA

1.369b, ¡Ay, lunita!..., 1951, Ángel E. Lasala, E♯4–G♯5, High, Clara Oyuela, RA BA10405, UCA

1.369c, Dicen que andan diciendo..., 1951, Cancionero popular, C♯4–E5, Med-high, Nilda Muller, RA BA10405, UCA

1.370, *Cantares*

1.370a, 1. Coplas, 1953, Alfredo R. Bufano, E4–F♯5, Med-high, Carlos López Buchardo, RA BA10838, UCA

1.370b, 2. Serrana, 1953, Alfredo R. Bufano, G4–D5, Med-high, Carlos López Buchardo, RA BA10838, UCA

1.370c, 3. Estoy en un verde prado, 1953, Alfredo R. Bufano, E♭4–F5, High, Carlos López Buchardo, RA BA10838, UCA

1.370d, 4. Cuyana, 1953, Alfredo R. Bufano, G♯4–E5, Med-high, Carlos López Buchardo, RA BA10838, UCA

1.371, Soledad, 1943, Orfila Bardesio, E♭4–G5, High, —, ACA, ZL

López Buchardo, Carlos, 1881–1948

1.372, Canción de ausencia, 1961, Gustavo Caraballo, C4–E♭5, Med, Marita, RA, UCA

1.373, Canción del niño pequeñito, 1949, Ida Réboli, C4–E♭5, Med, Carlitos Alfredo Fitte, RA, UCA

1.374, Canción de Perico, 1940, Fryda Schultz de Mantovani, B3–E5, Med, Frederick Fuller, RA, UCA

1.375, Canta tu canto, ruiseñor y vuela... (Soneto), 1949, Ignacio B. Anzoátegui, C4–G5, Med-high, Tina C. de Guido, RA, UCA

1.376, *Cinco canciones al estilo popular*

1.376a, Prendeditos de la mano, 1936, Miguel A. Camino, D♭4–F5, Med-high, Esther Llavallol de Roca; chamber orchestra accompaniment available [AW], GRic, UCA

1.376b, Si lo hallas, 1936, Miguel A. Camino, D♭4–E♭5, Med, —, GRic, UCA

1.376c, Frescas sombras de sauces, 1936, Anonymous, E4–A5, Med-high, Cayetano Troiani; chamber orchestra accompaniment available [AW], GRic, UCA

1.376d, Oye mi llanto, 1936, Miguel A. Camino, C♯4–E5, Med, Miguel Mastrogianni, GRic, UCA

1.376e, Malyaha la suerte mia, 1936, Miguel A. Camino, C4–A4, Med-high, Grassi

Díaz; chamber orchestra accompaniment available [AW], GRic, UCA

1.377, Copla criolla, 1938, Traditional poetry, F#4–G#5, Med-high, Conchita Badía, RA, UCA

1.378, Hormiguita (Canción infantil), 1925, Enrique Amorim, D4–F#5, Med-high, Dr. Benito Nazar Anchorena, GRic, UNLP

1.379, La canción desolada, 1925, Margarita Abella Caprile, E♭4–E♭5, Med-high, Antonieta Silveyra de Lenhardtson; text in French and Spanish, GRic, LBV

1.380, Lamento (Mírala como ha venido), 1938, Poesía popular, B3–C5, Med, Héctor Ruiz Díaz, RA, UCA

1.381, Querendona (Motivos serranos), 1938, Tilde Pérez Pieroni, D4–F#5, Med-high, Maestro Constantino Gaito, RA, UCA

1.382, *Seis canciones al estilo popular*

1.382a, Vidalita (Canción al estilo popular), 1925, Leopoldo Lugones, E♭4–G5, Med-high, María Barrientos, GRic, UCA

1.382b, Los puñalitos (Copla), 1925, Leopoldo Lugones, E4–G#5, Med-high, Gastón O. Talamon, GRic, UCA

1.382c, Desdichas de mi pasión... (Tonada), 1925, Leopoldo Lugones, D4–G#5, Med-high, Luis V. Ochoa, GRic, UCA

1.382d, Vidala, 1925, Gustavo Caraballo, D4–E5, Med, Entrique T. Susini, GRic, UCA

1.382e, Canción del carretero, 1925, Gustavo Caraballo, E♭4–G5, Med-high, Sarah Sagasta de Sagarna; Chamber orchestra accompaniment available [RA], GRic, UCA

1.382f, Jujeña, 1925, Victoriano Montes, D♭4–F#5, Med-high, In memory of Julián Aguirre, GRic, UCA

1.383, *Siete canciones infantiles*

1.383a, Este pajarito, 1938, Ida Réboli, D4–F5, Med, Dr. Antonio Sagarna, RA, UCA

1.383b, La casita del hornero, 1938, Ida Réboli, D4–G5, Med-high, Dr. Antonio Sagarna, RA, UCA

1.383c, El jardín de mi escuela, 1938, Ida Réboli, E♭4–E♭ (G)5, Med-high, Dr. Antonio Sagarna, RA, UCA

1.383d, Mi señorita, 1938, Ida Réboli, D4–E5, Med-high, Dr. Antonio Sagarna, RA, UCA

1.383e, El patio, 1938, Ida Réboli, C4–E5, Med, Dr. Antonio Sagarna, RA, UCA

1.383f, El canario, 1938, Ida Réboli, C4–D5, Med, Dr. Antonio Sagarna, RA, UCA

1.383g, El arco iris, 1938, Ida Réboli, D4–E♭5, Med, Dr. Antonio Sagarna, RA, UCA

Additional titles: Les roses de Noël; Petit Ynga; Porteñita [UCA]. Scordarmi di te..!!?? [CNMA]. La canción desolada [LBV]. A toute âme qui pleure... [ZL]. Nocturno; Pampeana; Pobres jazmines criollos [INM].

López de la Rosa, Horacio, 1933–1986

1.384, Canciones de Altisidora, op. 35, 1970, Miguel de Cervantes, C4–G5, Med-high, —, EAM, +

1.385, *Canciones pirenaicas*

1.385a, L'estridencia dels orgues..., 1962, Manolo Hugué, C#4–E♭5, Med, —, m, TC

1.385b, Cancó, 1962, Maria Manent, D4–C5, Med, —, m, TC

1.385c, La chanson de Marie-des-Anges, 1962, Jean Richepin, C4–E5, Med, —, m, TC

1.386, *Coplas de la paloma, op. 45*

1.386a, I. Paloma de la mañana, 1978–1979, Jorge Vocos Lescano and Horacio López, D4–E♭5, Med, Raúl Neumann, EAC, UCA

1.386b, II. El cielo hasta mi casa, 1978–1979, Jorge Vocos Lescano and Horacio López, C4–G5, Med, María Julia y mi hijas, EAC, UCA

1.386c, III. Así la paloma andaba, 1978–1979, Jorge Vocos Lescano and Horacio López, D♭4–G5, Med-high, Jorge Vocos Lescano, EAC, UCA

1.386d, IV. Cuando voy por la calle, 1978–1979, Jorge Vocos Lescano and Horacio

López, C4–E5, Med, Dora Berdichevsky, EAC, UCA

1.387, *Tres canciones americanas, op. 15*

1.387a, Villancico (Argentina), 1962, —, D4–G5, Med-high, —, RA BA11885, TC

1.387b, La campana (Ecuatoriana), 1962, —, C4–F5, Med, —, RA BA11885, TC

1.387c, Con una manzana verde (Araucana), 1962, —, D4–G5, Med-high, —, RA BA11885, TC

Additional titles: Homenaje (en el día del maestro) [CNMA]. *Dos canciones; Seis canciones* [+]. Sin dejar de sonreír [*Enciclopedia de la música argentina*].

Luzzatti, Arturo, 1875–1959

1.388, Ansiedad, 1948, José de Maturana, C#4–G5, Med-high, ZL

1.389, Coplas, 1946, Rafael Jijena Sánchez, F#4–F#5, Med-high, CLP

1.390, El jardín encantado, 1930, M. Abella Caprile, E♭4–G#5, Med-high, ZL

Additional titles: Deux mélodies [CNMA]. Au bord de la mer . . . [ZL]. Au paradis; Claro sol; Copla; Las golondrinas; Las rosas; Lied de la gracia triunfante; Madrigal; *Seis canciones* for voice and orchestra; Versos de otoño; Vesper [*Diccionario de la música española e hispanoamericana*].

Maiztegui, Isidro, 1905–1996

1.391, Cardo en flor (Canción criolla), 1950, Elena Areco, C4–G5, Med-high, ESar, UCA

1.392, El paraiso, 1948, Cordova Iturburu, D♭4–E♭5, Med, RA BA9956, UCA

1.393, Nocturno, 1944, B. Fernández Moreno, E♭4–G5, Med-high, —, IU

1.394, Nocturno en los muelles, 1951, Nicolás Guillén, B♭3–E5, Med, RA BA10390, CNMA

Additional titles: A Estrêla; Cuatro lagrimas; Duerme y no llores . . . ; En esta provincia de sueño y sangre; Esquinita Rosada; Este destino de mar y cielo; Lied; Los heraldos negros; Nanita María . . . ; ¿Quién me comprá una naranja?; Romancillo del niño moreno; Serranilla; Song; Un patio [IU]. Ahora que regreso . . . ; Nana del niño malo; *Seis poemas galegos;* Soy milonga del recuerdo [INM]. Canción 102 de Ora maritima; Canción criolla; Canción de cuna; Canciones juglarescas; *Cuatro canciones;* . . . del amor y soledad; Introducción y zamba; Larga noite da pedra; Qué pasa o redor de min; Sin niño; Tempo de chorar [*Diccionario de la música española e hispanoamericana*].

Maragno, Virtú, 1928–2004

1.395, *Baladas amarillas (Cuatro poemas de García Lorca)*

1.395a, Sobre el cielo de las margaritas ando, 1952, Federico García Lorca, D4–F#5, High, Francisco Maragno; chamber version also available, EAM 124, UCA

1.395b, En lo alto de aquel monte, 1952, Federico García Lorca, E4–G5, High, Zoraida Maragno; chamber version also available, EAM 124, UCA

1.395c, La tierra estaba amarilla, 1952, Federico García Lorca, G4–F#5, High, Poly Maragno; chamber version also available, EAM 124, UCA

1.395d, Dos bueyes rojos, 1952, Federico García Lorca, D♭4–A#5, High, Concepción Maragno; chamber version also available, EAM, 124, UCA

1.396, Canción de cuna para un niño ciego, 1952, Juan Pedro Ramos, E4–F#5, Med-high, —, EAM 68, UCA

1.397, *Tres canciones*

1.397a, Soneto para un tango, 1989, César Mermet, C#4–A♭5, Med-high, —, m, UCA

1.397b, Palabras sueltas, 1989, Jose Pedroni, A4–A♭5, High, —, m, UCA

1.397c, No te detengas alma sobre el borde, 1989, Juan L. Ortiz, C4–A5, Med-high, —, m, UCA

Additional titles: Blanca mariposa; Canción de bodas; Canción de cuna para Rosalía; Canciones marineras; Canción para la niña que no quiere dormir; Coplas con palomas; Dulzura; La loba; Mínima; Nievecita de los campos; Palabras sueltas; Romancillo del niño moreno; Rosa tu melancólica; Serranilla [*Enciclopedia de la música argentina*].

Massa, Juan Bautista, 1885–1938

1.398, Anhelo . . . , —, Emilio Ortiz Grognet, D♭4–G♭5, High, Matilde Duschenios de Ortiz de Guinea, RA BA6006, CNMA

1.399, Canción gitana, 1927, Felix E. Etcheverry, C4–F5, Med, Diego Ortiz Grognet, —, LBV

1.400, *Cinco piezas*

1.400a, En la ausencia, 1928, Félix E. Etcheverry, E4–A5, Med-high, Delia Dreyfus de Rossi, —, UCA

1.400b, La inicial, 1928, Felix E. Etcheverry, C♯4–E5, Med, Iris Sagarna, —, UCA

1.400c, Triste, 1928, Emilio Ortiz Grognet, C4–E♭5, Med-high, Ernestina G. de Siri, —, UCA

1.400d, Camino de plata, 1928, Arturo Capdevila, C4–G5, Med-high, Estela Jurado de Carrasco, —, UCA

1.400e, Desdén, 1928, Leopoldo Lugones, F4–F5, Med-high, Sadie Miller de Steinsleger, —, UCA

1.401, In dono, —, Italo Battelli, G4–G5, Med, Elsa Martinoli; text in Italian, GRic, UCA

1.402, Iorando p'adentro (Puneña), 1936, Jorge Rezzónico Berruet, D4–B♭5, High, Carlos López Buchardo, Brígida Frías de López Buchardo, RA BA12613, UCA

1.403, La madrecita, 1927, Felix E. Etcheverry, C4–E♭5, Med, Rosaura Libarona Brian, RA BA6147, UCA

1.404, Pasó . . . , 1932, Arturo Capdevila, D4–G5, High, Enriqueta Basavilbaso de Catelin, —, CNMA

1.405, Vidalita, —, Felix E. Etcheverry, C4–E♭5, Med-high, José A. Giménez, RA BA6771, CNMA

1.406, Visión, —, Rafael Obligado, F♯4–A5, High, Ofelia Locero Olmedo, —, CNMA

Additional titles: Serenata; Vidalita (II) [CNMA]. Yaraví [ZL]. Alba; A mi alma; Nenia [*Diccionario de la música española e hispanoamericana*]. Nuevo pericón y gato [CNC]. La visión del remanso (Leyenda) [RA].

Napolitano, Emilio Ángel, 1907–1989

1.407, Canción de cuna, op. 2 no. 1, 1939, Ataliva Herrera, A♭4–A♭5, High, A mi hijita Martha, RA BA7632, CNMA

1.408, Flor de cardón (Vidala), op. 2 no. 3, 1941, Ataliva Herrera, E♭4–G♭5, Med-high, Sofía Mendoza; optional duet, RA BA8254, CNMA

1.409, La canción del Saldan, op. 2 no. 2, 1946, Ataliva Herrera, D4–G5, Med-high, Piano reduction, originally for voice and chamber ensemble, RA BA9337, UCA

1.410, La Cenicienta (Canción), op. 6 no. 2, —, Gastón Figueira, C4–E♭5, Med-high, —, RA BA9108, CNMA

1.411, La mariposa (Canción), op. 6 no. 1, 1944, Gastón Figueira, B♭4–G♯5, High, Brígida Frías de López Buchardo, RA BA8920, CNMA

1.412, La suyuqueña (Chacarera), op. 8 no. 1, 1946, Edgardo Eneas Urtubey, E4–F♯5, High, Bertha P. de Bramanti Jauregui, RA, UCA

1.413, Picaflor (Zamba), op. 2 no. 4, 1953, Ataliva Herrera, G4–F5, Med-high, Isabel Marengo, RA BA8252, UCA

Additional titles: El "25 de Mayo"; Fruta silvestre; Mi canción; Patria; Serenata [RA].

Pahissa, Jaime, 1880–1969

1.414, El peregrino, 1957, Enrique Larreta, C♯4–C♯5, Med, Enrique Larreta, RA BA11485, CLP

1.415, *Seis canciones*

1.415a, 1. Añoranzas (L'Enyor), 1946, Jaime Pahissa, G4–G5, High, Line Stevenin; translation into Catalan by Carles Fages de Climent, RA BA9648, UCA

1.415b, 2. Canción del Pañuelo (Canco del mocador), 1946, Jaime Pahissa, F4–A♭5, High, Concepción Badia; translation into Catalan by Carles Fages de Climent, RA BA9648, UCA

1.415c, 3. Un abanico (Un ventall), 1946, Jaime Pahissa, G4–G5, High, María Isabel Curubeto Godoy; translation into Catalan by Carles Fages de Climent, RA BA9648, UCA

1.415d, 4. Canción de estudiante (Canço d'estudiant, serenata), 1946, Jaime Pahissa, F4–F5, High, A mi esposa Montserrat; translation into Catalan by Carles Fages de Climent, RA BA9648, UCA

1.415e, 5. La calesita, 1946, Germán Berdiales, E4–C♯5, Med, Pola Inschauspe de Berdiales; translation into Catalan by Carles Fages de Climent, RA BA9648, UCA

1.415f, 6. Canción de vendimia, 1946, Jaime Pahissa, D4–G5, Med-high, Bería López de Lachica; translation into Catalan by Carles Fages de Climent, RA BA9648, UCA

Additional titles: *Canciones populares catalanas* [UCA]. *Álbum de seis canciones; Baladas; Canço de fada; Canço de lladre; El bastó; El record; El vent de la tardor; En somnis; Invocació de Marçal Prior; La prometida; Liliana; Per un bés; Rosa; Tres baladas* [*Diccionario de la música española e hispanoamericana*].

Palma, Athos, 1891–1952

1.416, *8 Canciones salteñas*

1.416a, Y ese lunar que tienes... (El tapao), 1924, —, E4–C5, Med, Dictadas por María C. Bertolezzi de Oyuela, UCA

1.416b, En el barrio de arriba... (El día de las almas), 1924, —, F♯4–E5, Med-high, Dictadas por María C. Bertolezzi de Oyuela, GRic, UCA

1.416c, Yo soy una flor... (Los reyes en la montaña), 1924, —, F♯4–G5, Med-high, Dictadas por María C. Bertolezzi de Oyuela, GRic, UCA

1.416d, Malhaya de los morenos... (La quinta de los Grañas), 1924, —, E4–E5, Med-high, Dictadas por María C. Bertolezzi de Oyuela, GRic, UCA

1.416e, Oigo cocherito... (La reis y la leocaria), 1924, —, F4–F5, Med-high, Dictadas por María C. Bertolezzi de Oyuela, GRic, UCA

1.416f, Mi padre... (El brujo), 1924, —, F♯4–E5, Med-high, Dictadas por María C. Bertolezzi de Oyuela, GRic, UCA

1.416g, Canción quichua (El sucho), 1924, —, E4–E5, Med-high, Dictadas por María C. Bertolezzi de Oyuela, GRic, UCA

1.416h, Carnaval... (Las carpas), 1924, —, A4–F♯5, Med-high, Dictadas por María C. Bertolezzi de Oyuela, GRic, UCA

1.417, Canción de cuna (Canción a dos voces), 1921, Raúl Vila, D4–D5, Med, Optional duet, —, AW

1.418, El viento, 1920, Pedro Miguel Obligado, F♯4–F♯5, Med-high, Jeanne Dumas, SNM, UCA

1.419, ¡Es Navidad! (Canción a dos voces), 1924, Raúl Vila, D4–D5, Med, Optional duet, —, AW

1.420, Impresión (Canción escolar), 1921, Raúl Vila, C4–C5, Med, —, RA, AW

1.421, *La escuela de las flores*

1.421a, 1., 1921, Rabindranath Tagore, E♭4–G5, Med-high, —, SNM 9, UCA

1.421b, 2., 1921, Rabindranath Tagore, D4–F♯5, Med-high, —, SNM 9, UCA

1.421c, 3., 1921, Rabindranath Tagore, E♭4–E♭5, Med, —, SNM 9, UCA

1.422, Las tres toronjas (Para niños), 1956, Francisco Villaespesa, D♭4–D5, Med, —, RA BA11381, UCA

1.423, Mala (Yaraví), 1952, Agustín Dentone, C4–F5, Med-high, —, RA BA10576, UCA

1.424, *Mi canción*

1.424a, I., 1921, Rabindranath Tagore, B3–G5, Med-high, —, SNM 10, UCA

1.424b, II., 1921, Rabindranath Tagore, E4–F#5, Med-high, —, SNM 10, UCA

1.424c, III., 1921, Rabindranath Tagore, B3–F5, Med, —, SNM 10, UCA

1.425, Primavera (Canción a dos voces), 1921, Raúl Vila, D4–D5, Med, Optional duet, —, AW

1.426, Quiere a tu casita . . . (Canción escolar), 1921, Athos Palma, D♭4–E♭5, Med, —, —, AW

1.427, *Sueño del atardecer*

1.427a, I., 1926, Rafael de Diego, F4–G♭5, Med-high, —, GRic, UCA

1.427b, II., 1926, Rafael de Diego, E♭4–G5, High, —, GRic, UCA

1.428, *Tres canciones de cuna de estrella florida*

1.428a, Canción ligera, 1924, Ida Réboli, D4–C5, Med, —, RA BA9766, UCA

1.428b, Canción de pollitos con sueño, 1924, Ida Réboli, C4–C5, Med, —, RA BA9766, UCA

1.428c, Canción celeste, 1924, Ida Réboli, A3–C#5, Med, —, RA BA9766, UCA

1.429, Triste (Canción a dos voces), 1921, Raúl Vila, F4–D♭5, Med, —, —, AW

Additional titles: Cantique de la vierge; Caperucita; Chanson; El martillo; Elle avait trois couromes d'or; Elle l'enchaîna dans une grotte; Heures ternes; Ils ont tué trois petites filles; J'ai cherché trente ans . . . ; Le matin; Les septs filles d'Orlamonde; Les trois sœurs aveugles; *Trois chansons de Maurice Maeterlinck* [UCA]. Demain des l'aube; Un est venu dere . . .; XV Chansons de Maurice Maeterlinck [SADAIC]. Zamacueca [ZL]. Arpège; A toute âme qui pleure; Au jardin; Deux mélodies; Et s'il revenait un jour, que faut-il lui dire?; Glauche le luci; Les deux ombres; Les filles aux yeux bandés; Les trois sœurs aveugles ont leurs lampes d'or; Les trois sœurs ont voulu mourir; Otoño; Quand l'amant sortit; Romance; Soupir; Sur une croix du village; Vous avez allumé les lampes, oh!, le soleil dans le jardin [INM]. Gloria in excelsis Deo [*Diccionario de la música española e hispanoamericana*].

Panizza, Héctor, 1875–1967

1.430, Chanson galante, 1939, Armand Silvestre, E4–G♭5, High, Ad Amelia; text in French, RA BA7677, INM

1.431, Guitarra, 1942, Victor Hugo, C#4–G5, Med-high, Text in French, CNC, INM

1.432, *Neuf poésies de Paul Verlaine*

1.432a, I. Chanson d'automne, 1943, Paul Verlaine, B3–E♭5, Med, Text in French, RA BA8639, INM

1.432b, II. Green, 1943, Paul Verlaine, C4–F5, Med-high, Text in French, RA BA11223, UCA

1.432c, III. Colloque sentimental, 1943, Paul Verlaine, C4–G5, Med-high, Text in French, RA BA11222, UCA

1.432d, IV. En sourdine, 1943, Paul Verlaine, D4–G5, —, Text in French, RA, UCLA

1.432e, V. Sérénade, 1943, Paul Verlaine, B3–G5, Med, Text in French, RA BA11224, UCA

1.432f, VI. Mon rêve familier, 1943, Paul Verlaine, D4–G5, Med-high, Text in French, RA BA8636, INM

1.432g, VII. Ariettes oubliées (Canto y piano), 1943, Paul Verlaine, C4–F5, Med-high, Text in French, RA BA11221, CNMA

1.432h, VIII. A Clymène, 1943, Paul Verlaine, E♭4–G5, Med-high, Text in French, RA BA11193, UCA

1.432i, IX. Sagesse, 1943, Paul Verlaine, E♭4–G5, Med-high, Text in French, RA, BA8637, UCA

Additional titles: Canción de la bandera (Aurora) [UCA]. L'elogio della bocca; Medioevo latino [INM]. *Deux mélodies;* D'une prison; Escape [*Diccionario de la música española e hispanoamericana*].

Pasqués, Víctor, 1896–1961

1.433, *Dos laúdes*
1.433a, Laude L (Palabras filiales a la Virgen), Alfredo R. Bufano, C#4–G#5, Med-high, —, RA, CNMA
1.433b, El "Cola-blanca", Fermín Estrella Gutiérrez, D4–E5, Med-high, —, RA, ZL

1.434, *Seis Lieder*
1.434a, I. Lied del amor verdadero, Leopoldo Lugones, C4–B♭4, Med, A mi madre, Gaudiosi, ZL
1.434b, II. Lied del secreto dichoso, Leopoldo Lugones, D4–F5, Med-high, Albina Saggese de Macchiavelli, Gaudiosi, ZL
1.434c, III. Lied del misterio gentil, Leopoldo Lugones, F#4–G5, Med-high, Señorita María Nastri, Gaudiosi, ZL
1.434d, IV. Lied de la boca florido, Leopoldo Lugones, D4–F#5, Med-high, Señor Gastón O. Talamón, Gaudiosi, ZL
1.434e, V. Lied del viento y de la fuente, Leopoldo Lugones, C4–G#5, Med-high, Señor Raúl H. Espoile, Gaudiosi, ZL
1.434f, VI. Lied de los ojos amados, Leopoldo Lugones, F#4–A♭5, Med-high, A mi hermana Nélida, Gaudiosi, ZL

Additional titles: Tres canciones argentinas [SADAIC]. Campo argentina for soprano or tenor and chamber ensemble [ANA]. El cola blanca; Danza en el bosque; La cina; Novia del campo [RA].

Paz, Juan Carlos, 1897–1972

1.435, Abel, M. Machado, B3–A5, Med-high, CNMA

Pedrell, Carlos, 1878–1941

1.436, Alba, —, Rafael Obligado, B3–E♭5, Med-high, Clotilde Guillen, RA BA3682, UCA

1.437, *Cuatro canciones*
1.437a, Cállate, por Dios (Ah! tais-toi, par Dieu), 1926, Juan Ramón Jiménez, G4–G5, High, —, ME 1624, UCA
1.437b, Allá vienen las carretas, 1926, Juan Ramón Jiménez, F4–F5, Med-high, —, ME 1624, UCA
1.437c, En la mañana azul, 1926, Juan Ramón Jiménez, F#4–F5, Med-high, —, ME 1624, UCA
1.437d, Oración por las novias tristes, 1926, Juan Ramón Jiménez, G4–G#5, High, —, ME 1624, UCA

1.438, *De Castilla*
1.438a, I. Yo voy soñando caminos, 1919, Antonio Machado, C4–E♭5, Med, —, Breyer, CNMA
1.438b, II. Daba el reloj las doce..., 1919, Antonio Machado, C4–F5, Med-high, —, Breyer, CNMA
1.438c, III. Amada, el aura dice..., 1919, Antonio Machado, E♭4–F5, Med-high, —, Breyer, CNMA
1.438d, IV. Hoy buscarás en vano..., 1919, Antonio Machado, E4–E5, Med-high, —, Breyer, CNMA
1.438e, V. Dice la esperanza..., 1919, Antonio Machado, D♭4–E♭5, Med, —, Breyer, CNMA
1.438f, VI. Caballitos, 1919, Antonio Machado, D4–F5, Med-high, —, Breyer, CNMA

1.439, Ocaso, —, Rafael Obligado, D4–D5, Med, Clotilde Guillen, RA BA3680, UCA

Additional titles: Cantigas del buen amador [UCA]. C'était en avril...; Chansons tristes; *Cinco poemas vocales; Cinq poèmes de Paul Fort; Cuatro canciones argentinas;* Et s'il revenait un jour; *Hispaniques* (Nocturne; Paralleles; Montmartre y

Juan Tenorio) Les yeux qui songent; Ma mère l'oie; Pastorales; Sur l'eau [CNMA]. J'ai pleuré en rêve [INM]. Chanson pour endormir la peine; Le temps a laissé son manteau; Ma mère l'oye; Pour ce que plaisance est morte for voice and orchestra [*Diccionario de la música española e hispanoamericana*]. Aurora; Crepúsculo; Paysage; Voz extraña [RA].

Perceval, Julio, 1903–1963

1.440, *Cantares de Cuyo*

1.440a, I. Del rosal nace la rosa, 1945, Traditional poetry, F♯4–A5, High, Alberto Williams; popular texts collected by Juan Draghi Lucero, UNCA, —, UCA

1.440b, II. Triste me voy a los campos, 1945, Traditional poetry, C♯4–F♯5, Med-high, Alberto Williams; popular texts collected by Juan Draghi Lucero, UNCA, —, UCA

1.440c, III. De todo te acordarás, 1945, Traditional poetry, C♯4–F♯5, Med-high, Alberto Williams; popular texts collected by Juan Draghi Lucero, UNCA, —, UCA

1.440d, IV. Si acaso crees a mi alma, 1945, Traditional poetry, D4–F♯5, Med-high, Alberto Williams; popular texts collected by Juan Draghi Lucero, UNCA, —, UCA

1.440e, V. No se puede, no se puede, 1945, Traditional poetry, E♭4–F♯5, Med, Alberto Williams; popular texts collected by Juan Draghi Lucero, UNCA, —, UCA

1.440f, VI. Te he soñado, 1945, Traditional poetry, C4–F5, Med-high, Alberto Williams; popular texts collected by Juan Draghi Lucero, UNCA, —, UCA

1.440g, VII. Simpatías amorosas, 1945, Traditional poetry, C♯4–E♭5, Med, Alberto Williams; popular texts collected by Juan Draghi Lucero, UNCA, —, UCA

1.440h, VIII. La madrugada, 1945, Traditional poetry, C♯4–G5, Med-high, Alberto Williams; popular texts collected by Juan Draghi Lucero, UNCA, —, UCA

1.441, Poema de amor, 1944, Daniel Devoto, C4–G5, Med-high, María Teresa Maggi, CNC, *Antología de compositores argentinos, vol. VI*, UCA

Additional titles: Melodías; *Quatre sonnets spirituels*; Six chansons [INM]. Il était une fois; La chanson de Marie-des-Anges; Letanías de la Santísima Virgen; Quand sœur mort viendra l'heure [*Diccionario de la música española e hispanoamericana*].

Pinto, Alejandro, 1922–1991

1.442, *Cancionero y romancero de ausencias*

1.442a, I. De la contemplación, 1961, Miguel Hernández, C♯4–E♭5, Med, Also arranged for soprano, piano, clarinet, violin, and cello (1977), m, SADAIC

1.442b, II. ¿Para que me han parido, mujer?, 1961, Miguel Hernández, C4–F5, Med, Also arranged for soprano, piano, clarinet, violin, and cello (1977), m, SADAIC

1.442c, III. Ausencia, 1961, Miguel Hernández, C♯4–F5, Med, Also arranged for soprano, piano, clarinet, violin, and cello (1977), m, SADAIC

1.442d, IV. Cada vez mas presente, 1961, Miguel Hernández, B3–E5, Med, Also arranged for soprano, piano, clarinet, violin, and cello (1977), m, SADAIC

1.442e, V. No te asomes a la ventana, 1961, Miguel Hernández, B♭3–D5, Med, Also arranged for soprano, piano, clarinet, violin, and cello (1977), m, SADAIC

1.442f, VI. Cogedme, cogedme, 1961, Miguel Hernández, D♯4–E♭5, Med, Also arranged for soprano, piano, clarinet, violin, and cello (1977), m, SADAIC

1.442g, VII. ¿Qué pasa?, 1961, Miguel Hernández, F♯4–F♯5, Med, Also arranged for soprano, piano, clarinet, violin, and cello (1977), m, SADAIC

1.442h, VIII. Bocas de ira, 1961, Miguel Hernández, D4–F5, Med, Also arranged for soprano, piano, clarinet, violin, and cello (1977), m, SADAIC

1.442i, IX. Menos tu vientre, 1961, Miguel Hernández, B3–E♯5, Med, Also arranged for soprano, piano, clarinet, violin, and cello (1977), m, SADAIC

1.442j, X. Son mios, ¡Ay!, son mios, 1961, Miguel Hernández, G4–C♯5, Med, Also arranged for soprano, piano, clarinet, violin, and cello (1977), m, SADAIC

1.442k, XI. Quise despedirme más . . . , 1961, Miguel Hernández, B♭3–D5, Med, Also arranged for soprano, piano, clarinet, violin, and cello (1977), m, SADAIC

1.442l, XII. ¿Qué quiere el viento de enero . . . ?, 1961, Miguel Hernández, B3–F5, Med-high, Also arranged for soprano, piano, clarinet, violin, and cello (1977), m, SADAIC

1.442m, XIII. Cerca del agua te quiero llevar, 1961, Miguel Hernández, B3–E5, Med, Also arranged for soprano, piano, clarinet, violin, and cello (1977), m, SADAIC

1.442n, XIV. Dime desde alla abajo, 1961, Miguel Hernández, B♭3–B4, Med, Also arranged for soprano, piano, clarinet, violin, and cello (1977), m, SADAIC

1.442o, XV. Tristes guerras, 1961, Miguel Hernández, B♭3–F♯5, Med, Also arranged for soprano, piano, clarinet, violin, and cello (1977), m, SADAIC

1.442p, XVI. Déjame que me vaya, 1961, Hernández, C♯4–F5, Med, Also arranged for soprano, piano, clarinet, violin, and cello (1977), m, SADAIC

1.442q, XVII. La vejez de los pueblos, 1961, Miguel Hernández, B3–C5, Med, Also arranged for soprano, piano, clarinet, violin, and cello (1977), m, SADAIC

1.442r, XVIII. No, no hay carcel para el hombre, 1961, Miguel Hernández, B♭3–F♯5, Med, Also arranged for soprano, piano, clarinet, violin, and cello (1977), m, SADAIC

1.443, *Cinco pequeñas canciones judías*

1.443a, Vino (Vain), 1954, Kehos Klinger, D4–E5, Med, —, RA, IU

1.443b, Ven, Sol (Kum, Zun), 1954, Kehos Klinger, D4–E5, Med, —, RA, IU

1.443c, Estado yo aqui (Az ij bin do), 1954, Kehos Klinger, C♯4–G5, Med-high, —, RA, IU

1.443d, Muros (Vent), 1954, Kehos Klinger, D4–E5, Med, —, RA, IU

1.443e, ¡Que venga el leñador! (Zol kumen der heker!), 1954, Kehos Klinger, C4–F5, Med, —, RA, IU

1.444, *Tres canciones panameñas*

1.444a, Despedida, 1974, Tristan Solarte, C♯4–E♭5, Med-high, —, m, IU

1.444b, Trozo, 1974, Demetrio Herrera Sevillano, B3–E5, Med, —, m, IU

1.444c, Cumbia, 1974, José Franco, —, —, Narrated text, m, IU

Additional titles: Cinco pequeñas poesías de Haydée Waxman; ¿Dios, dónde te hallare?; ¿Escuchas?; Ocho miniaturas poéticas; Siete miniaturas poéticas [SADAIC]. *Árbol de Diana; Tiempo de Alejandra* (for voice and piano or for voice and chamber orchestra) [ANA]. *Tres canciones de amor a Frumet; Tres pequeñas poesías de Israel Aschendorf* [INM]. *Canción nocturna; Canciones primigenias; Cinco canciones del ghetto; Salmo 150; Seis pequeñas poesías* [Diccionario de la música española e hispanoamericana].

Pinto, Alfredo, 1891–1968

1.445, El arrepentío, 1941, Rosario Beltrán Núñez, G4–A♭5, High, A mi hijita Elsa, CNC, CNMA

Additional titles: 4 Chansons [RA]. *Trois chansons* [UCA]. *El alfanaje; Sole d'invierno* [SADAIC]. *Narcisses* [LBV]. *Allegresse; Amor de morenita; Com'api armoniose; Ella venne; Himno a la Llerena; I petali pispigliani; La danse de dieux; La danseuse; Les deux flûtes; L'orage favorable; Mattinatta; Solterito, buena vida; Tre canzoni; Toujours* [Diccionario de la música española e hispanoamericana].

Quaratino, Pascual, 1904–1973

1.446, Caja chayera, 1956, José Ramón Luna, E4–G5, Med-high, Mi Padre, RA BA11377, UCA

1.447, Canción para el niño en la cuna, 1944, C. Gonzalez Castillo, E♭4–F5, Med-high, Brigidita Frias de Lopez Buchardo, RA BA8876, ZL

1.448, Cerro, luna y aire, 1956, José Ramón Luna, D♯4–F5, Med-high, Guido Valcarenghi, RA BA11378, UCA

1.449, Duda, 1964, José Ramón Luna, E♭4–F5, Med-high, Nora Bloisse de Napolitano, RA BA12325, UCA

1.450, El flechazo (Canción en el estilo popular argentino), 1935, Amelia Monti, E4–F5, Med-high, Adelina Morelli, RA BA6902, UCA

1.451, La chucara, 1964, Rosario Beltrán Nuñez, E♭4–F5, Med-high, Floria Bloise, RA BA12324, UCA

1.452, Lamento indio (Vidala), 1938, María Carmen Cano, D♭4–F5, Med-high, Eugenia Harrison, RA BA7466, UCA

1.453, Machao, 1964, Jose Ramon Luna, F4–F5, Med-high, Francisco Lamattina, RA BA12326, UCA

1.454, Pampeana (Canción en el estilo popular argentino), 1934, Amelia Monti, C4–G5, Med-high, Tito Schipa, RA BA6873, UCA

1.455, Ronda del sol, 1947, Juan Bautista Grosso, C4–D5, Med-high, Carlos Enrique Castelli, RA BA9894, CNMA

1.456, *Tres canciones argentinas*

1.456a, Chismecito, 1941, Amelia Monti, D4–G♯5, Med-high, José Gil, —, UCA

1.456b, ¡Bien haya! . . . , 1941, Amelia Monti, D4–G5, Med-high, María Teresa Maggi, —, UCA

1.456c, El embrujao, 1941, Rosario Beltrán Nuñez, E♭4–G5, High, María Kareska, —, UCA

Additional titles: Alla luna [CNMA]. Guadiana; Plegaria del cerro; Siesta [*Diccionario de la música española e hispanoamericana*].

Rodríguez, Ricardo, 1877–1951

1.457, *Seis canciones*

1.457a, La calandria, 1953, Luis María Iglesias, A3–F5, Med-high, Luis María Iglesias, RA BA10884, TC

1.457b, Pajarito carpintero, 1953, Luis María Iglesias, C4–G5, Med-high, Luis María Iglesias, RA BA10884, ZL

1.457c, El picaflor, 1953, Luis María Iglesias, C♯4–F♯5, Med, Luis María Iglesias, RA BA10884, ZL

1.457d, La tacuarita, 1953, Luis María Iglesias, B3–D5, Med, Luis María Iglesias, RA BA10884, ZL

1.457e, El pescadito, 1953, Luis María Iglesias, D4–E♯5, Med, Luis María Iglesias, RA BA10884, ZL

1.457f, Las mariposas, 1953, Luis María Iglesias, E4–G♯5, Med-high, Luis María Iglesias, RA BA10884, ZL

Additional titles: Nueva salve [SADAIC]. No puede ser; Tendresse [ANA]. Automne; Blanca nieve; Canción a la música; Canción de cuna; Chanson déchirante; Duerme; El martillo; Fábula; La niña charlatana; La tos de la muñeca; L'aveu permis; Marcha escolar; Mía; Mon âme est une grappe de raisin; Ne dors pas; Prière; Tu sais; Vuela, vuela; Zapatitos de cristal [*Diccionario de la música española e hispanoamericana*].

Rosaenz, Elifio, 1916–

1.458, *Paisajes*

1.458a, Encanto, 1962, Leopoldo Lugones, F4–G♭5, Med-high, m, CNMA

1.458b, El lucero, 1962, Leopoldo Lugones, F♯4–F♯5, Med-high, m, CNMA

1.458c, Aurora, 1962, Leopoldo Lugones, E4–G♯5, High, m, CNMA

Additional titles: Pena India [*Diccionario de la música española e hispanoamericana*].

Sáenz, Pedro, 1915–1995

1.459, *Cinco canciones*
1.459a, 1. Por el campo, 1974, Miguel de Unamuno, C#4–F#5, Med-high, Ernesto Halffter, UME, UCA
1.459b, 2. Uno ojos dulces, 1974, Miguel de Unamuno, E4–F5, Med-high, Ernesto Halffter, UME, UCA
1.459c, 3. En la ribera, 1974, Miguel de Unamuno, D♭4–F#5, Med-high, Ernesto Halffter, UME, UCA
1.459d, 4. De noche, 1974, Miguel de Unamuno, D4–E5, Med-high, Ernesto Halffter, UME, UCA
1.459e, 5. Echa la copla, coplero, 1974, Miguel de Unamuno, D4–E♭5, Med, Ernesto Halffter, UME, UCA

1.460, *Seis canciones*
1.460a, Aquí está tu medio amante, 1986, Poetry from traditional Argentine songs, D4–E♭5, Med, Teresa Berganza, UME, ZL
1.460b, Vida mía, ya me voy, 1986, Poetry from traditional Argentine songs, D4–D5, Med-high, Teresa Berganza, UME, ZL
1.460c, La viuda que se casa, 1986, Poetry from traditional Argentine songs, D4–E♭5, Med, Teresa Berganza, UME, ZL
1.460d, Aquel pajarito triste, 1986, Poetry from traditional Argentine songs, D#4–F#5, Med-high, Teresa Berganza, UME, ZL
1.460e, Te quiero más que a mis ojos, 1986, Poetry from traditional Argentine songs, E4–F5, Med-high, Teresa Berganza, UME, ZL
1.460f, Así como todo muda, 1986, Poetry from traditional Argentine songs, G4–F#5, Med-high, Teresa Berganza, UME, ZL

1.461, *Tres canciones*
1.461a, I. Esa canción, 1959, Miguel Ángel Rondano, D4–F#5(A5), High, Lucía Bordelois, RA BA11749, +
1.461b, II. Madrigal, 1959, Miguel Ángel Rondano, C4–F#5, Med, Lucía Bordelois, RA BA11749, +
1.461c, III. Idilio, 1959, Miguel Ángel Rondano, D4–F5, Med-high, Lucía Bordelois, RA BA11749, +

Additional titles: Ave María; Canciones argentinas; Cinco poemas de Alberti; Dos canciones humorísticas [Diccionario de la música española e hispanoamericana].

Sammartino, Luis, 1888–1973

1.462, Agua del cielo, —, Carlos Fernández Shaw, D4–D5, Med, Luis V. Ochoa Poggi, —, AW
1.463, A la luna (Canción de cuna), —, Raúl Vila, C4–D5, Med-high, —, —, SADAIC
1.464, Alborada, —, Raúl Vila, D4–G5, Med-high, Adelina Morelli, —, SADAIC
1.465, Arroyito de nostalgia (Zamba), 1944, Juan Bautista Grosso, D4–E♭5, Med-high, —, CLSRL, CNMA
1.466, Azucenita del campo (Zamba), 1947, Juan Bautista Grosso, F#4–G5, Med-high, Mariano Olivares, RA BA9775, LBV
1.467, ¡Buen viaje!, —, Amado Nervo, E4–C#5, —, Meda los niños de la Escuela Jose Manuel Estrada Poggi, —, AW
1.468, ¡Caballito pampa!, 1956, Arsenio Cavillo Sinclair, C4–F5, Med-high, Ricardo Rodriguez, RA BA11408, CNMA
1.469, Caminito de sol, —, Pedro Juan Vignale, C4–D5, Med-high, Ricarde Bullé, —, AW
1.470, Campo de Buenos Aires, —, Andrés del Pozo, D4–G5, High, —, m, ZL
1.471, Cuando muere la tarde, —, Juan Juncos, D4–E5, Med-high, —, —, LBV

1.472, *De mi patria*
1.472a, Triste, 1946, Juan Bautista Grosso, B3–G5, Med-high, Gastón Figueira, RA BA9390, LBV
1.472b, Milonga, 1946, Juan Bautista Grosso, C4–G5, Med-high, Gastón Figueira, RA BA9390, LBV
1.472c, Gato, 1946, Juan Bautista Grosso, B3–G5, Med-high, Gastón Figueira, RA BA9390, LBV

1.473, Dolor serrano (Triste), 1947, Juan Bautista Grosso, F4–F5, Med-high, Pablo Scolari, CLSRL, LBV

1.474, El arriero serrano (Zamba), 1941, Marcos J. Ferraris, E4–F♯5, Med-high, Inés Mariani, RA BA11998, SADAIC

1.475, El poncho, 1934, Arsenio Cavillo Sinclair, C4–G5, Med-high, César Stiattesi, M. Calvello, CNMA

1.476, El sol de tu querer (Zamba), 1944, Juan Bautista Grosso, E4–E5, Med-high, —, CLSRL, CNMA

1.477, El viejo cacique, —, Juan Bautista Grosso, D4–F5, Med-high, —, m, ZL

1.478, Este es el viento, —, Andrés del Pozo, C♯4–G♯5, Med-high, —, m, ZL

1.479, La rosa, —, Adela Fautrier, E♭4–A♭5, High, —, —, SADAIC

1.480, Los camalotes (Zamba), —, Ernesto J. Etcheverry, B3–E5, Med, —, RA BA8035, LBV

1.481, Luna y suspiros (Vals), —, Juan Bautista Grosso, C4–E5, Med, —, —, SADAIC

1.482, Mariposas, —, Olivia von Frankenberg Martinez, D4–G♯5, High, —, m, SADAIC

1.483, Messaggio d'amore, —, A. C. Petri, F♯4–F5, Med-high, Al maestro Gaetano Radiente Ortelli; text in Italian, —, SADAIC

1.484, Mi vallecito florido (Zamba), 1947, Juan Bautista Grosso, D4–E♭5, Med, Ángel Escobal Bavio, CLSRL, LBV

1.485, Noche de luna, —, Luis Arena, C4–F5, Med, —, —, SADAIC

1.486, *Pampa, sierra y sol (Canciones y danzas de mi tierra)*

1.486a, 1. Nocturno pampeano (Triste), 1948, Juan Bautista Grosso, C4–E♭5, Med-high, Augusta Tarnassi de Palma, ESar, CNMA

1.486b, 2. Pregunto a mi guitarra (Gato), 1948, Juan Bautista Grosso, E♯4–E5, Med-high, José M. Peralta, ESar, CNMA

1.486c, 3. Mañana con sol (Tonada), 1948, Juan Bautista Grosso, C4–E5, Med-high, Bruno Bonfiglioli, ESar, CNMA

1.486d, 4. La huella gaucha (Huella), 1948, Juan Bautista Grosso, C♯4–E5, Med-high, Alfredo del Pozzo, ESar, CNMA

1.486e, 5. El río de montaña (Zamba), 1948, Juan Bautista Grosso, C4–D5, Med, Enrique Mariani, ESar, CNMA

1.486f, 6. Queja Coya (Vidala), 1948, Juan Bautista Grosso, C4–E5, Med, Carlos R. Larrimbo, ESar, CNMA

1.487, Parabola, —, Elio del Giglio, E4–G5, Med-high, Dionisio di Fonzo, —, SADAIC

1.488, *Rimas de Bécquer*

1.488a, Rima XVII, 1911, Gustavo Adolfo Bécquer, C4–E5, Med, Mario Rossegger Ortelli, —, SADAIC

1.488b, Rima XVIII, 1911, Gustavo Adolfo Bécquer, E4–G♯5, Med-high, Augusto Demaldé Ortelli, —, SADAIC

1.488c, Amor eterno, 1911, Gustavo Adolfo Bécquer, E4–F♯5, Med-high, A . . . ., Ortelli, —, SADAIC

1.489, Vorrei, —, Umberto Romanelli, F♯4–A5, Med-high, Umberto Romanelli; text in Italian, David Poggi, SADAIC

Additional titles: A la ronda del mar; En los valles de tus ojos (Zamba) [CNMA]. Los ojos de mi morena; Madrecita; Perfume de nostalgia [SADAIC]. Amor moreno; Morir bailando; Val [*Diccionario de la música española e hispanoamericana*]. ¡A una flor!; El overito; Hogar Carlos Spada (hijo) [CNC]. Aquí estoy (Chacarera); Canción del tucu-tucu; Ensueño embriagador (Vals); Primavera; Sueña Rosaflor [RA].

Sciammarella, Valdo, 1924–

1.490, *Canciones de amor*

1.490a, 1. El amor de las flores (Canción), 1979, Traditional Argentine *coplas*, D4–G5, High, Carlos López Buchardo, m, UCA

1.490b, 2. Canta la morena (Romance), 1979, Traditional Argentine *coplas*, D4–G5, Med-high, Carlos López Buchardo, m, UCA

1.490c, 3. El amor melancólico (En estilo de Vidala), 1979, Traditional Argentine *coplas*, C4–A♭5, Med-high, Carlos López Buchardo, m, UCA

1.490d, 4. El amor pícaro (Gato), 1979, Traditional Argentine *coplas*, C4–G5, Med-high, Carlos López Buchardo, m, UCA

1.491, *Cantigas de amigo*

1.491a, I., 1951, Francisco Javier, D4–A♭5, Med-high, A J. L. y E. R., Barry, UCA

1.491b, II., 1951, Francisco Javier, B♯3–G♯5, Med-high, A J. L. y E. R., Barry, UCA

1.491c, III., 1951, Francisco Javier, B3–G5, Med-high, A J. L. y E. R., Barry, UCA

1.491d, IV., 1951, Francisco Javier, F♯4–A5, Med-high, A J. L. y E. R., Barry, UCA

1.491e, V., 1951, Francisco Javier, F♯4–A5, High, A J. L. y E. R., Barry, UCA

1.491f, VI., 1951, Francisco Javier, C4–E♭5, Med-high, A J. L. y E. R., Barry, UCA

1.491g, VII., 1951, Francisco Javier, D4–G♯5, Med-high, A J. L. y E. R., Barry, UCA

1.491h, VIII., 1951, Francisco Javier, F4–F5, Med-high, A J. L. y E. R., Barry, UCA

1.492, *Cantos de melancolía*

1.492a, I. Mi voz, 1978, J. J. Castro, G3–A5, Med-high, Juán José Castro; two sets included in this collection, m, UCA

1.492b, II. Grito, 1978, J. J. Castro, B3–G5, Med-high, Juán José Castro; two sets included in this collection, m, UCA

1.493, *Cantos de melancolía*

1.493a, I. Soñé un canto, 1978, J. J. Castro, B♭3–G5, Med-high, Juán José Castro; two sets included in this collection, m, UCA

1.493b, II. Todos me piden que cante, 1978, Traditional text, A3–G5, Med, Juán José Castro; two sets included in this collection, m, UCA

1.493c, III. Melancolía, 1978, Rubén Darío, B♭3–A♭5, Med-high, Juán José Castro; two sets included in this collection, m, UCA

1.494, *Cuatro canciones*

1.494a, I. El instante, 1989, Francisco Luis Bernárdez, G3–F4, Med, —, m, UCA

1.494b, II. Si al mecer . . . , 1989, Gustavo Adolfo Bécquer, D4–F♯5, Med, —, m, UCA

1.494c, III. Volverán . . . , 1989, Gustavo Adolfo Bécquer, C4–G♭5, Med-high, —, m, UCA

1.494d, IV. Hoy como ayer, . . . , 1989, Gustavo Adolfo Bécquer, B♭3–G♯5, Med-high, —, m, UCA

1.495, Mon cœur, —, Rafael Insausti, E4–A5, Med-high, Text in French, IU,

1.496, *Romancillos de la colonia*

1.496a, I. Muerte de Elena, 1958, Traditional texts, A3–G♭5, Med, —, RA BA11617, +

1.496b, II. Delgadina, 1958, Traditional texts, B3–G5, Med, —, RA BA11617, +

1.496c, III. El galán y la calavera, 1958, Traditional texts, A3–F♯5, Med, —, RA BA11617, +

1.496d, IV. Escogiendo novia, 1958, Traditional texts, B3–G5, Med, —, RA BA11617, +

1.496e, V. Muerte del señor don Gato, 1958, Traditional texts, G3(B3)–A5, Med, —, RA BA11617, +

Additional titles: Campesina; Canción; *Dos canciones de ausencia* [INM]. Cánticos rituales; Las canciones de Anna-Sao [*Enciclopedia de la música argentina*].

Serrano Redonnet, Ana, 1910–1993

1.497, *Seis aires argentinos*

1.497a, Canción de la guagua (Arrorró indio), 1939, Rafael Jijena Sánchez, F4–F5, Med, EAM, UCA

1.497b, Yaveñita, 1939, Domingo Zerpa, G4–E5, Med-high, EAM, UCA

1.497c, Bagualita (Aire salteño), 1939, Letra popular, E4–E5, Med-high, EAM, UCA

1.497d, Una copla, 1939, Letra popular, E4–E5, Med, EAM, UCA

1.497e, Llorando (Aire de Vidala), 1939, Bernardo Canal Feijoó, C4–C5, Med, EAM, UCA

1.497f, Triste estoy (Aire de Yaraví), 1939, Rafael Jijena Sánchez, E4–E5, Med, EAM, UCA

1.498, Yaraví, 1965, Rubén A. Vela, C4–D5, Med, EAM 138, IU

Siccardi, Honorio, 1897–1963

1.499, Canción de los sembradores, 1943, María Alicia Domínguez, A3–D5, Med-high, —, RA, +

1.500, Canción para la abuela (Canzone per la nonna), 1940, Leonidas Barletta, E♭4–A♭5, Med-high, Josefina Leoni de Bigi; translated into Spanish by H. Siccardi, RA, +

1.501, *Dos canciones de Amado Villar*

1.501a, I. Primavera del campamento (Primavera d'accampamento), 1937, Amado Villar, D4–G5(A5), Med-high, Nilda Muller; translated into Spanish by H. Siccardi, RA, +

1.501b, II. Camino para la sonrisa de una muchacha (Cammino pel sorriso d'una ragazza), 1937, Amado Villar, D♭4–G5, High, Rosa Gonzalez Campos; translated into Spanish by H. Siccardi, RA, +

1.502, *Dos piezas*

1.502a, Desolación, 1929, Leopoldo Lugones, D♭4–D♭5, —, Italian translation by H. Siccardi, RA BA7371, +

1.502b, Melancolía, 1929, Leopoldo Lugones, F♯4–G♯5, —, Italian translation by H. Siccardi, RA BA7371, +

1.503, Romance con lejanías, 1940, Mastronardi, C♯4–G♯5, Med, Luis A. Barberis, Agustina Martinez de Barberis; translated into Spanish by H. Siccardi, RA, +

1.504, *Tríptico floral*

1.504a, I. Flor de tuna, 1944, Justo G. Dessein Merlo, G4–A♭5, High, —, CNC, CNMA

1.504b, II. Flor de durazno, 1944, Justo G. Dessein Merlo, F♯4–G♯5, High, —, CNC, CNMA

1.504c, III. Flor de ceibo, 1944, Justo G. Dessein Merlo, A3–F♯5, High, —, CNC, CNMA

Additional titles: El patito jugetón; Esperanza; Han llovido tus ojos... [INM]. A Juan María Gutiérrez; Ave María; Canto del huésped; Canzone; Caridad; *Cuatro melodías*; Degli occhi redenti; Desde allá, desde el fondo de mi alma; Dolor sin palabras; *Dos villancicos*; El carretiere (Pascoli); La lluvia no dice nada; Los caminos se cruzan; Me diste tu amistad; Momento; Niebla; Primavera; Tambo; *Tres canciones*; *Tres líricas para Amada*; Tu nombre for contralto and clarinet; Tus cuatro romanzas; Villancico [*Diccionario de la música española e hispanoamericana*]. Cuatro poesías de Horacio Rega Molina; Quattro liriche italiane [*Enciclopedia de la música argentina*].

Souviron, Yvette, 1914–

1.505, Al banco solitario, 1955, Yvette Souviron, D♭4–F5, Med-high, TR, *The Latin American Art Song*, +, LC

1.506, Carnavalito, 1990, Yvette Souviron, A3–A5, Med-high, TR, *The Latin American Art Song*, +, LC

1.507, Gaucho mensajero, 1990, Yvette Souviron, D4–A5, High, m, LC, —

Additional titles: Belle mer; Canto Gitano; Co-co-ro-có; Cousin; Do I dare?; Habanera; Irulia; La belle françoise; L'écho de Paris; Palomitay; Poema de Neruda; Poème; Tango argentino; Vidalita [LC].

Spena, Lita, 1904–1989

1.508, Agüita clara, Julia Crespo, G4–E5, Med-high, IU
1.509, Bailecito, Pedro Juan Vignale, E♭4–E5, Med, IU
1.510, Caminito de la sierra, Jullia Crespo, E4–B5, Med-high, IU
1.511, Camino de tu capricho (Zamba canción), Horacio Guillén, D4–G5, Med-high, IU
1.512, Canción, Carlos Mingo, E♭5–F♯5, Med-high, IU
1.513, Coplas al Tulumaya, Alfredo R. Bufano, G4–B♭5, High, IU

1.514, *Coplas jujeñas*
1.514a, I., —, D4–E5, Med, IU
1.514b, II., —, G4–G5, Med-high, IU
1.514c, III., —, F♯4–F♯5, Med-high, IU
1.514d, IV., —, E4–G♯5, Med-high, IU
1.514e, V., —, G4–E♭5, Med, IU
1.514f, VI., —, E4–A5, Med-high, IU
1.514g, VII., —, F4–F5, Med-high, IU
1.514h, VIII., —, E♭4–F5, Med-high, IU
1.514i, IX., —, F♯4–F♯5, Med-high, IU
1.514j, X., —, E4–G5, Med-high, IU

1.515, *Dos tonadas cuyanas*
1.515a, I. Corazón más no llores, Anonymous, D4–G5, Med-high, IU
1.515b, II. Canción de cuna, Anonymous, G4–A♭5, High, IU

1.516, Paloma del aire (Canción criolla), Horacio Guillén, F4–G5, Med-high, IU
1.517, Romance de las tres ranas, Jorge Jantus, C♯4–C♯5, Med, IU
1.518, Ronda con sabor a mar, Julia Crespo, D4–E5, Med, IU

Additional titles: Canción de la Vendimia [CNMA]. Preludios [SADAIC]. La brise vagabonde; Printemps plein d'indolence; Seuil de la vrai jeunesse … [IU]. Coplas del querer; Gato; Lluvia; Paisaje [*Diccionario de la música española e hispanoamericana*].

Stiatessi, César, 1881–1934

1.519, Atardecer (Zamba-Canción), Santiago Stagnaro, E4–A5, Med-high, Juan de Diós Filiberto, —, UCA

1.520, *Canciones argentinas*
1.520a, Triste, Luis Agote, D4–G5, High, —, SNM 16, UCA
1.520b, ¿Qué ansías?, Amado Nervo, F♯4–A5, High, —, SNM 17, UCA
1.521, El ave marina, Leopoldo Lugones, E4–A5, Med-high, —, SNM 19, CNMA
1.522, En el templo, E. Morales, E4–G5, Med-high, —, SNM 18, CNMA
1.523, Sfinge (Pagina d'album), Humberto Romanelli, D4–G5, High, A "Bibelot" Ortelli, —, TC
1.524, Silenzio ci vuole (Stornello popolare), Twelfth-century text, E♭4–G♭5, Med-high, Text in Italian, —, TC

Additional titles: Nostalgia (Triste) [CNMA]. Las campanas [*Diccionario de la música española e hispanoamericana*].

Suffern, Carlos, 1901–1991

1.525, *Con el alba en las manos*
1.525a, 1. La vertiente, 1956–1966, Antonio Requeni, E♭4–A5, Med-high, —, m, IU
1.525b, 2. Dulce engaño, 1956–1966, Antonio Requeni, D♭4–G5, Med-high, —, m, IU
1.525c, 3. Lluvia con sol, 1956–1966, Antonio Requeni, G4–B♭5, High, —, m, IU
1.525d, 4. Verano, 1956–1966, Antonio Requeni, E♭4–G♯5, High, —, m, IU

1.526, *Deux estampes japonaises*
1.526a, 1. Le chevalier amoureux, 1928, Anonymous, A3–G♯5, Med-high, —, m, UCA
1.526b, 2. Prés la ville de Ioba, 1928, Anonymous, D4–G5, Med-high, —, m, IU

1.527, En mi soledad, 1946, Fryda Schultz de Mantovani, C4–G5, Med, Lola V. M. de Puente, RA BA9656, IU

1.528, La lavandera, 1946, Fernán Silva Valdez, D4–F♯5, Med-high, A mi madre, RA BA9336, UCA

1.529, Por los campos verdes, 1936, Juana de Ibarbourou, D4–D5, Med, Para Huguita Romero Fernández, —, UCA

1.530, *Tres baladas de Liliencron*

1.530a, Al trote, 1946, Detlev von Liliencron, D4–F♯5, Med, —, m, IU

1.530b, Muerto en las mieses, 1946, Detlev von Liliencron, C♯4–F5, Med-high, —, m, IU

1.530c, Correría mañanera, 1946, Detlev von Liliencron, D4–F♯5, Med-high, —, m, IU

Additional titles: Seuil de la vrai jeunesse [IU]. Binnesegemen; Canción (Los astros son rondas de niños); Ciclo de la noche; Cipreses de jardín; Erakles; Espíritu sutil; La canción de la virgen; Luna; Mañana de enero; Mandoline; Melopea para el viejo pastor de Sicilia; Minnelied Tagewise; Seis canciones de cuna para Natacha; Silencio; Tres cantigas de Alfonso el Sabio for voice and piano or guitar; Trois poèmes d'André Gide; Yo me era mora moraima [*Diccionario de la música española e hispanoamericana*]. Ciclo de la noche; De "La flauta de caña"; Dos canciones infantiles; Héraclès [*Enciclopedia de la música argentina*].

Terzián, Alicia, 1934–

1.531, *Canciones para niños*

1.531a, I. Canción cantada, 1956, Federico García Lorca, D4–G5, Med-high, —, m, UCA

1.531b, II. Canción tonta, 1956, Federico García Lorca, C4–E♭5, Med, —, m, UCA

1.531c, III. Canción china en Europa, 1956, Federico García Lorca, D4–G5, Med-high, —, m, UCA

1.531d, IV. Cancioncilla sevillana, 1956, Federico García Lorca, E4–E♭5, Med, —, m, UCA

1.532, *Tres retratos*

1.532a, I. Debussy, 1954, Federico García Lorca, D♭4–E♭5, Med, —, m, UCA

1.532b, II. Juan Ramón Jiménez, 1954, Federico García Lorca, E4–E5, Med, —, m, UCA

1.532c, III. Verlaine, 1954, Federico García Lorca, D♯4–(E5)G♯5, Med, —, m, UCA

1.533, Tristeza, 1956, Lord Byron, C4–G♭5, Med-high, A mi Diana, m, UCA

Additional titles: Dos canciones; Embryo no. 5 de Imágenes cósmicas I for voice and violin; Tres canciones [*Diccionario de la música española e hispanoamericana*].

Torrá, Celia, 1884–1962

1.534, Abandono, 1932, Carmen Latino, D4–G5, Med-high, Antonieta Silveyra de Lenhardson, SNM, UCA

1.535, Cantar de arriero, —, Rafael Jijena Sánchez, D4–F♯5, Med, María Escudero Ortelli, —, CNMA

1.536, Changuito (Canción infantil), 1952, Adela Christensen, D4–B4, Med, Al jardín de infancia "Mitre"; may be accompanied by drum or tambourine, RA, UCA

1.537, Milonga del destino, —, Fernán Silva Valdés, D4–F5, Med-high, —, —, UCA

1.538, *Seis coplas*

1.538a, 1. Por los campos de la Patria, —, —, E4–G5, Med-high, —, m, IU

1.538b, 2. La copla es copla si nace..., —, —, F4–E♭5, Med, —, m, IU

1.538c, 3. No hay una pena más pena, —, —, F4–F5, Med-high, —, m, IU

1.538d, 4. Dale a mi copla, Dios mío, —, —, D♯4–E♭5, Med-high, —, m, IU

1.538e, 5. Mi patria para vivir, —, —, G4–E♭5, Med-high, —, m, IU

1.538f, 6. Maizales de Buenos Aires, —, —, F4–F5, Med-high, —, m, IU

1.539, Vida, vidita..., —, Rafael Jijena Sánchez, F4–F5, Med-high, María Antonieta Silveyra de Lenhardson Ortelli, —, CNMA

Additional titles: Himno a la paz; Himno a la raza; La campana; Las palomitas; Mi reloj; *Tres canciones* [UCA]. La señora semana; Los amigos [ANA]. Cacharros y ponchitos; Capillas; Crepuscular; Otoño; Quisiera eternizarme; Visión de paz [*Diccionario de la música española e hispanoamericana*]. A la patria; Alborada; El aguila; Himno del liceo; La gallina ponedora; Marcha patriótica; Oración a la bandera; Primavera [CNC]. El sauce; Oh María, Virgo pía [RA].

Torre Bertucci, José, 1888–1970

1.540, *Cuatro canciones*
1.540a, I. Melancolía, 1919, Pablo Cavestany, E4–G5, Med-high, A Ninon Vallin, Breyer Hermanos, UCA
1.540b, II. Madrigal, 1919, Pablo Cavestany, D♭4–F5, Med-high, —, Breyer Hermanos, UCA
1.540c, III. Madrigal, 1919, Pablo Cavestany, E4–F5, Med-high, —, Breyer Hermanos, UCA
1.540d, IV. El indiecito de Pichi-Mahuida, 1919, Pablo Cavestany, D4–F♯5, Med, —, Breyer Hermanos, UCA

1.541, *Tres poemas*
1.541a, I. Soledad, 1927, Rafael Alberto Arrieta, C♯4–G♯5, Med-high, —, SNM, UCA
1.541b, II. Canción ingenua, 1927, Rafael Alberto Arrieta, C4–G♯5, High, —, SNM, UCA
1.541c, III. El retorno, 1927, Rafael Alberto Arrieta, F♯3–A5, Med-high, —, SNM, UCA

Troiani, Cayetano, 1873–1942

1.542, *Canciones infantiles*
1.542a, La cabrita blanca, 1928, Mercedes y Avelina Peyro, E♭4–D5, Med, Raúl H. Espoile, RA BA7225, UCA
1.542b, Mis soldaditos, 1928, Mercedes y Avelina Peyro, C4–D5, Med, Emity Carlitos, RA BA7225, UCA
1.542c, El indiecito, 1928, Mercedes y Avelina Peyro, D4–D5, Med, Athos Palma, RA BA7225, UCA
1.542d, La provincianita (Zamba), 1928, Mercedes y Avelina Peyro, D4–D5, Med, Luis V. Ochoa, RA BA7225, UCA
1.542e, Canción, 1928, Mercedes y Avelina Peyro, D♭4–D♭5, Med, Señorita Mercedes Peydro, RA BA7225, UCA
1.542f, Los conejitos, 1928, Mercedes y Avelina Peyro, C4–D5, Med, Tinite Inesita, RA BA7225, UCA
1.542g, Leyenda, 1928, Mercedes y Avelina Peyro, D4–D5, Med, Ricardo Rodriguez, RA BA7225, UCA
1.542h, Canción de cuna, 1928, Mercedes y Avelina Peyro, D4–D5, Med, José André, RA BA7225, UCA

1.543, *Sonrisas (Canciones infantiles)*
1.543a, La escuelita nacional, 1933, Rafael Jijena Sánchez, C4–D♯5, Med, Miguel Mastrogianni, GRic CT518, UCA
1.543b, Arroyito, 1933, Miguel A. Camino, C4–C5, Med, José Gil, GRic CT518, UCA
1.543c, Canción de cuna (Nenito mio), 1933, Marcos Liebovich, D4–E♭5, Med, Franco Alfano, GRic CT518, UCA
1.543d, Amemos la vida (Vidalita), 1933, Ignotus, C4–E♭5, Med, Ignotus, GRic CT518, UCA
1.543e, Vamos a cantar (Zamba), 1933, Teresa Jurado, E4–E5, Med, Franquito, GRic CT518, UCA
1.543f, Canción de los niños bajo la lluvia, 1933, Rafael Jijena Sánchez, B3–C♯5, Med, Inés M. de Costantini, GRic CT518, UCA
1.543g, Campanillas, 1933, Teresa Jurado, E4–D5, Med, Corradino d'Agnillo, GRic CT518, UCA
1.543h, Ya llega la aurora, 1933, Teresa Jurado, D4–D♭5, Med, Mario Rossegger, GRic CT518, UCA
1.543i, A mamita, 1933, Germán Berdiales, D4–D5, Med, Señorita Amelidi Bacco, GRic CT518, UCA

Additional titles: Douze mélodies [UCA]. Cantan los niños; Canzonetta; Nostalgia [*Diccionario de la música española e hispanoamericana*].

Ugarte, Floro, 1884–1975

1.544, Balada del lobo, la niña y el ángel, 1935, Alfredo R. Bufano, D4–E5, Med, A los niños; designed for a children's choir but may also be sung as a solo, RA BA11017, UCA

1.545, *Baladas argentinas*
1.545a, I. Bajo el parral, 1918, —, D♯4–G5, Med-high, —, SNM 11, UCA
1.545b, II. Día de fiesta, 1918, —, D♭4–G5, Med-high, —, SNM 11, UCA
1.545c, III. Soledad pampeana, 1918, —, C4–F♯5, Med-high, —, SNM 11, UCA

1.546, Caballito criollo, 1928, Belisario Roldán, F4–G5, Med-high, María de Pini de Chrestia, CLSRL, UCA
1.547, El murciélago, 1923, Manuel Ugarte, D4–G5, Med, —, SNM, UCA
1.548, La barca, 1925, Manuel Ugarte, D4–A5, High, —, —, UCA
1.549, La shulca, 1934, Rafael Jijena Sánchez, D4–F5, Med-high, —, CLSRL, UCA
1.550, Le plus gai des lieds, 1918, Paul Fort, F4–B♭5, Med-high, Text in French, SNM 12, UCA

1.551, *Melodies, op. 14*
1.551a, I. Le Bohémien, 1917, Paul Fort, E4–G5, Med-high, Text in French, —, UCA
1.551b, II. J'ai des p'tites fleurs bleues, 1917, Paul Fort, E4–F♯5, Med-high, Text in French, —, UCA
1.551c, III. L'heure mystíque, 1917, Paul Fort, D4–G5, Med-high, Text in French, —, UCA

1.552, Naides, 1954, Agustín Dentone, D4–E♭5, Med-high, Olga, RA BA11004, UCA
1.553, Ofrenda, 1934, Miguel A. Camino, F4–G5, Med-high, —, CLSRL, UCA
1.554, Revelación, 1958, Ernesto Morales, C4–F♯5, Med-high, —, RA BA11663, UCA

Urteaga, Irma, 1929–

1.555, *Cánticos para soñar*
1.555a, Canción de cuna para mi corazón solitario, 1993, Ofelia Sussel-Marie, E♭4–G5, Med-high, Graciela Pera; accompaniment also arranged for string orchestra, m, UCA
1.555b, Canto de nodriza, 1993, Eva Frías, E4–G5, Med-high, Graciela Pera; accompaniment also arranged for string orchestra, m, UCA
1.555c, Vocalise, 1993, —, E4–E5, Med, Graciela Pera; accompaniment also arranged for string orchestra, m, UCA
1.555d, Capullito, 1993, Ofelia Sussel-Marie, F♯4–F♯5, Med-high, Graciela Pera; accompaniment also arranged for string orchestra, m, UCA

1.556, *Enigma de la palabra*
1.556a, I. Oscuro fuego, 1993, Antonio Requeni, C♯3–G4, High, Augusto Morales, m, IU
1.556b, II. Las palabras, 1993, Antonio Requeni, C♯3–F4, High, Augusto Morales, m, IU

Additional titles: Existenciales [UCA].

Williams, Alberto, 1862–1952

1.557, *Canciones de la pampa y la sierra, op. 82*
1.557a, 1. Niebla en la pampa, 1919, Alberto Williams, B3–F♯5, Med-high, José María Ramos Mejía, Gurina, UCA
1.557b, 2. Canción de las hojas, 1919, Alberto Williams, C4–A♭5, High, Emma Rosa Ferrrán, Gurina, UCA
1.557c, 3. Canción pasional, 1919, Alberto Williams, C4–A♭5, Med-high, Amanda Campodónico, Gurina, UCA
1.557d, 4. La neblina, 1919, Alberto Williams, B♭3–A♭5, Med-high, Amanda Campodónico, Gurina, UCA
1.557e, 5. El lago, 1919, Alberto Williams, B♭3–B♭5, High, Enriqueta Basavilbaso de Catelín, Gurina, UCA
1.557f, 6. Canción primaveral, 1919, Alberto

Williams, D4–A5, Med-high, Elcira Rosso, Gurina, UCA

1.557g, 7. Estrella doble, 1919, Alberto Williams, C♯4–G5, Med-high, Elvira Küker de Tjarks, Gurina, UCA

1.557h, 8. Anhelos, 1919, Alberto Williams, C♯4–G♯5, High, —, Gurina, UCA

1.557i, 9. Canción de amor, 1919, Alberto Williams, B♭3–A♭5, Med-high, María de Pini de Chrestia, Gurina, UCA

1.557j, 10. Milonga calabacera, 1919, Alberto Williams, D4–F5, Med-high, Luis Benvenuto, Gurina, UCA

1.558, *Canciones incaicas, op. 45*

1.558a, I. Quena, 1909, Alberto Williams, D4–G♯5, High, Félia Litvinne; orchestration available, Gurina, UCA

1.558b, II. Yaraví, 1909, Alberto Williams, B♭3–G♯5, Med-high, Félia Litvinne; orchestration available, Gurina, UCA

1.558c, III. Vidalita, 1909, Alberto Williams, E♯4–A♭5, Med-high, Félia Litvinne; orchestration available, Gurina, UCA

1.559, *Canciones incásicas (en el estilo popular), op. 57*

1.559a, I. Hayno (Canción de otoño), 1912, Alberto Williams, B♭3–G5, Med-high, Emilia Strömberg, Gurina, UCA

1.559b, II. Hayno (Las semillas del cardo), 1912, Alberto Williams, D♭4–G♭5, Med-high, Emilia Strömberg, Gurina, UCA

1.559c, III. Hayno (Al caer la tarde), 1912, Alberto Williams, C4–G5, Med-high, Emilia Strömberg, Gurina, UCA

1.560, *Diez canciones, op. 22 & 42*

1.560a, 1. La pena, 1890, Alberto Williams, C♯4–E5, Med, Enrique de Vedia, Gurina, UCA

1.560b, 2. Mi derrotero, 1890, Alberto Williams, C♯4–G5, Med-high, Enrique de Vedia, Gurina, UCA

1.560c, 3. Canción otoñal, 1899, Alberto Williams, D4–G♯5, Med-high, Enrique de Vedia, Gurina, UCA

1.560d, 4. Ondulación etérea, 1899, Alberto Williams, C4–F5, Med-high, Enrique de Vedia, Gurina, UCA

1.560e, 5. Las nubes de mi mente, 1899, Alberto Williams, F♯4–F♯5, Med-high, Enrique de Vedia, Gurina, UCA

1.560f, 6. Enjambre, 1899, Alberto Williams, C4–G5, Med-high, Enrique de Vedia, Gurina, UCA

1.560g, 7. La urna, 1899, Alberto Williams, C♯–F♯5, Med-high, Enrique de Vedia, Gurina, UCA

1.560h, 8. Al través de mi ventana, 1899, Alberto Williams, D4–F5, Med-high, Enrique de Vedia, Gurina, UCA

1.560i, 9. Atracción, 1899, Alberto Williams, D4–A♭5, High, Enrique de Vedia, Gurina, UCA

1.560j, 10. Marina, 1899, Alberto Williams, C4–G5, Med-high, Enrique de Vedia, Gurina, UCA

1.561, *Rumores del parque*

1.561a, 1. Reclamo, 1947, Alberto Williams, B3–G♯5, Med-high, A mi dulce compañera, La Quena, INM

1.561b, 2. Apras eólicas, 1947, Alberto Williams, E♭4–A♭5, Med-high, A mi dulce compañera, La Quena, INM

1.561c, 3. Al llegar, 1947, Alberto Williams, C4–A♭5, Med-high, A mi dulce compañera, La Quena, INM

1.561d, 4. Nocturno en las frondas, 1947, Alberto Williams, E♭4–A♭5, Med-high, A mi dulce compañera, La Quena, INM

1.561e, 5. La siesta, 1947, Alberto Williams, D4–A♭5, Med-high, A mi dulce compañera, La Quena, INM

1.561f, 6. La madrugada, 1947, Alberto Williams, C4–A♭5, High, A mi dulce compañera, La Quena, INM

1.561g, 7. Atardecer en el parque, 1947, Alberto Williams, C4–G5, High, A mi dulce compañera, La Quena, INM

1.561h, 8. Titilar de estrellas, 1947, Alberto Williams, D♯4–G♯5, High, A mi dulce compañera, La Quena, INM

1.561i, 9. Vidalita del payador, 1947, Alberto Williams, F♯4–A5, High, A mi dulce compañera, La Quena, INM

1.561j, 10. Milonga para ti, 1947, Alberto

Williams, D4–A♭5, Med-high, A mi dulce compañera, La Quena, INM

1.562, *Veinte canciones escolares en el estilo popular, op. 67*

1.562a, Arrorró, 1913, Alberto Williams, D4–E5, Med, no. 6 of 20, Gurina, UCA

Additional titles: Canciones femeniles; La mirada de mi china (Milonga); Milonga del árbol; *Veinte canciones escolares* [UCA]. *Antiguas canciones italianas;* Diana; La hierra; Triste [CNMA]. *Canciones pasionales* [IU]. Canción de las hojas [ZL]. Bandada de canciones; *Canciones argentinas; Cuatro canciones patrióticas* [INM].

Zorzi, Juan Carlos, 1936–1999

1.563, A tí, 1958, Carols Marún, D4–A♭5, Med-high, Orchestral version available [LBV], m, SADAIC

1.564, El carpintero, —, Leopoldo Lugones, D4–E5, Med, Zulema Castello de Lasala, m, SACAIC

1.565, ¿Sabes tú?, —, Gustavo Adolfo Bécquer, E4–F5, Med, —, m, SADAIC

1.566, Tu amor de las entrañas me arranqué, —, Gustavo Adolfo Bécquer, D4–G5, Med-high, Orchestral version available [LBV], m, SADAIC

Additional titles: Canción de Arminda [SADAIC]. Despedida; Plegaria; ¿Qué zapatitos me pongo?; Tu c'est ma terra; Zamba para la libertad [*Diccionario de la música española e hispanoamericana*]. El pájaro carpintero [*Enciclopedia de la música argentina*].

PUBLISHERS

ACA, Academia Argentina de Musica
ANA, Academia Nacional de Bellas Artes
Arista, A.S. Arista
Barry, Barry & Cia.
Breyer, Breyer Hermanos
Bryant, Bryant Music Company
Choudens, Choudens, Paris
CLSRL, Casa Lottermoser S.R.L.
CNC, Comisión Nacional de Cultura
Correo Musical, Correo Musical Sud Americano
David Poggi, David Poggi é Hijo
De Francisco de Paula
Diario "La Razón"
EAC, Editorial Argentina de Compositores
EAM, Editorial Argentina de Música
ECCM, Ediciones del Consejo Central de la Música
ES, Éditions Maurice Senart
ESar, Editorial Saraceno
Garrot, Tasso y Vita
Gaudiosi, Roque Gaudiosi
Gordon, Manuel L. Gordon (Ritmo)
Grech, Louis Grech, Paris, 3034
GRic, G. Ricordi
Gurina, Gurina y Cía.
J. Feliú, Juan Feliú y hijos
JK, Julio Korn
LAGOS, Editorial Lagos
La Quena
m, manuscript
M. Calvello
ME, Éditions Max Eschig
Ortelli, Ortelli Hermanos
Otto Beines, Otto Beines & Hijo
PEN, Pendragon Press
RA, Ricordi Americana, S.A.E.C.
R/E, Ries & Erler
Revista musical
RL, Rouart Lerolle et Cie.
SNM, Sociedad Nacional de Música (see also GRic and AAC [Collections])
Stahl/Schirmer, Albert Stahl
TR, Tritó, S.L.
UME, Unión Musical Española
UNCA, Universidad Nacional de Cuyo
University Society, Inc.

COLLECTIONS

AAC, Asociación Argentina de Compositores (Ex-Sociedad Nacional de Música), Tel Juan Carlos Delli Quadri 011 54 11 4581 5282, http://welcome.to/compositores

AG, Andrés Gaos II (private collection)
ALW, Allison Weiss (private collection)
AW, Asociación Wagneriana, Libertad 836 5° Piso, 1012 Capital Federal, Buenos Aires, Argentina, Tel 011 54 11 4802 0309, Contact Gisela Campeon, Email wagneriana@infovia.com.ar
CLP, Conservatorio Provincial Gilardo Gilardi, Calle 49 no. 342 entre 1 y 2, 1900 La Plata, Argentina, Tel 011 54 0221 4210 2453
CMA, Carlos Manso (private collection)
CNMA, Conservatorio Nacional de Música y Arte Escénica "Carlos López Buchardo," Córdoba 2445, 1120 Capital Federal, Buenos Aires, Argentina, Tel 011 54 11 4961 0161/4736, Fax 011 54 11 4961 9618, Contact Natalie Cohan, Email scottishforestmoon@yahoo.com
INM, Instituto Nacional de Musicología Carlos Vega, México 564, 1097 Capital Federal, Buenos Aires, Argentina, Tel 011 54 11 4361 6520/6013, http://www.inmuvega.gov.ar, Contact Edgardo Pagliera, Email edropa@nortron.com.ar
IU, Irma Urteaga (private collection)
LBV, Lucio Bruno-Videla (private collection)
LC, Library of Congress, Performing Arts Reading Room, 101 Independence Ave., SE Room LM 113, James Madison Memorial Bldg, Washington, D.C. 20540–4710, Tel 202 707 5507, http://www.loc.gov/rr/perform
MF, Miguel Ficher (private collection)
RD, Rodolfo Daluisio (private collection)
SADAIC, Biblioteca de Música Argentina Blas Parera de la Sociedad Argentina de Autores y Compositores de Música, Lavalle 1547, 1048 Capital Federal, Buenos Aires, Argentina, Tel 011 54 11 4410 4867, 011 54 11 4446 2730
SLM, Silvana Luz Mansilla (private collection)
TC, Biblioteca del Teatro Colón, Viamonte 1168, 1010 Capital Federal, Buenos Aires, Argentina, Tel 011 54 11 4378 7137, Email biblioteca@teatrocolon.org.ar

UCA, Universidad Católica Argentina, Biblioteca de la Facultad de Artes y Ciencias Musicales, Avenida Alicia Moreau de Justo 1500, Edificio San Alberto Magno, Subsuelo, Puerto Madero, 1107 Capital Federal, Argentina, Tel 011 54 11 4349 0422, http://www2.uca.edu.ar/esp/sec-fmusica/esp/page.php?subsec=biblioteca, Contact Claudia De la Vega, Email claudia_delavega @uca.edu.ar, bibmusi@uca.edu.ar
UCLA, University of California Southern Regional Library Facility, Box 951388, 305 De Neve Drive, Los Angeles, California 90095-1388, Tel 310 206 2010, Fax 310 206 5074
UNLP, Universidad Nacional de la Plata, Escuela Superior de Bellas Artes, Diagonal 78, Número 680, 1900 La Plata, Argentina, Tel 011 54 21 423 5698/5756, 011 54 21 421 2456, Email fbadecanato @infovia.com.ar
ZL, Zulema Castello de Lasala (private collection)
+, LAMC (Latin American Music Center), Indiana University

SOURCES

(See bibliography for publication information)

Antología de compositores argentinos
Caicedo, *The Latin American Art Song: A Critical Anthology and Interpretive Guide for Singers*
Barreda, *Joya de canciones españolas*
Diccionario de la música española e hispanoamericana
Enciclopedia de la música argentina
Wilson, *The Art Song in Latin America: Selected Works by Twentieth-Century Composers*

OTHER RESOURCES FOR THE STUDY OF ARGENTINE ART SONG

Archivo General de la Nación, Leandro N. Alem 246, 1003 Capital Federal, Buenos Aires, Argentina, Tel 011 54 11 4331 5531/5533, Fax 011 54 11 4334 0065, http://www.mininterior.gov.ar/agn, Email archivo@mininterior.gov.ar

Argentmúsica, Estela Telerman, Beruti 3676, 3°B, 1425 Capital Federal, Buenos Aires, Argentina, Tel/Fax 011 54 11 4832 4097, Email argentmusica@fibertel.com.ar

Associación Argentina de Musicología, Att. Y. Velo, México 564, 1097 Capital Federal, Buenos Aires, Argentina, Email aamusicologia@yahoo.com

Biblioteca de la Facultad de Filosofía y Letras de la Universidad de Buenos Aires, Puán 480, 1406 Capital Federal, Buenos Aires, Argentina, Tel 011 54 11 4432 0840/2497 x173

Biblioteca Musical del Centro Cultural Recoleta, Junín 1930, 1° Piso, 1113 Capital Federal, Buenos Aires, Argentina, Tel 011 54 11 4803 4051

Biblioteca Nacional, Agüero 2480, 1425 Capital Federal, Buenos Aires, Argentina, Tel 011 54 11 4806 4684/4692/4693

Casa Piscitelli, San Martín 450, 1004 Capital Federal, Buenos Aires, Argentina, Tel 011 54 11 4394 1992, Fax 011 54 11 4394 2376, Email info@piscitelli.com

Conservatorio Superior de Música Manuel de Falla, Gallo 238, 2° Piso, 1193 Capital Federal, Buenos Aires, Argentina, Tel 011 54 11 4865 9005/9006/9007/9008

D.I.M.I. (Distribuidora Internacional de Música Impresa), Montevideo 181, 1019 Capital Federal, Buenos Aires, Argentina, Tel 011 54 11 4371 8103, Email dimi@sinectis.com.ar

Disquería/Librería Zival's, Avenida Callao 395, 1022 Capital Federal, Buenos Aires, Argentina, Tel 011 54 11 4371 7500/4374 0675

Fundación Ostinato, Dora De Marinis, http://www.ostinato.org, Email dmarinis@supernet.com.ar

Gourmet Musical, Leandro Donozo, http://www.gourmetmusical.com, Email mensajes@gourmetmusical.com

Instituto de Investigación Musicológica Carlos Vega, Universidad Católica Argentina, Avenida Alicia Moreau de Justo 1500, Edificio San Alberto Magno, Oficina 01, Puerto Madero, 1107 Capital Federal, Argentina, Tel 011 54 11 4338 0882, Fax 011 54 11 4338 0882, Contact Diana Fernández Calvo, Email diana_fernandezcalvo@uca.edu.ar

Museo Histórico Nacional, Defensa 1500, 1143 Capital Federal, Buenos Aires, Argentina, Tel 011 54 11 4307 4457/3157, Fax 011 54 11 4307 1182

Música Clásica Argentina, Ana María Móndolo, http://www.musicaclasica argentina.com, Email musica @musicaacademica.com

Universidad Nacional de La Plata, Escuela Superior de Bellas Artes, Diagonal 78, Número 680, 1900 La Plata, Argentina, Tel 011 54 21 423 6598/5756, 011 54 21 421 2456, Email fbadecanato@infovia.com.ar

For additional information regarding the music of Argentina, please visit the LAASA website (http://www.laasa.org).

2

Bolivia

Bolivia has a rich musical history with a strong Andean base and a nationalistic style that developed in the early twentieth century. Much of Bolivian art song reflects the broader trend of the native-influenced, European-trained Latin American composer by remaining Romantic in style while incorporating folk elements into its subjects and themes.[1]

Bolivia has one of the largest indigenous populations of all of the countries in Latin America.[2] Although the variety of peoples is great, the most numerous are the Quechua and the Aymara. Native and folk elements stemming from these traditions should be examined in depth when studying Bolivian song repertoire, as there are many implications that stretch beyond the typical Western way of thought. Specific instruments, for example, are tied not only to religious rites dealing with the earth and the seasons, but also to gender and to deeper Andean philosophies of existence.[3] These complex ideas can easily wind their way into European musical forms, but in the process the inherent musical and social meanings important to indigenous cultures and, directly or indirectly, to composers, may be masked.

Nationalistic composers, such as Eduardo Caba (1890–1953), incorporate Andean elements such as modal or pentatonic harmonic language and folk dance (rhythmic) elements into their works. Caba's song "Kapuri" is completely pentatonic and, like his song "Kori Killa," has Aymara words in the title and/or text.

Other composers, such as Alberto Villalpando (1940–), are more contemporary in style. Having studied with such diverse teachers as Alberto Ginastera, Aaron Copland, Olivier Messiaen, and Luigi Dallapiccola, Villalpando writes within a decidedly European tonal concept, but his works are more melodically abstract than his more nationalistic predecessors.⁴ Other contemporary composers worthy of mention are Agustín Fernández and Edgar Alandia Canipa, both members of *The Living Composers Project*, and Sergio Vargas, whose songs are difficult to find even in Bolivia, but are well worth the search.⁵

Caba, Eduardo, 1890-1953

2.1, Crespuscular (Cantar indio), ©1947, Mayorino Ferraría, E♭4-B♭5, High, —, CLSRL, —, CNMB

2.2, Flor de bronce (Canto indio), —, Ramun Katari, D4-A5, High, A Gastón O. Talamón, RA BA 7217, —, CNMB

2.3, Kapuri (La hilandera), —, Eduardo Caba, C4-G5, Med, —, RA BA9683, —, CNMB

2.4, Kori Killa (Luna de oro), —, Eduardo Caba, F4-A♭5, Med-high, —, RA BA9684, —, CNMB

Fernández, Agustín, 1958-

2.5, *El anillo*

2.5a, I. El niño mudo, 1976, Federico García Lorca, A3-C5, Low, —, TR, *The Latin American Art Song*, +

2.5b, II. Escena, 1976, Federico García Lorca, A♭3-G5, Med, —, TR, *The Latin American Art Song*, +

2.5c, III. Desposorio, 1976, Federico García Lorca, B♭3-A♭5, Low-med, —, TR, *The Latin American Art Song*, +

Gutiérrez Illanes, Emilio, 1925-

2.6, Brisas del lago (Barcarola india), —, Ernesto Eduardo, B3-F#5, Low-med, For soprano and piano, —, —, CNMB

2.7, Evocación a mi tierra, 1958, Emilio Gutiérrez Illanes, B3-F#5, Med-high, —, m, —, CNMB

2.8, Quejas, 1958, Emilio Gutiérrez Illanes, C4-G5, Med-high, —, m, —, CNMB

Halas, Oldřich, 1967-

2.9, *Cantos líticos*, Primera colección

2.9a, I. Cordillera, 1995, Guillermo Riveros Tejada, D4-E5, Med, A Adalbert Bohm; First collection, —, —, CNMB

2.9b, II. Cantafora I, 1995, Guillermo Riveros Tejada, D4-A♭5, Med-high, —, —, —, CNMB

2.9c, III. Piedra, 1995, Jaime Choque, C4-G5, Low-med, —, —, —, CNMB

Soriano Arce, Ramiro, 1956-

2.10, *Canciones sobre poemas de Armando Soriano Badani*

2.10a, Ausencia, 1974, Armando Soriano Badani, G4-G5, Med-high, —, —, —, CNMB

2.10b, Tristeza, 1975, Armando Soriano Badani, E3-E4, Med, Bass clef, —, —, CNMB

2.10c, Tu nombre en la distancia, 1977, Armando Soriano Badani, G4-G#5/A3-C5, —, Soprano/Contralto duet, —, —, CNMB

2.10d, Presencia plural, 1977, Armando Soriano Badani, D4-E5, Med, —, —, —, CNMB

2.10e, Calor de ayer, 1981, Armando Soriano Badani, F4-E♭5, Med, —, —, —, CNMB

Villalpando, Alberto, 1940–

2.11, *Canciones para soprano y piano*
2.11a, I. A un amigo, —, —, G_4–A_5, High, Soprano, —, —, —, CNMB
2.11b, II. El bambú de la ventana de Li Ts'e Yun, —, —, E_4–A_5, High, Soprano, —, —, —, CNMB
2.11c, III. Amor, —, —, F_4–$A\flat_5$, Med-high, Soprano, —, —, —, CNMB

PUBLISHERS

CLSRL, Casa Lottermoser S.R.L.
m, manuscript
RA, Ricordi Americana, S.A.E.C.
TR, Tritó, S.L.

COLLECTIONS

CNMB, Conservatorio Nacional de Música, La Paz, Bolivia
+, LAMC (Latin American Music Center), Indiana University

SOURCES

(See bibliography for publication information)
Caicedo, *The Latin American Art Song: A Critical Anthology and Interpretive Guide for Singers*

3

Brazil

Stela M. Brandão

According to Maria Sylvia Pinto, the Brazilian art song has existed since at least the eighteenth century.[1] The roots of Brazilian art song date from colonial times, when two original matrices developed from opposite streams. One, of European origin, stemmed from the Portuguese *moda*, favored at the aristocratic salons of Lisbon. Transported to Brazil by the end of eighteenth century, the *moda* transformed into the *modinha*, a style of romantic sentimental song in vernacular Portuguese, cultivated at first by the elite and the aristocracy.

The other matrix was the *lundu* (or *londu, landu, lundum, londum, landum*), and it originated in African dances brought to Brazil by African slaves. The *lundu* is a direct descendent of African *batuques*, percussion music performed by slaves in the back yards of plantation houses or in the clearings of the forests.[2] Little by little, the sensual and humorous *lundu* transformed into a solo song with syncopated melodic lines no longer accompanied by drums and clapping, but by guitar, clavier, and piano. The *lundu* was the first Black musical manifestation to be accepted by Brazilian society. The first classical composer to use a popular Brazilian *lundu* theme was Sigismund Neukomm, the pupil of Haydn who lived in Rio de Janeiro from 1816 to 1821. In 1819, he wrote the piece "O Amor Brasileiro (The Brazilian Love)—caprice pour le Pianoforte sur un Londû brésilien," whose manuscript is kept in the Paris Conservatory Library. This is the oldest record of a Brazilian popular theme being used in a composition of a classical nature.[3]

These two opposite matrices, in spite of their social antagonism, developed intimately together in Brazilian homes, influencing each other and crossing class borderlines. While the syncopated *lundu* climbed the social scale and reached the bourgeois salons, thus influencing the *modinha*, the sentimental *modinha* descended from aristocracy, exchanging the piano for the guitar as an accompanying instrument, to become a popular genre of national scope. Both types were sung in the vernacular language of Portuguese. The *lundu* and the *modinha* represent the main pillars over which the framework of Brazilian popular music was built.

Although these two genres constituted the quintessential national expression in song and almost all composers used them, the cultural establishment did not consider them to be truly artistic or serious enough for the concert stage. The Portuguese language itself was also not respected as an idiom for cultivated and educated musical expression. This sentiment, coupled with the tremendous influence of Italian opera, led the majority of nineteenth-century Brazilian classical composers to favor Italian texts. Antonio Carlos Gomes (1836–1896), the most important Brazilian composer of that period, lived most of his life in Italy and wrote in the purest Italian operatic style of his time. He also wrote songs with Portuguese texts, and was the author of one of the most celebrated Brazilian *modinhas* of all times, "Quem sabe?" However, even his Brazilian songs are considered more Italian than Brazilian in form and style.

In nineteenth-century Brazil, Italian and French were more commonly heard in recitals than any other languages. It was not until Alberto Nepomuceno (1864–1920) returned to his country under the influence of European nationalistic movements (especially those from Scandinavia) that Brazil started a steady movement toward an authentic musical identity.[4] Nepomuceno led the campaign to implement the vernacular Portuguese at the National Conservatory in Rio de Janeiro, launched his own compositions for voice with Portuguese texts, promoted concerts and recitals where songs were sung in Portuguese, and encouraged composers of his time to look for national sources of inspiration. Thus the marriage between national poetry and national music flourished in Brazil.

Many composers born in the nineteenth century reached their prime in the following century. Such is the case for the generation of composers including João Gomes de Araújo (1846–1943), Savino de Benedictis (1883–1971), Antônio Francisco Braga (1868–1945), Ernani Costa Braga (1888–1948), Paulo Florence (1864–1949), Francisco Mignone (1897–1986), Oscar Lorenzo Fernandez (1897–1948), Antonio de Assis Republicano (1897–1960), Hekel Tavares (1896–1969), and so many others, including the most prolific and well-known Brazilian composer, Heitor Villa-Lobos (1887–1959).

Although the Portuguese language is used in the majority of the songs listed, songs with texts in French, Italian, German, Spanish, Latin, and English are also included. The frequent use of the French language is due to historical and cultural affinities between Brazil and France, and also to French cultural dominance in the past, when composers and artists in general looked to Paris as the center for the arts. French was a second language for most Brazilian intellectuals until shortly before the middle of the twentieth century, and many composers felt at ease in this idiom (Ernani Braga, Babi de Oliveira, Helza Camêu, Villa-Lobos, Mignone, etc.). Native Indian and African languages also have their importance in the repertoire, for they are, together with Portuguese, the roots that formed Brazilian cultural identity, and are a part of the ethos that became the aim of the nationalistic inspiration.

Vasco Mariz has distinguished and named two trends in the Brazilian art song repertoire: the universalistic and the nationalistic.[5] The universalistic type encompasses the classical repertoire, which remained firmly rooted in European practice and style, turning away from folk influence or musical nationalism and toward twentieth-century European music, which was dominated by neoclassicism and serialism. Out of this independent and international style, Brazilian composers wrote music that is fully comparable in technique and expression with compositions written outside of Brazil.

A predominant nationalistic aesthetic can be observed throughout the catalog, but the great exponent of the Brazilian nationalistic school was, without any doubt, Heitor Villa-Lobos. While Villa-Lobos wrote music using various technical procedures, his "acclaim resulted essentially from the freshness of his creation, grounded in the folk and popular music of Brazil."⁶ His songs, inspired by and based on national sources, remain the quintessential representation of the Brazilian art song repertoire. Other nationalistic composers include Luciano Gallet, Francisco Mignone, O. Lorenzo Fernandez, Ernani Braga, A. Guerra Peixe, M. Camargo Guarnieri, José Siqueira, Dinorá de Carvalho, Waldemar Henrique, and all of those who followed the doctrine prophesied by Mário de Andrade, whose breakthrough occurred during the Week of Modern Art in São Paulo, in 1922.⁷

A counter-movement known as Música Viva was founded in 1939 by composer H. J. Koellreuter, who introduced the twelve-tone technique in Brazil. This movement greatly influenced an entire generation of Brazilian composers, among them Cláudio Santoro and Guerra Peixe, who later regained their nationalistic inspiration. Koellreuter paved the way for an independent and free approach to musical composition and for the Brazilian avant-garde, represented by Almeida Prado, Gilberto Mendes, Edino Krieger, and Jorge Antunes, among others.

Despite the tendency to follow modern trends, nationalistic ideas remain a strong and important influence on contemporary Brazilian artistic and intellectual life. Folk and popular roots are present in the music by contemporary composers such as Edmundo Villani-Côrtes, Ricardo Tacuchian, Marlos Nobre, Kilza Setti, Osvaldo Lacerda, Ernani Aguiar, Ernst Mahle, Marlos Nobre and others. These composers continue to drink from the prolific fountain of the folkloric and popular music of their country. Frequently one will see the words *modinha, côco, desafio,* or *toada,* derived from popular traditions, as subtitles of recently composed songs.

An overview of the preferences in poetry by Brazilian composers indicates that Manuel Bandeira (1886–1968), the principal literary figure of the Brazilian Modernism Movement and the author of free, colloquial, and unconventional verses, is the poet most frequently set to music. After Bandeira, the most commonly used poets are Carlos Drummond de Andrade (1902–1987), Cecília Meireles (1901–1964), Mário de Andrade (1993–1945), Ribeiro Couto (1898–1963), Ascenço Ferreira (1895–1965), and Ronald de Carvalho (1893–1935), all modernists. Vinicius de Morais (1913–1980), the poet of *bossa nova,* also appears in this catalog.⁸ Curiously, the works of insightful realist Machado de Assis (1839–1908), considered by many to be a paramount figure of Brazilian literature and a great master of language, have rarely been used, although he has figured in important partnerships with composers such as Alberto Nepomuceno.

This list would not be possible without the fundamental contribution of the *Guia da canção brasileira* (Brazilian Song Guide), organized by Professors Guida Borghoff and Luciana Monteiro de Castro, both from the Federal University of Minas Gerais (UFMG). The *Guia* is a very comprehensive map of the Brazilian art song repertory, listing all known national composers who wrote for voice and piano. Each song has its own entry with information such as dates, poet, cycles, general character of the song, vocal range, sources, publications, first renditions, recordings, and also historical and musicological notes. Not all entries have complete data and, for reasons of time and space, a selection was made for this publication.[9]

After the *Guia*, another important reference source is *A canção brasileira de câmara*, an anthological study by Vasco Mariz.[10] Mariz has been the only author to write more specifically about the Brazilian art song repertoire. He does not cite a comprehensive list of songs by each composer, but names the most important ones, bringing light to each composer's place within the historical context of Brazilian music.[11]

Aguiar, Ernani H. Chaves, 1950–

3.1, Anos estelares, 1970, Paulo Brand, —, BN

3.2, Bem-te-vi, 1970, Cecília Meireles, FBN/DIMAS 1999, BN

3.3, Cantilena, —, Gerson Valle, —, BN

3.4, Corpo da própria cantora, —, Gerson Valle, —, BN

3.5, Corpo de Cristo, —, Gerson Valle, —, BN

3.6, Corpo do povo, —, Gerson Valle, —, BN

3.7, Corre que corre..., 1970, Paulo Brand, —, BN

3.8, Quando amanhecer, 1970, Paulo Brand, —, BN

3.9, Receita para o amor, 1982, Marina Tricanico, m, BN, USP

3.10, Rotação, 1970, —, —, USP

Additional titles: Despedida; Folha; Só; Solidão.

Albuquerque, Armando Amorim, 1901–1986

3.11, Alto da bronze, 1970, Athos Damasceno Ferreira, B_3–G_5, —, MPA 1976, UFMG, UFRGS

3.12, Ar, 1947, Augusto Meyer, $C\sharp_4$–G_5, —, MPA 1976, UFMG, UFRGS

3.13, Clic-clic (Comadre rã), 1940, Augusto Meyer, D_4–E_5, —, MPA 1976, —

3.14, Lua boa, 1947, Augusto Meyer, D♭4–G5, —, MPA 1976, UFMG, UFRGS

3.15, Oração da Estrela Boieira, 1943, Augusto Meyer, C4–G5, Also available for low voice (mezzo or baritone): B♭3–E5, MPA 1976, UFRGS

3.16, Reflexos n'água, 1940, Athos Damasceno, E♭4–E♭5, —, MPA 1976, UFMG, UFRGS

3.17, Sapo, 1944–1948, Augusto Meyer, A3–A♭5, —, MPA 1976, UFMG, UFRGS

3.18, Serenata dotrefoá (Tríptico), 1940, Athos Damasceno Ferreira, B3–F5, —, MPA 1976, BN, UFRGS, USP, UFMG

3.19, *Sorriso interior*

3.19a, Ciência, 1956, Augusto Meyer, E♭4–A5, —, MPA 1976, UFMG

3.19b, Ironia, 1956, Augusto Meyer, E♭4–A5, —, MPA 1976, UFMG, UFRGS

3.19c, Arte, 1956, Augusto Meyer, —, —, MPA 1976, UFMG

3.19d, Escravo, 1956, Augusto Meyer, —, —, MPA 1976, UFMG, UFRGS

3.19e, Inquietação, 1956, Augusto Meyer, —, —, MPA 1976, UFMG, UFRGS

3.20, *Três canções*

3.20a, Chuva de setembro, 1973, Ruy Cirne Lima, E4–D5, —, UFRGS 1973, BN, UFRGS, USP

3.20b, Árbita, 1973, Augusto Meyer, B2–B3, —, UFRGS 1973, BN, UFRGS, USP

3.20c, Pobreza, 1973, Mário Quintana, C4–F♯5, —, UFRGS 1973, UFRGS

Almeida Prado, José Antônio Resende de, 1943–

3.21, Acalanto, —, —, —, TMV, USP

3.22, A Iara e o boto, 1998, —, —, —, UNICAMP

3.23, Café de la paix, 1993, José Aristodemo Pinotti, —, —, UNICAMP

3.24, Canção, —, Cecília Meireles, —, —, UNICAMP

3.25, Canção do amor perfeito, 1998, Cecília Meireles, A3–E5, m, UFMG, UNICAMP

3.26, Dois cantos, 1972, —, —, —, UNICAMP

3.27, Duas flautas, 1996, —, —, —, UNICAMP

3.28, *Espiral II*

3.28a, Antropologia, 1993, José Aristodemo Pinotti, —, —, UNICAMP

3.28b, Através do canal, 1993, José Aristodemo Pinotti, —, —, UNICAMP

3.28c, Começo, 1993, José Aristodemo Pinotti, —, —, UNICAMP

3.28d, Dia seguinte, 1993, José Aristodemo Pinotti, —, —, UNICAMP

3.28e, Espiral, 1993, José Aristodemo Pinotti, —, —, UNICAMP

3.28f, Fragmento, 1993, José Aristodemo Pinotti, —, —, UNICAMP

3.28g, Síntese, 1993, José Aristodemo Pinotti, —, —, UNICAMP

3.28h, Tua boca mágica, 1993, José Aristodemo Pinotti, —, —, UNICAMP

3.29, Instrumento, 1998, Cecília Meireles, —, —, UFMG

3.30, Lembranças do coração I, 1973, Milton Vaz de Camargo, C4–E5, TMV, UNICAMP

3.31, Lembranças do coração II, 1973, Milton Vaz de Camargo, —, TMV, UNICAMP

3.32, Lembranças do coração III, 1973, Milton Vaz de Camargo, —, TMV, UNICAMP

3.33, Livro brasileiro no.1, 1974, —, —, —, UNICAMP

3.34, *Livro brasileiro-II caderno: Três invocações mágicas*

3.34a, À Manhã, 1975, J. A. R. de Almeida Prado, —, —, UNICAMP

3.34b, À noite, 1975, J. A. R. de Almeida Prado, —, —, UNICAMP

3.34c, Ao sol, 1975, J. A. R. de Almeida Prado, —, —, UNICAMP

3.35, Modinha no. 1, 1961, Folklore, D4–D5, —, UNICAMP

3.36, Modinha no. 2, —, —, —, —, UNICAMP

3.37, Modinha no. 3, Devaneio, 1998, Darcy de Freitas, —, —, UFMG, UNICAMP
3.38, Modinha no. 4, Canção, 1998, —, —, —, UFMG, UNICAMP
3.39, Pinião, —, —, —, TMV, USP, UNICAMP

3.40, *Portrait de Nadia Boulanger*
3.40a, Cantique marin, 1972, Virgilio, —, TMV, UNICAMP
3.40b, La fleur ardente, 1972, Apollinaire, —, TMV, UNICAMP
3.40c, La lampe dans la nuit, 1972, Shakespeare, —, TMV, UNICAMP
3.40d, Le fruit ardent, 1972, Paul Valéry, —, TMV, UNICAMP
3.40e, L'île magique, 1972, Shakespeare, —, TMV, UNICAMP
3.40f, Les colonnes infinies, 1972, Paul Valéry, —, TMV, UNICAMP
3.40g, Les yeux desirés, 1972, Saint Jean de la Croix, —, TMV, UNICAMP

3.41, *Quatro motivos da rosa*
3.41a, Primeiro motivo da rosa, 1998, Cecília Meireles, —, —, UFMG, UNICAMP
3.41b, Segundo motivo da rosa, 1998, Cecília Meireles, —, —, UFMG, UNICAMP
3.41c, Terceiro motivo da rosa, 1998, Cecília Meireles, —, —, UFMG, UNICAMP
3.41d, Quarto motivo da rosa, 1998, Cecília Meireles, —, —, UFMG, UNICAMP

3.42, *Quatro poemas de Manuel Bandeira*
3.42a, Andorinha, 1998, Manuel Bandeira, —, —, UFMG, UNICAMP
3.42b, Belo, belo, 1998, Manuel Bandeira, —, —, UNICAMP
3.42c, A estrela, 1998, Manuel Bandeira, —, —, UNICAMP
3.42d, Teu nome, 1998, Manuel Bandeira, —, —, UNICAMP

3.43, Rosamor, 1965, Guilherme de Almeida, $D\sharp 4$–$E5$, —, UNICAMP
3.44, Trem de ferro, 1964, Manuel Bandeira, $B3$–$F5$, —, UNICAMP

3.45, *Tres canções*
3.45a, Bem-vinda, 1972, José Augusto Leonel Vieira, $C4$–$F\sharp 5$, TMV, UNICAMP
3.45b, Manhã molhada, 1973, Vera Xavier de Mendonça, $B\flat 3$–$D5$, TMV, UNICAMP
3.45c, O Luandê-Luá, 1972, José Augusto Leonel Vieira, $D4$–$F5$, TMV, UNICAMP, UFMG, USP

3.46, *Tres episódios de animais*
3.46a, Anta, 1974, J. A. R. de Almeida Prado, —, TMV, UNICAMP
3.46b, Sinimbu, 1973, J. A. R. de Almeida Prado, —, TMV, UNICAMP
3.46c, Tamanduá, 1974, J. A. R. de Almeida Prado, —, TMV, UNICAMP

3.47, *Trovas de muito amor para um amado senhor*
3.47a, A minha voz é nobre, 1963, Hilda Hilst, —, —, UNICAMP
3.47b, Trova de muito amor para um amado Senhor, —, Hilda Hilst, $C3$–$E4$, —, UNICAMP

Additional titles: Triptico celeste.

Antunes, Jorge de Freitas, 1942–

3.48, Acalanto II, 1965, Jorge Antunes, —, SEML, UnB
3.49, A canção que passa, 1984, Gerson Valle, —, SEML, UnB
3.50, A primeira desilusão, —, Jorge Antunes, —, SEML, UnB
3.51, Cabra da peste, 1964, Jorge Antunes, —, SEML, UnB

3.52, *Ciclo Rio Quatrocentão*
3.52a, Cadeirinha, —, Jorge Antunes, —, SEML, UnB
3.52b, Moleque de Rugendas, 1964, Jorge Antunes, —, SEML, UnB
3.52c, Pregões, 1964, Jorge Antunes, —, SEML, UnB

3.53, Exercício de prosódia, 1966, Olégario Mariano, $C4$–$G5$, SEML, UnB
3.54, Fuga da inspiração, 1965, Jorge Antunes, —, SEML, UnB

3.55, O lenço, 1965, Jorge Antunes, —, SEML, UnB

3.56, *Seis missivas: Series of six short songs for baritone and piano*

3.56a, CCBB 1995, negando apoio às mini-óperas, 1997, Jorge Antunes, —, SEML, UnB

3.56b, FBB 1996, negando apoio à ópera Olga, 1997, Jorge Antunes, —, SEML, UnB

3.56c, CCBB 1996, negando apoio às mini-óperas, 1997, Jorge Antunes, —, SEML, UnB

3.56d, CCBB 1996, negando informação dos nomes dos membros da comisão de sel projetos, 1997, Jorge Antunes, —, SEML, UnB

3.56e, BB 1997, negando apoio à ópera Olga, 1997, Jorge Antunes, —, SEML, UnB

3.56f, CCBB 1997, negando apoio às mini-óperas, 1997, Jorge Antunes, —, SEML, UnB

3.57, Seresta de amor, 1964, Jorge Antunes, C_4–F_5, SEML, UnB

3.58, Sonho de amor, 1963, Jorge Antunes, $G\sharp 4$–$G\sharp 5$, SEML, UnB

Barroso, Francisco Paurilo, 1894–1968

3.59, Acalanto, —, Aracy Martins, $B\flat 3$–G_5, AN 1964, BN

3.60, Ave Maria, —, —, —, AN 1964, BN

3.61, Chanson pour ton sommeil, —, Dulcinea Paraense, —, —, BN, UFMG

3.62, Dorme ... dorme ... filhinho, 1945, Paurillo Barroso, —, IML, LMT, BN, UNESP, UFMG

3.63, Historieta (Pastoral), —, Dulcinea Paraense, E_4–$B\flat 5$, LMT 1945, UFMG

3.64, Lembras-te, 1964, Mozart Soriano Aderaldo, —, AN, BN, UFMG

3.65, Mãe preta, 1942, Paurillo Barroso, E_4–$E\flat 5$, IV 1942, BN

3.66, Marcha nupcial, 1964, Sacred text, —, AN, BN

3.67, Meprise, —, Nadir Papi Saboya, —, —, BN

3.68, Ninando, 1959, Paurilo Barroso, —, IV, BN

3.69, O sonho da netinha, 1964, Paurillo Barroso, —, AN, BN

3.70, Para ninar, 1952, Paurillo Barroso, E_4–E_5, CEMB, BN, UFMG

3.71, Sonho atrevido, 1964, Paurillo Barroso, —, AN, BN

3.72, Tres hai-kai, 1964, Dulcinea Paraense, —, AN, BN

3.73, Tu, 1959, Paurillo Barroso, $C\sharp 4$–A_5, IV 1959, BN

3.74, Valsa proibida, 1946, —, —, CEMB, BN

Barrozo Netto, Joaquim Antônio, 1881–1941

3.75, Adeus (Fragmento de um episódio lírico), —, Sylvio Bevilacqua, —, B/Cia, BN, UFMG

3.76, A um coração, —, Barrozo Netto, —, —, BN, UFMG

3.77, Ballada, 1926, Carlos Coelho, —, SA, BN, UFMG

3.78, Canção da despedida, —, J.B. Mello e Souza, $C\sharp 4$–$C\sharp 5$, CW, BN, UFMG

3.79, Canção da felicidade (Modinha), —, Nosor Sanches, $D\sharp 3$–C_5, CW 1925, 1939, BN, UNESP, UFMG

3.80, Canção da saudade (Modinha), —, Popular text, —, CW, BN, USP

3.81, Canção de Lavinia, —, Osório Duque Estrada, —, EM, BN, USP

3.82, Canção do amor, —, William Gordon, —, CW, BN

3.83, Canção sertaneja, —, Mariinha Braga, —, CW, BN

3.84, Cantiga (Chanson), —, Luís Guimarães, —, AN 1956, 1972, BN, UNESP

3.85, Ceguinha, —, João de Deus, —, AN 1956, 1972, BN

3.86, Conseil pour l'homme, —, Le Comte d'Arschot, —, B/Cia, BN

3.87, Hymno ao estudo, —, Arthur Azevedo, —, B/Cia, BN

3.88, Hymno escolar, —, Antonio Salles, —, B/Cia, BN
3.89, Invocação à natureza, 1906, Sylvio Bevilacqua, —, B/Cia, BN, UFMG
3.90, Jesus, 1907, Thomaz Ribeiro, —, B/Cia, BN
3.91, Laura, —, Joaquim Antônio Barrozo Netto, —, —, UFMG
3.92, Olhos tristes, —, Luiz Edmundo, —, Castro Lima, UFMG
3.93, Oração da pobre, —, João de Deus, —, B/Cia, BN
3.94, Orfãzinha, —, Joaquim Antônio Barrozo Netto, —, —, UFMG
3.95, Perdão, felicidade!, —, —, —, SA, BN
3.96, Regresso ao Lar, —, Guerra Junqueiro, —, B/Cia, BN
3.97, Ritornello, —, Carlos Coelho, —, B/Cia, BN, UFMG
3.98, Salutaris, —, —, —, B/Cia, BN
3.99, Salve Miss Brasil, —, William Gordon, —, CW, BN
3.100, Saudade amiga, —, Joaquim Antônio Barrozo Netto, —, CW, BN, UFMG
3.101, Se eu morresse amanhã, —, Álvares de Azevedo, —, CW, BN, UFMG
3.102, Suprema angústia, —, Solfieri de Albuquerque, —, CW, BN
3.103, Tarantela, 1938, Vocalise, —, CW, BN
3.104, Uma saudade, —, —, —, CW, BN
3.105, Vozes da floresta, 1932, —, —, CW, BN

Benedictis, Savino de, 1883–1971

3.106, Ave Maria, 1964, Francisco R. Dordal, —, RB, BN
3.107, A voz do sino, —, Wenceslau de Queiroz, —, A. Di Franco, BN
3.108, Berceuse, 1964, M. Lermontorf, —, RB, BN
3.109, Canção do Beijo, 1965, Olavo Bilac, —, RB, BN
3.110, L'eche, —, Theodore Botrel, —, RB, BN
3.111, Hymno à escola, —, Francisca Júlia da e Júlio César da Silva Munster, —, —, BN
3.112, Hymno ao trabalho, —, Francisca Júlia da e Júlio César da Silva Munster, —, CWag, BN, UNESP
3.113, Hymno dos voluntários, —, G. Scavone, —, CWag, BN
3.114, Meu coração sonhador, —, Correa Junior, —, —, BN
3.115, Numa coluna (Ecrit sur une colonne), —, Francisco Karam, —, —, BN
3.116, Saudade, 1964, Correa Junior, —, RB, BN

3.117, *Três canções do folclore brasileiro*
3.117a, Bemteví (Lundu), —, Folklore, C♯4–E5, RA 1957, BN
3.117b, Puxa o melão sabiá (Desafio), —, Folklore, C4–E5, RA 1957, BN
3.117c, Toca a cantá, —, Folklore, F♯4–F♯5, RA 1957, BN

3.118, Tristeza, —, Correa Junior, —, CWag, BN

Bidart, Lícia de Biase, 1910–

3.119, Amanhecer, —, Carlos Drummond de Andrade, BN
3.120, Ave Maria, 1927, —
3.121, Brauna, —, Carlos Drummond de Andrade, BN
3.122, Canto da vida a chegar, —, —, USP
3.123, Canto jovem, —, —, USP
3.124, Máquina do tempo, —, Carlos Drummond de Andrade, BN
3.125, Nova canção do exílio, —, Carlos Drummond de Andrade, BN
3.126, Paremia de cavalo, —, Carlos Drummond de Andrade, BN

Additional titles: Canto da noite.

Bittencourt-Sampaio, Sérgio, 1945–

3.127, Acalanto, 1970, Nair Marques Lisboa de Freitas, —, BN, UFMG
3.128, Canção do mar, 2004, Cláudia Alencar, —, UFMG
3.129, Meus oito anos, 1998, Casimiro de Abreu, E4–B5, BN, UFMG
3.130, Veleiro, 1998, Adelina Bittencourt Sampaio, —, BN, UFMG

3.131, Vocalise em estilo romântico, —, No text, D♯4–D♭6, UFMG

Additional titles: Cantochão; Ilusões perdidas; Primavera.

Bocchino, Alceu Ariosto, 1918–

3.132, À Marília, 1937, Tomás Antônio Gonzaga, —, BN
3.133, Canção de inverno, —, Pery Borges, —, BN
3.134, Cantiga de ninar, 1956, Glauco de Sá Brit, —, BN, UFMG
3.135, Gauchinha, —, Antonio Rangel Bandeira, —, BN
3.136, Lamento dos pinheirais, 1956, Luíza de Araújo, RB, BN, UFMG
3.137, Maxima no.1, —, Pery Borges, —, BN
3.138, Nada, —, Aplecina do Carmo, —, BN
3.139, Nhanderu, —, Durval Borges, —, BN

Additional titles: As duas flores; Berceuse; Cantar; Despedida de Bento cego; *Duas canções do folclore* (Côco do Aeroplano Jaú, Não quero que ninguém me prenda); Do nosso amor guardo apenas; Era uma vez; Fragmento; Nanynoël; Que coisa!; Serenata napolitana.

Braga, Antônio Francisco, 1868–1945

3.140, Barcarola, —, Carlos Coelho, —, —, BN
3.141, Borboletas, —, Hermes Fontes, B3–E5, B/Cia, BN
3.142, Brinde (Fontoura Xavier), —, —, C♯4–F5, CW, BN, UFMG
3.143, Canção de Romeu, 1907, Olavo Bilac, —, VM, BN
3.144, Cancioneiro, —, Sylvio Moreaux, —, m, BN
3.145, Cantiga de amor, —, Luís Guimarães, D♯4–F♯5, B/Cia, BN, UFMG
3.146, Catita, —, Ovídio de Mello, —, VM, BN
3.147, Cântico das árvores, —, Olavo Bilac, C4–E♭5, Castro Lima, CW, BN, UFMG
3.148, Desejo, —, A. Gonçalves Dias, —, Manuel Antônio Guimarães, BN, UFMG
3.149, En nia lando, 1912, J. B. Mello e Souza, C4–C5, VM, BN
3.150, Gavião de penacho, —, Afonso Arinos, —, CW, BN, UFMG, UNESP
3.151, Lágrimas de cera, 1945, Machado de Assis, E♭4–E♭5, Cooperativa, BN
3.152, Moreninha, —, Murilo de Araujo, —, Ed. Associação Rio Grandense de Música, BN, UFMG
3.153, O poder das lágrimas, —, Luiz Barreto Murat, —, B/Cia, BN, UEMG
3.154, O trovador do sertão, —, Alexandre José de Melo Morais Filho, —, Castro Lima, CW, FBN/DIMAS 1998, BN
3.155, O vizir, —, Fagundes Varella, —, B/Cia, BN, UEMG
3.156, Prece, 1902, Floriano de Brito, —, VM 1902, BN, UEMG
3.157, Primavera d'alma, —, Solfieri de Albuquerque, —, B/Cia, BN
3.158, Recueillement, 1903, Charles Baudelaire, D♯4–A5, Campassi & Camin, BN
3.159, Romanza (Stecchetti), 1907, Carlos Coelho, D♯4–A♯5, VM, UFMG
3.160, Vecchio tema, 1905, Carlos Coelho, D♯4–B♯5, B/Cia 1905, BN
3.161, Velha canção, —, Hemetério dos Santos, —, B/Cia, BN
3.162, Virgens mortas, —, Olavo Bilac, E♭4–B5, VM 1907, BN, UFMG

Additional titles: Ave Maria; A visitação; Dá-me as pétalas de rosa; Les voix interieures; O tear; Trovita; Vilancete.

Braga, Ernani Costa, 1888–1948

3.163, *Boi surubim-Suite Cearense*
3.163b, Aboio, —, Ernani Braga, E♭4–A5, —, RB, BN, UFMG
3.164, Cantigas praianas, —, Vicente de Carvalho, E4–F♯5, —, AN, FB, BN
3.165, *Cinco canções nordestinas do folclore brasileiro*

3.165a, Capim di pranta, —, Folklore, E♭4–A♭5, —, RA, BN
3.165b, Engenho novo, —, Folklore, E4–F5, —, RA, BN
3.165c, Nigue-nigue-ninhas, —, Folklore, E4–E5, —, RA, BN
3.165d, O Kinimbá, —, Folklore, B2–F♯4, African Yoruba text, RA, BN, +
3.165e, São João-da-ra-rão, —, Folklore, E4–F5, —, RA, BN

3.166, Casinha pequenina, —, Popular text, D♯4–C5, —, RB 1961, RA, BN, UFMG
3.167, Desiludida, —, Vicente de Carvalho, F4–A5, —, AN, —, BN, +
3.168, La cloche fêlée, —, Charles Baudelaire, D♭4–G♯5, —, AN, BN
3.169, Maracatu, —, Ascenço Ferreira, E♭4–G5, —, RB, BN, UFMG
3.170, Meia canha (Canção gaúcha), —, Folklore, C♯4–F♯5, —, RB, BN, UFMG
3.171, Moreninha, 1934, Willy Lewin, D4–E5, —, CW 1934, BN
3.172, Tristesse de la lune, —, Charles Baudelaire, D4–E5, —, AN, BN, +
3.173, Velha canção, 1922, Moacyr Chagas, D4–G5, —, —, BN

Additional titles: Abaluaiê; *Boi surubi—Suite Cearense* (Meu canário verde; Cavalo marinho); Cancioneiro Gaúcho (no. 11, Velha gaita); Den bão; Desafio; Dona do meu coração; Gaúcho; L'Ascencion; Makoetá; Manhã; Ogundê-uarerê; Ogundê-xangodê; Oxum Aiacó; Prenda minha; Suspiros que vão e vem; Taieiras; Vou danado pra Catende.

Brandão, José Vieira, 1911–2002

3.174, Adivinhação, 1938, Martins d'Alvarez, —, CM, BN
3.175, Angústia, —, —, —, —, BN
3.176, À sombra verde dos coqueiros, —, Carlos Paula Barros, —, CM, BN
3.177, Canção à toa, —, Guilherme de Almeida, —, IV 1944, UNESP
3.178, *Duas canções brasileiras*

3.178a, Confidência, —, Helio Peixoto, —, —, BN
3.178b, O sabiá e a mangueira, 1929, Álvaro Moreira, —, —, BN
3.179, Cromo no. 1, —, Mário Queiroz Rodrigues, —, IV 1958, BN
3.180, Cromo no. 2, —, Mário Queiroz Rodrigues, —, IV 1958, BN
3.181, Matinta Perera, 1940, Sylvio Moreaux, —, —, BN
3.182, Paysage, —, Beatrix-Reynal, —, —, BN
3.183, Poemeto, 1938, Helio Peixoto, —, CM, BN
3.184, Prequeté, 1938, Cassiano Ricardo, —, Vieira Brandão 1948, BN
3.185, Prière pour tous, —, Beatrix Reynal, —, —, BN
3.186, Serei . . . serás, 1941, J. G. de Araujo Jorge, —, AN, BN
3.187, Só (ou Canção sozinha), 1990, Guilherme de Almeida, G4–F5, IV 1958, BN
3.188, Uyara, 1940, Sylvio Moreaux, —, CM, BN

Additional titles: Almas comuns; Ausência; Cantiga de ninar; Coração incerto; Depois da ausência; Dois amô; Eu te amo; Haicai; Música brasileira; Onda; Paráfrase de Ronsard; Pintura; Prece; *Quatro canções em lá menor* (1. Angústia, 2. Eu te amo, 3. Ngo-gay-ngi, 4. Nós); Silêncio; Soneto; Soneto ingles; Trova.

Camêu, Helza de Cordoville, 1903–1995

3.189, A cavalgada, 1928, Raimundo Correia, —, FBN/DIMAS 1999, BN
3.190, A hora cinzenta, 1933, Raul de Leoni, —, FBN/DIMAS 1999, BN, UFMG
3.191, A lenda, 1958, René Cavé, —, m, UFMG
3.192, A torre morta do ocaso, op. 21, no. 5, 1933, Raul de Leoni, B2–G4, m, BN
3.193, Bem-te-vi, 1935, —, —, m, UFMG
3.194, Chuva fina, matutina, op. 38, no. 2,

1958–1962, Cecília Meireles, —, FBN/
DIMAS 1999, BN, UFMG

3.195, *Cinco canções Franco-suíças*
3.195a, Elisabeau, 1950, Folklore, —, m, BN
3.195b, En ce gracieux temps d'estè, 1950,
Folklore, —, m, BN
3.195c, Était-il une heure, 1950, Folklore, —,
m, BN
3.195d, Sur nos monts, 1950, Folklore, —,
m, BN
3.195e, Tite Jeanneton, 1950, Folklore, —,
m, BN

3.196, *Cinco canções medievais*
3.196a, Chanson, 1962, Folklore, —, m, BN
3.196b, Chanson druidique, 1962, Folklore,
—, m, BN
3.196c, Chanson du troubadour Pons de
Capdeuil, 1962, Folklore, —, m, BN
3.196d, Chant de croisés, 1962, Folklore, —,
m, BN
3.196e, Serventois du trouvère Quenes de
Bethune sur la Croisade, 1962, Folklore,
—, m, BN

3.197, *Cinco peças para canto, op. 5*
3.197a, Cantiga Praiana, 1936, Vicente de
Carvalho, —, m, —
3.197b, A voz do mar, 1936, Vicente de
Carvalho, —, m, —
3.197c, Cantiga, 1936, Aldemar Tavares, —,
m, —
3.197d, Canção, 1936, Aldemar Tavares, —,
m, —
3.197e, A balada das folhas, 1936, Olegário
Mariano, E♭3–G♭4, m, BN, UFMG

3.198, Ciúme, 1943, José de Alencar, —, m,
UFMG
3.199, Entardecer, op. 44, no. 1, 1967, Helena
Kolody, —, m, BN, UFMG
3.200, Interior, 1967, Onestaldo de
Pennafort, —, FBN/DIMAS 1999, BN
3.201, Jangada, 1943, Édila Mangabeira, —,
m, UFMG
3.202, Juju, sossego (Acalanto), 1952,
Folklore, —, m, BN, UFMG

3.203, Modinha, op. 15, 1937, Menotti del
Picchia, —, m, UFMG
3.204, Modinha, op. 44, no. 3, 1968, Hilma
Cardoso, —, m, BN, UFMG
3.205, Noitinha, 1945, Florbela Espanca, D3–
F♯4, m, BN

3.206, *O livro de Maria Sylvia, op. 28*
3.206a, 1. Imagem, 1945, Manuel Bandeira,
E♯3–C♭5, m, UFMG
3.206b, 2. Espera inútil, 1945, Olegário
Mariano, —, m, UFMG
3.206c, 3. A toada da chuva, 1945, Olegário
Mariano, —, m, UFMG
3.206d, 4. Canção, 1945, Olegário Mariano,
—, m, BN, UFMG
3.206e, 5. Canção triste, 1945, Olegário
Mariano, —, m, UFMG

3.207, O pastor pequenino, op. 38, no. 1, 1958,
Cecília Meireles, —, FBN/DIMAS 1999,
BN, UFMG

3.208, *Poema da água, op. 35*
3.208a, 1. A água também nasce pequenina,
1958, Raul Machado, —, m, BN, UFMG
3.208b, 2. A água também tem a sua infância,
1958, Raul Machado, —, m, BN, UFMG
3.208c, 3. A água também tem adolescência,
1958, Raul Machado, —, m, BN, UFMG
3.208d, 4. A água também tem maturidade,
1958, Raul Machado, —, m, BN, UFMG
3.208e, 5. A água também tem sua velhice,
1958, Raul Machado, —, m, BN, UFMG
3.208f, 6. A água também sofre, 1958, Raul
Machado, —, m, BN, UFMG
3.208g, 7. A água também morre, 1958, Raul
Machado, —, m, BN, UFMG
3.208h, 8. Bendita pois seja a água divina,
1958, Raul Machado, —, m, BN, UFMG

3.209, *Quatro peças, op. 39*
3.209a, 1. Música eterna, 1958–1962, Helena
Kolody, D3–C♭5, m, BN, UFMG
3.209b, 2. A sombra no rio, 1958, Helena
Kolody, —, m, BN, UFMG
3.209c, 3. Rio de planície, 1958, Helena
Kolody, D3–B4, m, BN, UFMG

3.209d, 4. Prenúncio de outono, 1958, Helena Kolody, D♯3–B♯4, m, BN, UFMG

3.210, *Quatro poemas de Helena Kolody, op. 43*

3.210a, 1. Ilusão, 1966–1967, Helena Kolody, —, FBN/DIMAS 1999, BN, UFMG

3.210b, 2. Crepúsculo de abril, 1968, Helena Kolody, —, m, BN

3.210c, 3. Sobrevivência, 1966–1967, Helena Kolody, —, m, BN

3.210d, 4. Canto, —, Helena Kolody, —, m, BN

3.211, Queixas, 1928, Jonatas Serrano, —, m, UFMG

3.212, Risos de dor, 1917, Ilka Maia, —, m, UFMG

3.213, Saudade, 1929, Vicente de Carvalho, D3–E♭4, IV 1968, FBN/DIMAS 1999, BN, UFMG

3.214, Solidão, 1934, Ribeiro Couto, —, m, BN, UFMG

3.215, *Suite lírica, op. 25*

3.215a, 1. Desencanto, 1943, Manuel Bandeira, —, FBN/DIMAS 1999, BN, UFMG

3.215b, 2. Crepúsculo de outono, 1943, Manuel Bandeira, —, FBN/DIMAS 1999, BN, UFMG

3.215c, 3. Madrugada, 1943, Manuel Bandeira, C3–G4, m, UFMG

3.215d, 4. Madrigal, 1943, Manuel Bandeira, —, m, UFMG

3.215e, 5. A estrela, 1943, Manuel Bandeira, —, m, UFMG

3.215f, 6. Dentro da noite, 1943, Manuel Bandeira, D♯3–F4, m, UFMG

3.215g, 7. Confidência, 1943, Manuel Bandeira, D♯3–F4, m, UFMG

3.215h, 8. Ao crepúsculo, 1943, Manuel Bandeira, —, m, UFMG

3.216, *Três números de Bumba-meu-boi*

3.216a, Boi-ê, 1952, Folklore, —, m, BN

3.216b, Aboio, 1952, Folklore, —, m, BN

3.216c, Meu Guriaba, 1952, Folklore, —, m, BN

Additional titles: Amar; Ao mar, op. 8; Asi va el aire; Astério de Campos; A ti, flor do céu; Avôa-avôa; Balada romântica, op. 31, no. 2; Bem-me-quer; Bem-te-vi; Bilhete perdido; Cantarola de acordeão; Canto de Natal; Carcarola; Casa de palha; Chá preto, sinhá; Cismando; De leve; Dois pontos de Xangô; El rancho; Embolada; Eterna incógnita; Eu-â; Festa de Natal; Gavião penerô; Iaiá, você quer morrer?; Ma Malia; Meia-canha; Milagre, op. 26, no. 3; Morena cor de canela; Morte e canção; Na s'urucaia; Noturno, op. 31, no.1; Pinicapau; Plena gratia; *Quatro canções hebraicas* (Benvinda, chuva; A gangorra; Levanta-te, irmão; Mayim); Queres ver esta menina; Quiriri; Saudade; Se eu vivesse; Seu Joaquim; Silêncio, op. 26, no. 2; Tarde, op. 26, no. 1; Ta voix; *Tres cantos de roda* (O Cravo brigou com a rosa; O Limão; Pai Francisco); Trovas; Vela branca.

Campos, Lina Pires de, 1918–2003

3.217, Confissão, 1975, Alice Camargo Guarnieri, UFMG

3.218, Eu sou como aquela fonte, 1966, —, UFMG

3.219, Modinha, 1961, —, UFMG

3.220, Toada, 1961, —, UFMG

3.221, Você diz que me quer bem, 1960, —, UFMG

Additional titles: Embolada; Retrato.

Carvalho, Dinorá Gontijo de, 1895–1980

3.222, Acalanto, 1933, Cleómenes Campos, D4–D5, —, BN, UFMG, USP, UNICAMP

3.223, Água que passa, 1972, Paulo Bonfim, E4–C5, m, UNICAMP

3.224, Ausência, 1955, Suzanna de Campos, D4–E5, m, UNICAMP

3.225, Bamboleia, —, —, —, —, UNICAMP

3.226, Banzo, 1948, Menotti del Picchia, B3–F5, m, UNICAMP

3.227, Berceuse, —, Jacques D'Avray, C4–F5, m, UNICAMP

3.228, Canção do embalo, 1966, Cecília Meireles, B3–E5, m, UNICAMP

3.229, Canção ingênua, 1979, Milton Vaz de Camargo, F4–E5, m, UNICAMP

3.230, Coqueiro-coqueirá, 1948, Folklore, F4–E5, m, UNICAMP

3.231, É a ti flor do céu, 1960, Theodomiro Alves, B3–E5, m, UNICAMP

3.232, Ê-bango-bango-ê, 1948, Afro Brazilian Folklore, D4–A5, IV, BN, USP, UNICAMP

3.233, Epigrama número 9, 1964, Cecília Meireles, C♭4–G5, m, UNICAMP

3.234, Espelho, 1980, Jandyra Sounis Carvalho de Oliveira, —, —, UNICAMP

3.235, *Estampas de Vila Rica*

3.235a, Carmo, 1975, Carlos Drummond de Andrade, C4–A5, m, UNICAMP

3.235b, São Francisco de Assis, 1975, Carlos Drummond de Andrade, B♭2–G4, m, UNICAMP

3.236, Ideti (a menina preta que buscava Deus), 1970, Dioscoredes dos Santos, E4–G5, m, UNICAMP

3.237, Instantâneo do adeus, 1969, Elza Heloisa, —, m, UNICAMP

3.238, Mosaico, 1948, Geraldo Vidigal, F♯4–F♯5, m, UNICAMP

3.239, Noite de São Paulo, —, Guilherme de Almeida, —, m, BN, UNICAMP

3.240, Num imbaiá, 1960, Folklore, B♯4–E5, m, UNICAMP

3.241, O ar, 1972, Paulo Bomfim, D4–G♯5, m, UNICAMP

3.242, O fogo, 1975, Paulo Bonfim, D4–A5, m, UNICAMP

3.243, Onde estás, 1979, Alice Camargo Guarnieri, D♯4–F♯5, m, UNICAMP

3.244, O Pipoqueiro (pregão), 1933, Anonymous, C4–G5, IV, AN, BN, UFMG, USP, UNICAMP

3.245, Pau-piá, 1948, Afro-Brazilian Folklore, E4–G5, IV, BN, UNICAMP

3.246, Perdão, 1960, Milton Marques, D4–F♯5, m, UNICAMP

3.247, Pobre cego, 1948, Folklore of Maranhão, C4–G5, IV, BN, UFMG, UNICAMP

3.248, Presença, 1980, Jandyra Sounis Carvalho de Oliveira, —, —, UNICAMP

3.249, Quem sofre, 1948, Menotti del Picchia, —, m, UNICAMP

3.250, Quibungo tê-rê-rê, 1949, Folklore, C4–C5, IV, BN, UNICAMP

3.251, Quinguê-lê, 1975, Folklore, B3–F5, m, UNICAMP

3.252, Samaritana, 1972, Paulo Bonfim, —, m, UNICAMP

3.253, Sinal de terra, 1949, Cassiano Ricardo, D4–F5, m, UNICAMP

3.254, Sum-sum, 1960, Folklore, D♯4–A♯5, m, UNICAMP

3.255, Teu rosto azul, 1974, Fúlvia Lopes de Carvalho, D3–A♭4, m, UNICAMP

3.256, Uai ni-nim, 1973, Folklore, D4–F5, m, UNICAMP

3.257, Último retrato, 1949, Maria Franquini Neto, —, m, UNICAMP

3.258, Velas ao mar, 1940, Alberto de Oliveira, D4–E5, m, UNICAMP

Additional title: Menino mandú.

Carvalho, Eleazar, 1912–1996

3.259, Alma minha gentil, 1941, Luís de Camões, —, BN

3.260, Bohemio, —, Roberto Maury, SA, BN

3.261, Cabana de palha, —, Sylvio Moreaux, —, BN

3.262, Cantiga maritime, —, Calazans Campos, RB, BN, UFMG

3.263, Hino a Brasília, 1960, Arnold Bruver, IV, BN

3.264, Incompatibilidades, 1941, J. Artur, —, BN

Carvalho, Joubert Gontijo de, 1900–1977

3.265, Agonia, —, —, BN, UFMG

3.266, Há nos teus olhos, Joubert de Carvalho, —, UFMG

3.267, Olhos tristes, os teus olhos!, Oswaldo Santiago, VM, BN

3.268, Os olhos de Maria, Duque de Abramonte, Campassi & Camin, BN

3.269, Pierrot, Paschoal Carlos Magno, —, UFMG

3.270, Sacy Pererê (Toada sertaneja), Joubert de Carvalho, —, UFMG

3.271, Teus olhos . . . o outono, Jayme Tavora, CEMB, BN

3.272, Último tango, Duque de Abramonte, Campassi & Camin, BN

Additional titles: Jurity; Malaventurada; Pecado.

Castro, Ênio de Freitas, 1911–1975

3.273, A velha carta, Dámaso Rocha, RB, BN, UFMG, +

3.274, A vida, Olavo Bilac, CW, RB, BN, UFMG, +

3.275, Canção, Cecília Meireles, RB, BN, UFMG, +

3.276, Historieta, Guilherme Figueiredo, RB, BN, UFMG, +

3.277, Mar, Augusto Frederico Schmidt, RB, BN, UFMG, +

3.278, Meu clarim, meu tambor, Cleómenes Campos, RB, BN, UFMG, +

3.279, Ouve o canto da noite, Paulo Corrêa Lopes, RB, BN, UFMG, +

3.280, Por quê, Alceu Wamosy, RB, BN, UFMG, +

Cavalcanti, Nestor de Hollanda, 1949–

3.281, Projeto de carta, 1985, Carlos Drummond de Andrade, Monologue for baritone, with staging, EMV, +

Additional titles: Canção de natal; *Canções de amor* (Corças; Corpos presentes; Eles); *Canções póstumas* (Arrelias, baby, no. 2; Do cavalo do bandido; Lar, doce lar, no. 1); Cantada; Cissiparidade; Confissão; Implexo; Leoa; Mulher; Noite occidental; Pombos; Sideral, no. 13; Simbiose; Síntese; Epitáfio; O Filho do Homem; Madrugada; Minha pessoa; Noite azul; Noturno; Relógio; O sábio ou Quem sabe, sabe; *Três ais* (Aos donos do poder; Aos gananciosos; Aos legisladores); Um certo mar.

Cosme, Luis, 1908–1965

3.282, Acalanto, 1931, T. Tostes, Ed. Associação Rio Grandense de Música, BN, UFMG

3.283, Bombo, 1932, Athos Damasceno Ferreira, —, BN, UFMG, +

3.284, Gauchinha, 1932, J. Barros, —, BN

3.285, O menino atrasado, —, —, —, BN

3.286, *Três manchas gaúchas*

3.286a, Aquela China, 1931, Manuel Vargas Neto, —, BN

3.286b, Balada para os carreteiros, 1931, Augusto Meyer, —, BN

3.286c, Madrugada no campo, 1948, Cecília Meireles, m, BN, UFMG

3.287, *Três manchas para canto e piano*

3.287a, Cantiga, —, Cecília Meireles, —, BN

3.287b, Chorinho, —, Cecília Meireles, m, BN, UFMG

3.287c, Colonial, —, Augusto Meyer, —, BN

3.287d, Modinha, 1947, Cecília Meireles, m, BN

Costa, Alberto, 1886–1934

3.288, Canto da saudade (Adeus à Vila Aida), Alberto Costa, C4–G5, —, BN

3.289, Cisnes, Júlio Mário Salusse, —, m, BN

3.290, Serenata (O luar da minha terra), —, —, m, BN

Curitiba, Henrique de (Henrique Morozowicz Zbigniew), 1934–2008

3.291, Al teléfono 345 . . . (Berceuse para uma pequena espanhola), 1996–1999, —, —, HC 1999, UFPR

3.292, *Brisas do Sul*

3.292a, Catavento, —, Mário Quintana, —, —, UFPR

3.292b, Nuvens, 1997, Mário Quintana, —, —, UFPR

3.292c, Silêncios do céu, 1997, Mário Quintana, —, —, UFPR

3.292d, Tristeza, 1997, Mário Quintana, —, —, UFPR

3.293, Canção goiana, —, A. G. Ramos Jubé, —, —, UFPR

3.294, Para um mestre de canto, —, Henrique de Curitiba, G♭4–C6, HC 2002, UFPR

3.295, *Seis poemas de Helena Kolody*

3.295a, Âmago, 1999, Helena Kolody, —, HC/UFPR 2003, UFPR

3.295b, Cantar, 1999, Helena Kolody, —, HC/UFPR 2003, UFPR

3.295c, Cantiga de roda, 1999, Helena Kolody, —, HC/UFPR 2003, UFPR

3.295d, Nunca e sempre, 1999, Helena Kolody, —, HC/UFPR 2003, UFPR

3.295e, Viagem infinita, 1999, Helena Kolody, —, HC/UFPR 2003, UFPR

3.295f, Voz da noite, 1999, Helena Kolody, —, HC/UFPR 2003, UFPR

3.296, Solfeggietto, —, Martins Fontes, —, HC 2002, UFPR

3.297, Vocalize, 1993, —, F4–D♯6, HC 1993, UFPR

Additional titles: My Shining Star; Dizeres (cycle for bass and piano).

Diniz, Jaime Cavalcanti, 1924–1989

3.298, Trovas no. 1, 1957, Aldemar Tavares, B3–D5, BN

3.299, Trovas no. 2, 1957, Adelmar Tavares, D4–C5, BN

3.300, Trovas no. 3, 1957, Adelmar Tavares, C♯4–D5, BN

Ellmerich, Luis, 1913–1988

3.301, Abandono, —, Gastão Barroso, m, BN

3.302, *Evocação Paulista, 1st Album*

3.302a, Acalanto, —, Guilherme de Almeida, —, BN

3.302b, Rua Vilaça, —, Altino Bodesan, —, BN

3.302c, São Paulo antigo, —, V. de Serpa e Paiva, —, BN

3.303, *Evocação Paulista, 2nd Album*

3.303a, Brejeirice, —, Luiz Otavio, —, BN

3.303b, Elegia, —, Luis Ellmerich, —, BN

3.303c, Uma casinha paulista, —, I. V. S. e Paiva, —, BN

3.304, Evocação sertaneja, 1956, Euly Coqueiros, —, BN

Additional title: Trova brasileira.

Faria, Celeste Jaguaribe de Matos, 1873–1938

3.305, A morte da boneca, —, Celeste Jaguaribe, SA, BN

3.306, A pedra, —, Celeste Jaguaribe, CW 1935, BN, UFMG

3.307, Aquele amor, —, Celeste Jaguaribe, CW, UFMG

3.308, Berceuse, —, Celeste Jaguaribe, —, UFMG

3.309, Canção da velhinha, —, —, CW, —

3.310, Cromo (Chromo), —, Celeste Jaguaribe, CW 1935, BN, UFMG

3.311, Interrogação, 1929, Celeste Jaguaribe, m, BN

3.312, O jasmineiro, 1933, Celeste Jaguaribe, CW 1933, UFMG

3.313, Olhos azuis, 1916, Celeste Jaguaribe, VM 1916, BN

3.314, O poente, —, Celeste Jaguaribe, CW 1935, BN, UFMG

3.315, Rosas, —, Celeste Jaguaribe, CW 1935, BN, UFMG

3.316, Treva, penumbra e luz, —, —, —, BN, UFMG

3.317, Trovas, 1916, Celeste Jaguaribe, VM, BN

Additional titles: A noite; Covardia; Minha vida é assim; Num postal; O menino curioso; Penas de garça; Saudade; Tão só; Vida fugaz.

Fernandez, Oscar Lorenzo, 1897–1948

3.318, A saudade, op. 11, 1921, Luís Carlos da Fonseca Monteiro de Barros, $C\sharp4-F\sharp5$, IV, BN, UFMG

3.319, As estrelas, op. 21, 1923, Olavo Bilac, —, B/Cia, BN

3.320, A sombra suave, 1929, Tasso da Silveira, E4–E5, VM, BN, UFMG

3.321, As tuas mãos, 1935, Ronald de Carvalho, G4–G5, IV, BN, UFMG

3.322, A velha história (Modinha), 1928, Honório de Carvalho, E4–F5, CW, IV, BN, UFMG

3.323, Aveludados sonhos, 1947, Antonio Rangel Bandeira, E4–G5, IV, BN

3.324, Berceuse da onda que leva o pequenino náufrago, op. 57, 1928, Cecília Meireles, $E\flat4-F5$, RB, BN, UFMG, USP

3.325, Canção ao luar, 1933, Gaspar Coelho, C4–F5, CW, IV, BN, UFMG

3.326, Canção da fonte, 1936, Oscar Lorenzo Fernandez, D4–F5, IV, BN, UFMG

3.327, Canção do berço, op. 35, 1925, Antônio Corrêa de Oliveira, D4–E5, IV, B/Cia, BN, UFMG

3.328, Canção do mar, 1934, Manuel Bandeira, D4–G5, AN, BN, UFMG, +

3.329, Canção do violeiro, op. 38, 1926, Castro Alves, F4–G5, B/Cia, IV, BN

3.330, Canção sertaneja, op. 31, 1924, Eurico de Góes, $D\flat4-F5$, B/Cia, IV, BN, UFMG

3.331, Cisnes, op. 9, 1921, Julio Salusse, $B\flat4-G5$, AN, BN

3.332, Coração inquieto, —, Oscar Lorenzo Fernandez, E4–E5, IV, BN

3.333, Dentro da noite, —, Osório Dutra, $D4-E\flat5$, IV, BN, UFMG

3.334, *Dois epigramas, op. 36*

3.334a, 1. A vida, 1925, Luiz de Andrade Filho, —, RB, BN, UFMG

3.334b, 2. A primavera, 1925, Luiz de Andrade Filho, —, RB, BN, UFMG

3.335, *Duas canções, op. 17*

3.335a, 1. Noite cheia de estrelas, 1922, Adelmar Tavares, D4–E5, IV, B/Cia, BN, UFMG

3.335b, 2. Mãos frias, 1922, Adelmar Tavares, $C\sharp4-G5$, B/Cia, BN

3.336, Elegia da manhã, —, Ronald de Carvalho, $C\sharp4-E5$, IV, BN, UFMG, USP

3.337, Essa negra fulô, 1934, Jorge de Lima, —, RM, BN, UFMG

3.338, Macumba, 1926, Murilo Araujo, —, —

3.339, Madrigal, 1943, Octávio Kelly, $E\flat4-F5$, IV, BN, UFMG, UNESP

3.340, Meu coração, op. 41 (Modinha), 1926, J. B. Mello e Souza, $C\sharp4-F5$, B/Cia, BN, UFMG, +

3.341, Meu pensamento, 1934, Renato de Almeida, D4–F5, IV, BN

3.342, Noite de junho, 1933, Ronald de Carvalho, F4–F5, IV, BN, UFMG, +

3.343, Noturno, 1934, Eduardo Tourinho, —, AN, BN, UFMG, USP, +

3.344, Ó vida de minha vida (Modinha), —, Belmiro Braga, $E\flat4-G\flat5$, SA/AN, BN, UFMG

3.345, Samaritana da floresta, 1936, O. Lourenzo Fernandez, E4–F5, IV, BN, UFMG, +

3.346, Serenata, 1930, Menotti del Picchia, E4–E5, IV, BN

3.347, Solidão, 1922, Ribeiro Couto, D4–F5, IV, BN, UFMG

3.348, Tapera, 1929, Cassiano Ricardo, $E\flat4-F5$, IV, BN

3.349, Toada p'ra você, 1928, Mário de Andrade, $E\flat4-F5$, IV, BN, UFMG, +

3.350, Toi, op. 23, 1923, Leconte de Lisle, $C\sharp4-A5$, IV, BN, UFMG

3.351, Trovas de amor, 1947, Múcio Leão, C4–G5, IV, BN

3.352, Um beijo, 1920, Olavo Bilac, —, m, BN

3.353, Vesperal, 1946, Ronald de Carvalho, F4–F5, IV, BN, UFMG

Additional titles: Caminho da vida; O horizonte vazio; Surdina.

Figueiredo, Laura Onofre, , 1908–

3.354, Acalanto, —, A. S. de Mendonça Jr., UFMG

3.355, Acrostik, —, —, UFMG

3.356, Adeus, —, Sebastião Fonseca, UFMG
3.357, Amar, —, Maria Stella Quirino Marchini, UFMG
3.358, Amor, —, Horácio Paiva, UFMG
3.359, As duas rosas, —, Dylma Cunha de Oliveira, BN
3.360, Avec l'âme, —, Charles Adolphe, UFMG
3.361, Ave Maria, —, —, BN
3.362, A voz do mar, 1956, Lisette Villar de Lucena, UFMG
3.363, Cantiga para os olhos fechados, —, Dylma Cunha de Oliveira, BN
3.364, Castelo de sonhos, —, Dylma Cunha de Oliveira, BN
3.365, Equando ele voltar, —, Colombina, UFMG
3.366, Epigrama, —, Lluis Valeri, UFMG
3.367, Esquecimento, —, Dylma Cunha de Oliveira, BN
3.368, Fé, 1956, Izabel Vieira de Serpra e Paiva, UFMG
3.369, História curta, 1954, João Passos Cabral, UFMG
3.370, Meu violão, —, Sebastião Fonseca, UFMG
3.371, Oração a Santa Teresinha, —, Dylma Cunha de Oliveira, BN
3.372, Os nossos olhos, —, Virgínia Nuno Vilar, UFMG
3.373, Paisagem, —, Adélia Calil, UFMG
3.374, Pecado, —, Dylma Cunha de Oliveira, BN
3.375, Quadras no. 2, —, Virgínia Nuno Vilar, UFMG
3.376, Súplica, —, Sílvia Celeste de Campos, UFMG
3.377, Virtus, —, Lluis Valeri, UFMG

Figueiredo, Letícia Onofre de

3.378, Canção do berço, Alice Lobo, Bandeirante 1949, BN
3.379, Changô, Ascenço Ferreira, Bandeirante 1949, BN
3.380, *Duas cantigas de roda*
3.380a, Esta arte de cortar flores, Cecília Meireles, —, BN, UFMG
3.380b, Valentina, Cecilia Meireles, —, BN, UFMG
3.381, Poema das duas mãosinhas, Jorge de Lima, —, BN

Fiúza, Virginia Salgado, 1897–1987

3.382, Canção dramática, 1947, Maurice Maeterlinck, —, —, UFMG
3.383, Cantiga, 1943, Faustino Nascimento, C4–F5, IV, BN, UFMG
3.384, O adormecer, 1942, Virginia Salgado Fiúza, D3–G4, IV, UFMG
3.385, O tear, —, Olavo Bilac, —, —, BN
3.386, Toada das horas, —, Sylvio Moreaux, —, —, BN

Additional titles: Ambição de ventura; Canção triste; Enganos do coração; Quando de mim te despedes.

Florence, Paulo, 1864–1949

3.387, Anseio (Erwartung), —, Hermann Löns, B/Cia, BN, UNESP
3.388, Ao luar, —, Catulo da Paixão Cearense, —, BN
3.389, Ao pé de um túmulo, —, Auta de Souza, —, BN
3.390, Canção de berço, —, Maria Kahle, —, BN, UNESP
3.391, *Cinco canções internacionais*
3.391a, Exaltação, 1926, Múcio Teixeira, —, BN, UNESP
3.391b, My Love is Like a Red Rose, 1926, Robert Burns, —, BN, UNESP
3.391c, Le silence, —, Alfred de Vigny, —, BN, UNESP
3.392, *Cinco sonetos*
3.392a, O condenado à morte, —, Henri Bocage, —, BN
3.392b, Na capela, —, Antero de Quental, —, BN
3.392c, Sete anos de pastor, —, Luís de Camões, —, BN

3.392d, Velhas árvores, —, Olavo Bilac, —, BN

3.392e, Velhice, —, Virgínia Victorino, —, BN

3.393, Clytie, —, André Chenier, —, BN, UNESP

3.394, Die goldne Wiege, 1926, Hermann Löns, —, BN, UNESP

3.395, Foi assim o seu amor, —, —, —, BN, UNESP

3.396, In der Wüste, —, Nikolaus Lenau, —, UNESP

3.397, Juriti, —, Baptista Junior, —, BN

3.398, L'aveugle à la rose, —, Jacques D'Avray, Campassi & Camin, BN, UNESP

3.399, Lugar assombrado, 1926, Friedrich Hebel, Paulo Florence 1926, UNESP

3.400, *Melodias e canções*

3.400a, O anu, —, —, —, BN

3.400b, O coração, —, Antero de Quental, —, BN, UNESP

3.400c, Eu sou flor arremessada, —, —, —, BN

3.400d, O ignoto, —, Anonymous, —, BN

3.400e, Quero mana, —, Anonymous, —, BN

3.401, No jardim do mosteiro, —, Graciema Nobre, —, BN, UNESP, UFMG

3.402, Pour une statue de l'amour, —, Charles D'Orléans, —, BN, UNESP, UFMG

3.403, *Seis canções de Cléomenes Campos*

3.403a, Canção, —, Cléomenes Campos, —, BN

3.403b, Canção tímida, —, Cléomenes Campos, —, BN

3.403c, Flor de ruína, —, Cléomenes Campos, —, BN

3.403d, A resposta que ele me deu, —, Cléomenes Campos, —, BN

3.403e, Serenata, —, Cléomenes Campos, —, BN

3.403f, Escrito em minha vidraça, —, Cléomenes Campos, —, BN

3.404, Serpens, —, Michelangelo Buonarroti, —, BN, UNESP

3.405, *Três canções francesas*

3.405a, Chanson de Barbérine, —, Alfred de Musset, —, BN, UFMG

3.405b, Aveu, —, Alfred de Musset, B/Cia, BN, UNESP

3.405c, Mea culpa, —, Paul Géraldy, —, UNESP

3.406, Vá como vai!, —, Alberto de Oliveira, —, UFMG

Additional titles: Cinco canções internacionais (Quando cadran le foglie); Idílio.

Gallet, Luciano, 1893–1931

3.407, A casinha pequenina, 1927, Popular text, $C\sharp 4$–$B5$, Harmonization, CW, BN

3.408, Acorda donzela, 1928, —, —, Harmonization, —, BN, UFMG

3.409, Ai, que coração, 1924, Popular text, $D\sharp 4$–$E5$, Harmonization, CW, BN

3.410, Alanguissement, 1918, Roberto Gomes, —, SA, BN, +

3.411, A partida, 1919, Silva Ramos, —, —, SA, AN, BN, UFMG, +

3.412, A vida, —, Ronald de Carvalho, $C\sharp 4$–$F5$, —, SA, AN, +

3.413, *Canções populares brasileiras, Caderno I*

3.413a, Tayêyras, 1925, Folklore, $F4$–$E\flat 5$, Harmonization; other songs in group for mixed choir, —, BN, UFMG

3.414, *Canções populares brasileiras, Caderno II*

3.414a, Foi n'uma noite calmosa, 1925, Popular text, $C4$–$C5$, Harmonization; other songs in group for mixed choir, CW, BN

3.414b, Bambalelê, 1925, Folklore, $E4$–$E\flat 5$, Harmonization, CW, BN, +

3.415, *Canções populares brasileiras, Caderno III*

3.415a, Arrazoar, 1925, —, $F\sharp 4$–$D5$,

Harmonization; other songs in group for mixed choir, CW, BN

3.416, *Interpretações*
3.416a, Infância brasileira, 1928, Murilo Araujo, —, —, CW, BN
3.416b, Pai do mato, 1928, Mário de Andrade, —, —, CW, BN

3.417, Morena, morena, 1921, Popular text, C4–E5, Harmonization, Lino José Barbosa, CW, BN
3.418, Surdina, 1919, Paulo de Godoy, D#4–G5, —, SA/AN, BN, +
3.419, Xangô, 1928, —, —, Harmonization, CW, BN, +

Additional titles: Bela pastora; Canção dolente; *Canções populares brasileiras, Caderno I* (O luar do sertão; Toca zumba; Tutú Marambá); *Canções populares brasileiras, Caderno II* (Sertaneja); *Canções populares brasileiras, Caderno III* (Puxa o melão, sabiá; Eu vi amor pequenino); *Canções típicas brasileiras, Caderno I* (Ai, que coração, morena; A perdiz piou no campo); *Canções típicas brasileiras, Caderno II* (Iaiá, você quer morrer; Suspira, coração triste; Fotorototó); Castanha ligeira; Condessa; Le sonnet d'arvres; Maxixe; Olhos verdes; Quadras; Salomé.

Gnatalli, Radamés, 1906–1988

3.420, A casinha pequenina, 1940, Popular text, IV, BN, UFMG
3.421, Modinha, 1934, Manoel Bandeira, —, BN
3.422, Nhapopé (toada), 1955, Popular theme, Bandeirante 1956, BN
3.423, O Rei mandou me chamá, 1955, Folklore, Bandeirante 1956, BN
3.424, Tanto amor nunca mais, —, Mário Lago, —, BN
3.425, Teus olhos ... água parada, 1933, Radamés Gnatalli, —, BN
3.426, Toada, 1956, Alberto Ribeiro, —, BN

3.427, *Três poemas de Augusto Meyer*
3.427a, Gaita, 1931, Augusto Meyer, —, BN, UFMG
3.427b, Oração da estrela boieira, 1931, Augusto Meyer, —, BN, UFMG
3.427c, Violão, 1931, Augusto Meyer, —, BN, UFMG

Additional titles: Azulão; Letra para uma valsa romântica no.1; Letra para uma valsa romântica no. 2; Morena, morena; Oração; Para meu rancho; Poema relativo; Praiana; Prenda minha; Seis canções; Tayieras.

Grau, Affonso Martinez, 1897–1963

3.428, Alvorada do sertão, Catulo da Paixão Cearense, —, —, BN

3.429, *Canções líricas brasileiras, Album no. 1*
3.429a, A canção da vida, Astério de Campos, D4–E5, AN, SA, BN, UFMG
3.429b, Amor, Beatrix dos Reis Carvalho, C4–F5, IV, AN, BN, UFMG
3.429c, Balada, Renato Sóldon, D4–G5, AN, BN, UFMG
3.429d, Brasileirinha, Luiz Peixoto, C4–E5, IV, AN, BN, UFMG
3.429e, Meu velho Rio, Pádua de Almeida, B3–E5, AN, BN, UFMG
3.429f, Último sino, Murilo de Araújo, E4–A♭5, AN, BN, UFMG
3.429g, Única ventura, Renato Travassos, F4–G5, AN, BN, UFMG

3.430, Dez caboquinho ... (Impressão brasileira), Luiz Peixoto, C4–C5, AN, BN
3.431, Felicidade, Luiz Iglesias, —, —, BN
3.432, Hino ao governador da cidade, Manoel Bastos Tigre, —, Secretaria de Educação e Cultura 1949, BN
3.433, In extremis, Olavo Bilac, —, AN, BN
3.434, Não creias, Caramuru, —, A. Di Franco, BN

Guarnieri, Mozart Camargo 1907–1993

3.435, Acalanto para Luísa, 1983, Mozart Camargo Guarnieri, —, —, —, USP

3.436, A culpa de perder o teu afeto, 1941, Francisco Pati, —, —, —, USP

3.437, Acuti-paru, 1934, Amerindian text, —, —, —, USP

3.438, Adoração, 1956, Suzanna de Campos, D_4–$E\flat_5$, —, RB, BN, USP, +

3.439, À glória de São Paulo, —, Menotti del Picchia, —, —, —, USP

3.440, Amor mesquinho, 1976, Olga Lilian Castilho, —, —, —, USP

3.441, Amo-te muito, 1958, Popular text, —, —, RB, BN, USP, +

3.442, Amo-te sim, 1959, Rossine Camargo Guarnieri, —, —, —, USP

3.443, Aribu, —, Popular text, —, —, —, USP

3.444, As flores amarelas dos ipês, 1928, Antônio de Azevedo Marques, D_4–$F\sharp_5$, —, Irmãos Chiarato 1929, L. G. Miranda, BN, USP

3.445, Ave Maria, 1973, Latin text, —, —, —, USP

3.446, Brinquedo, —, Rossine Camargo Guarnieri, —, —, —, USP

3.447, Cabedelo, 1931, Manuel Bandeira, —, —, —, USP

3.448, Cadê minha pomba rola, 1947, —, —, —, —, USP

3.449, Canção, 1942, Vinícius de Moraes, —, —, —, USP

3.450, Canção das iaras, 1929, José Figueiredo de Sobral Jr., —, —, —, USP

3.451, Canção ingênua, 1959, Wadisa Rússio, $C\sharp_4$–F_5, —, Goldberg 2001, BN

3.452, Cantiga contraditória, 1929, Cleómenes Campos, —, —, —, USP

3.453, Cantiga da ausência, 1973, Rossine Camargo Guarnieri, —, —, —, USP

3.454, Cantiga da porteira, 1930, Rossine Camargo Guarnieri, —, —, —, USP

3.455, Cantiga de quem te quer, 1942, Correa Junior, —, —, —, USP

3.456, Cantiga noturna, 1928, José de Figueiredo Sobral Jr., —, —, L. G. Miranda, USP

3.457, Cantiga sentimental, 1929, Cleómenes Campos, —, —, L. G. Miranda, USP

3.458, Cantiga triste, 1939, Juvenal Galeno, —, —, —, USP

3.459, Carícia, —, Correa Junior, —, —, —, USP

3.460, *Cinco poemas de Alice*

3.460a, E agora ... só me resta a minha voz, 1954, Alice Camargo Guarnieri, E_4–$F\sharp_5$, —, RA, RB, UFMG, USP, +

3.460b, Não posso mais esconder que te amo, 1954, Alice Camargo Guarnieri, $C\sharp_4$–F_5, —, RA, RB, UFMG, USP, +

3.460c, Pedido, 1954, Alice Camargo Guarnieri, D_4–F_5, —, RA, RB, UFMG, USP, +

3.460d, Recolhi no meu coração a tua voz, 1954, Alice Camargo Guarnieri, C_4–F_5, —, RA, RB, UFMG, USP, +

3.460e, Promessa, 1954, Alice Camargo Guarnieri, —, —, RA, RB, UFMG, USP, +

3.461, Ciúme, 1929, Lavínia Abranches Viotti, —, —, —, USP

3.462, Constância, 1935, J. Martins Júnior, —, —, —, USP

3.463, Curuzibambo, 1969, Afro-Brazilian folklore, —, —, —, UFMG, USP

3.464, Declaração, 1943, Francisco Pati, —, —, RB, BN, UFMG

3.465, Den-Báu, 1932, Mozart Camargo Guarnieri, F_4–F_5, —, RB, Music Press, BN, UFMG, +

3.466, Desejo, 1982, Suzanna de Campos, —, —, —, USP

3.467, Desesperança, —, Irene Drummond, —, —, —, UFMG, USP

3.468, Deslumbramento, 1974, Nísia Nóbrega, —, —, —, USP

3.469, Despedida sentimental, —, Mário de Andrade, —, —, —, USP

3.470, Despeito, 1929, Heráclito Viotti, —, —, —, USP

3.471, De você, 1929, Lavínia Abranches Viotti, —, —, —, USP

3.472, *Dois poemas*

3.472a, Eu te esperei na hora silenciosa, 1942, Oneyda Alvarenga, —, —, —, USP

3.472b, Vieste enrolado no perfume dos manacás, 1942, Oneyda Alvarenga, —, —, —, BN

3.473, Dona Janaína, 1935, Manuel Bandeira, —, —, —, USP

3.474, *Duas canções*
3.474a, Agora, 1956, Sylvio Cavalcanti de Oliveira, E4–E5, —, RB, BN, USP
3.474b, Castigo, 1956, Sylvio Cavalcanti de Oliveira, D4–E5, —, RB, BN, USP

3.475, *Duas canções de Celso Brandt*
3.475a, Como o coração da noite, 1955, Celso Brandt, E4–D5, —, RB, BN, USP, +
3.475b, Meus pecados, 1955, Celso Brandt, D♯4–E5, —, RB, BN, USP, +

3.476, *Duas canções de Cleómenes Campos*
3.476a, Quando te vi pela primeira vez, 1939, Cleómenes Campos, —, —, Music Press 1942, RB, BN, UFMG

3.477, *Duas canções de Menotti del Picchia*
3.477a, Desesperança, 1972, Menotti del Picchia, —, —, —, USP
3.477b, Desespero, 1972, Menotti del Picchia, —, —, —, USP
3.477c, Epílogo, 1972, Menotti del Picchia, —, —, —, USP

3.478, *Duas canções de Renata*
3.478a, Oferta, 1967, Renata Pallottini, —, —, —, USP
3.478b, Saudade definitiva, 1967, Renata Pallottini, —, —, —, USP

3.479, *Duas canções de Sílvia Celeste de Campos*
3.479a, Ausência, 1958, Sílvia Celeste de Campos, —, —, —, UFMG, USP
3.479b, Eu digo a meu próprio coração, 1958, Sílvia Celeste de Campos, —, —, —, USP

3.480, *Duas canções de Suzanna de Campos*
3.480a, Beijaste os meus cabelos, 1958, Suzanna de Campos, —, —, —, UFMG, USP
3.480b, Penso em você, 1958, Suzanna de Campos, —, —, —, UFMG, USP

3.481, *Duas cantigas de amor*
3.481a, Não sei porque . . ., 1957, Rossine Camargo Guarnieri, —, —, —, USP
3.481b, Se eu pudesse . . ., 1957, Rossine Camargo Guarnieri, —, —, —, USP

3.482, Duas irmãs, 1931, Correa Junior, —, —, —, USP

3.483, *Duas miniaturas*
3.483a, A luz desse seu olhar tristonho, 1944, Adelmar Tavares, —, —, —, USP
3.483b, Vou vivendo a minha vida, 1944, Adelmar Tavares, —, —, —, USP

3.484, E fico a pensar, 1978, Iêda Schmaltz, —, —, —, USP

3.485, Elvira, escuta, 1958, Popular text, —, —, RB, BN, USP, +

3.486, Ê mô kanceô, 1971, —, —, —, —, USP

3.487, És a mais bela . . ., 1957, Antônio Rangel Bandeira, —, —, —, USP

3.488, És a totalmente amada, 1943, Tasso da Silveira, —, —, —, USP

3.489, És na minha vida, 1974, Manuel Bandeira, —, —, —, USP

3.490, Espera, 1952, Suzanna de Campos, —, —, —, USP

3.491, Esse vazio que nada enche, 1948, Sérgio Millet, —, —, —, USP

3.492, É uma pena, doce amiga, 1933, Mário de Andrade, —, —, —, USP

3.493, Eu sinto dentro do peito, 1961, Waldisa P. Rússio, —, —, —, USP

3.494, Eu te encontrei, 1982, Suzanna de Campos, —, —, —, USP

3.495, Foi o vento . . . foi a vida, 1945, Correa Junior, —, —, —, USP

3.496, Gosto de estar a teu lado, 1933, Mário de Andrade, —, —, —, USP

3.497, Intermezzo, 1973, Nísia Nóbrega, —, —, —, USP

3.498, Já hoje que aqui me vistes, 1942, —, —, —, —, USP

3.499, Lembranças do losango cáqui, —, Mário de Andrade, —, —, —, BN, USP
3.500, Libera-me, —, —, —, —, RB, BR 0002305, USP
3.501, Migalhas, 1976, —, —, —, —, USP
3.502, Minha terra, 1930, Rossine Camargo Guarnieri, —, —, —, USP
3.503, Música e letra de modinha, 1968, Afonso Arinos, —, —, —, UFMG, USP
3.504, Não sei..., 1956, Folklore, —, —, RB, USP
3.505, No fundo dos teus olhos, 1934, Armando de Oliveira, —, —, —, USP
3.506, O amor de agora, 1959, Dante Milano, —, —, —, USP
3.507, O impossível carinho, 1930, Manuel Bandeira, —, —, RB, AMP, Derosa, BN, USP, +
3.508, Oferta, 1977, Renata Pallottini, —, —, —, USP
3.509, O que podia ter sido, 1978, —, —, —, —, USP

3.510, *Para acordar teu coração*
3.510a, Quero dizer baixinho, 1951, Suzanna de Campos, —, —, RA, BN, USP, +
3.510b, Pensei em ti com doçura 1951, 1951, Suzanna de Campos, E♭4–G♭5, —, RA, BN, USP, +
3.510c, Porque estás sempre comigo, 1951, Suzanna de Campos, D♭4–F♭5, —, RA, BN, USP, +
3.510d, Eu gosto de você, 1951, Suzanna de Campos, E4–G5, —, RA, BN, USP, +
3.510e, Olha-me tão somente, 1951, Suzanna de Campos, D♯4–E5, —, RA, BN, USP, +
3.510f, Às vezes, meu amor, 1951, Suzanna de Campos, D4–D5, —, RA, USP, +
3.510g, Quero afagar-te o rosto docemente, 1951, Suzanna de Campos, —, —, RA, BN, USP, +
3.510h, Aceitei tua amizade, 1951, Suzanna de Campos, C4–F5, —, RA, BN, USP, +

3.511, Pena, 1980, —, —, —, —, USP
3.512, Poema interior, 1977, Renata Pallottini, —, —, —, USP

3.513, *Poemas da negra*
3.513a, Ai, momentos de físico amor, 1975, Mário de Andrade, D♯4–G5, —, Goldberg 2004, USP
3.513b, Estou com medo, —, Mário de Andrade, E♭4–E5, —, Goldberg 2004, USP
3.513c, Há o mutismo exaltado dos astros 1929, 1975, Mário de Andrade, C4–A5, —, Goldberg 2004, USP
3.513d, Lá longe, no sul, 1974, Mário de Andrade, D4–G5, —, Goldberg 2004, USP
3.513e, Lembrança boa, 1974, Mário de Andrade, C4–F5, —, Goldberg 2004, USP
3.513f, Na zona da mata, 1975, Mário de Andrade, C4–F5, —, Goldberg 2004, USP
3.513g, Não sei porque espírito antigo, 1929, Mário de Andrade, D4–F5, —, Goldberg 2004, USP
3.513h, Não sei porque os tetéus, 1974, Mário de Andrade, D♭4–G5, —, Goldberg 2004, USP
3.513i, Não sei se estou vivo, 1968, Mário de Andrade, C♯4–G, —, —, USP
3.513j, Nega em teu ser primário, 1929, Mário de Andrade, C♯4–E♯5, —, Goldberg 2004, USP
3.513k, Quando, 1934, Mário de Andrade, E4–E5, —, Goldberg 2004, USP
3.513l, Você é tão suave, 1934, Mário de Andrade, E4–E5, —, Goldberg 2004, USP

3.514, Porto seguro, 1939, Rossine Camargo Guarnieri, G4–A5, —, —, USP
3.515, Prelúdio no. 2, 1928, Guilherme de Almeida, F4–F5, —, RB, USP

3.516, *Quatro cantigas*
3.516a, A cantiga da mutuca, 1949, Folklore, D4–A5, Medium voice, RB, USP, +
3.516b, Cantiga, 1955, Folklore, A♭3–D♭5, Medium voice, RB, USP, +
3.516c, Não sei, —, Folklore, —, Medium voice, RA, +
3.516d, Vamos dar a despedida, 1956,

Folklore, E_4–E_5, Medium voice, RB, BN, +

3.517, *Quatro poemas de Macunaíma*
3.517a, Antianti é Tapejara, 1931, Mário de Andrade, —, —, —, USP, +
3.517b, Mandu sarará, 1931, Mário de Andrade, —, —, —, USP, +
3.517c, Rudá, rudá, 1931, Mário de Andrade, —, —, —, USP, +
3.517d, Sai aruê, 1931, Mário de Andrade, —, —, —, USP, +

3.518, Solidão, —, Ribeiro Couto, —, —, —, USP

3.519, Tanta coisa a dizer-te, 1939, Cleómenes Campos, D_4–D_5, —, RB, BN, UFMG, USP

3.520, Toada do Pai do Mato, 1928, Mário de Andrade, —, —, —, USP

3.521, *Três canções brasileiras*
3.521a, Quando embalada, 1948, Folklore, D_4–F_5, —, RB, AMP, BN, +
3.521b, Quebra o coco, menina, 1948, Juvenal Galeno, —, —, RB, BN, USP
3.521c, Vou-me embora, 1948, Folklore, B_3–F_5, Medium voice, RB, AMP, BN, USP, +

3.522, *Três epigramas*
3.522a, Pêndulo, 1968, Péricles Eugênio da Silva Ramos, —, —, —, USP
3.522b, Suspeita, 1968, Péricles Eugênio da Silva Ramos, —, —, —, USP
3.522c, Terra natal, 1968, Péricles Eugênio da Silva Ramos, —, —, —, USP

3.523, *Três poemas*
3.523a, Coração cosmopolita, 1939, Rossine Camargo Guarnieri, —, —, —, USP
3.523b, Tristeza, 1939, Rossine Camargo Guarnieri, E_4–$A\flat_5$, —, —, USP

3.524, *Treze canções de amor*
3.524a, Acalanto do amor feliz, 1936, Rossine Camargo Guarnieri, —, —, —, USP
3.524b, Canção do passado, 1936, Correa Junior, —, —, —, USP
3.524c, Canção tímida, 1937, Cleómenes Campos, —, —, —, USP
3.524d, Cantiga da tua lembrança, 1937, Rossine Camargo Guarnieri, —, —, —, USP
3.524e, Em louvor do silêncio, 1936, Correa Júnior, —, —, —, USP
3.524f, Milagre, 1936, Olegário Mariano, —, —, —, USP
3.524g, Ninguém mais, 1936, Cassiano Ricardo, —, —, —, USP
3.524h, Por que?, 1937, Mozart Camargo Guarnieri, F_4–F_5, —, —, USP
3.524i, Se você compreendesse, —, Rossine Camargo Guarnieri, —, —, —, USP
3.524j, Segue-me, 1937, Folklore, —, —, —, USP
3.524k, Talvez, 1937, Carlos Pastina, —, —, —, USP
3.524l, Você, 1936, Francisco de Mattos, —, —, —, USP
3.524m, Você nasceu, 1937, Rossine Camargo Guarnieri, —, —, —, USP

3.525, *Triptico de Yeda*
3.525a, Por toda a eternidade, 1967, Yeda Prates Bernis, —, —, —, USP
3.525b, Saudade, 1967, Yeda Prates Bernis, —, —, —, USP
3.525c, Paz, 1967, Yeda Prates Bernis, —, —, —, USP

3.526, Trovas de amor, 1928, Folklore, E_4–F_5, —, RB, Chiarato, BN, UFMG, +
3.527, Vai, azulão, —, Manuel Bandeira, $E\flat_4$–$E\flat_5$, —, AMP 1944, RB, FBN/DIMAS 1998, BN, USP
3.528, Vocalise, 1977, —, —, —, —, USP

Guerra Peixe, Antonio 1914–1993

3.529, Amo as interrogações, —, Sônia Maria Vieira, —, m, BN
3.530, A solidão e sua porta, —, Carlos Pena Filho, —, m, BN
3.531, *Canções de Débora*
3.531a, Juntos amamos, —, Pierre Weil, —, —, BN
3.531b, Nossos olhos, —, Pierre Weil, —, —, BN

3.531c, Tua boca diz que não, —, Pierre Weil, —, —, BN

3.532, *Cânticos serranos no. 1*
3.532a, Fala, 1970, Mário Fonseca, —, m, GRic 1970, BN
3.523b, Chuva miúda, 1970, Mário Fonseca, —, m, GRic 1970, BN
3.532c, Seremos dois, 1970, Mário Fonseca, —, m, GRic 1970, BN

3.533, *Cânticos serranos no. 2*
3.533a, Almas desoladoramente frias, —, Raul de Leoni, —, —, BN
3.533b, Confusão, —, Raul de Leoni, —, —, BN
3.533c, História antiga, —, Raul de Leoni, —, —, BN

3.534, *Cânticos serranos no. 3*
3.534a, Arrependimento, —, Reynaldo Chaves, —, —, BN
3.534b, Última ilusão, —, Reynaldo Chaves, —, —, BN

3.535, *Cânticos serranos no. 4*
3.535a, Prudência, 1991, Raul de Leoni, —, —, BN

3.536, *Cantigas do amor existencial*
3.536a, Nossos olhos, —, —, —, m, BN
3.536b, Tua boca diz que não, —, Pierre Weil, —, m, BN
3.536c, Juntos amamos, —, Pierre Weil, —, —, BN

3.537, Chuva miúda, 1970, Mário Fonseca, —, m, GRic, BN
3.538, Da fatalidade (Modinha), —, Sônia Maria Vieira, —, m, BN
3.539, Ê boi!, —, —, —, RB, UFMG, USP
3.540, E quando o amor chegar, —, Sônia Maria Vieira, —, m, BN
3.541, Eu ia nadá, —, Folklore (côco-de-martelo), C_4–$E\flat_5$, RB, BN
3.542, Felicidade, —, Jorge Faraj, —, —, BN
3.543, Fibra de herói, —, Teófilo de Barros, —, IV, BN
3.544, Linhas de catimbó, —, —, —, m, BN
3.545, Mamãe Emanjá (Marcha-baião), —, —, —, RB, UFMG

3.546, Maria do mar, —, José Mauro de Vasconcelos, —, RB, BN, UFMG
3.547, Nagô, nagô, nagô, —, —, —, RB, BN
3.548, Nêgo bola-sete, —, —, —, RB, BN
3.549, Nesta manhã, —, Elson Farias, A_3–F_5, m, UFMG
3.550, O canto do mar, —, José Mauro de Vasconcelos, —, RB, BN
3.551, O que sou, —, Sônia Maria Vieira, —, m, BN
3.552, Ô Vaqueiro, —, —, —, RB, BN
3.553, Poema, —, Jayme Griz, B_3–$F\sharp_5$, RB, BN
3.554, Provérbios no. 1, —, —, —, —, BN
3.555, Provérbios no. 2, —, —, —, —, BN
3.556, Provérbios no. 3, —, —, —, —, BN
3.557, Qualquer tempo, —, Carlos Drummond de Andrade, —, —, BN
3.558, Rapadura, —, Carlos Drummond de Andrade, B_3–$F\sharp_5$, RB, BN
3.559, Resta sim, é remover, —, Elson Farias, —, m, BN
3.560, Sinto e provo, —, Sonia Maria Vieira, C_4–C_5, IV, Ed. Opus, —
3.561, Suave, —, Sônia Maria Vieira, —, m, BN
3.562, Tempo de Amor (Modinha), —, Julieta de Andrade, B_3–$E\flat_5$, IV, Ed. Opus, BN
3.563, Teus olhos, —, Emilia Guerra-Peixe, —, m, BN
3.564, Toadas de Xangô, —, —, —, —, BN

3.565, *Três canções*
3.565a, Carreiros, 1955, Jayme Griz, $C\sharp_4$–F_5, RB, BN, USP
3.565b, Poema, —, Jayme Griz, B_3–$F\sharp_5$, RB, BN, USP
3.565c, Suspiros, —, Jayme Griz, D_4–F_5, RB, BN, USP

3.566, *Trovas alagoanas*
3.566a, A viola e a prima, 1955, Popular song, —, RB, +
3.566b, Tomara achar quem me diga, 1955, Popular song, —, RB, +
3.566c, Até nas flores se nota, 1955, Popular song, —, RB, +

3.566d, Nossa amor . . ., 1955, Popular song, —, RB, +

3.566e, Canoeiro, canoerio, 1955, Popular song, —, RB, +

3.567, *Trovas capixabas*

3.567a, Abaixai, ó limoeiro, —, Folklore from the state of Espírito Santo, F4–E♭5, RB, BN, +

3.567b, Ainda que o fogo apague, —, Folklore from the state of Espírito Santo, D4–D♯5, RB, BN, +

3.567c, O Lua que estás tão clara, —, Folklore from the state of Espírito Santo, D4–F5, RB, BN, +

3.567d, Tanto verso que eu sabia, —, Folklore from the state of Espírito Santo, D4–D5, RB, BN, +

3.567e, Vou-me embora, vou-me embora, —, Folklore from the state of Espírito Santo, E4–G5, RB 1955, BN, +

3.568, Utopia, —, Sônia Maria Vieira, —, m, BN

3.569, Vai torná a vortá (cateretê), —, Popular text, —, RB, BN

3.570, Vou-me embora pra Pasárgada, 1986, Manuel Bandeira, C♯4–E5, m, BN

Additional titles: Canção amiga; Cânticos serranos no. 4 (Vivendo).

Hartman, Ernesto Frederico (Sobrinho), 1970–

3.571, *Canções de Sônia Maria*

3.571a, Dorme sobre o meu seio, 2002, Fernando Pessoa, C4–G5, m, UFMG, UEMG

3.571b, Mais nada, 2004, Samuel Linsman, A♯3–F♯5, m, UFMG, UEMG

3.571c, Não digas nada, 2004, Vinícius de Moraes, —, m, UFMG, UEMG

3.571d, Soneto da separação, 2004, Vinícius de Moraes, —, m, UFMG, UEMG

3.572, Souvenir, 1992, Raimundo Corrêia, D4–G5, —, UFMG, UEMG

Henn, Natho 1901–1958

3.573, *Canções de Ofélia*

3.573a, How Should I Your True Love, William Shakespeare, m, BN

3.574, *Doze músicas para canto e piano*

3.574a, Assovio, —, MPA, BN, USP

3.574b, Balada triste, Alceu Wamosy, MPA, BN, USP

3.574c, Borralheira, Marieta Costa, MPA, BN, USP

3.574d, Canção do baú, Mário Quintana, MPA, BN, USP

3.574e, Cantiguinha, —, MPA, BN, USP

3.574f, Caravelas, Nilson Bertoline, MPA, BN, USP

3.574g, Outono, Rainer Maria Rilker, MPA, BN, USP

3.574h, Quero-quero, Manuel do Nascimento Vargas, MPA, BN, USP

3.574i, Tão simples, Lila Ripoll, MPA, BN, USP

3.574j, Trovas, Ovídio Chaves, MPA, BN, USP

3.574k, Vento, —, MPA, BN, USP

3.574l, Violão, João Otávio de Nogueira Leiria, MPA, BN, USP

Henrique, Waldemar, 1905–1995

3.575, Abaluaiê, 1948, Afro-Brazilian religious song, E♭4–E♭5, —, EBMP, FCGo, BN

3.576, ABC de lampião, 1948, Folklore, E4–E5, —, FCGo, —

3.577, Acalanto, 1960, Ruy Paratininga Barata, D♭4–E♭5, —, FCGo, BN

3.578, Adeus, 1960, Waldemar Henrique, D4–D5, —, FCGo, UFMG

3.579, Alegria, alegria (Carimbó), —, Waldemar Henrique, —, —, FCGo, UFMG

3.580, Boi-Bumbá, 1934, Waldemar Henrique, C4–C5, —, USP, IV, BN, UFMG

3.581, Bôto, 1978, Waldemar Henrique, B3–D4, —, FCGo, BN, UFMG

3.582, Cabocla malvada, 1932, Vladimir Emanuel, B3-D4, —, FCG0, BN, UFMG

3.583, Canção do Siriry (Ciranda), 1934, —, B3-E5, —, FCG0, —

3.584, Canção nômade, 1931, Waldemar Henrique, C4-G5, —, FCG0, UFMG

3.585, *Canções marinhas*

3.585a, Vela que passou, 1936, Violeta Branca, B3-D5, —, IV, FCG0, BN, UFMG

3.586, Chorinho, 1932, Waldemar Henrique, C4-D5, —, FCG0, —

3.587, Cobra grande (Canção amazônica), 1934, João de Jesus Paes Loureiro, D4-D5, —, FCG0, UFMG

3.588, Côco perenuê, 1936, João de Jesus Paes Loureiro, D♭4-E♭5, —, RA, FCG0, BN, UFMG

3.589, É Maracatu, —, Waldemar Henrique, C4-D♭5, —, FCG0, —

3.590, Entretanto, eu canto, —, Maria Lúcia Godoy, E4-F♯5, —, FCG0, UFMG

3.591, Essa negra fulô, 1935, Jorge de Lima, A3-F5, —, RB, FCG0, BN, UFMG

3.592, Exaltação, 1934, Valentina Biosca Gonzalez, C4-D5, —, IV, RB, FCG0, BN, UFMG

3.593, Fiz da vida uma canção (valsa), 1930, Waldemar Henrique, E♭4-G5, —, IV, FCG0, UFMG

3.594, Hei de morrer cantando, —, Waldemar Henrique, D♭4-D♭5, —, IV, FCG0, BN, UFMG

3.595, Hei de seguir teus passos: maracatú, —, —, —, —, m, EBMP, UFMG, +

3.596, Hino aos Arcanjos São Miguel e São Gabriel, 1960, Raymundo de Souza Moura, B3-B4, —, FCG0, BN, UFMG

3.597, Juriti (Canção amazônica), 1936, Jorge Hurley, A3-B♭4, —, IV, FCG0, BN, UNESP

3.598, *Lendas amazônicas*

3.598a, Curupira, —, Waldemar Henrique, B3-E5, —, EM, FCG0, BN, UFMG

3.598b, Foi Bôto, sinhá!, 1933, Antônio Tavernard, E4-A♯5, —, EM, FCG0, BN, UFMG

3.598c, Manhã-nungára, 1935, Waldemar Henrique, D4-E5, —, FCG0, UFMG

3.598d, Matinta-perêra, —, Antônio Tavernard, —, —, EM, BN, UFMG, UNESP

3.598e, Minha amada tão longe, 1945, Alfonsus de Guimarães Filho, E4-F5, —, EM, FCG0, BN

3.598f, Tamba-tajá (Canção amazônica), 1934, Waldemar Henrique, C4-D5, —, EM, FCG0, BN, UFMG, UNESP

3.598g, Uirapuru (Canção amazônica-valsinha do Marajóa, 1934, Mara Costa Pereira, D4-D5, —, EM, FCG0, UFMG, USP

3.599, Mamãi preta, 1934, Paulo McDowell, —, —, FCG0, —

3.600, Meu "boi" vai-se embora, 1936, Folklore, —, —, EM, FCG0, BN

3.601, Minha terra, 1923, Waldemar Henrique, C♯4-E5, —, IV, FCG0, BN, UFMG, UNESP

3.602, Morena (Chula marajoara), 1930, Waldemar Henrique, D4-♯5, —, FCG0, UFMG

3.603, Noite de São João, 1935, Unknown, C4-C5, —, FCG0, —

3.604, O passo da ema, 1934, —, —, —, FCG0, —

3.605, O seringueiro, 1937, Popular text, E4-D5, Harmonization, FCG0, UFMG

3.606, Passarinho da lagoa, 1933, —, —, —, FCG0, —

3.607, *Pássaro da terra*

3.607a, Caçador (Tema do), 1978, João de Jesus Paes Loureiro, E4-D5, —, FCG0, —

3.607b, Coro (Do solo calcinado), 1978, João de Jesus Paes Loureiro, —, —, FCG0, —

3.607c, Donzela (Eu nasci no amor perfeito), 1978, João de Jesus Paes Loureiro, E4-C5, —, FCG0, UFMG

3.607d, Lundú dos caboclos, 1978, João de Jesus Paes Loureiro, —, —, FCG0, —

3.607e, Pássaro da terra, 1978, João de Jesus Paes Loureiro, E4-G5, —, FCG0, UFMG

3.607f, Teotônio, 1978, João de Jesus Paes Loureiro, —, —, FCGo, —

3.608, Remadores seringueiros, —, Álvaro Maia, D4–D5, —, FCGo RB, UFMG

3.609, Rolinha, —, Waldemar Henrique, C4–E5, —, RB 1954/1964/1965, BN, UFMG

3.610, Senhora Dona Sancha, 1932, Gastão Vieira, C4–E5, —, RJ: Ed. Bras. De Música Popular, BN

3.611, Sonho de curumim, 1934, —, —, —, FCGo, —

3.612, Tema de Jovino, 1978, Waldemar Henrique, C♯3–C♯5, —, FCGo, UFMG

3.613, Tema de triste, 1978, Waldemar Henrique, C♯4–D5, —, FCGo, —

3.614, Tema Severino (Tema teatral), 1958, —, —, —, FCGo, —

3.615, Tem pena da nega (Batuque amazônico), 1933, Antônio Tavernard, D4–C5, —, EM, FCGo, BN

3.616, Trem de Alagoas, 1939, Ascenço Ferreira, C4–D5, —, RB 1943/1952/1961, FCGo, BN, USP

3.617, *Três pontos rituais*
3.617a, Sem-seu (Candomblé de Ilhéus), 1952, Waldemar Henrique, —, —, RB, FCGo, BN
3.617b, Aba-lógum, —, Afro-Brazilian religious song, C♯4–E5, —, RB, FCGo, BN
3.617c, No jardim de Oeira, 1948, Waldemar Henrique, D4–E5, —, RB, FCGo, BN, UFMG

3.618, Uma canção de amor, 1989, João de Jesus Paes Loureiro, C4–F5, —, FCGo, UFMG

3.619, Violeiro da estrada, 1936, Popular text, C4–E5, —, FCGo, —

Additional titles: Abaluaiê-cô; Alcova zul; Alfama; Amar de longe ... ; Amor! Amor!; Ao te deixar; Boi canarinho; Boi tungão; Boquinha mimosa; Cadê os guerreiros; Farinhada; Felicidade; Fugi só pra vortá; Gesta primitiva; Hei de seguir teus passos; Jacaré com pirarucu; Japiym; Jongo; Lavagem do Bomfim; Lírio roxo; Lundu da negrinha; Macumba; Mãe Catirina; Mãe do terreiro; Menina, me dá teu remo; Menino, quem foi teu Mestre?; Minha canção do mosqueiro; Min orixá Xangô; Moreninha, Mururé; Na fazenda Jutlândia; Nau da Bahia; Negra dengosa; Negro véio; Olero-ô; Oração ao negrinho do pastoreio; Ouve esta prece que a viola te oferece; Pahy-tuna; Pitomba madura; Pororoca; Primavera; Quando a saudade acorda; Quiriru; Rito Palikur; Romance; Rosa leiteira; Soneto; Sonho de Paricá; Tapioca quentinha; Tem pena da nega; Teu corpo Moreno; Ui rapuru; Vamos embora pro engenho; Vem, Maria; Você não casa comigo.

Jabor, Najla (Maia de Carvalho Najla Jabor), 1915–2001

3.620, Alucinação, José Alfredo Maia de Carvlaho, —, IV, BN, BDB

3.621, A palavra de Deus, Stela Dubois, —, Guanabara, BN, USP

3.622, A semente é a dor amor, Roque Martins, —, —, BN, UFMG, USP

3.623, Assim falou o poeta, Guanabara, —, —, BN, USP

3.624, Ave Maria, Sacred text; Latin, —, CVG, BN

3.625, Balada no. 1: Teus Olhos, Beni Carvalho, —, —, BN

3.626, Balada no. 2: Raimundo de Brito, —, —, RB, BN, USP

3.627, Barcarola, op. 92, Dilma Cunha Oliveira, —, —, BN

3.628, Batuque no. 1, Silvio Morceaux, —, —, BN

3.629, Batuque no. 2, Hilda Reis Capucci, G3–E♭5, RB, BN, USP

3.630, Berceuse, op. 11, —, —, —, USP

3.631, Canção bárbara, Olga Mayer, —, RB, BN, USP

3.632, Canção de amor, Iveta Ribeiro, —, RB, BN, USP

3.633, Canção dos olhos, Guanabara, —, —, USP
3.634, Canção do trovador, José Alfredo Maia de Carvalho, —, RB, BN, USP
3.635, Canção simples, op. 83 (Berceuse), Nóbrega de Siqueira, —, —, BN
3.636, Copo de cristal, Agrippino Grieco, —, Seresta, BN, UFMG, USP, BDB
3.637, Desejo, op. 47, Iveta Ribeiro, —, —, BN
3.638, Gato preto, Nóbrega de Siqueira, —, —, BN
3.639, Noturno com palavras, José Alfredo Maia de Carvalho, —, EM, BN, UFMG, USP
3.640, Noturno no. 3, Rosa menina, —, —, EM, USP
3.641, Novo amor, op. 65 (Berceuse), Aracy Rivera de Rezende, —, EM, BN, UFMG, USP
3.642, Oração à esperança, Leopoldo Braga, —, —, BN
3.643, O sonho, J. Benedito Silveira Peixoto, —, IV, BN, USP, BDB
3.644, Pode entrar saudade, E. Mangione Jr., C_4-E_b5, RB, BN, USP
3.645, Romance, op. 11, Iveta Ribeiro, —, RB, BN
3.646, Romance, op. 13, Iveta Ribeiro, —, —, BN
3.647, Romance, op. 3, Sérgio Murilo, —, —, BN
3.648, Romance, op. 56, Iveta Ribeiro, —, —, BN
3.649, Romance, op. 6, José Guilherme de Araújo Jorge, —, —, BN

3.650, *Suite de seis peças*
3.650a, Louco devaneio, Alda Pereira Pinto, B_b3-C_5, Musicália, —
3.650b, Um adeus (no. 3), Alda Pereira Pinto, C_4-F_5, Musicália, —
3.650c, A um poeta (no. 5), Alda Pereira Pinto, B_3-B_4, Musicália, —

3.651, Teus olhos (Balada no. 1), Beni Carvalho, E_b3-G_5, m, OMB

3.652, Toada no. 1: Brasileira, Iveta Ribeiro, —, —, BN
3.653, Toada no. 2: Morena, Carlos Paulo Barros, —, —, BN
3.654, Toada no. 3: Não sei viver sem ti, Diva Jabor, —, —, BN, UFMG, USP
3.655, Toada no. 4: Amor, Carlos Paula Barros, —, —, BN
3.656, Toada no. 5: Quando o amor vem, Antônio Siqueira, —, —, BN
3.657, Único amor, op. 65 (Berceuse), Elora Possolo, —, —, BN

Additional title: Sou assim.

Kiefer, Bruno, 1923–1987

3.658, Canção da garoa, 1976, Mário Quintana, D_4-F_5, USP/SDP, BN, UFMG, UFRJ

3.659, *Canções do vento*
3.659a, Quem me dirá quem sou?, 1971, Fernando Pessoa, —, USP/SDP, BN
3.659b, O vento é quando?, 1971, Carlos Nejar, —, USP/SDP, BN
3.659c, Canção para uma valsa lenta, 1958, Mário Quintana, —, USP/SDP, BN
3.659d, Cantiga de São Francisco, 1978, Lara de Lemos, E_4-G_5, —, UFMG
3.659e, Contemplo o lago mudo, 1957, Fernando Pessoa, —, —, UFMG
3.659f, Elegia, 1971, Ribeiro Couto, —, USP/SDP, BN, UFMG
3.659g, No ouro sem fim da tarde morta, —, Fernando Pessoa, —, m, BN
3.659h, Palavras de anjo, 1979, Armindo Trevisan, —, —, UFMG
3.659i, Sol nulo dos dias vãos, 1958, Fernando Pessoa, —, USP/SDP, BN, UFMG

Additional titles: O menino doente; Relógio morre; *Três sonetos de Drummond* (Carta; Legado; Os poderes infernais).

Koellreuter, Hans Joachin, 1915–2005

3.660, A tarde, 1943, Menotti del Picchia, —, —, LMT, BN

3.661, Cantos de Kulka, 1964, Georg Kulka, —, —, Edition Modern, —

3.662, *Noturnos para voz media y piano*

3.662a, I., 1945, Oneyda Alvarenga, G$\sharp$3–F5, Medium voice, ECIC, BN, EMB, +

3.662b, II., 1945, Oneyda Alvarenga, B3–F5, Medium voice, ECIC, BN, EMB, +

3.662c, III., 1945, Oneyda Alvarenga, C$\sharp$4–F5, Medium voice, ECIC, BN, EMB, +

3.662d, IV., 1945, Oneyda Alvarenga, A$\sharp$3–B$\flat$4, Medium voice, ECIC, BN, EMB, +

3.662e, V., 1945, Oneyda Alvarenga, G$\sharp$3–E5, Medium voice, ECIC, BN, EMB, +

3.663, Poema, 1943, Oneyda Alvarenga, —, —, —, BN

3.664, Puebla, 1942, Ronald de Carvalho, C$\sharp$3–F$\sharp$4, —, IML, BN, EMB

3.665, Sonho de uma noite de verão, 1943, Ronald de Carvalho, C$\sharp$4–G$\sharp$5, —, LMT, BN, UFBA, EMB

3.666, Tanka II, 1973, Shutaro Mukai, —, —, Novas Metas, —

Krieger, Edino, 1928–

3.667, Balada do desesperado, 1954, —, —, —, UFRJ

3.668, Desafio, 1955, Manuel Bandeira, —, LK Produções Artísticas, BN

3.669, Tem piedade de mim, 1947, Antônio Rangel Bandeira, C4–G$\sharp$5, LK Produções Artísticas, BN, UFMG

3.670, Tu e o vento, 1954, Adelmar Tavares, —, m, BN

Additional titles: Canção do violeiro; Legado; Poderes infernais; *Três canções de Nicholas Guillén* (Canción china a dos voces; Canción del regreso; El negro mar); *Três sonetos de Drummond* (Carta; Legado; Poderes infernais).

Lacerda, Osvaldo Costa de, 1927–

3.671, Acalanto para minha mãe, 1986, Rossine Camargo Guarnieri, —, FBN/DIMAS, —, BN, USP

3.672, Alguém bateu à minha porta, 1988, Maria José V. Homem de Mello, —, FBN/DIMAS, —, BN, USP

3.673, Amargura, —, Fernando Bortoli, —, FBN/DIMAS, —, BN

3.674, A um passarinho, 1968, Vinicius de Morais, —, FBN/DIMAS, —, BN, USP

3.675, Ausência, 1954, Renato Lacerda, A3–F5, RB, FBN/DIMAS, —, BN, USP, EMB

3.676, A valsa, 1973, Casimiro de Abreu, D$\sharp$4–G5, Novas Metas, —, USP, UNESP

3.677, Basta de ser o outro, 1986, Paulo Bonfim, —, FBN/ DIMAS, —, BN, USP

3.678, Beijos mortos, 1992, Martins Fontes, —, —, —, USP

3.679, Bilhete àquela que ainda está por nascer, 1979, Paulo Bonfim, —, FBN/DIMAS, —, BN, USP

3.680, Boca, 1982, Carlos Drummond de Andrade, B3–E5, FBN/DIMAS, —, BN, USP

3.681, Canção à toa, 1988, Guilherme de Almeida, —, FBN/DIMAS, —, BN, USP

3.682, Canção do dia inútil, 1986, Ribeiro Couto, —, m, —, BN, USP

3.683, Canção do exílio, 1991, Antonio Gonçalves Dias, —, m, —, BN, USP

3.684, *Canções de Ofélia*

3.684a, And Will He Not Come Again?, 1980, William Shakespeare, D$\sharp$4–F5, m, —, BN

3.684b, How Should I Your True Love, 1980, William Shakespeare, E4–F5, m, —, BN

3.684c, To-morrow is Saint Valentine's Day, 1980, William Shakespeare, F$\flat$4–G5, m, —, BN

3.685, Cantiga, op. 8, no. 2, 1953, Manuel Bandeira, —, m, —, BN

3.686, Cantiga I, 1964, Manuel Bandeira, D4–G5, m, —, BN

3.687, Cantiga II, 1964, Manuel Bandeira, —, m, —, BN, USP

3.688, Cantiga de ninar escrava, 1970, Antônio Rangel Bandeira, —, —, —, BN, USP

3.689, Cantiga de viúvo, 1975, Carlos

Drummond de Andrade, —, FBN/DIMAS, —, BN, USP

3.690, Carnaval do desamor, 1982, Ilka Brunhilde Laurito, —, m, —, BN, USP

3.691, Castigo de amor, 1991, —, —, —, —, USP

3.692, *Cinco trovas*

3.692a, À noite, quando me deito, 1965, Folklore, $C4-G5$, m, —, BN

3.692b, Chamaste-me tua vida, 1965, Folklore, $E4-G5$, m, —, BN

3.692c, Eu quero bem..., 1965, Folklore, $C\sharp4-G5$, m, —, BN

3.692d, Fui no livro do destino, 1965, Folklore, $C4-G5$, m, —, BN

3.692e, Se eu fosse pé de pau, 1965, Folklore, $D\sharp4-F\sharp5$, m, —, BN

3.693, Contrição, 1987, Gregório de Matos, —, m, —, BN, USP

3.694, Dá-me as pétalas de rosa, 1988, Olavo Bilac, $D\sharp4-G5$, m, —, BN, USP

3.695, Delírio vão, —, Antônio Rangel Bandeira, —, m, —, BN

3.696, Desafio, 1953, Folklore, —, m, —, BN, USP

3.697, Desejos de doente, 1991, Francisco Otaviano, —, m, —, BN USP

3.698, Em uma frondosa roseira, —, Tomás Antônio Gonzaga, —, m, —, BN

3.699, Farei o que tu fizeres, 1991, Domingos Caldas Barbosa, —, m, —, BN, USP

3.700, Felicidade, 1951, Manuel Bandeira, —, FBN/DIMAS, —, BN, USP

3.701, Ladainha, 1970, Cassiano Ricardo, $A3-D\sharp5$, —, —, BN

3.702, Lamentação da hora perdida, 1985, —, —, —, —, USP

3.703, Lembrança de amor, —, Vicente de Carvalho, —, —, —, BN, USP

3.704, Lira, —, Antônio Gonçalves Dias, —, m, —, BN

3.705, Mandaste a sombra de um beijo, 1962, Manuel Bandeira, —, —, —, BN, USP

3.706, Marilia de Dirceu, 1965, Tomás Antônio Gonzaga, —, RB, —, BN, UFMG

3.707, Martírio, 1968, Junqueira Freire, —, FBN/DIMAS, —, BN, USP

3.708, Menina, minha menina, —, Gustavo Barroso, $C4-D5$, Novas Metas, —, BN, EMB

3.709, Minha carta a você, 1971, J. B. Silveira Peixoto, —, m, —, BN, USP

3.710, Minha mãe, 1986, Guilherme de Almeida, $D4-F5$, m, —, USP

3.711, Minha Maria, op. 1, no. 2, 1971, Castro Alves, $F4-G\flat5$, m, —, BN, USP

3.712, Mistério, 1985, Afonso Lopes de Almeida, —, m, —, BN, USP

3.713, Modinha, 1953, Fagundes Varela, $E\flat4-G5$, m, —, BN

3.714, Moinho, 1970, Cassiano Ricardo, $D4-G\sharp5$, m, —, BN, USP

3.715, Mozart no céu, 1991, Manuel Bandeira, $E\flat4-F5$, TR, *The Latin American Art Song*, BN, USP

3.716, Murmúrio, 1965, Cecília Meireles, $C\sharp4-F\sharp5$, m, —, BN, USP

3.717, Noturno, 1951, Vicente de Carvalho, $C4-F5$, m, —, BN

3.718, O alcoviteiro, —, Antônio Rangel Bandeira, —, m, —, BN

3.719, O atropelado, 1986, —, —, —, —, USP

3.720, O menino doente, 1949, Manuel Bandeira, $B3-F5$, Novas Metas, TR, *The Latin American Art Song*, BN, UFMG, USP

3.721, O relógio, 1984, Marina Tricânico, —, —, —, BN, USP

3.722, Outra voz, outra paisagem, —, Paulo Bonfim, —, m, —, BN, USP

3.723, Poema tirado de uma notícia de jornal, 1964, Manuel Bandeira, $C3-F5$, RB, —, BN, UFMG, USP

3.724, Poemeto erótico, 1951, Manuel Bandeira, $D3-F5$, TR, *The Latin American Art Song*, BN

3.725, Ponto de Oxalá, 1970, Afro-Brazilian religious text, —, —, —, BN

3.726, Porque?, 1968, Guilherme de Almeida, —, FBN/DIMAS, —, BN, USP

3.727, Prece, 1987, Gregório de Matos, —, —, —, BN, USP

3.728, Promessa, 1990, Alice Camargo Guarnieri, —, m, —, BN

3.729, Quando entardece, op. 1, no. 1, 1949, Vicente de Carvalho, —, EM, FBN/DIMAS, —, BN, USP

3.730, Quando ouvires o pássaro, —, Cassiano Ricardo, —, FBN/DIMAS, —, BN

3.731, *Quatro miniaturas de Adelmar Tavares*

3.731a, A luz desse olhar tristonho, —, Adelmar Tavares, E4–G♯5, RB, —, BN

3.731b, Não chega bem ao meu ombro, —, Adelmar Tavares, E4–G♯5, RB, —, BN, EMB

3.731c, Ando triste, —, Adelmar Tavares, D4–G5, RB, —, BN

3.731d, Dei-te os sonhos de minh'alma, —, Adelmar Tavares, E4–F♯5, RB, —, BN

3.732, Queixa da moça arrependida, 1968, Ribeiro Couto, F4–G♯5, —, —, BN, USP

3.733, Receita para o amor, 1982, Marina Tricânico, D4–F5, m, —, UNICAMP

3.734, Relance, 1982, —, —, —, —, USP

3.735, Retrato, 1970, Cecília Meireles, D♯4–F5, FBN/DIMAS, —, BN, USP

3.736, Rotação, 1970, Cassiano Ricardo, D♭4–G5, m, —, UNESP

3.737, Sabença, 1970, Folklore, —, FBN/DIMAS, —, BN, USP

3.738, Se eu morresse amanhã, 1991, —, —, —, —, USP

3.739, Seresta antiga, 1989, Anonymous, —, —, —, USP

3.740, Só tu, 1987, —, —, —, —, USP

3.741, Teus olhos, —, —, —, —, , USP

3.742, Trovas de amigo, —, Gustavo Barroso, E4–G♯5, Novas Metas, —, BN, EMB

3.743, Tudo o mais são penas, 1970, Cassiano Ricardo, A♭3–D5, RB, —, USP

3.744, Uma nota, uma só mão, 1967, Carlos Drummond de Andrade, —, m, —, USP

3.745, Vida, que és o dia de hoje, 1988, —, —, —, —, USP

3.746, *Viola de Lereno*

3.746a, Declaração de Lereno, 1991, Domingos Caldas Barbosa, —, —, —, USP

3.746b, Efeitos da saudade, 1991, Domingos Caldas Barbosa, —, —, —, USP

3.746c, Amar não é brinco, 1991, Domingos Caldas Barbosa, —, —, —, USP

3.746d, É bem feito, torne a amar, 1991, Domingos Caldas Barbosa, —, —, —, USP

3.747, Você, 1971, —, —, —, —, USP

Additional titles: A maldição; Ave Maria; Conselhos de amor; Descrente do amor; É bem Feito, torne a amar; Eco e o descorajado; Louvação da embolada tordilha; Ninguém mais; No circo; O herói que matara o reizinho; São Francisco; Saudade; Serenata sintética; Valsa brasileira.

Lemos, Artur Iberê de, 1901–1967

3.748, A canção de Romeu, —, Olavo Bilac, —, BN

3.749, A frauta de bamboo, —, Anonymous, —, BN

3.750, A vida dessas meninas, op. 19, —, Rogério de Miranda, —, BN

3.751, Canção árabe, —, Olavo Bilac, —, BN, UFMG

3.752, Canto à divina mãe bem-amada, —, Artur Iberê de Lemos, —, BN

3.753, Canto de Ofélia, op. 14, —, Luiz Andrade Filho, —, BN

3.754, Confissão, op. 34a, —, Yedda Lemos, —, BN

3.755, Crepúsculo de ouro, —, Felix Pacheco, —, BN

3.756, Desejo, 1925, Antonio Lemos Sobrinho, m, BN

3.757, *Duas elegias místicas*

3.757a, Oração, 1943, Luiz Andrade Filho, —, BN

3.757b, Sentença, 1943, Luiz Andrade Filho, —, BN

3.758, Ismália, op. 46a, 1943, Alphonsus de Guimarães, —, BN, +

3.759, Língua Portuguesa, —, Olavo Bilac, m, BN

3.760, Madrigal, —, Bastos Tigre, —, BN

3.761, *Momentos líricos*

3.761a, Balada do pingo d'água, 1918, Ribeiro Couto, SA, BN, UFMG

3.762, *Momentos líricos (Álbum no. 1)*
3.762a, Fides, —, G. Pascoli, SA, BN, UFMG
3.762b, Sonhando, —, Artur Iberê de Lemos, SA, BN, UFMG

3.763, Música brasileira, —, Olavo Bilac, —, BN

3.764, Noite de encantos, —, Teófilo da Fonseca, —, BN

3.765, O amanhecer, op. 16, —, Rogério de Miranda, —, BN

3.766, O vale, op. 17, —, Olavo Bilac, —, BN

3.767, Poema da saudade, op. 30a, —, Artur Iberê Lemos, —, BN

3.768, Poemas azuis, —, Sylvio Moreaux, —, BN

3.769, Quando cruzamos no caminho, op. 39, —, —, —, BN

3.770, Reflexões, —, Alma Cunha de Miranda, —, BN

3.771, Rosa do meu sonho, —, Ciro Costa, —, BN

3.772, Seio de Deus, —, Artur Iberê de Lemos, —, BN, UFMG

3.773, *Triptico de amor, op. 54*
3.773a, Vem comigo, op. 54, no. 1, —, Cherubina Rojas Ovalle de Carvalho, —, BN
3.773b, Céu azul, op. 54, no. 2, —, Cherubina Rojas Ovalle de Carvalho, —, BN
3.773c, Noite mansa, op. 54, no. 3, —, Cherubina Rojas Ovalle de Carvalho, —, BN

3.774, Valsa-canção, op. 35b, —, —, —, BN
3.775, Vento noturno, op. 12, —, —, —, BN

Additional titles: A nossa esperança; O mistério do amor; Prelúdio ao Samândhi; Serenata, canção de amor; Um sonho.

Lima, João de Souza 1898–1982

3.776, As neblinas, —, Guilherme de Almeida, —, RB, BN

3.777, A viagem, —, N. N., D4–A5, IV, BN

3.778, Dei a você!, —, Ilza das Neves, C4–F5, IV, BN

3.779, Divagação, 1959, Neyde Bonfiglioli Trussardi, C$\sharp$4–G$\sharp$5, IV, BN, UFMG

3.780, Guerra insondável, —, Neyde Bonfiglioli Trussardi, E3–G4, IV, BN

3.781, La belle aux fleurs, —, Jacques d'Avray, E$\sharp$4–G$\sharp$5, IV, BN

3.782, Lágrimas brancas, —, Yara Ferraz, D4–F5, IV, BN

3.783, Mosteiro, 1959, Neyde Bonfiglioli Trussardi, —, IV, BN, UFMG

3.784, No passar dos anos, 1961, Neyde Bonfiglioli Trussardi, —, IV, BN, UFMG

3.785, Numa concha, —, Olavo Bilac, —, CEMB, BN

3.786, Revelação, —, Ilza das Neves, F$\sharp$4–F$\sharp$5, IV, BN

Additional title: Ah! Si je pouvais.

Mahle, Ernst, 1929–

3.787, Ave Maria, 1972, —, —, Soprano, —, UFMG, EMPEM

3.788, Campanário de São José, 1972, Cassiano Ricardo, —, Baritone or Mezzo, —, EMPEM

3.789, Cântico do sol (da Missa de São Francisco), 1976, —, —, Low, —, EMPEM

3.790, Categiró, 1967/72, Cassiano Ricardo, —, Baritone or Mezzo, m, BN, UFMG, EMPEM

3.791, Cidadezinha, 1997, Mário Quintana, —, Soprano, —, EMPEM

3.792, *Cinco canções*
3.792a, A realidade e a imagem, 1961, Manuel Bandeira, —, Med-low, —, EMPEM
3.792b, A onda, 1961, Manuel Bandeira, —, Med, —, EMPEM
3.792c, Cantiga, 1961, Manuel Bandeira, —, Med-low, —, EMPEM

3.792d, Lenda brasileira, 1961, Manuel Bandeira, —, Med-low, —, EMPEM

3.792e, Tema e variações, 1961, Manuel Bandeira, —, Med-low, —, EMPEM

3.793, D. Janaína, 1997, Manuel Bandeira, —, Baritone, —, EMPEM

3.794, E agora José?, 1971, Carlos Drummond de Andrade, G3–E♭5, —, m, ECA/USP, BN, UFMG, EMPEM

3.795, Elegia, 1980, Ribeiro Couto, —, Tenor, —, EMPEM

3.796, Leilão de jardim, 1971, Cecília Meireles, —, Soprano, —, BN, USP, EMPEM

3.797, Meditação (da Missa de São Paulo), 1979, —, —, Soprano, —, EMPEM

3.798, O menino doente, 1961, Manuel Bandeira, —, Mezzo, —, EMPEM

3.799, O pato, —, Vinícius de Moraes, —, Tenor, —, EMPEM

3.800, Oração (de Missa de São Francisco), —, —, —, Low, —, EMPEM

3.801, O relógio, 1984, Vinícius de Moraes, —, Soprano, —, EMPEM

3.802, Os sinos, 1980, Manuel Bandeira, —, Baritone or Mezzo, —, EMPEM

3.803, Para uma cigarra, 1965, Cecília Meireles, F4–B♭5, —, —, USP, EMPEM

3.804, Quadras ao gosto popular, 1981, Fernando Pessoa, —, Baritone, —, EMPEM

3.805, Queixa da moça arrependida, 1972, Ribeiro Couto, —, Soprano, —, USP, EMPEM

3.806, Rosamor, 1966, Guilherme de Almeida, —, Soprano or Tenor, —, BN, USP, EMPEM

3.807, Rotação, —, —, E4–G5, —, —, UFMG, EMPEM

3.808, Salmo 127, 1972, —, —, Alto, —, UFMG, EMPEM

Massarini, Renzo, 1896–1975

3.809, A casinha pequenina, —, —, RB, BN

3.810, A saudade dos provincianos, —, Cleómenes Campos, IV, BN, UFMG

3.811, Azulão, 1942, Manuel Bandeira, FBN/DIMAS 1999, BN, UFMG

3.812, Cidadezinha qualquer, —, Carlos Drummond de Andrade, FBN/DIMAS 1999, —

3.813, Dos coplas para canto y piano, —, —, Forlivesi 1928, BN

3.814, *Due Madrigali*

3.814a, Brunetta, —, —, RM 1937, BN

3.814b, Morrir vorrei, —, —, RM 1937, BN

3.815, Jogo negro, —, —, RB, BN

3.816, Ode a Cassandre, —, Pierre de Ronsard, —, BN

3.817, Prece de chuva, —, —, RB, BN

3.818, Quando te vi pela primeira vez, —, Cleómenes Campos, —, BN, UFMG

3.819, *Quatro canti Veronesi*

3.819a, Anoma cara, —, —, RM 1934, —

3.819b, O Dio del cielo, —, —, RM 1934, —

3.819c, Signor Sergento, —, —, RM 1934, —

3.819d, Ve la conto e ve la canto, —, —, RM 1934, BN

3.820, Sette liriche, —, —, Pizzi 1922, BN

3.821, Tristeza no céu, —, Carlos Drummond de Andrade, FBN/DIMAS 1999, —

3.822, Ueremen, —, —, EM 1944, BN

Maul, Otávio, 1901–1974

3.823, Dúvida, —, Carlos Maul, UFMG

3.824, É assim que eu faço, 1943, Idalina Peçanha Dias, UFMG

3.825, Epigrama, —, Carlos Maul, UFMG

Additional titles: Canção da felicidade; Cena rústica; É bom sonhar; Madrigal a uns olhos negros; *Três poemas tupi-guaranis* (Cairé, mãe adorada; Ah! Se eu fosse um passarinho; Invocação a Rudá).

Mendes, Gilberto, 1922–

3.826, A festa, 1999, —, —, USP

3.827, Amplitude, 1999, —, —, USP

3.828, A tecelã, 1955, —, m, USP

3.829, Canção simples, 1957, —, m, USP

3.830, *Canções*

3.830a, A hora cinzenta, 1951, Raul de Leoni, m, USP

3.830b, Adolescência, 1952, Raul de Leoni, —, USP

3.830c, Confusão, 1952, Raul de Leoni, m, USP

3.830d, Felicidade I, 1951, Raul de Leoni, —, USP

3.830e, Felicidade II, 1951, Raul de Leoni, —, USP

3.830f, Ingratidão, 1952, Raul de Leoni, m, USP

3.831, Desencanto, 1966, Maria José A. Rezende, m, UFMG, USP

3.832, Desencontros, 1995, —, —, USP

3.833, Dizei, senhora, 1966, —, m, USP

3.834, Episódio, 1949, —, m, USP

3.835, Fenomenologia da certeza, 1995, —, —, USP

3.836, Finismundo—A última viagem I, 1993, —, m, USP

3.837, Lagoa, 1957, Carlos Drummond de Andrade, —, UFMG, USP

3.838, Lamento, 1956, —, m, USP

3.839, Luz mediterrânea—no olvido do tempo, 1995, —, —, USP

3.840, Mais uma vez, 1999, —, —, USP

3.841, O apocalipse: A mulher e o dragão, 1967, —, m, USP

3.842, O pai do universo, 1997, Fragment of Bahgavadad Gita, —, USP

3.843, O trovador, 1993, —, m, USP

3.844, Peixes de prata, 1955, —, —, USP

3.845, Poeminha poemeto poemeu poesseu poessua da flor, 1984, —, m, USP

3.846, Sol de Maiakovski, 1995, —, —, USP

3.847, Sonho póstumo, 1955, —, m, USP

3.848, Sugestões do crepúsculo, 1951, —, m, USP

3.849, TVgrama 1, 1995, —, —, USP

Additional title: Ex-ode.

Mignone, Francisco de Paula, 1897–1986

3.850, A boneca de cristal, —, Jacques d'Avray (José de Freitas Valle), —, m, BN

3.851, A bonequinha de seda (Canção das mães pretas), 1936, Narbal Fontes, C_4–F_5, EM 1936, FBN/DIMAS 1999, BN

3.852, Achado, 1949, Goethe, translated into Portuguese by Pedro Mourão, —, FBN/DIMAS 1999, BN

3.853, A Dolorida, 1943, Folklore, D_4–G_5, CEMB 1948, —

3.854, A estrela, 1942, Manuel Bandeira, —, EM 1950, BN

3.855, A folhinha de pimenta, —, —, —, CEM, 1948, UFMG

3.856, Alma adorada, 1918, —, $D\flat_4$–$G\flat_5$, EM 1951, BN

3.857, A sombra, 1932, Judas Isgorogota (Agnelo Rodrigues de Melo), $G\sharp_3$–C_5, EM, BN

3.858, Assombração, —, Sybika (Sylvia Autuori), —, Derosa, BN

3.859, As treis pinta (sic), 1941, Meton de Alencar, $C\sharp_4$–F_5, m, BN

3.860, Ave Maria, —, —, D_4–G_5, EM, —

3.861, A vendedora de violetas, —, Ribeiro Couto, —, RJ 1941, BN

3.862, Ballade frivole, —, Jacques d'Avray (José de Freitas Valle), —, EM, BN

3.863, Bella Granada, —, Alberto Vicente Garcia, —, RB, BN, UFMG

3.864, Canção (1a. versão), —, Murilo Miranda, —, —, BN

3.865, Canção (2a. versão), —, Murilo Miranda, —, —, BN, UFMG

3.866, Canção da liberdade, 1945, Ary Kerner, —, IV, BN, UNESP

3.867, Cânticos de Obaluaiê, 1934, African text (Nagô), $E\flat_4$–$B\flat_5$, EM 1951, IML, BN, UNESP, EMB

3.868, Cantiga de ninar, —, Sybika (Sylvia Autuori), —, EM 1964, BN, UFMG, +

3.869, Cantiga de viúvo, 1938, Carlos Drummond de Andrade, D_4–F_5, CW, BN

3.870, Cantiga do ai, —, Mário de Andrade, $C\sharp_4$–$A\flat_5$, RB, —

3.871, Canto de Negros, 1934, Sybika (Sylvia Autuori), $F\sharp_4$–$F\sharp_5$, Derosa 1934, CEMB, EBMMC 1943, BN, UFMG, UNESP, OMB, +

3.872, Dengues da Mulata Desinteressada, 1938, Ribeiro Couto, —, —, BN

3.873, Desafio, 1942, Manuel Bandeira, —, LMT 1945, BN

3.874, Desfolho a vida, —, Guilherme de Almeida, —, —, BN

3.875, Devoção, 1933, —, —, m, BN

3.876, Dois amô, 1961, Nelson Vaz, C4–G5, EM 1964, BN, UNESP

3.877, Dorme-dorme, 1930, Sibyka (Sylvia Autuori), D4–E5, Derosa, UFMG

3.878, El clavelito en tus lindos cabellos, 1932, —, —, CW, UFMG

3.879, Embolada do Brigadeiro, —, Manuel Bandeira, —, FBN/DIMAS 1999, BN

3.880, Extase, 1928, Jean Lahor (Henri Cazalis), —, —, BN

3.881, Farândola das horas, —, José Maria Goulart de Andrade, —, M, BN

3.882, Festa na Bahia, 1953, Ribeiro Couto, —, EM 1963, FBN/DIMAS 1998, BN

3.883, Flor andaluza, 1930, Alberto Vicente Garcia, D4–G5, RB, BN, UNESP

3.884, Imagem, —, Manuel Bandeira, —, EM, BN

3.885, Improviso no. 1, 1932, Francisco Mignone, D♭4–B♭5, CW 1934, BN, UFMG

3.886, Io non ho che l'amor del mio tesor, 1932, —, —, m, BN

3.887, La signora del fuoco, 1919, Jacques d'Avray (José de Freitas Valle), —, —, BN

3.888, Lagoa, —, Carlos Drummond de Andrade, —, FBN/DIMAS 1999, BN

3.889, Las mujeres son las moscas, 1928, —, —, RM 1928, FBN/DIMAS 1998, BN, UNESP

3.890, *Les Rubaiyat*

3.890a, Ah! Ma bien aimée, —, Omar Khayyan, —, m, BN

3.890b, L'esperance de ce monde, —, Omar Khayyan, —, m, BN

3.890c, Et cette herbe délicieuse, —, Omar Khayyan, —, m, BN

3.890d, Et le desert sera mon paradis, —, Omar Khayyan, —, m, BN

3.890e, Oh! Viens avec le vieux Khayyam, —, Omar Khayyan, —, m, BN

3.890f, Regarde la rose qui fleurit près de nous, —, Omar Khayyan, —, m, BN

3.891, Luar do Sertão, —, —, —, EM, BN

3.892, Madrigal, —, Yde Schloembach Blumenschein ("Colombina"), —, —, BN

3.893, *Mais cinco canções*

3.893a, Canção do vento, 1969, Jeny de Lima, —, RJ 1969, BN

3.893b, Luar do rio, 1969, Jeny de Lima, —, —, BN

3.893c, Na curva do caminho, 1969, Jeny de Lima, —, —, BN

3.893d, Ninho desfeito, 1969, Jeny de Lima, —, —, BN

3.893e, Velhos amigos, 1969, Jeny de Lima, —, —, BN

3.894, *Maracatu do Chico Rei* (Ballet)

3.894a, Quizomba, 1932, —, B♭3–F5, EM 1949, RJ 1980, BN, UFMG

3.894b, Maracatú do Chico Rei Uandala-iê, 1932, —, C4–G5, EM 1950, BN

3.895, Marinero, porque no has venido?, —, —, —, m, BN

3.896, Mariz, —, —, —, —, BN

3.897, Ma scovario non potrò, —, —, —, m, BN

3.898, Morena, morena (Harmonization), 1936, Catulo da Paixão Cearense, D♭4–G♭5, IML, CEMB, 1952, BN, UFMG

3.899, Noche clara y estrellada, —, —, —, EM, BN

3.900, No meio do caminho, 1938, Carlos Drummond de Andrade, E4–F5, CW, BN, EMB

3.901, Nossa Senhora da Neve, 1953, Osório Dutra, —, FBN/DIMAS 1999, BN

3.902, Nostalgia, —, Osório Dutra, —, m, BN

3.903, O anjo da guarda, —, Manuel Bandeira, —, —, BN

3.904, O doce nome de você, 1941, João Guimarães, —, EM 1941, BN, +

3.905, O que fizeram do Natal, —, Carlos Drummond de Andrade, —, CW, BN

3.906, Outro improviso, 1943, Manuel Bandeira, $E\flat 4$–$A\flat 5$, CW 1957, BN

3.907, Papai Noel, —, —, —, CEMB 1948, BN

3.908, Pardonnez-moi, —, Béatriz Reynal, —, IV, BN

3.909, Passarinho está cantando, —, Portuguese folklore, $F4$–$G5$, IML, BN, EMB

3.910, *Poema das cinco canções*

3.910a, Canção da ruazinha desconhecida, 1962, Mário Quintana, —, FBN/DIMAS 1999, BN, OMB

3.910b, Canção do baú, 1962, Mário Quintana, —, FBN/DIMAS 1999, BN, OMB

3.910c, Canção do vento e da chuva, 1962, Mário Quintana, —, FBN/DIMAS 1999, BN, OMB

3.910d, Canção para uma valsa lenta, 1962, Mário Quintana, —, FBN/DIMAS 1999, BN, OMB

3.910e, Canção da garoa, 1962, Mário Quintana, —, FBN/DIMAS 1999, BN, OMB

3.911, Poema para Manuel Bandeira, 1964, Murillo Miranda, —, EM 1964, BN

3.912, ¿Por qué lloras, morenita?, —, —, —, CW 1933, BN

3.913, Porquoi mentir, —, Béatrix Reynal, —, IV, BN

3.914, Pregão, p1949, —, —, —, BN

3.915, Quadras, —, Onestaldo de Pennafort Caldas, —, EM 1951, Derosa, BN, UFMG

3.916, Quadrilha, 1938, Carlos Drummond de Andrade, $E4$–$E5$ (original)/$F4$–$G5$ (High), CW, FBN/DIMAS 1999, BN, UFMG

3.917, Quando na roça anoitece, 1930, Ricardo Alves Guimarães, —, —, BN

3.918, Quando uma flor desabrocha (Toada), 1937, Popular text from Portugal, $F4$–$G5$, CEMB, BN, UNESP, UFMG, +

3.919, *Quatro líricas*

3.919a, Berimbau, 1942, Manuel Bandeira, —, LMT 1945, BN

3.919b, Cantiga, 1938, Manuel Bandeira, $D4$–$F5$, RB, BN

3.919c, Dentro da noite, 1938, Manuel Bandeira, $D4$–$F5$, RB, BN

3.919d, Dona Janaína, 1938, Manuel Bandeira, $E4$–$G5$, RB, BN, UFMG

3.920, *Quatro líricas*

3.920a, O menino doente, 1938, Manuel Bandeira, $E\natural 4$–$E\flat 5$, RB, BN, EMB

3.920b, Pousa a mão na minha testa, 1943, Manuel Bandeira, —, LMT 1945, BN

3.920c, Solau do desamado, 1943, Manuel Bandeira, $E4$–$F5$, LMT 1945, BN

3.921, *Quatro líricas brasileiras*

3.921a, Dissesste..., 1952, Gabriel de Lucena, $B3$–$E5$, EM 1963, —

3.921b, Nós, 1952, Gabriel de Lucena, $C3$–$F5$, EM 1963, —

3.921c, Tu, 1952, Gabriel de Lucena, $A3$–$F5$, EM 1963, —

3.921d, Você, 1952, Gabriel de Lucena, $B3$–$F5$, EM 1963, —

3.922, Ricordi?, —, Gerolamo Bottoni, —, —, BN

3.923, Rudá! Rudá!, —, Mário de Andrade, —, FBN/DIMAS, 1999, BN

3.924, Se tu soubesses, 1966, —, —, m, BN

3.925, *Seis líricas para canto e piano*

3.925a, Amor, 1932, Yde Schloenbach Blumenschein ("Colombina"), $E\flat 4$–$G\sharp 5$, L. G. Miranda, BN

3.925b, Fim de romance, 1932, Yde Schloenbach Blumenschein ("Colombina"), $C\sharp 4$–$G5$, L. G. Miranda, BN

3.925c, Júri do coração, 1932, Yde Schloenbach Blumenschein ("Colombina"), $E4$–$F\sharp 5$, L. G. Miranda, BN

3.925d, Musa que passa, 1932, Yde Schloenbach Blumenschein ("Colombina"), $E4$–$G5$, L. G. Miranda, BN

3.925e, Teu nome, 1932, Yde Schloenbach Blumenschein ("Colombina"), E4–G5, EM 1964, L. G. Miranda, BN, UFMG

3.926, Seresta, 1964, Murillo Miranda, D♯4–G5, EM 1964, UFMG

3.927, *Sete líricas*
3.927a, Asas! Oh, loucura dos vôos, —, Oneyda Alvarenga, —, m, BN
3.927b, Doçura de manhãzinha fresca, —, Oneyda Alvarenga, —, m, BN
3.927c, Eu queria cair na tua vida, —, Oneyda Alvarenga, —, m, BN
3.927d, Eu te esperei na hora silenciosa, —, Oneyda Alvarenga, —, m, BN
3.927e, Nunca sinto inveja, —, Oneyda Alvarenga, —, m, BN
3.927f, Queimada pelo sol desvairada, —, Oneyda Alvarenga, —, m, BN
3.927g, Vento que corropia, —, Oneyda Alvarenga, —, m, BN

3.928, Si vous saviez, 1944, Béatrix Reynal, E♭4–B♭5, EM 1949, BN
3.929, Sonho póstumo, 1917, Vicente de Carvalho, —, —, BN

3.930, *Três cantos populares espanhóis*
3.930a, A tu puerta están cantando, 1928, Spanish popular text, F♯4–G5, EM 1941, BN
3.930b, Salta, niña, en mi barquilla, 1928, —, D4–A♭5, EM 1941, BN
3.930c, Si quieres que yo te quiera, 1928, —, F4–B♭5, EM 1941, BN

3.931, *Triptico da saudade*
3.931a, Quando a saudade voltar, —, F. Célio Monteiro, —, FBN/DIMAS 1999, BN
3.931b, Quando eu não conhecia a saudade, —, F. Célio Monteiro, —, —, BN
3.931c, Se eu sei o que é saudade, —, F. Célio Monteiro, —, FBN/DIMAS 1999, BN

3.932, Trovas, —, Onestaldo de Pennafort, —, EM 1951, Derosa, BN, UFMG
3.933, Trovas de amor, —, Popular text, —, CEMB 1952, BN
3.934, Tuas mãos, —, —, —, —, BN

3.935, Uma cabocla, dois caboclos e um violão, —, Nelson Abreu, —, —, BN
3.936, Valse presque noble et sentimentale, —, —, —, —, BN
3.937, Vento balançava aquela rosa tão de leve, 1932, —, —, EM, BN
3.938, Vento da manhã, —, Álvaro Madaia, —, m, BN
3.939, Violão do capadócio, —, Béatrix Reynal, —, IV, BN
3.940, Violão do capadócio, —, Ribeiro Couto, —, FBN/DIMAS 1999, BN

Additional titles: A coieita; A menina boba; Bella princesa del norte; Canção do tropeiro; Canto do maior amor; En un Carmen granadino; Modinha; Por questa tornerà; Sei felice mio tesor l'ardor che mi strugge.

Miranda, Ronaldo, 1948

3.941, Cantares, 1969–1984, Walter Mariani, —, —, BN, UFMG, UEMG
3.942, Retrato, 1969, Cecília Meireles, C♯4–F♯5, —, BN, UFMG, USP
3.943, Segredo, 1973, Carlos Drummond de Andrade, —, USP/SDP, BN, UFMG
3.944, Soneto da separação, 1969, Vinícius de Moraes, B♭3–E♭5, —, BN, UFMG, USP

3.945, *Três canções simples*
3.945a, Cotidiano, 1980–1984, Orlando Codá, —, —, BN
3.945b, Noite e dia, 1980–1984, Orlando Codá, —, —, BN
3.945c, Visões, 1980–1984, Orlando Codá, —, —, BN

Additional title: Desenho leve.

Nepomuceno, Alberto, 1864–1920

3.946, A Grinalda, op. 31, no. 1, 1903, Carlhos Magalhães Azevedo, —, USP 2004, —, USP
3.947, Aime-moi, 1911, Emilie Arnal, D♯4–F♯5, USP 2004, —, BN, UFMG, USP
3.948, A jangada, 1920, Juvenal Galeno, —, USP 2004, —, BN, UFMG, USP, +

3.949, Amo-te muito, op. 12, no. 2, 1894, João de Deus Ramos, C_4–G_5, USP 2004, —, BN, UFMG, USP

3.950, Anoitece, op. 34, no. 2, 1904, Adelina A. Lopes Vieira, $B_{\sharp}3$–$F_{\sharp}5$, AN, VM, SA, USP 2004, —, BN, UFMG, USP

3.951, Ao amanhecer, op. 34, no. 1, 1904, Ana Nogueira Batista, D_4–G_5, AN, VM, SA, USP 2004, —, BN, UFMG, USP, +

3.952, Au jardin des rêves, 1895, Henri Piazza, C_4–F_5, VM, SA, USP 2004, —, BN, UFMG, USP

3.953, Ave Maria, 1911, Latin text, D_4–E_5, AN, USP 2004, —, BN, UFMG, USP

3.954, Canção, op. 30, no. 2, 1903, Fontoura Xavier, D_4–G_5, AN, SA, USP 2004, —, BN, UFMG, USP

3.955, Canção da ausência, 1915, Hermes Fontes, F_4–G_5, USP 2004, TR 2005, *The Latin American Art Song*, BN, UFMG, USP

3.956, Canção de amor (Liebeslied), 1902, Condessa Ana Antonia Amadei, $C_{\sharp}4$–$F_{\sharp}5$, VM, SA, AN, FBN/DIMAS 1998, USP 2004, —, BN, UFMG, USP

3.957, Canção do rio, 1917, Domingos Magarinos, D_4–$E_{\flat}5$, USP 2004, —, BN, UFMG, USP

3.958, Candura, 1908, Rabindranath Tagore, E_4–$F_{\sharp}5$, B/Cia, USP 2004, —, BN, UFMG, USP

3.959, Cantigas (A Guitarra), —, Branca de Gonta Colaço, D_4–E_5, B/Cia, EM, USP 2004, —, BN, UFMG, USP, +

3.960, Cantilena, 1902, Coelho Netto, C_4–$E_{\flat}5$, B/Cia, EM, USP 2004, —, BN, UFMG, USP

3.961, Canto nupcial, 1907, Biblical text (Ruth 1:16–17), $D_{\sharp}4$–F_5, VM, SA, USP 2004, —, BN, UFMG, USP

3.962, Cantos da sulamita, 1897, Múcio Teixeira, D_4–F_5, USP 2004, —, BN, UFMG, USP

3.963, Conselho, 1918, Visconde de Pedra Branca, C_4–F_5, B/Cia, —, BN, UFMG

3.964, Coração indeciso, op. 30, no. 1, 1903, Frota Pessoa, $D_{\sharp}4$–$F_{\sharp}5$, VM 1916, AN 1926, FBN/DIMAS 1998, USP 2004, —, BN, UFMG, USP, +

3.965, Coração triste, op. 18, no. 1, 1899, Machado de Assis, D_4–G_5, AN, VM, SA, USP 2004, TR 2005, *The Latin American Art Song*, BN, UFMG, USP, +

3.966, Der wunde Ritter, op. 20, no. 1, 1817–1821, Heinrich Heine, D_4–A_5, VM, SA, USP 2004, —, BN, UFMG, USP

3.967, Désirs d'hiver, 1894, Maurice Maeterlinck, $D_{\sharp}4$–$B_{\sharp}5$, VM, SA, USP 2004, —, BN, UFMG, USP, +

3.968, Despedida, op. 31, no. 2, 1903, Carlos Magalhães de Azeredo, $E_{\flat}4$–G_5, USP 2004, —, BN, UFMG, USP

3.969, Desterro, 1894, Olavo Bilac, B_3–E_5, FBN/DIMAS 1998, USP 2004, —, BN, UFMG, USP

3.970, Dolor supremus, op. 21, no. 2, 1901, Osório Duque Estrada, D_4–F_5, AN, FBN/DIMAS, USP 2004, —, BN, UFMG, USP

3.971, Dor sem consolo, op. 32, no. 2, 1904, Conde Affonso Celso, C_4–$E_{\flat}5$, m (autograph) at BN, SA, VM, USP 2004, —, BN, UFMG, USP

3.972, Drömd lycka, 1893, —, C_4–C_5, m (autograph) at BN, USP 2004, —, BN, UFMG, USP

3.973, Einklang, 1894, Nikolaus Lenau, $B_{\flat}3$–$C_{\flat}5$, FUNARJ 2000, USP 2004, —, BN, UFMG, USP

3.974, Epitalâmio, 1897, Antônio Salles, $C_{\sharp}3$–$F_{\sharp}4$, USP 2004, —, BN, UFMG, USP

3.975, Filomela (Philomela), op. 18, no. 2, p1899, Raimundo Correia, D_4–B_5, VM, SA, AN, FBN/DIMAS 1998, USP 2004, —, BN, UFMG, USP

3.976, Flores, 1908, Rabindranath Tagore, Portuguese version by Plácido Barbosa, E_4–A_5, B/Cia, FBN/DIMAS 1998, USP 2004, —, BN, USP

3.977, Gedicht, 1894, Nikolaus Lenau, —, m, —, BN

3.978, Herbst, 1894, Nikolaus Lenau, —, USP 2004, —, UFMG, USP

3.979, Hidrófana, 1901, Luís Guimarães

Filho, —, USP 2004, —, BN, UFMG, USP

3.980, Il flotte dans l'air (La chanson du silence), 1895, Henri Piazza, F4–F♭5, VM, SA, USP 2004, —, BN, UFMG, USP

3.981, Ingemisco, —, Sacred text; Latin, E4–A♭5, USP 2004, —, BN, UFMG, USP

3.982, Le miracle de la sémence, 1916–17, Jacques d'Avray (José de Freitas Valle), B3–E♭5, SA, FBN/DIMAS 1998, USP 2004, —, BN, UFMG, USP

3.983, Le miroir d'or, 1895, Henri Piazza, E4–G♯5, USP 2004, —, BN, UFMG, USP

3.984, Les yeux élus, 1895, Henri Piazza, D4–F5, VM, USP 2004, —, BN, USP, +

3.985, Luz e névoa, 1915, Hermes Fontes, E♭4–F5, B/Cia, USP 2004, —, UFMG, USP

3.986, Madrigal, op. 17, no. 2, 1894, Luís Guimarães Filho, B♭3–F5, Moreira de Sá, VM, SA, USP 2004, —, UFMG, USP, +

3.987, Mater dolorosa, 1894, Gonçalves Crespo, D♯4–D5, B/Cia, EM, USP 2004, —, BN, UFMG, USP

3.988, Medroso de amor (Moreninha), op. 17, no. 1, 1894, Juvenal Galeno, D4–F5, VM, AN, USP 2004, —, BN, UFMG, USP, +

3.989, Morta (Trovas do Norte), 1896, Antônio Salles, D4–D5, FBN/DIMAS 1998, USP 2004, —, BN, UFMG, USP

3.990, Nossa velhice, 1909, Emilio de Menezes, D4–A5, B/Cia, USP 2004, —, BN, UFMG, USP

3.991, Numa concha, 1913, Olavo Bilac, F♭4–G♭5, VM, SA, USP 2004, —, BN, UFMG, USP

3.992, Ocaso, 1911, Thomas Lopes, C4–F5, VM, USP 2004, —, BN, UFMG, USP

3.993, Olha-me!, 1913, Olavo Bilac, D4–G♭5, SA, VM, USP 2004, —, BN, UFMG, USP

3.994, Oração ao diabo, op. 20, no. 2, 1899, Orlando Teixeira, F3–C4, SA, AN, FBN/DIMAS 1998, USP 2004, —, BN, UFMG, USP, +

3.995, Ora dize-me a verdade, op. 12, no. 1, 1894, João de Deus, B3–E♭5, VM, SA, USP 2004, —, BN, UFMG, USP

3.996, Oraison, op. 11 no. 2, 1894, Maurice Maeterlinck, B3–F5, VM, SA, USP 2004, —, BN, UFMG, USP

3.997, O salutaris hostia, —, Latin text, D4–E5, USP 2004, —, BN, UFMG, USP

3.998, O sono, 1901, Antonio Gonçalves Dias, D4–B5, USP 2004, —, BN, UFMG, +

3.999, O wag es nicht, 1894, Nikolaus Lenau, C♯4–F♯5, USP 2004, —, BN, UFMG, USP

3.1000, Perché, 1888, Aleardo Aleardi, E♭3–F4, USP 2004, —, USP

3.1001, Razão e amor, 1911, —, C4–F5, CW, USP 2004, —, BN, UFMG, USP

3.1002, Sempre!, op. 32, no. 1, 1904, Conde Affonso Celso, C♯4–F♯5, USP 2004, —, BN, UFMG, USP

3.1003, Sehnsucht nach vergessen, 1894, Nikolaus Lenau, E4–G♭5, USP 2004, —, USP

3.1004, Serenata di un moro, 1889, Heinrich Heine, —, m, —, BN, UFMG, USP

3.1005, Soneto, op. 21 no. 3, 1901, Henrique Coelho Netto, E4–G5, AN, VM, SA, USP 2004, —, BN, UFMG, USP, +

3.1006, Sonhei, op. 19, no. 1, 1899, Heinrich Heine, B3–E5, USP 2004, —, BN, UFMG, USP

3.1007, Trovas, 1901, Osório Duque Estrada, F♭4–B♯5, AN, VM, SA, USP 2004, —, BN, UFMG, USP

3.1008, Trovas, op. 29, no. 2, 1901, Carlos Magalhães de Azeredo, E♭4–F5, AN, VM, SA, USP, 2004, —, BN, UFMG

3.1009, Tu és o sol, op. 14, no. 2, 1894, Juvenal Galeno, C4–F5, B/Cia, USP 2004, —, BN, UFMG, USP, +

3.1010, Turqueza, op. 26, no. 1, 1901, Luís Guimarães Filho, D♭4–G♭5, USP 2004, FUNARJ 2000, —, UFMG, USP

3.1011, Wiege sie sanft, o Schlaf, 1894, Nikolaus Lenau, D4–F5, USP 2004, —, USP

3.1012, Xácara, op. 20, no. 1, —, Rolando Teixeira, C4–G5, AN, VM, USP 2004, —, BN, UFMG, +

Additional titles: Blomma; Cantiga triste;

Cativeiro; Chanson de Gelisette; Rispondi; Saudade.

Nobre, Marlos (Marlos Nobre de Almeida), 1939-

3.1013, Amazônia III, op. 91, 2002, Marlos Nobre, —, Baritone, Text based on names of birds from the Amazon, EMNB 2005, —

3.1014, *Beiramar, op. 21*
3.1014a, Estrela do Mar, 1966, Marlos Nobre, —, Bass/Baritone, Based on folklore of Bahia, EMNB 2005, BN, UFMG
3.1014b, Iemanjá oto, 1966, Marlos Nobre, —, Bass/Baritone, Based on folklore of Bahia, EMNB 2005, BN, UFMG
3.1014c, Ogum de lê, 1966, Marlos Nobre, —, Bass/Baritone, Based on folklore of Bahia, EMNB 2005, BN, UFMG

3.1015, Dengues da Mulata Desinteressada, 1966, Ribeiro Couto, D4–G5, Soprano, —, IV, BN, USP, UFMG
3.1016, Dia da Graça, op. 32a, 1968, Glauber Rocha, —, Soprano, —, EMNB 2005, —

3.1017, *Kleine Gedichte, op. 90*
3.1017a, Du hast Diamanten und Perlen, 2000, Heinrich Heine, —, Baritone, —, EMNB 2005, —
3.1017b, Hat sie sich denn nie geäussert, 2000, Heinrich Heine, —, Baritone, —, EMNB 2005, —
3.1017c, In mein gar zu dunkles Leben, 2000, Heinrich Heine, —, Baritone, —, EMNB 2005, —
3.1017d, Sie haben heut' abend Gesellschaft, —, Heinrich Heine, —, Baritone, —, EMNB 2005, —
3.1017e, Sie liebten sich beide, 2000, Heinrich Heine, —, Baritone, —, EMNB 2005, —
3.1017f, Teurer Freund!, 2000, Heinrich Heine, —, Baritone, —, EMNB 2005, —
3.1017g, Werdet nur nicht ungeduldig, 2000, Heinrich Heine, —, Baritone, —, EMNB 2005, —

3.1018, *Llanto por Ignácio Sanchez Mejías, 93a*
3.1018a, Alma ausente, 2002, Federico García Lorca, —, Baritone, —, EMNB 2005, —
3.1018b, Cuerpo presente, 2002, Federico García Lorca, —, Baritone, —, EMNB 2005, —
3.1018c, La cogida y la muerte, 2002, Federico García Lorca, —, Baritone, —, EMNB 2005, —
3.1018d, La sangre derramada, 2002, Federico García Lorca, —, Baritone, —, EMNB 2005, —

3.1019, Modinha, op. 23a, 1966, Marcos Konder Reis, —, Soprano, —, EMNB 2005, —
3.1020, Monólogo do tempo, op. 56c, 1982, Simón Bolívar (Mi delirio del Chimborazo), —, Baritone, —, EMNB 2005, —
3.1021, O canto multiplicado, op. 38a, 1972/2003, Carlos Drummond de Andrade, —, Soprano, —, EMNB 2005, +
3.1022, O canto multiplicado, op. 38b, 1972/2002, Carlos Drummond de Andrade, —, Baritone, —, EMNB 2005, +
3.1023, Poema V (Raio de luz) op. 94, no. 5, 2002, Marlos Nobre, —, Soprano, —, EMNB 2005, —
3.1024, Poema XIII (Raio de luz) op. 94, no. 13, 2002, Marlos Nobre, —, Baritone, —, EMNB 2005, —

3.1025, *Poemas da negra, op. 10*
3.1025a, Lembrança boa, op. 10, no. 3, 1962, Mário de Andrade, —, Soprano, —, EMNB 2005, —
3.1025b, Quando, 1962, Mário de Andrade, —, Soprano, —, EMNB 2005, —
3.1025c, Você é tão suave, 1962, Mário de Andrade, —, Soprano, —, EMNB 2005, —

3.1026, *Praianas, op. 18*
3.1026a, Canoeiro, op. 18, no. 1, 1965, Marlos Nobre, —, Soprano, —, EMNB 2005, —

3.1026b, O mar, op. 18, no. 2, 1965, Marlos Nobre, —, Soprano, —, EMNB 2005, —

3.1026c, Janaína, op. 18, no. 3, 1965, Marlos Nobre, —, Soprano, —, EMNB 2005, —

3.1027, *Três canções, op. 9*

3.1027a, Maracatu, op. 9, no. 1, 1962, Ascenço Ferreira, —, Soprano, —, EMNB 2005, BN

3.1027b, Teu nome, op. 9, no. 2, —, Manuel Bandeira, —, Soprano, —, EMNB 2005, BN

3.1027c, Boca de forno, op. 9, no. 3, 1962, Manuel Bandeira, —, Soprano, —, EMNB 2005, BN

3.1028, *Três trovas, op. 6*

3.1028a, Trova no. 1 (Lundu), 1961, Aldemar Tavares, F4–F5, Soprano, —, TMV 1973, EMNB 2005, —

3.1028b, Trova no. 2 (Modinha), 1961, Aldemar Tavares, F4–F5, Soprano, —, TMV 1973, EMNB 2005, —

3.1028c, Trova no. 3 (Final), 1961, Aldemar Tavares, F4–F5, Soprano, —, TMV 1973, EMNB 2005, —

Oliveira, Babi de (Idalba Leite de Oliveira), 1908–1993

3.1029, Águas paradas, 1964, Mario Faccini, —, —, BN

3.1030, A sereia do mar, —, Oliveira Ribeiro Neto, —, AN, UFMG

3.1031, Balada da confiante espera, —, Átila Guterres Casses, —, —, BN

3.1032, Caboclo do rio (Toada), —, Babi de Oliveira, B♭3–C5, IV 1958, UFMG

3.1033, Canção do amor distante, —, Alma Cunha de Miranda, —, IV, UFMG

3.1034, Cantares de Pernambuco, —, Ricardina Ione, E♭4–E♭5, EM 1964, UFMG

3.1035, Deixa estar, —, Babi de Oliveira, C♯4–E♭5, AN 1959, Guanabara 1980, UFMG

3.1036, Diálogo elegante, —, Oliveira Ribeiro Neto, —, —, BN

3.1037, Estrela azul, —, Silvio Moreaux, —, LMT 1949, UFMG

3.1038, É vontade de te ver, —, Babi de Oliveira, D4–F5, IV, BDB

3.1039, Gaivota, —, Babi de Oliveira, —, LMT 1944, BN, UFMG

3.1040, Há sempre uma palavra, —, Leonor Posada, —, —, BN, UFMG

3.1041, Missa do galo, —, Deodato Meyer, C4–C5, —, UFMG

3.1042, Mormaço na varanda, —, Oliveira Ribeiro Neto, —, —, BN

3.1043, O jasmineiro, —, Babi de Oliveira, —, —, BN

3.1044, Os teus olhos, os meus olhos, —, —, —, —, UFMG

3.1045, Polquinha, 1969, Babi de Oliveira, C4–E♭5, Marajoara, —

3.1046, Praias de minha terra, 1972, Babi de Oliveira, D4–D5, IV, UFMG

3.1047, Presságios, —, Menotti del Picchia, —, —, BN

3.1048, Quando te vinha buscar, —, Deodato Mayar (Mário Faccini), —, —, BN

3.1049, Recado, —, Babi de Oliveira, —, —, BN

3.1050, Recomendação, —, Índia Rego, F4–G♭5, IV, UFMG

3.1051, Se te esqueceres de mim, —, Armando Fernandes, —, —, BN

3.1052, Singela canção de Maria, —, Mário Faccini, Tenor, EM 1954, UFMG

3.1053, Teus olhos, —, Sylvio Moreaux, —, —, BN

3.1054, Teus olhos são como a noite, —, Mário Faccini, —, —, BN

3.1055, Toada da saudade, —, Alma Cunha de Miranda, —, —, BN

3.1056, Tormenta, —, Babi de Oliveira, —, —, BN

3.1057, Tra-la-la-la, —, Ricardina Ione, —, Seresta 1973, UFMG

3.1058, Triolets, —, Átila Guterres Casses, —, —, BN

3.1059, Vamo saravá (ponto das baianas, —, Popular theme, —, EM 1952, UFMG

3.1060, Vela branca, —, Babi de Oliveira, —, —, BN

3.1061, Xangô, meu Orixá, —, —, F4–F5, Guanabara, UFMG

Additional titles: A moda da Rita; Amor de outono; Anda a roda; A palavra que eu não disse; Atavismo; Belém do Pará; Bom dia, felicidade; Cahimbo do sertão; Canção de ninar; Canção para teus olhos; Canção praiana; Chá de coitado; Contradições; Coqueiro vai balançar; Festa de Ogum; Invernia; Janaína; La vie; Madrigal; Mapinguari; Maria Macambira; Muiraquitã; Nana nani; Não esqueci; O que fui, o que serei?; Peixinho do mar; Poema para tuas mãos; Prece; Quem por Pitanga passou; Relógio parado; Rio enamorado; Rosa dos ventos; Rosa morena; Saia; Seresta da ilusão; Seresta da saudade; Sonhar é bom; Sonho; Ternura; Teu nome; Trovas; Tua música, doce lembrança; Tu, dulce poema; Vagamente; Yo te amo tanto.

Oswald, Henrique José Pedro Maria Carlos Luis, 1852–1931

3.1062, Ad una rondinella, 1874, —, m, USP
3.1063, Aos sinos, 1916, Olavo Bilac, —, BN, UFRJ, USP
3.1064, Ave!, 1902, S. Monte, —, USP
3.1065, Ave Maria, 1872, —, —, USP
3.1066, Berceuse, 1879, L. Gasperini, —, USP
3.1067, Canção, 1903, —, m, USP
3.1068, Cantiga boêmia, —, Olegário Mariano, —, USP
3.1069, Canto da coroação, 1919, —, m, USP
3.1070, Habanera, 1898, —, —, USP
3.1071, Il neo, —, —, —, UFRJ
3.1072, Mendigo!, —, —, m, USP
3.1073, Minha Estrela, —, Esther Ferreira Viana, —, USP, UFRJ
3.1074, Pater noster, —, —, —, UFRJ
3.1075, Romanza, 1903, L. Gasperini, —, USP

Additional title: A mia madre.

Otaviano, João (João Otaviano Gonçalves), 1892–1962

3.1076, Anoitecer, Popular text, VM, IV, BN
3.1077, Canção, Gonçalves Crespo, IV, —
3.1078, Lua branca (Harmonização), Francisca Gonzaga, IV, —
3.1079, Não, Honório de Carvalho, IV, BN
3.1080, Nhapopé, —, IV, —
3.1081, Os rios, Olavo Bilac, —, BN
3.1082, Rio abaixo, Olavo Bilac, —, BN
3.1083, Uma barquinha branca, Adelmar Tavares, IV, —

Additional titles: A roda do engenho; Meu coração; O meu anjo; Paixão; Por que; Soneto.

Ovalle, Jaime Rojas de Aragón y, 1894–1955

3.1084, Azulão, Manuel Bandeira, $D\flat4$–$E\flat5$, IV, AN, FBN/DIMAS, PI, —
3.1085, Berimbau, op. 4, Manuel Bandeira, —, SA, AN, BN
3.1086, Modinha, op. 5, Manuel Bandeira, —, IV, SA, BN, +
3.1087, Poema, op. 33, Onestaldo de Pennafort, —, SA, BN

3.1088, *Três cantos nativos, op. 3*
3.1088a, Unianguripê, op. 3, no. 1, —, —, —, BN, UFMG
3.1088b, Macumbebê, op. 3, no. 2, —, —, —, BN, UFMG
3.1088c, Papae Curumiassú, op. 3, no. 3, —, —, m, BN

3.1089, *Três pontos de santo*
3.1089a, Chariô, op. 10 no. 1, Afro-Brazilian religious text, —, IV, SA, BN, UFMG
3.1089b, Aruanda, op. 10 no. 2, Afro-Brazilian religious text, $B3$–$A5$, IV, SA, BN, UFMG
3.1089c, Estrela do mar, op. 10 no. 3, Afro-Brazilian religious text, —, IV, SA, BN, UFMG

3.1090, Zé Raymundo, op. 1, Olegário Mariano, —, FBN/DIMAS, BN

Additional titles: Festival; Invocação; Oração e dança.

Pádua, Newton de Menezes, 1894–1966

3.1091, Canção sentimental, Cleómenes Campos, UFMG

3.1092, O menino doente, Manuel Bandeira, UFMG

3.1093, Sinos, Manuel Bandeira, UFMG

Additional titles: Acalanto; A causa; Canção triste; Ciclo da mãe preta; Felicidade; Hino ao criador; Tanta falta eu sinto de você; Tia Ana.

Picchi, Acchile, 1951–

3.1094, Ai que riso me dá, —, Popular text collected by César das Neves, —, —, Hamonization, —, UFMG

3.1095, Allegro, op. 84, —, Vinicius de Morais, —, —, —, —, UFMG

3.1096, Amo-te, op. 62, —, Vicente de Carvalho, —, —, —, —, UFMG

3.1097, Azulão, op. 56, —, Manuel Bandeira, —, —, —, —, UFMG

3.1098, Berceuse, op. 84, 1987, Helena Ferraz, —, —, —, m, UFMG

3.1099, *Buquê de trovas, op. 148*

3.1099a, As almas, op. 148, no. 1, 2003, Belmiro Braga, $C\sharp 4$–$G\sharp 5$, —, —, —, UFMG

3.1099b, Custo, op. 148, no. 2, —, José Fonseca Duarte, $C4$–$E\flat 5$, —, —, —, UFMG

3.1099c, Sonho, op. 148, no. 3, —, Popular text, $D4$–$E5$, —, —, —, UFMG

3.1099d, Duas coisas, op. 148, no. 4, —, Albertina Carvalho, $D4$–$D5$, —, —, —, UFMG

3.1099e, Tarde triste, op. 148, no. 5, —, Demóstenes Cristino, $D\flat 4$–$E\flat 5$, —, —, —, UFMG

3.1099f, Encontrei-te, op. 148, no. 6, —, Isabelita Pinto Ferreira, $D\sharp 4$–$E\sharp 5$, —, —, —, UFMG

3.1099g, Momento, op. 148, no. 7, —, Cleómenes Campos, $F4$–$F5$, —, —, —, UFMG

3.1099h, Perfume triste, op. 148, no. 8, —, Menotti del Picchia, $E4$–$E5$, —, —, —, UFMG

3.1099i, Retrato, op. 148, no. 9, —, Albertina de Castro Borges, $D4$–$C\sharp 5$, —, —, —, UFMG

3.1099j, Perdidos, op. 148, no. 10, —, Popular text, $C4$–$E5$, —, —, —, UFMG

3.1099k, Ortografia, op. 148, no. 11, —, Gonçalves Crespo, $D\sharp 4$–$G5$, —, —, —, UFMG

3.1099l, O canto e o choro, op. 148, no. 12, —, Lilinha Fernandes, $D4$–$G5$, —, —, —, UFMG

3.1099m, Ameaça, op. 148, no. 13, 2003, Djalma Andrade, $E4$–$F5$, —, —, —, UFMG

3.1099n, Vontade, op. 148, no. 14, —, Augusto Linhares, $D4$–$D5$, —, —, —, UFMG

3.1099o, Furinhos, op. 148, no. 15, —, Luiz Eduardo, $B3$–$F5$, —, —, —, UFMG

3.1099p, Barco à margem, op. 148, no. 16, 2003, Yde Schloenbach Blumenschein ("Colombina"), $D4$–$F5$, —, —, —, UFMG

3.1099q, Sevilhana, op. 148, no. 17, —, Alberto Ferreira, $E4$–$E5$, —, —, —, UFMG

3.1099r, Cabeça, op. 148, no. 18, 2003, Laurindo Rabelo, $C4$–$F5$, —, —, —, UFMG

3.1099s, Adoração, op. 148, no. 19, 2003, Popular text, $D4$–$F5$, —, —, —, UFMG

3.1099t, Santo Antonio, op. 148, no. 20, —, Popular text, $D\sharp 4$–$D\sharp 5$, —, —, —, UFMG

3.1099u, Sofrer, op. 148, no. 21, —, Luiz Homero de Almeida, $D4$–$D5$, —, —, —, UFMG

3.1099v, Dia e noite, op. 148, no. 22, —, Vicente de Carvalho, $B\flat 3$–$D5$, —, —, —, UFMG

3.1099w, Lembrar/ esquecer, op. 148, no. 23, —, Fileman L. Amador, $F4$–$F5$, —, —, —, UFMG

3.1099x, Relógio, op. 148, no. 24, —, Nilo

Aparecido Pinto, C♯4–E♭5, —, —, —, UFMG

3.1099y, Longe de ti, op. 148, no. 25, —, Paulo Bonfim, D4–G♭5, —, —, —, UFMG

3.1099z, Aflição, op. 148, no. 26, 2003, Alcides Carneiro, C4–E♭5, —, —, —, UFMG

3.1099aa, Canção perdida, op. 148, no. 27, —, Paulo Freitas, C4–G♭5, —, —, —, UFMG

3.1099bb, Por piedade, op. 148, no. 28, —, Domingos Caldas Barbosa, E♭4–G♭5, —, —, —, UFMG

3.1099cc, Morena encanto, op. 148, no. 29, —, Ernesto da Silva Guimarães, D4–E♭5, —, —, —, UFMG

3.1099dd, Traço profundo, op. 148, no. 30, —, Djalma Andrade, C4–E5, —, —, —, UFMG

3.1099ee, Buquê saudades de Bastos Tigre (I), op. 148 no. 31, —, Costa e Silva, E♭4–F5, —, —, —, UFMG

3.1099ff, Saudades de Bastos Tigre (II), op. 148, no. 32, —, Bastos Tigre, E♭4–F5, —, —, —, UFMG

3.1099gg, Fala o poeta, op. 148, no. 33, —, Lindauro Gomes, D4–B4, —, —, —, UFMG

3.1100, Canção das morenas, —, Popular text, —, —, —, —, UFMG

3.1101, Cantiga do mar, op. 97, 1989, Manuel Bandeira, —, —, —, —, UFMG

3.1102, Caravana, op. 116, no. 3, 1994, Acchile Picchi, —, —, —, —, UFMG

3.1103, Chanson d'automne, op. 167, —, Paul Verlaine, —, —, —, —, UFMG

3.1104, *Cinco haikais, op. 112*

3.1104a, Infância, op. 112, no. 1, 1990, Guilherme de Almeida, —, —, —, —, UFMG

3.1104b, Cigarra, op. 112, no. 2, —, Guilherme de Almeida, —, —, —, —, UFMG

3.1104c, Quiriri, op. 112, no. 3, —, Guilherme de Almeida, —, —, —, —, UFMG

3.1104d, O haikai, op. 112, no. 4, 1990, Guilherme de Almeida, —, —, —, —, UFMG

3.1104e, O lago dos haikais, op. 112 no. 5, 1990, Guilherme de Almeida, —, —, —, —, UFMG

3.1105, *Comboio de corda (Modinhas), Volume I: 1990–1992*

3.1105a, 1. Dor, —, Castro Alves, —, —, —, —, UFMG

3.1105b, 2. Quando eu morrer, —, Laurindo Rabelo, —, —, —, —, UFMG

3.1105c, 3. Evocação, —, Helena Ferraz, —, —, —, —, UFMG

3.1105d, 4. Buquê, —, José Bandeira, —, —, —, —, UFMG

3.1105e, 5. Chama, —, Bastos Tigre, —, —, —, —, UFMG

3.1106, *Comboio de corda (Modinhas), Volume II: 1990–1992*

3.1106a, 1. Mágoa, 1990–1992, Eduardo Kemp, —, —, —, —, UFMG

3.1106b, 2. Moldura, 1990–1992, Cleómenes Campos, —, —, —, —, UFMG

3.1106c, 3. Gotas de pranto, 1990–1992, Lilinha Fernandes, —, —, —, —, UFMG

3.1106d, 4. Autopsicografia, 1990–1992, Fernando Pessoa, —, —, —, —, UFMG

3.1106e, 5. A flor e o lago, 1990–1992, J. de Lemos, —, —, —, —, UFMG

3.1107, *Doze cantigas sensíveis, op. 99*

3.1107a, Abandono, —, Maíra, —, —, —, —, UFMG

3.1108, *Duas canções de Drummond*

3.1108a, Cidadezinha qualquer, op. 151, no. 1, —, Carlos Drummond de Andrade, —, —, —, —, UFMG

3.1108b, Moinho, op. 151, no. 2, —, Carlos Drummond de Andrade, —, —, —, —, UFMG

3.1109, *Duas canções de Gisele Ganade*

3.1109a, Etéreo, op. 118, no. 1, 1997–1998, Gisele Ganade, —, —, —, —, UFMG

3.1109b, Escadas da Penha, op. 118, no. 2, —, Gisele Ganade, —, —, —, —, UFMG

3.1110, *Duas canções de Virginia Victorino, (Tríptico de Virgínia Victorino), op. 141*
3.1110a, 1. Aleluia, 1993–2001, Virgínia Victorino, —, —, —, —, UFMG
3.1110b, 2. Meia-Noite, 1993–2001, Virgínia Victorino, —, —, —, —, UFMG

3.1111, *Duas trovas para Luíza, op. 125*
3.1111a, 1. Goteira do coração, —, Celina Fereira, —, —, —, —, UFMG
3.1111b, 2. Duas aves, —, Carlyle Martin, —, —, —, —, UFMG

3.1112, *Harmonização de Acchile Picchi de canção do Cancioneiro de músicas populares de César das Neves*
3.1112a, Á Dália (Dança de roda), —, Popular text, —, —, —, —, UFMG
3.1112b, A partida, —, Soares de Passos, —, —, —, —, UFMG
3.1112c, A saloia (Canção), —, Angelo Frondoni/ José da Silva Mendes Leal, —, —, —, —, UFMG
3.1112d, Cruel saudade (Modinha), —, Manuel José Vidigal, —, —, Harmonization, —, UFMG
3.1112e, Despedida de Coimbra (Barcarola), —, Popular text, —, —, —, —, UFMG
3.1112f, Márcia bela (Modinha), —, Popular text, —, —, —, —, UFMG
3.1112g, Melodia popular d'anadia (Fado), —, Popular text, —, —, —, —, UFMG
3.1112h, Moqueca (Lundu), —, Popular text, —, —, —, —, UFMG
3.1112i, Oh querida, eu goto de ti (Cantiga), —, Popular text, —, —, —, —, UFMG
3.1112j, Os pratos na cantareira (Dança), —, Popular text, —, —, —, —, UFMG
3.1112k, Os teus olhos (Canção), —, Almeida Garrett, —, —, —, —, UFMG
3.1112l, Ru-chu-chu (Cantiga das ruas), —, Popular text, —, —, —, —, UFMG
3.1112m, Trovas e danças no. 1, —, Popular text, —, —, —, —, UFMG
3.1112n, Trovas e danças no. 2, —, Popular text, —, —, —, —, UFMG
3.1112o, Yayá (Lundu), —, Popular text, —, —, —, —, UFMG

3.1113, Inspiração súbita, 2000, Mário de Andrade, —, —, —, —, UFMG
3.1114, Madrigal muito fácil, op. 129, —, Manuel Bandeira, —, —, —, —, UFMG
3.1115, Neblina, op. 106, 1989, Ilka Brunhilde Laurito, —, —, —, —, UFMG
3.1116, O coração, op. 136, —, Castro Alves, —, —, —, —, UFMG
3.1117, O ipê e você, op. 127, —, Mário de Andrade, —, —, —, —, UFMG
3.1118, Olhos verdes, op. 155, —, Vicente de Carvalho, C4–F5, —, —, —, UFMG
3.1119, Perdi minha liberdade, op. 61, —, Marina Tricânico, C4–F5, —, —, —, UFMG
3.1120, Prece, op. 157, —, José Albano, C4–F5, —, —, —, UFMG
3.1121, Queixa, op. 126, 1997, Vicente Carvalho, —, —, —, —, UFMG

3.1122, *Ramo de rumos, op. 166*
3.1122a, 1. Algo, —, Paulo Bonfim, —, Soprano, —, —, UFMG
3.1122b, 2. Litania, —, Paulo Bonfim, —, Mezzo, —, —, UFMG
3.1122c, 3. Simplicidade, —, Paulo Bonfim, —, Soprano/Mezzo, —, —, UFMG

3.1123, Redondilha, op. 130, —, Luís de Camões, —, —, —, —, UFMG
3.1124, Roseira, op. 63, —, Vicente de Carvalho, —, —, —, —, UFMG
3.1125, Talvez, op. 117, 1995, Alphonsus de Guimarães, —, —, —, —, UFMG
3.1126, Teu nome, op. 116, no. 1, —, Manuel Bandeira, —, —, —, —, UFMG
3.1127, Timidez, op. 52, —, Cecília Meireles, —, —, —, UFMG

3.1128, *Três canções de Chico Moura*
3.1128a, 1. Valsinha, —, Chico Moura, —, —, —, —, UFMG
3.1128b, 2. Canção da brisa (I), —, Chico Moura, —, —, —, —, UFMG
3.1128c, 3. Canção da brisa (II), —, Chico Moura, —, —, —, —, UFMG

3.1129, *Três trovas de Manuel Bandeira, op. 114*

3.1129a, Trova 1, op. 114, no. 1, —, Manuel Bandeira, —, —, —, —, UFMG

3.1129b, Trova 2, op. 114, no. 2, —, Manuel Bandeira, G4–E5, —, —, —, UFMG

3.1129c, Trova 3, op. 114, no. 3, —, Manuel Bandeira, F#4–E5, —, —, —, UFMG

3.1130, *Três trovas de Mário de Andrade*, op. 169

3.1130a, 1. Barquinho esguio, op. 169, no. 1, —, Mário de Andrade, —, —, —, —, UFMG

3.1130b, 2. Menina de fita e renda, op. 169, no. 2, —, Mário de Andrade, —, —, —, —, UFMG

3.1130c, 3. Quem te viu... op. 169, no. 3, —, Mário de Andrade, —, —, —, —, UFMG

3.1131, *Triptico de Virginia Victorino*

3.1131c, 3. Não sei, op. 118, 1993–2001, Virgínia Victorino, —, —, See *Duas canções de Virginia Victorino, op. 141* (entry 3.1112, above) for op. 118, nos. 1–2, —, UFMG

3.1132, Vocalise, op. 47, —, No text, —, —, —, —, UFMG

Additional titles: A mariposa, op. 98, no.3; Canção do bêbado, op. 20; Caveira, op. 21; Danza, op. 16; Desafogo; Desinfeliz, op. 81; *Doze cantigas sensíveis, op. 99, volume I* (1. A Saudade é uma tristeza, 2. Saudade és ressonância, 3. Queres saber, doce amada, 4. Saudade, lâmpada acesa, 5. Melhor morrer de saudades, 6. Fadário); *Doze cantigas sensíveis, op. 99, volume II* (1. Mágoas, 2. Vazio, 3. Sobre o busto ela trazia, 10 Só, 11. Abandono, 12. Gosto de ti, ó chuva, nos beirados); *Duas canções de Geraldo Pinto Rodrigues, op. 79; Duas canções de Vinícius de Moraes, op. 83*; Estudo sobre temas populares, op. 9; *Harmonização de Acchile Picchi de canção do Cancioneiro de músicas populares de César das Neves* (Meu anjo, escuta); Lugar-comum, op. 45; Melodia, op. 116 no. 2; Música de fundo, op. 68; Num leque, op. 51; Salmo XXIII, op. 89; Sedução, op. 123; Sete canções de Helena, op. 59; Sino, op. 54; *Três sonetos, op. 57; Três trovas, op. 50; Treze cantigas tonais, op. 98, volume I* (1. Saudade, 2. Olhos nos olhos, 3. A mariposa, 4. Cantiga, 5. O amor e o canto, 6. Noturno); *Treze cantigas tonais, volume II* (7. Dentro da noite, 8. Tão pouco, 9. Quadra I, 10. Quadra II, 11. Árvore triste, 12. Alfa et Omega, 13. Clavis Aurea); Vagabondo, op. 64 (For solo voice); Vocação, op. 91; *Vou morrendo devagar (5 Trovas), op. 80*.

Pimenta, Altino, 1921–2003

3.1133, A bela e a fera, 1994, Altino Pimenta, C4–A5, UFPA, BN, UFMG, UFPA

3.1134, Canção da chuva, —, Sylvio Moreaux, D4–E5, UFPA, BN, UFMG, UFPA

3.1135, Canjerê (Canto do caboclo), 1991, Altino Pimenta, D4–F5, UFPA, BN, UFMG, UFPA

3.1136, Chora coração, —, Altino Pimenta, E4–G5, UFPA, BN, UFMG, UFPA

3.1137, Contigo, 1993, Gustavo J. de Souza, C#4–F5, UFPA, BN, UFMG, UFPA

3.1138, Estrela, 1943, Altino Pimenta, A4–F5, UFPA, UFMG, UFPA

3.1139, Igreja de Arrabalde, 1993, —, E4–G5, —, UFMG

3.1140, Ressonâncias, —, Altino Pimenta, C#4–G#5, UFPA, BN, UFMG, UFPA

3.1141, Romance da inconfidência, 1990, Cecília Meireles, D4–F5, UFPA, BN, UFMG, UFPA

3.1142, Romancello, 1988, Altino Pimenta, D4–G5, UFPA, BN, UFMG, UFPA

3.1143, Soneto à lua, —, Bruno de Menezes, C#4–G5, UFPA, BN, UFMG, UFPA

3.1144, Súplica, 1993, Milton Camargo, E4–G5, UFPA, BN, UFMG, UFPA

3.1145, Toada da Canoa, 1993, Altino Pimenta, —, UFPA, BN, UFMG, UFPA

3.1146, Uirapuru e o violão, —, Altino Pimenta, —, —, UFMG

3.1147, Vela morena, —, Alex Fiúza de Melo, F4–G5, UFPA, BN, UFMG, UFPA

Additional titles: Apresentação; A uma gaivota; Canto para Astor Piazzolla; Ecos Selvagens; Lundu Marajoara; Poema dos olhos da amada; Saci Pererê.

Rebello, Arnaldo, 1905–1984

3.1148, Cantigas, Adelmar Tavares, E♭4–A♭5, RB, —

3.1149, Dorme, dorme coração, Arnaldo Rabello, F4–F5, RB, BN, UFMG

3.1150, Quase seresta, Menezes de Oliva, D4–G5, RB, —

3.1151, Na partida, Luiz Otávio, C4–F5, RB, —

3.1152, Ninguém faz falta a ninguém, Beatriz dos Reis Carvalho, —, —, UFMG

3.1153, Toada Baré, —, C4–G5, RB, BN, USP

Additional titles: Amigo abandonado; Canção breve; Canção do Rio Mar; Marapatá; Na espera sem fim; Noites sem caminho; Rondó; Saudade ajuda a viver; Unidunitê.

Republicano, Antonio de Assis, 1897–1960

3.1154, Ave Maria, —, —, —, CO, —

3.1155, Candomblé, 1951, —, D4–A5, AN, BN, UFMG, +

3.1156, Desejo, —, Achilles Alves, —, —, BN

3.1157, Magdala, 1926, Silveira Netto, —, VM, BN

3.1158, O amor e a morte, —, Pereira da Silva, —, VM, BN

Additional titles: As mãos de Branca; Canção de Jaíra; Onde a ventura mora.

Ripper, João Guilherme, 1959–

3.1159, Rio desvelo, 1996, João Guilherme Ripper, BN, UFMG

Additional titles: Canção antiga; Libera me.

Santoro, Claudio Franco de Sá, 1919–1989

3.1160, *A menina boba: Quatro canções para canto e piano/Dos canciones para canto y piano, extraidas de los poemas de Oneyda Albarenga, A menina boba*

3.1160a, A menina exausta I, 1945, Oneyda Alvarenga, —, Mezzo, ECIC, ESav, BN, UnB, ACCS

3.1160b, A menina exausta II, 1944, Oneyda Alvarenga, C4–E♭5, Mezzo, ESav, UnB, EMB, ACCS, +

3.1160c, A menina exausta III, 1944, Oneyda Alvarenga, B3–F5, Mezzo, ECIC 1945, ESav, BN, UnB, ACCS, +

3.1160d, Asa ferida, no. IV, —, Oneyda Alvarenga, B♭3–F♯5, Mezzo, ECIC 1945, ESav, BN, UnB, ACCS

3.1160e, A menina exausta, no. XII, 1944, Oneyda Alvarenga, —, —, m, ACCS

3.1161, Amor que partiu, 1958, Vinícius de Moraes, C4–E♭5, —, ESav, BN, UFMG, UnB, ACCS

3.1162, A uma mulher, 1956, Celso Brandt, D♭4–F5, —, RB, ESav, BN, EMB, ACCS

3.1163, Berceuse, 1958, —, —, Med, —, ACCS

3.1164, Breve serenata, —, Cassiano Nunes, —, —, —, ACCS

3.1165, Canção (I), 1957, No text, —, High, —, ACCS

3.1166, Canção (II), 1957, No text, —, Mezzo, —, ACCS

3.1167, Canção, 1961, No text, —, High, —, ACCS

3.1168, Canção, 1966, No text, —, Med, —, ACCS

3.1169, Canção da fuga impossível, 1953, Ary de Andrade, C♯4–B5, —, RB, ESav, BN, UFMG, UnB, EMB, ACCS

3.1170, *Canções de Amor (1a. série)*

3.1170a, 1. Ouve o silêncio, 1958, Vinícius de Moraes, D♭4–G5, Med-low, ESav, BN, UFMG, UnB, EMB, ACCS

3.1170b, 2. Acalanto da rosa, 1958, Vinícius de Moraes, C4–E♭5, Med-low, —, BN, UFMG, UnB, ACCS

3.1170c, 3. Bem pior que a morte, —,

Vinicius de Moraes, F♯3–A4, Low, ESav, BN, UFMG, UnB, EMB, ACCS

3.1170d, 4. Balada da flor da terra, 1958/60, Vinicius de Moraes, D♭4–F♯5, Med-low, ESav, BN, UFMG, UnB, EMB, ACCS

3.1170e, 5. Amor que partiu, 1957/58, Vinícius de Moraes, —, Med-low, ESav, BN, UFMG, UnB, EMB, ACCS

3.1171, *Canções de amor* (2a. série)

3.1171a, 1. Jardim noturno, 1957, Vinícius de Moraes, C4–F5, Med-low, ESav, BN, UFMG, UnB, EMB, ACCS

3.1171b, 2. Pregão da saudade, 1959, Vinicius de Moraes, G3–E5, Med-low, ESav, BN, UFMG

3.1171c, 3. Alma perdida, 1958/59, Vinícius de Moraes, B♭3–A5, —, ESav, BN, UFMG, UnB, ACCS

3.1171d, 4. Em algum lugar, 1957/58, Vinicius de Morais, D♭4–E♭5, —, —, BN, UFMG, UnB, EMB, ACCS

3.1171e, 5. A mais dolorosa das histórias, 1958, Vinicius de Moraes, D♭4–C5, Med, ESav, BN, UFMG, UnB, EMB, ACCS

3.1172, Chanson de la liberté, 1957, Cláudio Santoro, —, Med, ESav, ACCS

3.1173, Chanson de la mélancholie, 1958, Cláudio Santoro, —, Mezzo, ESav, ACCS

3.1174, Chanson du Marron, 1959, Françoise Jonquière, —, Med, ESav, ACCS

3.1175, *Ciclo Brecht*

3.1175a, Das Lied von der wolke Nacht, 1974, Bertold Brecht, —, High, ESav, —

3.1176, Elegia, 1951, Lila Ripol, —, Med, RB, ESav, BN, ACCS

3.1177, Eu não sei, 1966, Ribeiro da Costa, D♭4–E5, Med, ESav, UFMG, ACCS

3.1178, Hino do Amazonas, 1980, Jorge Tufic, —, Med, ESav, ACCS

3.1179, Irremediável canção, 1953, Ary de Andrade, D4–A5, —, RB, ESav, BN, UnB, EMB, ACCS

3.1180, La nuit n'est jamais complète, 1958, Paul Éluard, —, Low, ESav, ACCS

3.1181, La prière du marchand de sable, 1958, Françoise Jonquière, —, —, ESav, ACCS

3.1182, Levavas a madrugada, 1956, Ary de Andrade, D♭4–E♭5, —, RB, ESav, BN, UFMG, ACCS

3.1183, Liebes Lied (with piano and magnetic tape), 1974, Bertold Brecht, —, Med, ESav, ACCS

3.1184, Marguerite, 1947, Louis Aragon, —, Bass, —, ACCS

3.1185, Meu amor me disse adeus, 1960, Gisele Santoro, —, Mezzo, ESav, ACCS

3.1186, Meu destino, 1956, Celso Brant, D4–F5, —, RB, ESav, ACCS

3.1187, Náiades (Soneto), 1983, Luís de Camões, —, —, ESav, ACCS

3.1188, Não te digo adeus, 1948, Jorge Amado, D4–F5, —, RB, ESav, BN, UFMG, UnB, EMB

3.1189, No meio fio da rua, 1960, Jeanete H. Alimonda, —, Med, —, ACCS

3.1190, O cavalinho de pau, 1958, Cláudio Santoro, —, Med-low, ESav, ACCS

3.1191, O cravo brigou com a rosa, 1955, Folklore, —, —, —, ACCS

3.1192, *O soldado*

3.1192a, 1. A colina, 1988, Alexis Zakythinos, —, Med, ESav, ACCS

3.1192b, 2. O soldado menino de ontem, 1988, Alexis Zakythinos, —, Med, ESav, ACCS

3.1192c, 3. O soldado recruta, 1988, Alexis Zakythinos, —, Med, ESav, ACCS

3.1192d, 4. O soldado do amor, 1988, Alexis Zakythinos, —, Med, ESav, ACCS

3.1192e, 5. O soldado de fogo, 1988, Alexis Zakythinos, —, Med, ESav, ACCS

3.1192f, 6. O soldado guardião dos caminhos, 1988, Alexis Zakythinos, —, Med, ESav, ACCS

3.1192g, 7. O soldado obediente, 1988, Alexis Zakythinos, —, Med, Esav, ACCS

3.1192h, 8. O soldado inválido, 1988, Alexis Zakythinos, —, Med, ESav, ACCS

3.1192i, 9. O soldado nu, 1988, Alexis Zakythinos, —, Med, ESav, ACCS

3.1193, Poema, 1950, Nair Bathista, E♭4–A5, —, RB, ESav, BN, UFMG, ACCS

3.1194, *Quatro canções da madrugada*
3.1194a, 1. Aspiração, 1982, Cassiano Nunes, B3–G♯5, —, ESav, UnB, EMB, ACCS
3.1194b, 2. Breve serenata, 1982, Cassiano Nunes, D4–A♭5, —, ESav, UFMG, UnB, EMB, ACCS
3.1194c, 3. Improviso, 1982, Cassiano Nunes, C4–F♯5, —, ESav, UFMG, UnB, EMB, ACCS
3.1194d, 4. Noturno no. 1, 1982, Cassiano Nunes, E♭4–F♯5, —, ESav, BN, UFMG, UnB, ACCS

3.1195, *Três canções populares*
3.1195a, 1. Luar de meu bem, 1958, Vinicius de Moraes, B♭3–G5, Low, ESav, BN, UFMG, UnB, EMB, ACCS
3.1195b, 2. Amor em lágrimas, 1957, Vinícius de Moraes, B3–F♯5, —, ESav, UFMG, UnB, EMB, ACCS
3.1195c, 3. Cantiga do ausente, 1958, Vinicius de Moraes, B♭3–F5, —, ESav, BN, UFMG, UnB, EMB, ACCS

3.1196, *Tríptico*
3.1196a, 1. Vigília, 1985, Da Costa e Silva, —, Med, ESav, —
3.1196b, 2. Fragmento para um réquiem, 1985, Da Costa e Silva, —, Med, ESav, ACCS
3.1196c, 3. O amante, 1985, Da Costa e Silva, —, Med, ESav, —

3.1197, Tu vais ao mar, 1961, Cláudio Santoro, —, Mezzo, ESav, ACCS

3.1198, Volar y volar, 1958, Nicolás Guillén, —, Med, ESav, ACCS

3.1199, Wanderers Nachtlied, 1989, J. Wolfgang von Goethe, —, Med, ESav, ACCS

Setti, Kilza (de Castro Lima), 1932–

3.1200, Acre-Nocturno, —, —, —, —, m, USP
3.1201, A Estrela, 1961, Manuel Bandeira, E♭4–G5, —, m, USP
3.1202, Cantiga, 1960, —, —, —, m, USP

3.1203, *Cantorias Paulistas*
3.1203a, 1. Ponto de terreiro, 1962, Folklore, D♯4–C5, —, m, USP
3.1203b, 2. Samba-lenço, 1962, Folklore, D4–D5, —, m, USP

3.1204, Distâncias, 1957, Alice Camargo Guarnieri, D4–E5, —, m, USP

3.1205, *Dois poemas de Geir Campos*, 1962, Geir Campos, —, —, m, USP

3.1206, Lua cheia, 1959, Cassiano Ricardo, E4–E5, —, m, USP

3.1207, Na palma da mão uma estrela, 1963, Ricardo Tavares de Lima, B♭3–E♭5, —, m, USP

3.1208, Os olhos do meu benzinho, 1955, —, —, —, m, USP

3.1209, Poema da tua luz, 1962, Rossine Camargo Guarnieri, D4–G5, —, m, USP

3.1210, Quadrinhas, 1956, Sílvio Romero, —, —, m, USP

3.1211, Raro dom, 1958, Suzanna de Campos, D4–E5, —, m, USP

3.1212, Serenata, 1966, Vicente de Carvalho, D4–E5, —, m, USP

3.1213, *Três lembranças do folclore infantil*
3.1213a, 1. Jogo do Tantanguê, 1961, Folklore, F4–G5, (from *Cantos populares do Brasil* by Silvio Romero), m, USP
3.1213b, 2. Jogo da lua nova, 1961, Folklore, F4–F5, (from *Cantos populares do Brasil* by Silvio Romero), m, USP
3.1213c, 3. Jogo de Varisto, 1961, Folklore, D4–A5, (from *Cantos populares do Brasil* by Silvio Romero), m, USP

3.1214, Trova de muito amor para um amado senhor, 1961, Hilda Hilst, E4–G5, —, m, USP

3.1215, Você gosta de mim, 1959, Sílvio Romero, —, —, m, USP

Siqueira, José de Lima, 1907–1985

3.1216, Acalanto, —, Manuel Bandeira, —, SAI, EDM, BN, UFMG

3.1217, Andorinha, 1952, Manuel Bandeira, A5–G5, SAI, BN, EMB
3.1218, Boca de forno, —, Manuel Bandeira, —, SAI, BN, UFMG
3.1219, Cantiga para ninar, —, Luiz Otávio, —, EDM, BN
3.1220, Debussy, —, Manuel Bandeira, —, SAI, BN, UFMG
3.1221, Desejo, —, Ronald de Carvalho, —, SA, BN, UFMG
3.1222, Desilusão, —, Guerra Durval, —, CW, BN, UFMG
3.1223, Ela era virgem, —, —, —, EDM, BN
3.1224, Folhas soltas, 1968, Lúcia Aizim, —, —, BN
3.1225, Irene no céu, 1948, Manuel Bandeira, —, —, BN
3.1226, The Island, —, Doris Dreyer, —, —, BN, UFMG
3.1227, Kessy, —, Albert Renart, —, AN, UFMG
3.1228, Longe de ti, —, —, —, EDM, BN
3.1229, Macumba do Pai Zusé, —, Manuel Bandeira, —, SAI, BN
3.1230, Madrigal, —, Manuel Bandeira, D$\sharp$4–F5, EDM, AN, BN, UFMG, USP, +
3.1231, Meu cavalo pimpão, —, Lúcia Aizim, G4–F5, —, BN
3.1232, Meu engenho d'Humaitá, —, —, —, EDM, BN
3.1233, Meu limão, meu limoeiro, —, Folklore, G$\flat$4–B$\flat$5, —, BN
3.1234, Mulher rendeira, —, Folklore, —, —, BN
3.1235, Na rua do sabão, —, Manuel Bandeira, —, —, BN
3.1236, Nada tenho, —, Luiz Otávio, —, —, BN
3.1237, Nós, —, Augusto Linhares, —, —, BN
3.1238, O impossível carinho, —, Manuel Bandeira, —, —, BN

3.1239, *Oito canções populares brasileiras*
3.1239a, 1. Benedito pretinho, —, Olegário Mariano, E4–E5, EDM, JLS, BN, UFMG
3.1239b, 2. Vadeia caboclinho, —, Olegário Mariano, D4–G5, —, BN, UFMG
3.1239c, 3. Loanda, —, Ascenço Ferreira, E4–F$\sharp$5, EDM, JLS, BN, UFMG
3.1239d, 4. Maracatu, —, Ascenço Ferreira, F4–F$\sharp$5, EDM, JLS, BN, UFMG
3.1239e, 5. Foi numa noite calmosa, —, Popular text, E4–E5, EDM, JLS, BN, UFMG
3.1239f, 6. Nesta rua, —, Folklore, D4–A5, EDM, JLS, BN, UFMG
3.1239g, 7. A dança do sapo, —, Folklore, F$\sharp$4–A$\sharp$5, EDM, JLS, BN, UFMG
3.1239h, 8. Natiô, —, Typical song of the Parecis indigenous people, B4–D5, EDM, JLS, BN, UFMG

3.1240, O trem de ferro, —, Manuel Bandeira, —, —, BN
3.1241, Ranchinho desfeito, —, —, —, EDM, BN
3.1242, Reminiscência, —, Raul Machado, —, EDM, BN
3.1243, Saudade é uma fogueira, —, Luiz Otávio, A4–F5, SAI, BN

3.1244, *Três canções para canto e piano*
3.1244a, 1. Balança eu, 1956, Raul Machado, G4–E5, EDM, BN, UFMG, USP
3.1244b, 2. Indiscrição, 1949, Raul Machado, —, —, BN, UFMG, USP
3.1244c, 3. Meu barco é veleiro, —, Olegário Mariano, —, —, BN, UFMG, USP

3.1245, Trovas, —, Luiz Otávio, —, —, BN
3.1246, Vai meu suspiro, —, —, —, EDM, BN
3.1247, Você, —, Augusto Linhares, F$\sharp$4–E5, EDM, AN, RB, BN, UFMG, USP

Additional titles: Adormecida; Canção desolada; Candomblé no. 3; Cigana; Ciranda, cirandinha; Giranda.

Souza, Oswaldo de, 1904–1995

3.1248, Aruanda, Folklore, —, —, RB, —
3.1249, Chuva com sol, Folklore, B3–C$\sharp$5, Motive of the "Jararaca" dance from Rio Grande do Norte, EM 1942, —

3.1250, *Cinco canções*

3.1250a, 1. Yemanjá, Afro-Brazilian ritualistic text and Oswaldo de Souza, D4–D5, —, RB, —

3.1250b, 2. Jurupanã (Coco), Folklore, A3–D5, —, RB, —

3.1250c, 3. Cantiga, Folklore, D♯4–D5, —, RB, —

3.1250d, 4. Gavião Penerô, —, —, —, RB, —

3.1250e, 5. Protesto, Sylvio Moreaux, C4–E5, —, RB, —

3.1251, *Duas canções praianas*

3.1251a, 1. Praieira, Oswaldo de Souza, C4–F5, —, RB, UFMG

3.1251b, 2. Sereia do mar, Oswaldo de Souza, —, —, RB, UFMG

3.1252, Gavião penerô (Coco), Folklore, B3–D♭5, —, RB, —

3.1253, Esconde esses teus olhos, —, —, —, RB, UFMG

3.1254, Pingo d'água, Folklore, C4–E♭5, —, RB, UFMG

3.1255, Querer bem não é pecado, —, —, —, EM 1942, —

3.1256, Retiradas (Cena-nordestina), Oswaldo de Souza, F4–C5, —, RB, —

Tacuchian, Ricardo, 1939–

3.1257, A Estrela, —, Manuel Bandeira, —, —, UFMG

3.1258, A Federico, 1973, Carlos Drummond de Andrade, —, —, BN, USP, UFMG

3.1259, A Rosa, 1966, Folklore, C♯4–F5, ECA/USP, USP, UFMG

3.1260, Auiê autiá, 1965, Indigenous theme collected by Roquete Pinto, B4–F♯5, ECA/USP, USP, UFMG

3.1261, A um passarinho, —, Vinicius de Moraes, —, —, BN

3.1262, Berimbau, —, Manuel Bandeira, —, ECA/USP, BN, USP, UFMG

3.1263, Canção de ninar, 1965, Popular text from Alagoas, E4–E5, ECA/USP, BN, USP, UFMG

3.1264, Cantiga, 1964, Manuel Bandeira, —, ECA/USP, BN, USP, UFMG

3.1265, Escondumba-a-rê, —, Theme collected by L. H. Corrêa de Azevedo, —, —, UFMG

3.1266, Hai Guetaza, —, Indigenous theme collected by Roquete Pinto, —, ECA/USP, USP, UFMG

3.1267, Lá em cima daquele morro, —, —, —, —, USP, UFMG

3.1268, Menina me dá teu remo (Côco), —, Theme collected by Luciano Gallet, 1927–1928, —, ECA/USP, USP, UFMG

3.1269, Ontem, hoje, amanhã, —, —, —, ECA/USP, USP, UFMG

Additional title: Assim cantava o Baiá.

Tavares, Heckel, 1896–1969

3.1270, Amendoim torradinho (Cenas cariocas), —, Joracy Camargo, —, —, —, SA, BN

3.1271, Aracy-Fox: Menina de cinema, —, Max-Mix, —, —, —, CW, BN

3.1272, A rendeira, —, Joracy Camargo, C4–D5, —, —, SA, AN, BN, +

3.1273, Azulão, —, Luiz Peixoto, A3–E5, —, —, IV, BN

3.1274, Bahia, 1930, Álvaro Moreyra, —, —, —, SA, BN, UNESP, +

3.1275, Bonequinha de seda, —, Joracy Camargo, —, —, —, EM 1946, BN

3.1276, Caboclo bom, —, Raul Pederneiras, —, —, —, IV, —

3.1277, Caixinha de música (Cenas infantis), —, Luiz Peixoto, —, —, —, SA, BN

3.1278, *Canções brasileiras*

3.1278a, 1. Meu amor tão bom, —, Popular text, —, —, —, DNIC, BN, USP

3.1278b, 2. Na minha terra tem, —, Luiz Peixoto, B3–D5, —, —, DNIC, VM, IV, BN, USP

3.1278c, 3. Cantigas dos sertanejos cuiabanos, —, Folklore, —, —, Harmonization of theme collected by Roquete Pinto, DNIC, EM, —

3.1278d, 4. Casa de caboclo, —, —, —, —, —, DNIC, BN

3.1278e, 5. Banzo, —, Murilo Araujo, C4–E♭5, —, —, DNIC, EM, BN, USP

3.1279, Cantiga de leito, —, Lobão Filho, —, —, —, VM, IV, BN, UNESP

3.1280, Cantiga de Nossa Senhora, —, Luiz Peixoto, —, —, —, IV, BN

3.1281, Casa de caboclo (Série regional), —, Luiz Peixoto, D4–E5, —, —, IV, VM, DNIC, BN, USP, UNESP

3.1282, *Cenas coloniais, 1870*

3.1282a, 1. Acalanto, 1930, Joracy Camargo, D4–A4, —, —, AN, SA, BN, UNESP, UFMG

3.1282b, 2. Carnaval, —, Joracy Camargo, D4–E5, —, —, AN, SA, BN, UNESP

3.1282c, 3. O leilão, —, Joracy Camargo, D4–E5, —, —, AN, SA, BN, UNESP

3.1283, Chove-chuva!, —, Ascenço Ferreira, —, —, —, VM, BN

3.1284, Côco de minha terra (Biá-tá-tá), 1930, Jorge D'Altavilla, —, —, —, EM 1930, —

3.1285, Comendo bola, —, Luiz Peixoto, —, —, —, VM, BN

3.1286, Dança negra, —, Sodré Viana, —, —, —, EM 1911, BN

3.1287, Despedida (Modinha sertaneja), —, Gastão Penalva, —, —, —, VM, BN

3.1288, Dona Domitilla, —, Álvaro Moreyra, —, —, —, VM, BN

3.1289, Eita Brasil, —, Jayme D'Altavilla, D4–D5, —, —, IV, VM, BN

3.1290, E nada mais!, —, Adelmar Tavares, —, —, —, CW, BN

3.1291, Engenho d'água, —, Lobão Filho, —, —, —, IV, —

3.1292, Escoteiro pequenino, —, Jorge Lima, —, —, —, IV, —

3.1293, Estrela pequenina, —, Luiz Peixoto, —, —, —, VM, IV, —

3.1294, Eu vi uma lagartixa, 1928, Folklore, —, —, —, CW, BN

3.1295, Faz isso comigo não (Toada), —, Luiz Peixoto, C4–D5, —, —, SA, AN, BN, UFMG

3.1296, Festa, —, Luiz Peixoto, C♯4–D5, —, —, EM 1935, BN

3.1297, Funeral d'um rei Nagô (Canto do Alufá), —, Murilo Araujo, E3–B4, —, —, EM, BN, UNESP, UFMG, +

3.1298, Guacyra (Baião), —, Joracy Camargo, E♭4–F5, —, —, A Melodia, EM, —

3.1299, Lavandeirinha, —, Olegário Mariano, —, —, —, VM, IV, BN

3.1300, Lua cheia, A, —, Joracy Camargo, —, —, —, VM, IV, BN

3.1301, Mamãe-preta (Lullaby), —, Paulo Mendes, C♯4–B4, —, —, VM, IV, BN, BDB

3.1302, Mãos Frias, —, Adelmar Tavares, —, —, —, IV, VM, BN

3.1303, *Maracatús: Três fragmentos*

3.1303a, 1. Invocação (Maracatú), —, Ascenço Ferreira, D4–B5, —, —, IV, BN, UFMG

3.1303b, 2. Oração e dança, —, Ascenço Ferreira, A3–B4, —, —, IV, BN, UFMG

3.1303c, 3. Festival (Maracatu), 1940, Ascenço Ferreira, D4–C♯5, —, —, IV, BN, UFMG

3.1304, Maria Rosa (Série regional), —, Luiz Peixoto, —, —, —, VM, IV, CVG, BN

3.1305, O carreiro, —, Olegário Mariano, —, —, —, IV, —

3.1306, O preto velho Cambindo, —, Joracy Camargo, —, —, —, SA, BN

3.1307, O que eu queria dizer ao seu ouvido, —, Mendonça Júnior, D4–E5, —, —, A Melodia, EM, BN

3.1308, *O sapo dourado (Suite infantil)*

3.1308a, 1. Sapo, —, Waldemar Henrique, —, —, —, —, BN

3.1308b, 2. O Rei, —, Waldemar Henrique, —, —, —, —, BN

3.1308c, 3. O Vassalo, —, Waldemar Henrique, —, —, —, —, BN

3.1308d, 4. Mestre Escola, —, Waldemar Henrique, —, —, —, —, BN

3.1308e, 5. Gisella, —, Waldemar Henrique, —, —, —, —, BN

3.1308f, 6. Fada azul, —, Waldemar Henrique, —, —, —, —, BN

3.1308g, 7. O príncipe, —, Waldemar Henrique, —, —, —, —, BN

3.1309, Os oinho d'ela, —, —, —, —, —, IV, —

3.1310, Papa curumiassu (Tema indígena), —, Parecis Indians, D4–F5, —, —, SA, BN, UFMG

3.1311, Papaizinho, —, Flavio de Andrade, —, —, —, VM, IV, BN

3.1312, *Raças: sobre a raça africana no Brasil*
3.1312a, 1. P'rá sinhozinho drumi, —, Luiz Peixoto, —, —, —, SA, BN
3.1312b, 2. Navio negreiro, —, Luiz Peixoto, —, —, —, SA, BN
3.1312c, 3. No Pegi de Ochossi, —, Luiz Peixoto, —, —, —, SA, BN

3.1313, Sabiá, —, Joracy Camargo, D4–E5, —, —, IV, VM, BN, UNESP

3.1314, Sussuarana, —, Luiz Peixoto, —, —, —, CW, BN, UNESP

3.1315, Toada (Série regional), —, Joracy Camargo, —, —, —, SA, BN

3.1316, *Três canções brasileiras I*
3.1316a, 1. A rendeira, —, Joracy Camargo, —, Low voice, —, SA, AN, +
3.1316b, 2. Madrugada, —, Gastão Penalva, C4–D5, Low voice, —, SA, BN, +
3.1316c, 3. Saudade, —, Luiz Peixoto, C♯4–B5, Low voice, —, SA, AN, BN, UFMG, +

3.1317, *Três canções brasileiras II*
3.1317a, 1. O boiadeiro, —, Olegário Mariano, —, —, —, SA, BN, UFMG
3.1317b, 2. Uma toada, —, Olegário Mariano, —, —, —, SA, AN, BN, UFMG
3.1317c, 3. A rendeira, —, Olegário Mariano, —, —, —, IV, VM, BN, UFMG

3.1318, *Três canções brasileiras (3a. série: Das cenas infantis)*
3.1318a, 1. Mamãezinha que estás no céu!..., —, Álvaro Moreyra, D♭4–A♭5, —, —, IV, VM, BN, UFMG
3.1318b, 2. A menina quer saber..., —, Álvaro Moreira, A♯3–B4, —, —, IV, VM, BN, UFMG
3.1318c, 3. O realejo, —, Álvaro Moreyra, E4–D5, —, —, IV, VM, BN, UFMG

3.1319, *Três canções modernas*
3.1319a, 1. Sapo-cururu, —, Olegário Mariano, —, —, —, Campassi & Camin, —
3.1319b, 2. Felicidade, —, Dante Milano, —, —, —, Campassi & Camin, BN
3.1319c, 3. Papai Noel, —, Olegário Mariano, —, —, —, Campassi & Camin, BN

3.1320, *Três canções modernas (1a. série)*
3.1320a, 1. Felicidade, —, Luiz Peixoto, B3–D5, —, —, IV, VM, BN, UFMG, UNESP
3.1320b, 2. Era aquilo só, —, Luiz Peixoto, B3–B4, —, —, IV, VM, BN, UFMG, UNESP
3.1320c, 3. Me deu uma vontade de chorar, —, —, A3–B4, —, —, IV, VM, BN, UFMG, UNESP

3.1321, *Três canções modernas (2a. série)*
3.1321a, 1. Tenho uma raiva de vancê, —, Luiz Peixoto, —, —, —, IV, VM, BN
3.1321b, 2. Dedo mindinho, —, Luiz Peixoto, —, —, —, IV, VM, BN
3.1321c, 3. No nosso tempo de colégio, —, Luiz Peixoto, —, —, —, IV, VM, BN

3.1322, *Três côcos (Sobre temas Pernambucanos)*
3.1322a, 1. Benedito pretinho, 1971, Olegário Mariano, E4–C5, —, —, AN, SA, BN, UFMG, +
3.1322b, 2. Vadeia cabocolinho, 1971, Olegário Mariano, A3–D5, —, —, SA, +
3.1322c, 3. O meu barco é veleiro, 1971, Olegário Mariano, C4–A4, —, —, SA, +

3.1323, *Três danças sertanejas (Côcos)*
3.1323a, 1. Dança de caboclo, 1934, Popular text, C4–D5, —, —, VM, IV, BN, UFMG
3.1323b, 2. Humaitá, 1934, Popular text, D4–D5, —, —, VM, IV, BN, UFMG
3.1323c, 3. Engenho novo, 1928, Folklore of the northeast, C4–B5, —, Harmonization, VM, IV, BN, UFMG

Additional titles: Favela; Você.

Terraza, Emilio, 1929–

3.1324, *Duas peças*
3.1324a, O legado, 1980, Cassiano Nunes, E♭4–A♭5, ECA/USP, UnB
3.1324b, Uma folha . . . outra folha, 1981, Cassiano Nunes, G♯4–G5, ECA/USP, UnB

Toni, George Olivier, 1926–

3.1325, *Canções Brejeiras*
3.1325a, Canção evocativa, 1954, Afro-Brazilian text collected by Silvio Romero, C4–G5, Novas Metas, USP
3.1325b, Chora morena, 1953, Popular text, D4–D5, Novas Metas, USP
3.1325c, Eu bem sei, 1952, —, C4–F5, Novas Metas, USP
3.1325d, Trova, 1953, Belmiro Braga, D4–D5, Novas Metas, USP

Tupinambá, Marcelo (Fernando Álvares Lobo), 1889–1953

3.1326, Canção da guitarra, 1928, Aplecina do Carmo, F4–G5, Campassi & Camin, CEMB, BN
3.1327, Candonga (Batuque), 1929, Ary Machado, A3–D5, IML, BN
3.1328, Canção dos pescadores, —, Ana Amélia de Queiroz Carneiro de Mendonça, D♭4–F5, AN, BN
3.1329, Minha'lma, —, J. Malta, E4–G5, IML, BN
3.1330, Rabicho, —, Olegário Mariano, C4–D5, IML, BN

Additional titles: Asas do Jaú; O cigano; O matuto; O pião; Serenata d'amor; Tristeza de caboclo; Viola cantadera.

Vasconcellos Corrêa, Sérgio Oliveira de, 1934–

3.1331, Camoniana no. 1 (Sete anos de pastor), —, —, —, —, UNESP
3.1332, Cantiga, 1964, Paulo Bonfim, —, AN 1976, BN, UFMG, BDB

3.1333, Chora Mané, não chora, 1959, Sílvio Romero, —, —, UNESP
3.1334, Eu cantador, —, —, —, —, UNESP
3.1335, Lamento, 1956, João Aciolly, E4–F♯5, RB 1956, UNESP
3.1336, Lá vai São Francisco, 1970, Vinícius de Moraes, —, —, BN, UNESP
3.1337, Louvação, 1995, Manuel Bandeira, —, —, UNESP
3.1338, Oração a Tupãssy, 1979, Pe. José de Anchieta, —, —, UNESP
3.1339, Que bobagem, meu filho, 1996, Mário de Andrade, —, —, UNESP
3.1340, Tenho medo do vento, 1956, João Acciolly, —, —, UNESP
3.1341, Velha modinha, —, Popular text collected by Silvio Romero, —, AN 1974, BN, UNESP

Veiga Jardim, Oswaldo (Oswaldo da Veiga Jardim Neto)

3.1342, Apresentação (Introduction), 1980, Cecília Meirelles, A♭3–A5, Phonoart 2000, UFMG
3.1343, Canção quase melancólica (Quasi-melancholic song), 1981, Cecília Meirelles, D♭4–E5, Phonoart 2000, UFMG
3.1344, Os amantes sem dinheiro (Penniless lovers), 1991, Eugênio de Andrade, B3–A5, Phonoart 2000, UFMG
3.1345, Sem título (Untitled), —, Carlos Drummond de Andrade, —, Phonoart 2000, UFMG

Velasquez, Glauco, 1884–1914

3.1346, A bella, 1907, Luís Guimarães, —, BN, UFMG, UFRJ
3.1347, A Berenice, op. 13, 1905, Barão de Paranapiacaba, m (autograph), BN, UFRJ
3.1348, A casa do coração, —, Introduction by Luciano Gallet, FBN/DIMAS 1998, BN
3.1349, A fada negra, op. 77, 1910, Antero de Quental, —, BN, UFRJ

3.1350, Alma minha gentil, op. 107, —, Luís de Camões, m, BN

3.1351, Amor vivo, op. 79, 1910, Antero de Quental, m, BN, UFRJ

3.1352, Anália (Romance), 1905, José Eloy Ottoni, m, BN, UFRJ

3.1353, As letras, 1906, Fagundes Varela, VM 1915, BN, UFRJ

3.1354, Ave Maria (1a.), op. 5, 1908, —, m, BN, UFRJ

3.1355, A virgem santíssima, 1910, Antero de Quental, m, BN, UFRJ

3.1356, Borboleta, op. 10, 1905, Aly, m, BN, UFRJ

3.1357, Canto d'amore, —, —, FBN/DIMAS 1998, BN

3.1358, Chanson d'amour, op. 24, 1905, —, m, BN, UFRJ

3.1359, Fatalità, op. 96, 1912, —, FBN/DIMAS 1998, BN, UFRJ

3.1360, Ici-bas, op. 46, 1906, René-François Sully-Prudhomme, VM 1916, BN, UFRJ

3.1361, J'ai voulu, op. 26, 1906, Mauricio Tubert, m, BN, UFRJ

3.1362, L'amour naissant, op. 51, 1910, Paul Bourget, m, BN, UFRJ

3.1363, La feuille, 1905, Antoine Vincent Arnault, m, BN, UFRJ

3.1364, Le livre de la vie, op. 16, 1905, Alphonse de Lamartine, m, BN, UFRJ

3.1365, Mal secreto, op. 45, 1907, Raimundo Corrêa, m, BN, UFRJ

3.1366, Mi se spezza la testa (Romanza), op. 33, 1906, —, m, BN, UFRJ

3.1367, Mors, amor, op. 73, 1910, Antero de Quental, m, BN, UFRJ

3.1368, Na capela, 1910, Antero de Quental, VM 1915, BN, UFRJ

3.1369, Não sabes?, op. 3, 1904, —, m, BN, UFRJ

3.1370, Nell'aria della sera umida e molle, op. 55, 1908, Lorenzo Stecchetti (Olindo Guerrini), m, BN, UFRJ

3.1371, Ouvir estrelas, op. 13, 1905, Olavo Bilac, m, BN, UFRJ

3.1372, Padre Nosso, 1908, —, SA 1903, BN, UFRJ

3.1373, Salutaris, 1902, —, m, BN, UFRJ

3.1374, Segredo, op. 15, 1905, —, m, BN, UFRJ

3.1375, Serenata, op. 75, —, —, m, BN

3.1376, Sete anos de pastor, op. 108, 1913, Luís de Camões, m, BN

3.1377, Seus olhos, op. 20, —, Antonio Gonçalves Dias, m, BN, UFRJ

3.1378, Soeur Beatrice, cantique (2nd act), 1913, —, m, BN

3.1379, Soledades, op. 21, 1905, Eusébio Blasco, VM 1915, BN, UFRJ

3.1380, Spes ultima Dea, op. 43, 1907, Lorenzo Stecchetti (Olindo Guerrini), VM 1918, BN, UFRJ

3.1381, Storia breve, op. 66, 1912, Ada Negri, m, BN, UFRJ

3.1382, Un desiderio, 1912, Milli, m, BN, UFRJ

3.1383, Un organetto suona per la via, op. 56, 1908, Lorenzo Stecchetti (Olindo Guerrini), m, BN, UFRJ

3.1384, Vita, op. 8, 1905, S. B. Lan, m, BN, UFRJ

Vianna, Fructuoso de Lima, 1896–1976

3.1385, Ave Maria, 1966, —, $F\sharp4–C6$, —, m, —, BN

3.1386, Canção da Jamaica, —, Manuel Bandeira, —, —, m, —, BN

3.1387, Desencanto, 1948, Manuel Bandeira, —, —, m, —, BN

3.1388, Madrigal, 1955, Palestrina (translation by Guilherme de Almeida), —, —, m, —, BN

3.1389, Modinha, —, —, —, —, m, —, USP

3.1390, Peregrinos do Joazeiro, 1955, Popular text, $E4–A\sharp5$, —, m, —, BN

3.1391, Refrão do mutum, 1932, Popular text, —, —, m, —, BN

3.1392, Resume of Life, 1966, Regina Chagas Pereira, —, —, m, —, BN

3.1393, *Seis canções trovadorescas*

3.1393a, 1. Relíquia apócrifa (Canção trovadoresca no. 1), 1951, Guilherme de Almeida, $D\sharp4–B5$, —, m, —, BN

3.1393b, 2. Cantar galego (Canção trovadoresca no. 2), 1951, Guilherme de Almeida, —, —, m, —, BN

3.1393c, 3. Partir e ficar (Canção trovadoresca no. 3), 1951, Guilherme de Almeida, —, —, m, —, BN

3.1393d, 4. Bailia (Canção trovadoresca no. 4), 1951, Guilherme de Almeida, —, —, m, —, BN

3.1393e, 5. Vilancete (canção trovadoresca no. 5), 1951, Guilherme de Almeida, —, —, m, —, BN, UFMG

3.1393f, 6. Cantiga dos olhos que choram (Canção trovadoresca no. 6), 1951, Guilherme de Almeida, —, —, m, —, BN, UFMG, USP

3.1394, Sem—fim (Modinha), 1938, Popular text, D#4–G5, —, —, *Viva Música!*, BN, UFMG

3.1395, Sonâmbula, 1928, Augusto de Lima, D4–C6, —, L. G. Miranda 1930, —, BN, UFMG

3.1396, Toada no. 3, 1930, Carlos Drummond de Andrade, E4–B#5, Toadas nos. 1,2,4,5,6, and 7 for solo piano, L. G. Miranda 1931, —, BN

3.1397, Un ami, 1957, Regina Chagas Pereira, —, —, m, —, BN, USP

Additional titles: Chula paroara; Sabiá.

Vieira, José Carlos do Amaral (José Carlos do Amaral Vieira Filho), 1952–

3.1398, A bailarina, op. 134, no. 5, 1979, Cecília Meireles, —, —, m, JCAV

3.1399, Ai Deus, eu é!, op. 54, 1969, D. Denis, —, —, m, JCAV

3.1400, Caminhando, op. 121, 1979, Dayse Ferraz, Mezzo, —, m, JCAV

3.1401, Canção da esperança, op. 85, 1976, A. L. Almeida Prado, Medium, —, m, JCAV

3.1402, *Cinco poemas de outono, op. 136*

3.1402a, 1. Caminhando (op. 121), 1979, Dayse Ferraz, Mezzo, —, —, JCAV

3.1402b, 2. Funeral de ilusões (op. 120), 1979, Dayse Ferraz, Mezzo, —, —, JCAV

3.1402c, 3. Ida e volta (op. 118), 1979, Dayse Ferraz, Mezzo, —, —, JCAV

3.1402d, 4. Lembrando (op. 114), 1979, Dayse Ferraz, Mezzo, —, —, JCAV

3.1402e, 5. Gratidão (op. 124), 1979, Dayse Ferraz, Mezzo, —, —, JCAV

3.1403, Com'estou d'amor ferida, op. 55, 1969, D. Afonso Sanches, —, —, m, JCAV

3.1404, Em meu coração fycays, op. 45, 1969, Rui Gonçalves de Castello Branco, —, Original version for voice and clavicembalo, m, JCAV

3.1405, Funeral de ilusões, op. 120, 1979, Paulo Fraletti, Mezzo, —, m, JCAV

3.1406, Gratidão, 1979, Dayse Ferraz, Mezzo, —, m, JCAV

3.1407, Ida e volta, op. 118, 1979, A. L. de Almeida Prado, Mezzo, —, m, JCAV

3.1408, Ja sempr'en coita viverei, op. 38, 1968, —, —, Original version for voice and clavicembalo, —, JCAV

3.1409, Lais de Leonoreta, op. 53, 1969, João Lobeira, —, —, m, JCAV

3.1410, Laudate Dominum, Psalm 16, op. 226, 1987, Latin text, Mezzo, Originally version for mezzo-soprano and string quartet, m, JCAV

3.1411, Lembrando, op. 114, 1978, Dayse Ferraz, Mezzo, —, m, JCAV

3.1412, Nebel, op. 119, 1979, Nikolaus Lenau, High, —, m, JCAV

3.1413, O meu amigo na guarda, op. 56, 1969, D. Afonso Sanches, —, —, m, JCAV

3.1414, O mudo falante, op. 184, 1984, —, Soprano, —, m, JCAV

3.1415, *Ou isto ou aquilo, op. 134*

3.1415a, 1. Pescaria, 1979, Cecília Meireles, Soprano, —, m, JCAV

3.1415b, 2. Moda da menina trombuda, 1979, Cecília Meireles, Soprano, —, m, JCAV

3.1415c, 3. Tanta tinta, 1979, Cecília Meireles, Soprano, —, m, JCAV

3.1415d, 4. Leilão de jardim, 1979, Cecília Meireles, Soprano, —, m, JCAV

3.1415e, 5. O mosquito escreve, 1979, Cecília Meireles, Soprano, —, m, JCAV

3.1415f, 6. Ou isto ou aquilo, 1979, Cecília Meireles, —, —, m, JCAV

3.1415g, 7. Ou isto ou aquilo, 1979, Cecília Meireles, —, —, m, JCAV

3.1416, Piedade, Cristo, op. 41, 1968, —, —, —, m, JCAV

3.1417, Poemas da vida e da morte, op. 110, 1978, Dayse Ferraz, Mezzo, —, m, JCAV

3.1418, Se eu tiver que partir . . . op. 90, —, A. L. Almeida Prado, —, —, m, JCAV

3.1419, Sonho póstumo, 1968, Vicente de Carvalho, Alto, —, m, JCAV

3.1420, Súplica para ser feliz, op. 158, 1981, Pe. Humberto Porto, —, —, m, JCAV

3.1421, Tua memória, op. 243, 1989, Nilde Caputi, Soprano, —, m, JCAV

3.1422, Um momento qualquer, op. 108, 1978, Dayse Ferraz, —, —, m, JCAV

3.1423, *Veinte poemas de amor y una canción desesperada, op. 179 B*

3.1423a, Cuerpo de mujer, 1983, Pablo Neruda, Mezzo, —, m, JCAV

3.1423b, En su llama mortal, 1983, Pablo Neruda, Mezzo, —, m, JCAV

3.1423c, Ah vastedad de pinos, 1983, Pablo Neruda, Mezzo, —, m, JCAV

3.1423d, Es la mañana llena de tempestad, 1983, Pablo Neruda, Mezzo, —, m, JCAV

3.1423e, Para mi corazón basta tu pecho, 1983, Pablo Neruda, Mezzo, —, m, JCAV

3.1423f, Puedo escribir los versos, 1983, Pablo Neruda, Mezzo, —, m, JCAV

3.1423g, La canción desesperada, 1983, Pablo Neruda, Mezzo, —, m, JCAV

3.1423h, Te recuerdo, op. 270, 1993, Pablo Neruda, —, —, m, JCAV

3.1424, Vengo otra vez a ti, op. 122, 1979, Facunde Recalde, Soprano, —, m, JCAV

3.1425, Veni Creator Spiritus, op. 241, 1989, Latin text, Baritone, —, m, JCAV

3.1426, Victoria, op. 109, 1978, A. L. de Almeida Prado, Soprano, —, m, JCAV

Villa-Lobos, Heitor, 1887–1959

3.1427, A cegonha, 1915, Aníbal Teófilo, $E\flat 4$–$F5$, —, —, AN, BN, EMB

3.1428, Amor y perfidia, 1918, Spanish song, $E4$–$A5$, —, —, AN, BN, +

3.1429, As filhas de Maria, 1926, Dante Milano, $E\flat 4$–$F5$, —, —, SMP, BN, Columbia University, +

3.1430, Ave Maria (no. 6), —, Sacred text, Latin, $F4$–$F5$, Medium voice, With organ or piano; originally for voice and string quartet, SA, AN, FB, +

3.1431, Ave Maria (19), —, Sacred text, Latin, $F4$–$F5$, High voice (soprano), With organ or piano, AN, SA, FB, +

3.1432, A virgem, 1913, Anthero de Quental, $B\flat 3$–$G5$, —, —, SA, MVL

3.1433, A voz do povo, Grito de guerra, 1942, Epaminondas Villalba Filho (Pen name of Heitor Villa-Lobos), $C4$–$G5$, —, —, m, MVL

3.1434, *Bachianas brasileiras, no. 5*

3.1434a, Aria (Cantilena), 1938, Ruth V. Corrêa, $E4$–$B\flat 5$, High, Reduction for soprano and piano by the composer; originally for soprano and 8 celli, ME, AMP, BN, MVL, EMB, +

3.1434b, Dansa (Martelo), 1945, Manuel Bandeira, $D4$–$A5$, High, Reduction for soprano and piano by the composer; riginally for soprano and 8 celli, ME, AMP, BN, MVL, EMB, +

3.1435, Big-Ben, 1948, E. Villalba Filho (HVL), $E\flat 4$–$G5$, —, —, SMP, Peer Musikverlag, Columbia University, +

3.1436, Canção árabe, 1914, Honório de Carvalho, —, —, —, AN, BN

3.1437, Canção das águas claras, 1956, Gilberto Amado, $C4$–$B5$, —, Originally for voice and orchestra; reduction for voice and piano by the composer, ME, +

3.1438, Canção de cristal, 1950, Murilo Araujo, $B3$–$G5$, —, —, ME, BN, UFMG, EMB, +

3.1439, Canção do poeta do século XVIII,

1918, Alfredo Ferreira, D4–F5, —, —, IV, SMP, BN, MVL, +

3.1440, Canção dos artistas, 1919, Raul Pederneiras, —, —, —, VV, —

3.1441, *Canções de cordialidade, no. 1*
3.1441a, 1. Feliz aniversário, 1945, Manuel Bandeira, —, —, —, m, BN
3.1441b, 2. Boas festas, 1945, Manuel Bandeira, —, —, —, m, BN
3.1441c, 3. Feliz Natal, 1945, Manuel Bandeira, —, —, —, m, BN
3.1441d, 4. Feliz Ano Novo, 1945, Manuel Bandeira, —, —, —, m, BN
3.1441e, 5. Boas vindas, 1945, Manuel Bandeira, —, —, —, m, BN

3.1442, *Canções indígenas*
3.1442a, 1. Pai do Mato (Native Indian text), —, Mário de Andrade, E4–F5, Medium voice, —, SMP, MVL, +
3.1442b, 2. Ualalocê (Parecis Legend), 1930, Indigenous words, —, —, —, m, BN, MVL
3.1442c, 3. Kamalô, 1930, Mário de Andrade and Native Indian texts, —, —, —, SMP, MVL

3.1443, *Canções típicas brasileiras (Chanson brésiliennes)*
3.1443a, 1. Mokocê-cê-maká, —, Indian lullaby song collected by E. Roquette Pinto, B3–G5, —, —, ME, BN, UFMG
3.1443b, 2. Nozani-ná, 1919, Indian theme collected by E. Roquette Pinto, E4–C5, —, —, ME, BN, UFMG
3.1443c, 3. Papae curumiassu, 1919, Popular song of Pará, G3–E5, —, —, ME, BN, UFMG
3.1443d, 4. Xangô, 1919, Afro-Brazilian text, G4–D5, —, —, ME, FBN/DIMAS, BN, UFMG
3.1443e, 5. Estrela é lua nova, 1919, Afro-Brazilian traditional text, D4–D5, —, —, ME, BN, MVL
3.1443f, 6. Viola quebrada, 1919, Mário de Andrade, E4–5, —, —, ME, BN
3.1443g, 7. Adeus Ema (Desafio), —, Popular theme from north of Minas Gerais, D4–E5, —, —, ME, BN
3.1443h, 8. Pálida Madona (Modinha antiga), 1919, Popular poem, C4–D5, —, —, ME, BN
3.1443i, 9. Tu passaste por este jardim, —, Catulo da Paixão Cearense, A3–F5, —, Harmonization of a theme by Alfredo Dutra, ME, BN
3.1443j, 10. Cabôca de Caxangá (Embolada from the north), 1919, Catulo da Paixão Cearense, —, —, Mixed voices, ME, MVL
3.1443k, 11. Pássaro fugitivo, 1935, Folklore collected by Severino Rangel, C4–E5, —, —, m, ME, BN
3.1443l, [12. Itabaiana]
3.1443m, 13. Onde o nosso amor nasceu, —, —, —, —, —, m, MVL

3.1444, Cascavel, 1917, Costa Rego Júnior, C♯4–F5, —, —, AN, BN, NYPL, +

3.1445, *Coleção brasileira*
3.1445a, 1. Tempos atrás, 1923, Godofredo da Silva Telles, A♭4–G, —, —, SA, BN
3.1445b, 2. Tristeza, 1923, Godofredo da Silva Telles, F♯4–G5, —, —, AN, FB, BN

3.1446, Confidência, 1908, Honório de Carvalho, E4–G5, —, —, AN, FB, BN
3.1447, Coração inquieto, 1948, Sylvio Moreaux, E4–D5, —, —, m, MVL
3.1448, Desejo, —, Guilherme de Almeida, —, —, —, AN, BN
3.1449, Dime perché, 1901, P. de Tasso, —, —, —, m, BN
3.1450, Dinga-donga, 1949, H. Villa-Lobos, F4–G5, —, —, IV, SMP, MVL, +

3.1451, *Duas paisagens (Deux paysages)*
3.1451a, 1. Manhã na praia, 1946, Carlos Sá, E4–G5, —, —, ME, BN
3.1451b, 2. Tarde na glória, 1946, Carlos Sá, E4–G5, —, —, ME, BN

3.1452, *Epigramas irônicos e sentimentais*
3.1452a, 1. Eis a vida, 1921, Ronald de Carvalho, E4–F♯5, —, —, SA, AN, FB, BN

3.1452b, 2. Inútil epigrama, 1921, Ronald de Carvalho, F♭4–F5, —, —, SA, AN, FB, BN

3.1452c, 3. Sonho de uma noite de verão, 1921, Ronald de Carvalho, —, Medium voice, —, SA, AN, FB, BN, +

3.1452d, 4. Epigrama, 1921, Ronald de Carvalho, F♭4–F5, —, —, SA, BN

3.1452e, 5. Perversidade, 1921, Ronald de Carvalho, D4–C5, —, —, SA, AN, FB, BN, +

3.1452f, 6. Pudor, 1921, Ronald de Carvalho, G4–E5, —, —, SA, BN, +

3.1452g, 7. Imagem, 1921, Ronald de Carvalho, E♭4–D♭5, —, —, SA, AN, FB, BN

3.1452h, 8. Verdade, 1921, Ronald de Carvalho, G4–E5, —, —, SA, FB, BN, +

3.1453, Eu te amo, 1956, Dora Vasconcellos, D♯4–A5, —, Reduction for voice and piano by the composer; originally for voice and orchestra, ME, BN, MVL, +

3.1454, Festim pagão, 1919, Ronald de Carvalho, E4–F♯5, —, —, SA, AN, FB, BN

3.1455, Fleur fanée, op. 18, 1913, A. Gallay, A♯3–F5, —, —, AN, BN, NYPL, +

3.1456, *Forest of the Amazon/Canções da floresta do Amazonas* (Excerpt)/Green Mansion

3.1456a, Canção do amor, 1958, Dora Vasconcellos, B3–A5, —, Reduction for voice and piano by the composer; originally for voice and orchestra, m, BN, MVL, +

3.1456b, Melodia sentimental, 1958, Dora Vasconcellos, B3–A5, —, Reduction for voice and piano by the composer; originally for voice and orchestra, FBN/DIMAS, BN, MVL, +

3.1456c, Tarde azul, 1958, Dora Vasconcellos, E4–G5, —, Reduction for voice and piano by the composer; originally for voice and orchestra, m, MVL

3.1456d, Veleiros, 1958, Dora Vasconcellos, B3–E5, —, Reduction for voice and piano by the composer; originally for voice and orchestra, m, BN, MVL, +

3.1456e, Cair da tarde, 1958, Dora Vasconcellos, —, Soprano, Reduction for voice and piano by the composer; originally for voice and orchestra, FBN/DIMAS, BN, MVL, +

3.1457, *Historietas*

3.1457a, 1. Solidão, 1920, Ribeiro Couto, E4–F♯5, High voice, Portuguese text, MMP, CM, AN, FB, BN, +

3.1457b, 2. Lune d'octobre, 1920, —, E4–E5, High voice, French text, MMP, CM, BN, +

3.1457c, 2.b O novelozinho de linha, 1920, —, E4–F5, High voice, Portuguese text, MMP, CM, AN, FB, BN, +

3.1457d, 3. Le petit peloton de fil, —, —, —, High voice, French text, MMP, +

3.1457e, 4. Hermione et les bergers, 1920, Albert Samain, D4–G5, High voice, French text, MMP, CM, NA, FB, BN, +

3.1457f, 5. Jous sans retard, car vite s'écoule la vie, —, —, —, High voice, French text, MMP, +

3.1457g, 6. Le marché, —, —, —, High voice, French text, MMP, +

3.1458, Il nome di Maria, 1915, Lorenzo Stechetti, B2–E4, —, —, AN, SA, FB, BN

3.1459, Jardim fanado, 1955, Amarylio Albuquerque, —, Soprano, —, ME, +

3.1460, Les mères, op. 45, 1914, Victor Hugo, C4–E♯5, —, —, AN, FB, BN, +

3.1461, Louco, 1913, J. Cadilhe, A3–F5, —, —, —, BN

3.1462, *Magdalena: A Musical Adventure*

3.1462a, 1. My Bus and I, 1947, Robert Wright and George Forrest, C4–F5, —, —, AN, VLM, BN, MVL

3.1462b, 2. The Emerald Song, 1947, George Forrest and Robert Wright, B3–G5, —, —, VLM, BN, MVL

3.1462c, 3. Bonsoir, Paris!, 1948, Robert Wright and George Forrest, F4–G5, —, —, VLM, MVL

3.1462d, 4. Food for Thought, 1947, George

Forrest and Robert Wright, C_4–G_5, —, —, VLM, MVL

3.1462e, 5. Magdalena, 1947, George Forrest and Robert Wright, $E\flat_4$–$E\flat_5$, —, —, AN, VLM, BN, MVL

3.1462f, 6. The Singing Tree, 1947, George Forrest and Robert Wright, D_4–F_5, —, —, VLM, MVL

3.1462g, 7. Scène de Paris, 1947, George Forrest and Robert Wright, —, —, —, AN, VLM, BN, MVL

3.1463, Mal secreto, 1912, Raimundo Correa, B_3–F_5, —, —, AN, FB, BN, +

3.1464, *Miniaturas*

3.1464a, 1. Cromo no. 2, 1916, B. Lopes, —, —, —, AN, —

3.1464b, 2. A viola, 1916, Sílvio Romero, E_4–F_5, —, —, AN, +

3.1464c, 3. Cromo no. 3, 1916, Abilio Barreto, —, —, —, AN, —

3.1464d, 4. Sonho, —, A. Guimarães, —, —, —, AN, —

3.1464e, 5. Japonesas, 1912, Luiz Guimarães Filho, F_4–G_5, —, —, AN, FB, +

3.1464f, 6. Sino da aldeia, —, Antonio Maria C. de Oliveira, —, —, —, —, +

3.1465, *Modinhas e canções, Album I*

3.1465a, 1. Canção do marinheiro, 1936, Gil Vicente, E_4–B_5, High voice, —, MMP, AN, IV, BN, MVL, +

3.1465b, 2. Lundu da Marquesa de Santos, 1938, Viriato Corrêa, F_4–B_5, High voice, —, MMP, AN, ME, IV, BN, MVL, +

3.1465c, 3. Cantilena, 1938, Folklore collected by Sodré Viana, —, High voice, —, MMP, AN, ME, IV, BN, +

3.1465d, 4. A gatinha parda, 1938, Children's theme from the nineteenth century, $E\flat_4$–C_5, High voice, —, MMP, AN, ME, IV, BN, UFMG, +

3.1465e, 5. Remeiro de S. Francisco, 1941, Folklore from St. Francis River in Bahia, collected by Sodré Viana, F_4–F_5, —, Harmonization, ME, IV, BN, MVL

3.1465f, 6. Nhapopé, 1933, Popular text, $C\sharp_4$–B_4, High voice, —, MMP, AN, ME, IV, BN, MVL, +

3.1465g, 7. Evocação, 1933, Sylvio Salema, D_4–$A\flat_5$, High voice, —, MMP, AN, ME, IV, BN, MVL, +

3.1466, *Modinhas e canções, Album II*

3.1466a, 1. O pobre peregrino, 1943, Popular text collected by E. Villalba-Filho (HVL), E_4–E_5, —, —, ME, BN

3.1466b, 2. Vida formosa, 1943, Popular text, D_4–A_5, —, —, ME, BN

3.1466c, 3. Nesta rua, 1943, Folklore, E_4–A_5, —, —, ME, BN

3.1466d, 4. Mando tiro, tiro lá, 1943, Popular Text, G_4–G_5, —, —, ME, BN

3.1466e, 5. João cambuête, 1943, Popular text, E_4–E_5, —, —, ME, BN

3.1466f, 6. Na corda da viola, 1943, Folklore, E_4–A_5, —, —, ME, BN

3.1467, Noite de luar, 1912, Baptista Junior, G_4–F_5, —, —, SA, FB, BN, +

3.1468, Oiseau blessé d'une flèche, op. 10, 1913, La Fontaine, C_4–E_5, —, —, AN, FB, BN, +

3.1469, Poema de Itabira, 1943, Carlos Drummond de Andrade, A_3–G_5, —, Reduction for voice and piano; originally for voice and orchestra, ME, BN, +

3.1470, Poème de l'enfant et de sa mère, 1923, E. Villalba Filho (HVL), —, —, Reduction for voice and piano, ME, BN, +

3.1471, Poema de palavras, 1957, Dora Vasconcellos, D_4–A_5, —, Reduction for voice and piano; originally for voice and orchestra, ME, BN, +

3.1472, Samba clássico, 1950, E. Villalba Filho (HVL), E_4–G_5, —, Reduction for voice and piano; originally for voice and orchestra, ME, BN, +

3.1473, *Serestas*

3.1473a, 1. Pobre cega, 1926, Álvaro Moreira, D_4–D_5, Medium voice, —, AN, FB, MMP, BN, UFMG, +

3.1473b, 2. Anjo da guarda, 1926, Manuel

Bandeira, E4–E5, Medium voice, —, AN, FB, MMP, BN, UFMG, +

3.1473c, 3. Canção da folha morta, 1926, Olegário Mariano, E4–F5, Medium voice, —, AN, FB, MMP, BN, UFMG, +

3.1473d, 4. Saudade da minha vida, 1926, Dante Milano, F#4–F5, Medium voice, —, AN, FB, MMP, BN, +

3.1473e, 5. Modinha, 1926, Manduca Piá (Pen name of Manuel Bandeira), C#4–F5, Medium voice, —, AN, FB, MMP, BN, UFMG, +

3.1473f, 6. Na paz do outono, 1925, Ronald de Carvalho, D4–E5, Medium voice, —, AN, FB, MMP, BN, UFMG, +

3.1473g, 7. Cantiga do viúvo, 1926, Carlos Drummond de Andrade, F4–G5, Medium voice, —, AN, FB, MMP, BN, UFMG, +

3.1473h, 8. Canção do carreiro, 1926, Ribeiro Couto, E4–F5, Medium voice, —, AN, FB, MMP, BN, +

3.1473i, 9. Abril, 1926, Ribeiro Couto, E4–F#5, Medium voice, —, AN, MMP, BN, +

3.1473j, 10. Desejo, —, —, —, Medium voice, —, MMP, +

3.1473k, 11. Redondilha, 1926, Dante Milano, C4–E5, Medium voice, —, AN, FB, MMP, BN, UFMG, +

3.1473l, 12. Realejo, 1926, Medium voice, E4–D5, —, —, AN, FB, MMP, BN, UFMG, +

3.1473m, 13. Serenata, 1943, David Nasser, D4–G♭5, Medium voice, —, MMP, ME, MVL, +

3.1473n, 14. Vôo, —, Abgar Renault, —, Medium voice, —, MMP, AN, ME, BN, +

3.1474, Sertão no estio (Cantico brasileiro), 1919, Arthur Lemos, E4–A5, Medium voice, —, AN, FB, MVL, +

3.1475, Sete vezes, 1958, Dora Vasconcellos, F4–A5, —, Reduction for voice and piano; Originally for voice and orchestra, ME, CEMB, +

3.1476, *Três poemas indígenas*

3.1476a, Canide ioune-sabath-Ave Amarela, 1926, After an Indian theme collected by Jean de Léry in 1553, D4–A4, —, —, ME, +

3.1476b, Teirú, 1926, Indian theme collected by Roquette Pinto, B3–G5, —, —, ME, MVL, +

3.1476c, Iara, 1926, Mário de Andrade, D4–G♭5, —, —, ME, MVL, +

3.1477, Vira, 1926, Portuguese popular text, E♭4–G5, —, —, ME, MVL, Columbia University, +

3.1478, Vocalise, —, Alphonse Leduc, B3–G#5, —, —, —, MVL

Villani-Côrtes, Edmundo, 1930–

3.1479, Alma da natureza, 1991, Júlio Bellodi, D4–A5/ B3–F#5, —, —, m, UFMG

3.1480, A saudade, 1961, Geralda Armond, —, —, —, m, USP/V-C

3.1481, Ave Maria, 1996, Latin text, D4–F5, —, —, m, USP/V-C

3.1482, Baile imaginário, 1990, Júlio Bellodi, C#4–G5, —, —, m, USP/V-C

3.1483, Balada dos 15, 1988, Júlio Bellodi, —, —, —, m, USP/V-C

3.1484, Canção da indiazinha, 1987, Cecília Meirelles, C#4–E5, —, —, m, USP/V-C

3.1485, Canção da menina triste, 1963, E. Villani-Cortes, —, —, —, m, USP/V-C

3.1486, Canção de Carolina, 1990, Júlio Bellodi, B♭3–F5, —, —, m, USP/V-C

3.1487, Casulo, 1992, Júlio Bellodi, C4–E♭5, —, —, m, USP/V-C

3.1488, Choro urbano, 1979, Júlio Bellodi, C4–G♭5, —, —, m, USP/V-C

3.1489, *Ciclo Cecília Meireles*

3.1489a, 1. Cântico XXV, 1987, Cecília Meirelles, D♭4–E5, —, —, m, USP/V-C

3.1489b, 2. Do caçador feliz, —, Cecília Meirelles, —, —, —, m, USP/V-C

3.1489c, 3. Imaginário serenata, —, Cecília Meirelles, —, —, —, m, USP/V-C

3.1489d, 4. Da música de Maria Ifigênia, 1987, Cecília Meirelles, D4–G5, —, —, m, USP/V-C

3.1489e, 5. Motivo, —, Cecília Meirelles, —, —, —, m, USP/V-C

3.1490, Confissão, 1979, E. Villani-Cortes, —, —, —, m, USP/V-C

3.1491, Confissões, 1982, Laerte Freire, D4–G5, —, —, m, UFMG, USP

3.1492, Desalento, 1967, Laerte Ferreira, —, —, —, m, UFMG

3.1493, Do caçador feliz, 1987, Cecília Meirelles, D4–F5, —, —, m, USP/V-C

3.1494, Em cantos do Brasil, 1993, Júlio Bellodi, —, —, —, m, USP/V-C

3.1495, Encontro, —, Edmundo Villani-Côrtes, —, —, —, m, USP/V-C

3.1496, Espelhos, 2004, Mônica Côrtes, A3–D5, —, —, m, USP/V-C

3.1497, Eterna música, 1991, Júlio Bellodi, D4–B♭5, —, —, m, USP/V-C

3.1498, Fonte eterna, 1975, Laerte Freire, D4–A♭5, —, —, m, USP/V-C

3.1499, Imaginária serenata, 1987, Cecília Meirelles, D4–G5, —, —, m, USP/V-C

3.1500, Minha saudade, 2003, Lula Côrtes, —, —, —, m, USP/V-C

3.1501, Modinha da moça de antes, 1994, Luciano Garcez, D♯4–G5, —, —, m, USP/V-C

3.1502, Motivo, 1985, Cecília Meirelles, C♯4–G♯5, —, —, m, USP/V-C

3.1503, Não viveu quem não ficou, 1999, —, —, —, —, m, USP/V-C

3.1504, Na sua ausência, 1979, E. Villani-Cortes, —, —, —, m, USP/V-C

3.1505, Oferenda, 1999, João da Cruz, C♯4–D♯5, —, —, m, UFMG, USP/V-C

3.1506, Olá, 1979, E. Villani-Côrtes, —, —, —, m, —

3.1507, O laço, 1979, E. Villani-Côrtes, —, —, —, m, USP/V-C

3.1508, O passarinho da praça da matriz, 1994, E. Villani-Cortes, D4–A♭5/ A♯2–E4, Soprano/Baritone, —, m, UFMG, USP/V-C

3.1509, O tesouro, 1980, E. Villani-Cortes, —, —, —, m, USP/V-C

3.1510, Papagaio azul, 1961, E. Villani-Cortes, D4–F♯5, —, —, m, UFMG, USP/V-C

3.1511, Para você, por mim, 2004, Itagiba Kuhlmann, —, —, —, m, USP/V-C

3.1512, Poema, 1962, Affonso Romano de Sant'Anna, D♭4–A5, —, —, m, USP/V-C

3.1513, Praia dos encantos, 1980, E. Villani-Côrtes, —, —, —, m, USP/V-C

3.1514, Prefiro, 2002, Itagiba Kuhlmann, D4–E♭5, —, —, m, USP/V-C

3.1515, *Prelúdio das cinco miniaturas brasileiras*

3.1515a, Para sempre, 1998, E. Villani-Cortes, C4–G5, —, Original theme, m, USP/V-C

3.1516, Presente, 1990, Júlio Bellodi, —, —, —, m, USP/V-C

3.1517, Quando eu morrer, 1993, Mário de Andrade, D4–E5, —, —, m, UFMG, USP

3.1518, Renascença, 1979, E. Villani-Cortes, D4–G5, —, —, m, UFMG, USP

3.1519, Restituo estas chaves, 2002, Carlos Drummond de Andrade, G3–D5, —, —, m, USP/V-C

3.1520, Retrato da alma, 2001, Mônica Côrtes, B3–E5, —, —, m, USP/V-C

3.1521, Rio de ternura, —, E. Villani-Cortes, —, —, —, m, USP/V-C

3.1522, Rua aurora, 1993, Mário de Andrade, C4–F5, —, —, m, UFMG, USP

3.1523, São Paulo, 1995, Júlio Bellodi, G♯3–E♭5, —, —, m, USP/V-C

3.1524, Saudade, 1963, E. Villani-Cortes, —, —, —, m, USP/V-C

3.1525, Sem nome, 2002, Mônica Côrtes, G3–E♭5, —, —, m, USP/V-C

3.1526, Se procurar bem, 2002, Carlos Drummond de Andrade, B3–E♭5, —, —, m, USP/V-C

3.1527, Sequência, 1991, Marília Freidenson, B3–G5, —, —, m, UFMG, USP

3.1528, Seu olhar, 1956, E. Villani-Cortes, —, —, —, m, USP/V-C

3.1529, Sina de cantador, 1990, Júlio Bellodi, C4–E5/C♯4–B♭5, —, —, m, USP/V-C

3.1530, Só o amor ficou, 1962, E. Villani-Cortes, —, —, —, m, USP/V-C

3.1531, Só sim, 1980, E. Villani-Côrtes, —, —, —, m, USP/V-C

3.1532, Tuas mãos, 1957, Unknown, —, —, —, m, USP/V-C

3.1533, Uma estrela brilhou, 1964–1966, —, —, —, —, m, USP/V-C

3.1534, Valsinha de roda, 1979, E. Villani-Cortes, B3–F5, —, —, m, UFMG, USP

3.1535, Vento serrano, 2000, Francisco Moura Campos, D4–B♭5, —, —, m, USP/V-C

3.1536, Vocalise, 1978, No text, E4–A♯5, —, —, m, UFMG, USP

3.1537, Você, 1958, E. Villani-Côrtes, —, —, —, m, USP/V-C

3.1538, Você não sabe, 2002, Curt Côrtes, —, —, —, m, USP/V-C

3.1539, Volta, 1979, E. Villani-Cortes, —, —, —, m, USP/V-C

Widmer, Ernst, 1927–1990

3.1540, *Cinco canções*. op. 124

3.1540a, Entre-estrelas, 1980, Antonio Brasileiro, Soprano, m, —, EWG

3.1540b, Viola do Amor, 1980, Antonio Brasileiro, Soprano, m, —, EWG

3.1540c, Cidade, 1980, Fernando da Rocha Peres, Soprano, m, —, EWG

3.1540d, Meu povo, meu poema, 1980, Ferreira Gullar, Soprano, m, —, EWG

3.1540e, Proposição, 1980, J. C. Teixeira Gomes, Soprano, m, —, EWG

3.1541, *Dezesseis melodias do passado com acompanhamento novo, First album*

3.1541a, 1. Araponga errante, 1986–1987, Castro Alves, High, m, —, EWG

3.1541b, 2. Garça parda leviana, 1986–1987, Folklore, High, m, —, EWG

3.1541c, 3. Ô viageiro, 1986–1987, Folklore, High, m, —, EWG

3.1541d, 4. Na beira da praia, 1986–1987, Folklore, High, m, —, EWG

3.1541e, 5. Bendito, 1986–1987, Folklore, High, m, —, EWG

3.1541f, 6. Ô seu marinheiro, 1986–1987, Folklore, High, m, —, EWG

3.1541g, 7. Da pinheira nasce a pinha, 1986–1987, Folklore, High, m, —, EWG

[7a. Interlúdio for solo piano]

3.1541h, 8. As duas flores, 1986–1987, Castro Alves, High, m, —, EWG

3.1541i, 9. Se eu fora poeta, 1986–1987, Folklore, High, m, —, EWG

3.1541j, 10. Na praia deserta, 1986, Folklore, High, m, —, EWG

3.1541k, 11. Amanhã (first version), 1986–1987, Gonçalves Dias, High, —, —, EWG

3.1541l, 12. Amanhã (second version), 1986–1987, Gonçalves Dias, High, m, —, EWG

3.1541m, 13. As saudades do meu bem, 1986–1987, Folklore, High, m, —, EWG

3.1541n, 14. Courana, 1986–1987, Folklore, High, m, —, EWG

3.1541o, 15. Qual quebra, 1986–1987, Folklore, High, m, —, EWG

3.1541p, 16. Linda entre mil, 1986–1987, Folklore, High, m, —, EWG

3.1542, *Dezesseis melodias do passado com acompanhamento novo, Second Album*

3.1542a, 1. As duas flores (Modinha), 1986–1987, Castro Alves, High, m, —, EWG

3.1542b, 2. Morena, morena (Modinha), 1986–1987, Folklore, High, m, —, EWG

3.1542c, 3. Sonhei, 1986–1987, Folklore, High, m, —, EWG

3.1542d, 4. As saudades do meu bem, 1986–1987, Folklore, High, m, —, EWG

3.1542e, 5. Eu sou como a garça triste, 1986–1987, —, High, m, —, EWG

3.1542f, 6. Frio manto de estrelas bordado, 1986–1987, Folklore, High, m, —, EWG

3.1542g, 7. Courana, 1986–1987, Folklore, High, m, —, EWG

3.1542h, 8. Se eu fora poeta, 1986–1987, Folklore, High, m, —, EWG

3.1542i, 9. Amanhã, 1986–1987, Gonçalves Dias, High, m, —, EWG

3.1543, *Dos muchachas, op. 13*

3.1543a, La Lola, op. 13, no. 1, 1955, Federico García Lorca, High, m, —, EWG

3.1543b, Amparo, op. 13, no. 2, 1955, Federico García Lorca, High, m, —, EWG

3.1544, Europa, França e Bahia, 1967, Gastão Neves, Soprano, m, —, EWG

3.1545, Incerto nexo, op. 86, 1975, Fernando Pessoa, Med, m, —, EWG

3.1546, *Quatro canções sobre poemas brasileiros para voz aguda e piano*
3.1546a, 1. Se eu me sentasse agora, 1960, Júlia Santos, High, Soprano or Tenor, m, —, EWG
3.1546b, 2. Eu diferente da vida, 1960, Júlia Santos, High, Soprano or Tenor, m, —, EWG
3.1546c, 3. A moça e o Trem, 1960, João Cabral de Melo Neto, High, Soprano or Tenor, m, —, EWG
3.1546d, 4. Variações sem tema, 1960, João Cabral de Melo Neto, High, Soprano or Tenor, —, —, EWG

3.1547, Tiradentes, 1989, Dantas Motta, Baritone, m (incomplete), —, EWG

3.1548, *Três ciclos de quatro canções, op. 32, I*
3.1548a, 1. A criança, 1964, Fernando Pessoa, High, Soprano or Tenor, m, —, EWG
3.1548b, 2. Cantiga, 1964, Manuel Bandeira, High, Soprano or Tenor, m, —, EWG
3.1548c, 3. A imagem e a realidade, 1964, Manuel Bandeira, High, Soprano or Tenor, m, —, EWG
3.1548d, 4. A um passarinho, 1964, Vinicius de Moraes, High, Soprano or Tenor, m, —, EWG

3.1549, *Três ciclos de quatro canções, op. 32, II*
3.1549a, 1. Anedota Búlgara, 1964, Carlos Drummond de Andrade, Med-low, m, P. Bastianelli, —, EWG
3.1549b, 2. Massacre, 1964, Carlos Drummond de Andrade, Med-low, Contralto or Baritone, m, P. Bastianelli, —, EWG
3.1549c, 3. Poético, 1964, Vinicius de Moraes, Med-low, Contralto or Baritone, m, P. Bastianelli, —, EWG
3.1549d, 4. Lenta, descansa, 1964, Fernando Pessoa, Med-low, Contralto or Baritone, m, P. Bastianelli, —, EWG

3.1550, *Três ciclos de quatro canções, op. 32, III*
3.1550a, 1. Cidadezinha qualquer, 1964, Carlos Drummond de Andrade, High, Soprano or Tenor, m, *Art, Revista da Escola de Música e Artes Cênicas*, EWG
3.1550b, 2. No meio do caminho, 1964, Carlos Drummond de Andrade, High, Soprano or Tenor, m, —, EWG
3.1550c, 3. Festa no brejo, 1964, Carlos Drummond de Andrade, High, Soprano or Tenor, m, —, EWG
3.1550d, 4. Toada do amor, 1964, —, Soprano or Tenor, —, —

3.1551, Triptico para os oitenta anos de C. D. A. [Carlos Drummond de Andrade], op. 137, 1982, Carlos Drummond de Andrade, —, FUNARTE/UFBA, —, EWG

PUBLISHERS

A. Di Franco
A. Melodia
AMP, Associated Music Publishers, Inc.
AN, Artur Napoleão
Bandeirante, Bandeirante Editora Musical
B/Cia, Viuva Bevilacqua & Cia
Campassi & Camin
Castro Lima, Castro Lima & C
CEMB, Casas Editoras Musicais Brasileiras Reunidas
Chiarato, S. Chiarato
CM, Casa Mozart
CMP, Consolidated Music Publishers
CO, Casa Oliveira
Cooperativa, Cooperativa Ed. Dos Compositores e Músicos Profissionais
CVG, Casa Viúva Guerreiro/Ed. E.A. Viúva Guereiro & Cia
CW, Carlos Wehrs & Cia
CWag, Casa Wagner
Derosa
DNIC, Departamento Nacional da Indústria e Comércio
EBMMC, Edwin B. Marks Music Corp.
EBMP, Editorial Brasileira de Música Popular
ECA/USP, (see under Collections, this chapter)

ECIC, Editorial Cooperativa Inter-Americana de Compositores
Edições Associação Rio Grandense de Música
Edition Modern
EDM, Edição de Musica
EM, Editorial Mangione S.A.
EMNB, Editora Música Nova do Brasil
EMV, Edição Música Viva
ESAV, Edition Savart
FB, Fermata do Brasil
FBN/DIMAS, Fundação Biblioteca Nacional
FCGo, Fundação Carlos Gomes
Forlivesi, A. Forlivesi, G. C. Edizioni Musicali
FUNARJ, Fundação Nacional das Artes
FUNARTE, Fundação Nacional de Artes
Goldberg, Goldberg Edições Musicais
GRic, G. Ricordi
Guanabara, Musicais Guanabara
HC, H. de Curitiba
HC/UFPR, H. de Curitiba for UFPR (see under Collections, this chapter)
IML, Ed. Impressora Moderna Ltda
Irmãos Chiarato
IV, Irmãos Vitale & Cia
JLS, J.L. Siqueiria-Liuros Didácticoas e Músicas
L.G. Miranda
Lino José Barbosa
LK Produções Artísticas
LMT, Ed. Litero Musical Tupy Ltda
m, manuscript
Manuel Antônio Guimarães
Marajoara, Edições Musicais Marajoara
ME, Éditions Max Eschig
MMP, Ludwig Masters Music Publications
Moreira de Sá
MPA, Movimento
Music Press
Musicália, Musicália/A Cultura Musical
Novas Metas
Paulo Florence
P. Bastianelli, Piero Bastianelli
Peer Musikverlag, Peermusic Classical GmBH
Phonoart
PI, Peer International Corporation
Pizzi, Pizzi e C.
RA, Ricordi Americana, S.A.E.C.
RB, Ricordi Brasileira
RJ, Rio de Janeiro (place of publication)
RM, Ricordi Milano
SA, Sampaio Araujo & Cia
SAI, Sociedade Artistica Internacional
SEML, Sistrum Edições Musicais Ltda
Seresta, Seresta Edições Musicais
SMP, Southern Music Publishing, Inc.
SP, São Paulo (place of publication)
TMV, Tonos Musik Verlag
TR, Tritó, S.L.
UFBA, Universidade Federal da Bahia
UFPA, Universidad Federal do Pará
USP, Editora da Universidade de São Paulo
USP/SDP, USP Serviço de Difusão de Partituras
Vieira Brandão
VLM, Villa-Lobos Music Corporation
VM, Vieira Machado & Cia
VV, Vicente Vitale

COLLECTIONS

ACCS, Associação cultural Claudio Santoro, www.claudiosantoro.art.br/Santoro/accs.html (accessed 10 March 2007).
BDB, Biblioteca Demonstrativa de Brasília (Brasilia Demonstrative Library)
BN, Fundação Biblioteca Nacional (the National Library) is the official library of Brazil. Also the oldest library in Brazil, it is located in Rio de Janeiro and is the receptor and registrar of all copyrights in the country. DIMAS (Divisão de Música e Arquivo Sonoro) is responsible for the musical archives.
Columbia University, The Gabe M. Weiner Music and Arts Library, Columbia University, New York, New York
ECA/USP, Escola de Comunicação e Artes da Universidade de São Paulo (School of Arts and Communication, University of São Paulo)

EMB, Escola de Música de Brasília (Music School of Brasília)

EMPEM, Escola Municipal de Música de Piracicaba (City Music School of Piracicaba), São Paulo State, www.empem.org.br (accessed 10 March 2007)

EWG, Ernst Widmer Gesellschaft, Postfach 2638 CH 5001 Aarau, Tel ++0041 (0) 62-822 40 52, Fax 0041 (0) 62-827 12 72, Email mail@ernstwidmer.ch

JA, Works by Jorge Antunes are available directly through the composer, Email antunes@unb.br.

JCAV, Works by José Carlos do Amaral Vieira are available directly through the composer, Email amvieira@netpoint.com.br, or through Ponteio Publishing, Inc., http://www.ponteio.com (accessed 10 March 2007)

OL, Works by Osvaldo Lacerda are also available through http://www.correiomusical.com.br (accessed 10 March 2007).

MVL, Museo Villa-Lobos, Rua Soracaba 200, Botafogo-Rio di Janeiro, R.J., CEP 22271-110-Brasil, Tel/Fax 55-21 2266.1024/3894/3845

NYPL, New York Public Library for the Performing Arts, New York, New York.

OMB, Ordem Dos Músicos do Brasil, Secretaria de Edução e Cultura (Secretary of Education and Culture, State of Rio de Janeiro)

Secretaria de Educação e Cultura, Secretaria de Educação e Cultura (Secretary for Education and Culture, State of Rio de Janeiro)

UEMG, Universidade do Estado de Minas Gerais (State University of Minas Gerais), Belo Horizonte, Brazil

UFBA, Universidade Federal da Bahia (Federal University of the State of Bahia), Salvador, Brazil

UFMG, Universidade Federal de Minas Gerais (Federal University of Minas Gerais), Belo Horizonte, Brazil (UFMG hosts the online resource *Guia da canções brasileiras,* the fundamental source for this chapter's catalog).

UFPA, Universidade Federal do Pará (Federal University of the State of Pará), Belém, Brazil

UFPR, Universidade do Paraná (Federal University of the State of Paraná), Curitiba, Brazil

UFRGS, Universidade Federal do Rio Grande do Sul (Federal University of Rio Grande do Sul), Porto Alegre, Brazil

UFRJ, Universidade Federal do Rio de Janeiro, Rio de Janeiro, Brazil

UnB, Universidade de Brasília (Federal University of Brasilia), located in the federal capital, Brasilia, DF

UNESP, Universidade Estadual de São Paulo (State University of São Paulo), São Paulo, Brazil

UNICAMP, Universidade Estadual de Campinas (City University of Campinas), São Paulo State, Centro de Documentação de Música Contemporânea, Coleção Almedio Prado (Center for Documentation of Contemporary Music, Almeido Prado Collection)

USP, Universidade de São Paulo (City University of São Paulo), São Paulo, São Paulo

USP/V-C, The music of Edmundo Villani-Côrtes, Professor of Composition at the University of São Paulo (USP), is available directly through the composer, http://www.villani-cortes.tom.mus.br (accessed 10 March 2007).

+, LAMC (Latin American Music Center), Indiana University

SOURCES

(See main bibliography for publication information)

Art, Revista da Escola de Música e Artes Cênicas 15 (April 1987): 77–80

Borghoff and Castro, *Guia da canções brasileiras* (online resource)

Caicedo, *The Latin American Art Song: A Critical Anthology and Interpretive Guide for Singers*

Mariz, *A canção brasileira de câmera*

Viva Música!

ADDITIONAL BIBLIOGRAPHY

Antunes, Jorge. Interview by Stela M. Brandão via email communication. University of Brasília (UnB), Brasília, DF, Brazil, 4 November, 2006.

——. *Jorge Antunes: Catálogo de obras*. SISTRUM Edições Músicais, 1976.

Araujo, Mozart de. *A modinha e o lundu no século XVIII*. São Paulo: Ricordi Brasileira, 1963.

Béhague, Gerard. *Heitor Villa-Lobos: The Search for Brazil's Soul*. Institute of Latin American Studies, University of Texas at Austin, 1993.

Brandão, Stela Maria Santos. Collection of Brazilian Art Songs, Scores. New York, New York, 2007.

Carvalho, Flávio de. *Canções de Dinorá de Carvalho: Uma análise interpretativa*. Campinas, São Paulo: Editora da Unicamp, 2001.

Corrêa, Sérgio Nepomuceno Alvim. *Alberto Nepomuceno: Catálogo geral*. Rio de Janeiro: FUNARTE/Instituto Nacional de Música/Projeto Memória Musical Brasileira, 1985.

——. *Lorenzo Fernandez: Catálogo geral*. Rio de Janeiro: RIOARTE, 1992.

Filho, Claver. *Waldemar Henrique: O canto da Amazônia*. Rio de Janeiro: FUNARTE, 1978.

Itaú Cultural Institute "Panorama, Poesia e Crônica." 2007. http://www.itaucultural.org.br, accessed 3 March 2007.

Kiefer, Bruno. *Música e dança popula: Sua influência na música erudita*. Porto Alegre: Movimento, 1990.

Lacerda, Osvaldo. Program notes to *Ouvindo Osvaldo Lacerda* (compact disc). Performed by Eudóxia De Barros, Denise De Freitas, Sávio Sperandio, and Mario Balzi. [São Paulo]: Academia Brasileira de Música. ABM Digital Recording, 2003.

Marcondes, Marcos A. *Enciclopédia da música brasileira: Popular, erudita e folclórica*. 2nd. ed. São Paulo: Art Editora: Publifolha, 1998.

Mariz, Vasco. *Cláudio Santoro*. Rio de Janeiro: Editora Civilização Brasileira S.A., 1994.

——. *Francisco Mignone: O homem e a obra*. Rio de Janeiro, R.J.: FUNARTE, Editora da Universidade do Rio de Janeiro, 1997.

Museu Villa-Lobos. *Villa-Lobos, sua obra*, 3rd ed. Rio de Janeiro, 1989.

Nobre, Marlos. *Marlos Nobre*. http://marlosnobre.sites.uol.com.br, accessed 3 March 2007.

Nogueira, Ilza. Interview by Stela M. Brandão via email communication on the works of Ernst Widmer. University of Paraiba, Brazil, 25 January 2007.

Pereira, José Ricardo. Interview by Stela M. Brandão via email communication on the works of Ernani Braga. Northern University of Arizona, Flagstaff, Arizona, 20 February 2007.

Pignatari, Dante, ed. *Alberto Nepomuceno: Canções para voz e piano*. São Paulo, S.P.: Editora da Universidade de São Paulo, 2004.

Pimenta, Altino Rosauro Salazar. *Altino Pimenta: Composições para canto e piano*. Belém: Editora Universitária, Universidade Federal do Pará, 1994.

Pinto, Maria Sylvia. *A Canção brasileira: Da modinha à canção de câmara*. Rio de Janeiro: Companhia Brasileira de Artes Gráficas, 1985.

Prado, Almeida. Program notes to *Canções de Almeida Prado* (compact disc). Performed by Victoria Kerbauy, soprano and Almeida Prado, piano. Marcelo Spínola, producer. [São Paulo]: Spy Artes Digitais, ca. 2004.

Salles, Vicente, Augusto Teixeira, Felipe Andrade Silva, and Jorge Santos Souza. *Waldemar Henrique: Canções*. Belém: Secretaria de Estado da Educação, Fundação Carlos Gomes, 1996.

Santoro, Gisèle, and Raffaello Santoro. *Associação Cultural Claudio Santoro*. 2007. http://www.claudiosantoro.art.br/Santoro/accs.html, accessed 3 March 2007.

Silva, Luciano Simões. Interview by Stela M. Brandão via email communication on the works of Edmundo Villani-Côrtes. Toronto, Canada, 13 November, 2006.

Verhaalen, Marion. *Camargo Guarnieri: Expressões de uma vida*. Translated by Vera Silvia Camargo Guarnieri. São Paulo: Editora da Universidade de São Paulo/Imprensa Oficial, 2001.

4

Chile

The same trends appear in Chilean music as in Bolivian music: folk and European influences, and later, contemporary tendencies—all of which combine to create a rich body of colorful and diverse music. The *Revista musical chilena*, a musicological journal devoted entirely to Chile, is probably the most current source of information on this body of work.[1]

Gerard Béhague writes that nationalism has met with some skepticism from Chilean composers, most notably Domingo Santa Cruz (1899–1977), perhaps due to the fact that the Chilean people do not feel as connected to folk and popular traditions as people in other areas of Latin America do.[2] Santa Cruz's argument, however, seems to have been that Chilean music should be set apart for its quality, which should reflect the particular Chilean persona, and not for its incoporation of elements seen from the outside world as exotic or different.[3]

Santa Cruz's songs do represent the quality for which he hoped, and are deliberately lacking in elements that could be labeled Andean or folk-influenced. His major song cycles *Cuatro poemas* and *Cantos de soledad* exhibit Impressionistic and atonal tendencies, while the songs in *Canciones del mar* are more neoclassical in their exploration of counterpoint, fugue, and canon combined with polytonal harmonies.[4]

Greater nationalistic tendencies are illustrated in the songs of Pedro Humberto Allende (1885–1959), whose settings of popular poetry are more traditional in terms of tonality and form. Allende represents the opposite end of the spectrum from Santa Cruz in that he was one of the first people to collect actual examples of Mapuche (Araucanian Indian) music.[5] The folk music itself is complicated and varies by region and tribe, but in general it is non-Western in harmonic language and overall conception, and a small part of a much larger "symbolic communication" process.⁶

The post-Impressionistic works of Jorge Urrutia Blondel (1905–1981) and the dissonant, polytonal writing of Alfonso Letelier (1912–1994) are predecessors to the important works of Juan Orrego-Salas (1919–). Not only a prolific contemporary composer but also an active musicologist, Orrego-Salas was the first director of the Latin American Music Center at Indiana University, and continues to be an important proponent of Latin American music worldwide.

Allende, Pedro Humberto, 1885–1959

4.1, *Seis cantos infantiles*
4.1a, I. Este niñito compró un huevito, 1940, Traditional poetry, B3–B4, Low, —, TR, *The Latin American Art Song*, +
4.1b, II. Tutito hagamos ya, 1940, Traditional poetry, D4–A4, Low, —, TR, *The Latin American Art Song*, +
4.1c, III. Pimpín sarabín, 1940, Traditional poetry, D4–B4, Low, —, TR, *The Latin American Art Song*, +
4.1d, IV. Mañana es domingo, 1940, Traditional poetry, D4–E♭5, Med, —, TR, *The Latin American Art Song*, +
4.1e, V. Cotón colorado, 1940, Traditional poetry, B3–F5, Med, —, TR, *The Latin American Art Song*, +
4.1f, VI. Comadre Rana, 1940, Traditional poetry, A3–D5, Low, —, TR, *The Latin American Art Song*, +

Amengual Astaburuaga, René, 1911–1954

4.2, Caricia, p1935, —, D4–A5, High, Mezzo, —, IEM, —, +

Botto Vallarino, Carlos, 1923–2004

4.3, *Songs of Love and Solitude*, op. 12, 1959–1960, James Joyce, —, —, —, —, —, +

Carmona, Oscar, 1975–

4.4, Ausencias, 1995–1997, Cecilia Carmona, —, Soprano, —, —, LCP, —

García, Fernando, 1930–

4.5, Bestiario, 1987, Nicolás Guillén, —, Soprano, —, —, LCP, —
4.6, *Buenas maneras*, 2004, Ómar Lara, —, Baritone, —, —, LCP, —
4.7, *Cantos de otoño*, 1969, Andrés Sabella, Federico García Lorca, —, Tenor (1969), Soprano (1984), Two versions, —, LCP, —
4.8, *Cuatro apuntes líricos*
4.8a, 1., 2005, Sonia Luz Carrillo, —, Female voice, —, —, LCP, —
4.8b, 2., 2005, Alberto Pérez, —, Female voice, —, —, LCP, —
4.8c, 3., 2005, César Vallejo, —, Female voice, —, —, LCP, —
4.8d, 4., 2005, Vicente Huidobro, —, Female voice, —, —, LCP, —
4.9, *Cuatro recitativos*, 1987, Ómar Lara, —, Bass, Original version as *Decires de espanto y amor* for Soprano (1986), —, LCP, —
4.10, *Decires de espanto y amor*, 1986, Ómar Lara, —, Soprano (1986), Bass (1987),

Two versions; also as *Cuatro recitativos*, —, LCP, —

4.11, El espejo de agua, 1983, Vicente Huidobro, —, Bass (1983), Baritone (1992), Two versions, —, LCP, —

4.12, Himno de la CUT, 1963, —, —, —, Original version for choir, —, LCP, —

4.13, Poemas en tiempos de guerra, 2004, Vicente Huidobro, —, Tenor, —, —, LCP, —

4.14, Retazos de poesía, 2001, Vicente Huidobro, —, Alto, —, —, LCP, —

4.15, *Sabelliades a Ruiseñor Rojo*, 1972, Andrés Sabella, —, Tenor, —, —, LCP, —

4.16, *Tres canciones para una bandera*, 1965, Andrés Sabella, —, Tenor, —, —, LCP, —

4.17, *Tres recitativos breves*, 1982, Sonia Luz Carrillo, —, Soprano, —, —, LCP, —

Guarello Finlay, Alejandro, 1951–

4.18, Mis caballos suben despacio, 1983, H. Vogel (Obra homónima), —, Soprano, —, m, LCP, —

4.19, Reyerta, 1979, Federico García Lorca, —, Tenor, —, IEM, LCP, —

4.20, Romance de la Luna, Luna, 1977, Federico García Lorca, —, Soprano, —, IEM, LCP, —

Isamitt, Carlos, 1887–1974

4.21, Quietud, 1930, —, —, —, —, IEM, —, +

Leng, Alfonso, 1884–1974

4.22, Cima, 1922, Gabriela Mistral, B3–D♯5, Low, —, IEM, —, +

Letelier, Alfonso, 1912–1994

4.23, *Canciones antiguas*

4.23a, I. [Al alba venid buen amigo . . .], 1951, Fifteenth- and sixteenth-century Spanish poems, A3–F5, Med, —, PAU, —, +

4.23b, II. [Enemiga le soy madre . . .], 1951, Fifteenth- and sixteenth-century Spanish poems, F♯3–F♯5, Low-med, —, PAU, —, +

4.23c, III. [Mios fueron mi corazón], 1951, Fifteenth- and sixteenth-century Spanish poems, C4–E5, Med, —, PAU, —, +

4.24, *Tres canciones*

4.24a, Balada, op. 10, 1936, Gabriela Mistral, B♭3–F♯5, Med-high, —, IEM, —, +

4.24b, Canción, op. 13, 1935, Manuel Arellano, C♯4–G♭5, Med-high, —, IEM, —, +

4.24c, Otoño, op. 8, 1934, Gabriela Mistral, C4–A♭5, High, —, IEM, —, +

Montecino, Alfonso, 1924–

4.25, *Cinco canciones*

4.25a, Serenata, op. 14, 1953, Federico García Lorca, —, Med, —, m, —, +

4.25b, ¡Ay!, 1953, Federico García Lorca, —, Med, —, m, —, +

4.25c, Mi niña se fue a la mar, 1953, Federico García Lorca, —, Med, —, m, —, +

4.25d, Cazador, 1953, Federico García Lorca, —, Med, —, m, —, +

4.25e, A Irene García, 1953, Federico García Lorca, —, Med, —, m, —, +

4.25f, Sorpresa, 1946, Federico García Lorca, D♭4–G5, Med-high, —, m, —, +

4.26, *Cuatro canciones*

4.26a, La fe del ciego, 1950, Popular Chilean poetry, A3–G5, Med, —, PAU, —, +

4.26b, Todo el mundo me murmura, 1950, Popular Chilean poetry, F4–F5, Med, —, PAU, —, +

4.26c, Ausencia, 1950, Popular Chilean poetry, D4–C♯5, Med, —, PAU, —, +

4.26d, Dicen que el mundo es redondo, 1950, Popular Chilean poetry, B3–F♯5, Med-high, —, PAU, —, +

4.27, Todo es ronda, 1945, Gabriela Mistral, D4–E5, Med, —, IEM, —, +

Morel, Marcelo, 1928–1983

4.28, *Canciones de la soledad*

4.28e, 5. Noche, 1959, Federico García Lorca, B♭3–G5, High, A mis hijos; Constanza, IEM, —, +

4.28f, 6. Alba, 1959, Federico García Lorca, B4–G5, High, A mis hijos; Marcelo, IEM, —, +

4.28g, 7. Tierra, 1959, Federico García Lorca, E♭4–F♯5, Med-high, A mis hijos; Patricia, IEM, —, +

Orrego-Salas, Juan, 1919–

4.29, *Alabanzas a la Virgen, op. 49*

4.29a, Cantiga, 1959, Josef de Valdivielso, F♯4–A5, High, Soprano, A Carmen; Compuesta para celebrar la Navidad del año 1960, IEM, —, +

4.29b, Villancico, 1959, Anonymous text of Cáceres, F♯4–G♯5, High, Soprano, A Juan Felipe, IEM, —, +

4.29c, Pascalle, 1959, Anonymous text of Cáceres, A♭3–G♯5, High, Soprano, A Juan Cristian, IEM, —, +

4.29d, Alborado, 1959, Anonymous text of Cáceres, F♯4–G♯5, High, Soprano, A Juan Miguel, IEM, —, +

4.29e, Ofrenda, 1959, Anonymous text of Cáceres, F4–A5, High, Soprano, A Francisca, IEM, —, +

4.30, *El Alba del Alhelí, op. 29*

4.30a, 1. Prólogo, 1950, Rafael Alberti, F♯4–G5, Med-high, Soprano, Dedicated to Clara Oyuela, PI, "Rafael Alberti and Chilean Composers", +

4.30b, 2. La novia, 1950, Rafael Alberti, E4–G5, Med-high, Soprano, Dedicated to Clara Oyuela, PI, "Rafael Alberti and Chilean Composers", +

4.30c, 3. El pregón, 1950, Rafael Alberti, E♭4–A5, High, Soprano, Dedicated to Clara Oyuela, PI, "Rafael Alberti and Chilean Composers", +

4.30d, 4. La flor del Candil, 1950, Rafael Alberti, F4–A♭5, High, Soprano, Dedicated to Clara Oyuela, PI, "Rafael Alberti and Chilean Composers", +

4.30e, 5. La gitana, 1950, Rafael Alberti, E4–A♭5, High, Soprano, Dedicated to Clara Oyuela, PEN, PI, "Rafael Alberti and Chilean Composers," *The Art Song in Latin America*, +

4.30f, 6. El pescador sin dinero, 1950, Rafael Alberti, E♭4–G♭5, Med-high, Soprano, Dedicated to Clara Oyuela, PI, "Rafael Alberti and Chilean Composers", +

4.30g, 7. Madrigal del peine perdido, 1950, Rafael Alberti, F♯4–A5, Med-high, Soprano, Dedicated to Clara Oyuela, PI, "Rafael Alberti and Chilean Composers", +

4.30h, 8. El farolero y su novia, 1950, Rafael Alberti, F♯4–F♯5, Med-high, Soprano, Dedicated to Clara Oyuela, PI, "Rafael Alberti and Chilean Composers", +

4.30i, 9. ¡Al puente de la golondrina!, 1950, Rafael Alberti, F♯4–A5, High, Soprano, Dedicated to Clara Oyuela, PI, "Rafael Alberti and Chilean Composers", +

4.30j, 10. Castilla tiene castillos, 1950, Rafael Alberti, F♯4–A5, High, Soprano, Dedicated to Clara Oyuela, PI, "Rafael Alberti and Chilean Composers", +

4.31, *Psalms, op. 74*

4.31a, Lord, give ears to my words (V), 1977, Biblical text, (E2)A♭3–D4, Med, Baritone, To John Williams; English text, m, —, +

4.31b, The earth is the Lord's (XXIV), 1977, Biblical text, B3–F4, Med-high, Baritonee, To John Williams; English text, m, —, +

4.31c, Unto Thee I lift my soul (XXV), 1977, Biblical text, G2–D4, Med, Baritone, To John Williams; English text, m, —, +

4.31d, Sing a new song (XXXIII), 1977, Biblical text, B♭3–F4, Med-high, Baritone, To John Williams; English text, m, —, +

4.31e, Praise the Lord (CXLVIII), 1977, Biblical text, B3–E4, Med-high, Baritone, To John Williams; English text, m, —, +

Riesco, Carlos, 1925–

4.32, *Sobre los ángeles*

4.32a, Canción del ángel sin suerte, 1955–

1959, Rafael Alberti, —, —, —, PAU, "Rafael Alberti and Chilean Composers", +

4.32b, El ángel de los números, 1955–1959, Rafael Alberti, —, —, —, PAU, "Rafael Alberti and Chilean Composers", +

4.32c, El ángel bueno, 1955–1959, Rafael Alberti, —, —, —, PAU, "Rafael Alberti and Chilean Composers", +

4.32d, El ángel ángel, 1955–1959, Rafael Alberti, —, —, —, PAU, "Rafael Alberti and Chilean Composers", +

4.32e, El ángel ceniciento, 1955–1959, Rafael Alberti, —, —, —, PAU, "Rafael Alberti and Chilean Composers", +

Santa Cruz, Domingo, 1899–1977

4.33, *Canciones del mar, op. 29*

4.33a, I. Rocas, 1952, Domingo Santa Cruz, C4–G5, High, Soprano, —, m, —, +

4.33b, II. Amanecer junto al mar, 1952, Domingo Santa Cruz, C#4–A5, High, Soprano, —, m, —, +

4.33c, III. Olas, 1952, Domingo Santa Cruz, C#4–A♭5, High, Soprano, —, m, —, +

4.33d, IV. Balada de la animita, 1952, Domingo Santa Cruz, D4–F#5, High, Soprano, —, m, —, +

4.33e, V. Lejanía, 1952, Domingo Santa Cruz, C4–A5, High, Soprano, —, m, —, +

4.33f, VI. Plenilunio, 1952, Domingo Santa Cruz, B♭3–A5, High, Soprano, —, m, —, +

4.33g, VII. Ante el mar, 1952, Domingo Santa Cruz, D♭4–G5, Med-high, Soprano, —, m, —, +

4.33h, VIII. Pinos de costa, 1952, Domingo Santa Cruz, D♭4–A♭5, High, Soprano, —, m, —, +

4.33i, IX. La noche, 1952, Domingo Santa Cruz, D♭4–G5, Med-high, Soprano, —, m, —, +

4.33j, X. Gaviotas, 1952, Domingo Santa Cruz, E♭4–G5, High, Soprano, —, m, —, +

4.33k, XI. Reflejos, 1952, Domingo Santa Cruz, D4–A5, High, Soprano, —, m, —, +

4.33l, XII. Desde lo alto, 1952, Domingo Santa Cruz, D4–A5, High, Soprano, —, m, —, +

4.34, *Cantos de soledad, op. 10*

4.34a, I. Dolor, 1926–1927, Domingo Santa Cruz, F4–G5, High, —, IEM, —, +

4.34b, II. Madre mía, 1926–1927, Domingo Santa Cruz, C#4–B5, High, —, IEM, —, +

4.34c, III. Canción de cuna, 1926–1927, Domingo Santa Cruz, F4–E5, Med, —, IEM, —, +

4.35, *Cuatro poemas, op. 9*

4.35a, Árbol muerto, 1927, Gabriela Mistral, B3–E5, Med, —, m, —, +

4.35b, Piececitos, 1927, Gabriela Mistral, E♭4–G♭5, Med, —, m, —, +

4.35c, Tres árboles, 1927, Gabriela Mistral, D♭4–G#5, Med-high, —, m, —, +

4.35d, La lluvia lenta, 1927, Gabriela Mistral, C4–A5, High, —, m, —, +

Schidlowsky, León, 1931–

4.36, *Drei Liebeslieder*, 1953, Georg Trakl, —, —, —, —, LCP, —

4.37, Estudiante baleado, 1967, Fernando Rojas, —, —, —, —, LCP, —

4.38, *Tres canciones de amor*, 1963, —, —, Tenor, —, —, LCP, —

4.39, *Tres poemas*, 1955, Federico García Lorca, Vicente Huidobro, —, —, —, —, LCP, —

4.40, *Zwei Lieder*, 1962, Georg Trakl, —, Tenor, —, —, LCP, —

4.41, *Zwei Lieder vom Tode*, 1954, —, —, —, —, —, LCP, —

Urrutia Blondel, Jorge, 1905–1981

4.42, *Tres poemas de Gabriela Mistral, op. 20*

4.42a, Yo no tengo soledad, 1938–1942, Gabriela Mistral, D4–A5, High, —, IEM, —, +

4.42b, Hallazgo, 1938–1942, Gabriela Mistral, D4–A5, High, —, IEM, —, +

4.42c, Corderito, 1938–1942, Gabriela Mistral, D♭4–G5, High, —, IEM, —, +

PUBLISHERS

IEM, Instituto de Extensión Musical
m, manuscript
PAU, Pan American Union
PEN, Pendragon Press
PI, Peer International Corporation
TR, Tritó, S.L.

COLLECTIONS

+, LAMC (Latin American Music Center), Indiana University

SOURCES

(See bibliography for publication information)
Caicedo, *The Latin American Art Song: A Critical Anthology and Interpretive Guide for Singers*
LCP, *The Living Composers Project* (online resource)
Orrego-Salas, "Rafael Alberti and Chilean Composers"
Wilson, *The Art Song in Latin America: Selected Works by Twentieth-Century Composers*

5

Colombia

Ellie Anne Duque

The history of art song in Colombia logically mirrors that of other art music. If limited to the development of songs with piano accompaniment during the nineteenth and twentieth centuries, the Colombian art song displays the same stylistic features found in early Romantic music: nationalistic tendencies, chromatically enhanced musical writing of the late nineteenth century, followed by neoclassicism and experiments with tonality and sound characteristic of other twentieth-century music. However, it must be pointed out that the list of art songs included in the present volume is relatively small when compared to the list of songs composed in Europe or the United States during the same period of time.

The breadth of the repertoire is constricted by various factors. One such factor is the general lack of publications: musical editions are few in Colombia and publishing efforts are short-lived, making it difficult to locate compositions, which mainly survive in personal archives. Few, if any, song anthologies have been published in the country. Another factor is the predominance of popular songs inspired by national airs, accompanied by string instruments (guitar, tiple, bandola, harp, cuatro, etc.) that basically improvise the accompaniment.

In a way, the art song genre has been imposed upon the Colombian repertoire from the outside (as a European nineteenth-century concept) and does not embrace the more popular expressions. Colombian song is imbued with national sentiment, not only about the country itself but also its music, people, customs, and landscape. Poetry for songs is chosen with sentiment and sentimentality in mind and, to a great extent, the urgency of its expression has impaired the notion of musical experimentation and growth through song.

The mid- and late-nineteenth-century song repertoire was mainly located in periodical publications. The first lithographed music pieces to be printed in Colombia date from 1848. For the twentieth-century repertoire, the collection at the Centro de Documentación Musical of the Ministry of Culture proves to be the most reliable source. Nevertheless, the Centro does not have the complete works of all Colombian composers, and many valuable song collections cannot be included in our present list, as researchers and performers would be seriously hampered when pursuing a copy of the song.

Many of the songs composed by artists of nationalistic tendencies are still considered paradigmatic of the Colombian song and are heard in recitals. Such is the case with the pieces written by Jesús Bermúdez Silva, José Rozo Contreras and Adolfo Mejía. Contemporary Colombian composers have noticeably abandoned the practice of art songs, as can be seen in the following catalog. A particular example is Blas Atehortúa, one of the most prolific Colombian composers of the second half of the twentieth century. Although he has over two hundred opus numbers, he has placed a great deal of attention on the oratorio and the cantata and has only written twelve songs, none of which are published.

The first symphonies and quartets were produced in Colombia at the beginning of the twentieth century, and composers spent great efforts on learning musical forms and orchestration, forgoing the composition of songs. Many of the younger composers favor the purely instrumental medium or have concentrated in the new world of electronically produced sound.

Bermúdez Silva, Jesús, 1884–1969

5.1, Canción de la tarde, —, Martín H. Cortés, D♯4–G5, High, Soprano or Tenor, Soprano or Tenor, —, *Mundo al día* no. 2241 (julio 25 de 1931), CDM

5.2, Ilusión, ca. 1946, Enrique Ortega Arredondo, G4–A5, High, Soprano or Tenor, ICC, *Música colombiana*, CDM

Biava, Pedro, 1902–1973

5.3, La imagen de tu perfil, rondó, —, José A. Calcaño, B3–F5, Med, Soprano, —, ICC, *Música colombiana*, CDM

5.4, Triste, muy tristemente, —, Rubén Darío, D4–F5, Med, —, ICC, *Música colombiana*, CDM

Calvo, Luis Antonio, 1882–1945

5.5, Amapola, —, Unknown, E4–B5, High, —, Navia, —, CDM

5.6, Cuando caigan las hojas, —, Stecchetti, Trad. Ismael Enrique Arciniegas, D4–A5, High, —, —, *Mundo al día* no. 2081 (enero 2 de 1931), CDM

5.7, En la playa, 1930, Luis Antonio Calvo, C♯4–B4, Low, —, TR, *The Latin American Art Song*, +

5.8, Gitana, 1930, Luis Antonio Calvo, G♯4–F♯5, Med-high, —, TR, *The Latin American Art Song*, +

5.9, La orden de Lázaro, romanza, —, Eduardo López, F4–F5, High, —, Navia ©1925, —, CDM

5.10, Never more, canción, —, Adolfo León Gómez, F4–E5, Med, —, —, *Revista cromos* no. 103 (febrero 19 de 1921), CDM

Escobar, Luis Antonio, 1925–1993

5.11, Fugueta a dos voces, —, León de Greiff, E4–A5, High, —, ICC, *Música colombiana*, CDM

Espinosa, Luis Carlos, 1919–1990

5.12, Amanecer, 1953, Helcías Martán, A4–F♯5, Med, Soprano, —, ICC, *Música colombiana*, CDM

5.13, Búsqueda, —, Helcías Martán, D4–E5, Med, Soprano, —, ICC, *Música colombiana*, CDM

Figueroa, Luis Carlos, 1923–

5.14, Berceuse, 1945, Luis Carlos Figueroa, E4–D5, Med, A Maruja Rengifo Salcedo, PEN, *The Art Song in Latin America*, CDM, +

Hasler, Johann, 1972–

5.15, Dunkelheit, 1993, J. Hasler, —, —, —, m, —, +

5.16, No me censuren ni riñan, 1993, —, —, —, Russian text, m, —, +

5.17, Shibumú, 1993, Ingrid Uribe, —, —, —, m, —, +

Lara, Gustavo Adolfo, 1955–

5.18, Canción de un azul imposible, —, Porfirio Barba Jacob, A♭3–D♯5, Med, —, ICC, *Música colombiana*, CDM

5.19, Síntesis, —, Porfirio Barba Jacob, A3–B4, Med, —, ICC, *Música colombiana*, CDM

León, Jaime, 1921–

5.20, A ti, 1977, José Asunción Silva, G4–G5, Med, A mi querida esposa Beatriz, TR, *The Latin American Art Song*, +

5.21, Cuando lejos, muy lejos, 1977, Julio Flórez, E♭4–A♭5, Med-high, —, TR, *The Latin American Art Song*, +

5.22, La campesina, —, Isabel Lleras Restrepo, D4–A5, High, —, PEN, *The Art Song in Latin America*, CDM, +

5.23, Serenata, 1977, José Asunción Silva, C♯4–E5, Med, —, TR, *The Latin American Art Song*, +

Mojica Mesa, Raúl, 1928–1991

5.24, Danza de los alcaravanes, —, Raúl Mojica Mesa, C4–D5, Med, Temática sobre el canto y rítmico movimiento del

Alcaraván, ICC, *Música colombiana*, CDM

Morales Pino, Pedro, 1863-1926

5.25, Serenata, en la mayor para canto y piano, —, Leopoldo Lugones, E4-A5, High, —, Navia ©1930, —, CDM

Murillo Chapull, Emilio, 1880-1942

5.26, Canción mística, —, Julio Flórez, D4-D5, Med, —, —, *Magasin de musique du conservatoire* ©1904, CDM

Neuman, Hans Federico, 1917-1992

5.27, Rumbo estelar, —, Andrés Pardo Tovar, D4-E5, Med, —, ICC, *Música colombiana*, CDM

Nova Sondag, Jacqueline, 1935-1975

5.28, A veces un no niega, 1966, Pedro Salinas, C4-G#5, High, —, PEN, *The Art Song in Latin America*, CDM, +

Pineda Duque, Roberto, 1910-1977

5.29, La espera, —, F. Zapata Lillo, C3-F4, Low, Baritone, A Luis Méndez, ICC, *Música colombiana*, CDM

Posada Amador, Carlos, 1908-1993

5.30, A fin de que los vientos . . ., —, Otto de Greiff, D4-A5, High, —, ICC, *Música colombiana*, CDM

Rozo Contreras, José, 1894-1976

5.31, A te (Romanza), —, Silvio Palmieri, D3-E4, Med, —, de Sants ©1928, —, CDM

5.32, Caracola, p1958, Carlos López Narváez, C4-E5, Med, —, —, —, CDM

5.33, Día de diciembre (Romanza), —, Carlos Villafañe, E4-A5, High, A la memoria de mi madre, ICC, *Música colombiana*, CDM

5.34, En el brocal (Romanza), —, Ismael Enrique Arciniegas, D4-G5, High, —, —, *Mundo al día* no. 2988 (agosto 4 de 1934), CDM

5.35, Victoria (Canción colombiana), —, Pedro A. Gómez Naranjo, C4-A5, High, —, EMA, —, CDM

Tena, José María, 1895-1952

5.36, Romance de la niña negra, —, Luis Cané, E4-F5, Med, —, ICC, *Música colombiana*, CDM

Uribe Holguín, Guillermo, 1880-1971

5.37, Hay un instante en el crepúsculo, —, Guillermo Valencia, D4-B5, High, —, BPCAC, *Tres canciones de Guillermo Uribe Holguín*, CDM

5.38, Las garzas, op. 44, —, Emilio Oribe, —, —, —, BLA, —, +

5.39, Nupcial, —, José Asunción Silva, D4-G5, High, —, BPCAC, *Tres canciones de Guillermo Uribe Holguín*, CDM

5.40, Rimas, —, León de Greiff, E4-A5, High, —, BPCAC, *Tres canciones de Guillermo Uribe Holguín*, CDM

Valencia, Antonio María, 1902-1952

5.41, Ai-je fait un rêve?, —, Heinrich Heine, C♭4-G5, High, —, CC, *Imagen y obra de Antonio María Valencia*, CDM

5.42, Arrurrú, soneto lírico, —, José Eustasio Rivera, C4-F5, High, —, CC, *Imagen y obra de Antonio María Valencia*, CDM

5.43, Canción de cuna vallecaucana, —, Unknown, E4-F5, High, —, CC, *Imagen y obra de Antonio María Valencia*, CDM

5.44, Est-il mort?, —, Francis Carco, E4-D5, Med, —, CC, *Imagen y obra de Antonio María Valencia*, CDM

5.45, Iremos a los Astros . . ., —, Otto de Greiff, D4-E5, Med, —, CC, *Imagen y obra de Antonio María Valencia*, CDM

5.46, La luna sobre el agua de los lagos, —, Otto de Greiff, B3-G5, High, —, CC,

Imagen y obra de Antonio María Valencia, CDM

5.47, Tarde maravillosa, —, Otto de Greiff, C4-G5, High, —, CC, *Imagen y obra de Antonio María Valencia,* CDM

5.48, Tres días hace que Nina dormida en su lecho está, —, Otto de Greiff, D4-G5, High, —, CC, *Imagen y obra de Antonio María Valencia,* CDM

Velasco, Jerónimo, 1885-1963

5.49, Bajo la luna, serenata, —, Francisco Giraldo, C4-G♯5, High, —, Rodríguez 1912, —, CDM

5.50, Canción de las hadas, —, Jorge Isaacs, B3-G5, High, —, Buffet, Crampton et Cie. 1923, —, CDM

5.51, Se va la barca, pasillo, —, Unknown, D4-A5, High, —, —, *Colombia artística,* Año II no. 11 (abril 1909), CDM

Vidal, Gonzalo, 1863-1946

5.52, Crepuscular, romanza para canto y piano, —, Gabriel Latorre, C4-G5, High, —, SEC, *Gonzalo Vidal, Antología,* CDM

5.53, ¡Hacia el mar!, himno patriótico, —, Ernesto González, C4-F5, High, —, SEC, *Gonzalo Vidal, Antología,* CDM

5.54, Serenata de amor, aire de danza, —, J. M. Trespalacios, E4-F5, High, —, —, *Revista musical* (1900), CDM

Villalobos, Alejandro, 1875-1938

5.55, Ensueños, romanza para soprano, —, Gregorio Consuegra, C4-B5, High, —, —, *Tierra nativa* no. 75 Año II (Junio 23 de 1928), CDM

Yepes, Gustavo

5.56, Admonición a los impertinentes, —, León de Greiff, E♭4-B♭5, High, —, —, *Canciones para voz y piano,* CDM

5.57, A una dama, —, León de Greiff, D4-E5, Med-high, —, —, *Canciones para voz y piano,* CDM

5.58, A veces, —, Antonio Carvajal, E4-A5, High, Dedicada a Beatriz Mora, —, *Canciones para voz y piano,* CDM

5.59, Canción ligera, —, León de Greiff y Gustavo Yepes, C4-A♭5, High, —, —, *Canciones para voz y piano,* CDM

5.60, Día de diciembre, pasillo, —, Carlos Villafañe, G4-G5, High, —, —, *Canciones para voz y piano,* CDM

5.61, Futuro, —, Porfirio Barba Jacob, E4-G5, Med, —, —, *Canciones para voz y piano,* CDM

5.62, La niña de la guitarra, —, Carlos Castro Saavedra, E4-G5, High, —, PEN, *Canciones para voz y piano, The Art Song in Latin America,* CDM, +

5.63, Son, —, León de Greiff, E4-G5, High, —, —, *Canciones para voz y piano,* CDM

5.64, Soneto, —, Luis Carlos López, G4-G5, Med, —, —, *Canciones para voz y piano,* CDM

5.65, Soneto de la guirnalda de rosas, —, Federico García Lorca, C4-B♭5, High, —, —, *Canciones para voz y piano,* CDM

5.66, Tarde de verano, —, Luis Carlos López y Gustavo Yepes, D4-F5, Med-high, —, —, *Canciones para voz y piano,* CDM

5.67, Te has ido, —, Antonio Llanos, E4-A5, High, —, —, *Canciones para voz y piano,* CDM

5.68, ? [En la alameda de ese jardín, ...], —, León de Greiff y Gustavo Yepes, D4-E5, Med-high, —, —, *Canciones para voz y piano,* CDM

Zamudio, Daniel, 1885-1952

5.69, Para ti (Lied), —, Unknown, F4-E5, Med, Soprano, —, ICC, *Música colombiana,* CDM

PUBLISHERS

BLA, Boletín Latinoamericano de Música
BPCAC, Bogotá Patronato Colombiano de Artes y Ciencias
Buffet, Cramption et Cie.
CC, Corporación para la Cultura de Sants
EMA, Edizioni Musicale Armonia
ICC, Instituto Colombiano de Cultura
m, manuscript
Navia
PEN, Pendragon Press
Rogríguez
SEC, Secretaría de Educación y Cultura
TR, Tritó, S.L.

COLLECTIONS

CDM, Centro de Documentación Musical (Bogotá)
+, LAMC (Latin American Music Center), Indiana University

SOURCES

(See bibliography for additional publication information)
Bonilla, *Música colombiana: La canción culta*
Caicedo, *The Latin American Art Song: A Critical Anthology and Interpretive Guide for Singers*
Colombia artística
Gómez-Vignes, *Imagen y obra de Antonio María Valencia*
Magasin de Musique du Conservatoire
Mundo al día
Revista cromos
Revista musical
Rodríguez, Gonzalo Vidal, *Antología*
Tierra nativa
Uribe Holguín, *Tres canciones de Guillermo Uribe Holguín*
Wilson, *The Art Song in Latin America: Selected Works by Twentieth-Century Composers*
Yepes, *Canciones para voz y piano (voz alta)*

6

Costa Rica

Art music in Costa Rica before the nineteenth century was primarily used in religious worship as part of Catholicism.[1] Native Costa Rican composers first began composing art music in the nineteenth century, and by the second half of the century, the musical life of Costa Rica was largely shaped by European influences. The domination of Italian opera brought foreign opera companies on tour through San José, and teachers from Europe were brought in as music educators.[2]

There were several different types of vocal compositions prevalent at the end of the nineteenth century and the beginning of the twentieth. Songs for educational purposes, such as those by José Joaquín Vargas Calvo (1879–1956), José Daniel Zuñiga Zeledón (1889–1981), and Alcides Prado Quesada (1900–1984), proved to be important not only for music education but also for Costa Rican nationalism.[3] The main composers of art song during this time were Julio Fonseca and Julio Mata Oreamuno. Fonseca was considered to be a nationalistic composer, although his style is basically Romantic and Impressionistic in conception.

Music in Costa Rica was able to flourish in a way that it could not in other Latin American countries, due to government funding. In the 1940s, the Orquesta Sinfónica Nacional de Costa Rica and the Conservatorio Nacional de Música (now the Escuela de Artes Musicales de la Universidad de Costa Rica) were founded.[4]

Costa Rican composers in general use less folk material than other Latin American composers, perhaps in part because they are generally of European descent.[5] Traditional folk music, which comes primarily from the northwest region of Guanacaste, has typical rhythmic and melodic elements as well as instruments.

Important figures extending into the latter part of the twentieth century include Carlos Enrique Vargas (1919–1998), Benjamin Gutiérrez Sáenz (1937–), Bernal Flores (1937–), Rocío Sanz Quirós (1934–1993), Dolores Castegnaro (1900–1979), Ricardo Ulloa Barrenechea (1928–), and Jorge Luis Acevedo Vargas (1943–). The anthology *Canciones costarricenses* contains a selection of songs by the aforementioned composers that vary in texture, range, style, and difficulty. Published by the University of Costa Rica (CEDIM), the anthology is also available in the United States through interlibrary loan from Tulane University and Eastern Illinois University.[6]

Acevedo, Medardo Guido, 1913-2007

6.1, Canto a cañas, —, Medardo Guido Acevedo, A3–D5, Low-med, Arr. Jorge Acevedo Vargas, UCR, *Antología de música guanacasteca*, —

6.2, Despedida, —, Medardo Guido Acevedo, C#4–F#5, Med-high, Arr. Jorge Acevedo Vargas, UCR, *Antología de música guanacasteca*, —

6.3, Junto al tempisque (Danza), —, Medardo Guido Acevedo, C4–F5, Med-high, Arr. Jorge Acevedo Vargas, UCR, *Antología de música guanacasteca*, —

Acevedo, Medardo Guido and Guillermo Chaves

6.4, Espíritu guanacasteco, —, Medardo Guido Acevedo, C4–D5, Med, Arr. Jorge Acevedo Vargas, UCR, *Antología de música guanacasteca*, —

Acevedo, Medardo Guido and José Ortiz

6.5, Bagaceñista, —, Medardo Guido Acevedo, A3–D5, Low-med, Arr. Jorge Luis Acevedo Vargas, UCR, *Antología de música guanacasteca*, —

Acevedo Jácamo, Pasión

6.6, Pasión (Aire de pasillo guanacasteco), —, Roberto Arce, —, MC, *Música tradicional costarricense*, —

Acevedo Vargas, Jorge Luis, 1943-

6.7, Los amanezqueros, —, Jorge Acevedo Vargas, C4–D5, Med, Arr. Jorge Acevedo Vargas, UCR, *Antología de música guanacasteca*, —

6.8, Quijonguito, —, Jorge Acevedo Vargas, C4–D5, Med, Arr. Gerardo Duarte R., UCR, *Antología de música guanacasteca*, —

Alfagüell, Mario, 1948-

6.9, 30 *Canciones para la patria de ayer y mañana, op. 81*, 1996, —, —, —, —, —, LCP, —

6.10, *Canción integrata, op. 18*, 1982, —, —, Female voice, —, —, LCP, —

6.11, *Serenata, op. 33*, 1989, —, —, Soprano, Juan Rulfo, —, LCP, —

6.12, *Siete canciones amerindias, op. 165a*, 2005, —, —, Soprano, Indigenous Costa Rican texts, —, LCP, —

Aráuz, Ramiro

6.13, Bienvenido y el barroso, —, Medardo Guido Acevedo, C4–E5, Med, Arr. Jorge Acevedo Vargas, UCR, *Antología de música guanacasteca*, —

Bonilla Chavarria, Jesus, 1912–

6.14, Noche en la selva, —, Guillermo Ortiz S., —, —, —, ED, *La patria canta*, +

Campabadal G., Roberto, 1881–?

6.15, En Puntarenas (Popular), —, Lisímaco Chavarría, —, —, —, ED, *La patria canta*, +

Campos Chanto, Alirio

6.16, Caminamos, 1978, Emma Gamboa, E4–F5, Med-high, —, m, MEP, *Ciclo de 26 canciones y 2 corales*, —

6.17, Como abejas, 1978, Emma Gamboa, D4–D5, Med, —, m, MEP, *Ciclo de 26 canciones y 2 corales*, —

6.18, Comunión de luna, 1978, Emma Gamboa, E4–F♯5, Med-high, —, m, MEP, *Ciclo de 26 canciones y 2 corales*, —

6.19, De aquellos días, 1978, Emma Gamboa, D♭4–G5, Med-high, —, m, MEP, *Ciclo de 26 canciones y 2 corales*, —

6.20, ¿Donde estás?, 1978, Emma Gamboa, D4–G5, Med-high, —, m, MEP, *Ciclo de 26 canciones y 2 corales*, —

6.21, El morir de la rosa, 1978, Emma Gamboa, E♭4–F5, Med-high, —, m, MEP, *Ciclo de 26 canciones y 2 corales*, —

6.22, En el huerto, 1978, Emma Gamboa, D♭4–F5, Med-high, —, m, MEP, *Ciclo de 26 canciones y 2 corales*, —

6.23, Enigma, 1978, Emma Gamboa, E4–E5, Med, —, m, MEP, *Ciclo de 26 canciones y 2 corales*, —

6.24, Estrella perdida, 1978, Emma Gamboa, C4–F5, Med-high, —, m, MEP, *Ciclo de 26 canciones y 2 corales*, —

6.25, Flor invisible, 1978, Emma Gamboa, E♭4–F5, Med-high, —, m, MEP, *Ciclo de 26 canciones y 2 corales*, —

6.26, Hoy..., 1978, Emma Gamboa, C4–D5, Med, —, m, MEP, *Ciclo de 26 canciones y 2 corales*, —

6.27, Manglar, agua y cielo, 1978, Emma Gamboa, D4–G5, Med-high, —, m, MEP, *Ciclo de 26 canciones y 2 corales*, —

6.28, Mi corazón..., 1978, Emma Gamboa, D♯4–C5, Med, —, m, MEP, *Ciclo de 26 canciones y 2 corales*, —

6.29, Mi oración, 1978, Emma Gamboa, D♭4–E5, Med, —, m, MEP, *Ciclo de 26 canciones y 2 corales*, —

6.30, Nadie percibe, 1978, Emma Gamboa, C4–C5, Med, —, m, MEP, *Ciclo de 26 canciones y 2 corales*, —

6.31, Nuestro instante, 1978, Emma Gamboa, C4–G5, Med-high, —, m, MEP, *Ciclo de 26 canciones y 2 corales*, —

6.32, Pequeño oasis, 1978, Emma Gamboa, C4–E5, Med, —, m, MEP, *Ciclo de 26 canciones y 2 corales*, —

6.33, Plenilunio, 1978, Emma Gamboa, C4–G5, Med-high, —, m, MEP, *Ciclo de 26 canciones y 2 corales*, —

6.34, Rosa en la nieve, 1978, Emma Gamboa, C4–G♭5, Med-high, —, m, MEP, *Ciclo de 26 canciones y 2 corales*, —

6.35, Si tú..., 1978, Emma Gamboa, D4–F♯5, Med-high, —, m, MEP, *Ciclo de 26 canciones y 2 corales*, —

6.36, Soledad, 1978, Emma Gamboa, E4–G5, Med-high, —, m, MEP, *Ciclo de 26 canciones y 2 corales*, —

6.37, Solo quisiera, 1978, Emma Gamboa, E4–G♭5, Med-high, —, m, MEP, *Ciclo de 26 canciones y 2 corales*, —

6.38, Tendido, 1978, Emma Gamboa, D♭4–F5, Med, —, m, MEP, *Ciclo de 26 canciones y 2 corales*, —

6.39, Tengo, 1978, Emma Gamboa, F4–E♭5, Med, —, m, MEP, *Ciclo de 26 canciones y 2 corales*, —

6.40, Todo fue así, 1978, Emma Gamboa, E4–G5, Med-high, —, m, MEP, *Ciclo de 26 canciones y 2 corales*, —

6.41, Todos creen..., 1978, Emma Gamboa, D4-G5, Med-high, —, m, MEP, *Ciclo de 26 canciones y 2 corales*, —

Castegnaro, Dolores, 1900-1979

6.42, La casita, —, —, B4-E5, Low-med, —, CEDIM, *Antología canciones costarricenses*, —

6.43, Panis angelicus, 1934, Sacred, C4-E♭5, Med, —, CEDIM, *Antología canciones costarricenses*, —

Chaves Torres, Rafael, 1839-1907

6.44, Duelo de la patria (Marcha fúnebre), —, —, —, —, —, ED, *La patria canta*, +

Cubillo, Saturnino

6.45, Morena linda (Callejera), —, Adán Guevara, —, —, —, MC, *Música tradicional costarricense*, —

Desconocido [Unknown]

6.46, El coyotillo (Callejera), —, —, —, —, —, MC, *Música tradicional costarricense*, —

6.47, Indio enamorado (Danza típica), —, —, —, —, —, MC, *Música tradicional costarricense*, —

6.48, Pajarito Chichiltote, —, —, —, —, —, MC, *Música tradicional costarricense*, —

6.49, Serenata del Indio (Danza), —, —, —, —, —, MC, *Música tradicional costarricense*, —

Dijeres, Rafael de la O

6.50, Brisas norteñas (Vals), MC, *Música tradicional costarricense*

Fonseca G., Julio, 1885-1950

6.51, América, 1933, Juan de la Cruz Varela, —, —, Arr. voice and piano, ED, LAGOS, *La patria canta*, +

6.52, Amor ti chiedi, 1904, A. Murciano, E4-B♭5, High, Italian text, Spanish version underneath, CEDIM, *Antología canciones costarricenses*, —

6.53, Balada a la Santísima Virgen, 1932-

6.54, Canto de las Repúblicas Centroamericanas, —, Carmen Lira, —, —, —, ED, *La patria canta*, +

6.55, Cincuenta cánticos sagrados

6.55a, Cogiendo café (Dramatizable), José María Zeledón Brenes, —, —, —, —, MC, *Música tradicional costarricense*, —

6.55b, La garza herida, 1919, Rogelio Sotela, C4-D5, Med, —, CEDIM, *Antología canciones costarricenses*, —

6.55c, ¡Oh Costa Rica!, —, J. J. Salas Perez, —, —, —, ED, *La patria canta*, +

Additional titles: Al nombre de María; Es todo pura, canción religiosa; Historia trunca; Invocación (Ave María); Romanza; Solo un amor; Triunfó tu gracia

Guadamuz de la O., Isidro

6.56, El negrito de Esquipulas (Parrandero), —, Isidro Guadamuz de la O., B3-D5, Med, Arr. Gerardo Duarte R., UCR, *Antología de música guanacasteca*, —

6.57, Los dos Jinetes, —, Isidro Guadamuz de la O., C4-E♭5, Med, Arr. Gerardo Duarte R., UCR, *Antología de música guanacasteca*, —

Guadamuz de la O., Teodoro

6.58, Fiesta en Santa Cruz, Teodoro Guadamuz, C4-D5, Med, Arr. Gerardo Duarte R., UCR, *Antología de música guanacasteca*

6.59, La Soncoyeña, Teodoro Guadamuz, C4-F5, Med-high, Arr. Gerardo Duarte R., UCR, *Antología de música guanacasteca*

6.60, Nandayureña, Teodoro Guadamuz, F4-F5, Med-high, Arr. Gerardo Duarte R., UCR, *Antología de música guanacasteca*

Gutiérrez, Carlos Ma.

6.61, Alajueleña (Punto popular), —, León Vargas, —, —, —, MC, *Música tradicional costarricense*, —

Gutiérrez Sáenz, Benjamín, 1937–

6.62, *Tres canciones para soprano*
6.62a, I. Quisiera ser..., 1977, Alfredo Espino, E♭4–A5, High, —, CEDIM, *Antología canciones costarricenses*, —
6.62b, II. Por la senda oscura yo camino..., 1977, Alfredo Espino, C4–B♭5, High, Original version for soprano and orchestra; piano arrangement by the composer, CEDIM, *Antología canciones costarricenses*, —
6.62c, III. ¡Quizás ya no venga...!, 1977, Alfredo Espino, B♭3–A♭5, High, —, CEDIM, *Antología canciones costarricenses*, —

Herra Rodríguez, Luis Diego, 1952–

6.63, *Salgamos al amor*
6.63a, He aquí el líquido puro de mi amor, 1996, Jorge Debravo, D4–F♯5, Med-high, CEDIM, *Antología canciones costarricenses*, —
6.63b, Salmo a la tierra animal de tu vientre, 1996, Jorge Debravo, D4–G5, Med-high, CEDIM, *Antología canciones costarricenses*, —
6.63c, ¡Salgamos al amor, hermano hombre!, 1996, Jorge Debravo, D♯4–G5, Med-high, CEDIM, *Antología canciones costarricenses*, —

6.64, Sobre el gavilán, —, Bribrí, B3–B5, High, CEDIM, *Antología canciones costarricenses*, —

Mata Bonilla, Félix, 1935–1980

6.65, Canciones, ©2005, Ed. Zamira Barquero, Enrique Cordero, —, —, —, UCR, —, —
6.66, Silencio, —, Julián Marchena, B3–D5, Low, —, CEDIM, *Antología canciones costarricenses*, —
6.67, Vuelo supremo, —, Julián Marchena, C4–G5, Med-high, —, CEDIM, *Antología canciones costarricenses*, —

Mata Oreamuno, Julio, 1899–1969

6.68, Campana mayor, 1958, Rafael Hiliodoro Valle, E♭4–F5, Med, —, CEDIM, *Antología canciones costarricenses*, —
6.69, Dime ensueño, dime, 1925, —, D4–G5, Med, —, CEDIM, *Antología canciones costarricenses*, —
6.70, Mujeres de Costa Rica, —, Julio Mata Oreamuno, —, —, —, ED, *La patria canta*, +

Monestel Zamore, Alejandro, 1865–1950

6.71, Ave María, p1900, Sacred, C4–G♯5, Med-high, —, CEDIM, *Antología canciones costarricenses*, —
6.72, La cosecha, —, Manuel González Zeledón, E4–F5, Med-high, —, CEDIM, *Antología canciones costarricenses*, —

Murilló M., Claudio

6.73, Canto patriótico, —, Napoleon Quesada S., —, —, —, ED, *La patria canta*, +

Pizarro, Daniel

6.74, La lluvia, María Leal de Noguera, C4–C5, Med, Arr. Gerardo Duarte R., UCR, *Antología de música guanacasteca*, —

Prado Quesada, Alcides, 1900–1984

6.75, A la marimba guanacasteca (Danza), —, Carmen C. de Prado, —, —, —, MC, *Música tradicional costarricense*, —
6.76, Mi Costa Rica (Corrido), —, Alcides Prado Quesada, —, —, —, ED, *La patria canta*, +

Rodríguez Caracas, Manuel, 1904–

6.77, He guardado (Callejera), —, Aristides Baltodano, —, —, —, ED, *La patria canta,* +

Sanz Quirós, Rocío, 1934–1993

6.78, A unos ojos, 1970, Rubén Darío, D4–G5, Med-high, Para Oki María, CEDIM, *Antología canciones costarricenses, Canciones para canto y piano,* +

6.79, *Canciones de la noche*
6.79a, Prólogo (La guitarra) y la noche amiga, —, Rocío Sanz, D4–G#5, High, A María Luisa Rangel, UCR- CEDIM, *Canciones para canto y piano,* +
6.79b, Campana, —, Rocío Sanz, E♭4–G5, Medi-high, —, CEDIM, *Canciones para canto y piano,* +
6.79c, La noche murmura, —, Rocío Sanz, C#4–F#5, Med-high, —, CEDIM, *Canciones para canto y piano,* +
6.79d, Tiempo de noche, —, Rocío Sanz, D4–F#5, Med-high, —, CEDIM, *Canciones para canto y piano,* +
6.79e, Epílogo- "Guitarra sola", —, Rocío Sanz, D4–B5, High, —, CEDIM, *Canciones para canto y piano,* +

6.80, *Cinco canciones de Brecht (La buena mujer de Sezúan)*
6.80a, Canción a la viuda Shin (Escena 7), 1963–1964, Bertold Brecht, D4–E♭5, Med, —, CEDIM, *Canciones para canto y piano,* +
6.80b, Canción de Shen-te ante los dioses, 1963–1964, Bertold Brecht, C4–G5, Med, —, CEDIM, *Canciones para canto y piano,* +
6.80c, Canción de las tardes tristes (Escena 3), 1963–1964, Bertold Brecht, D4–G5, Med, —, CEDIM, *Canciones para canto y piano,* +
6.80d, Canción del agua, 1963–1964, Bertold Brecht, D4–F5, Med, —, CEDIM, *Canciones para canto y piano,* +
6.80e, Entracto cantado- Shenta se transforma en Shui-ta, 1963–1964, Bertold Brecht, E4–A5, —, —, CEDIM, *Canciones para canto y piano,* +

6.81, *Cinco canciones de verano*
6.81a, Prégon, —, —, —, Mezzo-soprano, —, LAC, —
6.81b, Verano largo, —, —, —, Mezzo-soprano, —, LAC, —
6.81c, Tormento, —, —, —, Mezzo-soprano, —, LAC, —
6.81d, Nocturno, —, —, —, Mezzo-soprano, —, LAC, —
6.81e, Soy el verano, —, —, —, Mezzo-soprano, —, LAC, —

6.82, *Cinco canciones para niños*
6.82a, Campanita, 1962, Carlos Luis Sáenz, D4–E5, Med, —, CEDIM, *Canciones para canto y piano,* +
6.82b, Las campanas de San Juan, 1962, Carlos Luis Sáenz, E4–E5, Low, Para Iván, CEDIM, *Canciones para canto y piano,* +
6.82c, Cunera, 1962, Carlos Luis Sáenz, B♭3–G5, Med, Para Li Gabriela, CEDIM, *Canciones para canto y piano,* +
6.82d, Sólo por cantar, 1962, Carlos Luis Sáenz, B♭3–G♭5, Low, Para Rodrigo Mendoza, CEDIM, *Canciones para canto y piano,* +
6.82e, Cabanavenú, 1962, Carlos Luis Sáenz, C#4–F5, Low, —, CEDIM, *Canciones para canto y piano,* +

6.83, *Tres canciones de Ariel (La Tempestad)*
6.83a, I. [A estas aúreas arenas llegáos, . . .], 1964, William Shakespeare, D4–D5, Low, —, CEDIM, *Canciones para canto y piano,* +
6.83b, II. [De tu padre, . . .], 1964, William Shakespeare, C4–B♭4, Low, —, CEDIM, *Canciones para canto y piano,* +
6.83c, III. [Cual abeja los pétalos . . .], 1964, William Shakespeare, B♭3–B♭4, Low, —, CEDIM, *Canciones para canto y piano,* +

Ulloa Barrenechea, Ricardo, 1928-

6.84, Cantar, 1971, Ricardo Ulloa Barrenechea, C4–B4, Low, Written for soprano Amelia Barquero, CEDIM, *Antología canciones costarricenses*, —

6.85, Cantar del campesino, 1978, Ricardo Ulloa Barrenechea, E4–B6, High, Written for soprano Amelia Barquero, CEDIM, *Antología canciones costarricenses*, —

Ureña Morales, José Joaquín

6.86, Caminito del maizal (Canción típica), —, J. Joaquín Ureña Morales, —, —, —, ED, *La patria canta*, +

Villegas, Sacramento

6.87, Caminito de mi huerto, —, Rodolfo Salazar, C4–D5, Med, Arr. Gerardo Duarte R., UCR, *Antología de música guanacasteca*, —

Zúñiga Rovira, Héctor, 1913-

6.88, El burro'e chilo, —, Héctor Zúñiga, C4–D5, Med, Arr. Jorge Acevedo V., UCR, *Antología de música guanacasteca*, —

Zúñiga Zeledón, José Daniel, 1889-1981

6.89, Auroral, —, Ramon Leiva C., —, —, —, ED, *La patria canta*, +

6.90, Caña dulce (Canción popular), —, J. J. Salas Perez, —, —, —, ED, *La patria canta*, +

6.91, Carretera costanera (Popular), —, —, —, —, —, MC, *Música tradicional costarricense*, —

6.92, Carreterita (Popular), —, José Daniel Zúñiga Zeledón, —, —, —, MC, *Música tradicional costarricense*, —

6.93, Costa Rica (Corrido tico), —, José Daniel Zúñiga Zeledón, —, —, —, MC, *Música tradicional costarricense*, —

6.94, El boyero, —, J. J. Salas Perez, —, —, —, ED, *La patria canta*, +

6.95, Gitana (Tango-canción), —, J. Daniel Zúñiga Zeledón, —, —, —, ED, *La patria canta*, +

6.96, La Noche Buena (Canción tradicional de Navidad), —, José María Alfaro C., —, —, —, ED, *La patria canta*, +

6.97, Las playas del coco (Vals), —, José Daniel Zúñiga Zeledón, —, —, —, MC, *Música tradicional costarricense*, —

6.98, La tristeza del güetar, —, Carlos Soto Monge, —, —, Premiada en los juegos florales de 1963, ED, *La patria canta*, +

6.99, Mi patria (Marcha), —, José Daniel Zúñiga Zeledón, —, —, —, MC, *Música tradicional costarricense*, —

6.100, Nandayure (Capricho chorotega), —, José Ramírez Saizar, —, —, —, ED, *La patria canta*, +

6.101, Nandayureña, —, —, —, —, —, ED, *La patria canta*, +

6.102, Oración de duelo, —, Rogelio Sotela B., —, —, —, ED, *La patria canta*, +

6.103, Pensamiento (Marcha premiada en concurso), —, Spanish poet, —, —, —, ED, *La patria canta*, +

6.104, Romancillo del beso, —, Moises Vincenzi, —, —, —, ED, *La patria canta*, +

6.105, Sinfonía matinal, —, Carlos Mora Barrantes, —, —, —, ED, *La patria canta*, +

6.106, Tardes de noviembre (Barcarola), —, Fabio Rojas Díaz, —, —, —, ED, *La patria canta*, +

PUBLISHERS

CEDIM, Escuela de Artes Musicales
ED, Editor Danzuni
LAC, Liga de Compositores de México
LAGOS, Editorial Lagos
m, manuscript
MC, Ministerio de Cultura, Juventud y Deportes
MEP, Ministerio de Educación Pública
UCR, Editorial de la Universidad de Costa Rica

COLLECTIONS

+, LAMC (Latin American Music Center), Indiana University

SOURCES

(See bibliography for publication information)

Acevedo Vargas, *Antología de música guanacasteca*

Barquero, *Antología canciones costarricenses*

Campos Chanto, *Ciclo de 26 canciones y 2 corales*

LCP, *The Living Composers Project* (online resource)

Sanz Quiros, *Canciones para canto y piano*

Zuñiga Zeledón, *La patria canta: Música y canciones, autores de Costa Rica*

Zuñiga Zeledón, *Música tradicional costarricense*

7

Cuba

It was during the transition from the eighteenth to the nineteenth century that a distinctly Cuban music, although influenced by Spain and Africa, began to develop.[1] During this time, Cuba was host to performances of *zarzuela* and opera (crucial to the development of Cuban song), and concert music became increasingly popular as composer Manuel Saumell (1817–1870) began writing the first examples of Cuban art music.[2] By the second half of the nineteenth century, composer Ignacio Cervantes (1847–1905) was incorporating Cuban rhythmic elements into larger art forms.[3]

The early twentieth century brought a revolutionary interest in Cuba's African roots, leading to *Afrocubanismo* and the new voice of Cuban nationalism.[4] In 1923, the young revolutionaries formed a group composed of poets, musicians, and artists. The movement, led by Amadeo Roldán (1900–1939) and Alejandro García Caturla (1906–1940), was called the Grupo Minorista. Roldán and Caturla explored the incorporation of Afro-Cuban instruments and rhythms into large forms and in combination with Impressionistic and neoclassical elements. Caturla especially was able to master the juxtaposition of Afro-Cubanism with various mestizo folk elements, including Creole folklore, to create a unique style of his own.[5]

There was great political turmoil in Cuba at the turn of the century, including a U.S. military occupation, but in the first half of the twentieth century, Cuban music began to make an impression on the outside world.[6] It was during this period that Ernesto Lecuona (1895–1963), composer of the famous "La comparsa," brought one of the first Latin orchestras to the United States. For the first time, people in North

America and Western Europe heard Cuban sounds. This had tremendous implications for the rise of professional popular music and jazz. "La comparsa" was considered revolutionary when it premiered in 1912, due to the fantastic incorporation of Cuban elements. Lecuona's famous song "Malagueña" debuted at the Roxy Theatre in New York City in 1927. Both songs exist in almost any possible arrangement of instruments, in addition to the voice and piano versions included in this catalog.[7]

José Ardévol Gimbernat (1911–1981) was the leading composer of the 1930s and 1940s. A prolific composer, he first chose a neoclassical style of composition but later turned to more experimental atonal and twelve-tone methods. Still in search of a more solid foundation for Cuban music, he started a "Cuban school" of composers known as the Grupo de Renovación Musical. Among his contemporaries were Gisela Hernández (1912–1971), who was a member of the Grupo, and Joaquín María Nin-Culmell (1908–2004).[8]

The next generation of composers includes Ardévol's pupils Hilario González (1920–1999) and Argeliers León (1918–), who stayed with Afro-Cubanism. Composers Juan Blanco (1920–), Aurelio de la Vega (1925–), Carlos Fariñas (1934–2002), Julián Orbón (1925–1991), Leo Brouwer (1939–), and Tania León (1943–) exhibit a diversity of compositional styles and their works encompass many areas of composition, including film scores and electroacoustic music.[9]

Composers listed on *The Living Composers Project* with songs on their works list include Sergio Barroso (1946–), Irina Escalante Chernova (1977–), Orlando Jacinto García (1954–), Eduardo Morales Caso (1969–), Mónica O'Reilly-Viamontes (1975–), and José María Vitier (1954–).[10]

Ardévol Gimbernat, José, 1911–1986

7.1, ¡Ay señora, mi vecina!, 1960, Nicolás Guillén, F4–A5, High, —, SMP, —, +

Avilés, Danilo, 1948-

7.2, *Tres poemas minimos*
7.2a, I. Brizna, pequeño tallo, —, —, —, —, —, EMC, —
7.2b, II. Brisa que apenas mueve, —, —, —, —, —, EMC, —
7.2c, III. Punto de luz, suspenso lampo, —, —, —, —, —, EMC, —

Barroso, Sergio, 1946-

7.3, El ángel desengañado, 1963, Rafael Alberti, —, Alto, —, —, LCP, —
7.4, Grietas, 1965, Xiomara Funes, —, Soprano, —, —, LCP, —
7.5, *Tres canciones azules*, 1963, Rafael Alberti, —, Soprano, —, —, LCP, —
7.6, *Tres canciones grises*, 1963, Federico García Lorca, —, Alto, —, —, LCP, —

Escalante Chernova, Irina, 1977-

7.7, *Tres canciones*, —, —, —, —, —, —, LCP, —

García, Orlando Jacinto, 1954-

7.8, Ascending from the abyss, 2004, —, —, Mezzo, Mezzo and tape (CD), —, LCP, —
7.9, Canción (para mi niño), 1990, —, —, Soprano or mezzo, —, PEN, LCP, *The Art Song in Latin America*, +
7.10, Music for Nada, 1990, —, —, Soprano, Soprano and tape (or CD), —, LCP, —
7.11, Sitio Sin Nombre, 1990, —, —, Soprano, Soprano and tape (CD), —, LCP, —
7.12, Song no. 2, 1991, —, —, Soprano, Soprano, —, LCP, —
7.13, Voces en la distancia, 2003, —, —, Soprano, Soprano and piano, —, LCP, —

García Caturla, Alejandro, 1906–1940

7.14, Bito Manué, 1930, Nicolás Guillén, C♯4–G♯5, High, —, ES, PEN, *The Art Song in Latin America*, +
7.15, Yambambó, 1933, Nicolás Guillén, —, —, —, ES, —, +

González, Hilario, 1920–1999

7.16, Canción de Cleia (Quasi griega), ©1992, Guilherme Figueiredo, D4–F5, Med, A Carmen Arencibia, FVES, —, +

7.17, *Ciclo de canciones*
7.17a, He vivido horas sin igual (Hesitation waltz), ©1992, Claude Andre Puget, B3–F5, Med, A Fernando Gómez, FVES, —, +
7.17b, Rema tu bote (Quasi spiritual), 1952, William Saroyan, B♭2–F4, Med-high, Bass clef, A Carlos Márquez, FVES, —, +
7.17c, Entre casados de honor (Quasi punto), ©1992, Miguel de Cervantes, D4–E♭5, Med, A Juana Sujo, FVES, —, +
7.17d, [Oíd Efebos y atletas]
7.17e, Matinal tristeza (Lied), 1948, Juan Liscano, B♭2–E4, Med, A Juan Liscano, FVES, —, +
7.17f, El balandro (Balada), 1957, Manuel Felipe Rugeles, C4–B♭5, High, A Juan Liscano, FVES, —, +
7.17g, Cortejo (Criolla-Bolero), 1982, Miguel Otero Silva, B3–A♭5, High, A Juan Liscano, FVES, —, +

7.18, Liscano, —, —, —, Bass clef, —, FVES, —, +

Hernández, Gisela, 1912–1971

7.19, *Nueve canciones*
7.19a, Mi corazón lo tragó el mar, 1943, Mirta Aguirre, —, —, A Juan Liscano, EBC, —, +
7.19b, Única mar, 1943, Mirta Aguirre, —, —, A Juan Liscano, EBC, —, +
7.19c, Sólo por el rocío, 1944, Federico García Lorca, —, —, A Juan Liscano, EBC, —, +

7.19d, Huerto de marzo, 1944, Federico García Lorca, —, —, A Juan Liscano, EBC, —, +

7.19e, Romancillo, 1944, Federico García Lorca, —, —, A Juan Liscano, EBC, —, +

7.19f, Tránsito, 1945, Rabindranath Tagore, —, —, A Juan Liscano, EBC, —, +

7.19g, Deprisa tierra, deprisa, 1947, Juan Ramón Jiménez, —, —, A Juan Liscano, EBC, —, +

7.19h, Diálogo, 1955, Dulce María Loynaz, —, —, A Juan Liscano, EBC, —, +

7.19i, Voy a medirme el amor, 1958, Dulce María Loynaz, —, —, A Juan Liscano, EBC, —, +

7.20, Sólo por el rocío, 1964, Federico García Lorca, D4–E5, Med, A Manuel de Falla, TR, *The Latin American Art Song*, +

7.21, Tránsito, 1964, Rabindranath Tagore, B♭3–G5, Med, —, TR, *The Latin American Art Song*, +

Lecuona, Ernesto, 1895–1963

7.22, Andalucía, ©1928, Ernesto Lecuona, C4–C6, High, —, HL, *Always in My Heart*, —

7.23, Canto Karabalí, ©1929, Ernesto Lecuona, E4–C♯5(A5), Med-high, —, HL, *Always in My Heart*, —

7.24, Damisela encantadora, ©1935, Ernesto Lecuona, E♭4–G5, Med-high, —, HL, *Always in My Heart*, —

7.25, Juventud, ©1960, Ernesto Lecuona, E4–G5, Med-high, —, HL, *Always in My Heart*, —

7.26, La comparsa, ©1929, Ernesto Lecuona, B3–G♯5, Med, —, HL, *Always in My Heart*, —

7.27, Malagueña, ©1928, Ernesto Lecuona, E4–A5, Med-high, —, HL, *Always in My Heart*, —

7.28, María La O, ©1931, Ernesto Lecuona, B♭3–G5, Med-high, —, HL, *Always in My Heart*, —

7.29, Noche azul, ©1929, Ernesto Lecuona, C4–A5, Med-high, —, HL, *Always in My Heart*, —

7.30, Por eso te quiero, ©1936, Ernesto Lecuona, D4–F5, Med, —, HL, *Always in My Heart*, —

7.31, Siboney, ©1929, Ernesto Lecuona, D4–G5, Med-high, —, HL, *Always in My Heart*, —

7.32, Siempre en mi corazón, ©1942, Ernesto Lecuona, D4–F5, Med, —, HL, *Always in My Heart*, —

Nin-Culmell, Joaquín María, 1908–2004

7.33, *Cinco canciones tradicionales españolas*

7.33a, 1. Tres morillas me enamoran en Jaén, 1971, —, —, —, —, ME, +

7.33b, 2. Si tu madre quiere un rey, 1971, —, —, —, —, ME, +

7.33c, 3. En el café de Chinitas, 1971, —, —, —, —, ME, +

7.33d, 4. Este galapaguito: nana, 1971, —, —, —, —, ME, +

7.33e, 5. Tengo los ojos azules, 1971, —, —, —, —, ME, +

7.34, *Deux chansons populaires cubaines*

7.34a, I. Canción de cuna afro-cubana, 1985–1990, Traditional Text, —, —, —, Med, In memoriam mes cousins les Castellanos, —, ME, —, —, —, +, —

7.34b, II. La niña de Guatemala (Guajira romance), 1985–1990, José Marti, —, —, —, Med-high, —, —, ME, +

7.35, *Douze chansons populaires de Catalogne / Dotze cançons populars de Catalunya*

7.35a, La mar de Déu, 1952–1953, —, —, —, —, Medium voice, Catalan text, —, ME 6963, +

7.35b, El ram de la passió, 1952–1953, —, —, —, —, Medium voice, Catalan text, —, ME 6963, +

7.35c, La dama d'Aragó, 1952–1953, —, —, —, —, Medium voice, Catalan text, —, ME 6963, +

7.35d, El testament d'Amelia, 1952–1953, —, —, —, Medium voice, Catalan text, —, ME 6963, +

7.35e, La Paula i en Jordi, 1952–1953, —, —,

—, —, Medium voice, Catalan text, —, ME 6963, +

7.35f, L'hostal de la peira, 1952–1953, —, —, —, —, Medium voice, Catalan text, —, ME 6963, +

7.35g, Muntanyes regalades, 1952–1953, —, —, —, —, Medium voice, Catalan text, —, ME 6963, +

7.35h, Canço del lladre, 1952–1953, —, —, —, —, Medium voice, Catalan text, —, ME 6963, +

7.35i, El pardal quan s'ajocava, 1952–1953, —, —, —, —, Medium voice, Catalan text, —, ME 6963, +

7.35j, La filla del marxant, 1952–1953, —, —, —, —, Medium voice, Catalan text, —, ME 6963, +

7.35k, Mariagneta, 1952–1953, —, —, —, —, Medium voice, Catalan text, —, ME 6963, +

7.35l, Els fadrins de Sant Boi, 1952–1953, —, —, —, —, Medium voice, Catalan text, —, ME 6963, +

7.36, *Quatre chansons populaires de Catalogne/Cuatro canciones populares de Cataluña*

7.36a, Rossinyol que vas a França, 1960, —, —, —, —, Medium voice, Catalan text, —, ME 7224, +

7.36b, L'hermosa Antonia, 1960, —, —, —, —, Medium voice, Catalan text, —, ME, +

7.36c, El pobre alegre, 1960, —, —, —, —, Medium voice, Catalan text, —, ME, +

7.36d, La gata i el belitre, 1960, —, —, —, —, Medium voice, Catalan text, —, ME, +

7.37, *Quatre chansons populaires de L'Andalousie/Cuatro canciones populares de Andalucía*

7.37a, Anda jaleo, 1960, —, Federico García Lorca, —, —, High voice, —, ME, +

7.37b, Los cuatro muleros, 1960, —, Federico García Lorca, —, —, High voice, —, ME, +

7.37c, Debajo de la hoja, 1960, —, Federico García Lorca, —, —, High voice, —, ME, +

7.37d, Seguidillas Sevillanas, 1960, —, Federico García Lorca, —, —, High voice, —, ME, +

7.38, *Quatre chansons populaires de Salamanque/Cuatro canciones populares de Salamanca*

7.38a, Los mozos de Monleón, ©1964, —, —, —, —, High voice, —, —, ME, +

7.38b, Y se muriu el burru, ©1964, —, —, —, —, High voice, —, —, ME, +

7.38c, Los ojos de mi morena, ©1964, —, —, —, —, High voice, —, —, ME, +

7.38d, Ah! tienes mi corazón, ©1964, —, —, —, —, High voice, —, —, ME, +

7.39, *Seis canciones populares sefardíes*

7.39a, Yo boli de foja en foja, 1986, —, —, —, —, High voice, Ladino text; In memoriam omnium martyrum iudaeorum, —, ME 8606, +

7.39b, Adonenu, elohenu, 1986, —, —, —, —, High voice, Ladino text; In memoriam omnium martyrum iudaeorum, —, ME 8606, +

7.39c, La rosa enflorece, 1986, —, —, —, —, High voice, Ladino text; In memoriam omnium martyrum iudaeorum, —, ME 8606, +

7.39d, Ya salió de la mar, 1986, —, —, —, —, High voice, Ladino text; In memoriam omnium martyrum iudaeorum, —, ME 8606, +

7.39e, Mi suegra la negra, 1986, —, —, —, —, High voice, Ladino text; In memoriam omnium martyrum iudaeorum, —, ME 8606, +

7.39f, Secretos quero descuvrir, 1986, —, —, —, —, High voice, Ladino text; In memoriam omnium martyrum iudaeorum, —, ME 8606, +

7.40, Si ves un mote de espumas, 1985–1990, José Monti, —, —, —, —, Baritone and piano, —, ME, +

7.41, *Trois poèmes/Tres poemas de Gil Vicente*, ©1955, Gil Vicente, —, —, —, —, —, —, ME, +

O'Reilly Viamontes, Mónica, 1975–

7.42, *Epitafios*, 1999, Yanella Duarte, —, —, —, —, LCP, —

7.43, Luz, 1999, Yanella Duarte, —, —, —, —, LCP, —

Puebla, Carlos Manuel, 1917–1989

7.44, Hasta siempre, —, —, —, —, —, UOC, —, —

Roldán, Amadeo, 1900–1939

7.45, *Motivos del son*, —, —, —, —, —, —, —, —

7.45a, Negro bembón, 1934, Nicolás Guillén, —, Med-high, Arr. voice and piano, originally 8 songs for high voice and 11 instruments (1930), AMC, —, +

7.45b, Ayé me dijeron negro, ©1934, Nicolás Guillén, —, Med-high, Arr. voice and piano, originally 8 songs for high voice and 11 instruments (1930), AMC, —, +

7.45c, Sigue, ©1934, Nicolás Guillén, —, Med-high, Arr. voice and piano, originally 8 songs for high voice and 11 instruments (1930), AMC, —, +

Sánchez de Fuentes, Eduardo, 1874–1944

7.46, Canto de esclavos (Cuba 1870), 1927, Poesía popular, C4–G5, Med, —, TR, *The Latin American Art Song*, +

7.47, Deseo (Canción cubana), 1927, Eduardo Sánchez de Fuentes, E4–F5, Med, —, TR, *The Latin American Art Song*, +

Tomás, Guillermo M, 1868–1933

7.48, El pino y la palmera, —, —, —, Medium voice, —, EBN, —, +

7.49, ¡No! Canto de esperanza, —, —, —, Medium voice, —, EBN, —, +

Ubieta Gómez, Enrique, 1934–

7.50, Himno agrario, —, Nicolás Guillén, —, Medium voice, —, INRA, —, —

Vega, Aurelio de la, 1925–

7.51, El encuentro, 1950, Rabindranath Tagore, —, —, m, —, +

Additional titles: La fuente infinita.

Vitier, José María, 1954–

7.52, Agnus Dei, 1992, —, —, —, —, —, LCP, —

7.53, Canción de otoño, 2001, Rubén Darío, —, —, —, —, LCP, —

7.54, Romanza de los adolescentes, 1992, Juan Clemente Zenea, —, —, —, —, LCP, —

7.55, Se dice cubano, 1993, José Martí, —, —, —, —, LCP, —

7.56, Silvia, 2002, Amaury Pérez, —, —, Version of piano work, —, LCP, —

7.57, Suite de canciones infantiles no. 1, 1977, Mirta Aguirre, —, —, —, —, LCP, —

7.58, Suite de canciones infantiles no. 2, 1983, Mirta Aguirre, —, —, —, —, LCP, —

PUBLISHERS

AMC, American Music Center
EBC, Ediciones de Blanck
EBN, Ediciones de la Biblioteca Nacional José Marti
EMC, Editorial Musical de Cuba
ES, Éditions Maurice Senart
FVES, Fundación Vicente Emilio Sojo
HL, Hal Leonard Corporation
INRA, Dirección de Relaciones Públicas del INRA
ME, Éditions Max Eschig
m, manuscript
PEN, Pendragon Press
SMP, Southern Music Publishing Company, Inc.
TR, Tritó, S.L.
UOC, Universidad de Oriente

COLLECTIONS

+, LAMC (Latin American Music Center), Indiana University

SOURCES

(See bibliography for additional publication information)

Caicedo, *The Latin American Art Song: A Critical Anthology and Interpretive Guide for Singers*

LCP, *The Living Composers Project* (online resource)

Plácido Domingo—Always in My Heart: The Songs of Ernesto Lecuona

Wilson, *The Art Song in Latin America: Selected Works by Twentieth-Century Composers*

8

Dominican Republic

The Dominican Republic, Cuba, and Puerto Rico are often designated as "Caribbean Latin America," and, especially in discussions about music, are kept separate from the rest of the islands on the basis of their predominant use of the Spanish language. While it makes sense to divide the Caribbean according to gross cultural differences, over time the smaller islands have become marginalized and are rarely included in studies of music from Latin America. It is important to note that there are geographic, cultural, and musical connections, both among the small and large islands and between the Caribbean islands and the rest of Latin America. Furthermore, given the long history of things African or Black being negatively perceived (Africanism and *hispanidad*), society today must be careful to uphold all expressions of Caribbean culture and ethnicity equally.[1]

The Dominican Republic occupies the eastern two-thirds of the island of Hispaniola, which it shares with Haiti. The relationship between ethnicity and cultural identity is a complex one with many social and political implications, and language is often used as the basic defining feature of culture, identity, and even region.[2]

Dominican music is a part of Dominican identity, and features a blend of native-influenced Spanish and African music. African influences are most apparent in the use of percussion, specifically of long drums, and the use of various types of social and narrative songs.[3]

The Republic's government supports and encourages music—the capital city has a symphony orchestra, a National Conservatory was established in 1941, and in 1944, the government sponsored a composition contest for local musicians, with a grand prize of $1000 (USD).[4]

Juan Bautista Alfonseca (1810–1875) was one of the first to use national folklore in his compositions, and is known as "the father of Dominican music."[5]

Composers using national music as a base but in large forms were José de Jesús Ravelo (1876–1951), the incredibly prolific Augusto Vega (1885–?), and Gabriel del Orbe (1888–?).[6] Other notable composers from the twentieth century include Enrique Mejía Arredondo (1901–1951), Enrique de Marchena Dujarric (1908–1988), and Ninón Lapeiretta de Brouwer (1907–1989). Current composer Ana Silfa Finke (1949–) has songs listed in her works list on *The Living Composers Project*.[7]

Pierret Villanueva, Florencia, 1932–

8.1, Cancionero juvenil dominicano, —, Children's Songbook, —, PAU, —, +

Silfa Finke, Ana, 1949–

8.2, La fuente, 1976, Porfirio Herrera, High, Soprano, —, LCP, —
8.3, Meciendo, 1973, Gabriela Mistral, High, Soprano, —, LCP, —

PUBLISHERS

PAU, Pan American Union

COLLECTIONS

+, LAMC (Latin American Music Center), Indiana University

SOURCES

(See bibliography for publication information)
LCP, *The Living Composers Project* (online resource)

9

Ecuador

According to author John L. Walker, the main barriers to the success of art music in Ecuador are a lack of government support and the overall poverty from which the composers come, a lack of performing forces, and a lack of music publishing.[1] Composers in Ecuador can be classified in several ways, although the most common seems to be according to generation.[2] Most are nationalistic in the sense that they strive for a voice that is specifically "Ecuadorian," and most incorporate traditional nationalistic tendencies, such as the use of indigenous (Quechua, Incan, or Amazonian) elements. Although several efforts have been made to preserve indigenous musical traditions, little can be found from before the 1860s. Musicologist Pablo Guerrero has played an important role in preserving traditional music, and also founded the Corporación Musicología Ecuatoriana (CONMUSICA).[3]

Previous composers of the twentieth century such as Segundo Luis Moreno (1882–1972) and Luis H. Salgado (1903) set the pace for nationalism in Ecuadorian music. The former was also an important figure in the collection of popular and indigenous music, and in his own compositions used indigenous Ecuadorian melodies and folk rhythms within a European Romantic harmonic language.[4] Salgado also used native themes and indigenous musical elements, perhaps paving the way for the important contributions of Gerardo Guevara (1930–), who incorporated traditional Amazonian rhythms into his works.[5] Guevara continues to be an integral figure, striving to preserve Amazonian elements in Ecuadorian music.

The composers during the first third of the twentieth century contributed in various ways to Ecuador's music. Ángel Honorario Jiménez was an important figure in the leftist worker's movement during the 1930s and 1940s. Néstor Cueva Negrete created a new system of musical notation called Nescueván, and Corsino Durán created folk-like tunes reminiscent of Andean music, which Guerrero called "recreations or stylizations."[6]

Others, like Pedro Pablo Traversari (1874–1956), used a more neo-Romantic approach indicative of European training. Experimental composers from Ecuador exist as well, such as Mesías Maiguashca (1938–), who studied at the Eastman School of Music (University of Rochester, New York) and worked with Karlheinz Stockhausen.[7] The latest generation of composers includes Milton Estévez (1947–), Arturo Roda (1951–), and Diego Luzuriaga (1955–).[8]

Guevara, Gerardo, 1930–

9.1, Yaraví, —, César Monroy, B3–G5, Med-high, PEN, *The Art Song in Latin America*, +

Luzuriaga, Diego, 1955–

9.2, 2 *Canciones infantiles*, 1982, —, —, Medium voice, —, LCP, —
9.3, Mademoiselle Satan, 1982, Jorge Carrera Andrade, —, Baritone, —, LCP, —

Paredes Herrera, Francisco, 1891–1952

9.4, *Mélodies populaires indiennes*
9.4a, Méjico (Himno), 1923, —, —, —, CMC, —
9.4b, Ferreira (Tango), 1923, —, —, —, CMC, —

Additional title: Durán, Sixto María (from *Mélodies populaires indiennes*) [CMC].

PUBLISHERS

CMC, Castellanos-Molino Corporation
PEN, Pendragon Press

COLLECTIONS

+, LAMC (Latin American Music Center), Indiana University

SOURCES

(See bibliography for publication information)
LCP, *The Living Composers Project* (online resource)
Wilson, *The Art Song in Latin America: Selected Works by Twentieth-Century Composers*

10

El Salvador

El Salvador is sorely under-represented in the existing literature. Although several attempts have been made to correct this problem, there remains a noticeable gap in the area of research and published compositions. A committee was established in 1942 with the hopes of rectifying this situation; however, the results were unsatisfactory. A further attempt was made by María de Baratta with Jeremías Mendoza in the two-volume publication *Cuzcatlán típico: Ensayo sobre etnofonía de El Salvador, folklore, folkwisa, y folkway*. Nicolas Slonimsky's forward-looking announcement of the committee's initial study in his 1945 publication proved overly optimistic, although Baratta's work seems to be an improvement.[1] Slonimsky discusses El Salvador briefly, but the country is completely missing from Béhague's *Music in Latin America*.[2] From the existing literature, the following conclusions can be drawn: the instruments and dances common to Central America in general, such as the danza, pasillo, and marcha, are prevalent in El Salvador; and the nineteenth-century musical scene was dominated by Italian musicians, who brought leadership and education in the Western style with them. The first orchestra, the Sociedad Orquestal Salvadoreña, was also directed by an Italian, Antonio Gianoli.[3]

Some earlier composers, who in general incorporate indigenous melodies into their music, include Ciriaco Jesús Alas (1866–?), a voice teacher who seems to have written mostly larger scale works; the Italian-schooled Domingo Santos (1892–?); María Mendoza de Baratta (1890–1978), an important figure in the preservation of El Salvadorian culture; and the composer and voice teacher José Napoleón Rodríguez (1901–).[4]

Modern composers from this country also exist, such as serialist Gilberto Orellana (1942–).[5] German Gustavo Cáceres (1954–), another important modern composer and conductor, was educated in the United States but returned to El Salvador to maintain important positions in the musical life there.[6] His numerous vocal compositions are listed in this catalog, and he is currently the only El Salvadorian member of *The Living Composers Project*.[7]

Cáceres, German Gustavo, 1954–

10.1, *Cartas interdimensionales*
10.1a, I. [Las estrellas binarias . . .], 2004, Juana Rosa Pita, A3–G5, High, —, —, LCP, —
10.1b, II. [Los poemas que al verbo se resisten . . .], 2004, Juana Rosa Pita, A3–G5, High, —, —, LCP, —
10.1c, III. [Estos ojos que ahora están mirando . . .], 2004, Juana Rosa Pita, B♭3–G♯5, High, —, —, LCP, —

10.2, *Cuatro canciones para soprano y piano*
10.2a, I. Si un niño muere en la guerra, 1981, Álvaro Menéndez-Leal, B3–A♯5, High, Soprano, —, PEN, *The Art Song in Latin America*, +
10.2b, II. Apunte, 1981, Álvaro Menéndez-Leal, C4–G♯5, High, Soprano, —, —, LCP, —
10.2c, III. Canción de cuna, 1981, Álvaro Menéndez-Leal, F4–A5, High, Soprano, —, —, LCP, —
10.2d, IV. Preguntas, 1981, Álvaro Menéndez-Leal, B♭3–A5, High, Soprano, —, —, LCP, —

10.3, *Cuatro canciones para soprano y piano*
10.3a, I. [Sos un sueño . . .], 1999, —, C♯4–F5, High, Soprano, —, —, LCP, —
10.3b, II. [Cuando haya tomado . . .], 1999, —, B3–F♯5, High, Soprano, —, —, LCP, —
10.3c, III. [Si alguna vez . . .], 1999, —, B3–G♯5, High, Soprano, —, —, LCP, —
10.3d, IV. [Adios de deo clausurar . . .], 1999, —, C4–A5, High, Soprano, —, —, LCP, —

10.4, *Elegía de junio*
10.4a, I. Fin de un sueño, 2005, Cristóbal Humberto Ibarra, A♯3–F♯5, Med, —, —, LCP, —
10.4b, II. Alta noche, 2005, Cristóbal Humberto Ibarra, A♯3–F♯5, Med, —, —, LCP, —
10.4c, III. Llora un niño, 2005, Cristóbal Humberto Ibarra, G3–G5, Med, —, —, LCP, —
10.4d, IV. Madrugada, 2005, Cristóbal Humberto Ibarra, B3–G5, Med, —, —, LCP, —
10.4e, V. La euforia nos nace y muere adentro, 2005, Cristóbal Humberto Ibarra, F♯4–G5, Med-high, —, —, LCP, —

10.5, *El señor de la casa del tiempo*
10.5a, I. [Pero cómo habríamos de permanecer aquí . . .], 1996, Ricardo Lindo, B3–A♭5, High, Soprano, —, —, LCP, —
10.5b, II. [Desciende, gris, de las olas lentas del aire . . .], 1996, Ricardo Lindo, C4–G♯5, High, Soprano, —, —, LCP, —
10.5c, III. [Ceniza, lluvia, vino, . . .], 1996, Ricardo Lindo, C♯4–G5, High, Soprano, —, —, LCP, —

10.5d, IV. [¿Y quién eres, ... ?], 1996, Ricardo Lindo, C♯4–G♯5, High, Soprano, —, —, LCP, —

10.6, In Memoriam Elisa Huezo Paredes: Yo tengo que decir mi palabra, 2004, —, G♯3–G5, Med-high, —, —, LCP, —

10.7, *Llama y espina: Tres sonetos para soprano y piano*
10.7a, I. Metamorfosis, 2004, —, C4–A♭5, High, —, —, LCP, —
10.7b, II. Revelación, 2004, —, C4–G♯5, Med-high, —, —, LCP, —
10.7c, III. Profecía, 2004, —, E4–A5, High, —, —, LCP, —

10.8, *Siete canciones*
10.8a, I. [Quiero hundir la mirada en el vacío ...], 1999, Mariana Sansón Argüello, C4–A5, High, Soprano, —, —, LCP, —
10.8b, II. [Me atormentan las voces ...], 1999, Mariana Sansón Argüello, C4–G5, Med-high, Soprano, —, —, LCP, —
10.8c, III. [La corriente continuaba ...], 1999, Mariana Sansón Argüello, A♯3–G♯5, High, Soprano, —, —, LCP, —
10.8d, IV. [He tomado los gestos ...], 1999, Mariana Sansón Argüello, C4–F♯5, Med-high, Soprano, —, —, LCP, —
10.8e, V. [Y sé por dónde voy ...], 1999, Mariana Sansón Argüello, C4–G♯5, Med-high, Soprano, —, —, LCP, —
10.8f, VI. [Estoy continuando al aire que me sigue ...], 1999, Mariana Sansón Argüello, D♯4–G♯5, High, Soprano, —, —, LCP, —
10.8g, VII. [He pasado a otros mundos ...], 1999, Mariana Sansón Argüello, D4–A5, High, Soprano, —, —, LCP, —

10.9, *Tres canciones epigramáticas*
10.9a, I. Ileana, 1979, Ernesto Cardenal, B3–A5, High, Soprano, —, —, LCP, —
10.9b, II. La noche, 1979, Ernesto Cardenal, B♭3–A5, High, Soprano, —, —, LCP, —
10.9c, III. Detrás del Monasterio Junto al Camino, 1979, Ernesto Cardenal, C♯4–B5, High, Soprano, —, —, LCP, —

10.10, *Tres canciones para soprano y piano*
10.10a, I. [Empolvado de seda ...], 1995, Francisco Morales Eró, C♯4–G♯5, High, Soprano, Para Siri Rico, —, LCP, —
10.10b, II. [Me mataron en la víspera de tu silencio ...], 1995, Francisco Morales Eró, B3–G5, High, Soprano, Para Siri Rico, —, LCP, —
10.10c, III. [Se te llenó la vida lentamente de mar ...], 1995, Francisco Morales Eró, C4–G5, High, Soprano, Para Siri Rico, —, LCP, —

Additional titles: María Mendoza de Baratta (1890–1978): Can-calagui-tunal; La campana llora; Los tecomatillos. Esteban Servellón (1921–2003): Les violons de l'Automne; Un rancho y un lucero.

PUBLISHERS

PEN, Pendragon Press

COLLECTIONS

+, LAMC (Latin American Music Center), Indiana University

SOURCES

LCP, *The Living Composers Project* (online resource)
Wilson, *The Art Song in Latin America: Selected Works by Twentieth-Century Composers*

Guatemala

Before the Spanish conquest, Guatemala was a part of the heart of Mayan civilization. Mayans still occupy half of Guatemala, maintaining the traditions of the Mayan religion. Mayan music is an integral part of the culture, and musical events center around a calendar that combines dates from the Roman Catholic religion with Mayan agricultural cycles. Guatemala is also home to Arawak and Carib descendants (descendants of African slaves brought over by the Spaniards) and to Spanish-speaking Ladinos, although it took until the 1920s for African rhythms to begin to work their way into Guatemalan music.[1]

The nineteenth century saw the influence of European art and art forms, as was typical in other regions of Latin America, but also the elevation of local or popular music as it became fashionable at elite events. In 1859, the Teatro Oriente opened, featuring great Italian operas of the time and touring Italian opera companies, many of whose European-trained musicians chose to stay in Guatemala. The Italian-born Juan Aberle, who became the first head of El Salvador's National Conservatory of Music, spent time in Guatemala before eventually settling in El Salvador.[2]

Much of the Guatemalan folk music has been catalogued and classified by musicologist and composer Jesús Castillo.[3] In general, Guatemalan composers from the middle of the nineteenth century and into the beginning of the twentieth century followed the same trends as did composers in other areas of Latin America—the quest for national identity within the context of European art forms resulted in the incorporation of native elements into otherwise Romantic or Impressionistic music. Composers exemplifying this type of composition include

Jesús Castillo (1877–1946), Ricardo Castillo (1894–1967), Salvador Ley (1907–1985), and Enrique Solares Echeverría (1910–). Ley wrote over fifty songs, a limited number of which are available in manuscript form from the Latin American Music Center at Indiana University.

As with the Costa Rican composers, a handful of Guatemalan composers have focused on educational songs. These include Jesús María Alvarado (1896–1977), whose numerous songs for children were published in several books,[4] and José Castañeda (1898–), whose children's songs have also been published. Some of Miguel Sandoval's (1903–1953) settings of folk songs from Spain and Latin America are included in this catalog.

Other composers have employed more modern techniques, such as José Castañeda, who experimented with polytonality, microtonality, and serialism, and José Sarmientos (1931–), who also used serial techniques.[5]

Ley, Salvador, 1907–1985

11.1, Balada del tiempo mozo, 1940, Enrique Gonzales Martínez, —, Med-high, —, m, —, +

11.2, Copla triste (Elegy), 1940, Enrique Gonzales Martínez, D4–F5, Med, —, EBMMC, PEN, *The Art Song in Latin America*, +

11.3, Der Krieg, 1950, Matthias Claudius, —, Med-high, German text; score text illegible, m, —, +

11.4, *Tres canciones sobre poemas de Enrique Gonzáles Martinez*

11.4a, Lumen, 1940, Enrique Gonzales Martínez, —, Medium voice, —, m, —, +

11.4b, Victoria sobre el tiempo, 1940, Enrique Gonzales Martínez, —, Medium voice, —, m, —, +

11.4c, Diafanidad, 1940, Enrique Gonzales Martínez, —, Medium voice, —, m, —, +

11.5, Yo pienso en tí, 1963, José Batres Montúfar, —, Med-high, —, m, —, +

Marroquín, José Sabre, 1900–1995

11.6, Canción de cuna a Patricia, 1955, José Agüeros, D4–E5, Med, —, PI, —, +

Sandoval, Miguel, 1903–1953

11.7, A casinha pequenina, —, Brazilian folk song, arr. Sandoval, —, —, —, GSch 41941, —, —

11.8, Adelita, —, Mexican folk song, arr. Sandoval, —, —, —, GSch 41941, —

11.9, A la orilla del palmar, —, Mexican folk song, arr. Sandoval, —, —, —, GSch 41941, —

11.10, A las montañas iré, —, Bolivian folk song, arr. Sandoval, —, —, —, GSch 41941, —

11.11, Así amo yo (Cueca), ©1949, Chilean folk song, arr. Sandoval, E4–F♯5, Med, —, GSch 41941, —

11.12, ¡Ay, ay, ay!, —, Chilean folk song, arr. Sandoval, —, —, —, GSch 41941, —

11.13, *Cantos de España*
11.13a, Romería Mariana, ©1954, —, —, Medium voice, —, GRic, —
11.13b, En casa del tío Vicente, ©1954, —, —, Medium voice, —, GRic, —
11.13c, Charrada, ©1954, —, —, Medium voice, —, GRic, —
11.13d, Nostalgia, ©1954, —, —, Medium voice, —, GRic, —
11.13e, Soleá, ©1954, —, —, Medium voice, —, GRic, —
11.13f, Caminito de Avilés, ©1954, —, —, Medium voice, —, GRic, —

11.14, Cielito lindo, —, Mexican folk song, arr. Sandoval, —, —, —, GSch 41941, —
11.15, Coco de los Santos, —, Panamanian folk song, arr. Sandoval, —, —, —, GSch 41941, —
11.16, Cuatro milpas, —, Mexican folk song, arr. Sandoval, —, —, —, GSch 41941, —
11.17, El mishito, —, Guatemalan folk song, arr. Sandoval, —, —, —, GSch 41941, —
11.18, El tecolote, —, Mexican folk song, arr. Sandoval, —, —, —, GSch 41941, —
11.19, En Cuba, —, Cuban folk song, arr. Sandoval, —, —, —, GSch, 41941, —
11.20, Eres tu (Bolero), —, —, —, —, —, SMP, —
11.21, Joropo, ©1950, —, —, —, —, TPC, —
11.22, La golondrina, —, Mexican folk song, arr. Sandoval, —, —, —, GSch 41941, —
11.23, La malagueña, —, Mexican folk song, arr. Sandoval, —, —, —, GSch 41941, —
11.24, Lament: Vocalise
11.25, La paloma, —, Mexican folk song, arr. Sandoval, —, —, —, GSch, 41941, —
11.26, Las mañanitas, —, Mexican folk song, arr. Sandoval, —, —, —, GSch 41941, —
11.27, La tarde era triste, —, Folk song, arr. Sandoval, —, —, —, GSch 4194, —
11.28, Lullaby, ©1952, —, D4–E5, Med, —, GRic, —
11.29, Madrigal, —, —, A3–E4, Low, Baritone, —, GSch, *The Second Book of Baritone/Bass Solos, Part II*, —

11.30, Mis flores, —, Colombian folk song, arr. Sandoval, —, —, —, GSch 41941, —
11.31, Por un beso de tu boca (Bambuco), ©1949, Colombian folk song, arr. Sandoval, E4–F5, Med, —, GSch 41941, —
11.32, Pregúntale a las estrellas, —, Folk song, arr. Sandoval, —, —, —, GSch 41941, —
11.33, Río, río, —, Chilean folk song, arr. Sandoval, —, —, —, GSch 41941, —
11.34, Riqui, Riqui, Riquirrán, —, Venezuelan folk song, arr. Sandoval, —, —, —, GSch 41941, —
11.35, Serenata gitana, —, —, —, —, —, GSch, *Great Art Songs of Three Centuries*, —
11.36, Sin tu amor, p1939, —, —, —, —, GSch, *50 Art Songs from the Modern Repertoire*, —
11.37, Te quiero porque te quiero, —, Mexican folk song, arr. Sandoval, —, —, —, GSch 41941, —
11.38, Una vez clavelina, —, Argentinean folk song, arr. Sandoval, —, —, —, GSch 41941, —
11.39, Vidalita, ©1949, Argentinian folk song, arr. Sandoval, G♯4–G♯5(A5), Med-High, —, GSch 41941, —

Additional titles: Ricardo Castillo (1894–1967): *Cuatro canciones guatemaltecas*; Nudo ciego; Vocalice Maya. Julián González (1870–1898): Melodía. Joaquín Orellana (1935–): *Three Songs*. Jorge Alvaro Sarmientos de León (1931–): *Seis cantos de esperanza*; *Eighteen Songs*. Enrique Solares Echeverría (1910–): Prayer; Cradle Song; Olivereto de Ferm; El Ciprés de silos; Cosecha de la amistad; Miguel Sandoval: Besos obscuros (Canción); Ciruja (Tango); Cocaina; Primavera (One Step).

PUBLISHERS

EBMMC, Edward B. Marks Music Corporation
GRic, G. Ricordi
GSch, G. Schirmer, Inc.
m, manuscript
PEN, Pendragon Press
PI, Pier International Corporation
SMP, Southern Music Publishing Company, Inc.
TPC, Theodore Presser Co.

COLLECTIONS

+, LAMC (Latin American Music Center), Indiana University

SOURCES

(See bibliography for additional publication information)

50 Art Songs from the Modern Repertoire
Boytim, *The Second Book of Baritone/Bass Solos, Part II*
Taylor, *Great Art Songs of Three Centuries*
Wilson, *The Art Song in Latin America: Selected Works by Twentieth-Century Composers*

12

Haiti

Jean-Ronald LaFond

The development of the Haitian *mélodie* is not unlike that of many national art songs, particularly those from other Latin American countries. The early Haitian composer experienced a search for identity between two extremes: 1) reaching for the elevated status of the French composer, whose model naturally had a profound influence on the Haitian musical psyche by virtue of the French colonization of Haiti; and 2) finding a formal musical language based on the rich folkloric influences of Haitian *Vodou,* Hispanic America, the English and Dutch Caribbean, as well as Haitian folk melodies, a folk song hybrid of the French folk song and Afro-Haitian melodic and rhythmic sources.

It is important to note that art music of various forms existed from as far back as the eighteenth century, when Haiti, then named Saint Domingue, enjoyed the status of the most valued and most lucrative of the French colonies. The *Dialogue créole* by Michel-Étienne Descourtilz is included here as the one vocal example that survives from this period. It is not a traditional art song, but a quasi-operatic scene for two voices and keyboard (probably harpsichord or fortepiano). It is conceivable that the French library system may contain additional works, composed by inhabitants of Saint Domingue who returned to France during the revolutionary period between 1790 and 1804, when Haiti won its independence from France.

The subsequent development of art music genres slowed down during most of the nineteenth century as the first Black republic struggled to establish a working government while naturally warding off both potential French retaliation and a potential American invasion. Haiti's close proximity to the United States, where slavery was practiced, incited the African Americans who saw uniformed Haitian regiments assist the American colonies in defeating the British, particularly in Savannah, Georgia. Despite the participation of Haitian troops in the American Revolutionary Wars (albeit under the French flag), the United States did not recognize Haiti as a sovereign nation until the early 1860s, after Lincoln delivered the Emancipation Proclamation. By the late nineteenth century, amateur musicians from the Haitian upper class had composed a fair amount of music, including songs. Both imitations of the French *mélodie* and folk-inspired songs, usually in the form of vocal *méringues*, were being composed.[1] Meanwhile, these amateur composers, mostly pianists, also wrote a significant number of *méringues* for solo piano. The celebrated folk song "Choucoune" by Mauléar Monton (1855, New Orleans–1895, Port-au-Prince) is one of the early *méringues*. Other early *méringues* are found by Fernand Frangeul (1872–1911) and Henri Étienne (dates unknown).

Werner Jaegerhuber (1900–1953), a Haitian of German parentage, is responsible for the first musicological study of Haitian *Vodou* musical traditions, and subsequently arranged twenty-four of the standard ceremonial songs for voice and piano in a collection entitled *Offrandes vaudouesques* (Vodou Offerings). This seminal work led to the composition of the *Messe vaudouesque*, a controversial setting of the Catholic Mass utilizing *Vodou* melodic and rhythmic styles. In a country that had become politically Catholic, this was a bold move, and had art music played an important role in Haitian culture, this piece might have caused a great stir. Jaegerhuber also wrote more European-style songs, including some in the German language. The French settings are exclusively from Haitian poets.

Jaegerhuber's work influenced many of the affluent Haitians who were musically trained to try their hands at composition. Among them are Frantz Casséus, a guitar virtuoso, who made his Carnegie Hall debut in the 1950s, and Carmen Brouard (1909–2005), the most accomplished Haitian composer until recent years. Casséus contributed much more to the development of the guitar in Haiti than he did to that of songs. However, he was a first-class musician and his *Haïtianesques*, a collection of four folk songs in Haitian creole, for voice and guitar, raised the bar significantly for Haitian art music composition. Brouard was trained at the Paris Conservatory and was strongly influenced by the late works of Fauré. Her songs show an economy of material and a refined harmonic language, expertly interweaving a traditional European language with a profound knowledge of Haitian musical folk elements. A very serious personality, her choice of poetry was usually of a dark, melancholic nature. Her extensive body of work encompasses several sets of songs, including *Reflets d'âme* (six songs), *Cinq interprétations d'Omar Khayyam*, and *Cinq chants funèbres* (five songs).

Throughout the 150-year history of the modern Haitian art song, many composers have produced excellent pieces that add to the amalgam of the Haitian song output, but none were as completely dedicated to the art of music as Jaegerhuber and Brouard. It is important to remember that other than those two, none until the late twentieth century can be labeled a professional musician. The most interesting songs from this group come from Ferrère Laguerre, Justin Elie, Solon Verrett, Ludovic Lamothe, and Edouard Woolley.

The turbulent political climate of Haiti in the twentieth and twenty-first centuries caused the professional training of Haitian musicians to occur abroad. Many of them have chosen to formally study composition. The most successful one is the young Haitian-American, Daniel Roumain, who is enjoying a prolific career in New York City. Others include the Haitian-Canadian David Bontemps (1978–), the French Haitian Amos Coulanges, the Haitian-American Jean-Ronald LaFond, and the Canadian-American Claude Dauphin, a musicologist-composer and professor of music at the Université de Québec à Montréal, who undertook to assemble all the Haitian art music he could find in one place, making it all accessible to a wider public. The Canadian-American singer-composer Robert Grenier, professor at the University of South Carolina, has given hundreds of hours of his time in order to edit many of the Haitian manuscripts in the collection of Haitian scores at the Université de Québec à Montréal.

Few of the Haitian art songs have been published, and those that have been published have not been reissued. The Société des Recherches et de Diffusion de la Musique Haïtienne acts as custodian of the collection of musical scores in the music library of the Université de Québec à Montréal and promotes performances of Haitian musical works. The organization is overseen by Dr. Claude Dauphin, who continues to seek out Haitian works of music that may have been displaced or presumed lost through many years of political and social turmoil. Dr. Dauphin and the Société constitute the primary resource for Haitian art music.

Anonymous

12.1, Ti Zando, —, —, Med, —, m, —, SRDMH

12.2, Vous êtes belle, —, —, Med, —, m, —, SRDMH

Blain, Iphares

12.3, Dodo titit', —, Folk, Med, —, m, —, SRDMH

Bontemps, David, 1978–

12.4, *Deux mélodies*

12.4a, Que tal?, —, Marie-Ange Jolicœur, Med, Baritone, —, m, —, SRDMH (M-BOND-Qu-11)

12.4b, Tes yeux sont des adieux, —, Marie-Ange Jolicœur, Med, Baritone, —, m, —, SRDMH (M-BOND-Qu-12)

12.5, Il a neigé, —, Marie-Ange Jolicœur, Med, Baritone, —, m, —, SRDMH (M-BOND-Il-14)

Borno, Louis (Luigi Francesco)

12.6, Hymne du bicentenaire, 1904, —, Med, Medium voice, Accompaniment by Justin Cie Elie, Lithographique, Port-au-Prince, Haiti, —, SRDMH (M-BORL-Hyl-02)

Brouard, Carmen, 1909–2005

12.7, Chant spirituel, 1996, Sri Aurobindo, Med-high, Medium voice, —, m, fsRG, SRDMH

12.8, *Cinq chants funèbres*

12.8a, Le corbillard, 1984, Émile Nelligan, Med-high, Medium voice, —, m, fsRG, SRDMH

12.8b, Les corbeaux, 1984, Émile Nelligan, Med-high, Medium voice, —, m, fsRG, SRDMH

12.8c, Les carmélites, 1984, Émile Nelligan, Med-high, Medium voice, —, m, fsRG, SRDMH

12.8d, Le tombeau de la négresse, 1984, Émile Nelligan, Med-high, Medium voice, —, m, fsRG, SRDMH

12.8e, Marches funèbres, 1984, Émile Nelligan, Med-high, Medium voice, —, m, fsRG, SRDMH

12.9, *Cinq interprétations d'Omar Khayyam*

12.9a, Sur la terre bariolée, 1960, Omar Khayyam, Med-high, Medium voice, —, m, fsRG, SRDMH

12.9b, Je ne peux apercevoir le ciel, 1960, Omar Khayyam, Med-high, Medium voice, —, m, fsRG, SRDMH

12.9c, Un peu de pain!... Un peu d'eau fraîche, 1960, Omar Khayyam, Med-high, Medium voice, —, m, fsRG, SRDMH

12.9d, Il te versera sa chaleur, 1960, Omar Khayyam, Med-high, Medium voice, —, m, fsRG, SRDMH

12.9e, Pourquoi, 1960, Omar Khayyam, Med-high, Medium voice, —, m, fsRG, SRDMH

12.10, Haïti ma jolie..., 1985, Nadine Magloire, Med, Medium voice, —, m, —, SRDMH

12.11, Nuit, 1995, Pierre Julien, High, Soprano, —, m, —, SRDMH

12.12, *Reflets d'âme*

12.12a, Devant le couchant, 1934, Renée Vivien, Med-high, Medium voice, —, m, fsRG, SRDMH (M-BROC-Re-02)

12.12b, Plus qu'ennuyée, 1934, Marie Laurencin, Med-high, Medium voice, —, m, fsRG, SRDMH (M-BROC-Re-02)

12.12c, Mes larmes, 1934, Heinrich Heine (Aus Meinen Thränen Sprießen), Med-high, Medium voice, —, m, fsRG, SRDMH (M-BROC-Re-02)

12.12d, Prière de Madame Elizabeth à sa prison, 1934, —, Med-high, Medium voice, —, m, fsRG, SRDMH (M-BROC-Re-02)

12.12e, Quand je serai mort, 1934, Carl Brouard, Med-high, Medium voice, —, m, fsRG, SRDMH (M-BROC-Re-02)

12.12f, Prière, 1934, Carl Brouard, Med-high, Medium voice, —, m, fsRG, SRDMH (M-BROC-Re-02)

12.13, *Soirs*

12.13a–12.13d, 1.–4., 1993, Charles Baudelaire, Med-high, Medium voice, —, m, fsRG, SRDMH

12.14, *Temps*

12.14a–12.14d, 1.–4., 1995, Pierre Julien, Med-high, Medium voice, —, m, fsRG, SRDMH

Casséus, Frantz, 1915–1993

12.15, *Haïtienesques*

12.15a, Adieu foulards, —, Folk (Martinique), Med-high, Medium-High, —, FCP, —, SRDMH

12.15b, Fi nan bois, —, Folk, Med-high, Medium-High, —, FCP, —, SRDMH

12.15c, Asotô, —, Traditional (*Vodou*), Med-high, Medium-High, —, FCP, —, SRDMH

12.15d, Se gran maten, —, Folk, Med-high, Medium-High, —, FCP, —, SRDMH

Dauphin, Claude, 1949–

12.16, Folklores harmonisés, op. 7, 1975–1977, Folk, Med-high, Medium-High, —, m, —, SRDMH

Desmangles, Édouard

12.17, *Pièces pour chant et piano*

12.17a, Message, 1939–1941, V. Wilder, Med-high, Medium-High, —, m, —, SRDMH

12.17b, Il pleure dans mon cœur, 1939–1941, Paul Verlaine, Med-high, Medium-High, —, m, —, SRDMH

12.17c, Élégie, 1939–1941, F. Jammes, Med-high, Medium-High, —, m, —, SRDMH

12.17d, Chanson triste, 1939–1941, Jean Lahore, Med-high, Medium-High, —, m, —, SRDMH

12.17e, J'ai presque peur, 1939–1941, Paul Verlaine, Med-high, Medium-High, —, m, —, SRDMH

Elie, Justin, 1883–1931

12.18, Lorsque je serai vieux et que tu seras vieille, —, Georges Sylvain, Med-high, Medium-high, —, m, —, SRDMH

Frangeul, Fernand, 1872–1911

12.19, A l'hè qui lé, —, Folk, Med, Medium, —, Facsimile Éditions Frangeul, —, SRDMH

12.20, Sous le ciel bleu, 1905, Maurice De Brache, Med, Medium, —, m, Facsimile Éditions Frangeul, —

Héraux, Jules, 189?–1960

12.21, Volonté, 1949, Jean Brierre, Med, Medium, Photocopy of edited score, Édition Exposition du bicentenaire, —, SRDMH

Jaegerhuber, Werner, 1900–1953

12.22, Chanson Jean Brierre, —, —, —, Unknown facsimile, m, —, SRDMH (M-JAEW-Ch-03)

12.23, Chansons folkloriques d'Haïti, 1945, Unknown, —, Unknown photocopy of manuscript; Valrio Canez, editor, —, —, SRDMH (M-JAEW-Ch-04)

12.24, Claire de lune, —, Louis Borno, —, Unknown photocopy of manuscript, m, —, SRDMH (M-JAEW-Cl-06)

12.25, *Offrandes vodouesques* (original title: *Complaintes haïtiennes*)

12.25a, A legba, 1945, Folk, Med-high, Medium-High, —, RGAHM, fsRG, SRDMH (M-JAEW-Of-29)

12.25b, Bouclé noué, 1945, Folk, Med-high, Medium-High, —, RGAHM, fsRG, SRDMH (M-JAEW-Of-29)

12.25c, Agoué Ta Royo, 1945, Folk, Med-high, Medium-High, —, RGAHM, fsRG, SRDMH (M-JAEW-Of-29)

12.25d, Moin tandé youn cannon, 1945, Folk, Med-high, Medium-High, —, RGAHM, fsRG, SRDMH (M-JAEW-Of-29)

12.25e, C'est jodi moin nan lanmè, 1945, Folk, Med-high, Medium-High, —, RGAHM, fsRG, SRDMH (M-JAEW-Of-29)

12.25f, Solè oh, 1945, Folk, Med-high, Medium-High, —, RGAHM, fsRG, SRDMH (M-JAEW-Of-29)

12.25g, Siba oh, 1945, Folk, Med-high, Medium-High, —, RGAHM, fsRG, SRDMH (M-JAEW-Of-29)

12.25h, Erzulie oh, 1945, Folk, Med-high, Medium-High, —, RGAHM, fsRG, SRDMH (M-JAEW-Of-29)

12.25i, Vling sou Vling, 1945, Folk, Med-high, Medium-High, —, RGAHM, fsRG, SRDMH (M-JAEW-Of-29)

12.25j, Barré, 1945, Folk, Med-high, Medium-High, —, RGAHM, fsRG, SRDMH (M-JAEW-Of-29)

12.25k, Laza oh, 1945, Folk, Med-high, Medium-High, —, RGAHM, fsRG, SRDMH (M-JAEW-Of-29)

12.25l, Dambala oh, 1945, Folk, Med-high, Medium-High, —, RGAHM, fsRG, SRDMH (M-JAEW-Of-29)

12.25m, Yo ouè bo mio couè, 1945, Folk, Med-high, Medium-High, —, RGAHM, fsRG, SRDMH (M-JAEW-Of-29)

12.25n, Missiyé Ouèzan, 1945, Folk, Med-high, Medium-High, —, RGAHM, fsRG, SRDMH (M-JAEW-Of-29)

12.25o, Onimba, 1945, Folk, Med-high, Medium-High, —, RGAHM, fsRG, SRDMH (M-JAEW-Of-29)

12.25p, Vévélo, 1945, Folk, Med-high, Medium-High, —, RGAHM, fsRG, SRDMH (M-JAEW-Of-290

12.25q, Simbi, 1945, Folk, Med-high, Medium-High, —, RGAHM, fsRG, SRDMH (M-JAEW-Of-29)

12.25r, Gros loa moin, 1945, Folk, Med-high, Medium-High, —, RGAHM, fsRG, SRDMH (M-JAEW-Of-29)

12.25s, Erzulie, 1945, Folk, Med-high, Medium-High, —, RGAHM, fsRG, SRDMH (M-JAEW-Of-29)

12.25t, Guédé Nibo, 1945, Folk, Med-high, Medium-High, —, RGAHM, fsRG, SRDMH (M-JAEW-Of-29)

12.25u, Guédé Zareigné, 1945, Folk, Med-high, Medium-High, —, RGAHM, fsRG, SRDMH (M-JAEW-Of-29)

12.25v, Erzulie malade, 1945, Folk, Med-high, Medium-High, —, RGAHM, fsRG, SRDMH (M-JAEW-Of-29)

12.25w, Erzulie eh, 1945, Folk, Med-high, Medium-High, —, RGAHM, fsRG, SRDMH (M-JAEW-Of-29)

12.25x, Bouclé noué, 1945, Folk, Med-high, Medium-High, —, RGAHM, fsRG, SRDMH (M-JAEW-Of-290

12.26, O mort, vieux capitaine, 1943, Charles Baudelaire, High, High, —, m, fsRG, SRDMH (M-JAEW-Om-34)

12.27, Puisque le ciel t'envoie, —, —, Med-high, Medium-High, —, m, fsRG, SRDMH (M-JAEW-Pu-39)

12.28, Seigneur, lorsque viendra, 1952, Dominique Hyppolite, Med-high, Medium-High, —, m, fsRG, SRDMH (M-JAEW-Pu-39)

12.29, *Trois chansons d'après des textes d'Ida Faubert*
12.29a, Quand on vous dira, 1951, Ida Faubert, Med-high, Medium-High, —, m, fsRG, SRDMH (M-JAEW-Tr-57)
12.29b, Amour, 1951, Ida Faubert, Med-high, Medium-High, —, m, fsRG, SRDMH (M-JAEW-Tr-57)
12.29c, Nirvana, 1951, Ida Faubert, Med-high, Medium-High, —, m, fsRG, SRDMH (M-JAEW-Tr-57)

LaFond, Jean-Ronald, 1965–

12.30, *Trois chansons vodouesques*
12.30a, Agué Ta Royo, 2004, Traditional (*Vodou*), Med, Medium, Finale score edited by the composer, m, —, SRDMH
12.30b, Fèy ô, 2004, Traditional (*Vodou*), Med, Medium, Finale score edited by the composer, m, —, SRDMH
12.30c, Ezili malad, 2004, Traditional (*Vodou*), Med, Medium, Finale score edited by the composer, m, —, SRDMH

Laguerre, Ferrère, 1935–1983

12.31, Comme un profil perdu, —, Henry Torres, High, High, —, m, —, SRDMH (M-LAGF-Co-03)
12.32, Trois rondes haïtiennes, —, Folk, High, High, —, m, —, SRDMH (M-LAGF-Tr-07)

Lamothe, Ludovic, 1882–1953

12.33, Billet, —, Vieux Damoclès, Med-high, Medium-High, Photocopy of edited score, Imprimerie Roeder, Paris, France, —, SRDMH (LAML-Bi-02(sd))

Monton, Mauléar, 1855–1898

12.34, Choucoune, —, Oswald Durand, Med-high, Medium-High, Photocopy of edited score, Édition Alphonse, Montreuil, —, SRDMH (M-MONM-Ch-02)

Ricourt, Volvick

12.35, Souvenances et souffrances (Méringue), —, —, Med-high, Medium-High, Arr. Augustin Brunot, m, —, SRDMH

Salnave, Dépestre

12.36, Canta mi corazón (Chante mon cœur), 1934, Ida Faubert, Med, Medium, Photocopy of manuscript edition, Digoudé Diodet, Paris, —, SRDMH

Verrett, Alexandre

12.37, Hymne aux héros, 1956, J. Dieudonné Lubin, Med, Medium, —, m, —, SRDMH

Verrett, Solon, 1912–1992

12.38, Ave Maria (Méditation), —, Traditonal (Catholic), Med, Medium, —, m, —, SRDMH
12.39, Ave Maria (Prière), —, Traditonal (Catholic), Med, Medium, —, m, —, SRDMH
12.40, Claire de lune, —, Marcel Dauphin, Med, Medium, —, m, —, SRDMH (M-VERS-CdL-01)

Woolley, Édouard, 1916–1991

12.41, *A l'ombre de tes ailes*
12.41a, Le jardin, —, Mary Marquet, Med-high, Medium-High, —, m, fsRG, SRDMH
12.41b, Lettres, —, Mary Marquet, Med-high, Medium-High, —, m, fsRG, SRDMH
12.41c, Féminité, —, Mary Marquet, Med-high, Medium-High, —, m, fsRG, SRDMH
12.41d, Sérénitié, —, Mary Marquet, Med-high, Medium-High, —, m, fsRG, SRDMH
12.41e, Chères mains, —, Jean Gillet, Med-high, Medium-High, —, m, fsRG, SRDMH

12.41f, J'ai ta tête sur mon épaule, —, Jean Gillet, Med-high, Medium-High, —, m, fsRG, SRDMH

12.41g, Berceuse à la bien-aimée (Vocalise-étude), —, Vocalise, Med-high, Medium-High, —, m, fsRG, SRDMH

12.41h, Similitude, —, Kyouco, Med-high, Medium-High, —, m, fsRG, SRDMH

12.41i, Pêche d'ombres, —, Georges Dessoudeix, Med-high, Medium-High, —, m, fsRG, SRDMH

12.41j, Pour ton visage, —, Marie-Louise Dromart, Med-high, Medium-High, —, m, fsRG, SRDMH

12.42, O salutaris hostia, —, Traditonal (Catholic), —, —, m, —, SRDMH

PUBLISHERS

RGAHM, Robert Grenier for Agence Haïtienne de Musique

FCP, Franco Columbo Publications

m, manuscript

COLLECTIONS

SRDMH, Société des Recherches et de Diffusion de la Musique Haïtienne, Université de Québec à Montréal

SOURCES

fsRG, Finale score edited by Robert Grenier

13

Honduras

There is little evidence of art music in Honduras. In reference works, Honduras is left out, and there seems to be little evidence on internet sources; in fact, the Latin American Network Information Center (LANIC) does not have one link to anything related to Honduras. Slonimsky covers the country in five paragraphs, surmising that there is little professional activity and that the country's musical life is sustained mainly by military bands and popular music.[1]

Of the few composers covered in *Latin American Classical Composers: A Biographical Dictionary*, even fewer wrote secular art music, and there is almost no evidence of song composition.[2] The surviving song of Manuel de Adalid y Gamero (1872–1947), "Voces de la tarde," is held in a collection of papers in the Latin American Library at Tulane University.[3]

Adalid y Gamero, Manuel de, 1872-1947

13.1, Voces de la tarde (Canción de cuna), 1929, Manuel de Adalid y Gamero, —, TUL

Mejía, Joaquín Orellana, 1937-

13.2, Los pobres (Five Songs), 1986–1987, Roberto Sosa, Soprano, Includes intermezzo for piano, JM

PUBLISHERS

JM, Josef Marx/McGinnis & Marx Music Publishers

COLLECTIONS

TUL, Tulane University, Latin American Library (online resource)

14

Jamaica

Searches for sources on Jamaican music will generally lead to information on the popular genre of reggae. However, classical music by Jamaican composers, while difficult to find, does exist. Although the findings on art songs by Jamaican composers thus far are admittedly few, there is evidence of activity, and several internet sources will lead ambitious singers to more information.

There is confusion regarding composer delimitations, as many composers who identify themselves as Jamaican either were not born in Jamaica or no longer live there. In the interest of inclusion, this chapter includes composers who identify themselves as being of Jamaican heritage, regardless of place of birth or current residence.

A wonderful source of information on Jamaican music is the website entitled "Jamaica's Classical Musicians."[1] While it is not always clear whether or not the composers included on this website wrote art songs following the scope of this study, it does serve as a basis for information on these composers. This site includes composers Oswald Russell (1933–); Noel DeCosta (1929–), who was born in Nigeria to Jamaican parents and whose work incorporates African, West Indian, and African American folk traditions; and Frederic H. Cowen (1852–1935), some of whose three hundred songs can be obtained through the personal collection of Christopher Parker, who currently resides in the United Kingdom.[2]

This chapter includes the song cycles of Richard Thompson (1954–), who, like Noel DeCosta, was born in Nigeria to Jamaican parents and identifies himself as Jamaican. His songs contain lyric vocal lines with a wide range, and complex piano accompaniments which combine with the voice to create rich textures that are both beautiful and interesting.

Thompson, Richard, 1954–

14.1, *Dream Variations*
14.1a, I, too, sing America, 2004, Langston Hughes, F♯4–G5*, Med-high, Tenor, Dedicated to Darryl Taylor, MMB
14.1b, The Negro speaks of rivers, 2004, Langston Hughes, E4–A5, High, Tenor, Dedicated to Darryl Taylor, MMB
14.1c, Monotony, 2004, Langston Hughes, A4–G5, Med-high, Tenor, Dedicated to Darryl Taylor, MMB
14.1d, A Black Pierrot, 2004, Langston Hughes, F4–A♭5, Med-high, Tenor, Dedicated to Darryl Taylor, MMB
14.1e, Dream variations, 2004, Langston Hughes, F4–A♭5, High, Tenor, Dedicated to Darryl Taylor, MMB
*Ranges in this cycle are listed in treble clef; however, the cycle is intended to be sung by a tenor.

14.2, *The Shadow of Dawn: Five Poems by Paul Laurence Dunbar*
14.2a, 1. Dawn, 1999, Paul Laurence Dunbar, E4–G5, High, Soprano, —, MMB
14.2b, 2. Love's apotheosis, 1999, Paul Laurence Dunbar, E4–G5, High, Soprano, —, MMB
14.2c, 3. We wear the mask, 1999, Paul Laurence Dunbar, E♭4–G♭5(B♭5), High, Soprano, —, MMB
14.2d, 4. One life, 1999, Paul Laurence Dunbar, B3–G5, Med-high, Soprano, —, MMB
14.2e, 5. Sympathy, 1999, Paul Laurence Dunbar, F4–G♭5, Med-high, Soprano, —, MMB

PUBLISHERS

MMB, MMB Music, Inc.

15

Mexico

Prior to the twentieth century, art music in Mexico was influenced by Italian opera and characterized by salon-style compositions, especially piano pieces incorporating national dances and songs.[1] What followed was a plethora of important and prolific composers, each playing a valuable part not only in Mexican music itself, but also with regard to the reception of Mexican music in the larger world.

The Mexican Revolution in 1910 sparked a wave of nationalism, and composers began to incorporate elements of native Indian and Mestizo cultures into their music. Tonality and structure remained Romantic in nature, and continued to mimic the salon composition in form.[2] Manuel M. Ponce (1882–1948) paved the way, with a compositional style that varied over the decades from Romantic to Impressionistic and later incorporated dissonant harmonies within a consonant framework.[3] His songs, such as the famous "Estrellita," written in 1912 and published in 1914, exemplify his ideal balance between popular and more modern trends. As a nationalist, he used actual folk material, Indian subject matter, and Mexican elements such as cross-rhythms (specifically hemiola) and alternating duple and triple figures indicative of typical Mexican dances.[4] In addition to folk song arrangements and sixty-eight songs in the salon tradition that lean toward a more popular style, Ponce also published song cycles such as *Tres poemas de Mariano Brull, Cuatros poemas de Francisco A. de Icaza, Seis canciones arcaicas, Tres poemas de Enrique Gonzáles Martínez, Three Poems by Rabindranath Tagore,* and *Tres poemas de Lermontow.*[5]

Carlos Chávez (1988–1978), although not as prolific in writing vocal music as Ponce was, is considered by many to be one of the most important figures in Mexican music and a leading proponent of nationalism.[6] Writing during what he claimed was the Aztec Renaissance and Indianist movement in the arts (1920–1934), he was a champion of the nationalist movement.[7] Chávez felt that Aztec music typified the complete and most profound state of the Mexican soul. He identified the defining elements of Aztec melody as a preference for thirds and fifths, use of the pentatonic scale, and the absence of semitones.[8] Chávez later moved into a more modern neoclassic polytonal style. He became a strong proponent of new music and an important figure in the development of Mexican musical life. He founded the Orquesta Sinfónica de México in 1928 and remained its primary conductor until 1949. He also served as director of the Conservatorio Nacional de Música de Mexico and the Instituto Nacional de Bellas Artes.[9]

Silvestre Revueltas (1899–1940), also a nationalistic composer, was inspired by popular and folk elements of contemporary society, which he incorporated into a neoclassical structure along with a modern use of tonality. His vocal lines are generally lyrical in conception, and some compositions, like *Dos canciones* and *Cinco canciones de niños,* are partnered with hypnotically repetitive figures in the accompaniments featuring interesting dissonances.

Other important song composers associated with Mexico include Spanish-born Rodolfo Halffter (1900–1987), Jésus Bal y Gay (1905–1993), and María Teresa Prieto (1910–1982), and native Mexican composers Luis Sandi (1905–1996) and Blas Galindo Dimas (1910–1993). Composer Simón Tapia Colmán (1906–1933) was also born in Spain but is associated with Mexico.

It is important to note that Mexico has a very rich tradition of songs that fall into the popular category but which can easily be incorporated into a classical recital program. Considered by many to be standards of the tenor repertoire alongside Italian classics such as "Cor 'ngrato" and "O sole mio," these songs are generally lyrical in nature with some sort of dramatic (high and loud or high, soft, and sweet) finish. Of the songs falling into this category, some of the most popular are "Jurame" by María Grever (1885–1951) and "Granada" by Agustín Lara (1900–1970).[10] To include them all in this catalog would be virtually impossible (María Grever alone wrote over eight hundred songs); however, most are readily available through popular music sources and publishers such as Southern Music Publishing and Peer International Corporation.

It is also worth checking *The Living Composers Project* website for a glimpse at this generation of Mexican composers, particularly Enrique González-Medina (1954–), who has numerous songs that are easily accessible through the website.[11]

Adomián, Lan, 1905–1979

15.1, *Dos canciones*
15.1a, Vengan vientos, ©1974, Teodoro Cesarman, —, Medium, —, EMM-CA, —, +
15.1b, Charada, ©1974, Teodoro Cesarman, —, Medium, —, EMM-CA, —, +

15.2, *Dos nanas*
15.2a, I. A la nana blanca que se fue a la mar, 1969, Juan Rejano, A3–E5, Low-med, —, EMM-CA, —, +
15.2b, II. Que se va a dormir . . ., 1969, Juan Rejano, A3–F5, Low-med, —, EMM-CA, —, +

Ayala Pérez, Daniel, 1906–1975

15.3, *Cuatro canciones*
15.3a, I. Nostalgía, 1947, Juan Ramón Jiménez, D4–F5, Med, —, ECIC, —, +
15.3b, II. Abril, 1947, Juan Ramón Jiménez, F4–G♭5, Med-high, —, ECIC, —, +
15.3c, III. Otoño último, 1947, Juan Ramón Jiménez, D♭4–G5, Med-high, —, ECIC, —, +
15.3d, IV. Soledad, 1947, Juan Ramón Jiménez, D4–F5, Med, —, ECIC, —, +

Bal y Gay, Jesús, 1905–1993

15.4, *Cuatro piezas*
15.4a, Canción, 1941, Emilio Prados, F4–G5, Med, —, EMM, —, +
15.4b, La plenitud, 1940, Juan Ramón Jiménez, E4–A5, Med-high, —, EMM, —, +
15.4c, Nana del niño malo, 1942, Rafael Alberti, D♭4–F5, Med, —, EMM, —, +
15.4d, A la luna feliz, 1941, Juan Ramón Jiménez, F4–G5, Med-high, —, EMM, —, +

Bañuelas, Roberto, 1931–

15.5, *Tres canciones españolas: para canto y piano*
15.5a, I. Es verdad, 1971, Federico García Lorca, E4–G5, Med-high, —, EMM-CA, —, +
15.5b, II. Las seis cuerdas, 1971, Federico García Lorca, E4–F♯5, Med-high, —, EMM-CA, —, +
15.5c, III. Romance de la Luna, Luna, 1971, Federico García Lorca, C♯4–G♯5, Med-high, —, EMM-CA, —, +

Chávez, Carlos, 1899–1978

15.6, Canto a la tierra, 1946, Enrique Gonzales Martínez, C4–D5, Low-med, A la Escuela Nacional de Agricultura de Chapingo, EMM, —, +

15.7, *Dos canciones*
15.7a, Todo, 1942, Ramón López Velarde, C4–F5, Med, Mezzo- soprano or baritone, —, B/H, —, +
15.7b, North Carolina blues, 1942, Xavier Villaurrutia, C4–F5, Med, Mezzo- so-

prano or baritone, —, B/H, PEN, *The Art Song in Latin America* (1998), +

15.8, Du bist wie eine Blume, 1919, Heinrich Heine, D4–B♭5, High, —, m, —, LPALC, NAM

15.9, Estrellas fijas, 1919, Asunción Silva, D4–B♭5, High, —, m, —, LPALC, NAM

15.10, Extase, 1918, Victor Hugo, E4–F5, Med, —, m, —, NAM, LPALC

15.11, Inutil epigramma, 1919, Ronald de Carvalho, G4–G♯5, High, —, m, —, LPALC, NAM

15.12, La casada infiel, 1941, Federico García Lorca, C4–E♯5, Low-med, Mezzo or baritone, —, EMM, SMP, —, +

15.13, Nocturno de la estatua, —, —, C4–G♯5, High, —, m, —, LPALC, NAM

15.14, Nocturno en que nada se oye, —, —, F4–F♯5/A4–E5, Low-med, —, m, —, LPALC, NAM

15.15, Nocturno sueño, —, —, B4–D5, Low-med, —, m, —, LPALC, NAM

15.16, Primer nocturno, —, —, C4–G♭5, Med, —, m, —, LPALC, NAM

15.17, *Tres exágonos*

15.17a, Exágono I, 1923, Carlos Pellicer, A4–G♭5, High, —, m, —, LPALC, NAM

15.17b, Exágono II, 1923, Carlos Pellicer, G♯4–F5, High, —, m, —, LPALC, NAM

15.17c, Exágono III, 1923, Carlos Pellicer, A4–B♭5, High, —, m, —, LPALC, NAM

15.18, *Three poems/Tres poemas*

15.18a, Segador, 1938, Carlos Pellicer, F4–F♭5, Med, —, GSch, —, +

15.18b, Hoy no lució la estrella de tus ojos, 1938, Salvador Novo, C4–C♯5, Med, —, GSch, —, +

15.18c, Nocturna rosa, 1938, Villaurrutia, D4–G5, Med, —, GSch, —, +

Elías, Manuel de, 1939–

15.19, Canciones del ocaso, 1988, Manuel de Elías, —, Mezzo, Version for mezzo and orchestra (1992) available, —, —, LCP

15.20, Las erupciones, 1959, Salvador Díaz Mirón, —, Alto, —, —, —, LCP

15.21, Salmodia, 2003, —, —, Mezzo, —, —, —, LCP

15.22, *Siete canciones para niños*, 1988, Manuel de Elías, —, Soprano, —, —, —, LCP

15.23, Vocalise, 1994, —, —, Baritone, —, —, —, LCP

Galindo Dimas, Blas, 1910–1993

15.24, *Cinco canciones a la madre muerta*, ©1994, —, —, —, —, EMM-Serie B no. 28, —, +

15.25, *Dos canciones*

15.25a, Arullo, 1944, Alfonso del Río, D4–F5, Med, A la Niña del Retrato, EMM-Serie B no. 3, —, +

15.25b, Madre mía, cuando muera, 1944, Rubén M. Campos, E4–E5, Med, —, EMM-Serie B no. 3, —, +

15.26, Fuensanta, ©1968, Ramón López Velarde, F♯4–F♯5, Med-high, Irma González, EMM-CA, —, +

15.27, *Tres canciones*

15.27a, Jicarita, 1939, Alfonso del Río, F♯4–E5, Med, —, ArMP, EMM-Serie B no. 18, —, +

15.27b, Mi querer pasaba el río, 1939, Elías Nandino, F4–G5, Med-high, —, ArMP, EMM-Serie B no. 18, —, +

15.27c, Paloma blanca, 1939, Blas Galindo, E4–E5, Med, —, ArMP, EMM-Serie B no. 18, —, +

Gomezanda, Antonio, 1894–1961

15.28, Vieja danza: sobre un antiguo tema mexicano, ©1931, —, Medium voice or for solo left hand, EIMG, —, +

González-Medina, Enrique, 1954–

15.29, *Bajacalifornianos*, op. 28 and op. 28a, Book III from the *Baja California Songbook*

15.29a, 1. En mañanas como ésta, —, José

Javier Villaroel, —, Low, Bass (Op. 28a), Also version for tenor (op. 28), —, LCP, —

15.29b, 2. Entendimiento, —, José Javier Villaroel, —, Low, Bass (Op. 28a), Also version for tenor (op. 28), —, LCP, —

15.29c, 3. Elegía frente al mar, —, José Javier Villaroel, —, Low, Bass (Op. 28a), Also version for tenor (op. 28), —, LCP, —

15.29d, 4. Mis abuelos, —, José Javier Villaroel, —, Low, Bass (Op. 28a), Also version for tenor (op. 28), —, LCP, —

15.29e, 5. Tijuana, —, José Javier Villaroel, —, Low, Bass (Op. 28a), Also version for tenor (op. 28), —, LCP, —

15.30, *Siete poemínimos, op. 9*, 1995, Efraín Huerta, —, High voice, Also versions for voice and chamber orchestra, —, LCP, —

15.31, Vorrei baciarti, O fillis, op. 4, 1991, Giambattista Marino, —, Tenor, Italian text, —, LCP, —

Grever, María, 1885–1951

15.32, Júrame (Tango), —, —, (B3)C4–F5(G5), Med, —, SMP, —, +

Additional titles: Despedida, Rataplan [GSch].

Halffter, Rodolfo, 1900–1987

15.33, Desterro, op. 31: para canto y piano, 1967, Xosé M. Álvarez Blázquez, F4–G#5, Med, Text in Galician, EMM-CA, —, +

15.34, *Dos sonetos, op. 15: para canto y piano*

15.34a, Miró Celia una rosa..., 1940–1946, Sor Juana Inés de la Cruz, B♭3–E♭5, Med, —, EMM, UME, —, +

15.34b, Feliciano me adora, 1940–1946, Sor Juana Inés de la Cruz, D4–E5, Med, —, EMM, UME, —, +

15.35, *Marinero en tierra, op. 27: para canto y piano*

15.35a, 1. Qué altos los balcones..., ©1963, Rafael Alberti, D4–G5, High, —, RA BA12199, —, +

15.35b, 2. Casadita, ©1963, Rafael Alberti, D4–G5, High, —, RA BA12199, —, +

15.35c, 3. Siempre que sueño las playas..., ©1963, Rafael Alberti, F#4–F#5, Med, —, RA BA12199, —, +

15.35d, 4. Verano, ©1963, Rafael Alberti, E4–F#5, High, —, RA BA12199, —, +

15.35e, 5. Gimiendo por ver el mar..., ©1963, Rafael Alberti, A4–G5, High, —, RA BA12199, —, +

Hernández Moncada, Eduardo, 1899–1995

15.36, *Canciones al estilo de mi tierra*

15.36a, Tropical, 1958, Agustín Delgado, —, High voice, —, EMM-Serie B no. 25, —, +

15.36b, Dame pápiro de luna, 1958, Jorge Ramón Juárez, —, High voice, —, EMM-Serie B no. 25, —, +

15.36c, Es de noche, te estoy viendo, —, Librado Basilio, —, High voice, —, EMM-Serie B no. 25, —, +

15.36d, Madrugada, —, Jorge Saldaña, —, High voice, —, EMM-Serie B no. 25, —, +

15.36e, Canción costeña, —, Carlos McGregor Giociniti, —, High voice, —, EMM-Serie B no. 25, —, +

Additional titles: Cuatro fragmentos de San Juan de la Cruz; Tres sonetos de sor Juana.

Ibarra, Federico, 1946–

15.37, *Dos canciones para soprano y piano*

15.37a, Canción arcaica para niños, 1979, Federico García Lorca, E4–G5, High, —, EMM-Serie B no. 21, —

15.37b, La ermita, 1965, Anonymous fifteenth-century text, C4–A♭5, Med, —, EMM-Serie B no. 21, —

Jiménez Mabarak, Carlos, 1916–1994

15.38, *Seis canciones para cantar a los niños*

15.38a, 1. Din don, 1962, Carlos Luis Sáenz, D4–E♭5, Med, —, RA BA12196, —, +

15.38b, 2. La casa, 1962, Carlos Luis Sáenz, D4–G♯5, Med, —, RA BA12196, —, +

15.38c, 3. La vieja Inés, 1962, Carlos Luis Sáenz, D4–G5, Med-high, —, RA BA12196, —, +

15.38d, 4. Ron-ron, 1962, Carlos Luis Sáenz, E4–F♯5, Med-high, —, RA BA12196, —, +

15.38e, 5. El niño azul, 1962, Carlos Luis Sáenz, C♯4–F♯5, Med-high, —, RA BA12196, —, +

15.38f, 6. El alacrán, 1962, Carlos Luis Sáenz, D♭4–F5, Med, —, RA BA12196, —, +

15.39, *Tres canciones breves*

15.39a, 1. Queja, 1939, —, —, —, —, EMM-Serie B no. 30, —, +

15.39b, 2. Nocturno (de Rafael Solana), 1939, —, —, —, —, EMM-Serie B no. 30, —, +

15.39c, 3. Canción de primavera, 1939, —, —, —, —, EMM-Serie B no. 30, —, +

Kuri Aldana, Mario, 1931–

15.40, *Canciones españolas*

15.40a, Nana, ©1997, Lope de Vega, —, —, —, EMM-Serie B no. 29, —, +

15.40b, Niña, limón, limonero, ©1997, A. Khoury, —, —, —, EMM-Serie B no. 29, —, +

15.40c, La más bella niña, ©1997, Luis de Góngora, —, —, —, EMM-Serie B no. 29, —, +

15.40d, En el corazón del sueño, ©1997, Federico García Lorca, —, —, —, EMM-Serie B no. 29, —, +

15.40e, Canción nuestra, ©1997, Luis Cernuda y A. Khoury, —, —, —, EMM-Serie B no. 29, —, +

15.40f, Madrigal, ©1997, Gutierre de Cetina, —, —, —, EMM-Serie B no. 29, —, +

15.40g, Como sa mu trista, ©1997, Luis de Góngora, —, —, —, EMM-Serie B no. 29, —, +

Ladrón de Guevara, Raúl, 1934–2006

15.41, *Dos nocturnos para voz y piano*

15.41a, Blanca noche, —, Rosalba Pérez Priego, B3–E♭5, Med, A Cecilia y Mónica, LAC, —

15.41b, Testimonio, 1979, Rosalba Pérez Priego, A3–E5, Low-med, —, LAC, —

Lara, Agustín, 1900–1970

15.42, Granada (Fantasía española), ©1932, Agustín Lara, D4–F5, Med, English text by Dorothy Dodd, PI, —, +

Additional titles: Album No. 1 (Aventurera, Clavel sevillano, Cortesana, Despierta, Gotas de amor, Monísima, Muchacha, Mujer, Páginas rotas, Rosa, Si yo pudiera, Solo tú) [SMP, PI et al.].

Lara, Ana, 1959–

15.43, Déjame soñar tu sueño, 1998, —, —, Mezzo, —, —, LCP, —

15.44, Llévame a donde quieras, 1999, —, —, Mezzo, —, —, LCP, —

Lavalle García, Armando, 1924–1994

15.45, *Tres canciones para voz y piano*

15.45a, La niña ausente, 1980, Neftalí Beltrán, D4–F♯5, Med, Soprano, A María Luisa Rangel, LAC, —

15.45b, Botoncito, 1980, Gabriela Mistral, C4–G5, Med-high, Soprano, A Alda Segovia, LAC, —

15.45c, Canción que es llanto en el mar, 1980, Enrique Gonzales Martínez, D4–F5, Med-high, Mezzo, —, LAC, —

Lavista, Mario, 1943–

15.46, *Dos canciones, op. 2*

15.46a, Palpar, 1966, Octavio Paz, A♭3–F♯5, Med-high, Mezzo, A Rosa Martha; voice and piano or harpsichord; non-traditional notation, EMM-Serie B no. 11, —

15.46b, Reversible, 1966, Octavio Paz, A♭3–G5, Med-high, Mezzo, A Juan Vicente Melo; Voice and piano or harpsichord; non-traditional notation, EMM-Serie B no. 11, —

15.47, Hacia el comienzo, 1988, Octavio Paz, —, —, Originally for mezzo and orchestra, —, LCP, —

15.48, Pañales y sonajas, Lullaby for Elisa, 1999, Untexted, —, Mezzo, Prepared piano, diapers, and rattles, —, LCP, —

15.49, *Tres canciones chinas*, 1993, Li-Po and Wang Wei (Tang Dynasty), —, Mezzo, Trans. Marcela San Juan and Gariel Zaid, —, LCP, —

Lobato, Domingo, 1920–

15.50, *Siete cantos breves: para soprano y piano*
15.50a–15.50f, 1.–6., ©1983, José Juan Tablada, —, Soprano, —, EMM-Serie B no. 19, —, +

Paredes, Hilda, 1957–

15.51, Anachronic Songs, 1979, Ted Hughes and Ramón López, —, —, —, —, LCP, —

Ponce, Manuel, 1882–1948

15.52, *Canciones mejicanas para niños*
15.52a, I. La primavera, —, José D. Frias, E_4–E_5, Low-med, —, ZP, —, +
15.52b, II. La luna, —, José D. Frias, $D\sharp_4$–$D\sharp_5$, Low-med, —, ZP, —, +
15.52c, III. La aurora, —, José D. Frias, $E\flat_4$–F_5, Med, —, ZP, —, +
15.52d, IV. La lluvia, —, José D. Frias, E_4–E_5, Med, —, ZP, —, +

15.53, *Cantos infantiles: para los jardines de niños*
15.53a, Himno a la madre, —, Rosaura Zapata, —, Medium voice, —, ESEB, —, +

15.54, *Cuatros poemas de Francisco A. de Icaza (De la vida honda y de la emoción fugitiva), op. 37*
15.54a, I. De oro, 1936, Francisco A. de Icaza, D_4–E_5, Med, —, SMP, —, +
15.54b, II. La sombra, 1936, Francisco A. de Icaza, E_4–F_5, Med, —, SMP, —, +
15.54c, III. La fuente, 1936, Francisco A. de Icaza, E_4–F_5, Med, —, SMP, —, +
15.54d, IV. Camino arriba, 1936, Francisco A. de Icaza, E_4–$F\sharp_5$, Med, —, SMP, —, +

15.55, *Dos poemas de B. Dávalos*
15.55a, Cerca de tí, ©1961, Baica Dávalos, D_4–A_5, High, —, PI, —, +
15.55b, Lejos de tí, ©1961, Baica Dávalos, —, High, —, PI, —, +

15.56, Espera, ©1949, Manuel M. Ponce, D_4–E_5, Med, —, PI, —, +

15.57, Estrellita, ©1951, Manuel M. Ponce, Multiple keys, —, Original for low voice; transcription for voice and guitar available [RA], SMP, EBMMC, —, +

15.58, Insomnio, —, —, —, Medium voice, —, PI, —, +

15.59, Palomita, —, —, —, —, —, PEN, PI, *The Art Song in Latin America*, +

15.60, *Seis canciones arcaicas (Seis poemas arcaicos), op. 35*, —, —, —, Medium voice, —, —, —
15.60a, I. Más quiero morir, por veros..., ©1943, Juan del Encina, D_4–F_5, Med-high, —, ECIC, —, +
15.60b, II. Zagaleja del casar..., ©1943, Anonymous, E_4–G_5, Med-high, —, ECIC, —, +
15.60c, III. De las sierras, ©1943, Juan del Encina, E_4–G_5, Med, —, ECIC, —, +
15.60d, IV. Sol, sol, gi, gi..., —, —, —, —, —, ECIC, —, +
15.60e, V. Desciendo el valle..., —, —, —, —, —, ECIC, —, +
15.60f, VI. Tres morillas..., —, —, —, —, —, ECIC, —, +

15.61, *Seis canciones populares mejicanas, op. 7*
15.61a, 1. Palomita, ©1958, Popular text, D_4–G_5, Med, Mexican popular folk songs; arr. Ponce, PI, —, +
15.61b, 2. La peña, ©1958, Popular text, F_4–$E\flat_5$, Med, Mexican popular folk songs; arr. Ponce, PI, —, +
15.61c, 3. Joven divina, ©1958, Popular text,

B3–E5, Med, Mexican popular folk songs; arr. Ponce, PI, —, +

15.61d, 4. Qué pronto, ©1958, Popular text, —, —, Mexican popular folk songs; arr. Ponce, PI, —, +

15.61e, 5. China del alma, ©1958, Popular text, —, —, Mexican popular folk songs; arr. Ponce, PI, —, +

15.61f, 6. Hace ocho meses, ©1958, Popular text, —, —, Mexican popular folk songs; arr. Ponce, PI, —, +

15.62, Serenata mejicana, ©1915, Manuel M. Ponce, C4–G5, Med-high, —, PI, —, +

15.63, *Tres poemas de Enrique Gonzáles Martínez*

15.63a, I. Nocturno de las rosas, 1938, Enrique Gonzales Martínez, C4–F5, Low-med, —, ECIC, —, +

15.63b, II. Onda, 1938, Enrique Gonzales Martínez, C♯–E5, Low-med, —, ECIC, —, +

15.63c, III. La despedida, 1938, Enrique Gonzales Martínez, C♯4–E5, Low-med, —, ECIC, —, +

Prieto, María Teresa, 1910–1982

15.64, Ave Maria, —, —, —, —, Voice and piano or organ, EMM-Serie B no. 9, —, +

15.65, *Canciones modales*

15.65a, I. Si ves el ciervo herido (en modo dórico), ©1963, Juana Inés de la Cruz, D4–F5, Med, —, EMM-Serie B no. 8, —, +

15.65b, II. Sonatina (en modo frígio), ©1963, Juana Inés de la Cruz, E4–F5, Med, —, EMM-Serie B no. 8, —, +

15.65c, III. De extremadura a Léon (en modo lidio), ©1963, Alejandro Casona, D4–F5, Med, —, EMM-Serie B no. 8, —, +

15.65d, IV. Esta verde hierba... (en modo mixolidio), ©1963, María Teresa Prieto, D4–A5, High, —, EMM-Serie B no. 8, —, +

15.65e, V. Cristo en la tarde... (en modo eólico), ©1963, Carlos Bousoña Prieto, E4–A5, High, —, EMM-Serie B no. 8, —, +

15.65f, VI. Quién dijo acaso...? (en modo jónico), ©1963, Vicente Aleixandre, D4–A5, High, —, EMM-Serie B no. 8, —, +

15.66, *Cuatro canciones para canto y piano*

15.66a, Dios te otorgó la gracia, ©1971, María Teresa Prieto, D4–G♭5, High, —, EMM-Serie B no. 13, —, +

15.66b, Canzón da noite do afiador, ©1971, Augusto Casas, F♯4–G♯5, High, —, EMM-Serie B no. 13, —, +

15.66c, Cantiga, ©1971, Alvaro Cunquiero, D4–G♯5, High, —, EMM-Serie B no. 13, —, +

15.66d, Oración de quietud (Poema sinfónico), ©1971, María Teresa Prieto, C4–G5, Med-high, —, EMM-Serie B no. 13, —, +

15.67, *Odas celestes*

15.67a, I. Oda celeste, ©1952, Carlos Bousoña Prieto, G♯4–A5, High, —, EMM-Serie B no. 5, —, +

15.67b, II. Cantad, pájaros, ©1952, Vicente Aleixandre, B♭3–A5, High, —, EMM-Serie B no. 5, —, +

15.67c, III. Mirando las altas cumbres, ©1952, María Teresa Prieto, D4–G5, Med-high, —, EMM-Serie B no. 5, —, +

15.67d, IV. Les peupliers de Kéranroux, ©1952, Charles Le Goffic, D4–G5, High, —, EMM-Serie B no. 5, —, +

15.67e, V. Le colibri, ©1952, Georges Boutelleau, E♭4–F♯5, High, —, EMM-Serie B no. 5, —, +

Revueltas, Silvestre, 1899–1940

15.68, Canto de una muchacha negra, 1938, Langston Hughes, G3–E♭5, Low, —, EBMMC, —, +

15.69, *Cinco canciones de niños*

15.69a, Caballito, 1938, Federico García Lorca, G3–E♭5, Low, Also available for voice and chamber ensemble [SMP],

EBMMC, PEN, *The Art Song in Latin America*, +

15.69b, Canción tonta, 1938, Federico García Lorca, F♯4–E5, Med, Also available for voice and chamber ensemble [SMP], EBMMC, PEN, *The Art Song in Latin America*, +

15.69c, Las cinco horas, 1938, Federico García Lorca, E4–E5, Med, Also available for voice and chamber ensemble [SMP], EBMMC, PEN, *The Art Song in Latin America*, +

15.69d, 4. Canción de cuna, ©1945, —, —, —, Also available for voice and chamber ensemble [SMP], GSch, —

15.69e, 5. El lagarto, ©1945, —, —, —, Also available for voice and chamber ensemble [SMP], GSch, —

15.70, *Dos canciones*

15.70a, I. Amiga que te vas, 1936–1937, Ramón López Velarde, B3–E5, Low, —, ECIC, —, +

15.70b, II. Caminando, 1936–1937, Nicolás Guillén, D3–F4, Med-high, Bass clef, ECIC, —, +

15.71, Dúo para pato y canario, 1931, Daniel Castañeda, C4–A5, High, —, SMP, —, +

15.72, El tecolote, —, Daniel Castañeda, E♭4–G5, High, —, SMP, —, +

15.73, Ranas, —, Daniel Castañeda, E4–G♯5, Med-high, —, SMP, —, +

Rodríguez, Marcela, 1951–

15.74, *Adúltera, enemiga: ciclo de ocho canciones de Juan Ruíz de Alarcón*

15.74a, Cierra el labio, 1992, Juan Ruiz de Alarcón, —, High voice, Soprano or Tenor, With harpsichord, m, —, +

15.74b, Que adornada primavera, 1992, Juan Ruiz de Alarcón, —, High voice, Soprano or Tenor, With harpsichord, m, —, +

15.74c, Tiempo, lugar y ventura, 1992, Juan Ruiz de Alarcón, —, High voice, Soprano or Tenor, With harpsichord, m, —, +

15.74d, Tente liviana, 1992, Juan Ruiz de Alarcón, —, High voice, Soprano or Tenor, With harpsichord, m, —, +

15.74e, Yo, señora, 1992, Juan Ruiz de Alarcón, —, High voice, Soprano or Tenor, With harpsichord, m, —, +

15.74f, Lo que con la boca niego, 1992, Juan Ruiz de Alarcón, —, High voice, Soprano or Tenor, With harpsichord, m, —, +

15.74g, Pluguiera a Dios, 1992, Juan Ruiz de Alarcón, —, High voice, Soprano or Tenor, With harpsichord, m, —, +

15.74h, Hame contado Don Diego, 1992, Juan Ruiz de Alarcón, —, High voice, Soprano or Tenor, With harpsichord, m, —, +

Rolón, José 1883–1945

15.75, *Dibujos sobre un puerto*

15.75a, I. El alba, ©1968, José Gorostiza, C4–G5, Med-high, —, EMM-Serie B no.12, —, +

15.75b, II. La tarde, ©1968, José Gorostiza, D4–F5, Med-high, —, EMM-Serie B no.12, —, +

15.75c, III. Nocturno, ©1968, José Gorostiza, D4–G5, Med-high, —, EMM-Serie B no.12, —, +

15.75d, IV. Elegía, ©1968, José Gorostiza, D4–A5, Low, —, EMM-Serie B no.12, —, +

15.75e, V. Cantarcillo, ©1968, José Gorostiza, D4–G5, Med-high, —, EMM-Serie B no.12, —, +

15.75f, VI. El faro, ©1968, José Gorostiza, D4–G5, Med-high, —, EMM-Serie B no.12, —, +

15.75g, VII. Oración, ©1968, José Gorostiza, D4–G5, Med-high, —, EMM-Serie B no.12, —, +

15.76, Naufragio, —, Salvador Novo, —, —, —, —, CENIDIM, —

Sandi, Luis, 1905–1996

15.77, *Cuatro canciones de amor*

15.77a, La hora tranquila, ©1954, Anonymous (Poesía árabe), D♭4–A♭5, High, —, EMM, —, +

15.77b, La batalla, ©1954, Anonymous (Poesía árabe), G4–A♭5, High, —, EMM, —, +

15.77c, Y pensar que pudimos . . ., ©1954, Lopez Velarde, D4–A♭5, High, —, EMM, —, +

15.77d, Pregón submarino, ©1954, Rafael Alberti, F♯4–G♯5, High, —, EMM, —, +

15.78, *Diez Haikais*

15.78a, El pavo real, 1933, José Juan Tablada, E♭4–F5, Med, —, EMM-Serie B no. 1, —, +

15.78b, Las abejas, 1933, José Juan Tablada, D4–C5, Low-med, —, EMM-Serie B no. 1, —, +

15.78c, El sauz, 1933, José Juan Tablada, G♯4–E5, Med, —, EMM-Serie B no. 1, —, +

15.78d, El abejorro, 1933, José Juan Tablada, D4–D5, Low-med, —, EMM-Serie B no. 1, —, +

15.78e, Las toninas, 1933, José Juan Tablada, F4–G♯5, Med-high, —, EMM-Serie B no. 1, —, +

15.78f, Caballo del diablo, 1933, José Juan Tablada, F4–F5, Med, —, EMM-Serie B no. 1, —, +

15.78g, El caimán, 1933, José Juan Tablada, F4–F5, Med, —, EMM-Serie B no. 1, —, +

15.78h, La mariposa, 1933, José Juan Tablada, C4–E5, Med, —, EMM-Serie B no. 1, —, +

15.78i, Peces voladores, 1933, José Juan Tablada, G♯4–B♭5, High, —, EMM-Serie B no. 1, —, +

15.78j, El bambú, 1933, José Juan Tablada, F♯4–F♯5, Med, —, EMM-Serie B no. 1, —, +

15.79, *Poemas del amor y de la muerte*

15.79a, I. Quién no ha amado nunca . . ., 1966, Epígrafes griegos y Rabaiyat de Omar Khayyam, D4–E5, Med, —, EMM-Serie B no. 10, —, +

15.79b, II. Bien amada . . ., 1966, Epígrafes griegos y Rabaiyat de Omar Khayyam, B♭3–G♭5, Med, —, EMM-Serie B no. 10, —, +

15.79c, III. Aquí, con un pedazo de pan . . ., 1966, Epígrafes griegos y Rabaiyat de Omar Khayyam, A3–G♭5, Med, —, EMM-Serie B no. 10, —, +

15.79d, IV. ¡Qué mezquino el corazón . . . !, 1966, Epígrafes griegos y Rabaiyat de Omar Khayyam, G3–E5, Low, —, EMM-Serie B no. 10, —, +

15.79e, V. Rodopis, . . ., 1966, Epígrafes griegos y Rabaiyat de Omar Khayyam, G3–F♯5, Low, —, EMM-Serie B no. 10, —, +

15.79f, VI. ¡Ah, gocemos . . . !, 1966, Epígrafes griegos y Rabaiyat de Omar Khayyam, B3–D5, Med, —, EMM-Serie B no. 10, —, +

15.79g, VII. Vine al mundo, . . ., 1966, Epígrafes griegos y Rabaiyat de Omar Khayyam, C4–G5, Med, —, EMM-Serie B no. 10, —, +

15.79h, VIII. ¡Ah llenad las copas!, 1966, Epígrafes griegos y Rabaiyat de Omar Khayyam, A3–E♭5, Low, —, EMM-Serie B no. 10, —, +

15.79i, IX. Todo es un ajedrez . . ., 1966, Epígrafes griegos y Rabaiyat de Omar Khayyam, G♯3–A5, Low, —, EMM-Serie B no. 10, —, +

15.79j, X. Un instante de reposo . . ., 1966, Epígrafes griegos y Rabaiyat de Omar Khayyam, B♭3–D♭5, Low, —, EMM-Serie B no. 10, —, +

15.79k, XI. ¡Oh, luna! . . ., 1966, Epígrafes griegos y Rabaiyat de Omar Khayyam, B♭3–G♭5, Low-med, —, EMM-Serie B no. 10, —, +

15.79l, XII. Cuando hayamos muerto . . ., 1966, Epígrafes griegos y Rabaiyat de Omar Khayyam, D4–E♭5, Low-med, —, EMM-Serie B no. 10, —, +

Tapia Colmán, Simón, 1906–1993

15.80, *Los días de la voz: cuatro poemas para canto y piano*

15.80a, En mi nocturno sueño, 1980, Margarita López Portillo, —, High voice, —, LAC, —, +

15.80b, Tu, 1980, Margarita López Portillo, —, High voice, —, LAC, —, +
15.80c, Oh sutil invisible, 1980, Margarita López Portillo, —, High voice, —, LAC, —, +
15.80d, Como lámpara eterna, 1980, Margarita López Portillo, —, High voice, —, LAC, —, +

Téllez Oropeza, Roberto, 1909–2001

15.81, *Cuatro cantos: para voz y piano*
15.81a, No corras, ©1980, Griselda Álvarez, —, Medium voice, —, LAC, —, —, +
15.81b, Asfixia, ©1980, Griselda Álvarez, —, Medium voice, —, LAC, —, —, +
15.81c, Amor, ©1980, Griselda Álvarez, —, Medium voice, —, LAC, —, —, +
15.81d, Lluvia...lluvia, ©1980, Griselda Álvarez, —, Medium voice, —, LAC, —, —, +

PUBLISHERS

ArMP, Arrow Music Press
B/H, Boosey and Hawkes Inc.
EBMMC, Edwin B. Marks Music Corp.
ECIC, Editorial Cooperativa Interamericana de Compositores
EIMG, Ediciones del Instututo Musical Gomezanda
EMM, Ediciones Mexicanas de Música
EMM-CA, Ediciones Mexicanas de Música, Colección Arion
ESEB, Ediciones de la Secretaría de Educación Pública
GSch, G. Schirmer
LAC, Liga de Compositores de México
m, manuscript
PEN, Pendragon Press
PI, Peer International Corporation
RA, Ricordi Americana, S.A.E.C.
SMP, Southern Music Publishing, Inc.
UME, Unión Musical Española
ZP, Zimmermann Print

COLLECTIONS

CENIDIM, Centro Nacional de Investigación, Documentación e Información Musical "Carlos Chávez"
LPALC, Library of the Performing Arts, Lincoln Center, New York, New York
NAM, National Archives of Mexico, Mexico City, Mexico
+, LAMC (Latin American Music Center), Indiana University

SOURCES

(See bibliography for publication information)
LCP, *The Living Composers Project* (online resource)
Wilson, *The Art Song in Latin America: Selected Works by Twentieth-Century Composers*

16

Nicaragua

Nicaragua is another Central American country virtually left off of the publication map with respect to art music. Rich in folk history, it is home to Maya and Quiché musical traditions and has many native songs and dances. Nicaraguan native instruments, like those of El Salvador, are common to the rest of Central America.[1] As in South America, native ancient cultures have combined with colonial forms of Catholicism to create a blend of religions and cultures. Native dances and rhythms are maintained in the art music, although there has been relatively little activity in the twentieth and early twenty-first centuries, probably due in part to the outstanding political situation.

Luis A. Delgadillo (1887–1961) is the lone musical figure discussed in most of the secondary literature.[2] A prolific composer and an important musical figure on many levels, he taught many of the next generation of Latin American musicians.[3] He served as the General Director of the Cultura Musical of Nicaragua, and taught in Mexico City, Mexico, and Panama City, Panama. He returned to Nicaragua in 1945.[4] Delgadillo is mentioned in Béhague's *Music in Latin America*, together with a handful of Guatemalan composers, as an example of a composer whose style combines indigenous, mestizo, and African influences within a Romantic and/or Impressionistic context.[5]

It is worth noting that the writer Rubén Darío (1867–1916), whose texts are extremely popular with art song composers from all over Latin America, was from Nicaragua.

Delgadillo, Luis Abraham, 1887–1961

16.1, *21 Romanzas*

16.1k, No. 11, 1917, Rubén Darío, SSMC

Additional titles: Ciento cincuenta cantos escolares; Five Waltzes; Seven Popular Songs.

PUBLISHERS

SSMC, Sherman Square Music Company

17

Panama

The native dances and songs of Panama are as diverse as its people—from the indigenous and African tribes of the jungle and the coast to those who live in the cosmopolitan center of Panama City.[1] Most indigenous Panamanian music retains elements similar to those found in pre-Colombian music, and is as deeply rooted in cultural and religious or ritual meaning as the music of many Andean cultures.[2] Influences range from Aztec and Mayan to African, and artifacts evidencing musical life exist from as far back as AD 1300–1500.[3]

Probably the most well-known composer and important musical figure from Panama was Roque Cordero (1917–2008). He was an experimental composer in the sense that he wrote using both traditional and more modern techniques (including serialism), and defined nationalism according to the sincerity of the composer's intentions. Cordero believed that native elements such as rhythm and melody flourished through a composer's ability to keep a broad world view of music.[4]

Among the few Panamanian composers recognized in current publications, not many are known for song composition.[5] Narciso Garay (1876–1953) was one of them, although he is known mainly for his book on Panamanian folk music.[6] Few songs are published or easily accessible; however, there are some songs by Ricardo Fábrega (1905–1973), more popular in vein, that are available and included in this catalog, and there is a website for the current generation of Panamanian composers where singers can contact composers directly to access scores.[7]

Fábrega, Ricardo, 1905–1973

17.1, El chichemito (Guaracha panameña), ©1942, —, PI/SMP

17.2, Panamá viejo (Bolero canción), ©1930s, Medium voice, Imp. Acción Católica (Panamá)

17.3, Una noche tropical (Serenata), —, —, PAU-LAMB

Additional titles: Gonzalo Brenes (1907–2003), [*Song Cycle One*]; [*Song Cycle Two*]. Eduardo Charpentier de Castro (1927–), Para entonces. Narciso Garay (1876–1953).

PUBLISHERS

PAU-LAMB, Pan American Union, Latin-American Music Bureau

PI/SMP, Peer International/Southern Music Publishing Company, Inc.

18

Paraguay

Paraguay, like the rest of the countries in South America, has a complicated and fascinating history—even its isolated, land-locked status was not enough to keep it safe from colonization. Although the physical evidence of indigenous musical life is relatively sparse due to the nomadic nature of the people, careful records were kept in the seventeenth century by the incoming Jesuits, who documented how they used music to convert the native population.[1]

Indigenous music was used for ritual, religion, and celebration. Timothy L. Watkins writes that although there were fewer African slaves in Paraguay than in other areas of South America, musical elements from the ritual or religious music of these populations did open new avenues for African-influenced (and later African-Brazilian) Paraguayan music.[2] The more traditional indigenous music (Native American as opposed to African) is based on the pentatonic scale, which under the influence of the Spanish later changed to the Western European scale, mainly the minor mode.[3] The nineteenth century brought European salon genres, which were incorporated into a "tropical" rhythmic language (that is, the delaying of strong beats in a measure to create the feeling of a relaxed mixed meter), and the dominance of the guitar as a primary instrument.[4]

Important Paraguayan musical figures include Agustín Pío Barrios (1885–1944), a composer of primarily guitar music; José Asunción Flores (1904–1972); Carlos Lara Bareiro (1914–1987), a composer mainly of large-scale works and an important figure in helping to create the first symphony orchestra in Paraguay; and Juan Max Boettner (1899–1958), author of the book *Música y músicos del Paraguay*.[5]

Paraguay seems to be a country with a strong musical history but lacking a solid body of art music; if it exists, there is little evidence of it in the United States. Although Boettner composed songs, it is not clear if these could be considered art songs or if they were more popular in style. Either way, they are not accessible, so they are not included in this catalog. Some songs by contemporary Paraguayan composer Daniel Luzko (1966–) are listed on *The Living Composers Project*, and one song cycle is included below, giving Paraguay a presence, however sparse, in this study.[6]

Luzko, Daniel, 1966–

18.1, *Three Songs/Tres canciones con texto de John Thurman*
18.1a, I. Paining the talus, 1996, John Thurman, B2–G4, Tenor, LCP
18.1b, II. On the beach, 1996, John Thurman, E♭3–G4, Tenor, LCP
18.1c, III. Featureless, 1996, John Thurman, C3–A♭4, Tenor, LCP

SOURCES

(See bibliography for publication information.)
LCP, *The Living Composers Project* (online resource)

19

Peru

José-Luis Maúrtua

The development of Peruvian art song in the twentieth century is strongly tied to the compositional outputs of Peruvian composers Cárlos Sánchez Málaga (1904–1995), Theodoro Valcárcel (1900–1942), Roberto Carpio Valdés (1900–1986), French-Belgian composer Andrés Sas (1900–1967), and German composer Rudolph Holzmann (1910–1992). Also important from previous generations are Peruvian Luis Duncker Lavalle (1874–1922) and Italian Renzo Bracesco (1888–1982).

Sas and Holzmann included Peruvian folk elements in their music, otherwise European in nature. Sas's songs presented mostly pentatonic and modal melodic designs with strong Romantic tendencies. His titles and texts, like Sánchez Málaga's and Holzmann's, were written in proper Spanish. This changed with composers like Theodoro Valcárcel and his nephew Edgar Valcárcel (1932–). Strongly identified with the music from their native highlands, the Valcárcels used original Quechua titles and texts in their compilations of Andean music and in many of their original compositions as well. Their songs are based mainly on folk rhythms and dances from the Andean regions.[1]

The compositional foundations laid down by Sánchez Málaga, Valcárcel, Sas, and Holzmann produced composers like Enrique Iturriaga (1918–), Celso Garrido-Lecca (1926–), Luis Antonio Meza (1931–), Enrique Pinilla (1927–1989), Francisco Pulgar Vidal (1929–), and Edgar Valcárcel, among others. Most of these composers pursued further studies in Europe and in the United States with teachers like Honegger, Ginastera, Messiaen, Malipiero, Maderna, Dallapiccola, Ussachevsky, and Copland. Consequently, the music written by Peruvian composers of this generation made extensive use of twentieth-century compositional techniques, including the use of quartal and quintal harmonies, open dissonance, and serial and aleatory principles. The Andean and urban elements on which the music is based were transformed and modernized, although their original character is almost always preserved. Titles and texts still resemble the typical Peruvian sentiment, either in Quechua or in Spanish.

Art songs written by Peruvian composers, regardless of their generation, are still fairly difficult to obtain even in the twenty-first century. Some important sources are the Latin American Music Centers at the Catholic University of Lima (Peru), the Catholic University of America in Washington, D.C., and Indiana University; the National Symphony Orchestra Library at Lima's Museo de la Nación, and the National Conservatory (Peru) Library. Other contemporary composers worthy of mention are Aurelio Tello, Teófilo Alavarez-Alvarez and Carlos Fernández Sosaya.

Bisetti, Alejandro, 1932–

19.1, El poeta a su amada, op. 8, —, —, —, —, —, m, —, +

Bracesco, Renzo, 1888–1982

19.2, Canción de cuna incaica, 1954, —, —, Soprano, —, m, —, +

Carpio Valdés, Roberto, 1900–1986

19.3, Canciones, —, —, —, —, —, INCP, —, —

Duncker Lavalle, Luis, 1874–1922

19.4, *Seven Compositions*
19.4g, 7. Lágrimas (Romanza), p1964, Pablo Neruda, C4–G5, Med, First six movements for solo piano, CNMP, —, +

Holzmann, Rudolph, 1910–1992

19.5, *Tres madrigales*
19.5a, Lamento lento, 1944, Pablo Neruda, D4–A♭5, Med-high, —, EAM, —, +
19.5b, Fantasma, 1944, Pablo Neruda, D♭4–B5, High, —, EAM, —, +
19.5c, Madrigal escrito en invierno, 1944, Pablo Neruda, C4–G5, High, —, EAM, —, +

Pinilla, Enrique, 1927–1989

19.6, Molle, molle (Popular song from Cuzco, Peru), ©1955, —, —, —, Arr. voice and piano, m, —, +
19.7, Saucecito, palma verde (Popular song from Conchucos-Huari, Peru), ©1955, —, —, —, Arr. voice and piano, m, —, +
19.8, Tarde de la noche vengo (Popular song from Cuenca, Ecuador), ©1955, —, —, —, Arr. voice and piano, m, —, +

19.9, Tristezas (Popular song from Cuenca, Ecuador), ©1955, —, —, —, Arr. voice and piano, m, —, +

Sánchez Málaga, Carlos, 1904–1995

19.10, *Dos Lieder*
19.10a, Medrosamente ibas, 1937, Luis Fabio Xammar, D4–G5, High, —, m, —, -, +
19.10b, Te seguiré, 1937, Luis Fabio Xammar, C♯4–F5, Med, —, m, —, +

Sarabia Quiroz, M. Nicolás

19.11, *Cancionero del niño peruano*
19.11a–11aa, 1–27, 1965, Pedro Barrantes Castro, —, —, —, m, —, +

Sas, Andrés, 1900–1967

19.12, *Canciones simbólicas, op. 14*
19.12a, Melodía, 1931, Daniel Castañeda, —, —, —, BLA, —, +
19.12b, Quenas, 1931, Daniel Castañeda, —, —, —, —, —, +

19.13, *Cuatro melodías*
19.13a, Triolet, 1941, Manuel González Prada, E♭4–G♭5, Med, Para la señora Helen Harrison Mills, PI, —, +
19.13b, La fuente, 1941, María Weisse de Sabogal, C♯4–G♯5, Med-high, Para la señora María Luisa Vertiz de Lange, PI, —, +
19.13c, Melodía II, 1931, Daniel Castañeda, D4–E5, Med, Para Dominto Santa Cruz, PI, —, +
19.13d, Amanecer, 1930, Enrique Bustamante y Ballivián, D4–G5, Med-high, Para la señora Elizabeth Sprague Smith, for voice and flute, PI, —, +

Tello, Aurelio, 1951–

19.14, Canción de cuna para despertar a un negrito, 2000, Nicolás Guillén, —, Mezzo, —, —, LCP, —

Valcárcel, Edgar, 1932–

19.15, *Homenaje a Masías*
19.15a, I. Imillita, 1968, Traditional poetry, D4–G5, Med-high, A Augusto Masías, TR, *The Latin American Art Song*, +
19.15b, II. Amaneciendo, 1968, Traditional poetry, E4–A5, High, —, TR, *The Latin American Art Song*, +

Valcárcel, Theodoro, 1900–1942

19.16, *Tahwa Inka'j Tak'y-nam*
19.16a, I. Suray surita, 1930, Traditional Quechua poetry, E♭4–C6, High, A Don Rafael Larco Herrera, Text in Quechua, TR, *The Latin American Art Song*, +
19.16b, II. H'acuchu! (¡Vámonos!), 1930, Traditional Quechua poetry, E♭4–B♭5, High, —, Text in Quechua, TR, *The Latin American Art Song*, +
19.16c, III. W'ay! (¡Ayes!), 1930, Traditional Quechua poetry, D4–B♭5, High, —, Text in Quechua, TR, *The Latin American Art Song*, +
19.16d, IV. Chililin-uth'aja (Campanita de mi pueblo), 1930, Traditional Quechua poetry, E4–G5, High, —, Text in Quechua, TR, *The Latin American Art Song*, +

PUBLISHERS

BLA, Boletín Latinoamericano de Música
CNMP, Conservatorio Nacional de Música de Peru
EAM, Editorial Argentina de Música
INCP, Instituto Nacional de Cultura
m, manuscript
PI, Peer International Corporation
TR, Tritó, S.L.

COLLECTIONS	SOURCES
+, LAMC (Latin American Music Center), Indiana University	(See bibliography for publication information) Caicedo, *The Latin American Art Song: A Critical Anthology and Interpretive Guide for Singers* LCP, *The Living Composers Project* (online resource)

20

Puerto Rico

With an ethnographic history similar to that of Cuba and the Dominican Republic, Puerto Rico has a diverse cultural composition.[1] Formerly a colony of Spain, it is now a commonwealth of the United States, although it maintains its own strong national identity and Spanish remains the primary language. It is important to note that there is a passionate nationalistic movement for independence in Puerto Rico regarding its status with the United States.[2]

The nationalistic quality of Puerto Rican music comes from the use of folk and traditional music, often through the use of native instruments such as the cuatro and tiple and forms such as the *décima* and the *seis*.[3] Spanish and Afro-Cuban influences are also evident.[4]

There is a very high quality of music education on the island, and composers are of the highest caliber. Several universities, a national conservatory, a national orchestra, and many other professional ensembles help to ensure the high quality of music performance and music education.

Héctor Campos Parsi (1922–1998) is probably the best known Puerto Rican composer of nationalistic music, although he later turned to neoclassicism, atonality, and serialism.[5] Narciso Figueroa (1906–2004), of the famous Figueroa family of musicians, wrote several beautiful songs that are both contemporary in feel yet traditional in style. Luis Manuel Alvarez (1939–) and Ernesto Cordero (1946–), both composers and guitarists who have taught at the University of Puerto Rico, also wrote songs that are both lyrical and interesting. Rafael Aponte Ledée (1938–) is a particularly prolific composer writing in a more modern style. Also worthy of mention are Raymond Torres-Santos (1958–), Jack Delano (1914–1998), and Amaury Veray (1922–1995).

In 1986, the National Association of Puerto Rican Composers published a song anthology, readily available through interlibrary loan in the United States. It features a diverse and comprehensive body of literature, and includes songs for both voice and piano and voice and guitar. In his prologue, composer and guitarist Leonardo Egúrbida points out that the inclusion of songs accompanied by guitar is important both to the composers who wrote them as well as to the society for which they were written.[6]

Alvarez, Luis Manuel, 1939–

20.1, Canción tonta, 1962, García Lorca, E4–E5, Med, —, ANCPR, *La canción de arte*, +

20.2, Media luna, —, García Lorca, C4–C♯5, Med, —, ANCPR, *La canción de arte*, +

Aponte Ledée, Rafael, 1938–

20.3, Calla niño, calla, 1961, Traditional poetry, D♯4–B4, Low, A Enrique Massó, TR, *The Latin American Art Song*, +

20.4, Cuando voy a la aldea, 1963, Traditional poetry, G4–G5, Med-high, A Alfredo Romero, TR, *The Latin American Art Song*, +

20.5, Éstas lágrimas tan bellas, 1963, —, E♭4–G5, Med, —, ANCPR, *La canción de arte*, +

20.6, Zarzamora con el tronco gris, 1963, Federico García Lorca, B♭3–G♭5, Med, —, TR, *The Latin American Art Song*, +

Cabrer, Carlos R., 1950–

20.7, Canción, 1985, Jesús Tomé, D♭4–E♭5, Med, —, ANCPR, *La canción de arte*, +

Campos Parsi, Héctor, 1922–1998

20.8, Columnas y círculos, 1968, —, —, Soprano, Graphic notation, m, —, +

20.9, *Puntos cubanos*

20.9a, 1. Muerta, 1960, Luis Llorens Torres, C4–F♯5, Med-high, —, ICP, —, +

20.9b, 2. Mi rancho, 1960, Luis Llorens Torres, E4–F♯5, Med-high, —, ICP, —, +

20.9c, 3. Madrugada, 1960, Luis Llorens Torres, D4–F5, Med-high, —, ICP, —, +

20.9d, 4. Vida criolla, 1960, Luis Llorens Torres, E4–G5, Med-high, —, ICP, —, +

Additional titles: Los paréntesis; Majestad negra; Nana; *Tres poem[a]s de Corretjer*.

Cordero, Ernesto, 1946–

20.10, La hija del viejo Pancho, 1974, Luis Llorens Torres, D4–G5, Med, A Aura Robledo, ANCPR, *La canción de arte*, +

20.11, Pregunta, 1974, Nimia Vicens, D4–F♯5, Med, A Elaine Arandes, ANCPR, *La canción de arte*, +

20.12, Si quieres comprender, 1974, Juan Antonio Corretjer, A4–F5, Med, A Margarita Castro Alberty, ANCPR, PEN, *La canción de arte, The Art Song in Latin America*, +

20.13, Voz del güiro, 1967, Andrés Castro Ríos, F4–G5, Med, A Luisita Rodríguez, ANCPR, *La canción de arte,* +

Delano, Jack, 1914–1998

20.14, *Tres cancioncitas del mar*
20.14a, 1. Los catañecitos, 1963, Nimia Vicens, C4–F♯5, Med, —, ANCPR, *La canción de arte,* +
20.14b, 2. ¡A navegar!, 1963, Ester Feliciano Mendoza, C4–F♯5, Med, —, ANCPR, *La canción de arte,* +
20.14c, 3. Cantarcillo marinero, 1963, Carmelina Vizcarrondo, C♯4–F♯5, Med, —, ANCPR, *La canción de arte,* +

Dueño Colón, Braulio, 1854–1934

20.15, La terruca, ©1962, Virgilio Dávila, —, Medium voice, —, ICP, —, +
20.16, Serenata española, ©1963, Virgilio Dávila, —, Medium voice, —, ICP, —, +

Figueroa, Narciso, 1906–2004

20.17, *Impresiones boriquenses*
20.17a, Friquitín, 1976, J. A. Dávila, D4–F♯5, Med, —, ANCPR, *La canción de arte,* +

20.18, *Suite bucolicas infantiles*
20.18a, Silencio, 1972, Ángeles Pastor, D♯4–G♯5, Med-high, —, ANCPR, *La canción de arte,* +

20.19, *Tres poemas de José de Diego*
20.19a, El ojo de agua, 1975, José Diego, D♭4–F♯5, Med-high, —, ANCPR, *La canción de arte,* +
20.19b, El canto de las piedras, 1975, José Diego, C4–G5, Med-high, —, —, —, MH
20.19c, Isla, 1975, José Diego, C4–F5, Med-high, —, —, —, MH

Additional title: *Cuatro décimas*

Martínez, José Daniel, 1956–

20.20, *Tres canciones*
20.20a, La sed del agua, 1976, Manuel Joglar Cacho, C4–G5, Med-high, —, ANCPR, *La canción de arte,* +

Ramírez, Luis Antonio, 1923–

20.21, Llegó un Jíbaro a San Juan, 1963, Luis Llorens Torres, G4–G5, Med, —, ANCPR, *La canción de arte,* +
20.22, Lucero de Alba, 1963, Luis Llorens Torres, D4–F♯5, Med, —, ANCPR, *La canción de arte,* +
20.23, Vida criolla, 1963, Luis Llorens Torres, E4–F♯5, Med-high, —, ANCPR, *La canción de arte,* +

Ríos Ovalle, Juan, 1863–1928

20.24, Amor bendito (Dance), —, M. Dessuse, —, Medium voice, ICP, —, +

Sierra, Roberto, 1953–

20.25, *Cinco poemas aztecas*
20.25a, 1. ¿Qué es la poesía?, 1994, Aztec poetry, translated by Roberto Sierra, A4–G♯5, Med-high, High voice, —, Subito, —
20.25b, 2. La vida pasa..., 1994, Aztec poetry, translated by Roberto Sierra, E4–A5, Med-high, High voice, —, Subito, —
20.25c, 3. Poema de la conquista, 1994, Aztec poetry, translated by Roberto Sierra, E♭4–A♭5, Med-high, High voice, —, Subito, —
20.25d, 4. La amistad, 1994, Aztec poetry, translated by Roberto Sierra, E4–A5, Med-high, High voice, —, Subito, —
20.25e, 5. Gozo efímero, 1994, Aztec poetry, translated by Roberto Sierra, F♯4–A5, High, High voice, —, Subito, —

20.26, *Rimas*
20.26a, I. ["¿Qué es poesía?"...], 1996, Gustavo Adolfo Bécquer, F♯4–E5, Med, Medium voice, —, Subito, —
20.26b, II. [Por una mirada, un mundo;...], 1996, Gustavo Adolfo Bécquer, E4–D♯5, Med, Medium voice, —, Subito, —
20.26c, III. [Yo sé cuál el objeto de tus suspiros es;...], 1996, Gustavo Adolfo

Bécquer, C#4–F#5, Med, Medium voice, —, Subito, —
20.26d, IV. [Los suspiros son aire, . . .], 1996, Gustavo Adolfo Bécquer, E4–G#5(E5), Med, —, Subito, —
20.26e, V. [Mi vida es un erial: . . .], 1996, Gustavo Adolfo Bécquer, F#4–F5, Med, —, Subito, —

Torres-Santos, Raymond, 1958–

20.27, *Ciclo de canciones para mezzo-soprano y piano*
20.27a, Andando de noche sola, 1977, Juan Antonio Corretjer, C4–G5, Med, —, ANCPR, *La canción de arte*, +

Vázquez, Carlos Alberto, 1952–

20.28, Madrigal, 1985, José Luis Véga, D4–G5, Med-high, —, ANCPR, *La canción de arte*, +
20.29, Yo no sé, 1970, Traditional poetry from Nahuas, Méjico, D4–F#5, Med, —, TR, *The Latin American Art Song*, +

Veray, Amaury, 1922–1995

20.30, *Tres canciones*
20.30a, 1. Solo he sembrado en tu alma, 1968, David Ortiz, C4–E5, Med, A Luisita Rodríguez, ANCPR, *La canción de arte*, +
20.30b, 2. Cuando se te llenen los ojos de lejanía, 1968, David Ortiz, B3–G#5, Low-med, A Luisita Rodríguez, ANCPR, *La canción de arte*, +
20.30c, 3. He vestido con encajes de espuma, 1968, David Ortiz, B3–B5, High, A Luisita Rodríguez, ANCPR, *La canción de arte*, +

PUBLISHERS

ANCPR, Asociación Nacional de Compositores de Puerto Rico
ICP, Instituto de Cultura Puertorriqueña
m, manuscript
PEN, Pendragon Press
Subito, Subito Music Publishing, Inc. (ASCAP)
TR, Tritó, S.L.

COLLECTIONS

MH, —, Maya Hoover (private collection)
+, LAMC (Latin American Music Center), Indiana University

SOURCES

(See bibliography for publication information)
Caicedo, *The Latin American Art Song: A Critical Anthology and Interpretive Guide for Singers*
Wilson, *The Art Song in Latin America: Selected Works by Twentieth-Century Composers*
Wilson and Hopkin, *La canción de arte en Puerto Rico: Selected Works by Twentieth-Century Composers*

Uruguay

As in other countries in Latin America, the nineteenth-century musical scene in Uruguay was primarily dominated by Italian opera and other Europe musical genres.[1] As nationalism became an important factor in the twentieth century, Uruguayan music continued to follow broader trends in Latin American art music, specifically the incorporation of folklore elements within a European harmonic framework.

During the first few decades of twentieth century, music in Uruguay tended to follow European models. Composers like César Cortinas and Luis Sambucetti wrote in typical European forms, setting Italian and French texts that have since become canonized by the songs of composers such as Gabriel Fauré and Claude Debussy.

The primary composers heading the nationalistic movement were Alfonso Broqua (1876–1946) and Félix Eduardo Fabini (1882–1950). They, along with the Italian-born Vicente Ascone (1897–1979), used native Indian themes, melodic motives, and traditional rhythms (for instance, Chase points out Fabini's use of the the Andean *yaraví* in his song "Triste").[2] These nationalistic composers, including Luis Cluzeau Mortet (1889–1957), seemed to also follow the popular compositional path from Romanticism and Impressionism to a more romantic nationalism.[3]

Other noteworthy Uruguayan composers include Carlos Pedrell (1878–1941), Carlos Estrada (1909–1970), and non-nationalist composers César Cortinas (1890–1918) and Carmen Barradas (1888–1963).[4] Carlos Pedrell was the nephew of Felipe Pedrell, an important figure in Spanish music. He studied with his uncle in Madrid and Barcelona and then went on to continue his education in Paris. Pedrell later became part of the musical life in Argentina, serving as an administrator in the Buenos Aires school system and as a professor at the University of Tucumán.[5] His works are included in this volume as part of the chapter on Argentina.

Ascone, Vicente, 1897–1979

21.1, *Cinco canciones al estilo popular rioplatense*

21.1a, Aquí me pongo a cantarte (Tonada), —, Fernán Silva Váldes, E_4–E_5, Med, Dedicada a Jorge Alorta, EC E.C. 157, *Los compositores del Uruguay*, TUL

21.1b, Huella, —, Fernán Silva Váldes, C_4–D_5, Med, Dedicada a Jorge Alorta, EC E.C. 157, *Los compositores del Uruguay*, TUL

21.1c, Vidalita del querer, —, Fernán Silva Váldes, D_4–D_5, Med, Dedicada a Jorge Alorta, EC E.C. 157, *Los compositores del Uruguay*, TUL

21.1d, Caballito criollo (Gato), —, Fernán Silva Váldes, D_4–$E\flat_5$, Med, Dedicada a Jorge Alorta, EC E.C. 157, *Los compositores del Uruguay*, TUL

21.1e, Como las frutas del monte (Aire de chacarera), p1955, Fernán Silva Valdés, C_4–D_5, Med, A Jorge Algorta, CNMU, EC E.C. 157, *Los compositores del Uruguay*, TUL, +

Broqua, Alfonso, 1876–1946

21.2, ¡Ay, mi vida!, —, Alfonso Broqua, D_4–F_5, Med, —, TR, *The Latin American Art Song*, +

Calcavecchia, Benone, 1886–1953

21.3, Visione del Gange (Romanza hindú), —, Luigi Morandi, A_4–$B\flat_5$, Med-high, Dedicada a la Srta. Juanita Fabini, EC E.C. 157, *Los compositores del Uruguay*, TUL

Cervetti, Sergio, 1940–

21.4, *El triunfo de la muerte*, 1993, Circe Maia, —, —, In 6 movements, m, —, +

Cluzeau Mortet, Luis, 1889–1957

21.5, Canto de chingolo (Vidalita), —, Fernán Silva Váldes, D_4–$F\sharp_5$, Med, A la señorita María Lavinia Piccioli, EC E.C. 157, *Los compositores del Uruguay*, TUL

21.6, En la copa de los montes, —, Carlos César Lenzi, $F\sharp_4$–F_5, Med, A Julieta F. Telles de Menezes, EC E.C. 157, *Los compositores del Uruguay*, TUL

21.7, Mar de luna, ©1941, Carlos César Lenzi, $C\sharp_4$–$G\flat_5$, Med-High, —, ECIC, —, +

21.8, Río indígena, —, Andrés Lerena Acevedo, B_3–$F\sharp_5$, Med, A Alma Reyles, EC E.C. 157, *Los compositores del Uruguay*, TUL

21.9, *Tríptico criollo*

21.9a, Tarde de verano, —, Fernán Silva Valdés, D_4–G_5, Med, —, EC E.C. 157, *Los compositores del Uruguay*, TUL

21.9b, Rancho solo, —, Fernán Silva Valdés, D_4–E_5, Med, —, EC E.C. 157, *Los compositores del Uruguay*, TUL

21.9c, La canción de la moza de los ojos pardos, —, Fernán Silva Valdés, D_4–$E\flat_5$, Med, —, EC E.C. 157, *Los compositores del Uruguay*, TUL

21.10, *Tríptico primaveral*

21.10a, La noche blanca de luna, 1923, Luis Barbé Pérez, C_4–E_5, Med, —, EC E.C. 157, *Los compositores del Uruguay*, TUL

21.10b, Se oye tu risa en la tarde, 1923, Luis Barbé Pérez, E4–F♯5(G5), Med, —, EC E.C. 157, *Los compositores del Uruguay*, TUL

21.10c, Languidece, 1923, Luis Barbé Pérez, E4–G♯5, Med, —, EC E.C. 157, *Los compositores del Uruguay*, TUL

Cortinas, César, 1890–1918

21.11, À *Madame la Princesse Marie Lubomirska*

21. 11a, À une étoile, 1910, Alfred de Musset, D♭4–G♭5, Med-High, —, CNMU, —, +

21.12, À *Mademoiselle Rita Wouters*

21.12a, Berceuse, 1913, Alfred de Musset, E4–A5, Med-High, —, CNMU, —, +

21.13, Chanson d'automne, 1912, Paul Verlaine, E4–G♯5, Med, À Monsieur Antonio Bianchi, EC E.C. 157, *Los compositores del Uruguay*, TUL

21.14, Printemps, 1912, Jules Barbier, D4–G5(B♭5), Med, —, EC E.C. 157, *Los compositores del Uruguay*, TUL

21.15, Rappelle-toi, 1911, Alfred de Musset, E4–B♭5, High, À Madame la Comtesse Hélène Lutke, EC E.C. 157, *Los compositores del Uruguay*, TUL

Dente, Domingo, 1896–1974

21.16, Cantares criollos, —, Scarzolo Travieso, E♭4–G5, Med, Dedicada a Elvira Orengo, EC E.C. 157, *Los compositores del Uruguay*, TUL

21.17, Reliquia, 1923, Domingo Dente, F4–B♭5, High, Italian text, EC E.C. 157, *Los compositores del Uruguay*, TUL

21.18, Risposta, —, Domingo Dente, G4–A5, High, Italian text, EC E.C. 157, *Los compositores del Uruguay*, TUL

21.19, Sombras (Canción criolla), —, Raimundo Radaelli, A4–G♯5, Med-high, —, EC E.C. 157, *Los compositores del Uruguay*, TUL

Dentone, Raúl Roberto, 1892–1948

21.20, Adiós, op. 20, no. 1 (Canción triste para canto y piano), Agustín Chalar, B♭3–C6, Med-high, Dedicada a mi madre, EC, E.C. 157, *Los compositores del Uruguay*, TUL

Estrada, Carlos, 1909–1970

21.21, Caminos tristes, 1935, —, —, High, —, ECIC, —, +

21.22, Cruauté, op. 38, 1951, Tristan Richepin, E4–B♭5, High, À Germán Denis Barreiro; French text, CNMU, —, +

21.23, Duermen las nubes, op. 26, 1945, —, D4–G5, Med, A la Sra. Clara Oyuela, CNMU, —, +

21.24, Pièce de circonstance, op. 33, 1949, Jean Cocteau, E4–E5, Med, À Martha Fornella; French text, CNMU, —, +

21.25, Rocío, 1930, —, E♭4–D♭5, Med, A la señora Hélène Derambune, EC E.C. 157, *Los Compositores del Uruguay*, TUL, +

21.26, Pastor, pastor, ya viene la luna, 1940, —, D4–C5, Low-med, A Gonzalo, PN, —, +

Fabini, Félix Eduardo, 1882–1950

21.27, Duerme muñeca, ©1930, Avelina Baños, —, —, —, MECU, —

21.28, El grillo, 1927, Fernando Nebel, F♯4–F♯5, Med, —, EC E.C. 157, *Los compositores del Uruguay*, TUL

21.29, El nido, 1923, Fernán Silva Váldes, F4–A5, Med, —, EC E.C. 157, *Los compositores del Uruguay*, TUL

21.30, El poncho, 1925, Fernán Silva Váldes, C4–G5, Med, —, EC E.C. 157, *Los compositores del Uruguay*, TUL

21.31, El tala, 1927, Lorenzo Laborde, E4–G5, Med, —, BLA, EC E.C. 157, *Los compositores del Uruguay*, TUL, +

21.32, Flores del monte, 1927, F. Eduardo Fabini, D4–G5, Med, A la señora María V. De Müller, EC E.C. 157, *Los compositores del Uruguay*, TUL

21.33, La güeya, 1926, José María Alonso y

Trelles, "El viejo Pancho", D4–G5, Med, A María Delia Corchs, EC E.C. 157, *Los compositores del Uruguay*, TUL

21.34, Luz mala, 1924, José María Alonso y Trelles, "El viejo Pancho", D4–F♯5, Med, A Enrique Caroselli, EC E.C. 157, TR, *Los compositores del Uruguay, The Latin American Art Song*, TUL, +

21.35, Remedio, 1925, José A. Trelles, "El viejo Pancho", A3–D♯5, Med, —, EC E.C. 157, *Los compositores del Uruguay*, TUL

21.36, Triste [Triste no. 4], 1925, Elías Regules, C4–F5, Med, —, CNMU, PEN, TR, EC E.C. 157, *Los compositores del Uruguay, The Art Song in Latin America, The Latin American Art Song*, TUL, +

Additional titles: Canción del labrador (Canto escolar); El barquito; Himno al mar; Himno de juventud estudiantil; Hormiguita negra; La lluvia; Vaquita colorada.

Giucci, Carlos, 1906–1958

21.37, Atardecer, op. 6, ©1960, Manuel García de la Llera, D4–A5, Med, —, CNMU, EC E.C. 157, *Los compositores del Uruguay*, TUL, +

21.38, Lejos, ©1960, Américo Idoyaga, D4–F5, Med, —, CNMU, EC E.C. 157, *Los compositores del Uruguay*, TUL, +

Grasso, Gerardo, 1864–1937

21.39, ¡Oh madre mia! (Vidalita), —, —, D4–F♯5, Med, —, EC E.C. 157, *Los compositores del Uruguay*, TUL

Ipuche Riva, Pedro, 1924–1996

21.40, *Distante álamo*

21.40a, Disfraz, 1960, Julio J. Casal, D4–A5, Med-high, —, CNMU, —, +

21.40b, Vieja palabra, 1960, Julio J. Casal, E♭4–G5, Med-high, —, CNMU, —, +

21.40c, Vengo desde mi sombra para verte, 1960, Julio J. Casal, D4–G5, Med-high, —, CNMU, —, +

Mondino, Luis Pedro, 1903–1974

21.41, La vidalita, —, Juan C. Welker, E♭4–F5, Med, —, EC E.C. 157, *Los compositores del Uruguay*, TUL

Morales de Villegas, Socorrito, 1896–1992

21.42, La flecha, —, Fernán Silva Váldes, C♯4–G♯5, Med, A la Sra. María V. de Müller, EC E.C. 157, *Los compositores del Uruguay*, TUL

21.43, Mi testamento, —, José A. de Trelles ("El viejo Pancho"), D4–G5, Med, Al baritono uruguayo Sr. Víctor Damiani, EC E.C. 157, *Los compositores del Uruguay*, TUL

Peyrallo, Félix, 1882–1933

21.44, Aleluya (Romanza para tenor), —, Luis G. Urbina, C4–G5, Med, —, EC E.C. 157, *Los compositores del Uruguay*, TUL

Ribeiro, León Julio Alfredo, 1854–1931

21.45, Adiós (Romanza para soprano o tenor), —, Manuel Muñoz y Maines, F4–B♭5, High, Soprano or Tenor, —, EC E.C. 157, *Los compositores del Uruguay*, TUL

Rodríguez Socas, Ramón, 1890–1957

21.46, Mensaje (Romanza), —, Rodríguez Marín, D♯4–G5, Med-high, Soprano or Tenor, —, EC E.C. 157, *Los compositores del Uruguay*, TUL

Sambucetti, Luis, 1860–1926

21.47, Ninon (Romance), —, Alfred de Musset, F♯4–F♯5, Med, French text, EC E.C. 157, *Los compositores del Uruguay*, TUL

21.48, Non posso amarti (Romanza), —, M. Muñoz y Pérez, E♭4–A5, High, Italian text, EC E.C. 157, *Los compositores del Uruguay*, TUL

21.49, Toujours!! (Ognor) (Mélodie pour chant), —, René-François Sully-Prudhomme, D♭4–D♭5, Med, French text with Italian version, EC E.C. 157, *Los compositores del Uruguay*, TUL

Segu, José, 1873–1960

21.50, Cómo los pájaros, 1921, Andrés Lerena Acevedo, D4–F♯5, Med, A Sara Duce Astenco, EC E.C. 157, *Los compositores del Uruguay*, TUL

21.51, Tristesse, 1925, Alfred de Musset, D4–F♯5, Med, French text, EC E.C. 157, *Los compositores del Uruguay*, TUL

Serebrier, José, 1938–

21.52, Canción sin nombre y sin palabras, no. 1, 1956, No text, E♭4–B♭5, High, —, SMP, —, +

Storm, Ricardo, 1930–2000

21.53, Anochecer en el campo, ©1958, Pedro Dodero, C♯4–A5, Med-high, —, CNMU, —, +

Tosar Errecart, Héctor, 1923–2002

21.54, *Seis canciones sobre "El barrio de Santa Cruz" de José María Pemán*

21.54a, 1. El barrio misterioso, 1942, José María Pemán, E4–E♭5, Med, —, ECIC, —, +

21.54b, 2. Cantarcillo del aire ligero (Callejón del agua), 1942, José María Pemán, E4–G5, Med-high, —, ECIC, —, +

21.54c, 3. Fuente, 1942, José María Pemán, F4–G5, High, —, ECIC, —, +

21.54d, 4. Calle de la pimienta, 1942, José María Pemán, F♯4–E♭5, Med, —, ECIC, —, +

21.54e, 5. Cantar (Barrio adentro), 1942, José María Pemán, E4–G5, Med, —, ECIC, —, +

21.54f, 6. Villancico del sol de las cinco, 1942, José María Pemán, C♯4–E5, Med, —, ECIC, —, +

Additional titles: Santórsola, Guido (1904–1994): Aspirar; Duérmete pequeño; Imágenes musicales; Obediencia.

PUBLISHERS

BLA, Boletín Latinoamericano de Música
CNMU, Conservatorio Nacional de Música
EC, Editorial Campos
ECIC, Editorial Cooperativa Interamericana de Compositores
MECU, Ministerio de Educación y Cultura de Uruguay
m, manuscript
PEN, Pendragon Press
PN, Pierre Noël, Éditeur
SMP, Southern Music Publishing, Inc.
TR, Tritó, S.L.

COLLECTIONS

+, LAMC (Latin American Music Center), Indiana University
TUL, Tulane University (online resource)

SOURCES

(See bibliography for publication information)
Caicedo, *The Latin American Art Song: A Critical Anthology and Interpretive Guide for Singers*
Huertas, *Los compositores del Uruguay: Su obra lírica, 1860–1960*
Wilson, *The Art Song in Latin America: Selected Works by Twentieth-Century Composers*

22

Venezuela

Kathleen L. Wilson

An overview of Venezuelan art song in the twentieth century must begin with Vicente Emilio Sojo (1887–1974) and Juan Bautista Plaza (1898–1965), who were primarily responsible for the nationalist movement in Venezuela that had begun ten years earlier in other parts of Latin America. Both pedagogues and composers, they drew their inspiration from Afro-Venezuelan and Andean folk songs, rhythms, and dances, and they influenced several generations of Venezuelan composers to follow. Vicente Emilio Sojo collected and arranged well over one hundred Venezuelan folk songs, but his influence as a teacher of composition was his enduring legacy. Juan Bautista Plaza also collected and catalogued folk songs, and wrote several didactic works in addition to compositions for piano, chorus, and solo voice. His *Siete canciones venezolanas* are excellent examples of the nationalist school in Venezuela, using dance rhythms such as the *joropo* and *vals* and texts that evoke the Venezuelan countryside. His harmonies are neo-Romantic, with some influence from the French Impressionists (a style which would have been familiar to composers and audiences in the 1920s in Latin America).

Reynaldo Hahn (1875–1947) was born in Venezuela and immigrated to France at age three. As part of the late Romantic tradition of French *chanson* composers, his music lies outside of the Latin American school of nationalism. Other composers of the early nationalistic style in Venezuela include Moisés Moleiro (1904–1979), Angel Sauce (1911–), Inocente Carreño (1919–), Carlos Teppa (1923–), Gonzalo Castellanos

Yumar (1926–), Modesta Bor (1926–1998), and José Luis Muñoz (1928–1982). These composers graduated from the music school established by Sojo, but Castellanos also traveled to Paris, Teppa to New York and Italy, and Muñoz to Poland, while Bor studied in Russia with Kachaturian.

This essentially European post-Romantic/Impressionistic style with nationalistic influences of folk songs and dances prevailed until the 1960s, when many Latin American composers began to experiment with new compositional styles, having been influenced by U.S. and European composers using alleatoric, electronic and non-diatonic systems. One of the most important composers of this period is pianist and composer Alexis Rago (1930–). He began his musical education in Caracas and later studied at the Peabody Conservatory in Baltimore, in Vienna and Rome, and he immigrated to London in 1969. He has received many prestigious international awards for his performances as well as his compositions. His cycle *Rapasgotori* for tenor and piano, commissioned by the Venezuelan Cultural Council, is a decided departure from the harmonic language of his predecessors. While not as experimental as some of his international contemporaries, Rago uses extended harmonies and shows the influence of minimalism in these songs. Rago has also written several operas. Alberto Grau (1937–) is best known as a conductor and has made an international name for himself as such. One of Venezuela's leading choral conductors and pedagogues, he founded the Schola Cantorum of Caracas and has won national and international awards for his compositions as well. Having studied with Sojo and Plaza, Grau's choice of texts and use of lyricism evoke a nationalistic quality, while his harmonic language is more dissonant.

A younger generation of Venezuelan song composers includes Beatriz Bilbao (1951–), Victor Varela (1955–), Marianella Machado (1959–), and Ricardo Lorenz (1961–). Varela studied electronic music and has had his compositions performed in the Caribbean and Europe, while Bilbao, Machado, and Lorenz studied at Indiana University with Juan Orrego-Salas. Lorenz was appointed director of the Indiana University Latin American Music Center and has had his compositions performed in the United States and Europe as well as in Latin America.

Venezuelan art song—and by extension Latin American art song—tends to be lyrical in nature, written for medium voices and therefore accessible to most voice types, heavily informed by dance rhythms, and based on nationalistic and often socio-political texts. Suggestions for performance include paying close attention to the dance form that often defines a song's structure. The tempos, syncopations and hemiolas inherent in these dance forms—*vals, merengue,* and *joropo,* for example—must be carefully observed. Note the very effective use of *joropo* rhythms in Alexis Rago's "Glosa de Beatriz" and in the *vals* pattern of Juan Plaza's "Por estos cuatro caminos."[1] Keeping in mind the original instrumentation of a setting's folk song equivalent will also allow the pianist and the singer to make more informed musical decisions. These instruments would likely have included the guitar, cuatro (a small four-string guitar-like instrument), the harp, and/or various percussion instruments such as the tambor and maracas. Note the song "Guitarra" by Modesta Bor, with its programmatic guitar-like flourishes in the piano, found very often in Latin American art song. The texts too are often socio-political in nature, and careful study of the texts, mood, and sometimes double entendres are essential for a successful performance of these songs.

This very rich body of repertoire is becoming increasingly available with new anthologies and bibliographic resources such as this reference work. Kudos go to publishers and singer-scholars who are helping to make this very important body of work available to performers, coaches, teachers, and wider audiences.

Avella, Vicente, 1970–

22.1, *Between Two Gardens* (song cycle), 1994, —, —, Soprano, —, —, —, LCP

22.2, *Canciones de arena,* 2000, —, —, Mezzo, —, —, —, LCP

Bor, Modesta, 1926–1998

22.3, *Segundo ciclo de romanzas y canciones: para contralto y piano*

22.3a, I. Si el silencio fuera mío, 1984, Andrés Eloy Blanco, G3–F5, Low, Contralto, —, FVES, TR, *The Latin American Art Song,* +

22.3b, II. Coplas venezolanas, 1984, Andrés Eloy Blanco, B3–C♯5, Low, Contralto, —, FVES, TR, *The Latin American Art Song,* +

22.3c, III. Suspiro cuando te miro, 1984, Andrés Eloy Blanco, G3–D5, Low, Contralto, —, FVES, TR, *The Latin American Art Song,* +

22.3d, IV. Pregón, 1984, Andrés Eloy Blanco, G3–D5, Low, Contralto, —, FVES, TR, *The Latin American Art Song,* +

22.4, *Tríptico sobre poesía cubana: para canto y piano*
22.4a, Guitarra, 1965, Nicolás Guillén and Emilio Ballagas, C♯4–F♯5, Med, —, FVES, —, +
22.4b, Canción de cuna para dormir un negrito, 1965, Nicolás Guillén and Emilio Ballagas, C4–D5, Low, —, FVES, —, +
22.4c, Nocturno en los muelles, 1966, Nicolás Guillén and Emilio Ballagas, E4–G♯5, Med-high, —, FVES, —, +

Carreño, Inocente, 1919–

22.5, *12 Canciones*, —, —, —, —, —, m, —, +

Castellanos Yumar, Gonzalo, 1926–

22.6, Rosal, 1958, Juan Ramón Jiménez, —, High voice, EGEC, —, +

Estévez, Antonio, 1916–1988

22.7, Arrunango (Canción de cuna indígena), 1970, Héctor Guillermo Villalobos, C4–E5, Med, A mi esposa Flor, TR, *The Latin American Art Song*, +

Estrella de Mescoli, Blanca, 1915–1986

22.8, *Ciclo de canciones*
22.8a, Luna, —, Manuel Felipe Rugeles, —, —, —, CMVC-FVES, —
22.8b, Cita, —, Manuel Felipe Rugeles, —, —, —, CMVC- FVES, —
22.8c, Por los caminos de Zorca, —, Manuel Felipe Rugeles, —, —, Dedicada a Fedora Alemán, CMVC-FVES, —
22.8d, Lunar, —, Manuel Felipe Rugeles, —, —, A Gladys Róo de Rotondaro, CMVC-FVES, —
22.8e, La caña la están cortando, —, —, —, —, —, CMVC-FVES, —
22.8f, Gotitas de agua (Canción de cuna), —, —, —, —, —, CMVC-FVES, —
22.8g, Jardín de ensueño, 1950, Blanca Estrella de Mescoli, —, —, Dedicada a Mari Méscoli, CMVC-FVES, —
22.8h, Soledad, —, Luz Machado, —, —, —, CMVC-FVES, —
22.8i, El silencio, —, A. Eloy Blanco, —, —, —, CMVC-FVES, —

Grau, Alberto, 1937–

22.9, *Tríptico*
22.9a, Creciente, —, Manuel Felipe Rugeles, —, Mezzo-soprano or baritone, —, FVES, —
22.9b, Aria triste, —, Juan Ramón Jiménez, —, Mezzo-soprano, With flute and piano, FVES, —

Moleiro, Moisés, 1904–1979

22.10, *Nueve canciones*
22.10a, Recuerdo, p1961, Moisés Moleiro, F3–E4, Med-high, Bass clef, IN, —, +
22.10b, Otoño, p1961, Fernando Paz Castillo, F♯4–F♯5, Med, —, IN, —, +
22.10c, Estrella, p1961, Pedro Rivera, B♭4–F5, Med, —, IN, —, +
22.10d, En el parque, p1961, Moisés Moleiro, E4–G5, Med, —, IN, —, +
22.10e, Crepuscular, p1961, F. Lazo Martí, C4–E5, Med, —, IN, —, +
22.10f, Extasis, p1961, Rabindranath Tagore, D4–E5, Med, —, IN, —, +
22.10g, Canción de otoño, p1961, Paul Verlaine, D4–E5, Med, —, IN, —, +
22.10h, Vigilia, p1961, Moisés Moleiro, D4–F5, Med, —, IN, —, +
22.10i, Tonada, p1961, Moisés Moleiro, F4–G♭5, Med-high, —, IN, —, +

22.11, Romance, —, Rodolfo Moleiro, —, Medium voice, —, m, —, +

Muñoz, José Luis, 1928–1982

22.12, Canciones de mi juventud, —, José Luis Muñoz, —, High voice, —, PAC, —, +

22.13, *Canciones populares*
22.13a, Ilusión, —, José Luis Muñoz, —, Medium voice, —, PAC, —, +

22.13b, Teresita, —, José Luis Muñoz, —, Medium voice, —, PAC, —, +

Plaza, Juan Bautista, 1898–1965

22.14, Negra está la noche, 1926, Rabindranath Tagore, $A3–A\flat 5$, Med-high, —, TR, *The Latin American Art Song*, +

22.15, *Obras para canto y piano*

22.15a, La fuente abandonada, 1933, F. Paz Castillo, $E\flat 4–A\flat 5$, Med-high, —, PAC, —, +

22.15b, Tarde, 1940, Otto D'Sola, $E4–G5$, Med-high, —, PAC, —, +

22.15c, Claro rayo de luna, 1924, Jacinto Fombona Pachano, $G4–A5$, Med-high, —, PAC, —, +

22.15d, Pájaros en el alba, 1956, Manuel Felipe Rugeles, $C4–G5$ ($C6$), Med, —, PAC, —, +

22.15e, La luna es entre las nubes (de Las Pastorales), 1958, Juan Ramón Jiménez, $E\flat 4–G5$, Med-high, —, PAC, —, +

22.15f, En el camino (de Aromas de Leyenda), 1951, Ramón del Valle-Inclán, $D4–F5$, Med, —, PAC, —, +

22.15g, Cantar margariteño, 1942, Pedro Rivera, $C4–A\flat 5$, Med-high, —, PAC, —, +

22.15h, Cuando el camino me fatiga, 1953(56?), Rabindranath Tagore, $D\flat 4–F5$, Med, —, PAC, TR, *The Latin American Art Song*, +

22.16, *Siete canciones venezolanas: Suite para canto y piano*

22.16a, Yo me quedé triste y mudo, 1932, Luis Barrios Cruz, $D4–G5$, Med, Cuaderno I, PAC, —, +

22.16b, La noche del Llano Abajo, 1932, Luis Barrios Cruz, $C4–F5$, Med, Cuaderno I, PAC, PEN, *The Art Song in Latin America*, +

22.16c, Cuando el caballo se para, 1932, Luis Barrios Cruz, $C4–F5$, Med, Cuaderno I, PAC, TR, *The Latin American Art Song*, +

22.16d, Hilando el copo del viento, 1932, Luis Barrios Cruz, $D4–F5$, Med, Cuaderno I, PAC, PEN, *The Art Song in Latin America*, +

22.16e, Por estos cuatro caminos, 1932, Luis Barrios Cruz, $E4–F\sharp 5$, Med, Cuaderno II, PAC, PEN, *The Art Song in Latin America*, +

22.16f, La sombra salió del monte, 1932, Luis Barrios Cruz, $(A4)C\sharp 4–G5$, Med, Cuaderno II, PAC, —, +

22.16g, Palma verde, garza blanca, 1932, Luis Barrios Cruz, $D4–G5$, Med-high, Cuaderno II, PAC, —, +

Additional titles: Barcarola; Canción de cuna para mi nieta; *Due liriche* (Serenata, Incantissimo); Elegía; La preghiera dei bimbi; L'infinito; Le soir descend sur nous; Preghiera; Salve Regina; Si tu savais; Sinfonía en gris mayor; Tantum ergo (voice and organ)

Rago, Alexis, 1930–

22.17, *Rapasgotori*

22.17a, Soneto del cielo, ©1980, Luis Pastori, —, Tenor, —, FVES, —, +

22.17b, Soneto del purgatorio, ©1980, Luis Pastori, —, Tenor, —, FVES, —, +

22.17c, Soneto del infierno, ©1980, Luis Pastori, —, Tenor, —, FVES, —, +

22.17d, Ángel ciego, ©1980, Luis Pastori, —, Tenor, —, FVES, —, +

22.17e, Glosa para hablar mal del amor, ©1980, Luis Pastori, —, Tenor, —, FVES, —, +

22.17f, El pozo, ©1980, Luis Pastori, —, Tenor, —, FVES, —, +

22.17g, La glosa de los ríos, ©1980, Luis Pastori, —, Tenor, —, FVES, —, +

22.17h, Ah, quién tuviera una nube, ©1980, Luis Pastori, —, Tenor, —, FVES, —, +

22.17i, Glosa de Beatriz, ©1980, Luis Pastori, —, Tenor, —, FVES, —, +

22.17j, Regreso, ©1980, Luis Pastori, —, Tenor, —, FVES, —, +

22.17k, Siempre crece un pino, ©1980, Luis Pastori, —, Tenor, —, FVES, —, +

22.18, *Tres canciones populares*
22.18a, Canción de cuna para la tarde, —, R. Rojas, —, —, —, FVES, —
22.18b, Canto triste, —, R. Rojas, —, —, —, FVES, —
22.18c, De qué vale decirlo, —, R. Rojas, —, —, —, FVES, —

Sojo, Vicente Emilio, 1887–1974

22.19, Aguinaldos populares venezolanos para la Noche Buena, ©1945, —, —, —, Carols arranged for voice and piano by Vicente Emilio Sojo, EME, —, +

PUBLISHERS

CMVC-FVES, Colección Músicos Venezolanos Contemporaneos
EGEC, Ediciones de la Gobernación del Estado Carabobo
EME, Ediciones del Ministerio de Educación
FVES, Fundación Vicente Emilio Sojo
IN, Imprenta Nacional
m, manuscript
PAC, Ediciones Padre Antolin Company
PEN, Pendragon Press
TR, Tritó, S.L.

COLLECTIONS

+, LAMC (Latin American Music Center), Indiana University

SOURCES

(See bibliography for additional publication information)
Caicedo, *The Latin American Art Song: A Critical Anthology and Interpretive Guide for Singers*
LCP, *The Living Composers Project* (online resource)
Wilson, *The Art Song in Latin America: Selected Works by Twentieth-Century Composers*

Appendix A

Countries and Regions in Latin America

Caribbean Islands

Antigua and Barbuda
Aruba
Bahamas
Barbados
Cayman Islands
Cuba
Dominica
Dominican Republic
Grenada
Guadeloupe
Haiti
Jamaica
Martinique
Puerto Rico
Saint Barthélemy
Saint Kitts and Nevis
Saint Lucia
Saint Vincent and the Grenadines
Trinidad and Tobago
Turks and Caicos Islands
Virgin Islands

Central America

Belize
Costa Rica
El Salvador
Guatemala
Honduras
Nicaragua
Panama

North America

Mexico

South America

Argentina
Bolivia
Brazil
Chile
Colombia
Ecuador
French Guiana
Guyana
Paraguay
Peru
Suriname
Uruguay
Venezuela

Appendix B

Statistics by Geographic Region

Statistics in Tables 1–4 from *The World Factbook*, a public domain web publication of the CIA (Central Intelligence Agency), https://www.cia.gov/library/publications/the-world-factbook (figures from 2007 website unless otherwise indicated).

Table 1. Caribbean Islands

	Population[1]	Ethnicity	Religion	Language	Government Type	Independence Status
Antigua and Barbuda	85,632	black 91%, mixed 4.4%, white 1.7%, other 2.9%	Anglican 25.7%, Seventh-Day Adventist 12.3%, Pentecostal 10.6%, Moravian 10.5%, Roman Catholic 10.4%, Methodist, Baptist, Church of God, other Christian	English (official), local dialects	constitutional monarchy with a parliamentary system of government	1 November 1981 (from U.K.)
Aruba	103,065	mixed white/Caribbean Amerindian 80%	Roman Catholic 80.8%, Protestant 9%, Hindu, Muslim, Confucian, Jewish	Dutch (official), Papiamento (a Spanish, Portuguese, Dutch, English dialect), English (widely spoken), Spanish (2000 census)	parliamentary democracy	none (part of the Netherlands)
Bahamas	309,156	black 85%, white 12%, Asian and Hispanic 3%	Baptist 35.4%, Anglican 15.1%, Roman Catholic 13.5%, Pentecostal 8.1%, Church of God 4.8%, Methodist 4.2%, other Christian 15.2%, none or unspecified 2.9%, other 0.8% (2000 census)	English (official), Creole (among Haitian immigrants)	constitutional parliamentary democracy	10 July 1973 (from U.K.)
Barbados	284,589	black 90%, white 4%, Asian and mixed 6%	Protestant 63.4% (Anglican 28.3%, Pentecostal 18.7%, Methodist 5.1%, other 11.3%), Roman Catholic 4.2%, other Christian 7%, none 20.6%, other 4.8%	English	parliamentary democracy	30 November 1966 (from U.K.)

1. Population figures based on July 2009 estimate.

continued on next page

Table 1 continued

	Population	Ethnicity	Religion	Language	Government Type	Independence Status
Cayman Islands	49,035	mixed 40%, white 20%, black 20%, expatriates of various ethnic groups 20%	Church of God 26%, United Church (Presbyterian and Congregational) 11.8%, Roman Catholic 11%, Baptist 8.7%, Seventh-Day Adventist 8.2%, Anglican 5.7%, Pentecostal 5.3%, other	English	British crown colony	none (overseas territory of the U.K.)
Cuba	11,451,652	white 65.1%, mulatto and mestizo[2] 24.8%, black 10.1%	nominally 85% Roman Catholic prior to Castro assuming power; Protestants, Jehovah's Witnesses, Jews, and Santeria also represented	Spanish	communist state	20 May 1902 (from Spain 10 December 1898; administered by the U.S. from 1898 to 1902)
Dominica	72,660	black 86.8%, mixed 8.9%, Carib Amerindian 2.9%, white 0.8%, other	Roman Catholic 61.4%, Seventh-Day Adventist 6%, Pentecostal 5.6%, Baptist 4.1%, Methodist 3.7%, Church of God 1.2%, Jehovah's Witnesses 1.2%, other	English (official), French patois	parliamentary democracy	3 November 1978 (from U.K.)
Dominican Republic	9,650,054	mixed 73%, white 16%, black 11%	Roman Catholic 95%, other 5%	Spanish	democratic republic	27 February 1844 (from Haiti)
Grenada	90,739	black 82%, mixed black and European 13%, European and East Indian 5%, and trace of Arawak/Carib Amerindian	Roman Catholic 53%, Anglican 13.8%, other Protestant 33.2%	English (official), French patois	parliamentary democracy	7 February 1974 (from U.K.)

2. Mestizo refers to mixed white and Amerindian; mulatto refers to mixed white and black ethnicity.

Guadeloupe[3]	452,776	black or mulatto 90%, white 5%, East Indian, Lebanese, Chinese less than 5%	Roman Catholic 95%, Hindu and pagan African 4%, Protestant 1%	French (official) 99%, Creole patois	NA	none (overseas department of France)
Haiti	9,035,536	black 95%, mulatto and white 5%	Roman Catholic 80%, Protestant 16% (Baptist 10%, Pentecostal 4%, Adventist 1%, other 1%), none 1%, other 3% (note: roughly half of the population practices Voodoo)	French (official), Creole (official)	republic	1 January 1804 (from France)
Jamaica	2,825,928	black 91.2%, mixed 6.2%, other	Protestant 62.5% (Seventh-Day Adventist 10.8%, other Church of God 8.3%, Baptist 7.2%, New Testament Church of God 6.3%, Church of God in Jamaica 4.8%, Church of God of Prophecy 4.3%, Anglican 3.6 %, other Christian 7.7), Roman Catholic 2.6%, other	English, English patois	constitutional parliamentary democracy	6 August 1962 (from U.K.)
Martinique‡	436,131	African and African-white-Indian mixture 90%, white 5%, East Indian and Chinese less than 5%	Roman Catholic 85%, Protestant 10.5%, Muslim 0.5%, Hindu 0.5%, other 3-5% (1997)	French, Creole patois	NA	none (overseas department of France)

3. As of 2009, Guadeloupe, Martinique, and French Guiana are no longer listed individually in *The World Factbook*. Together with Reunion (an island in the Indian Ocean), they are listed under the domain of France as overseas departments. Their combined statistics include population: 1,908,017; ethnicities: black, white, mulatto, East Indian, Chinese, and Amerindian; religions: Roman Catholic, Protestant, Hindu, Muslim, Buddhist, and pagan; languages: French and Creole patois; government type: republic (France). Saint Barthélemy seceded from Guadeloupe in 2003 and in 2007, it became an overseas department of France.

continued on next page

Table 1 continued

	Population	Ethnicity	Religion	Language	Government Type	Independence Status
Puerto Rico	3,971,020	white (mostly Spanish origin) 80.5%, black 8%, Amerindian 0.4%, Asian 0.2%, mixed and other 10.9%	Roman Catholic 85%, Protestant and other 15%	Spanish, English	commonwealth	none (unincorporated, organized territory of the U.S. with commonwealth status)
Saint Kitts and Nevis	40,131	predominantly black; some British, Portuguese, and Lebanese	Anglican, other Protestant, Roman Catholic	English	parliamentary democracy	19 September 1983 (from U.K.)
Saint Lucia	160,267	black 82.5%, mixed 11.9%, East Indian 2.4%, other	Roman Catholic 67.5%, Seventh-Day Adventist 8.5%, Pentecostal 5.7%, Anglican 2%, Evangelical 2%, other Christian 5.1%, Rastafarian 2.1%, other 1.1%, unspecified 1.5%, none 4.5% (2001 census)	English (official), French patois	parliamentary democracy	22 February 1979 (from U.K.)
Saint Vincent and the Grenadines	104,574	black 66%, mixed 19%, East Indian 6%, European 4%, Carib Amerindian 2%, other 3%	Anglican 47%, Methodist 28%, Roman Catholic 13%, Hindu, Seventh-Day Adventist, other Protestant 12%	English, French patois	parliamentary democracy	27 October 1979 (from U.K.)
Trinidad and Tobago	1,229,953	Indian (South Asian) 40%, African 37.5%, mixed 20.5%, other 1.2%, unspecified 0.8% (2000 census)	Roman Catholic 26%, Hindu 22.5%, Anglican 7.8%, Baptist 7.2%, Pentecostal 6.8%, other Christian 5.8%, Muslim 5.8%, Seventh-Day Adventist 4%, other 10.8%, unspecified 1.4%, none 1.9% (2000 census)	English (official), Caribbean Hindustani (dialect of Hindi), French, Spanish, Chinese	parliamentary democracy	31 August 1962 (from U.K.)

	Population	Ethnicity	Religion	Language	Government Type	Independence Status
Turks and Caicos Islands	22,942	black 90%, mixed, European, or North American 10%	Baptist 40%, Anglican 18%, Methodist 16%, Church of God 12%, other 14% (1990)	English (official)	NA	none (overseas territory of the U.K.)
Virgin Islands	109,825	black 76.2%, white 13.1%, Asian 1.1%, other 6.1%, mixed 3.5% (2000 census)	Baptist 42%, Roman Catholic 34%, Episcopalian 17%, other 7%	English 74.7%, Spanish or Spanish Creole 16.8%, French or French Creole 6.6%, other 1.9% (2000 census)	NA	none (organized, unincorporated territory of the U.S. with policy relations between the Virgin Islands and the U.S. under the jurisdiction of the Office of Insular Affairs, U.S. Department of the Interior)

Table 2. Central America

	Population	Ethnicity	Religion	Language	Government Type	Independence Status
Belize	307,899	mestizo 48.7%, Creole 24.9%, Maya 10.6%, Garifuna 6.1%, other 9.7% (2000 census)	Roman Catholic 49.6%, Protestant 27% (Pentecostal 7.4%, Anglican 5.3%, Seventh-Day Adventist 5.2%, Mennonite 4.1%, Methodist 3.5%, Jehovah's Witnesses 1.5%), other 14%, none 9.4% (2000)	English (official), Creole, Mayan dialects, Garifuna (Carib), German, other	parliamentary democracy	21 September 1981 (from U.K.)
Costa Rica	4,253,877	white (including mestizo) 94%, black 3%, Amerindian 1%, Chinese 1%, other 1%	Roman Catholic 76.3%, Evangelical 13.7%, Jehovah's Witnesses 1.3%, other Protestant 0.7%, other 4.8%, none 3.2%	Spanish (official), English	democratic republic	15 September 1821 (from Spain)
El Salvador	7,185,218	mestizo 90%, white 9%, Amerindian 1%	Roman Catholic 57.1%, Protestant 21.2%, Jehovah's Witnesses 1.9%, Mormon 0.7%, other (2003 est.)	Spanish, Nahua (among some Amerindians)	republic	15 September 1821 (from Spain)

continued on next page

Table 2 continued

	Population	Ethnicity	Religion	Language	Government Type	Independence Status
Guatemala	13,276,517	mestizo (mixed Amerindian-Spanish, locally called "Ladino") and European 59.4%, K'iche 9.1%, Kaqchikel 8.4%, Mam 7.9%, Q'eqchi 6.3%, other Mayan 8.6%, indigenous non-Mayan 0.2%, other 0.1% (2001 census)	Roman Catholic, Protestant, indigenous Mayan beliefs	Spanish 60%, Amerindian languages 40% (23 officially recognized Amerindian languages, including Quiche, Cakchiquel, Kekchi, Mam, Garifuna, and Xinca)	constitutional democratic republic	15 September 1821 (from Spain)
Honduras	7,792,854	mestizo (mixed Amerindian and European) 90%, Amerindian 7%, black 2%, white 1%	Roman Catholic 97%, Protestant 3%	Spanish, Amerindian dialects	democratic constitutional republic	15 September 1821 (from Spain)
Nicaragua	5,891,199	mestizo 69%, white 17%, black 9%, Amerindian 5%	Roman Catholic 58.5%, Evangelical 21.6%, Moravian 1.6%, Jehovah's Witnesses 0.9%, other 1.7%, none 15.7% (2005 census)	Spanish 97.5% (official), Miskito 1.7%, other 0.8% (1995 census) (note: English and indigenous languages on Atlantic coast)	republic	15 September 1821 (from Spain)
Panama	3,360,474	mestizo 70%, Amerindian and mixed (West Indian) 14%, white 10%, Amerindian 6%	Roman Catholic 85%, Protestant 15%	Spanish (official), English 14% (many Panamanians bilingual)	constitutional democracy	3 November 1903 (from Colombia; independence from Spain 28 November 1821)

Table 3. North America

Mexico	111,211,789	mestizo (Amerindian-Spanish) 60%, Amerindian or predominantly Amerindian 30%, white 9%, other 1%	Roman Catholic 76.5%, Protestant 6.3% (Pentecostal 1.4%, Jehovah's Witnesses 1.1%, other 3.8%), other (2000 census)	Spanish, various Mayan, Nahuatl, and other regional indigenous languages	federal republic	16 September 1810 (from Spain)

Table 4. South America

Argentina	40,913,584	white (mostly Spanish and Italian) 97%, mestizo, Amerindian or other non-white groups 3%	nominally Roman Catholic 92% (less than 20% practicing), Protestant 2%, Jewish 2%, other 4%	Spanish (official), English, Italian, German, French	republic	9 July 1816 (from Spain)
Bolivia	9,775,246	Quechua 30%, mestizo 30%, Aymara 25%, white 15%	Roman Catholic 95%, Protestant (Evangelical Methodist) 5%	Spanish (official), Quechua (official), Aymara (official), other	republic (Bolivia's constitution defines it as a "Social Unitarian State")	6 August 1825 (from Spain)
Brazil	198,739,269	white 53.7%, mulatto 38.5%, black 6.2%, other (includes Japanese, Arab, Amerindian) 0.9%, unspecified 0.7% (2000 census)	Roman Catholic (nominal) 73.6%, Protestant 15.4%, Spiritualist 1.3%, Bantu/Voodoo 0.3%, other 1.8%, unspecified 0.2%, none 7.4% (2000 census)	Portuguese (official), Spanish, German, Italian, Japanese, English, a large number of Amerindian languages	federal republic	7 September 1822 (from Portugal)

continued on next page

Table 4 continued

	Population	Ethnicity	Religion	Language	Government Type	Independence Status
Chile	16,601,707	white and white-Amerindian 95.4%, Mapuche 4%, other indigenous groups 0.6% (2002 census)	Roman Catholic 70%, Evangelical 15.1%, Jehovah's Witnesses 1.1%, other Christian 1%, other 4.6%, none 8.3%	Spanish, Mapundungun, German, English	republic	18 September 1810 (from Spain)
Colombia	45,644,023	mestizo 58%, white 20%, mulatto 14%, black 4%, mixed black-Amerindian 3%, Amerindian 1%	Roman Catholic 90%, other 10%	Spanish	republic	20 July 1810 (from Spain)
Ecuador	14,573,101	mestizo 65%, Amerindian 25%, Spanish and others 7%, black 3%	Roman Catholic 95%, other 5%	Spanish (official), Amerindian languages (especially Quechua)	republic	24 May 1822 (from Spain)
French Guiana‡	199,509	black or mulatto 66%, white 12%, East Indian, Chinese, Amerindian 12%, other 10%	Roman Catholic	French	overseas department of France	none (overseas department of France)
Guyana	772,298	East Indian 43.5%, black (African) 30.2%, mixed 16.7%, Amerindian 9.1%, other 0.5% (2002 census)	Hindu 28.4%, Pentecostal 16.9%, Roman Catholic 8.1%, Anglican 6.9%, Seventh-Day Adventist 5%, Methodist 1.7%, Jehovah's Witnesses 1.1%, other Christian 17.7%, Muslim 7.2%, other (2002 census)	English, Amerindian dialects, Creole, Caribbean Hindustani (a dialect of Hindi)	republic	26 May 1966 (from U.K.)

Paraguay	6,995,655	mestizo (mixed Spanish and Amerindian) 95%, other 5%	Roman Catholic 90%, Protestant 6.2%, other Christian 1.1%, other (2002 census)	Spanish (official), Guarani (official)	constitutional republic	14 May 1811 (from Spain)
Peru	29,546,963	Amerindian 45%, mestizo 37%, white 15%, black, Japanese, Chinese, and other 3%	Roman Catholic 81%, Seventh-Day Adventist 1.4%, other Christian 0.7%, other 0.6%, unspecified or none 16.3% (2003 est.)	Spanish (official), Quechua (official), Aymara, and a large number of minor Amazonian languages	constitutional republic	28 July 1821 (from Spain)
Suriname	481,267	Hindustani (known locally as "East Indians") 37%, Creole (mixed white and black) 31%, Javanese 15%, "Maroons" 10%, Amerindian 2%, Chinese 2%, white 1%, other 2%	Hindu 27.4%, Protestant 25.2% (predominantly Moravian), Roman Catholic 22.8%, Muslim 19.6%, indigenous beliefs 5%	Dutch (official), English (widely spoken), Sranang Tongo (Surinamese, sometimes called Taki-Taki, is the native language of Creoles and much of the younger population, and lingua franca among others), Caribbean Hindustani (a dialect of Hindi), Javanese	constitutional democracy	25 November 1975 (from the Netherlands)
Uruguay	3,494,382	white 88%, mestizo 8%, black 4%, Amerindian (practically nonexistent)	Roman Catholic 47.1%, non-Catholic Christians 11.1%, nondenominational 23.2%, Jewish 0.3%, atheist or agnostic 17.2%, other (2006)	Spanish, Portunol, or Brazilero (Portuguese-Spanish mix on the Brazilian frontier)	constitutional republic	25 August 1825 (from Brazil)
Venezuela	26,814,843	Spanish, Italian, Portuguese, Arab, German, African, indigenous people	nominally Roman Catholic 96%, Protestant 2%, other 2%	Spanish (official), numerous indigenous dialects	federal republic	5 July 1811 (from Spain)

Appendix C

Publishers

A. Di Franco[1]	São Paulo, Brazil
A. Melodia	São Paulo, Brazil
ACA	Academia Argentina de Musica
	Buenos Aires, Argentina
AHM	Agence Haïtienne de Musique
	Port-au-Prince, Haiti
Albert Stahl	Berlin, Germany
Alfred Publishing	Alfred Publishing Company, Inc.
	16320 Roscoe Blvd., Suite 100
	P.O. Box 10003
	Van Nuys, Calif. 91410-0003, U.S.A.
	www.alfred.com
AMC	American Music Center
	30 W. 26th St., Suite 1001
	New York, N.Y. 10010-2011, U.S.A.
AMP	Associated Music Publishers, Inc.
	New York, N.Y., U.S.A.
AN	Arthur Napoleão
	Sampaio Araujo Co. (see SA)
	122 Avenida Rio Branco
	Caixa Postal 536
	Rio de Janeiro, Brazil
ANA	Academia Nacional de Bellas Artes
	Buenos Aires, Argentina
ANCPR	Asociación Nacional de Compositores de Puerto Rico
	Apartado 22481, Estación UPR
	Río Piedras, Puerto Rico 00931

1. No current information found; probably no longer in existence.

PUBLISHERS

Arista	A.S. Arista
	Buenos Aires, Argentina
	Montevideo, Uruguay
ArMP	Arrow Music Press
	New York, N.Y., U.S.A.
Bandeirante	Bandeirante Editora Musical
	São Paulo, Brazil
Barry & Cia	Montevideo 264
	Buenos Aires, Argentina
B/Cia	Viuva Bevilacqua & Cia
	Rua de Ouvidor
	Rio de Janeiro, Brazil
B/H	Boosey and Hawkes, Inc.
	35 East 21st Street, Floor 9
	New York, N.Y. 10010, U.S.A.
	Tel 212-358-5361
	Fax 212-358-5309
	www.boosey.com
BLA	Boletín Latinoamericano de Música
	Casilla de Correo 540
	Montevideo, Uruguay
BPCAC	Bogotá Patronato Colombiano de Artes y Ciencias
	Colombia
Breyer	Breyer Hermanos
	Bolivar 1610, Florida 414
	Buenos Aires, Argentina
Bryant	Bryant Music Company
	New York, N.Y., U.S.A.
Buffet, Crampton et Cie.	Paris, France
CA	Colección Arion/Ediciones Mexicanas de Música, A.C.
	Avenida Juárez 18-206
	México
Campassi & Camin	São Paulo, Brazil
	(now Casa Editoras Musical Brasileira; see CEMB)
Castro Lima	Castro Lima & C
	Rio de Janeiro, Brazil
CC	Corporación para la Cultura
	Cali, Colombia

APPENDIX C

CEDIM	Escuela de Artes Musicales
	Universidad de Costa Rica
	San Pedro de Montes de Oca
	San José, Costa Rica
	Fax 224-5025
	Email higiniof@cariari.ucr.ac.cr
CEMB	Casas Editoras Musicais Brasileiras Reunidas
	(now owned by IV; see below)
	Rio de Janeiro and São Paulo, Brazil
Chiarato	S. Chiarato
	São Paulo, Brazil
Choudens	Choudens
	30, Boulevard des Capucines
	Paris, France
CLSRL	Casa Lottermoser S.R.L.
	Rivadavia 851
	Buenos Aires, Argentina
CM	Casa Mozart
	Avenida Rio Branco, 118
	Rio de Janeiro, Brazil
CMC	Castellanos-Molino Corporation
CMP	Consolidated Music Publishers
	24 East 22nd Street
	New York, N.Y. 10010-6146, U.S.A.
CMVC-FVES	Colección Musicos Venezolanos Contemporaneos
	Division of FVES (see below)
	Caracas, Venezuela
CNC	Comisión Nacional de Cultura
	Buenos Aires, Argentina
CNMP	Conservatorio Nacional de Música de Peru
	Lima, Peru
CNMU	Conservatorio Nacional de Música
	Montevideo, Uruguay
CO	Casa Oliveira
	Rua da Carioca, 70-Centro
	Rio de Janeiro-RJ 2005008, Brazil
	Tel 011 55 21 2222-0290
Cooperativa	Cooperativa Ed. Dos Compositores e Músicos Profissionais
	Rio de Janeiro, Brazil
Correo Musical	Correo Musical Sud Americano
	Buenos Aires, Argentina

PUBLISHERS

CVG	Casa Viúva Guerreiro/Ed. E.A. Viúva Guereiro & Cia
	Rio de Janeiro, Brazil
CW	Carlos Wehrs & Cia
	Rio de Janeiro, Brazil
CWag	Casa Wagner
	São Paulo, Brazil
David Poggi	David Poggi é Hijo
	Artes 418
	Buenos Aires, Argentina
De Francisco de Paula	Avenida de Mayo 1053
	Buenos Aires, Argentina
Derosa	São Paulo, Brazil
de Sants	Rome
Diario "La Razón"	Buenos Aires, Argentina
DNIC	Departamento Nacional da Indústria e Comércio
	Rio de Janeiro, Brazil
EAC	Editorial Argentina de Compositores
	Buenos Aires, Argentina
EAM	Editorial Argentina de Música
	Bartolomé Mitre 1568
	Buenos Aires, Argentina
EBC	Ediciones de Blanck
	Havana, Cuba
EBMMC	Edward B. Marks Music Corp.
	136 W. 57th St.
	New York, N.Y. 10019, U.S.A.
EBMP	Editorial Brasileira de Música Popular
	Brazil
EBN	Ediciones de la Biblioteca Nacional José Marti
	Apartado No. 3
	Havana, Cuba
EC	Editorial Campos
	Uruguay
ECCM	Ediciones del Consejo Central de la Música
	Dirección General de Bellas Artes
	(Ministerio de Instrucción Pública)
	Buenos Aires, Argentina
ECIC	Editorial Cooperativa Interamericana de Compositores
	Montevideo, Uruguay
	c/o SMP (see below)

ED	Editor Danzuni	
	Costa Rica	
	Edições Associação Rio Grandense de Música	
	Edition Modern	
EDM	Edição de Música	
	Moscow	
EGEC	Ediciones de la Gobernación del Estado Carabobo	
	Valencia, Venezuela	
EIMG	Ediciones del Instututo Musical Gomezanda	
	Mexico	
EM	Editorial Mangione S.A.	
	São Paulo, Brazil	
EMA	Edizioni Musicale Armonia	
	Rome, Italy	
EMC	Editorial Musical de Cuba	
	Havana, Cuba	
EME	Ediciones del Ministerio de Educación	
	Caracas, Venezuela	
EMM	Ediciones Mexicanas de Musica	
	Avenida Juarez 18	
	Mexico, D.F.	
EMM-CA	See CA, above	
EMNB	Editora Música Nova do Brasil	
	Rio de Janeiro, Brazil	
EMV	Edição Música Viva	
	Caixa Postal 3846, Rio de Janeiro, Brazil	
ES	Éditions Maurice Senart	
	20, rue du Dragon	
	Paris, France	
ESar	Editorial Saraceno	
	Pujol 1325	
	Buenos Aires, Argentina	
ESav	Editions Savart	
	SQN107-BL.H-Apt. 204	
	Brasilia-DF, Brazil	
ESEB	Ediciones de la Secretaria de Educación Pública	
	Mexico, D.F.	
FB	Fermato do Brasil	
	Editores de Músicas	
	Av. Ipiranga, 1123	
	São Paulo, Brazil	

FBN/DIMAS	Fundação Biblioteca Nacional
	Divisão de Música e Arquivo Sonoro
	Rio de Janeiro, Brazil
FCGo	Fundação Carlos Gomes
	Belém, Pará, Brazil
FCP	Franco Columbo Publications
	New York, N.Y., U.S.A.
Forlivesi	A. Forlivesi, G.C. Edizioni Musicali
	Florence, Italy
FUNARJ	Fundação Nacional das Artes
	Rio de Janeiro, Brazil
FUNARTE	Fundação Nacional de Artes
	Palácio da Impresna, 16, térreo
	Rio de Janeiro, Brazil
FVES	Fundación Vicente Emilio Sojo
	Caracas, Venezuela
Garrot, Tasso y Vita	Serrano 2163
	Buenos Aires, Argentina
Gaudiosi	Roque Gaudiosi
	Ediciones Musicales Argentinas
	Calle Salta 1160
	Buenos Aires, Argentina
Goldberg	Goldberg Edições Musicais
	São Paulo, Brazil
Gordon	Manuel L. Gordon (Ritmo)
	Diagonal 7° Norte 1006 Esq. 5
	La Plata, Argentina
Grech	Louis Grech
	15, Chaussée d'Autin et 40, blvd. Haussmann
	Paris, France
GRic	G. Ricordi (see RA)
	Milan, Italy; Buenos Aires, Argentina;
	New York, N.Y., U.S.A.
GSch	G. Schirmer, Inc.
	257 Park Avenue South, 20th floor
	New York, N.Y. 10010, U.S.A.
	212-254-2100
	www.schirmer.com
Guanabara	Musicais Guanabara
	Rio de Janeiro, Brazil
Gurina	Gurina y Cía
	Buenos Aires, Argentina
HC	H. de Curitiba
	Curitiba, Londrina, Brazil

HL	Hal Leonard Corporation
	7777 W. Bluemound Rd., P.O. Box 13819
	Milwaukee, Wis. 53213, U.S.A.
	www.halleonard.com
ICC	Instituto Colombiano de Cultura
	Subdirrección de Bellas Artes
	Centro de Documentación Musical
	Colombia
ICP	Instituto de Cultura Puertorriqueña
	San Juan, Puerto Rico
IEM	Instituto de Extensión Musical
	Universidad de Chile
	Compania 1264
	Santiago, Chile
IML	Ed. Impressora Moderna Ltda
	São Paulo, Brazil
IN	Imprenta Nacional
	Caracas, Venezuela
INCP	Instituto Nacional de Cultura
	Lima, Peru
INRA	Dirección de Relaciones Públicas del INRA
	Havana, Cuba
Irmãos Chiarato	São Paulo, Brazil
IV	Irmãos Vitale & Cia
	Rua Franca Pinca 42
	São Paulo, Brazil
J. Feliú	Juan Feliú y Hijos
	Carlos Pellegrini 440
	Buenos Aires, Argentina
JK	Julio Korn
	Moreno 2034
	Buenos Aires, Argentina
JLS	J.L. Siqueiria-Liuros Didácticos e Músicas
	Largo de São Franciso, 26-S/1612
	Rio de Janeiro, Brazil
JM	Josef Marx/McGinnis & Marx Music Publishers
	236 West 26th St., No. 11S
	New York, N.Y. 10001-6736, U.S.A.
LAC	Liga de Compositores de México
	Apartado Postal M-2904
	México
LAGOS	Editorial Lagos
	Talcahuano 638
	Buenos Aires, Argentina

PUBLISHERS

LAMB	Latin American Music Bureau (see PAU)
	Division of the Pan American Union, Washington, D.C., U.S.A.
La Quena	La Quena Casa de Música S.R.L.
	Viamonte 859
	Buenos Aires, Argentina
L.G. Miranda	S.I.L.G. Miranda
	Brazil
Lino José Barbosa	Rio de Janeiro, Brazil
LK Produções Artisticas	Rio de Janeiro, Brazil
LMT	Ed. Litero Musical Tupy Ltda
	São Paulo, Brazil
Manuel Antônio Guimarães	Rio de Janeiro, Brazil
Marajoara	Edições Musicais Marajoara
	Rio de Janeiro, Brazil
MC	Ministerio de Cultura, Juventud y Deportes
	Dirección de Publicaciones
	San José, Costa Rica
M. Calvello	Buenos Aires, Argentina
ME	Éditions Max Eschig
	48, rue de Rome
	Paris, France
MECU	Ministerio de Educación y Cultura de Uruguay
	Montevideo, Uruguay
MEP	Ministerio de Educación Pública
	Departamento de Publicaciones
	Costa Rica
MMB	MMB Music, Inc.
	Contemporary Arts Building
	3526 Washington Avenue
	St. Louis, Mo. 63103-1019, U.S.A.
	Tel 1-314-531-9635/1-800-543-3771
	www.mmbmusic.com
MMP	Ludwig Masters Publications
	(formerly Masters Music Publications)
	6403 West Rogers Circle
	Boca Raton, Florida 33487, U.S.A.
	800-434-6340/561-241-6169
	Fax 561-241-6347
Moreira de Sá	Rio de Janeiro, Brazil
MPA	Movimento
	Porto Alegre, Brazil
Music Press	Brazil

APPENDIX C

Musicália	Musicália/A Cultura Musical
	Brazil
Navia	Bogotá, Colombia
Novas Metas	São Paulo, Brazil
Ortelli	Ortelli Hermanos
	Belgrano 2947
	Buenos Aires, Argentina
Otto Beines	Otto Beines & Hijo
	Calle Bartólome Mitre 1032
	Buenos Aires, Argentina
PAC	Ediciones Padre Antolin Company
	Caracas, Venezuela
PAU	Pan American Union
	17th St. and Constitution Avenue
	Washington, D.C. 20006, U.S.A.
PAU-LAMB	Pan American Union, Latin-American Music
	Bureau (see PAU)
Paulo Florence	São Paulo, Brazil
P. Bastianelli	Piero Bastianelli
Peer Musikverlag	Peermusic Classical GmBH
	Mühlenkamp 45-22303-Hamburg
	Hamburg, Germany
	Tel 011 49 40 278379-0
	Fax 011 49 20 278379-40
	www.peermusic-classical.de
PEN	Pendragon Press
	Stuyvesant, N.Y., U.S.A.
Phonoart	Macau, China
PI	Peer International Corporation
	810 7th Avenue, Floor 10
	New York, N.Y. 10019-5818, U.S.A.
Pizzi	Pizzi e C.
	Bologna, Italy
PN	Pierre Noël, Éditeur
	24, blvd. Poissonnière
	Paris, France
RA	Ricordi Americana, S.A.E.C.
	Tte. Gral. Juan D. Perón 1558, 1037 Capital Federal
	Buenos Aires, Argentina
	Tel 011-54-11-4371-9841/9842/9843
	Fax 011-54-11-4371-8791
	info@ricordiamericana.com.ar

PUBLISHERS

RB	Ricordi Brasileira
	Al. Barao de Limeira, 331
	São Paulo, Brazil
R/E	Ries & Erler
	Wandalenallee 8
	14052 Berlin, Germany
	011-49-30-8251049
RL	Rouart Lerolle et Cie.
	29, rue d'Astorg
	Paris, France
RM	Ricordi Milano
	Milan, Italy
Rodríguez	Bogotá, Colombia
SA	Sampaio Araujo & Cia
	Rio de Janeiro, Brazil
SAI	Sociedade Artistica Internacional
	Rio de Janeiro, Brazil
SEC	Secretaría de Educación y Cultura
	Medellín, Colombia
SEML	Sistrum Edições Musicais Ltda
	Brazil
Seresta	Seresta Edições Musicais
	São Paulo, Brazil
SMP	Southern Music Publishing Company, Inc.
	1619 Broadway
	New York, N.Y. 10019, U.S.A.
SNM	Sociedad Nacional de Música (see also GRic, above, and AAC Collections, chap. 1)
SSMC	Sherman Square Music Company
	New York, N.Y., U.S.A.
Stahl/Schirmer	See Albert Stahl
Subito	Subito Music Publishing, Inc. (ASCAP)
	New York, N.Y., U.S.A.
	www.subitomusic.com
TMV	Tonos Musik Verlag
	Darmstadt, Germany
TPC	Theodore Presser Co.
	1 Presser Place
	New York, N.Y. 10021, U.S.A.
TR	Tritó, S.L.
	Av. De la Catedral 3, 08002, Barcelona, Spain
	Tel 011-34-93-342-61-75
	Fax 011-34-93-302-26-70
	www.trito.es, info@trito.es

APPENDIX C

UCR	Editorial de la Universidad de Costa Rica
	Ciudad Universitaria "Rodrigo Facio"
	San José, Costa Rica
	Apdo. 75-2060, Fax 207-5257
	eucr@ns.vinv.ucr.ac.cr
UFBA	Universidade Federal da Bahia
	Salvador, Brazil
UFPA	Universidad Federal do Pará
	Brazil
UME	Unión Musical Española
	Carrera de San Jerónimo 26, Madrid
	(Associated Music Publishers)
	c/o G. Schirmer, Inc.
	3 East 43rd St., New York, N.Y. 10019, U.S.A.
UNCA	Universidad Nacional de Cuyo
	Mendoza, Argentina
	University Society, Inc. See GSch
	257 Park Avenue South, 20th floor
	New York, N.Y. 10010, U.S.A.
	Contact: Peter Herb, Tel 212-254-2100
UOC	Universidad de Oriente
	Departamento de Actividades Culturales
	Santiago, Chile
USP	Editora da Universidade de São Paulo
	São Paulo, Brazil
USP/SDP	USP Serviço de Difusão de Partituras
	São Paulo, Brazil
Vieira Brandão	Rio de Janeiro, Brazil
VLM	Villa-Lobos Music Corporation
	1538 Broadway
	New York, N.Y., U.S.A.
VM	Vieira Machado & Cia
	Rio de Janeiro and São Paulo, Brazil
VV	Vicente Vitale
	Irmãos Vitale, Ind. & Com. Ltda
	Rua da Quintanda 17-1°. Andar
	Rio de Janeiro, Brazil
ZP	Zimmermann Print

Appendix D

Suggested Repertoire

UNDERGRADUATE (BEGINNING STUDIES)

Carlos Guastavino (Argentina): *15 Canciones escolares*, fifteen limited-range songs, appropriate for both young men and women
Jayme Ovalle (Brazil): Azulão
Luis Carlos Figueroa (Colombia): Berceuse (Mezzo)
José Daniel Zúñiga Zeledon, ed., *La patria canta, música y canciones, autores de Costa Rica* (Costa Rica)
Bruce Trinkley, ed., *Nine Latin American Folk Songs* (Various), folk songs available in both Medium-Low and Medium-High keys: Vuela suspiro; A cantar a una niña; Mi mamá me aconsejaba; Nesta rua; Una tarde fesquita de Mayo; El Capotín; Al pasar por Sevilla

UNDERGRADUATE (INTERMEDIATE TO ADVANCED)

High

Carlos López Buchardo (Argentina): Canción del carretero (*Seis canciones al estilo popular*); Prendeditos de la mano (*Cinco canciones al estilo popular*); Canción de Perico
Pascual De Rogatis (Argentina): Vidala, from *Cinco canciones argentinas*
Gilardo Gilardi (Argentina): Canción de cuna india
Alberto Ginastera (Argentina): Canción al árbol del olvido (*Dos canciones, op. 3*)
Manuel Gómez Carrillo (Argentina): Huainito
Carlos Guastavino (Argentina): La rosa y el sauce; Pueblito, mi pueblo; *4 Canciones argentinas*
Abramah Jurafsky (Argentina): Copla (*Tres canciones*)
Alberto Williams (Argentina): Vidalita, from *Canciones incaicas, op. 45*; Milonga calabacera, from *Canciones de la pampa y la sierra, op. 82*
Oscar Lorenzo Fernandez (Brazil): Meu coração

Alberto Nepomuceno (Brazil): Canção da ausência
Heitor Villa-Lobos (Brazil): Lundu da Marquesa de Santos, from *Modinhas e canções, Album 1* (Soprano)
Jaime León (Colombia): La campesina; A ti
German Cáceres (El Salvador): Si un niño muere en la guerra, from *Cuatro canciones para soprano y piano* (Soprano)
Salvador Ley (Guatemala): Copla triste
Frantz Casséus (Haiti): Se gran maten, Asotô; both from *Haïtianesques*
Silvestre Revueltas (Mexico): *Cinco canciones de niños*
Rafael Aponte-Ledée (Puerto Rico): Cuando voy a la aldea; Éstas lágrimas tan bellas
Juan Bautista Plaza (Venezuela): *Siete canciones venezolanas*

Low

Carlos Guastavino (Argentina): Se equivocó la paloma; Pampamapa, from *12 Canciones populares*; *Flores argentinas*
Oscar Lorenzo Fernandez (Brazil): Dentro da noite (Mezzo)
Claudio Santoro (Brazil): Amor em lágrimas, from *Três canções populares* (Mezzo)
Pedro Humberto Allende (Chile): *Seis cantos infantiles*
Luis A. Calvo (Colombia): En la playa
Gisela Hernández (Cuba): Sólo por el rocío, from *Nueve canciones*
Ferrère Laguerre (Haiti): Trois rondes haïtiennes
Edouard Woolley (Haiti): Berceuse à la bien-aimée
Carlos Chávez (Mexico): *Three poems*
Blas Galindo Dimas (Mexico): *Tres canciones* (High or Low)
Carlos Jimenez Mabarak (Mexico): *Seis canciones para cantar a los niños* (High or Low)
Andrés Sas (Peru): *Cuatro melodías*
Modesta Bor (Venezuela): *Segundo ciclo de romanzas y canciones*

Advanced

Alberto Ginastera (Argentina): *Cinco canciones populares argentinas*
Agustín Fernández (Bolivia): *El anillo*
Alberto Villalpando (Bolivia): *Canciones para soprano y piano*
Osvaldo Lacerda (Brazil): Mozart no céu; Poemeto erótico; O menino doente
Francisco Mignone (Brazil): Quando uma flor desabrocha (Mezzo)
Alberto Nepomuceno (Brazil): Trovas (Mezzo)
Marlos Nobre (Brazil): Dengues da mulata desinteressada (Mezzo)
Heitor Villa-Lobos (Brazil): Aria (Cantilena), from *Bachianas brasileiras no. 5*, (Soprano); Melodia sentimental, from the *Forest of the Amazon Suite* (Soprano)
Juan Orrego-Salas (Chile): Multiple works
Jacqueline Nova Sondag (Colombia): A veces un no niega
German Cáceras (El Salvador): Multiple works

SUGGESTED REPERTOIRE

David Bontemps (Haiti): Que tal, from *Deux mélodies* (High baritone)
Carmen Brouard (Haiti) *Cinq chants funèbres;* Quand je serai mort; Plus qu'ennuyée; Prière de Mme. Elizabeth, from *Reflets d'âme*
Jean-Ronald LaFond (Haiti): Agué Ta Royo, Fèy ô; both from *Trois chansons vodouesques*
Rodolfo Halffter (Mexico): *Marinero en tierra*
Edgar Valcárcel (Peru): *Homenaje a Masías*
Amaury Veray (Puerto Rico): *Tres canciones*
Juan Bautista Plaza (Venezuela): Cuando el camino me fatiga, from *Obras para canto y piano;* Negra está la noche

For additional recommendations, please contact LAASA (http://www.laasa.org).

Notes

Introduction

1. Many new works are now available electronically directly through the composer. See *The Living Composers Project* in the bibliography (online resources).

2. A more complete list of online resources is found in the bibliography.

3. Juan A. Orrego-Salas was already calling for updates in published literature in the United States as early as the 1960s. See Orrego-Salas, "The Acquisition of Latin-American Books and Music," *Notes*, 2nd. ser., 22, no. 3 (Mar. 1966): 1008–1013.

4. Nicholas Slonimsky, ed., *Music of Latin America*. (New York: Thomas Y. Crowell, 1945; repr. Da Capo Press, 1972).

5. Gerard Béhague, *Music in Latin America: An Introduction* (Englewood Cliffs, N.J.: Prenctice-Hall, 1979).

6. Malena Kuss, ed., *Music in Latin American and the Caribbean: An Encyclopedic History*, vols. 1–2 (Austin: University of Texas Press, 2004–2005).

7. Miguel Ficher, Martha Furman Schleifer, and John M. Furman, eds., *Latin American Classical Composers: A Biographical Dictionary*, 2nd ed. (Latham, Md.: Scarecrow Press, 2002).

8. The end of the last millennium also ushered in several books of philosophical interest, some of which include Gerard Béhague's *Music and Black Ethnicity: The Caribbean and South America* (Miami: University of Miami North-South Center Press, 1994), Frances R. Aparicio's *Listening to Salsa: Gender, Latin Popular Music, and Puerto Rican Cultures* (Hanover, N.H.: University Press of New England, 1998), and *Tropicalizations: Transcultural Representations of Latinidad* (Hanover, N.H.: University Press of New England, 1997), a collection of essays edited by Frances Aparicio and Susana Chávez-Silverman.

9. *List of Latin American Music* (Washington, D.C.: Pan American Union, 1933).

10. *Music in Latin America: A Brief Survey*, Series on Literature—Art—Music 3 (Washington, D.C.: Pan American Union, 1945); and Gilbert Chase, *A Guide to the Music of Latin America*, 2nd ed. rev. (Washington, D.C.: Pan American Union, 1962).

11. *Music of Latin America,* 3rd ed. (Washington, D.C.: Pan American Union, 1963); this is a reprint of the third edition, which was originally published in 1953.

12. Pan American Union Music Section, *Composers of the Americas* (Washington, D.C.: Pan American Union, 1955–1979): nos. 1–19.

13. Ricardo Lorenz, ed.,with Luis R. Hernández and Gerardo Dirie, *Scores and Recordings at the Indiana University Latin American Music Center* (Bloomington: Indiana University Press, 1995).

14. Kerlinda Degláńs and Luis E. Pabón Roca, *Catálogo de música clásica contemporánea de Puerto Rico* (Río Piedras, Puerto Rico: Pro-Arte Contemporáneo, 1989).

15. Luis Fernando Lopes Lopes, "Sample Repertoire [for Fifth Annual Competition in the Performance of Music from Spain and Latin America (2002), sponsored by Indiana University's Latin American Music Center and the Embassy of Spain, Washington, D.C.]: Song Literature from Spain and Latin America," http://www.music.indiana.edu/som/lamc/competition_root/reserves/voice_songs_reserve.html (accessed 15 April 2009).

16. Enrique Alberto Arias, "Contemporary Argentinean Vocal Literature," *The NATS Journal* 41 (Jan/Feb 1985): 8–12.

17. Gilbert Chase, "Latin America," in Dennis Stevens, ed., *A History of Song* (New York: W.W. Norton, 1960), 304–322.

18. Jonathan Kulp, "Carlos Guastavino: The Intersection of Música culta and Música popular in Argentine Song," *Latin American Music Review/Revista de música latinoamericana* 24, no. 1 (Spring/Summer 2003): 42–61; John L. Walker, "The Younger Generation of Ecuadorian Composers, *Latin American Music Review/Revista de música latinoamericana* 22, no. 2 (Autumn/Winter 2001): 199–213; Marie Elizabeth Labonville, *Juan Bautista Plaza and Musical Nationalism in Venezuela* (Bloomington: Indiana University Press, 2007).

19. *Revista Argentina de musicología* (Buenos Aires, Argentina: Asociación Argentina de Musicología, 1996–); *Revista musical puertorriqueña* (San Juan, Puerto Rico: Instituto de Cultura Puertorriqueña, 1987–1990); *Revista musical de Venezuela* (Caracas: Consejo Nacional de la Cultura, 1980–); *Revista musical chilena* (Santiago: Facultad de Artes, Universidad de Chile 1973–), http://www.scielo.cl/scielo.php?pid=0716-2790&script=sci_serial (accessed 3 March 2007).

20. *Latin American Music Review/Revista de música latinoamericana* (Austin: University of Texas Press, 1980–), http://www.utexas.edu/utpress/journals/jlamr.html (accessed 3 March 2007).

21. Gerard Béhague, "Boundaries and Borders in the Study of Music in Latin America: A Conceptual Remapping," *Latin American Music Review/Revista de música latinoamericana* 21, no. 1 (Spring/Summer 2000): 16–30; Kazadi wa Mukuna, "Ethnomusicology and the Study of Africanisms in the Music of Latin America: Brazil," in *Turn Up the Volume! A Celebration of African Music,* ed. Jacqueline Cogdell DjeDje (Los Angeles: University of Los Angeles Fowler Museum of Cultural History, 1999): 182–185.

22. Vanda Lima Bellard Freire, "Panorama da musico latino-americana," *Anais 1: Encontro latino-americano de educação musical Salvador* (Brazil: Associação Brasileira de Educação Musical, 1997): 19–25; Benjamin Chamorro Yepez, "El camino de las sombras: La música de los Guahibo," *Culturas musicales del Mediterraneo y sus ramificaciones, Revista de musicología* 16, no. 4 (1993): 2113–2125.

23. UMI (University Microfilms) dissertation services is now a part of ProQuest Information and Learning; see http://www.proquest.com/products_umi/dissertations (accessed February 15, 2007).

24. Harry M. Switzer, "The Published Art Songs of Juan Bautista Plaza" (D.M.A. diss., University of Miami, 1985); Adriana Giarola, "João de Souza Lima: A Performer's Guide to the Songs for Voice and Piano" (D.M.A. diss., University of Washington, 1990) (not available from UMI); and Robert Gerald Magee, "The Solo Songs for Voice and Piano of Carlos Chavez" (D.M.A. diss., University of Southern Mississippi, 1989).

25. Deborah Rae Wagner, "Carlos Guastavino: An Annotated Bibliography of His Solo Vocal Works" (D.M.A. diss., Arizona State University, 1997); Jonathan Lance Kulp, "Carlos Guastavino: A Study of His Songs and Musical Aesthetics" (Ph.D. diss., University of Texas at Austin, 2001); and Roxane Marie LaCombe, "Carlos Guastavino's Song Cycles 'Las nubes' and 'Cuatro sonetos de Quevedo': The Relationship of Text and Music" (D.M.A. diss., University of Oklahoma, 2000).

26. Hugh F. Cardon, "A Survey of Twentieth-Century Mexican Art Song" (D.M.A. diss., University of Oregon, 1970).

27. Patricia Caicedo, *The Latin American Art Song: A Critical Anthology and Interpretive Guide for Singers* (Barcelona: Tritó, 2005), vi–xliii.

28. An attempt has been made to include all available information on each piece included in this catalog. The authors and collaborators have decided to include some pieces without range and tessitura for research purposes. This may especially apply to some songs that are directly available from composers or from other new music sources.

29. Estelle R. Jorgensen, *In Search of Music Education* (Urbana and Chicago: University of Illinois Press, 1997), 76–77.

30. The objective of this project was to collect a comprehensive and thorough representation of published and accessible manuscript editions of classical Latin American art songs from Central America, North America (Mexico), South America, and the Caribbean Islands. It was accomplished by working with main sources of this repertoire, namely collections such as the LAMC and the Pan American Union, with colleagues and scholars who are native to Latin America, composers, and other reliable sources (see bibliography). Other comparable sources have taken up to ten years to complete. In the interest of getting information to the public quickly, preparation of this volume has spanned only a few years.

31. See appendix A: List of Countries and Regions in Latin America. Composers are eligible for inclusion if they were born in Latin America or are/were otherwise identified as Latin American, and if they lived into the twentieth century. Non-

native composers may be considered Latin American if they have spent the majority of their professional lives in Latin America and are professionally or personally associated with that area.

32. Jorgensen, *In Search of Music Education*, 75. The idea of traditions is a concept that was explored by researchers at the University of Chicago in the mid-twentieth century as a way to analyze culture. Jorgensen identifies "great traditions" as "those that have developed an international following, and are revered as highly developed cultural products, complex, notated with an extensive written tradition, ethically elitist, and practiced mainly by professional artists."

33. A *zarzuela* is a Spanish form of opera or musical theater with spoken dialogue.

34. Andrés Sas, *Cuatro melodías* (Montevideo, Uruguay: Editorial Cooperativa Interamericana de Compositores, 1941).

1. Argentina

1. Singers interested in nineteenth-century composers may visit the website of the Latin American Art Song Alliance (http://www.laasa.org) for more information, where they will also find a listing of Argentine songs with accompaniments for instruments other than the piano. For pedagogical purposes, note that songs in this chapter with a medium-high tessitura often contain wide-ranging vocal lines, while songs with a medium tessitura generally possess easier melodies and more regular phrasing. See Other Resources for the Study of Argentine Song at the end of chapter 1 for more information on this repertoire.

2. Bolivia

1. Gerard Béhague, *Music in Latin America: An Introduction* (Englewood Cliffs, N.J.: Prentice-Hall, 1979), 173.

2. The U.N. agency's Social Panorama report on Latin America (2006) indicates that Bolivia, Mexico, Guatemala, and Peru have the largest indigenous populations. Reported in Daniela Estrada, "Latin America: Indigenous People Gaining Ground (On Paper)," in Inter Press Service News Agency, http://ipsnews.net (accessed 10 March 2007). See also Latin American and Caribbean Demographic Center (a division of the United Nations) at http://www.eclac.cl/celade (accessed 10 March 2007).

3. Max Peter Baumann, "Music and Worldview of Indian Societies in the Bolivian Andes," in *Music in Latin America and the Caribbean: An Encyclopedic History*, ed. Malena Kuss (Austin: University of Texas Press, 2004), vol. 1, 102.

4. Miguel Ficher, Martha Furman Schleifer, and John M. Furman, eds., *Latin American Classical Composers: A Biographical Dictionary*, 2nd ed. (Lanham, Md.: Scarecrow Press, 2002), 595.

5. *The Living Composers Project*, Dan Albertson and Ron Hannah, http://www

.composers21.com (accessed 14 January 2007). *The Living Composers Project* is "a non-profit database begun in 2000, which aims to provide composers, listeners, performers, and researchers with a source of information about the music of our time."

3. Brazil

1. Maria Sylvia Pinto, *A canção brasileira: Da modinha à canção de câmara* (Rio de Janeiro: Cia Brasileira de Artes Gráficas, 1985), 57.

2. Bruno Kiefer, *Música e dança popular: Sua influência na música erudita* (Porto Alegre: Movimento, 1990), 31.

3. Mozart de Araujo, *A modinha e o lundu no século XVIII* (São Paulo: Ricordi Brasileira, 1963), 9.

4. Nepomuceno is considered to be the father of Brazilian art song, and his work represents the starting point in the Brazilian chapter of this catalog.

5. Vasco Mariz, *A canção brasileira de câmara* (Rio de Janeiro: Livraria Francisco Alves Editora, 2002), 33.

6. Gerard Béhague, *Heitor Villa-Lobos: The Search for Brazil's Musical Soul* (Austin: Institute of Latin American Studies, University of Texas at Austin, 1993), 20.

7. The Week of Modern Art, led and organized by poet, writer, journalist, and musicologist Mário de Andrade, took place in 1922 in the Metropolitan Theater of São Paulo. It represented a major shift in Brazilian arts toward a nationalistic aesthetic. The Modern Movement, as it was called then, incited all artists to free themselves from old European models and instead, to look to their own country as a source of inspiration and reference. The new aesthetic project proclaimed the validation of Brazilian folklore and cultural roots as the path to achieve a true national identity in all artistic expression.

8. *Bossa nova* was born in Rio de Janeiro among young musicians looking for new ways to express their syncopated musicality together with lyric feelings and exquisite harmonies. It completely revolutionized Brazilian popular music by the end of 1950s. The influence of American jazz is clear in the harmony, but the subtle accented rhythm that innovated the way to play the samba became the ultimate trademark of modern Brazilian musicality. Among major luminaries of the *bossa nova* were composer Tom Jobim and poet Vinicius de Moraes.

9. The *Guia da canção brasileira* is a dynamic and ongoing project that is open to qualified contributions. This researcher has tried as much as possible to complement data on the selected composers with information drawn from her own private collection of scores and other sources. See http://www.grude.ufmg.br/musica/cancao Brasileira.nsf.

10. Mariz, *A canção brasileira de câmara.*

11. Personal communication with composer Jorge de Freitas Antunes (1942) allowed for the inclusion of his works in this publication. Acknowledgement is also due to Luciano Simões Silva, who contributed a comprehensive list of Edmundo Villani-Côrtes's songs, and to Professor Ilza Nogueira of the Federal University of Para-

iba, who provided the comprehensive list of Ernst Widmer's songs. Ernani Braga's list was enriched by the research of José Ricardo Pereira, from Northern Arizona University. Some composers, both living and passed—Marlos Nobre, Claudio Santoro, Radamés Gnatalli, Ernst Widmer, Ersnt Mahle, Villani-Cortes, Nestor de Holanda Cavalcanti, and Ronaldo Miranda—have their own catalogs published online. Also see additional bibliography at the end of chapter 3.

4. Chile

1. *Revista musical chilena* (Santiago: Facultad de Artes, Universidad de Chile 1973–), http://www.scielo.cl/scielo.php?pid=0716-2790&script=sci_serial (accessed 3 March 2007).
2. Gerard Béhague, *Music in Latin America: An Introduction* (Englewood Cliffs, N.J.: Prentice-Hall, 1979), 178.
3. *Buenos Aires musical* 12, no. 197 (1 October 1957): 7; quoted in Béhague, *Music in Latin America*, 178.
4. Béhague, *Music in Latin America*, 238 and 264.
5. Ibid., 179.
6. María Ester Grebe, "Amerindian Music of Chile," in *Music in Latin America and the Caribbean: An Encyclopedic History*, ed. Malena Kuss (Austin: University of Texas Press, 2004), vol. 1, 146.

6. Costa Rica

1. Bernal Flores, *La música en Costa Rica* (San José: Editorial Costa Rica, 1978), 30–34.
2. Ronald Sider, "Contemporary Composers in Costa Rica," *Latin American Music Review/Revista de música latinoamericana* 5, no. 2 (Autumn/Winter 1984): 263–276.
3. Manuel Matarrita, "An Analytical Study of Concerto for Piano and Orchestra, Op. 13, by Costa Rican Composer Carlos Enrique Vargas" (D.M.A. diss., Louisiana State University, 2004), 8. Some of these songs are included in this catalog, and many are appropriate choices for beginning singers. Also see appendix D for a list of suggested repertoire.
4. Ibid.
5. Sider, "Contemporary Composers in Costa Rica," 264.
6. WorldCat search results, http://www.worldcat.org (accessed 6 February 2007).

7. Cuba

1. For more on Cuban ethnicity, see Victoria Eli Rodríguez, "Cuban Music and Ethnicity: Historical Considerations," in *Music and Black Ethnicity: The Caribbean*

and South America, ed. Gerard Béhague, (Miami: University of Miami North-South Center Press, 1994), 91–108.

2. Olavo Alén Rodríguez, "Cuba," in *The Garland Handbook of Latin American Music,* ed. Dale A. Olsen and Daniel E. Sheehy (New York and London: Garland Publishing, 2000), 121.

3. Cervantes is considered by Béhague to be the most important nineteenth-century composer. See Gerard Béhague, *Music in Latin America: An Introduction* (Englewood Cliffs, N.J.: Prentice-Hall, 1979), 103.

4. Ibid., 147.

5. Ibid., 233 and 150–151.

6. See Benjamin Keen and Keith Hayes, "The Cuban Revolution," in *A History of Latin America,* 7th ed. (Boston and New York: Houghton Mifflin Co., 2004), 424–453.

7. See Ned Sublette, *Cuba and Its Music: From the First Drums to the Mambo* (Chicago: Chicago Review Press, 2004) and Rodríguez, "Cuba," 122.

8. Béhague, *Music in Latin America,* 151 and 256–258. Also see Miguel Ficher, Martha Furman Schleifer, and John M. Furman, eds., *Latin American Classical Composers: A Biographical Dictionary,* 2nd ed. (Lanham, Md.: Scarecrow Press, 2002), 392.

9. Béhague, *Music in Latin America,* 301. See also Ficher, Schleifer, and Furman, *Latin American Classical Composers,* 2002.

10. *The Living Composers Project* website, Don Albertson and Ron Hannah, http://www.composers21.com (accessed 10 March 2007).

8. Dominican Republic

1. See Martha Ellen Davis, "Music and Black Ethnicity in the Dominican Republic," in *Music and Black Ethnicity: The Caribbean and South America,* ed. Gerard Béhague (Miami: University of Miami North-South Center Press, 1994), 120, 121; and Victoria Eli Rodríguez, "Cuban Music an Ethnicity: Historical Considerations," ibid., 91–108.

2. Progressive discussions equate the two, as does Davis in "Music and Black Ethnicity," 119–120: "Ethnic diversity is national identity, and vice versa."

3. Ibid, 129.

4. Nicolas Slonimsky, *Music of Latin America* (New York: Thomas Y. Crowell, 1945; repr. Da Capo Press, 1972).

5. Ibid., 191; and Jacob Maurice Coopersmith, "Music and Musicians of the Dominican Republic: A Survey—Part II," *The Musical Quarterly* 31, no. 2 (April 1945): 212–226.

6. Coopersmith, "Music and Musicians of the Dominican Republic," 217. Orbe has supposedly written thirty art songs with texts by Fabio Fiallo deemed "excellent" by Coopersmith.

7. "Ana Silfa Finke," *The Living Composers Project* website, Don Albertson and Ron Hannah, http://www.composers21.com (accessed 10 March 2007).

9. Ecuador

1. John L. Walker, "The Younger Generation of Ecuadorian Composers," *Latin American Music Review/Revista de música latinoamericana* 22, no. 2 (Autumn/Winter 2001): 199 and 202.

2. This is the method used by Ecuadorian musicologist Pablo Guerrero (1962–); ibid.

3. Ibid.

4. Gerardo Guevara, "La música en el Ecuador," *Espejo* 7 (April 1983): 50, quoted in Walker, "The Younger Generation of Ecuadorian Composers," 200–201.

5. Gerard Béhague, *Music in Latin America: An Introduction* (Englewood Cliffs, N.J.: Prentice-Hall, 1979), 164.

6. Pablo Guerrero and Ketty Wong, *Corsino Durán Carrión* (Quito: Dirección General de Educación y Cultura, 1994), 42; in Walker, 201.

7. Béhague, *Music in Latin America*, 310.

8. See also Diego Luzuriaga, *Once canciones para voz media y guitarra (Eleven Songs for Medium Voice and Guitar)* (Oxford University Press, 2002).

10. El Salvador

1. María de Baratta and Jeremías Mendoza, *Cuzatlán típico: Ensayo sobre etnofonía de El Salvador, folklore, folkwisa, y folkway* (San Salvador: Minesterio de Culture, 1951); Nicolas Slonimsky, *Music of Latin America* (New York: Thomas Y. Crowell, 1945; repr. Da Capo Press, 1972), 280; and Ronald R. Smith, "Latin American Ethnomusicology: A Discussion of Central America and Northern South America," *Latin American Music Review/Revista de música latinoamericana* 3, no. 1 (Spring/Summer 1982): 4.

2. Gerard Béhague, *Music in Latin America: An Introduction* (Englewood Cliffs, N.J.: Prentice-Hall, 1979).

3. Slonimsky, *Music of Latin America*, 279.

4. It should be noted that it was the nineteenth-century Italian-born composer Juan Aberle who wrote the Salvadorian national anthem; see Miguel Ficher, Martha Furman Schleifer, and John M. Furman, eds., *Latin American Classical Composers: A Biographical Dictionary*, 2nd ed. (Lanham, Md.: Scarecrow Press, 2002), 11, 506, 58, and 474. María de Baratta served as the President of the Comisión de Investigación Folklore Nacional y Arte Nativo of the Ministerio de Educación Pública. See also n. 1, above.

5. Béhague, *Music in Latin America*, 308.

6. Ficher, Schleifer, and Furman, *Latin American Classical Composers*, 94.

7. "German Gustavo Cáceres," *The Living Composers Project*, Don Albertson and Ron Hannah, http://www.composers21.com (accessed 10 March 2007).

11. Guatemala

1. Linda O'Brien-Rothe, "Guatemala," in *The Garland Handbook of Latin American Music*, ed. Dale E. Olsen and Daniel E. Sheehy (New York: Garland Publishing, 2000), 175–176, 183, and 187–189.

2. Ibid., 189–190, and Miguel Ficher, Martha Furman Schleifer, and John M. Furman, eds., *Latin American Classical Composers: A Biographical Dictionary*, 2nd ed. (Lanham, Md.: Scarecrow Press, 2002), 1.

3. Nicolas Slonimsky, *Music of Latin America* (New York: Thomas Y. Crowell, 1945; repr. Da Capo Press, 1972), 201.

4. Jesús María Alvarado, *Canciones escolares guatemaltecas: Para todos los niños del mundo* (Guatemala: Editorial del Ministerio de Educación Pública "José de Pineda Ibarra", 1950), and *Nueva selección de cantos infantiles* (Mexico: Editorial Cultura, 1961).

5. Gerard Béhague, *Music in Latin America: An Introduction* (Englewood Cliffs, N.J.: Prentice-Hall, 1979), 308.

12. Haiti

1. The *méringue*, a folk dance developed in Haiti, spread to the rest of Latin America via the Dominican Republic and then Puerto Rico under the name *meringue*. *The New Grove Dictionary of Music and Musicians*, 2nd. ed., "Haiti", credits Haiti with the origin of this musical dance form.

13. Honduras

1. Nicolas Slonimsky, *Music of Latin America* (New York: Thomas Y. Crowell, 1945; repr. Da Capo Press, 1972), 212–213.

2. Miguel Ficher, Martha Furman Schleifer, and John M. Furman, eds., *Latin American Classical Composers: A Biographical Dictionary*, 2nd ed. (Lanham, Md.: Scarecrow Press, 2002). This source includes composers José Trinidad Reyes (1797–1855), Carlos Haertling (nineteenth century, dates vary by source; German-born composer of the national anthem), Guadalupe Haertling (1871–?), Manuel de Adalid y Gamero (1872–1947), Ignacio Villanueva Galeano (1885–?), Fernando Varela Borjas (1895–?), and Francisco R. Díaz Zelaya (1900–?).

3. Tulane University, Latin American Library website, http://www.tulane.edu/~latinlib/adalidcoll.html.edu (accessed 10 March 2007).

14. Jamaica

1. *Jamaica's Classical Musicians*, ©Joy Lumsden, 2004, http://www.joyousjam.com/jamaicaclassicalmusicians (accessed 18 February 2007).

2. Cowen's compositions are available at http://www.btinternet.com/~john.parker17/index.html (accessed 10 March 2007). Scores available through the webmaster, Christopher.Parker@dur.ac.uk, or parkermusic@btopenworld.com.

15. Mexico

1. Gerard Béhague, *Music in Latin America: An Introduction* (Englewood Cliffs, N.J.: Prentice-Hall, 1979), 98.
2. Ibid., 125.
3. Ibid., 232, and Gilbert Chase, "Latin America," in *A History of Song*, ed. Denis Stevens (New York and London: W.W. Norton and Co., 1960), 307.
4. Béhague, *Music in Latin America*, 126.
5. Chase, "Latin America," 308.
6. Ibid.
7. Gerard Béhague refers to this as the "so-called Aztec Renaissance"; see his *Music in Latin America*, 126 and 129. See also Béhague, "Mexico," in *Grove Music Online*, ed. Laura Macy, http://www.grovemusic.com (accessed 28 February 2007).
8. Robert M. Stevenson, *Music in Mexico: A Historical Survey* (New York: Thomas Y. Crowell, 1952), 6.
9. Béhague, *Music in Latin America*, 141 and 229; Miguel Ficher, Martha Furman Schleifer, and John M. Furman, eds., *Latin American Classical Composers: A Biographical Dictionary*, 2nd ed., (Lanham, Md.: Scarecrow Press, 2002), 135.
10. Grever, who was one of the most popular and prolific composers of Mexican popular song, studied in Paris with Claude Debussy (Ficher, Furman, and Furman, *Latin American Classical Composers*, 251). Most of this Mexican popular repertoire has been published by Southern Music Publishing/Peer International Corporation.
11. *The Living Composers Project*, Dan Albertson and Ron Hannah, http://www.composers21.com (accessed 14 January 2007).

16. Nicaragua

1. Nicolas Slonimsky, *Music of Latin America* (New York: Thomas Y. Crowell, 1945; repr. Da Capo Press, 1972), 254–255.
2. Miguel Ficher, Martha Furman Schleifer, and John M. Furman, eds., *Latin American Classical Composers: A Biographical Dictionary*, 2nd ed. (Lanham, Md.: Scarecrow Press, 2002) also has entries for Pablo Vega y Raudes (1850–1919), Fernando Luna (1853–1936), and Alejandro Vega Matus (1875–1937).
3. Ibid., 158.
4. Slonimsky, *Music of Latin America*, 260.
5. Gerard Béhague, *Music in Latin America: An Introduction* (Englewood Cliffs, N.J.: Prentice-Hall, 1979), 308.

17. Panama

1. See Ronald R. Smith, "Arroz Colorao: Los Congos of Panama," in *Music and Black Ethnicity: The Caribbean and South America*, ed. Gerard Béhague (Miami: University of Miami North-South Center Press, 1994), 239–266.

2. The Kuna, who live on the Archipiélago de las Mulatas islands off of the coast of Panama as well as in the heart of Panama City, have a fascinating musical culture. Velásquez writes that "[t]he concept of 'music' exists in Kuna language, but it is expressed in a composite formulation that names a dynamic process, as opposed to a static object." See Ronny Velásquez, "The Fundamental Role of Music in the Life of Two Central American Ethnic Nations: The Mískito in Honduras and Nicaragua, and the Kuna in Panama," in *Music in Latin America and the Caribbean: An Encyclopedic History*, ed. Malena Kuss (Austin: University of Texas Press, 2004), vol. 1, 212.

3. Dale A. Olsen, "Approaches to Musical Scholarship," in *The Garland Handbook of Latin American Music*, ed. Dale A. Olsen and Daniel E. Sheehy (New York: Garland Publishing, 2000), 7–8 and 16.

4. *Clave, revista musical venezolana* 5 (April 1957): 13, quoted in Gerard Béhague, *Music in Latin America: An Introduction* (Englewood Cliffs, N.J.: Prentice-Hall, 1979), 261.

5. As is the case with El Salvador, Panama's national anthem was written by an immigrant, the Spanish-born composer Santos Jorge (1870–1941). Panama's second national anthem, *Marcha Panama*, was written by Alberto Galimany (1889–?), also of Spanish origin. Miguel Ficher, Martha Furman Schleifer, and John M. Furman, eds., *Latin American Classical Composers: A Biographical Dictionary*, 2nd ed. (Lanham, Md.: Scarecrow Press, 2002), 288 and 213.

6. Ibid., 217. Garay's text, *Tradiciones y cantares de Panamá ensayo folklórico* (Brussels: Presses de l'Expansion Belge), was written in 1930.

7. "Compositores panameños," *Asociación guitarrística de Panamá*, http://www.fermatapub.com/Compositores.asp (accessed 14 January 2007). For more, see Jaime Ingram Jaén, "Apuntes para una historia de la música en Panamá (1903–2003)," *Istmo: Revisa virtual de estudios literarios y culturales centroamericanos* 7 (November–December 2003), http://www.denison.edu/collaborations/istmo/no7 (accessed 14 January 2007).

18. Paraguay

1. Timothy D. Watkins, "Paraguay," in *The Garland Handbook of Latin American Music*, Dale A. Olsen and Daniel E. Sheehy (New York: Garland Publishing, 2000), 288–289. The Jesuits used their own music as well as the Guaraní's own native music to carry out their mission work.

2. Ibid., 293.

3. Nicolas Slonimsky, *Music of Latin America* (New York: Thomas Y. Crowell, 1945; repr. Da Capo Press, 1972), 262.

4. Ibid., 263.

5. "Agustín Pío Barrios," "Carlos Lara Bareiro," "José Asunción Flores," *Revista digital artística paraguaya,* http://www.musicaparaguaya.org.py (accessed 10 March 2007); Juan Max Boettner, *Música y músicos del Paraguay* (Asunción: Edición de Autores Paraguayos Asociados, [1956?]).

6. "Daniel Luzko," *The Living Composers Project,* Dan Albertson and Ron Hannah, http://www.composers21.com (accessed 14 January 2007).

19. Peru

1. Rudolph Holzmann published a complete catalog of compositions by Theodoro Valcárcel in "Catálogo de la obra de Teodor Valcárcel (1902–1942)," *Boletín Bibliográfico* (Lima) 15, no. 12 (1942): 135–271. Holzmann also published an analytical essay on Valcárcel's music, as well catalogs of compositions by Daniel Alomía Robles, composer of El Cóndor Pasa, and by Alfonso de Silva and Vicente Stea; see his "Catálogo de las obras de Daniel Alomía Robles," (1871–1942), *Boletín bibliográfico* 15, no. 13:1/2 (1943): 25–78 and "Catálogo de las obras de Alfonso Silva y Vicente Stea," *Boletín bibliográfico* 15, no. 13:3/4 (1943): 242–252.

20. Puerto Rico

1. Héctor Vega Drouet, "Puerto Rico," in *The Garland Handbook of Latin American Music,* ed. Dale A. Olsen and Daniel E. Sheehy (New York and London: Garland Publishing, 2000), 134.

2. See Jose R. Bas García, "Puerto Rico Is a Colony," trans. Javier Hernández, *Magazine of Social Sciences of the UPR* 10 (March 1966), available at http://www.independencia.net/ingles/pr_is_a_colony.html (accessed 10 March 2007); and the Independent Puerto Rican Party's website, http://www.independencia.net/ingles/aboutind.html (accessed 10 March 2007).

3. See Vega Drouet, "Puerto Rico," 135–142.

4. For more on Puerto Rican and Cuban dance and rhythm relationships, see Gerard Béhague, *Music in Latin America: An Introduction* (Englewood Cliffs, N.J.: Prentice-Hall, 1979), 104–105.

5. Ibid., 309.

6. Leonardo Egúrbida, prologue to *"La canción de arte" en Puerto Rico* (Río Piedras, Puerto Rico: Asociación Nacional de Compositores de Puerto Rico, 1986).

21. Uruguay

1. Uruguay was invaded by Brazil in 1817 and remained occupied until Great Britain helped it gain independence. See Benjamin Keen and Keith Haynes, *A History*

of Latin America, 7th ed. (Boston and New York: Houghton Mifflin Co., 2004), 165, 193; and Nicholas Slonimsky, *Music of Latin America* (New York: Thomas Y. Crowell, 1945; repr. Da Capo, 1972), 283.

2. Gilbert Chase, "Latin America," in *A History of Song,* ed. Denis Stevens (New York and London: W.W. Norton and Co., 1960), 320; and Gerard Béhague, *Music in Latin America: An Introduction* (Englewood Cliffs, N.J.: Prentice-Hall, 1979), 221.

3. Béhague, *Music in Latin America,* 241.

4. Miguel Ficher, Martha Furman Schleifer, and John M. Furman, eds., *Latin American Classical Composers: A Biographical Dictionary,* 2nd ed. (Lanham, Md.: Scarecrow Press, 2002), 147 and 60.

5. Ibid., 429.

22. Venezuela

1. See Gerard Béhague, *Music in Latin America: An Introduction* (Englewood Cliffs, N.J.: Prentice-Hall, 1979); and Gerard Béhague, Jonathan D. Hill, and Walter Guido, "Venezuela," in *The New Grove Dictionary of Music and Musicians,* 2nd ed., ed. Stanley Sadie and John Tyrell (London, 2001) for examples of these rhythms.

Bibliography

50 Art Songs from the Modern Repertoire. New York: G. Schirmer, 1980.

Acevedo Vargas, Jorge Luis. *Antología de música guanasteca.* San José: Editorial Universidad de Costa Rica, 1981.

Alvarado, Jesús María. *Canciones escolares guatemaltecas: Para todos los niños del mundo.* Guatemala: Editorial del Ministerio de Educación Pública "José de Pineda Ibarra," 1950.

———. *Nueva selección de cantos infantiles.* Mexico: Editorial Cultura, 1961.

Anaya Arze, Franklin. *La música en Latinoamérica y en Bolivia.* Cochabamba, Bolivia: Editorial Serrano, 1994.

Anderson, William M., and Patricia Shehan Campbell, eds. *Multicultural Perspectives in Music Education.* 2nd ed. Reston, Va.: Music Educators National Conference, 1996.

Antología de compositores argentinos. Vol. 6. Buenos Aires: Comisión Nacional de Cultura, 1941.

Aparicio, Frances R. *Listening to Salsa: Gender, Latin Popular Music, and Puerto Rican Cultures.* Hanover, N.H.: University Press of New England, 1998.

Aparicio, Frances R., and Susana Chávez-Silverman, eds. *Tropicalizations: Transcultural Representations of* Latinidad. Hanover, N.H.: University Press of New England, 1997.

Araujo, Mozart de. *A modinha e o lundu no século XVIII.* São Paulo: Ricordi Brasileira, 1963.

Araújo, Samuel. "The Politics of Passion: The Impact of Bolero on Brazilian Musical Expressions." *Yearbook for Traditional Music* 31 (1999): 42–56.

Arias, Enrique Alberto. "Contemporary Argentinean Vocal Literature." *The NATS Journal* 41 (Jan/Feb 1985): 8–12.

Arizaga, Rodolfo. *Enciclopedia de la música argentina.* Buenos Aires: Fondo Nacional de las Artes, 1971.

Arizaga, Rodolfo, and Pompeyo Camps. *Historia de la música en la Argentina.* Buenos Aires: Ricordi Americana, 1990.

Art, Revista da Escola de Música e Artes Cênicas 15 (April 1987): 77–80. Salvador, Brazil: Universidade Federal da Bahia/Federal University of the State of Bahia.

Assies, Willem, Gemma van der Haar, and André J. Hoekema, eds. *The Challenge of Diversity: Indigenous Peoples and Reform of the State in Latin America.* Amsterdam: Thela Thesis, 1998.

Backus, Leroy M., III. "An Annotated Bibliography on Selective Sources on Jamaican Music." *The Black Perspective in Music* 8, no. 1 (Spring 1980): 35–53.

Baratta, María, and Jeremías Mendoza. *Cuzcatlán típico: Ensayo sobre etnofonía de El Salvador, folklore, folkwisa y folkway.* San Salvador: Ministerio de Cultura, 1951.

Barquero, Zamira, ed. *Antología canciones costarricenses.* San José, Costa Rica: CEDIM, Escuela de Artes Musicales, University of Costa Rica, 1998.

Barreda, Ernesto Mario. *Joya de canciones españolas.* Buenos Aires: Asociación Patriótica Española, 1942.

Bas García, Jose R. "Puerto Rico Is a Colony." Trans. Javier Hernández. *Magazine of Social Sciences of the UPR*, vol. 10 (March 1966). Available at http://www.independencia.net/ingles/pr_is_a_colony.html (accessed 10 March 2007), and the Independent Puerto Rican Party website, at http://www.independencia.net/ingles/aboutind.html (accessed 10 March 2007).

Baumann, Max Peter. *Cosmología y música en los Andes.* Madrid: Iberoamericana; Frankfurt am Main: Vervuert, 1996.

———. "Music and Worldview of Indian Societies in the Bolivian Andes." In *Music in Latin America and the Caribbean: An Encyclopedic History,* edited by Malena Kuss, vol. 1, 101–122. Austin: University of Texas Press, 2004.

Béhague, Gerard. *The Beginnings of Musical Nationalism in Brazil.* Detroit Monographs in Musicology 1. Detroit: Information Coordinators, 1971.

———. "Boundaries and Borders in the Study of Music in Latin America: A Conceptual Remapping." *Latin American Music Review/Revista de música latinoamericana* 21, no. 1 (Spring/Summer 2000): 16–30.

———. "Ecuadorian, Peruvian, and Brazilian Ethnomusicology: A General View." *Latin American Music Review/Revista de música latinoamericana* 3, no. 1 (Spring/Summer 1982): 17–35.

———. *Heitor Villa-Lobos: The Search for Brazil's Musical Soul.* Austin: Institute of Latin American Studies, University of Texas at Austin, 1993.

———. "Mexico." In *Grove Music Online,* edited by Laura Macy. http://www.grovemusic.com (accessed 28 February 2007).

———, ed. *Music and Black Ethnicity: The Caribbean and South America.* Miami: University of Miami North-South Center Press, 1994.

———. *Music in Latin America: An Introduction.* Englewood Cliffs, N.J.: Prentice-Hall, 1979.

———. *Performance Practice: Ethnomusicological Perspectives.* Westport, Conn.: Greenwood Press, 1984.

———. "Popular Musical Currents in the Art Music of the Early Nationalistic Period in Brazil, ca. 1870–1920." Ph.D. diss., Tulane University, 1966.

Béhague, Gerard, Jonathan D. Hill, and Walter Guido. "Venezuela." In *The New Grove Dictionary of Music and Musicians*, 2nd ed., edited by Stanley Sadie and John Tyrell. London: Macmillan, 2001.

Berrios-Miranda, Marisol. "The Significance of Salsa Music to National and Pan-Latino Identity." Ph.D. diss., University of California, Berkeley, 2000.

Bethell, Leslie. *A Cultural History of Latin America: Literature, Music and the Visual Arts in the 19th and 20th Centuries*. Cambridge: Cambridge University Press, 1998.

Boettner, Juan Max. *Música y músicos del Paraguay*. Asunción: Edición de Autores Paraguayos Asociados, [1956?].

Bolaños, Alvaro Félix, and Gustavo Verdesio, eds. *Colonialism Past and Present: Reading and Writing about Colonial Latin America Today*. Albany: State University of New York Press, 2002.

Bonilla, Stella, ed. *Música colombiana: La canción culta*. Bogotá: Instituto Colombiano de Cultura, 1992.

Boytim, Joan Frey. *The Second Book of Baritone/Bass Solos, Part II*. New York: G. Schirmer, Inc., 2004.

Brandão, Stela Maria Santos. "The Brazilian Art Song: A Performance Guide Utilizing Selected Works by Heitor Villa-Lobos." Ed.D. diss., Columbia University, 1999.

Caicedo, Patricia. "Del nacionalismo y la 'performance' en la canción artística latinoamericana." M.A. thesis, Universidad Complutense de Madrid, 2006.

———. *The Latin American Art Song: A Critical Anthology and Interpretive Guide for Singers*. Barcelona: Tritó, 2005.

Campos Chanto, Alirio. *Ciclo de 26 canciones y 2 corales*. San José: Ministerio de Educación Pública.

Cardon, Hugh F. "A Survey of Twentieth-Century Mexican Art Song." D.M.A. diss., University of Oregon, 1970.

Carpentier, Alejo. *Music in Cuba*. Minneapolis: University of Minnesota Press, 2001.

Casares Rodicio, Emilio, and José López-Calo, Ismael Fernández de la Cuesta, María Luz González Peña, eds. *Diccionario de la música española e hispanoamericana*. 10 vols. Madrid: Sociedad General de Autores y Editores, 1999–2002.

Cava, Roberto Sebastián. *Apuntes para una historia de la música latinoamericana desde una perspectiva histórico-cultural*. Buenos Aires: Ediciones Dunken, 1997.

Centeno, Jesus Manuel. "The Political-Musical Phenomenon in Puerto Rico: 1930–1975." Ph.D. diss., Rutgers, The State University of New Jersey–New Brunswick, 1996.

Chase, Gilbert. *Bibliography of Latin American Folk Music*. Washington, D.C.: The Library of Congress, Division of Music, 1942.

———. *A Guide to the Music of Latin America*. 2nd ed., rev. Washington, D.C.: The Pan American Union and The Library of Congress, 1962.

———. "Latin America." In *A History of Song*, edited by Denis Stevens, 304–322. New York: W.W. Norton, 1960.

———. *Latin American Music in 1940.* Cambridge, Mass.: Harvard University Press, 1940, 1941.

———. *Partial List of Latin American Music Obtainable in the United States with a Supplementary List of Books and a Selective List of Phonograph Records.* Washington, D.C.: Pan American Union, 1942.

Colombia artística. Serial publication. Bogotá, Colombia.

"Compositores panameños." *Asociación guitarrística de Panamá.* http://www.fermata pub.com/Compositores.asp (accessed 14 January 2007).

Coopersmith, Jacob Maurice. "Music and Musicians of the Dominican Republic: A Survey—Part II." *The Musical Quarterly* 31, no. 2 (April 1945): 212–226.

Cordero, Roque. "La música en Centroamerica y Panama." *Journal of Inter-American Studies* 8, no. 3 (July 1966): 411–418.

Cuadros-Pozo, Antonio Ernesto. "A History of Mexican Indians, Their Music and Its Influence on the Music of Carlos Chavez." M.A. thesis, California State University, Dominguez Hills, 1998.

Davis, Martha Ellen. "Music and Black Ethnicity in the Dominican Republic." In *Music and Black Ethnicity: The Caribbean and South America,* edited by Gerard Béhague, 119–155. Miami: University of Miami North-South Center Press, 1994.

DeCesare, Ruth. *90 Songs of the Americas: A Musical Introduction to the Varied Cultural Heritage of the Americas Compiled and Arranged by Ruth DeCesare.* Miami: Belwin Mills, 1993.

Degláns, Kerlinda, and Luis E. Pabón Roca. *Catálogo de música clásica contemporánea de Puerto Rico.* Río Piedras, Puerto Rico: Pro-Arte Contemporáneo, 1989.

Diaz Diaz, Edgardo. "Puerto Rican Affirmation and Denial of Musical Nationalism: The Cases of Campos Parsi and Aponte Ledee." *Latin American Music Review/Revista de música latinoamericana* 17, no. 1 (Spring/Summer, 1996): 1–20.

Donozo, Leandro. *Diccionario bibliográfico de la música argentina (y de la música en la Argentina).* Buenos Aires: Gourmet Musical Ediciones, 2006.

Egúrbida, Leonardo. Prologue to *"La canción de arte" en Puerto Rico.* Rio Piedras, Puerto Rico: Asociación Nacional de Compositores de Puerto Rico, 1986.

Elder, Jacob Delworth. "Evolution of the Traditional Calypso of Trinidad and Tobago: A Socio-Historical Analysis of Song-Change." Ph.D. diss., University of Pennsylvania, 1966.

Enciclopedia de la música argentina. Buenos Aires: Fondo Nacional de las Artes, 1971.

Estrada, Daniela. "Latin America: Indigenous People Gaining Ground (On Paper)." Inter Press Service News Agency. http://ipsnews.net (accessed 10 March 2007).

Estrada, Julio, and Susana Dultzin Dubín. *La música de México.* México: Instituto de Investigaciones Estéticas, Universidad Nacional Autónoma de México, 1984–1988.

Fern, Leila. *Selected References in English on Latin American Music.* Washington, D.C.: Pan American Union, 1944.

Ficher, Miguel, Martha Furman Schlieffer, and John M. Furman, eds. *Latin American*

Classical Composers: A Biographical Dictionary. 2nd ed. Lanham, Md. Scarecrow Press, 2002.

Fitzgibbon, Russell H. *Visual Outline of Latin American History*. New York and Toronto: Longmans, Green and Co., 1938.

Flores, Bernal. *La música en Costa Rica*. San José: Editorial Costa Rica, 1978.

Freire, Vanda Lima Bellard. "Panorama da Musico Latino-Americana." In *Anais 1: Encontro latino-americano de educação musical Salvado*, 19–25. Brazil: Associação Brasileira de Educação Musical, 1997.

Frontera, Nelida Munoz De. "A Study of Selected Nineteenth Century Puerto Rican Composers and Their Musical Output." 4 vols. Ph.D. diss., New York University, 1988.

Garay, Narciso. *Tradiciones y cantares de Panamá, ensayo folklórico*. Brussels: Presses de l'Expansion Belge, 1930.

García Acevedo, Mario. *La música argentina contemporánea*. Buenos Aires: Ediciones Culturales Argentinas, 1963.

———. *La música argentina durante el período de la organización nacional*. Buenos Aires: Ediciones Culturales Argentinas, 1961.

García Morillo, Roberto. *Estudios sobre música argentina*. Buenos Aires: Ediciones Culturales Argentinas, 1984.

Gesualdo, Vicente. *Breve historia de la música en la Argentina*. Buenos Aires: Editorial Claridad, 1998.

———. *Historia de la música en la Argentina*. 2 vols. Buenos Aires: Editorial Beta, 1961.

Giarola, Adriana. "João De Souza Lima: A Performer's Guide to the Songs for Voice and Piano." D.M.A. diss., University of Washington, 1990.

Giroux, Henry. *Impure Acts: The Practical Politics of Cultural Studies*. New York: Routledge, 2000.

Gómez, Zoila, and Victoria Eli Rodríguez. *Música latinoamericana y caribeña*. Ciudad de La Habana: Editorial Pueblo y Educación, 1995.

Gómez-Vignes, Mario, ed. *Imagen y obra de Antonio María Valencia*. Vol. 2. Cali: Corporación para la Cultura, 1991.

González Sol, Rafael. *Historia del arte de la música en El Salvador*. San Salvador: Imprenta Mercurio, 1940.

Gould, Cassius Wallace. "An Analysis of the Folk Music in the Oaxaca and Chiapas Areas of Mexico." Ph.D. diss., Northwestern University, 1954.

Grebe, Maria Ester."Amerindian Music of Chile." In *Music in Latin America and the Caribbean: An Encyclopedic History*, edited by Malena Kuss, vol. 1, 145–161. Austin: University of Texas Press, 2004.

———. *The Chilean Verso: A Study in Musical Archaism*. Trans. Bette Jo Hileman. Los Angeles: University of California Latin American Center, 1967.

Grebe Vicuna, Maria Ester. "El Tayil Mapuche, como categoria conceptual y medio de comunicación trascendente." *Inter-American Music Review* 10, no. 2 (Spring/Summer 1989): 69–76.

Green, Lucy. *Music, Gender, Education*. Cambridge: Cambridge University Press, 1997.

Griffin, Nigel, ed. and trans. *A Short Account of the Destruction of the Indies: Bartolomé de Las Casas*. Introduction by Anthony Pagden. London: Penguin Books, 1992.

Gross, Daniel R., ed. *Peoples and Cultures of Native South America: An Anthropological Reader*. New York: Doubleday/The Natural History Press, 1973.

Grove Music Online. Edited by Laura Macy. http://www.grovemusic.com (accessed 21 April 2008).

Guerrero, Pablo, and Ketty Wong. *Corsino Durán Carrión*. Quito: Dirreción General de Educación y Cultura, 1994.

Hague, Eleanor. *Latin American Music Past and Present*. Santa Ana, Calif.: The Fine Arts Press, 1934.

Hamlett, Robert Curtis. "An Investigation of Selected Colonial Latin American Vocal/Choral Works, Including Practical Performance Editions." Ph.D. diss., University of Southern Mississippi, 1986.

Hanke, Lewis. *The Spanish Struggle for Justice in the Conquest of America*. Boston and Toronto: Little, Brown and Co., 1965.

Hernández-Rios, Prisco. "Spanish and Portuguese Song at the End of the Middle Ages and the Beginning of the Renaissance (1466–1516): A Contextual Study." Ph.D. diss., University of Wisconsin at Madison, 1999.

Herrera, Rodrigo. "The Role of Classical Music in the Development of Nationalism and the Formation of Class in Quito, Ecuador." Ph.D. diss., University of Texas at Austin, 2000.

Holzmann, Rudolph. "Catálogo de la obra de Teodoro Valcárcel (1902–1942)." *Boletín bibliográfico* (Lima) 15, no. 12 (1942): 135–271.

———. "Catálogo de las obras de Alfonso Silva y Vicente Stea." *Boletín bibliográfico* (Lima) 15, no. 13:3/4 (1943): 242–252.

———. "Catálogo de las obras de Daniel Alomía Robles (1871–1942)." *Boletín bibliográfico* (Lima) 15, no. 13:1/2 (1943): 25–78.

Horna, Hernán. *La Indianidad: The Indigenous World before Latin America*. Princeton, N.J.: Markus Wiener Publishers, 2001.

Huertas, Julio César. *Los compositores del Uruguay: Su obra lírica, 1860–1960*. Uruguay: Editorial Campo, 1992.

Illari, Bernardo. "Ética, estética, nación: Las canciones de Juan Pedro Esnaola." *Cuadernos de música iberoamericana* 10 (2005): 137–223.

Ingram Jaén, Jaime. "Apuntes para una historia de la música en Panamá (1903–2003)." *Istmo: Revista virtual de estudios literarios y culturales centroamericanos*, no. 7 (November–December 2003). http://www.denison.edu/collaborations/istmo/no7 (accessed 14 January 2007).

Jacobson, Gloria Castiel. "The Life and Music of Ernesto Lecuona." Ph.D. diss., University of Florida, 1982.

Jorge, Bernarda. *La música dominicana, siglos XIX–XX*. Santo Domingo, R.D.: Editora de la Universidad Autónoma de Santo Domingo, 1982.

Jorgensen, Estelle R. *In Search of Music Education*. Urbana and Chicago: University of Illinois Press, 1997.
Joyce, Rosemary A. *Gender and Power in Prehistoric Mesoamerica*. Austin: University of Texas Press, 2001.
Keen, Benjamin, and Keith Haynes. *A History of Latin America*. 7th ed. Boston and New York: Houghton Mifflin Co., 2004.
Kicza, John E., ed. *The Indian in Latin American History: Resistance, Resilience, and Acculturation*. Rev. ed. Wilmington, Del.: Scholarly Resources, 2000.
Kiefer, Bruno. *Música e dança popular: Sua influência na música erudita*. Porto Alegre: Movimento, 1990.
Kimball, Carol. *Song: A Guide to Style and Literature*. Redmond, Wash.: Pst . . . Inc., 1996.
Kulp, Jonathan Lance. "Carlos Guastavino: A Study of His Songs and Musical Aesthetics." Ph.D. diss., University of Texas at Austin, 2001.
———. "Carlos Guastavino: The Intersection of Música culta and Música popular in Argentine Song." *Latin American Music Review/ Revista de música latinoamericana* 24, no. 1 (Spring/Summer 2003): 42–61
Kuss, Malena, ed. *Latin-American Music: An Encyclopedic History of Musics from South America, Central America, Mexico, and the Caribbean*. New York: Schirmer Books, 1999.
———, ed. *Music in Latin American and the Caribbean: An Encyclopedic History*. 2 vols. Austin: University of Texas Press, 2004–2008.
Labonville, Marie Elizabeth. *Juan Bautista Plaza and Musical Nationalism in Venezuela*. Bloomington: Indiana University Press, 2007.
———. "Musical Nationalism in Venezuela: The Work of Juan Bautista Plaza (1898–1965)." Ph.D. diss., University of California, Santa Barbara, 1999.
Lacombe, Roxane Marie. "Carlos Guastavino's Song Cycles 'Las Nubes' and 'Cuatro Sonetos de Quevedo': The Relationship of Text and Music." D.M.A. diss., University of Oklahoma, 2000.
Latin American Music Center. "Customized Catalog of Song Repertoire from the LAMC Database [Prepared in 2001]." Electronic file. Updated versions available by writing to lamc@indiana.edu; more information at http://www.music.indiana.edu/som/lamc/services/index.htm. See also LAMC listing under Online Resources, below.
Latin American Music Review/Revista de música latinoamericana. Online journal. Austin: University of Texas Press, 1980–. http://www.utexas.edu/utpress/journals/jlamr.html (accessed 3 March 2007).
Leclair, Charmaine Francoise. "The Solo and Chamber Music of Silvestre Revueltas." Ph.D. diss., University of Oregon, 1995.
Lekis, Lisa. "The Origin and Development of Ethnic Caribbean Dance and Music." Ph.D. diss., University of Florida, 1956.
León, Javier F. "The Politics of Afro-Peruvian Style: Music, History and the Reinvention of Difference." Ph.D. diss., University of Texas at Austin.

List of Latin American Music. Washington, D.C.: Pan American Union, 1933.

Lomax, Alan. *Folk Song Style and Culture.* Washington, D.C.: American Association for the Advancement of Science, 1968.

Lopes, Luiz Fernando Lopes. "Sample Repertoire [for Fifth Annual Competition in the Performance of Music from Spain and Latin America (2002), sponsored by Indiana University's Latin American Music Center and the Embassy of Spain, Washington, D.C.]: Song Literature from Spain and Latin America." Latin American Music Center. http://www.music.indiana.edu/som/lamc/competition_root/reserves/voice_songs_reserve.html (accessed 15 April 2009).

López Speziale, Carla D. "Ignacio Jerusalem: A Transcription of Selected Pieces for One and Two Soprano Voices." D.M.A. diss., Manhattan School of Music, 1998.

Lorenz, Ricardo, ed., with Luis R. Hernández and Gerardo Dirié. *Scores and Recordings at the Indiana University Latin American Music Center.* Bloomington: Indiana University Press, 1995.

Loza, Steven, ed. *Musical Cultures of Latin America: Global Effects, Past and Present.* Los Angeles: UCLA Ethnomusicology Publications, March 2003.

Lucas, Maria Elizabeth. "Directory of Latin American and Caribbean Music Theses and Dissertations (1984–1988)." *Latin American Music Review/Revista de música latinoamericana* 10, no. 1 (Spring/Summer 1989): 148–176.

Luzuriaga, Diego. *Once canciones para voz media y guitarra (Eleven Songs for Medium Voice and Guitar).* Oxford: Oxford University Press, 2002.

Machado-Echezuria, Marianella Perpetua. "'Así en la tierra como en el cielo': A Musical Approach to Poetry." Ph.D. diss., University of Cincinnati, 1998.

Magaldi, Cristina. *Music in Imperial Rio de Janeiro: European Culture in a Tropical Milieu.* Lanham, Md.: Scarecrow Press, 2004.

Magasin de Musique du Conservatoire. Serial publication. Paris.

Magee, Robert Gerald. "The Solo Songs for Voice and Piano of Carlos Chavez." D.M.A. diss., University of Southern Mississippi, 1989.

Manuel, Peter Lamarche, ed. *Essays on Cuban Music: North American and Cuban Perspectives.* Lanham, Md.: University Press of America, 1991.

———. "Latin America and the Caribbean." In *Popular Musics of the Non-Western World: An Introductory Survey,* 24–83. New York: Oxford University Press, 1988.

Mariñas Otero, Luis. "Panorama de la música hondureña." *Cuadernos hispanoamericanos: Revista mensual de cultura hispánica* (Madrid) 35 (julio 1958): 103.

Mariz, Vasco. *A canção brasileira de câmara.* Rio de Janeiro: Livraria Francisco Alves Editora, 2002.

Matarrita, Manuel. "An Analytical Study of Concerto for Piano and Orchestra, Op. 13, by Costa Rican Composer Carlos Enrique Vargas." D.M.A. diss., Louisiana State University, 2004. Available at http://etd.lsu.edu/docs/available/etd-06302004-182749/unrestricted/Matarrita_thesis.pdf (accessed 8 April 2009).

May, Elizabeth, ed. *Musics of Many Cultures: An Introduction.* Foreword by Mantle Hood. Berkeley, Los Angeles, and London: University of California Press, 1980.

McCoy, James A. "The *bomba* and *aguinaldo* of Puerto Rico as They Have Evolved from Indigenous, African, and European Cultures." Ph.D. diss., Florida State University, 1968.

Moore, Robin. "Directory of Latin American and Caribbean Music Theses and Dissertations since 1988." *Latin American Music Review/Revista de música latinoamericana* 14, no. 1 (Spring/Summer 1993): 145–171.

———. *Music and Revolution: Cultural Change in Socialist Cuba*. Berkeley: University of California Press, 2006.

———. *Nationalizing Blackness: Afrocubanismo and Artistic Revolution in Havana, 1920–1940*. Pittsburgh: University of Pittsburgh Press, 1997.

Morales, Ed. *The Latin Beat: The Rhythms and Roots of Latin Music from Bossa Nova to Salsa and Beyond*. Cambridge, Mass.: Da Capo Press, 2003.

Moreno González, Juan Carlos. *Datos para la historia de la música en el Paraguay*. Asunción: Dirección del Departamento de Enseñanza Secundaria y Profesional, Ministerio de Educación, 1953.

Moreno Rivas, Yolanda. *La composición en México en el siglo XX*. México: Cultura Contemporanea de México, 1994.

———. *Rostros del nacionalismo en la música mexicana: Un ensayo de interpretación*. México: Fondo de Cultura Económica, 1989.

Mukuna, Kazadi wa. "Ethnomusicology and the Study of Africanisms in the Music of Latin America: Brazil." In *Turn Up the Volume! A Celebration of African Music*, edited by Jacqueline Cogdell DjeDje, 182–185. Los Angeles: University of Los Angeles Fowler Museum of Cultural History, 1999.

Mundo al día. Serial publication. Bogotá, Colombia.

Music in Latin America: A Brief Survey. Series on Literature—Art—Music 3. Washington, D.C.: Pan American Union, 1945.

Music of Latin America. 3rd ed., reprint. Washington, D.C.: Pan American Union, 1963.

Nettl, Bruno. "American Indian Music North of Mexico: Its Styles and Areas." Ph.D. diss., Indiana University, 1953.

The New Grove Dictionary of Music and Musicians. 2nd ed. Edited by Stanley Sadie and John Tyrell. London: Macmillan, 2001.

O'Brien, Linda Lee. "Songs of the Face of the Earth: Ancestor Songs of the Tzutuhil-Maya of Santiago Atitlán, Guatemala." Ph.D. diss., University of California at Los Angeles, 1975.

O'Brien-Rothe, Linda. "Guatemala." In *The Garland Handbook of Latin American Music*, edited by Dale E. Olsen and Daniel E. Sheehy, 175–191. New York: Garland Publishing, 2000.

Ochoa, Ana Maria. "Plotting Musical Territories: A Comparative Study in Recontextualization of Andean Folk Musics in Colombia." Ph.D. diss., Indiana University, 1996.

Oliphant, Dave. *Nahuatl to Rayuela: The Latin American Collection at Texas*. Austin: Harry Ransom Humanities Research Center, University of Texas at Austin, 1992.

Olsen, Dale A., and Daniel E. Sheehy, eds. *The Garland Handbook of Latin American Music*. New York and London: Garland Publishing, 2000.
Orrego-Salas, Juan. "The Acquisition of Latin-American Books and Music," *Notes*, 2nd. ser., 22, no. 3 (Mar. 1966): 1008–1013.
———. *Involvement with Music: Music in Latin America*. New York: Harper, 1976.
———, ed. *Music from Latin America Available at Indiana University: Scores, Tapes and Records*. Bloomington: Latin American Music Center, School of Music, Indiana University, 1971.
———. "Rafael Alberti and Chilean Composers." Document submitted to Indiana University, 1977.
———. "Traditions, Experiment, and Change in Contemporary Latin America." *Latin American Music Review/Revista de música latinoamericana* 6, no. 2 (Autumn/Winter 1985): 152–165.
Pan American Union Music Section. *Composers of the Americas: Biographical Data and Catalogs of Their Works*. Vols. 1–19. Washington, D.C.: Pan American Union, 1955–1979.
Pinto, Maria Sylvia. *A canção brasileira: Da modinha à canção de câmara*. Rio de Janeiro: Cia Brasileira de Artes Gráficas, 1985.
Plácido Domingo—Always in My Heart: The Songs of Ernesto Lecuona. Milwaukee: Hal Leonard Corp, 1997.
Radin, Paul. *Indians of South America*. Garden City, N.Y.: Doubleday, Doran & Co., 1942.
Ramon y Rivera, Luis Felipe. "La décima musical en Venezuela y America hispana." *Revista musical de Venezuela* no. 27 (Jan.–Apr. 1989): 63–76.
Revista Argentina de musicología. Serial publication. Buenos Aires, Argentina: Asociación Argentina de Musicología, 1996–.
Revista cromos. Serial publication. Bogotá, Colombia.
Revista digital artística paraguaya. Online journal. "Agustín Pío Barrios," "Carlos Lara Bareiro," "José Asunción Flores." http://www.musicaparaguaya.org.py (accessed 10 March 2007).
Revista musical. Serial publication. Medellín, Colombia.
Revista musical chilena. Online journal. Santiago: Facultad de Artes, Universidad de Chile, 1973–. http://www.scielo.cl/scielo.php?pid=0716-2790&script=sci_serial (accessed 3 March 2007).
Revista musical de Venezuela. Serial publication. Caracas: Consejo Nacional de la Cultura, 1980–.
Revista musical puertorriqueña. Serial publication. San Juan, Puerto Rico: Instituto de Cultura Puertorriqueña, 1987–1990.
Roberts, John Storm. *The Latin Tinge: The Impact of Latin American Music on the United States*. 2nd ed. New York and Oxford: Oxford University Press, 1999.
Rodríguez, Luis C., ed. *Gonzalo Vidal, Antología*. Medellín: Secretaría de Educación y Cultura, 1997.
Rodríguez, Olavo Alén. "Cuba." In *The Garland Handbook of Latin American Music*,

edited by Dale A. Olsen and Daniel E. Sheehy, 116–133. New York and London: Garland Publishing, 2000.

Rodríguez, Victoria Eli. "Apuntes sobre la creación musical actual en Cuba." *Latin American Music Review/Revista de música latinoamericana* 10, no. 2 (Autumn/Winter, 1989): 287–297.

———. "Cuban Music and Ethnicity: Historical Considerations." In *Music and Black Ethnicity: The Caribbean and South America*, edited by Gerard Béhague, 91–108. Miami: University of Miami North-South Center Press, 1994.

Roy, Maya. *Cuban Music*. London: Latin America Bureau, 2002.

Saavedra, Leonora. "Of Selves and Others: Historiography, Ideology, and the Politics of Modern Mexican Music." Ph.D. diss., University of Pittsburgh, 2001.

Saavedra, Mariano. "Para la historia de la música en Honduras." *Honduras rotaria* 24:238 (diciembre 1967/enero 1968): 29–30, 32. Tegucigalpa: Los clubes rotarios de la República.

Sanz Quirós, Rocio. *Canciones para canto y piano*. Edited by Zamiro Barquero. San José, Costa Rica: CEDIM, Escuela de Artes Musicales, University of Costa Rica, 1995.

Sas, Andrés. *Cuatro melodías*. Montevideo, Uruguay: Editorial Cooperativa Interamericana de Compositores, 1941.

Schwartz-Kates, Deborah. "The *Gauchesco* Tradition as a Source of National Identity in Argentine Art Music (ca. 1890–1955)." Ph.D. diss., University of Texas at Austin, 1997.

Shalini, Puri. *Marginal Migrations: The Circulation of Cultures within the Caribbean*. Oxford: Macmillan Caribbean, 2003.

Sherzer, Joel. *Stories, Myths, Chants, and Songs of the Kuna Indians*. Austin: University of Texas Press, Teresa Lozano Long Institute of Latin American Studies, 2003.

Sider, Ronald R. "The Art Music of Central America: Its Development and Present State." Ph.D. diss., University of Rochester, 1967.

———. "Contemporary Composers in Costa Rica," *Latin American Music Review/Revista de música latinoamericana* 5, no. 2 (Autumn/Winter 1984): 263–276.

Slonimsky, Nicholas, ed. *Music of Latin America*. New York: Thomas Y. Crowell, 1945. Reprinted with new foreword and addenda by the author. New York: Da Capo Press, 1972.

Smith, Ronald R. "Arroz Colorao: Los Congos of Panama." In *Music and Black Ethnicity: The Caribbean and South America*, edited by Gerard Béhague, 239–266. Miami: University of Miami North-South Center Press, 1994.

———. "Latin American Ethnomusicology: A Discussion of Central America and Northern South America." *Latin American Music Review/Revista de música latinoamericana* 3, no. 1. (Spring/Summer 1982): 1–16.

Stevenson, Robert M. *Music in Mexico: A Historical Survey*. New York: Thomas Y. Crowell, 1952.

———. *La música en Quito*. 2nd ed. Quito: Banco Central del Ecuador, Centro de Investigación y Cultura, 1989.

Studies in Latin American Music. Serial publication. Metuchen, N.J.: Scarecrow Press, 1991–.

Sublette, Ned. *Cuba and Its Music: From the First Drums to the Mambo.* Chicago: Chicago Review Press, 2004.

———. *A Discography of Hispanic Music in the Fine Arts Library of the University of New Mexico.* Westport, Conn.: Greenwood Press, 1978.

Switzer, Harry M. "The Published Art Songs of Juan Bautista Plaza (Venezuela)." D.M.A. diss., University of Miami, 1985.

Tánchez, J. Eduardo. *La música en Guatemala: Algunos músicos y compositores.* Guatemala: Impresos Industriales, 1987.

Taylor, Bernard, ed. *Great Art Songs of Three Centuries.* New York: G. Schirmer, Inc., 1960.

Thompson, Leila Fern. *Selected List of Latin American Song Books and References for Guidance in Planning Programs of Music and Dance.* 7th ed. rev. Washington, D.C.: Pan American Union, 1949.

Tiemstra, Suzanne Spicer. *The Choral Music of Latin America: A Guide to Compositions and Research.* New York: Greenwood Press, 1992.

Tierra nativa. Serial publication. Bucaramanga, Colombia.

Titon, Jeff Todd. *Worlds of Music: An Introduction to the Music of the World's Peoples.* Belmont, Calif.: Schirmer/Thomson Learning, 2002.

Tompkins, William David. "Traditional Music of the Blacks of Coastal Peru." Ph.D. diss., University of California at Los Angeles.

Transcultural Music Review/Revista transcultural de música. Online journal. 1995–. http://www.sibetrans.com/trans/trans1/indice1.htm (accessed 3 March 2007).

Trinkley, Bruce, ed. *Nine Latin American Folk Songs.* Alfred Publishing Co., 2004.

Uribe Holguín, Guillermo. *Tres canciones de Guillermo Uribe Holguín.* Bogotá: Bogotá Patronato Colombiano de Artes, 1975.

Van Cott, Donna Lee, ed. *Indigenous Peoples and Democracy in Latin America.* New York: St. Martin's Press, 1994.

Vega, Aurelio de la. "Latin American Composers in the United States." *Latin American Music Review/Revista de música latinoamericana* 1, no. 2 (Autumn/Winter 1980): 162–175.

Vega Drouet, Héctor. "Puerto Rico." In *The Garland Handbook of Latin American Music*, edited by Dale A. Olsen and Daniel E. Sheehy, 134–144. New York and London: Garland Publishing, 2000.

Véjar Pérez-Rubio, Carlos. *Contrapuntos: Colegio de compositores latinoamericanos de música de arte, su nacimiento.* México: Archipiélago, 2000.

Velásquez, Ronny. "The Fundamental Role of Music in the Life of Two Central American Ethnic Nations: The Mískito in Honduras and Nicaragua, and the Kuna in Panama." In *Music in Latin America and the Caribbean: An Encyclopedic History*, edited by Malena Kuss, vol. 1, 193–230. Austin: University of Texas Press, 2004.

Veniard, Juan María. *Aproximación a la música académica argentina.* Buenos Aires: Ediciones de la Universidad Católica Argentina, 2000.

———. *La música nacional argentina (Influencia de la música criolla tradicional en la música académica argentina: relevamineto de datos históricos para su estudio).* Buenos Aires: Instituto Nacional de Musicología "Carlos Vega," 1986.

Viva Música! Online journal. 1994–1998. Rio de Janeiro, ©2005. http://www.vivamusica.com.br/english.php journal (accessed 10 March 2007).

Wagner, Deborah Rae. "Carlos Guastavino: An Annotated Bibliography of His Solo Vocal Works." D.M.A. diss., Arizona State University, 1997.

Walker, John L. "The Younger Generation of Ecuadorian Composers." *Latin American Music Review/Revista de música latinoamericana* 22, no. 2 (Autumn/Winter 2001): 199–213.

Wara Cespedes, Gilka. "New Currents in 'Música Folklórica' in La Paz, Bolivia." *Latin American Music Review/Revista de música latinoamericana* 5, no. 2 (Autumn/Winter 1984): 217–242.

Watkins, Timothy D. "Paraguay." In *The Garland Handbook of Latin American Music*, edited by Dale A. Olsen and Daniel E. Sheehy, 288–302. New York: Garland Publishing, 2000,

Weich-Shahak, Susana. "Music and Mythical Strata in Several Indian Cultures of South America: Four Indian Tribes of the Peruvian Forest—Yagua, Campa, Mashco and Orejón." Ph.D. diss., Tel-Aviv University.

Weiss, Allison. "A Guide to the Songs of Carlos López Buchardo (1881–1948)." M.A. thesis, University of Portland, 2005.

Wiarda, Howard J. *The Soul of Latin America: The Cultural and Political Tradition.* New Haven, Conn. and London: Yale University Press, 2001.

Wilson, Kathleen L. *The Art Song in Latin America: Selected Works by Twentieth-Century Composers.* Vox Musicae Series 1. Stuyvesant, N.Y.: Pendragon Press, 1998.

Wilson, Kathleen L., and Arden Hopkin. *La canción de arte en Puerto Rico: Selected Works by Twentieth-Century Composers.* Río Piedras, Puerto Rico: Asociación Nacional de Compositores de Puerto Rico, 1986.

Wong, Ketty. "Directory of Latin American and Caribbean Music Theses and Dissertations (1992–1998)." *Latin American Music Review/Revista de música latinoamericana* 20, no. 2 (Autumn/Winter 1999): 253–309.

Yepes, Gustavo. *Canciones para voz y piano (voz alta).* Medellín: Edición del compositor, 2003.

Yepez, Benjamin Chamorro. "El camino de las sombras: La música de los Guahibo," *Culturas musicales del Mediterraneo y sus ramificaciones, Revista de musicología* 16, no. 4 (1993): 2113–2125.

Zentner, Harry. *Prelude to Administrative Theory.* Calgary: Strayer Publications, 1973.

Zuñiga Zeledon, José Daniel, ed. *La patria canta: Música y canciones, autores de Costa Rica.* Costa Rica: Editor Danzuni, 1968.

———, ed. *Música tradicional costarricense:* San José, Costa Rica: Ministerio de Cultura, 1981.

ONLINE RESOURCES

Borghoff, Guida, and Luciana Monteiro Castro. *Guia da canções brasileiras. Resgate da canção brasileira.* Online database. Escola de Música, Departamento de Instrumentos e Canto, Universidade Federal de Minas Gerais, 2007. http://www.grude.ufmg.br/musica/cancaobrasileira.nsf (accessed 3 March 2007).

Center for World Indigenous Studies. ©1994–2007. http://www.cwis.org (accessed 13 January 2007).

Centro Nacional de Investicación, Documentación e Información Musical "Carlos Chávez" (CENIDIM). http: //www.cenart.gob.mx/centros/cenidim (accessed 16 April 2009).

CIA (Central Intelligence Agency). *The World Factbook.* https://www.cia.gov/cia/publications/factbook/index.html (accessed 10 March 2007).

Internet Resources for Latin America and the Caribbean—Music Resources Florida International University Libraries. http://library.fiu.edu/files/internet/subjects/caribbean/music1.html (accessed 10 March 2007).

Jamaica's Classical Musicians. ©Joy Lumsden, 2004. http://www.joyousjam.com/jamaicaclassicalmusicians (accessed 18 February 2007).

Latin American Art Song Alliance (LAASA). ©Latin American Art Song Alliance, 2007. http://www.laasa.org (accessed 3 March 2007).

Latin American Music Center at Indiana University (LAMC). Resource Center. Jacobs School of Music, Indiana University. http://www.music.indiana.edu/som/lamc (accessed 3 March 2007).

Latin American Network Information Center (LANIC). Austin, Texas, 2001. http://lanic.utexas.edu/las.html (accessed 13 January 2007).

Library of Congress Handbook of Latin American Studies (HLAS Online). http://memory.loc.gov/hlas (accessed 10 March 2007).

The Library of Congress Online Catalog. Online database. http://catalog.loc.gov (accessed 3 March 2007).

The Living Composers Project (LCP). Online database. Created by Dan Albertson and maintained by Ron Hannah; hosted by Kalvos and Damian's New Music Bazaar. http://www.composers21.com (accessed 3 March 2007).

Tulane University, Latin American Library website. http://www.tulane.edu/~latinlib (accessed 10 March 2007).

WorldCat (OCLC/Online Computer Library Center). Online database. © OCLC, 2001–2006. http://www.worldcat.org. (accessed 10 March 2007).

Contributors

Stela M. Brandão, soprano, studied at the Music School of Brasília, Brazil and went on to graduate with a Bachelor of Arts degree in singing and performance from the University of Brasília. In 1994, she received her Master of Music degree in vocal performance from the Conservatory of Music of Brooklyn College, New York. As a fellowship recipient of the Organization of the American States, Dr. Brandão received her Doctor of Education degree from the Music Education Doctoral Program at Teachers College, Columbia University.

Ellie Anne Duque is Professor of Music History and Director of the Office for Research at the Universidad Nacional de Colombia. She is editor of *Ensayos: Historia y teoría del arte,* a periodical published by the Instituto de Investigaciones Estéticas of the Universidad Nacional de Colombia, and co-editor of the *Página Web de Compositores Colombianos.*

Jean-Ronald LaFond, dramatic tenor, has more than thirty operatic roles in his repertoire and an equal number of oratorio roles. He earned a Doctor of Musical Arts and a Master of Music degree from the University of Michigan, and a Bachelor of Music degree from Westminster Choir College. LaFond currently holds master classes and teaches privately in New York City and Berlin.

José-Luis Maúrtua holds a Doctor of Music degree in composition from Florida State University, a Master of Music degree in composition from George Mason University, and a Bachelor of Music degree in composition from Carlos Valderrama Conservatory (Trujillo, Peru). He is currently Associate Professor of Composition and Theory at Central Michigan University and Director of the CMU Contemporary Music Ensemble. He is also Artistic Advisor and Guest Conductor of the Trujillo Bach Festival in Peru.

Allison L. Weiss, soprano, holds a Master of Arts degree in music from the University of Portland and a Master of Arts degree in Latin American studies from the University of Chicago. As a U.S. Fulbright Student Scholar in 2001, she lived in Buenos Aires for nine months, where she researched and performed Argentine art song. In 2003, she organized the Latin American Art Song Alliance (www.laasa.org) to promote the distribution and publication of Latin American art song.

Kathleen L. Wilson, soprano, has served as a Fulbright Scholar to Venezuela and as a United States Information Agency Cultural Specialist in Colombia. She is author of *The Art Song in Latin America* and appears on the CD *Elan*. Wilson holds a Master of Arts degree in musicology from the University of Arizona and a Doctorate in vocal pedagogy from Teachers College, Columbia University, and is currently Professor of Voice at Florida International University.

Index of General Subjects and Song Composers

Aberle, Juan, 162
Acevedo, Medardo Guido, 141
Acevedo Vargas, Jorge Luis, 141
Adalid y Gamero, Manuel de, 174
Adomián, Lan, 179
Aguiar, Ernani H. Chaves, 62–63
Aguirre, Julián, 1–2
Alas, Ciriaco Jesús, 159
Albano, Enrique, 4
Albuquerque, Armando Amorim, 63–64
Alcorta, Amancio, 1
Alfagüell, Mario, 141
Alfonseca, Juan Bautista, 156
Allende, Pedro Humberto, 128–29
Almeida Prado, A. L., 62
Almeida Prado, José Antônio Resende, 64–65
Alvarado, Jesús María, 163
Alvarez, Luis Manuel, 198–99
Amengual Astaburuaga, René, 129
André, José, 2, 4–6
Antunes, Jorge de Freitas, 62, 65–66
Aponte Ledée, Rafael, 198–99
Aráuz, Ramiro, 142
Ardévol Gimbernat, José, 149–50
Aretz, Isabel, 6–7
Arias, Enrique Alberto, xvi
Armesto, Jorge César, 2
Ascone, Vicente, 202–203
Assis Republicano, Antonio de, 61
Asunción Flores, José, 192
Atehortúa, Blas, 135
Avella, Vicente, 209
Avilés, Danilo, 150
Ayala Pérez, Daniel, 179
Aymara language, 56–57, 221, 223

Bal y Gay, Jesús, 178–79
Bañuelas, Roberto, 179
Baratta, María Mendoza de, 159
Bareiro, Carlos Lara, 192
Baron Supervielle, Suzanne, 3, 7
Barradas, Carmen, 202
Barroso, Francisco Paurilo, 66
Barroso, Sergio, 149–50
Barrozo Netto, Joaquim Antônio, 66–67
bataque (African musical form), 59
Bautista, Julián, 3, 7
Béhague, Gerard, xiv–xvi, 128, 159, 188
Bemberg, Hermann, 1, 8
Benedictis, Savino de, 61, 67
Bermúdez Silva, Jesús, 135–36
Biava, Pedro, 136
Bidart, Lícia de Biase, 67
Bilbao, Beatriz, 208
Bisetti, Alejandro, 195
Bittencourt-Sampaio, Sérgio, 67–68
Blain, Iphares, 169
Blanco, Juan, 149
Bocchino, Alceu Ariosto, 68
Boero, Felipe, 2, 9
Boettner, Juan Max, 192–93
Bonilla Chavarria, Jesus, 142
Bontemps, David, 168–69
Bor, Modesta, 208–10
Borghoff, Guida, 63
Borno, Louis (Luigi Francesco), 169
Botto Vallarino, Carlos, 129
Bracesco, Renzo, 194–95
Braga, Antônio Francisco, 61, 68
Braga, Ernani Costa, 61–62, 68–69
Brandão, José Vieira, 69

INDEX OF GENERAL SUBJECTS AND SONG COMPOSERS

Broqua, Alfonso, 202–203
Brouard, Carmen, 167–70
Brouwer, Leo, 149
Brouwer, Ninón Lapeiretta de, 156
Bruno-Videla, Lucio, 2

Caamaño, Roberto, 2, 10
Caba, Eduardo, 56–57
Cabrer, Carlos R., 199
Cabrera, Ana Schneider de, 3, 10–11
Cáceres, German Gustavo, 160–61
Caicedo, Patricia, xvii
Calcagno, Elsa, 3, 11
Calcavecchia, Benone, 203
Calvo, Luis Antonio, 136
Camêu, Helza, 61
Camêu, Helza de Cordoville, 69–71
Campabadal G., Roberto, 142
Campmany, Montserrat, 3, 12
Campos, Lina Pires de, 71
Campos Chanto, Alirio, 142–43
Campos Parsi, Héctor, 198–99
Camps, Pompeyo, 2, 12–13
Canipa, Edgar Alandia, 57
Cardon, Hugh F., xvii
Carmona, Oscar, 129
Carpio Valdés, Roberto, 194–95
Carreño, Innocente, 207, 210
Carrique, Ana, 3, 13–14
Carvalho, Dinorá Gontijo de, 62, 71–72
Carvalho, Eleazar, 72
Carvalho, Joubert Gontijo de, 72–73
Casella, Enrique Mario, 14–15
Casséus, Frantz, 167–68, 170
Castegnaro, Dolores, 141, 143
Castellanos Yumar, Gonzalo, 207–208, 210
Casteñeda, José, 163
Castillo, Jesús, 162
Castillo, Ricardo, 163
Castro, Ênio de Freitas, 73
Castro, José María, 15
Castro, Juan José, 16
Castro, Luciana Monteiro de, 63
Catalan language, 3, 12, 16, 38, 151–52
Cavalcanti, Nestor de Hollanda, 73
Cervantes, Ignacio, 148
Cervetti, Sergio, 203
Chase, Gilbert, xv–xvi
Chaves, Guillermo, 141
Chaves Torres, Rafael, 143
Chávez, Carlos, xvii, 177–80

Cimaglia Espinosa, Lía, 3, 16–17
Cluzeau Mortet, Luis, 202–204
Copland, Aaron, 56, 195
Cordero, Ernesto, 198–200
Cordero, Roque, 190
Cortinas, César, 202, 204
Cosme, Luis, 73
Costa, Alberto, 73
Coulanges, Amos, 168
Cowen, Frederic H., 175
Cubillo, Saturnino, 143
Cueva Negrete, Néstor, 158
Curitiba, Henrique de (Henrique Morozowicz Zbigniew), 73–74

Dagláns, Kerlinda, xv–xvi
Dallapiccola, Luigi, 56, 194.
Dauphin, Claude, 168–70
De Rogatis, Pascual, 2–3, 17
Debussy, Claude, 202
DeCosta, Noel, 175
Delano, Jack, 199–200
Delgadillo, Luis Abraham, 188–89
Dente, Domingo, 204
Dentone, Raúl Roberto, 204
Descourtilz, Michel-Étienne, 166
Desmangles, Édouard, 170
D'Espósito, Arnaldo, 17
Dijeres, Rafael de la O, 143
Diniz, Jaime Cavalcanti, 74
Drangosch, Ernesto, 18
Dublanc, Emilio, 2, 18–19
Dueño Colón, Braulio, 200
Duncker Lavalle, Luis, 194–95
Durán, Corsino, 158

Egúrbida, Leonardo, 199
Elías, Manuel de, 180
Elie, Justin, 168, 170
Ellmerich, Luis, 74
English language, 3, 8, 21, 31, 61, 131, 182, 215–23
Escalante Chernova, Irina, 149–50
Escobar, Luis Antonio, 136
Esnaola, Juan Pedro, 1
Espinosa, Luis Carlos, 136
Espoile, Raúl Hugo, 19–20
Estévez, Antonio, 210
Estrada, Carlos, 202, 204
Estrella de Mescoli, Blanca, 210
Étienne, Henri, 167

INDEX OF GENERAL SUBJECTS AND SONG COMPOSERS

Fabini, Félix Eduardo, 202, 204–205
Fábrega, Ricardo, 190–91
Faria, Celeste Jaguaribe de Matos, 74
Fariñas, Carlos, 149
Fauré, Gabriel, 202
Fernández, Agustín, 57
Fernandez, Oscar Lorenzo, 61–62, 75–76
Ficher, Jacobo, 2–3, 20
Ficher, Miguel, xv
Figueiredo, Letícia Onofre de, 76
Figueroa, Luis Carlos, 136
Figueroa, Narciso, 198, 200
Fiúza, Virginia Salgado, 76
Florence, Paulo, 61, 76–77
Flores, Bernal, 141
Fonseca G., Julio, 140, 143
Frangeul, Fernand, 167, 170
Freire, Vanda Lima Bellard, xvi–xvii
French language, 1–2, 5, 8, 12, 14–15, 19–21, 31, 35, 39, 46, 51, 60–61, 118, 166–68, 202, 204–207, 216–22
Furman, John M., xv

Gaito, Constantino, 2, 21
Galician language, 3, 10–11, 181
Galician-Portuguese language, 10
Galindo Dimas, Blas, 178, 180
Gallet, Luciano, 62, 77–78
Gaos, Andrés, 3, 21
Garay, Narciso, 190
García, Fernando, 129–30
García, Orlando Jacinto, 150
García Caturla, Alejandro, 148, 150
García Mansilla, Eduardo, 1, 21
García Morillo, Roberto, 22
García Robson, Magdalena, 22
Garrido-Lecca, Celso, 194
Giacobbe, Juan Francisco, 2, 23–24
Gianneo, Luis, 2, 24
Gianoli, Antonio, 159
Giarola, Adriana, xvii
Gil, José, 24
Gilardi, Gilardo, 2, 25
Ginastera, Alberto, 2, 26, 56, 194
Giucci, Carlos, 205
Gnatalli, Radamés, 78
Gomes, Antonio Carlos, 60
Gomes de Araújo, João, 61
Gómez Carrillo, Manuel, 26–27
Gomezanda, Antonio, 180
Gonzáles Martínez, Enrique, 179

González, Hilario, 149–50
González-Medina, Enrique, 180–81
Grasso, Gerardo, 205
Grau, Affonso Martinez, 78
Grau, Alberto, 208, 210
Grenier, Robert, 168
Grever, María, 178, 181
Grisolía, Pascual, 27
Guadamuz de la O., Isidro, 143
Guadamuz de la O., Teodoro, 143
Guarello Finlay, Alejandro, 130
Guarnieri, Mozart Camargo, 62, 78–82
Guastavino, Carlos, xvii, 2, 27–32
Guerra Peixe, Antonio, 82–84
Guerrero, Pablo, 157
Guevara, Gerardo, 157–58
Gutiérrez, Carlos Ma., 144
Gutiérrez Illanes, Emilio, 57
Gutiérrez Sáenz, Benjamin, 141, 144

Hahn, Reynaldo, 207
Halas, Oldřich, 57
Halffter, Rodolfo, 178, 181
Hargreaves, Francisco, 1, 32
Hartman, Ernesto Frederico (Sobrinho), 84
Hasler, Johannn, 136
Henn, Natho, 84
Henrique, Waldemar, 62, 84–86
Héraux, Jules, 170
Hernández, Gisela, 149–51
Hernández Moncada, Eduardo, 181
Herra Rodríguez, Luis Diego, 144
Holzmann, Rudolph, 194–95
Honegger, Arthur, 194

Ibarra, Federico, 181
Iglesias Villoud, Héctor, 32
Inzaurraga, Alejandro, 33
Ipuche Riva, Pedro, 205–206
Isamitt, Carlos, 130
Italian language, 3, 8, 14–15, 17, 20–21, 32, 37, 45, 48, 60–61, 140, 143, 162, 177–78, 181, 194, 202, 204–206, 221, 223
Iturriaga, Enrique, 194

Jabor, Naijla (Maia de Carvalho Najla Jabor), 86–87
Jacinto García, Orlando, 149
Jaegerhuber, Werner, 167, 170–72
Jiménez, Ángel Honorario, 157
Jiménez Mabarak, Carlos, 181–82

joropo (dance form), 208–209
Jurafsky, Abraham, 33–34

Kachaturian, Aram, 208
Kazadi wa Mukuna, xvi
Kiefer, Bruno, 87
Koellreuter, Hans Joachin, 62, 87–88
Krieger, Edino, 62, 88
Kulp, Jonathan Lance, xvi–xvii
Kuri Aldana, Mario, 182
Kuss, Malena, xv

Labonville, Marie Elizabeth, xvi
Lacerda, Osvaldo, 62
Lacerda, Osvaldo Costa de, 88–90
LaCombe, Roxane Marie, xvii
Ladrón de Guevara, Raúl, 182
LaFond, Jean-Roland, 168, 172
Laguerre, Ferrère, 168, 172
Lamothe, Ludovic, 168, 172
Lara, Agustín, 178, 182
Lara, Ana, 182
Lara, Gustavo Adolfo, 136
Lasala, Ángel E., 2, 34
Latin language, 79, 97–98, 115–16, 120
Lavalle García, Armando, 182
Lavista, Mario, 182–83
Lecuona, Ernesto, 148, 151
Lemos, Artur Iberê de, 90–91
Leng, Alfonso, 130
León, Argeliers, 149
León, Jaime, 136
León, Tania, 149
Letelier, Alfonso, 129–30
Ley, Salvador, 163
Lima, João de Souza, xvii, 91
Lobato, Domingo, 183
López Buchardo, Carlos, 1–2, 34–35
López de la Rosa, Horacio, 35–36
Lorenz, Ricardo, 208
lundu (Brazilian musical form), 59–60
Luzko, Daniel, 192–93
Luzuriaga, Diego, 158
Luzzatti, Arturo, 3, 36

Machado, Marianella, 208
Maderna, Bruno, 194
Magee, Robert Gerald, xvii
Mahle, Ernst, 62, 91–92
Maiguashca, Mesías, 158
Maiztegui, Isidro, 36
Malipiero, Gian Francesco, 194

Maragno, Virtú, 36
Marchena Dujarric, Enrique de, 156
Mariz, Vasco, 61, 63
Marroquín, José Sabre, 163
Martínez, José Daniel, 200
Massa, Juan Bautista, 37
Massarini, Renzo, 92
Mata Bonilla, Félix, 144
Mata Oreamuno, Julio, 140, 144
Maul, Otávio, 92
Mejía, Adolfo, 135
Mejía, Joaquín Orellana, 174
Mejía Arredondo, Enrique, 156
mélodie (French musical genre), 1
Mendes, Gilberto, 62, 92–93
Mendoza, Jeremías, 159
merengue (dance form), 209
méringue (Haitian song form), 167
Messiaen, Olivier, 56, 194
Meza, Luis Antonio, 194
Mignone, Francisco de Paula, 61–62, 93–96
Miranda, Rolando, 96
modinha (Brazilian musical form), 60
Mojica Mesa, Raúl, 136
Moleiro, Moisés, 207, 210
Mondino, Luis Pedro, 205
Monestel Zamore, Alejandro, 144
Montecino, Alfonso, 130
Monton, Mauléar, 167, 172
Morales Caso, Eduardo, 149
Morales de Villegas, Socorrito, 205
Morales Pino, Pedro, 137
Morel, Marcelo, 130–31
Moreno, Segundo Luis, 157
Muñoz, José Luis, 208, 210–11
Murillo, M. Claudio, 144
Murillo Chapull, Emilio, 137
Música Viva (Brazilian music movement), 62

Napolitano, Emilio Ángel, 37
Nepomuceno, Alberto, 60, 63, 96–98
Neukomm, Sigismund, 59
Neuman, Hans Federico, 137
Nin-Culmell, Joaquín María, 149, 151–52
Nobre, Marlos (Marlos Nobre de Almeida), 62, 99–100
Nova Sondag, Jacqueline, 137

Octaviano, João (João Otaviano Gonçalves), 101
Oliveira, Babi de (Idalba Leite de Oliveira), 61, 100–101
Orbe, Gabriel del, 156

INDEX OF GENERAL SUBJECTS AND SONG COMPOSERS

Orbón, Julián, 149
O'Reilly-Viamontes, Mónica, 149, 153
Orellana, Gilberto, 160
Orrego-Salas, Juan, 129, 131, 208
Ortiz, José, 141
Oswald, Henrique José Pedro Maria Carlos Luis, 101
Ovalle, Jaime Rojas de Aragón y, 101

Pabón Roca, Luis E., xv–xvi
Pádua, Newton de Menezes, 102
Pahissa, Jaime, 3, 37–38
Palma, Athos, 2, 38–39
Paredes, Hilda, 183
Paredes Herrera, Francisco, 158
Parker, Christopher, 175
Pasqués, Víctor, 40
Paz, Juan Carlos, 2, 40
Pedrell, Carlos, 40, 202–203
Pedrell, Felipe, 202
Peixe, A. Guerra, 62
Perceval, Julio, 2–3, 41
Peyrallo, Félix, 205
Picchi, Acchile, 102–105
Pierret Villaneuva, Florencia, 156
Pimenta, Altino, 105
Pineda Duque, Roberto, 137
Pinilla, Enrique, 194–96
Pinto, Alejandro, 2–3, 41–42
Pinto, Alfredo, 42
Pinto, Maria Sylvia, 59
Pío Barrios, Augustín, 192
Pizarro, Daniel, 144
Plaza, Juan Bautista, xvi–xvii, 207, 211
Ponce, Manuel M., 177, 183–84
Portuguese language. See Chapter 3 introduction and pertinent entries
Posada Amador, Carlos, 137
Prado Quesada, Alcides, 140, 144
Prieto, María Teresa, 178, 184
Puebla, Carlos Manuel, 153
Pulgar Vidal, Francisco, 194

Quaratino, Pascual, 3, 43
Quechua language, 56, 157, 194–96, 221–23
Quevedo y Villegas, Francisco de, xvii

Rago, Alexis, 208–209, 211–12
Ramírez, Luis Antonio, 200
Ravelo, José de Jesús, 156
Rebello, Arnaldo, 106
Republicano, Antonio de Assis, 106

Revueltas, Silvestre, 178, 184–85
Ribeiro, León Julio Alfredo, 205
Ricourt, Volvick, 172
Riesco, Carlos, 131–32
Ríos Ovalle, Juan, 200
Ripper, João Guilherme, 106
Roda, Arturo, 158
Rodríguez, José Napoleón, 159
Rodríguez, Marcela, 185
Rodríguez, Ricardo, 43
Rodríguez Caracas, Manuel, 145
Rodríguez Socas, Ramón, 205
Roldán, Amadeo, 148, 153
Rolón, José, 185
Rosaenz, Elifio, 43
Roumain, Daniel, 168
Rozo Contreras, José, 135, 137
Russell, Oswald, 175

Sáenz, Pedro, 44
Salgado, Luis H., 157
Salnave, Dépestre, 172
Sambucetti, Luis, 202, 205–206
Sammartino, Luis, 2, 44
Sánchez de Fuentes, Eduardo, 153
Sánchez Málaga, Carlos, 194, 196
Sandi, Luis, 178, 185–86
Sandoval, Miguel, 163–64
Santa Cruz, Domingo, 128, 132
Santoro, Claudio Franco de Sá, 62, 106–108
Santos, Domingo, 159
Sanz Quirós, Rocío, 141, 145
Sarabia Quiroz, M. Nicholás, 196
Sarmientos, José, 163
Sas, Andrés, 194, 196
Sauce, Angel, 207
Saumell, Manuel, 148
Schidlowsky, León, 132
Schleifer, Martha Furman, xv
Sciammarella, Valdo, 45–46
Segu, José, 206
Serebrier, José, 206
Serrano Redonnet, Ana, 3, 46–47
Setti, Kilza, 62
Setti, Kilza (de Castro Lima), 108
Siccardi, Honorio, 47
Sierra, Roberto, 200–201
Silfa Finke, Ana, 156
Siqueira, José de Lima, 62, 108–109
Slonimsky, Nicholas, xiv, 159
Sojo, Vicente Emilio, 207, 212
Solares Echeverría, Enrique, 163

Soriano Arce, Ramiro, 57
Souviron, Yvette, 3, 47
Souza, Oswaldo de, 109–10
Spena, Lita, 3, 48
Stiatessi, César, 3, 48
Stockhausen, Karlheinz, 158
Storm, Ricardo, 206
Suffern, Carlos, 48
Switzer, Harry M., xvii

Tacuchian, Ricardo, 62, 110
Tapia Colmán, Simón, 178, 186–87
Tavares, Heckel, 61, 110–12
Téllez Oropeza, Roberto, 187
Tello, Aurelio, 195–96
Tena, José María, 137
Teppa, Carlos, 207–208
Terraza, Emilio, 113
Terzián, Alicia, 2
Thompson, Richard, 175–76
Tomás, Guillermo M, 153
Toni, George Olivier, 113
Torrá, Celia, 3
Torre Bertucci, José, 50
Torres-Santos, Raymond, 199, 201
Tosar Errecart, Héctor, 206
Traversari, Pedro Pablo, 158
Troiani, Cayetano, 50
Tupinambá, Marcelo (Fernando Álvares Lobo), 113

Ubieta Gómez, Enrique, 153
Ugarte, Floro, 2, 51
Ulloa Barrenechea, Ricardo, 141, 146
Ureña Morales, José Joaquín, 146
Uribe Holguín, Guillermo, 137
Urrutia Blondel, Jorge, 129, 132
Urteaga, Irma, 2, 51
Ussachevsky, Vladimir, 194

Valcárcel, Edgar, 194, 196
Valcárcel, Theodoro, 194, 196
Valencia, Antonio María, 137–38

vals (dance form), 208–209
Varela, Victor, 208
Vargas, Carlos Enrique, 141
Vargas, Sergio, 57
Vargas Calvo, José Joaquín, 140
Vasconcellos Corrêa, Sérgio Oliveira de, 113
Vázquez, Carlos Alberto, 201
Vega, Augusto, 156
Vega, Aurelio de la, 149, 153
Veiga Jardim, Oswaldo (Oswaldo da Veiga Jardim Neto), 113
Velasco, Jerónimo, 138
Velasquez, Glauco, 113–14
Veray, Amaury, 199, 201
Verrett, Alexandre, 172
Verrett, Solon, 168, 172
Vianna, Fructuoso de Lima, 114–15
Vidal, Gonzalo, 138
Vieira, José Carlos do Amaral (José Carlos do Amaral Vieira Filho), 115–16
Villalobos, Alejandro, 138
Villa-Lobos, Heitor (Epaminondas Villalba Filho), 61–62, 116–20
Villalpando, Alberto, 56–58
Villani-Côrtes, Edmundo, 62, 120–22
Villegas, Sacramento, 146
Vitier, José María, 149, 153

Wagner, Deborah Rae, xvii
Walker, John L., xvi, 156
Watkins, Timothy L., 192
Widmer, Ernst, 122–23
Williams, Alberto, 2, 51–53
Woolley, Édouard, 168, 172–73

yaraví (Andean song form), 202
Yepes, Gustavo, 138
Yepez Chamorro, Benjamin, xvii

Zamudio, Daniel, 138
Zorzi, Juan Carlos, 53
Zúñiga Rovira, Héctor, 146
Zúñiga Zeledón, José Daniel, 140

Index of Poets and Text Sources

Catalog numbers are used as locators.

Abella Caprile, Margarita, 1.92, 1.379
Abreu, Casimiro de, 3.129, 3.676
Abreu, Nelson, 3.935
Acciolly, João, 3.1335, 3.1340
Acevedo, Medardo Guido, 6.1, 6.2, 6.3, 6.4, 6.5, 6.13
Adler, María Raquel, 1.7, 1.9
Adolphe, Charles, 3.360
African text, 3.867
Afro-Brazilian folklore, 3.232, 3.245, 3.463
Afro-Brazilian religious song, 3.575, 3.617b, 3.725, 3.1089, 3.1250a
Afro-Brazilian text, 3.1325a, 3.1443d, 3.1443e
Agote, Luis, 1.520a
Agüeros, José, 11.6
Aguirre, Julián, 1.3a, 1.3b, 1.3c
Aguirre, Mirta, 7.19a, 7.19b, 7.57, 7.58
Aizenberg, Guiche, 1.302c, 1.302h, 1.332, 1.341
Aizim, Lúcia, 3.1224, 3.1231
Ajalbert, Jean, 1.16j, 1.16k
Alarcón, Juan Ruiz de, 15.74
Albano, José, 3.1120
Alberti, Rafael, 1.223, 1.342, 1.346, 4.30, 4.32, 7.3, 7.5, 15.4c, 15.35, 15.77d
Albuquerque, Amarylio, 3.1459
Albuquerque, Solfieri de, 3.102, 3.157
Aldalur, Félix, 1.287, 1.292
Aleardi, Aleardo, 3.1000
Aleixandre, Vicente, 15.65f, 15.67b
Alencar, Cláudia, 3.128
Alencar, José de, 3.198
Alencar, Meton de, 3.859
Alfaro, José María, 6.96
Alimonda, Jeanete H., 3.1189

Allende Iragorri, Tomás, 1.1c, 1.236
Almeida, Afonso Lopes de, 3.712
Almeida, Guilherme de, 3.43, 3.177, 3.187, 3.239, 3.302a, 3.515, 3.681, 3.710, 3.726, 3.776, 3.806, 3.874, 3.1104, 3.1388, 3.1393, 3.1448
Almeida, Luiz Homero de, 3.1099u
Almeida, Pádua de, 3.429e
Almeida, Renato de, 3.341
Almeida Prado, A. L., 3.1401, 3.1407, 3.1418, 3.1426
Alonso y Trelles, José María, 21.33, 21.34
Alvarenga, Oneyda, 3.472, 3.662, 3.663, 3.927, 3.1160
Álvarez, Griselda, 15.81
Alvarez, Martins d', 3.174
Álvarez, Rodolfo, 1.8
Álvarez Blázquez, Xosé M., 15.33
Alves, Achilles, 3.1156
Alves, Castro, 3.329, 3.711, 3.1105a, 3.1116, 3.1541a, 3.1541h, 3.1542a
Alves, Theodomiro, 3.231
Alves Guimarães, Ricardo, 3.917
Aly, 3.1356
Amadei, Condessa Ana Antonia, 3.956
Amado, Gilberto, 3.1437
Amado, Jorge, 3.1188
Amador, Fileman L., 3.1099w
Amorim, Enrique, 1.378
Ana Amélia de Queiroz Carneiro de Mendonça, 3.1328
Anchieta, Pe. José de, 3.1338
Andersen, Hans Christian, 1.4d, 1.235
Andrade, Ary de, 3.1169, 3.1179, 3.1182
Andrade, Carlos Drummond de, 3.119, 3.121,

INDEX OF POETS AND TEXT SOURCES

3.124, 3.125, 3.126, 3.235a, 3.235b, 3.281, 3.557, 3.558, 3.680, 3.689, 3.744, 3.794, 3.812, 3.821, 3.837, 3.869, 3.888, 3.900, 3.905, 3.916, 3.943, 3.1021, 3.1022, 3.1108a, 3.1108b, 3.1258, 3.1345, 3.1396, 3.1469, 3.1473g, 3.1519, 3.1526, 3.1549a, 3.1549b, 3.1550a, 3.1550b, 3.1550c, 3.1551
Andrade, Djalma, 3.1099dd, 3.1099m
Andrade, Eugênio de, 3.1344
Andrade, Flavio de, 3.1311
Andrade, Julieta de, 3.562
Andrade, Mário de, 3.349, 3.416b, 3.469, 3.492, 3.496, 3.499, 3.513, 3.517, 3.520, 3.870, 3.923, 3.1025, 3.1113, 3.1117, 3.1130, 3.1339, 3.1442a, 3.1442c, 3.1443f, 3.1476c, 3.1517, 3.1522
Anzoátegui, Ignacio B., 1.375
Apollinaire, Guillaume, 1.23a, 3.40b
Arabic poetry, 15.77a, 15.77b
Aragon, Louis, 3.1184
Araújo, Luíza de, 3.136
Araujo, Murilo, 3.152, 3.338, 3.416a, 3.429f, 3.1278e, 3.1297, 3.1438
Araújo Jorge, José Guilherme de, 3.186, 3.649
Arce, Roberto, 6.6
Arciniegas, Ismael Enrique, 5.34
Areco, Elena, 1.391
Arellano, Manuel, 4.24b
Arena, Luis, 1.485
Argentinean coplas, 1.490a, 1.490b, 1.490c, 1.490d
Argentinean folk song, 1.64d, 1.257, 1.460, 11.38, 11.39
Arinos, Afonso, 3.150, 3.503
Aristodemo Pinotti, José, 3.28
Armond, Geralda, 3.1480
Arnal, Emilie, 3.947
Arnault, Antoine Vincent, 3.1363
Arrieta, Rafael Alberto, 1.141, 1.187, 1.541
Arschot, Comte d', 3.86
Artur, J., 3.264
Assis, Machado de, 3.151, 3.965
Audigier, G., 1.26b
Aurobindo, Sri, 12.7
Avray, Jacques D' (pen name of José de Freitas Valle), 3.227, 3.398, 3.781, 3.850, 3.862, 3.887, 3.982
Azevedo, Álvares de, 3.101
Azevedo, Arthur, 3.87
Azevedo, L. H. Corrêa de, 3.1265
Azevedo Marques, Antônio de, 3.444
Aztec poetry, 20.25

Ballagas, Emilio, 22.4a, 22.4b, 22.4c
Baltodano, Aristides, 6.77
Bandeira, Antônio Rangel, 3.135, 3.323, 3.487, 3.669, 3.688, 3.695, 3.718
Bandeira, José, 3.1105d
Bandeira, Manuel (Manduca Piá), 3.42, 3.44, 3.206a, 3.215, 3.328, 3.421, 3.447, 3.473, 3.489, 3.507, 3.527, 3.570, 3.668, 3.685, 3.686, 3.687, 3.700, 3.705, 3.715, 3.720, 3.723, 3.724, 3.792, 3.793, 3.798, 3.802, 3.811, 3.854, 3.873, 3.879, 3.884, 3.903, 3.906, 3.919, 3.920, 3.1027b, 3.1027c, 3.1084, 3.1085, 3.1086, 3.1092, 3.1093, 3.1097, 3.1101, 3.1114, 3.1126, 3.1129, 3.1201, 3.1216, 3.1217, 3.1218, 3.1220, 3.1225, 3.1229, 3.1230, 3.1235, 3.1238, 3.1240, 3.1257, 3.1262, 3.1264, 3.1337, 3.1386, 3.1387, 3.1434b, 3.1441, 3.1473b, 3.1473e, 3.1548b, 3.1548c
Baños, Avelina, 21.27
Barata, Ruy Paratininga, 3.577
Barba Jacob, Porfirio, 5.18, 5.19, 5.61
Barbé Pérez, Luis, 21.10
Barbier, Jules, 21.14
Barbieri, Vicente, 1.152
Bardesio, Orfila, 1.371
Barletta, Leonidas, 1.500
Barrantes Castro, Pedro, 19.11a
Barreto, Abilio, 3.1464c
Barrios, Segundo, 1.64b
Barrios Cruz, Luis, 22.16
Barros, Carlos Paula, 3.176, 3.653, 3.655
Barros, J., 3.284
Barros, Luís Carlos da Fonseca Monteiro de, 3.318
Barros, Teófilo de, 3.543
Barroso, Francisco Paurilo, 3.71
Barroso, Gastão, 3.301
Barroso, Gustavo, 3.708, 3.742
Basilio, Librado, 15.36c
Bathista, Nair, 3.1193
Batista, Ana Nogueira, 3.951
Batres Montúfar, José, 11.5
Battelli, Italo, 1.401
Baudelaire, Charles, 3.158, 3.168, 3.172, 12.13, 12.26
Bautista Grosso, Juan, 1.70, 1.102, 1.183, 1.455, 1.465, 1.466, 1.472, 1.473, 1.476, 1.477, 1.481, 1.484, 1.486
Bécquer, Gustavo Adolfo, 1.229, 1.488, 1.494b, 1.494c, 1.494d, 1.565, 1.566, 20.26
Bellodi, Júlio, 3.1479, 3.1482, 3.1483, 3.1486, 3.1487, 3.1488, 3.1494, 3.1497, 3.1516, 3.1523, 3.1529

INDEX OF POETS AND TEXT SOURCES

Beltrán, Neftalí, 15.45a
Beltrán Núñez, Rosario, 1.445, 1.451, 1.456c
Bemberg, Hermann, 1.29
Benarós, León, 1.203, 1.301, 1.302b, 1.302d, 1.302e, 1.3021, 1.303, 1.308, 1.312, 1.322, 1.324, 1.328, 1.335, 1.340, 1.344
Berdiales, Germán, 1.415e, 1.543i
Bernárdez, Francisco Luis, 1.61, 1.105, 1.108, 1.161a, 1.494a
Bernis, Yeda Prates, 3.525
Bertoline, Nilson, 3.574f
Bevilacqua, Sylvio, 3.75, 3.89
Bewer, Max, 1.188b
Bilac, Olavo, 3.109, 3.143, 3.147, 3.162, 3.274, 3.319, 3.352, 3.385, 3.392d, 3.433, 3.694, 3.748, 3.751, 3.759, 3.763, 3.766, 3.785, 3.969, 3.991, 3.993, 3.1063, 3.1081, 3.1082, 3.1371
Biosca Gonzalez, Valentina, 3.592
Bittencourt-Sampaio, Adelina, 3.130
Blanco, Andrés Eloy, 22.3a, 22.3b, 22.3c, 22.3d, 22.8i
Blasco, Eusébio, 3.1379
Blumenschein, Yde Schlöenbach (Columbina), 3.365, 3.892, 3.925, 3.1099p
Bocage, Henri, 3.392a
Bodesan, Altino, 3.302b
Bolívar, Simón, 3.1020
Bolivian folk song, 11.10
Bólseyro, Joyão, 1.57a
Bolseyro, Juyas, 1.149
Bonfim, Paulo, 3.223, 3.241, 3.242, 3.252, 3.677, 3.679, 3.722, 3.1099y, 3.1122, 3.1332
Borges, Durval, 3.139
Borges, Jorge Luis, 1.331
Borges, Pery, 3.133, 3.137
Borja, Cecilia, 1.260
Borno, Louis (Luigi Francesco), 12.24
Bortoli, Fernando, 3.673
Botrel, Theodore, 3.110
Bottoni, Gerolamo, 3.922
Bourget, Paul, 3.1362
Boutelleau, Georges, 15.67e
Brache, Maurice De, 12.20
Braga, Belmiro, 3.344, 3.1099a, 3.1325d
Braga, Leopoldo, 3.642
Braga, Mariinha, 3.83
Branca, Violeta, 3.585a
Branco, Rui Gonçalves de Castello, 3.1404
Brant, Celso (Celso Brandt), 3.475, 3.1162, 3.1186
Brasileiro, Antonio, 3.1540a, 3.1540b

Brazilian folklore, 3.247, 3.567, 3.1263, 3.1323c, 3.1443c, 3.1443g, 3.1465e, 11.7
Brazilian Indian/indigenous song, 3.437, 3.1443a, 3.1443b, 3.1476b
Brecht, Bertolt, 3.1175a, 3.1183, 6.80
Bribrí tradition, 6.64
Brierre, Jean, 12.21
Brito, Floriano de, 3.156
Broqua, Alfonso, 21.2
Brouard, Carl, 12.12e, 12.12f
Bru, Paul, 1.16i
Bruver, Arnold, 3.263
Bufano, Alfredo R., 1.83, 1.96, 1.103, 1.104, 1.107, 1.123, 1.252, 1.255, 1.370, 1.433a, 1.513, 1.544
Buonarroti, Michelangelo, 3.404
Burns, Robert, 1.4c, 3.391b
Bustamante y Ballivián, Enrique, 19.13d
Bustos, Julia, 1.69
Byron, Lord, 1.533

Caba, Eduardo, 2.3, 2.4
Cabral, João Passos, 3.369
Cadilhe, J., 3.1461
Calampelli, Susana, 1.164
Calcaño, José A., 5.3
Caldas, Onestaldo de Pennafort, 3.915
Caldas Barbosa, Domingos, 3.699, 3.746, 3.1099bb
Calil, Adélia, 3.373
Calvo, Luis Antonio, 5.7, 5.8
Camargo, Joracy, 3.1270, 3.1272, 3.1275, 3.1282, 3.1298, 3.1300, 3.1306, 3.1313, 3.1315, 3.1316a
Camargo, Milton Vaz de, 3.30, 3.31, 3.32, 3.229, 3.1144
Camino, Miguel A., 1.171a, 1.175d, 1.176, 1.204, 1.208, 1.376a, 1.376b, 1.376d, 1.376e, 1.543b, 1.553
Camões, Luís de, 3.259, 3.392c, 3.1123, 3.1187, 3.1350, 3.1376
Campos, Astério de, 3.429a
Campos, Calazans, 3.262
Campos, Cleómenes, 3.222, 3.278, 3.403, 3.452, 3.457, 3.476a, 3.519, 3.524c, 3.810, 3.818, 3.1091, 3.1099g, 3.1106b
Campos, Francisco Moura, 3.1535
Campos, Geir, 3.1205
Campos, Rúben M., 15.25b
Campos, Sílvia Celeste de, 3.376, 3.479
Campos, Suzanna de, 3.224, 3.438, 3.466, 3.480a, 3.480b, 3.490, 3.494, 3.510, 3.1211
Canal Feijoó, Bernardo, 1.497e

INDEX OF POETS AND TEXT SOURCES

Cané, Luis, 1.139, 1.143, 1.144, 1.147, 5.36
Cano, María Carmen, 1.452
Capdevila, Arturo, 1.72, 1.400d, 1.404
Caprile, M. Abella, 1.390
Capucci, Hilda Reis, 3.629
Caputi, Nilde, 3.1421
Caraballo, Gustavo, 1.128, 1.364, 1.372, 1.382d, 1.382e
Caramuru (Diogo Álvares Correia), 3.434
Carco, Francis, 5.44
Cardenal, Ernesto, 10.9a, 10.9b, 10.9c
Cardoso, Hilma, 3.204
Carmo, Aplecina do, 3.138, 3.1326
Carmona, Cecilia, 4.4
Carneiro, Alcides, 3.1099z
Carrera Andrade, Jorge, 9.3
Carriego, Evaristo, 1.78
Carrillo, Sonia Luz, 4.8a, 4.17
Carrizo, César, 1.35b
Carvajal, Antonio, 5.58
Carvalho, Albertina, 3.1099d
Carvalho, Beatrix dos Reis, 3.429b, 3.1152
Carvalho, Beni, 3.625, 3.651
Carvalho, Cherubina Rojas Ovalle de, 3.773
Carvalho, Fúlvia Lopes de, 3.255
Carvalho, Honório de, 3.322, 3.1079, 3.1436, 3.1446
Carvalho, José Alfredo Maia de, 3.620, 3.634, 3.639
Carvalho, Ronald de, 3.321, 3.336, 3.342, 3.353, 3.412, 3.664, 3.665, 3.1221, 3.1452, 3.1454, 3.1473f, 15.11
Carvalho, Vicente de, 3.164, 3.167, 3.197a, 3.197b, 3.213, 3.703, 3.717, 3.729, 3.929, 3.1096, 3.1099v, 3.1118, 3.1121, 3.1124, 3.1212, 3.1419
Casa, José Iglesias de la, 1.299
Casal, Julio J., 21.40a, 21.40b, 21.40c
Casas, Augusto, 15.66b
Cascallares Gutiérrez, Isabel, 1.110
Casona, Alejandro, 15.65c
Castañeda, Daniel, 15.71, 15.72, 15.73, 19.12
Castello Branco, Rui Gonçalves de, 3.1404
Castilho, Olga Lilian, 3.440
Castro, J. J., 1.492, 1.493a
Castro, Rosalía de, 1.58, 1.77, 1.158, 1.237
Castro Borges, Albertina de, 3.1099i
Castro Ríos, Andrés, 20.13
Castro Saavedra, Carlos, 5.62
Catholic traditional texts, 12.38, 12.39, 12.42
Cavé, René, 3.191
Cavestany, Pablo, 1.540a, 1.540b, 1.540c, 1.540d
Cavillo Sinclair, Arsenio, 1.468, 1.475

Cearense, Catulo da Paixão, 3.388
Celso, Conde Affonso, 3.971, 3.1002
Cernuda, Luis, 1.298a, 1.298b, 1.298c, 1.315, 1.327a, 1.327b, 1.327c, 15.40e
Cervantes, Miguel de, 1.384, 7.17c
Cesarman, Teodoro, 15.1a, 15.1b
Cetina, Gutierre de, 1.91, 15.40f
Chagas, Moacyr, 3.173
Chalar, Agustín, 21.20
Charras, Julián de, 1.52
Chavarría, Lisímaco, 6.15
Chaves, Ovidio, 3.574j
Chaves, Reynaldo, 3.534a, 3.534b
Chenier, André, 3.393
Chilean folk song, 4.26a, 4.26b, 4.26c, 4.26d, 11.11, 11.12, 11.33
Chirre Danós, R., 1.256a, 1.256b, 1.256c, 1.256d
Choque, Jaime, 2.9c
Chouhy Aguirre, Ana María, 1.329, 1.347
Christensen, Adela, 1.536
Cimino, 1.177
Cirne Lima, Ruy, 3.20a
Claudius, Matthias, 11.3
Clemente Zenea, Juan, 7.54
Cocteau, Jean, 21.24
Codá, Orlando, 3.945a, 3.945b, 3.945c
Coelho, Carlos, 3.77, 3.97, 3.140, 3.159, 3.160
Coelho, Gaspar, 3.325
Coelho Netto, Henrique, 3.1005
Colaço, Branca de Gonta, 3.959
Colombian folk song, 11.30, 11.31
Colombina (Yde Schloenbach Blumenschein), 3.365, 3.892, 3.925, 3.1099p
Consuegra, Gregorio, 5.55
Coppée, François, 1.26m, 1.26o
Coqueiros, Euly, 3.304
Cordero, Enrique, 6.65
Coria Peñaloza, Gabino, 1.175b, 1.175c, 1.175e, 1.280, 1.282
Corrêa, Ruth V., 3.1434a
Corrêa, Viriato, 3.1465b
Correia, Raimundo, 3.189, 3.572, 3.975, 3.1365, 3.1463
Corretjer, Juan Antonio, 20.12, 20.27a
Côrtes, Curt, 3.1538
Côrtes, Lula, 3.1500
Cortés, Martín H., 5.1
Côrtes, Mônica, 3.1496, 3.1520, 3.1525
Cortese, Nina, 1.325
Costa, Ciro, 3.771
Costa, Marieta, 3.574c
Costa, Ribeiro da, 3.1177

INDEX OF POETS AND TEXT SOURCES

Costa e Silva, Alberto Vasconcellos da, 3.1099ee, 3.1196a, 3.1196b, 3.1196c
Costa Pereira, Mara, 3.598g
Costa Rican folklore, 6.50
Couto, Ribeiro, 3.214, 3.347, 3.518, 3.659f, 3.682, 3.732, 3.761a, 3.795, 3.805, 3.861, 3.882, 3.940, 3.1015, 3.1457a, 3.1473h, 3.1473i
Crespo, Gonçalves, 3.987, 3.1077, 3.1099k
Crespo, Julia, 1.508, 1.510, 1.518
Cristino, Demóstenes, 3.1099e
Cruz, João da, 3.1505
Cruz, Sor Juana Inés de la, 15.34a, 15.34b, 15.65a, 15.65b
Cruz Varela, Juan de la, 6.51
Cuban folk song, 11.19
Cunha de Miranda, Alma, 3.770, 3.1033, 3.1055
Cunquiero, Alvaro, 15.66c

D'Altavilla, Jayme, 3.1289
D'Altavilla, Jorge, 3.1284
Damasceno, Athos, 3.16
Damoclès, Vieux, 12.33
Danel, Fernand, 1.26c
Daneri, M. A., 1.132
Darío, Rubén, 1.94a, 1.94g, 1.94h, 1.95, 1.214, 1.493c, 5.4, 6.78, 7.53, 16.1k, 188
Dauphin, Marcel, 12.40
Dávalos, Baica, 15.55a, 15.55b
Dávalos, Juan Carlos, 1.35a, 1.35c, 1.35e, 1.35f
Dávila, J. A., 20.17a
Dávila, Virgilio, 20.15, 20.16
Debravo, Jorge, 6.63a, 6.63b, 6.63c
Delavigne, Casimir, 1.27
Delgado, Agustín, 15.36a
Del Giglio, Elio, 1.487
Denis, D., 3.1399
Dentone, Agustín, 1.32, 1.33, 1.44, 1.45, 1.50, 1.79, 1.80, 1.81, 1.82, 1.84, 1.101, 1.109, 1.111, 1.115, 1.178, 1.179, 1.195, 1.197, 1.201, 1.266, 1.423, 1.552
Desbordes-Valmore, Marceline, 1.212, 1.213
Dessein Merlo, Justo G., 1.504a, 1.504b, 1.504c
Dessoudeix, Georges, 12.41i
Dessuse, M., 20.24
Deus, João de, 3.85, 3.93, 3.995
Devoto, Daniel, 1.441
Dias, Idalina Peçanha, 3.824
Díaz, Leopoldo, 1.36, 1.38, 1.40, 1.42, 1.46, 1.47, 1.48, 1.49, 1.53
Díaz Leguizamón, Héctor, 1.41
Díaz Mirón, Salvador, 15.20
Diego, José, 20.19a, 20.19b, 20.19c

Diego, Rafael de, 1.175a, 1.427a, 1.427b
Dios Peza, Juan de, 1.231
Dodero, Pedro, 21.53
Domingues Garcia, Aida Grisolia de, 1.294
Domínguez, María Alicia, 1.499
Dordal, Francisco R., 3.106
D'Orléans, Charles, 3.402
D'Ormeville, Carlo, 1.227
Dreyer, Doris, 3.1226
Dromart, Marie-Louise, 12.41j
Drummond, Irene, 3.467
D'Sola, Otto, 22.15b
Duarte, Yanella, 7.42, 7.43
Dubois, Stela, 3.621
Dunbar, Paul Laurence, 14.2
Duque Estrada, Osório, 3.81, 3.970, 3.1007
Durand, Oswald, 12.34
Durval, Guerra, 3.1222
Dutra, Osório, 3.333, 3.901, 3.902

Edmundo, Luiz, 3.92
Eduardo, Ernesto, 2.6
Eduardo, Luiz, 3.1099o
Eichendorff, Joseph Freiherr von, 1.4e
Elías Tarnassi, Ricardo de, 1.54
Éluard, Paul, 3.1180
Emanuel, Vladimir, 3.582
Encina, Juan del, 15.60a, 15.60c
Eneas Urtubey, Edgardo, 1.412
Espanca, Florbela, 3.205
Espino, Alfredo, 6.62a, 6.62b, 6.62c
Estrella Gutiérrez, Fermín, 1.171b, 1.367a, 1.367b, 1.367c, 1.433b
Etcheverry, Ernesto J., 1.480
Etcheverry, Félix E., 1.399, 1.400a, 1.400b, 1.403, 1.405
Ezcurra, María Magdalena de, 1.180

Faccini, Mário, 3.1029, 3.1052, 3.1054
Fages de Climent, Carles, 1.415, 1.415b, 1.415c, 1.415d, 1.415e, 1.415f
Failersleben, August Heinrich Hoffmann von, 1.191d
Faraj, Jorge, 3.542
Farias, Elson, 3.549, 3.559
Faubert, Ida, 12.29a, 12.29b, 12.29c, 12.36
Fautrier, Adela, 1.479
Feliciano Mendoza, Ester, 20.14b
Fereira, Celina, 3.1111a
Fernandes, Armando, 3.1051
Fernandes, Lilinha, 3.10991, 3.1106c
Fernandez, Oscar Lorenzo, 3.326, 3.345

INDEX OF POETS AND TEXT SOURCES

Fernández, Tristán, 1.184b
Fernández de la Puente, J. L., 1.51
Fernández Moreno, B., 1.393
Fernández Shaw, Carlos, 1.462
Ferraría, Mayorino, 1.37, 2.1
Ferraris, Marcos J., 1.474
Ferraz, Dayse, 3.1400, 3.1402, 3.1406, 3.1411, 3.1417, 3.1422
Ferraz, Helena, 3.1098, 3.1105c
Ferraz, Yara, 3.782
Ferreira, Alberto, 3.1099q
Ferreira, Alfredo, 3.1439
Ferreira, Ascenço, 3.169, 3.616, 3.1027a, 3.1239c, 3.1239d, 3.1283, 3.1303
Ferreira, Athos Damasceno, 3.11, 3.18, 3.283
Ferreira, Isabelita Pinto, 3.1099f
Ferreira, Laerte, 3.1492
Ferreira Viana, Esther, 3.1073
Figueira, Gastón, 1.410, 1.411
Figueiredo, Guilherme, 7.16
Filho, Carlos Pena, 3.530
Filho, Lobão, 3.1279, 3.1291
Filho, Luiz de Andrade, 3.334a, 3.334b, 3.753, 3.757a, 3.757b
Flórez, Julio, 5.21, 5.26
folklore, 3.35, 3.117, 3.165, 3.170, 3.195, 3.196, 3.202, 3.216, 3.230, 3.240, 3.250, 3.251, 3.254, 3.256, 3.413a, 3.414b, 3.423, 3.504, 3.516, 3.521a, 3.521c, 3.524j, 3.526, 3.541, 3.576, 3.600, 3.692, 3.696, 3.737, 3.853, 3.1191, 3.1203a, 3.1203b, 3.1213, 3.1233, 3.1234, 3.1239f, 3.1239g, 3.1259, 3.1278c, 3.1294, 3.1465c, 3.1466c, 3.1466f, 3.1541b, 3.1541c, 3.1541d, 3.1541e, 3.1541f, 3.1541g, 3.1541i, 3.1541j, 3.1541m, 3.1541n, 3.1541o, 3.1541p, 3.1542b, 3.1542c, 3.1542d, 3.1542f, 3.1542g, 3.1542h, 11.27, 11.32, 12.3, 12.15b, 12.15d, 12.16, 12.19, 12.25, 12.32. See also popular poetry, traditional poetry
Fombona Pachano, Jacinto, 22.15c
Fonseca, Mário, 3.523b, 3.532a, 3.532c, 3.537
Fonseca, Sebastião, 3.356, 3.370
Fonseca, Teófilo da, 3.764
Fonseca Duarte, José, 3.1099b
Fontes, Hermes, 3.141, 3.955, 3.985
Fontes, Martins, 3.296, 3.678
Fontes, Narbal, 3.851
Forrest, George, 3.1462
Fort, Paul, 1.550, 1.551
Fraletti, Paulo, 3.1405
Franco, José, 1.444c
Franco, Luis L., 1.363, 1.366

Frankenberg Martinez, Olivia von, 1.482
Freidenson, Marília, 3.1527
Freire, Junqueira, 3.707
Freire, Laerte, 3.1491, 3.1498
Freitas, Darcy de, 3.37
Freitas, Nair Marques Lisboa de, 3.127
Freitas, Paulo, 3.1099aa
Freitas Valle, José de (Jacques D'Avray), 3.227, 3.398, 3.781, 3.850, 3.862, 3.887, 3.982
Frías, Eva, 1.555b
Frías, José D., 15.52a, 15.52b, 15.52c, 15.52d
Frondoni, Angelo, 3.1112c
Funes, Xiomara, 7.4
Fusoni, Fernando, 1.31, 1.34c

Galeno, Juvenal, 3.458, 3.521b, 3.948, 3.988, 3.1009
Galindo, Blas, 15.27c
Gallay, A., 3.1455
Gallet, Luciano, 3.1268, 3.1348
Gamboa, Emma, 6.16, 6.17, 6.18, 6.19, 6.20, 6.21, 6.22, 6.23, 6.24, 6.25, 6.26, 6.27, 6.28, 6.29, 6.30, 6.31, 6.32, 6.33, 6.34, 6.35, 6.36, 6.37, 6.38, 6.39, 6.40, 6.41
Ganade, Gisele, 3.1109a, 3.1109b
Gaos, Andrés, 1.230, 1.234, 1.238, 1.239
Garcez, Luciano, 3.1501
García, Alma, 1.302g, 1.317, 1.333
García Lorca, Federico, 1.22, 1.24, 1.25, 1.56b, 1.155, 1.156, 1.157, 1.159, 1.160, 1.163, 1.243, 1.395, 1.531, 1.532, 2.5, 3.1018, 3.1543a, 3.1543b, 4.19, 4.20, 4.25, 4.28e, 4.28f, 4.28g, 4.39, 5.65, 7.6, 7.19c, 7.19d, 7.19e, 7.20, 7.37, 15.5, 15.12, 15.37a, 15.40d, 15.69, 20.1, 20.2, 20.6
García Mansilla, Daniel, 1.242
García Mansilla, Eduardo, 1.240, 1.241
Garrett, Almeida, 3.1112k
Gasperini, L., 3.1066, 3.1075
Gauna, R. G., 1.121
Gautier, Théophile, 1.89, 1.211
Géraldy, Paul, 3.405c
Giacobbe, Juan Francisco, 1.246a, 1.246b, 1.248, 1.250
Giannoni, Iverna Codina de, 1.196, 1.199
Gilardi, Gilardo, 1.262
Gille, Philippe, 1.26i, 1.26n
Gillet, Jean, 12.41e, 12.41f
Gimenez, Juan Ramón, 1.119
Giociniti, Carlos McGregor, 15.36e
Giraldo, Francisco, 5.49
Godoy, Maria Lúcia, 3.590

INDEX OF POETS AND TEXT SOURCES

Godoy, Paulo de, 3.418
Góes, Eurico de, 3.330
Goethe, 3.852
Goethe, Johann Wolfgang von, 1.4a, 3.852, 3.1199
Gomes, Lindauro, 3.1099gg
Gomes, Roberto, 3.410
Gómez, Adolfo León, 5.10
Gómez Naranjo, Pedro A., 5.35
Gonçalves Dias, Antônio, 3.148, 3.683, 3.704, 3.998, 3.1377, 3.1541k, 3.15411, 3.1542i
Góngora, Luis de, 15.40c, 15.40g
Gonzaga, Francisca, 3.1078
Gonzaga, Tomás Antônio, 3.132, 3.698, 3.706
Gonzales Bonorino, Elena Serry de, 1.67
Gonzales Martínez, Enrique, 11.1, 11.2, 11.4, 15.6, 15.45c, 15.63
Gonsáles Prada, Manuel, 19.13a
González, Ernesto, 5.53
González, Gilda Arabéhéty de, 1.219
Gonzalez Castillo, C., 1.447
González López, E. N., 1.35d, 1.55
González Zeledón, Manuel, 6.72
Gordon, William, 3.82, 3.99
Gorostiza, José, 15.75
Goulart de Andrade, José Maria, 3.881
Greiff, León de, 5.11, 5.40, 5.56, 5.57, 5.59, 5.63
Greiff, Otto de, 5.30, 5.45, 5.46, 5.47, 5.48
Grieco, Agrippino, 3.636
Griz, Jayme, 3.553, 3.565a, 3.565b, 3.565c
Guanabara tradition, 3.633
Guarnieri, Alice Camargo, 3.217, 3.243, 3.460, 3.728, 3.1204
Guarnieri, Rossine Camargo, 3.442, 3.446, 3.453, 3.454, 3.481a, 3.481b, 3.502, 3.514, 3.523a, 3.523b, 3.524a, 3.524d, 3.524i, 3.524m, 3.671, 3.1209
Guastavino, Carlos, 1.311
Guatemalan folk song, 11.17
Guerra-Peixe, Emilia, 3.563
Guevara, Adán, 6.45
Guillén, Horacio, 1.511, 1.516
Guillén, Nicolás, 1.394, 3.1198, 4.5, 7.1, 7.14, 7.15, 7.45a, 7.45b, 7.45c, 7.50, 15.70b, 19.14, 22.4a, 22.4b, 22.4c
Guimarães, Alphonsus de, 3.758, 3.1125, 3.1464d
Guimarães, João, 3.904
Guimarães Filho, Alfonsus de, 3.598e
Guimarães Filho, Luis, 3.84, 3.145, 3.979, 3.986, 3.1010, 3.1346, 3.1464e
Gullar, Ferreira, 3.1540d
Guterres Casses, Átila, 3.1031, 3.1058
Gutiérrez, Ricardo, 1.284

Hebel, Friedrich, 3.399
Heine, Heinrich, 1.4b, 1.97, 1.190e, 1.232, 3.966, 3.1004, 3.1006, 3.1017, 5.41, 12.12c, 15.8
Heloisa, Elza, 3.237
Henrique, Waldemar, 3.578, 3.579, 3.580, 3.581, 3.584, 3.586, 3.589, 3.593, 3.594, 3.598a, 3.598c, 3.598f, 3.601, 3.602, 3.609, 3.612, 3.613, 3.617a, 3.617c, 3.1308
Hernández, 1.442p
Hernández, Miguel, 1.151a, 1.151b, 1.442
Herrera, Ataliva, 1.407, 1.408, 1.409, 1.413
Herrera, Porfirio, 8.2
Herrera Sevillano, Demetrio, 1.444b
Hiliodoro Valle, Rafael, 6.68
Hilst, Hilda, 3.47a, 3.47b, 3.1214
Hiolivichc, C., 1.124
Hipólito Lobo, 1.64e, 1.64f
Holderlin, Friedrich, 1.185b
Huerta, Efraín, 15.30
Huertas, José G., 1.194
Hughes, Langston, 14.1, 15.68
Hughes, Ted, 15.51
Hugo, Victor, 1.210, 1.431, 3.1460, 15.10
Hugué, Manolo, 1.385a
Huidobro, Vicente, 4.8d, 4.11, 4.13, 4.14
Hurley, Jorge, 3.597
Hyppolite, Dominique, 12.28

Ibarbourou, Juana de, 1.337, 1.529
Ibarbourou, Juan, 1.15
Ibarra, Cristóbal Humberto, 10.4
Icaza, Francisco A. de, 15.54a, 15.54b, 15.54c, 15.54d
Idoyaga, Américo, 21.38
Iglesias, Luis María, 1.457, 3.431
Iglesias Villoud, Héctor, 1.184a
Ignotus, 1.543d
Indians, Parecis, 3.1310
Insausti, Rafael, 1.495
Inzaurraga, Alejandro, 1.360, 1.361a, 1.361b, 1.361c
Ione, Ricardina, 3.1034, 3.1057
Isaacs, Jorge, 5.50
Isgorogota, Judas (Agnelo Rodrigues de Melo), 3.857
Iturburu, Cordova, 1.392

Jabor, Diva, 3.654
Jammes, F., 12.17c
Jantus, Jorge, 1.517
Javier, Francisco, 1.491
Jean de la Croix, Saint, 3.40g

INDEX OF POETS AND TEXT SOURCES

Jijena Sánchez, Rafael, 1.62, 1.65c, 1.66, 1.88, 1.106, 1.113, 1.129, 1.131, 1.133, 1.172, 1.193, 1.389, 1.497a, 1.497f, 1.535, 1.539, 1.543a, 1.543f, 1.549
Jiménez, Juan Ramón, 1.437a, 1.437b, 1.437c, 1.437d, 7.19g, 15.3, 15.4b, 15.4d, 22.6, 22.9b, 22.15e
Joglar Cacho, Manuel, 20.20a
Jolicœur, Marie-Ange, 12.4a, 12.4b, 12.5
Jonquière, Françoise, 3.1174, 3.1181
Jordán, Juan Manuel, 1.205
Joyce, James, 4.3
Juan Vignale, Pedro, 1.469
Juárez, Jorge Ramón, 15.36b
Jubé, A. G. Ramos, 3.293
Julien, Pierre, 12.11, 12.14
Juncos, Juan, 1.471
Junior, Baptista, 3.397, 3.1467
Junior, Correa, 3.114, 3.116, 3.118, 3.455, 3.459, 3.482, 3.495, 3.524b, 3.524e
Júnior, J. Martins, 3.462
Júnior, Mendonça, 3.1307
Junqueiro, Guerra, 3.96
Jurado, Teresa, 1.543e, 1.543g, 1.543h

Kahle, Maria, 3.390
Karam, Francisco, 3.115
Katari, Ramun, 2.2
Kelly, Octávio, 3.339
Kemp, Eduardo, 3.1106a
Kerner, Ary, 3.866
Khayyam, Omar, 3.890, 12.9, 15.79
Khoury, A., 15.40b, 15.40e
Kinkel, Gottfried, 1.188c
Klinger, Kehos, 1.443
Klingsor, Tristan, 1.16f, 1.16g, 1.16h
Kolody, Helena, 3.199, 3.209, 3.210, 3.295
Kuhlmann, Itagiba, 3.1511, 3.1514
Kulka, Georg, 3.661
Kyouco, 12.41h

Laborde, Lorenzo, 21.31
Lacerda, Renato, 3.675
La Fontaine, Jean de, 3.1468
Lago, Mário, 3.424
Lahor, Jean (Henri Cazalis), 3.880
Lahore, Guislaine, 1.198
Lahore, Jean, 12.17d
Lamartine, Alphonse de, 1.359, 3.1364
Lan, S. B., 3.1384
Lara, Ómar, 4.6, 4.9, 4.10

Larreta, Enrique, 1.414
Lasker Schüler, Else, 1.56a, 1.56c
Latin text, 3.445, 3.953, 3.997, 3.1410, 3.1425, 3.1481
Latino, Carmen, 1.534
Latorre, Gabriel, 5.52
Laurencin, Marie, 1.23d, 12.12b
Laurito, Ilka Brunhilde, 3.690, 3.1115
Lazo Martí, Francisco, 22.10e
Leão, Múcio, 3.351
Leduc, Alphónse, 3.1478
Le Goffic, Charles, 15.67d
Leiria, João Octávio de Nogueira, 3.5741
Leiva, Ramon, 6.89
Lemos, Arthur, 3.1474
Lemos, J. de, 3.1106e
Lemos, Lara de, 3.659d
Lemos, Yedda, 3.754
Lenau, Nikolaus, 3.396, 3.973, 3.977, 3.978, 3.999, 3.1003, 3.1011, 3.1412
Lenzi, Carlos César, 21.6, 21.7
Leoni, Raul de, 3.190, 3.192, 3.533a, 3.533b, 3.533c, 3.535a, 3.830
Lerena Acevedo, Andrés, 21.8, 21.50
Lermontorf, M., 3.108
Léry, Jean de, 3.1476a
Lewin, Willy, 3.171
Liebovich, Marcos, 1.543c
Liliencron, Detlev von, 1.530
Lima, Augusto de, 3.1395
Lima, Jeny de, 3.893
Lima, Jorge de, 3.337, 3.591, 3.1292
Lima, Ricardo Tavares de, 3.1207
Lima Quintana, Hamlet, 1.302f, 1.302k, 1.316, 1.320
Lindo, Ricardo, 10.5a, 10.5b, 10.5c, 10.5d
Linhares, Augusto, 3.1099n, 3.1237, 3.1247
Linsman, Samuel, 3.571b
Li-Po, 15.49
Lira, Carmen, 6.54
Liscano, Juan, 7.17e
Lisle, Leconte de, 3.350
Llanos, Antonio, 5.67
Llera, Manuel García de la, 21.37
Lleras Restrepo, Isabel, 5.22
Llorens Torres, Luis, 20.9, 20.10, 20.21, 20.22, 20.23
Lobeira, João, 3.1409
Löns, Hermann, 3.387, 3.394
Lopes, B., 3.1464a
Lopes, Thomas, 3.992

INDEX OF POETS AND TEXT SOURCES

Lopes Vieira, Adelina A., 3.950
López, Eduardo, 5.9
López, Horacio, 1.386a, 1.386b, 1.386c, 1.386d
López, Luis Carlos, 5.64, 5.66
López, Ramón, 15.51
López Narváez, Carlos, 5.32
Lopez Palmero, M., 1.173
López Portillo, Margarita, 15.80a, 15.80b, 15.80c, 15.80d
López Velarde, Ramon, 15.7a, 15.26, 15.70a, 15.77c
Lopo, 1.57b
Loureiro, João de Jesus Paes, 3.587, 3.588, 3.607, 3.618
Loynaz, Dulce María, 7.19h, 7.19i
Lubin, J. Dieudonné, 12.37
Lucena, Gabriel de, 3.921a, 3.921b, 3.921c, 3.921d
Lucena, Lisette Villar de, 3.362
Lugones, Leopoldo, 1.1, 1.2, 1.13, 1.116, 1.174, 1.265, 1.267, 1.296, 1.382, 1.400e, 1.434, 1.458, 1.502a, 1.502b, 1.521, 1.564, 5.25
Lugones, Santiago M., 1.206a, 1.206b, 1.221
Luna, José Ramón, 1.446, 1.448, 1.449, 1.453

MacDougall, Hugo, 1.264
Machado, Antonio, 1.438
Machado, Ary, 3.1327
Machado, Luz, 22.8h
Machado, M., 1.153
Machado, Raul, 3.208, 3.1242, 3.1244a, 3.1244b
Madaia, Álvaro, 3.938
Madeleine, Jacques, 1.161
Maeterlinck, Maurice, 3.382, 3.967, 3.996
Magalhães de Azeredo, Carlhos, 3.946, 3.968, 3.1008
Magarinos, Domingos, 3.957
Magloire, Nadine, 12.10
Maia, Álvaro, 3.608
Maia, Circe, 21.4
Maia, Ilka, 3.212
Maíra, 3.1107a
Malinow, Inés, 1.348
Malta, J., 3.1329
Manent, Maria, 1.385b
Mangabeira, Édila, 3.201
Mangione, E., Jr., 3.644
Mantovani, Fryda Schultz de, 1.374, 1.527
Marchena, Julián, 6.66, 6.67
Marchini, Maria Stella Quirino, 3.357
Mariani, Walter, 3.941
Mariano, Olegário, 3.53, 3.197e, 3.206b, 3.206c, 3.206d, 3.206e, 3.524f, 3.1068, 3.1090, 3.1239a, 3.1239b, 3.1244c, 3.1299, 3.1305, 3.1317a, 3.1317b, 3.1317c, 3.1319a, 3.1319c, 3.1322a, 3.1322b, 3.1322c, 3.1330, 3.1473c
Mariéton, Paul, 1.261, 1.26r, 1.26t
Marín, Ernesto, 1.184c
Marín, José, 1.218
Marín, Rodríguez, 21.46
Marino, Giambattista, 15.31
Marques, Antônio de Azevedo, 3.444
Marques, Milton, 3.246
Marquet, Mary, 12.41a, 12.41b, 12.41c, 12.41d
Marrone, E. D., 1.289, 1.290, 1.297
Martán, Helcías, 5.12, 5.13
Martí, José, 7.34b, 7.55
Martin, Carlyle, 3.1111b
Martínez, Leonardo, 1.19, 1.20, 1.21
Martinique folklore, 12.15a
Martins, Aracy, 3.59
Martins, Roque, 3.622
Martí y Folguera, J., 1.87
Marún, Carols, 1.563
Mastronardi, Carlos, 1.503
Matos, Gregório de, 3.693, 3.727
Mattos, Francisco de, 3.5241
Maturana, José de, 1.388
Maul, Carlos, 3.823, 3.825
Maury, Roberto, 3.260
Mayar, Deodato (Mário Faccini), 3.1048
Mayer, Olga, 3.631
Mazzanti, José, 1.140a, 1.140b, 1.140c, 1.140d
McDowell, Paulo, 3.599
Meireles, Cecília, 3.25, 3.29, 3.41, 3.194, 3.207, 3.228, 3.233, 3.286c, 3.287a, 3.287b, 3.287d, 3.324, 3.716, 3.735, 3.796, 3.803, 3.942, 3.1127, 3.1141, 3.1342, 3.1343, 3.1398, 3.1415, 3.1484, 3.1489, 3.1493, 3.1499, 3.1502
Mello, Maria José V. Homem de, 3.672
Mello, Ovídio de, 3.146
Mello e Souza, J. B., 3.78, 3.149, 3.340
Melo, Alex Fiúza de, 3.1147
Mendes, Paulo, 3.1301
Méndez Cuesta, Concha, 1.192
Mendonça, A. S. de, Jr., 3.354
Mendonça, Vera Xavier de, 3.45b
Mendoza, Íñigo López de, 1.357
Menéndez-Leal, Álvaro, 10.2a, 10.2b, 10.2c, 10.2d
Menezes, Bruno de, 3.1143
Menezes, Emilio de, 3.990
Mermet, César, 1.397a
Mescoli, Blanca Estrella de, 22.8g

INDEX OF POETS AND TEXT SOURCES

Mexican folk song, 11.8, 11.9, 11.14, 11.16, 11.18, 11.22, 11.23, 11.25, 11.26, 11.37
Meyer, Augusto, 3.12, 3.13, 3.14, 3.15, 3.17, 3.19, 3.20b, 3.286b, 3.287c, 3.427a, 3.427b, 3.427c
Meyer, Deodato, 3.1041
Meyer, Friedrich Albert, 1.191c
Mignone, Francisco de Paula, 3.885
Milano, Dante, 3.506, 3.1319b, 3.1429, 3.1473d, 3.1473k
Millet, Sérgio, 3.491
Milli, 3.1382
Mingo, Carlos, 1.512
Miranda, Murillo, 3.864, 3.865, 3.911, 3.926
Miranda, Rogério de, 3.750, 3.765
Mistral, Gabriela, 1.165, 1.321, 1.336, 1.339, 1.343, 1.365, 4.22, 4.24a, 4.24c, 4.27, 4.35, 4.42, 8.3, 15.45b
Moleiro, Moisés, 22.10a, 22.10d, 22.10h, 22.10i
Moleiro, Rodolfo, 22.11
Monroy, César, 9.1
Montagne, Edmundo, 1.6
Monte, S., 3.1064
Monteiro, F. Célio, 3.931a, 3.931b, 3.931c
Montes, Victoriano, 1.382f
Monti, Amelia, 1.450, 1.454, 1.456a, 1.456b
Monti, José, 7.40
Mora Barrantes, Carlos, 6.105
Moraes, Vinícius de, 3.449, 3.571c, 3.571d, 3.674, 3.799, 3.801, 3.944, 3.1095, 3.1161, 3.1170, 3.1171, 3.1195a, 3.1195b, 3.1195c, 3.1261, 3.1336, 3.1548d, 3.1549c
Morais Filho, Alexandre José de Melo, 3.154
Morales, Ernesto, 1.522, 1.554
Morales Eró, Francisco, 10.10a, 10.10b, 10.10c
Morandi, Luigi, 21.3
Moreaux, Sylvio, 3.144, 3.181, 3.188, 3.261, 3.386, 3.628, 3.768, 3.1037, 3.1053, 3.1134, 3.1447
Moreyra, Álvaro, 3.178b, 3.1274, 3.1288, 3.1318a, 3.1318b, 3.1318c, 3.1473a
Motta, Dantas, 3.1547
Moura, Chico, 3.1128a, 3.1128b, 3.1128c
Moura, Raymundo de Souza, 3.596
Moya, Ismael, 1.43, 1.226, 1.276
Mukai, Shutaro, 3.666
Muñoz, José Luis, 22.12, 22.13a
Muñoz y Maines, Manuel, 21.45
Muñoz y Pérez, M., 21.48
Murat, Luiz Barreto, 3.153
Murciano, A., 6.52
Murilo, Sérgio, 3.647
Musset, Alfred de, 1.16c, 1.16d, 1.16e, 3.405a, 3.405b, 21.12a, 21.15, 21.47, 21.51

Nadir Papi Saboya, 3.67
Nalé Roxlo, Conrado, 1.5, 1.254, 1.288, 1.291, 1.293, 1.295
Nandino, Elías, 15.27b
Nascimento, Faustino, 3.383
Nasser, David, 3.1473m
Native Indian texts, 3.1442c
Navas, Juan de, 1.117
Nebel, Fernando, 21.28
Negri, Ada, 3.1381
Nejar, Carlos, 3.659b
Nelligan, Émile, 12.8
Neruda, Pablo, 1.323, 3.1423, 19.4g, 19.5a, 19.5b, 19.5c
Nervo, Amado, 1.146, 1.185c, 1.185d, 1.186a, 1.186b, 1.220, 1.249a, 1.249b, 1.467, 1.520b
Neto, João Cabral de Melo, 3.1546c, 3.1546d
Neto, Manuel Vargas, 3.286a
Neto, Maria Franquini, 3.257
Netto, Coelho, 3.960
Netto, Silveira, 3.1157
Neves, César das, 3.1094
Neves, Gastão, 3.1544
Neves, Ilza das, 3.778, 3.786
Nobre, Graciema, 3.401
Nóbrega, Nísia, 3.468, 3.497
Noguera, María Leal de, 6.74
Novillo Quiroga, Diego, 1.65d
Novo, Salvador, 15.18b, 15.76
Nunes, Cassiano, 3.1164, 3.1194a, 3.1194b, 3.1194c, 3.1194d, 3.1324a, 3.1324b

Obligado, Jorge, 1.169
Obligado, Pedro Miguel, 1.259, 1.418
Obligado, Rafael, 1.12, 1.406, 1.436, 1.439
Ocampo, Armand, 1.26c, 1.26d, 1.26e, 1.26k, 1.26p, 1.26s, 1.30
Ocampo, Silvina, 1.154, 1.274
Oliva, Menezes d, 3.1150
Oliveira, Alberto de, 3.258, 3.406
Oliveira, Antônio Corrêa de, 3.327
Oliveira, Antonio Maria C. de, 3.1464f
Oliveira, Armando de, 3.505
Oliveira, Dylma Cunha de, 3.359, 3.363, 3.364, 3.367, 3.371, 3.374, 3.627
Oliveira, Jandyra Sounis Carvalho de, 3.234, 3.248
Oliveira, Sylvio Cavalcanti de, 3.474a, 3.474b
Olivera, Rubén F. de, 1.120
Oribe, Emilio, 5.38
Oro, Eugenia de, 1.181
Ortega Arredondo, Enrique, 5.2

INDEX OF POETS AND TEXT SOURCES

Ortiz, Carlos, 1.17c
Ortíz, Carlos, 1.17a, 1.17b
Ortiz, David, 20.30a, 20.30b, 20.30c
Ortiz, Juan L., 1.397c
Ortiz Grognet, Emilio, 1.398, 1.400c
Ortiz S., Guillermo, 6.14
Otaviano, Francisco, 3.697
Otávio, Luiz, 3.303a, 3.1151, 3.1219, 3.1236, 3.1243, 3.1245
Otero Silva, Miguel, 7.17g
Ottoni, José Eloy, 3.1352

Pacheco, Felix, 3.755
Pahissa, Jaime, 1.415a, 1.415b, 1.415c, 1.415d, 1.415f
Paiva, Horácio, 3.358
Paixão Cearense, Catulo da, 3.428, 3.898, 3.1443i, 3.1443j
Palacios, Pedro B., 1.71
Palestrina, Giovanni P., 3.1388
Pallottini, Renata, 3.478a, 3.478b, 3.508, 3.512
Palmieri, Silvio, 5.31
Panamanian folk song, 11.15
Paraense, Dulcinea, 3.61, 3.63, 3.72
Paranapiacaba, Barão de, 3.1347
Pardo Tovar, Andrés, 5.27
Parecis song, 3.1239h
Pascoli, G., 3.762a
Passos, Soares de, 3.1112b
Pastina, Carlos, 3.524k
Pastor, Ángeles, 20.18a
Pastori, Luis, 22.17
Pati, Francisco, 3.436, 3.464
Paz, Octavio, 15.46a, 15.46b, 15.47
Paz Castillo, Fernando, 22.10b, 22.15a
Pederneiras, Raul, 3.1276, 3.1440
Pedra Branca, Visconde de, 3.963
Pedroni, José, 1.330, 1.397b
Pedro Ramos, Juan, 1.396
Peixoto, Helio, 3.178a, 3.183
Peixoto, J. Benedito Silveira, 3.643, 3.709
Peixoto, Luiz, 3.429d, 3.430, 3.1273, 3.1277, 3.1278b, 3.1280, 3.1281, 3.1285, 3.1293, 3.1295, 3.1296, 3.1304, 3.1312, 3.1314, 3.1316c, 3.1320a, 3.1320b, 3.1321
Pellicer, Carlos, 15.17a, 15.17b, 15.17c, 15.18a
Pemán, José María, 21.54
Peña, Jacobo, 1.202, 1.215, 1.217
Penalva, Gastão, 3.1287, 3.1316b
Pennafort Caldas, Onestaldo de, 3.200, 3.915, 3.932, 3.1087
Pereira, Regina Chagas, 3.1392, 3.1397

Pérez, Alberto, 4.8b
Pérez, Amaury, 7.56
Pérez Priego, Rosalba, 15.41a, 15.41b
Perrey, A., 1.138
Pessoa, Fernando, 3.571a, 3.659a, 3.659e, 3.659g, 3.659i, 3.804, 3.1106d, 3.1545, 3.1548a, 3.1549d
Pessoa, Frota, 3.964
Petri, A. C., 1.483
Peyro, Mercedes y Avelina, 1.542
Piá, Manduca (pen name of Manuel Bandeira), 3.42, 3.44, 3.206a, 3.215, 3.328, 3.447, 3.473, 3.489, 3.507, 3.527, 3.570, 3.668, 3.685, 3.686, 3.687, 3.700, 3.705, 3.715, 3.720, 3.723, 3.724, 3.792, 3.793, 3.798, 3.802, 3.811, 3.854, 3.873, 3.879, 3.884, 3.903, 3.906, 3.919a, 3.919b, 3.919c, 3.919d, 3.920a, 3.920b, 3.920c, 3.1027b, 3.1027c, 3.1084, 3.1085, 3.1086, 3.1092, 3.1093, 3.1097, 3.1101, 3.1114, 3.1126, 3.1129a, 3.1129b, 3.1129c, 3.1201, 3.1216, 3.1217, 3.1218, 3.1220, 3.1225, 3.1229, 3.1230, 3.1235, 3.1238, 3.1240, 3.1257, 3.1262, 3.1337, 3.1386, 3.1387, 3.1434b, 3.1441, 3.1473b, 3.1473e, 3.1548b, 3.1548c
Piazza, Henri, 3.952, 3.980, 3.983, 3.984
Picchia, Menotti del, 3.203, 3.226, 3.249, 3.346, 3.439, 3.477a, 3.477b, 3.477c, 3.660, 3.1047, 3.1099h
Pieroni, Tilde Pérez, 1.381
Pimenta, Altino, 3.1133, 3.1135, 3.1136, 3.1138, 3.1140, 3.1142, 3.1145
Piñero, Blanca, 1.189
Pinto, Alda Pereira, 3.650a, 3.650b, 3.650c
Pinto, E. Roquete, 3.1260, 3.1266, 3.1443a, 3.1443b, 3.1476b
Pinto, Nilo Aparecido, 3.1099x
Pita, Juana Rosa, 10.1a, 10.1b, 10.1c
Ponchon, Raoul, 1.23b
Ponferrada, Juan Oscar, 1.166, 1.167, 1.168, 1.170, 1.244a, 1.244b, 1.244c, 1.244d
popular poetry, 1.65e, 1.380, 1.497c, 1.497d, 3.80, 3.166, 3.407, 3.409, 3.414a, 3.417, 3.420, 3.422, 3.441, 3.443, 3.485, 3.569, 3.605, 3.619, 3.933, 3.1059, 3.1076, 3.1094, 3.1099c, 3.1099j, 3.1099s, 3.1099t, 3.1100, 3.1112a, 3.1112e, 3.1112f, 3.1112g, 3.1112h, 3.1112i, 3.1112j, 3.11121, 3.1112m, 3.1112n, 3.1112o, 3.1239e, 3.1278a, 3.1323a, 3.1323b, 3.1325b, 3.1390, 3.1391, 3.1394, 3.1443h, 3.1465f, 3.1466b, 3.1466d, 3.1466e, 7.46, 15.61. *See also* folklore, traditional poetry
popular song, 3.566

INDEX OF POETS AND TEXT SOURCES

Porto, Pe. Humberto, 3.1420
Portuguese folklore, 3.909, 3.918, 3.1477
Posada, Leonor, 3.1040
Possolo, Elora, 3.657
Pozo, Andrés del, 1.470, 1.478
Prado, Carmen C. de, 6.75
Prado Quesada, Alcides, 6.76
Prados, Emilio, 15.4a
Prieto, Carlos Bousoña, 15.65e, 15.67a
Prieto, María Teresa, 15.65d, 15.66a, 15.66d
Prudhomme, Sully, 1.26q
Puerto Rican poetry, 20.29
Puget, Claude Andre, 7.17a

Quechuan poetry, 19.16a, 19.16b, 19.16c, 19.16d
Queiroz, Wenceslau de, 3.107
Quental, Antero de, 3.392b, 3.400b, 3.1349, 3.1351, 3.1355, 3.1367, 3.1368, 3.1432
Quesada, Luis Alberto, 1.100a, 1.100b, 1.100c
Quesada, Napoleón, 6.73
Quevedo y Villegas, Francisco de, 1.98a, 1.98b, 1.98c, 1.98d, 1.314a, 1.314b, 1.314c, 1.314d
Quintana, Mário, 3.20c, 3.292, 3.658, 3.659c, 3.791, 3.910

Rabello, Arnaldo, 3.1149
Rabelo, Laurindo, 3.1099r, 3.1105b
Radaelli, Raimundo, 21.19
Raffo, Hortensia Margarita, 1.200a, 1.200b, 1.200c
Ramírez Saizar, José, 6.100
Ramos, João de Deus, 3.949
Ramos, Silva, 3.411
Rangel, Severino, 3.1443k
Réboli, Ida, 1.373, 1.383, 1.428a, 1.428b, 1.428c
Recalde, Facunde, 3.1424
Rega Molina, Mary, 1.112, 1.246c, 1.246d, 1.246e, 1.246f, 1.249c, 1.249d, 1.249e, 1.249f
Rego, Índia, 3.1050
Rego Júnior, Costa, 3.1444
Regules, Elías, 21.36
Reis, Marcos Konder, 3.1019
Rejano, Juan, 15.2a, 15.2b
Renard, Jules, 1.23c
Renart, Albert, 3.1227
Renault, Abgar, 3.1473n
Requeni, Antonio, 1.525a, 1.525b, 1.525c, 1.525d, 1.556a, 1.556b
Reynal, Beatriz, 3.182, 3.185, 3.908, 3.913, 3.928, 3.939
Rezende, Aracy Rivera de, 3.641
Rezende, Maria José A., 3.831

Rezzónico Berruet, Jorge, 1.402
Ribaux, A., 1.26h
Ribeiro, Alberto, 3.426
Ribeiro, Iveta, 3.632, 3.637, 3.645, 3.646, 3.648, 3.652
Ribeiro, Thomaz, 3.90
Ribeiro Neto, Oliveira, 3.1030, 3.1036, 3.1042
Ricardo, Cassiano, 3.184, 3.253, 3.348, 3.524g, 3.701, 3.714, 3.730, 3.736, 3.743, 3.788, 3.790, 3.1206
Ricardo Furlán, Luis, 1.307
Richepin, Jean, 1.4f, 1.385c
Richepin, Tristan, 21.22
Rilke, Rainer Marie, 3.574g
Río, Alfonso del, 15.25a, 15.27a
Ripoll, Lila, 3.574i, 3.1176
Riu, Francisco A., 1.64a
Rivas Jordán, María T. C. de, 1.137
Rivera, José Eustasio, 5.42
Rivera, Pedro, 22.10c, 22.15g
Riveros Tejada, Guillermo, 2.9a, 2.9b
Rocha, Glauber, 3.1016
Rocha Peres, Fernando da, 3.1540c
Rodrigues, Mário Queiroz, 3.179, 3.180
Rojas, Fernando, 4.37
Rojas, Ricardo, 1.286, 22.18a, 22.18b, 22.18c
Rojas Díaz, Fabio, 6.106
Roldán, Belisario, 1.130, 1.216, 1.546
Romanelli, Humberto, 1.489, 1.523
Romero, Sílvio, 3.1210, 3.1215, 3.1325a, 3.1333, 3.1341, 3.1464b
Rondano, Miguel Ángel, 1.461a, 1.461b, 1.461c
Ronsard, Pierre de, 3.816
Roque, Ant., 1.28
Rosario Cipriota, María, 1.273
Rugeles, Manuel Felipe, 7.17f, 22.8a, 22.8b, 22.8c, 22.8d, 22.9a, 22.15d
Rússio, Waldisa (Waldisa Rússio Camargo Guarnieri), 3.451, 3.493

Sá, Carlos, 3.1451a, 3.1451b
Sabella, Andrés, 4.7, 4.15, 4.16
Sabogal, María Weisse de, 19.13b
Sá Brit, Glauco de, 3.134
sacred texts, 3.66, 3.961, 3.981, 3.1430, 3.1431, 4.31, 6.43, 6.71. *See also* Catholic traditional texts
Sáenz, Carlos Luis, 6.82, 15.38
Sáenz, Hilario, 1.209
Salas Perez, J. J., 6.55c, 6.90, 6.94
Salazar, Rodolfo, 6.87
Saldaña, Jorge, 15.36d

Salema, Sylvio, 3.1465g
Sales, Enriqueta, 1.188a
Salinas, Pedro, 5.28
Salles, Antonio, 3.88
Salles, Antônio, 3.974, 3.989
Salusse, Julio, 3.331
Samain, Albert, 3.1457e
Sanches, D. Afonso, 3.1403, 3.1413
Sanches, Nosor, 3.79
Sansón Argüello, Mariana, 10.8
Santa Cruz, Domingo, 4.33, 4.34
Sant'Anna, Affonso Romano de, 3.1512
Santiago, Oswaldo, 3.267
Santillana, Marqués de, 1.358
Santoro, Gisele, 3.1185
Santos, Dioscoredes dos, 3.236
Santos, Hemetério dos, 3.161
Santos, Júlia, 3.1546a, 3.1546b
Saroyan, William, 7.17b
Scavone, G., 3.113
Schmaltz, Iêda, 3.484
Serpa e Paiva, Isabel Vieira de, 3.302c, 3.303c, 3.368
Serrano, Jonatas, 3.211
Serrano Redonnet, Ana, 1.261
Servetti Reeves, Y. C., 1.228
Shakespeare, William, 3.40c, 3.40e, 3.573a, 3.684a, 3.684b, 3.684c, 6.83a, 6.83b, 6.83c
Silva, Francisco, 1.309, 1.310, 1.326, 1.334, 1.338, 1.345
Silva, José Asunción, 5.20, 5.23, 5.39, 15.9
Silva, Júlio César da, 3.111, 3.112
Silva, Pereira da, 3.1158
Silva Guimarães, Ernesto da, 3.1099cc
Silva Mendes Leal, José da, 3.1112c
Silva Munster, Francisca Júlia da, 3.111, 3.112
Silva Ramos, Péricles Eugênio da, 3.522a, 3.522b, 3.522c
Silva Telles, Godofredo da, 3.1445a, 3.1445b
Silva Valdés, Fernán, 1.39, 1.73, 1.171c, 1.253, 1.270, 1.272a, 1.272b, 1.369a, 1.528, 1.537, 21.1, 21.5, 21.9a, 21.9b, 21.9c, 21.29, 21.30, 21.42
Silveira, Tasso da, 3.320, 3.488
Silveira Peixoto, J. B., 3.709
Silvestre, Armand, 1.26j, 1.430
Siqueira, Antônio, 3.656
Siqueira, Nóbrega de, 3.635, 3.638
Sobral, José Figueiredo de, Jr., 3.450, 3.456
Sobrinho, Antonio Lemos, 3.756
Solarte, Tristan, 1.444a
Sóldon, Renato, 3.429c

Soriano Aderaldo, Mozart, 3.64
Soriano Badani, Armando, 2.10
Sosa, Roberto, 13.2
Sotela, Rogelio, 6.55b, 6.102
Soto Monge, Carlos, 6.98
Souza, Auta de, 3.389
Souza, Gustavo J. de, 3.1137
Souza, Oswaldo de, 3.1251a
Souza Moura, Raymundo de, 3.596
Spanish poetry, 3.930a, 4.23a, 4.23b, 4.23c, 4.29b, 4.29c, 4.29d, 4.29e, 6.103
Stagnaro, Santiago, 1.519
Stecchetti, Lorenzo (Olindo Guerrini), 1.127, 1.134, 3.1370, 3.1380, 3.1383, 3.1458, 5.6
Sterbenburg, Mathilde Gräfin, 1.191b
Storni, Alfonsina, 1.263
Sully-Prudhomme, René-François, 3.1360, 21.49
Supervielle, Jules, 1.23e, 1.23f, 1.23g
Sussel-Marie, Ofelia, 1.555a, 1.555d
Sybika (Sylvia Autuori), 3.858, 3.868, 3.871, 3.877
Sylvain, Georges, 12.18

Tablada, José Juan, 15.50, 15.78
Tagore, Rabindranath, 1.125, 1.126, 1.135, 1.421a, 1.421b, 1.421c, 1.424a, 1.424b, 1.424c, 3.958, 3.976, 7.19f, 7.21, 7.51, 22.10f, 22.14, 22.15h
Tasso, P. de, 3.1449
Tavares, Aldemar, 3.197c, 3.197d, 3.298, 3.299, 3.300, 3.335a, 3.483a, 3.483b, 3.670, 3.731a, 3.731b, 3.731c, 3.731d, 3.1028a, 3.1028b, 3.1028c, 3.1083, 3.1290, 3.1302
Tavernard, Antônio, 3.598b, 3.598d, 3.615
Teixeira, Múcio Scévola Lopes, 3.391a, 3.962
Teixeira, Orlando, 3.994
Teixeira, Rolando, 3.1012
Teixeira Gomes, J. C., 3.1540e
Teófilo, Aníbal, 3.1427
Thurman, John, 18.1a, 18.1b, 18.1c
Tiempo, César, 1.224d
Tigre, Bastos, 3.760, 3.1099ff, 3.1105e
Tigre, Manuel Bastos, 3.432
Tomé, Jesús, 20.7
Torre, Antonio de la, 1.268a, 1.268b, 1.268c
Torres, Henry, 12.31
Torres Botet, J., 1.122a, 1.122b, 1.122c, 1.122d
Tostes, T., 3.282
Tourinho, Eduardo, 3.343
traditional poetry, 1.245a, 1.245b, 1.251a, 1.251b, 1.251d, 1.258, 1.271, 1.278, 1.377, 1.440, 1.493b, 1.496, 1.524, 3.1442b, 4.1, 7.34a, 19.15a, 19.15b, 20.3, 20.4. *See also* folklore, popular poetry

INDEX OF POETS AND TEXT SOURCES

Trakl, Georg, 4.36, 4.40
Travassos, Renato, 3.429g
Travieso, Scarzolo, 21.16
Trelles, José A., 21.35, 21.43
Trespalacios, J. M., 5.54
Trevisan, Armindo, 3.659h
Tricânico, Marina, 3.721, 3.733, 3.1119
Trussardi, Neyde Bonfiglioli, 3.779, 3.780, 3.783, 3.784
Tubert, Mauricio, 3.1361
Tufic, Jorge, 3.1178

Ugarte, Manuel, 1.279, 1.547, 1.548
Uhland, Ludwig, 1.185a, 1.190a, 1.190b, 1.190c, 1.190d, 1.190f, 1.191a
Unamuno, Miguel de, 1.459
Urbina, Luis G., 21.44
Uribe, Ingrid, 5.17

Valdivielso, Josef de, 4.29a
Valencia, Guillermo, 5.37
Valeri, Lluis, 3.366, 3.377
Valéry, Paul, 1.23h, 1.23i, 3.40d, 3.40f
Valladares, Leda, 1.285
Valle, Gerson, 3.49
Valle-Inclán, Ramón del, 22.15f
Vallejo, César, 4.8c
Varela, Fagundes, 3.713, 3.1353
Varela, Lorenzo, 1.313
Varella, Fagundes, 3.155
Vargas, León, 6.61
Vargas, Manuel do Nascimento, 3.574h
Vasconcelos, Dora, 3.1453, 3.1456, 3.1471, 3.1475
Vasconcelos, José Mauro de, 3.546, 3.550
Vaz, Nelson, 3.876
Vázquez Cey, Arturo, 1.68, 1.74, 1.222, 1.302a, 1.302j
Vega, Garcilaso de la, 1.145a, 1.145b, 1.145c
Véga, José Luis, 20.28
Vega, Lope de, 1.60a, 1.60b, 1.60c, 15.40a
Vela, Rubén A., 1.498
Velasco, Ricardo, 1.65b
Venezuelan folk song, 11.34
Verlaine, Paul, 1.4g, 1.16a, 1.16b, 1.432, 3.1103, 12.17b, 12.17e, 21.13, 22.10g
Viana, Sodré, 3.1286, 3.1465c
Vibert, Andrée, 1.114
Vicens, Nimia, 20.11, 20.14a
Vicente, Gil, 3.1465a, 7.41
Vicente Garcia, Alberto, 3.863, 3.883

Victorino, Virgínia, 3.392e, 3.1110a, 3.1110b, 3.1131c
Vidigal, Geraldo, 3.238
Vidigal, Manuel José, 3.1112d
Vieira, Adelina A. Lopes, 3.950
Vieira, Gastão, 3.610
Vieira, José Augusto Leonel, 3.45a, 3.45c
Vieira, Sonia Maria, 3.529, 3.538, 3.540, 3.551, 3.560, 3.561, 3.568
Vighi, Francisco, 1.142
Vigil, Constancio C., 1.75
Vignale, Pedro Juan, 1.509
Vigny, Alfred de, 3.391c
Vila, Raúl, 1.417, 1.419, 1.420, 1.425, 1.429, 1.463, 1.464
Vilar, Virgínia Nuno, 3.372, 3.375
Villaespesa, Francisco, 1.422
Villafañe, Carlos, 5.33, 5.60
Villafañe, Javier, 1.99
Villalobos, Héctor Guillermo, 22.7
Villa-Lobos, Heitor (Epaminondas Villalba Filho), 3.1466a, 3.1472
Villani-Côrtes, Edmundo, 3.1485, 3.1490, 3.1504, 3.1506, 3.1507, 3.1509, 3.1510, 3.1513, 3.1515a, 3.1518, 3.1521, 3.1524, 3.1528, 3.1530, 3.1531, 3.1534, 3.1537, 3.1539
Villar, Amado, 1.225, 1.501a, 1.501b
Villaroel, José Javier, 15.29a, 15.29b, 15.29c, 15.29d, 15.29e
Villaurrutia, Xavier, 15.7b, 15.18c
Vincenzi, Moises, 6.104
Viotti, Heráclito, 3.470
Viotti, Lavínia Abranches, 3.461, 3.471
Virgilio, 3.40a
Vivien, Renée, 12.12a
Vizcarrondo, Carmelina, 20.14c
Vocos Lescano, Jorge, 1.386a, 1.386b, 1.386c, 1.386d
Vodou tradition, 12.15c, 12.30a, 12.30b, 12.30c
Vogel, H., 4.18

Wamosy, Alceu, 3.280, 3.574b
Wang Wei, 15.49
Weil, Pierre, 3.531a, 3.531b, 3.531c, 3.536b, 3.536c
Welker, Juan C., 21.41
Wilder, V., 12.17a
Williams, Alberto, 1.557, 1.558, 1.559, 1.560, 1.561, 1.562a
Wright, Robert, 3.1462

INDEX OF POETS AND TEXT SOURCES

Xammar, Luis Fabio, 19.10a, 19.10b
Xavier, Fontoura, 3.954

Yupanqui, Atahualpa, 1.302i, 1.304

Zakythinos, Alexis, 3.1192
Zanné, Gerori, 1.93

Zanné, Jeronimo, 1.85, 1.86, 1.90
Zapata, Rosaura, 15.53a
Zapata Lillo, F., 5.29
Zeledón Brenes, José María, 6.55a
Zerpa, Domingo, 1.305, 1.497b
Zúñiga Zeledón, José Daniel, 6.92, 6.93, 6.97, 6.99

Index of Song and Song Cycle Titles

Catalog numbers in brackets are followed by page numbers. Titles of song cycles are shown in italics.

A água também morre [3.208g], 70
A água também nasce pequenina [3.208a], 70
A água também sofre [3.208f], 70
A água também tem a sua infância [3.208b], 70
A água também tem adolescência [3.208c], 70
A água também tem maturidade [3.208d], 70
A água também tem sua velhice [3.208e], 70
A bailarina, op. 134, no. 5 [3.1398], 115
A balada das folhas [3.197e], 70
A bela e a fera [3.1133], 105
A bella [3.1346], 113
A Berenice, op. 13 [3.1347], 113
A Black Pierrot [14.1d], 176
A boneca de cristal [3.850], 93
A bonequinha de seda (Canção das mães pretas) [3.851], 93
A canção da vida [3.429a], 78
A canção de Romeu [3.748], 90
A canção que passa [3.49], 65
A cantiga da mutuca [3.516a], 81
A casa do coração [3.1348], 113
A casinha pequenina [3.407], 77
A casinha pequenina [3.420], 78
A casinha pequenina [3.809], 92
A casinha pequenina [11.7], 163
A cavalgada [3.189], 69
A cegonha [3.1427], 116
A Clymène [1.432h], 39
A colina [3.1192a], 107
A criança [3.1548a], 123
A culpa de perder o teu afeto [3.436], 79
À Dália (Dança de roda) [3.1112a], 104
A dança do sapo [3.1239g], 109
A Dolorida [3.853], 93

A estas aúreas arenas llegáos... [6.83a], 145
A estrela [3.42c], 65
A estrela [3.215e], 71
A estrela [3.854], 93
A Estrela [3.1201], 108
A Estrela [3.1257], 110
A fada negra, op. 77 [3.1349], 113
A Federico [3.1258], 110
A festa [3.826], 92
A fin de que los vientos... [5.30], 137
A flor e o lago [3.1106e], 103
A folhinha de pimenta [3.855], 93
A frauta de bamboo [3.749], 90
A gatinha parda [3.1465d], 119
À glória de São Paulo [3.439], 79
A Grinalda, op. 31, no. 1 [3.946], 96
A hora cinzenta [3.190], 69
A hora cinzenta [3.830a], 93
A Iara e o boto [3.22], 64
A imagem e a realidade [3.1548c], 123
A Irene García [4.25e], 130
A jangada [3.948], 96
A la luna (Canción de cuna) [1.463], 44
A la luna feliz [15.4d], 179
A la marimba guanacasteca (Danza) [6.75], 144
A la nana blanca que se fue a la mar [15.2a], 179
A la orilla del palmar [11.9], 163
A la santé [1.23a], 7
A las montañas iré [11.10], 163
A legba [12.25a], 171
A lenda [3.191], 69
A l'hè qui lé [12.19], 170
A l'ombre de tes ailes [12.41], 172
A luz desse olhar tristonho [3.731a], 90

INDEX OF SONG AND SONG CYCLE TITLES

A luz desse seu olhar tristonho [3.483a], 80
À *Madame la Princesse Marie Lubomirska* [21.11], 204
À Mademoiselle Rita Wouters [21.12], 204
A mais dolorosa das histórias [3.1171e], 107
A mamita [1.543i], 50
A manhã [3.34a], 64
À Marília [3.132], 68
A menina boba: Quatro canções para canto e piano/ Dos canciones para canto y piano, extraidas de los poemas de Oneyda Albarenga, A menina boba [3.1160], 106
A menina exausta I [3.1160a], 106
A menina exausta II [3.1160b], 106
A menina exausta III [3.1160c], 106
A menina exausta, no. XII [3.1160e], 106
A menina quer saber..., [3.1318b], 112
A mi puerta has de golpear [1.245a], 22
A minha voz é nobre [3.47a], 65
A moça e o Trem [3.1546c], 123
A morte da boneca [3.305], 74
¡A navegar! [20.14b], 200
À noite [3.34b], 64
À noite, quando me deito [3.692a], 89
A onda [3.792b], 91
A palavra de Deus [3.621], 86
A partida [3.411], 77
A partida [3.1112b], 104
A Patay huele la luna [1.107b], 13
A pedra [3.306], 74
A primavera [3.334b], 75
A primeira desilusão [3.50], 65
A realidade e a imagem [3.792a], 91
A rendeira [3.1272], 110
A rendeira [3.1316a], 112
A rendeira [3.1317c], 112
A resposta que ele me deu [3.403d], 77
A Rosa [3.1259], 110
A Saint Blaise a la Zuecca [1.16d], 5
A saloia (Canção) [3.1112c], 104
A saudade [3.1480], 120
A saudade dos provincianos [3.810], 92
A saudade, op. 11 [3.318], 75
A semente é a dor amor, Roque Martins [3.622], 86
A sereia do mar [3.1030], 100
A solidão e sua porta [3.530], 82
A sombra [3.857], 93
A sombra no rio [3.209b], 71
A sombra suave [3.320], 75
À sombra verde dos coqueiros [3.176], 69

A tarde [3.660], 87
A te (Romanza) [5.31], 137
A tecelã [3.828], 92
A tí [1.563], 53
A tí [5.20], 136
A ti única [1.174], 17
A toada da chuva [3.206c], 70
A todas las albas [1.192], 18
A torre morta do ocaso, op. 21, no. 5 [3.192], 69
A tu puerta están cantando [3.930a], 96
A um coração [3.76], 66
A um passarinho [3.674], 88
A um passarinho [3.1261], 110
A um passarinho [3.1548d], 123
A um poeta (no. 5) [3.650c], 87
A uma mulher [3.1162], 106
A un amigo [2.11a], 58
A un árbol (Canción pampeana) [1.307], 29
A una coqueta [1.202], 19
A una dama [5.57], 138
À une étoile [21.11a], 204
A unos ojos [6.78], 145
A valsa [3.676], 88
A veces [5.58], 138
A veces un no niega [5.28], 137
A velha carta [3.273], 73
A velha história (Modinha) [3.322], 75
A vendedora de violetas [3.861], 93
A viagem [3.777], 91
A vida [3.274], 73
A vida [3.334a], 75
A vida [3.412], 77
A vida dessas meninas, op. 19 [3.750], 90
A viola [3.1464b], 119
A viola e a prima [3.566a], 83
A virgem [3.1432], 116
A virgem santíssima [3.1355], 114
¡A volar! [1.346b], 32
A voz do mar [3.197b], 70
A voz do mar [3.362], 76
A voz do povo, Grito de guerra [3.1433], 116
A voz do sino [3.107], 67
A xusticia pol-a-man (La justicia por su mano) [1.58a], 10
Abaixai, ó limoeiro [3.567a], 84
Aba-lógum [3.617b], 86
Abaluaiê [3.575], 84
Abandono [1.534], 49
Abandono [3.301], 74
Abandono [3.1107a], 103
ABC de lampião [3.576], 84

INDEX OF SONG AND SONG CYCLE TITLES

Abel [1.435], 40
Abendgang [1.191b], 18
Abismo de sed (Zamba) [1.302g], 28
Aboio [3.163b], 68
Aboio [3.216b], 71
Abril [3.1473i], 120
Abril [15.3b], 179
Abrojo Pampa (Milonga) [1.101], 13
Abuelita [1.11d], 5
Acalanto [3.21], 64
Acalanto [3.59], 66
Acalanto [3.127], 67
Acalanto [3.222], 71
Acalanto [3.282], 73
Acalanto [3.302a], 74
Acalanto [3.354], 75
Acalanto [3.577], 84
Acalanto [3.1216], 108
Acalanto [3.1282a], 111
Acalanto da rosa [3.1170b], 106
Acalanto do amor feliz [3.524a], 82
Acalanto II [3.48], 65
Acalanto para Luísa [3.435], 78
Acalanto para minha mãe [3.671], 88
Aceitei tua amizade [3.510h], 81
Acerico [1.330c], 31
Achado [3.852], 93
Achalay [1.62], 10
Acorda donzela [3.408], 77
Acre-Nocturno [3.1200], 108
Acrostik [3.355], 75
Acuti-paru [3.437], 79
Ad una rondinella [3.1062], 101
Adelina de paseo [1.24b], 7
Adelita [11.8], 163
Adeus [3.356], 76
Adeus [3.578], 84
Adeus (Fragmento de um episódio lírico) [3.75], 66
Adeus Ema (Desafio) [3.1443g], 117
Adieu foulards [12.15a], 170
Adiós [1.287], 27
Adiós (Romanza para soprano o tenor) [21.45], 205
Adiós, op. 20, no. 1 (Canción triste para canto y piano) [21.20], 204
Adiós, quebrachito blanco [1.304], 29
Adios de deo clausurar... [10.3d], 160
Adiós te digo (Vidala indígena) [1.64c], 11
Adivinhação [3.174], 69
Admonición a los impertinentes [5.56], 138
Adolescência [3.830b], 93

Adonenu, elohenu [7.39b], 152
Adoração [3.438], 79
Adoração, op. 148, no. 19 [3.1099s], 102
Adúltera, enemiga: ciclo de ocho canciones de Juan Ruíz de Alarcón [15.74], 185
Aflição, op. 148, no. 26 [3.1099z], 103
Agnus Dei [7.52], 153
Agonia [3.265], 72
Agora [3.474a], 80
Agoué Ta Royo [12.25c], 171
Agua de fuente [1.205a], 19
Agua del cielo [1.462], 44
Água que passa [3.223], 71
Águas paradas [3.1029], 100
Agué Ta Royo [12.30a], 172
Aguinaldos populares venezolanos para la Noche Buena [22.19], 212
Agüita clara [1.508], 48
¡Ah, gocemos...! [15.79f], 186
Ah, quién tuviera una nube [22.17h], 211
¡Ah llenad las copas! [15.79h], 186
Ah! Ma bien aimée [3.890a], 94
Ah! tienes my corazón [7.38d], 152
Ah vastedad de pinos [3.1423c], 116
Ahora sé [1.21b], 6
Ai, momentos de físico amor [3.513a], 81
Ai, que coração [3.409], 77
Ai Deus, eu é! op. 54 [3.1399], 115
Ai que riso me dá [3.1094], 102
Ai-je fait un rêve? [5.41], 137
Aime-moi [3.947], 96
Aime-moi!... [1.26a], 8
Ainda que o fogo apague [3.567b], 84
Al alba venid buen amigo... [4.23a], 130
Al banco solitario [1.505], 47
Al llegar [1.561c], 52
Al maestro que se fué [1.11c], 4
Al pampero (Décima) [1.10], 4
¡Al puente de la golondrina! [1.346f], 32
¡Al puente de la golondrina! [4.30i], 131
Al teléfono 345... (Berceuse para uma pequena espanhola) [3.291], 73
Al través de mi ventana [1.560h], 52
Al trote [1.530a], 49
Alabanzas a la Virgen, op. 49 [4.29], 131
Alajueleña (Punto popular) [6.61], 144
Álamo serrano [1.173], 17
Alanguissement [3.410], 77
Alba [1.436], 40
Alba [4.28f], 131
Alba con luna [1.252], 24
Alborada [1.464], 44

INDEX OF SONG AND SONG CYCLE TITLES

Alborado [4.29d], 131
Alegráos pastores [1.60a], 10
Alegria, alegria (Carimbó) [3.579], 84
Alegría de la soledad [1.327c], 30
Aleluia [3.1110a], 104
Aleluya (Romanza para tenor) [21.44], 205
Alférez [1.335e], 31
Algarrobo [1.19a], 6
Algo [3.1122a], 104
Alguém bateu à minha porta [3.672], 88
Allá vienen las carretas [1.437b], 40
Allegro, op. 84 [3.1095], 102
Alma adorada [3.856], 93
Alma ausente [3.1018a], 99
Alma da natureza [3.1479], 120
Alma mía (Estilo) [1.118], 14
Alma minha gentil [3.259], 72
Alma minha gentil, op. 107 [3.1350], 114
Alma perdida [3.1171c], 107
Almas desoladoramente frias [3.533a], 83
Alta está mi ventana sobre el mundo [1.224d], 20
Alta noche [10.4b], 160
Alto da bronze [3.11], 63
Alucinação [3.620], 86
Alvorada do sertão [3.428], 78
Amada, el aura dice ... [1.438c], 40
Âmago [3.295a], 74
Amalhaya ... [1.368b], 34
Amanecer [5.12], 136
Amanecer [19.13d], 196
Amanecer junto al mar [4.33b], 132
Amaneciendo [19.15b], 196
Amanhã [3.1542i], 122
Amanhã (first version) [3.1541k], 122
Amanhã (second version) [3.15411], 122
Amanhecer [3.119], 67
Amapola [5.5], 136
Amar [3.357], 76
Amar não é brinco [3.746c], 90
Amargura [3.673], 88
Amazônia III, op. 91 [3.1013], 99
Ameaça, op. 148, no. 13 [3.1099m], 102
Amemos [1.185d], 18
Amemos la vida (Vidalita) [1.543d], 50
Amendoim torradinho (Cenas cariocas) [3.1270], 110
América [6.51], 143
Amiga que te vas [15.70a], 185
Amo as interrogações [3.529], 82
Amor [1.288], 27
Amor [2.11c], 58
Amor [3.358], 76

Amor [3.925a], 95
Amor [15.81c], 187
Amor, Beatrix dos Reis Carvalho [3.429b], 78
Amor bendito (Dance) [20.24], 200
Amor em lágrimas [3.1195b], 108
Amor eterno [1.488c], 45
Amor mesquinho [3.440], 79
Amor que partiu [3.1161], 106
Amor que partiu [3.1170e], 107
Amor ti chiedi [6.52], 143
Amor vivo, op. 79 [3.1351], 114
Amor y perfidia [3.1428], 116
Amores cativos [1.77a], 11
Amo-te, op. 62 [3.1096], 102
Amo-te muito [3.441], 79
Amo-te muito, op. 12, no. 2 [3.949], 97
Amo-te sim [3.442], 79
Amour [12.29b], 172
Amparo, op. 13, no. 2 [3.1543b], 122
Amplitude [3.827], 92
Anachronic Songs [15.51], 183
Anália (Romance) [3.1352], 114
And Will He Not Come Again? [3.684a], 88
Anda jaleo [7.37a], 152
Andalucía [7.22], 151
Andando de noche sola [20.27a], 201
Ando triste [3.731c], 90
Andorinha [3.42a], 65
Andorinha [3.1217], 109
Anedota Búlgara [3.1549a], 123
Ángel ciego [22.17d], 211
Angústia [3.175], 69
Anhelo [1.305], 29
Anhelo ... [1.398], 37
Anhelos [1.557h], 52
Anjo da guarda [3.1473b], 119
Anochecer en el campo [21.53], 206
Anoitece, op. 34, no. 2 [3.950], 97
Anoitecer [3.1076], 101
Anoma cara [3.819a], 92
Añoranza con un adiós [1.289], 27
Añoranzas (L'Enyor) [1.415a], 38
Anos estelares [3.1], 63
Anseio (Erwartung) [3.387], 76
Ansiedad [1.388], 36
Anta [3.46a], 65
Ante el mar [4.33g], 132
Antianti é Tapejara [3.517a], 82
Antigüedad de cielo [1.290], 27
Antonino [1.249b], 23
Antropologia [3.28a], 64
Ao amanhecer, op. 34, no. 1 [3.951], 97

INDEX OF SONG AND SONG CYCLE TITLES

Ao crepúsculo [3.215h], 71
Ao luar [3.388], 76
Ao pé de um túmulo [3.389], 76
Ao sol [3.34c], 64
Aos sinos [3.1063], 101
Apegado a mí [1.343b], 31
Apras eólicas [1.561b], 52
Apresentação (Introduction) [3.1342], 113
Apunte [10.2b], 160
Aquel pajarito triste [1.460d], 44
Aquela China [3.286a], 73
Aquele amor [3.307], 74
Aquí, con un pedazo de pan . . . [15.79c], 186
Aquí está tu medio amante [1.460a], 44
Aquí me pongo a cantarte (Tonada) [21.1a], 203
Ar [3.12], 63
Aracy-Fox: Menina de cinema [3.1271], 110
Araponga errante [3.1541a], 122
Árbita [3.20b], 64
Árbol muerto [4.35a], 132
Arbolé Arbolé . . . (Andaluzas) [1.24h], 7
Aria (Cantilena) [3.1434a], 116
Aria triste [22.9b], 210
Aribu [3.443], 79
Ariettes oubliées [1.432g], 39
Arioso [1.27], 8
Aromito, flor de tusca . . . [1.324i], 30
Arrazoar [3.415a], 77
Arrependimento [3.534a], 83
Arrorró [1.271d], 26
Arrorró [1.562a], 53
Arrorró de la esposa [1.354], 33
Arroyito [1.543b], 50
Arroyito de nostalgia (Zamba) [1.465], 44
Arroyito serrano (Canción escolar) [1.306], 29
Arrunango (Canción de cuna indígena) [22.7], 210
Arrurrú, soneto lírico [5.42], 137
Arte [3.19c], 64
Aruanda [3.1248], 109
Aruanda op. 10 no. 2 [3.1089b], 101
Arullo [15.25a], 180
As almas, op. 148, no. 1 [3.1099a], 102
As duas flores [3.1541h], 122
As duas flores (Modinha) [3.1542a], 122
As duas rosas [3.359], 76
As estrelas, op. 21 [3.319], 75
As filhas de Maria [3.1429], 116
As flores amarelas dos ipês [3.444], 79
As letras [3.1353], 114
As neblinas [3.776], 91
As saudades do meu bem [3.1541m], 122
As saudades do meu bem [3.1542d], 122
As treis pinta (sic) [3.859], 93
As tuas mãos [3.321], 75
Às vezes, meu amor [3.510f], 81
Asa ferida, no. IV [3.1160d], 106
Asas! Oh, loucura dos vôos [3.927a], 96
Ascending from the abyss [7.8], 150
Asfixia [15.81b], 187
Así amo yo (Cueca) [11.11], 163
Así como todo muda [1.460f], 44
Así la paloma andaba [1.386c], 35
Asotô [12.15c], 170
Aspiração [3.1194a], 108
Assim falou o poeta [3.623], 86
Assombração [3.858], 93
Assovio [3.574a], 84
Atardecer (Zamba-Canción) [1.519], 48
Atardecer, op. 6 [21.37], 205
Atardecer en el parque [1.561g], 52
Até nas flores se nota [3.566c], 83
Atracción [1.560i], 52
Através do canal [3.28b], 64
Au jardin des rêves [3.952], 97
Auf eine Tänzerin [1.185a], 18
Auiê autiá [3.1260], 110
Aurora [1.458c], 43
Auroral [6.89], 146
Ausencia [1.442c], 41
Ausencia [2.10a], 57
Ausência [3.224], 71
Ausência [3.479a], 80
Ausência [3.675], 88
Ausencia [4.26c], 130
Ausencias [4.4], 129
Autopsicografia [3.1106d], 103
Ave! [3.1064], 101
Ave María [1.349], 32
Ave Maria [3.60], 66
Ave Maria [3.106], 67
Ave Maria [3.120], 67
Ave Maria [3.361], 76
Ave Maria [3.445], 79
Ave Maria [3.624], 86
Ave Maria [3.787], 91
Ave Maria [3.860], 93
Ave Maria [3.953], 97
Ave Maria [3.1065], 101
Ave Maria [3.1154], 106
Ave Maria [3.1385], 114
Ave Maria [3.1481], 120
Ave María [6.71], 144
Ave Maria [15.64], 184

294

INDEX OF SONG AND SONG CYCLE TITLES

Ave Maria (1a.), op. 5 [3.1354], 114
Ave Maria (19) [3.1431], 116
Ave Maria (Méditation) [12.38], 172
Ave Maria (no. 6) [3.1430], 116
Ave Maria (Prière) [12.39], 172
Avec l'âme [3.360], 76
Aveludados sonhos [3.323], 75
Aveu [3.405b], 77
¡Ay! [4.25b], 130
Ay, aljaba,flor de chilco . . . , 1970 [1.324k], 30
¡Ay, ay,ay!--Chilean folk song [11.12], 163
¡Ay, lunita! . . . [1.369b], 34
¡Ay, mi amor! [1.34b], 9
¡Ay, mi vida! [21.2], 203
Ay, que el alma [1.203], 19
Ay, que el alma [1.308], 29
Ay madre, nunca mal sentíu [1.57a], 10
¡Ay! ¡Mi amor! (Canción) [1.230], 21
¡Ay señora, mi vecina! [7.1], 150
Ayé me dijeron negro [7.45b], 153
Azúcar, malvones, menta . . . [1.225e], 20
Azucenita del campo (Zamba) [1.466], 44
Azul [1.79], 12
Azulão [3.811], 92
Azulão [3.1084], 101
Azulão [3.1273], 110
Azulão, op. 56 [3.1097], 102

Bachianas brasileiras, no. 5 [3.1434], 116
Bagaceñista [6.5], 141
Bagualita (Aire salteño) [1.497c], 46
Bahia [3.1274], 110
Baile [1.25c], 7
Baile imaginário [3.1482], 120
Bailecito [1.509], 48
Bailecito Navideño [1.80], 12
Bailia (Canção trovadoresca no. 1951 [3.1393d], 115
Bajacalifornianos, op. 28 and op.28a [15.29], 180
Bajo el parral [1.545a], 51
Bajo la luna, serenata [5.49], 138
Balada [1.164], 16
Balada [3.429c], 78
Balada, op. 10 [4.24a], 130
Balada a la Santísima Virgen [6.53], 143
Balada da confiante espera [3.1031], 100
Balada da flor da terra [3.1170d], 107
Balada de Don Amarillo [1.223a], 20
Balada de la animita [4.33d], 132
Balada de los mosquitos [1.223d], 20
Balada del amor que no se dijo [1.139], 15
Balada del jinete muerto [1.291], 27

Balada del lobo, la niña y el ángel [1.544], 51
Balada del tiempo mozo [11.1], 163
Balada do desesperado [3.667], 88
Balada do pingo d'água [3.761a], 91
Baladas dos 15 [3.1483], 120
Balada no. 1: Teus Olhos [3.625], 86
Balada no. 2: Raimundo de Brito [3.626], 86
Balada para os carreteiros [3.286b], 73
Balada que trajo un barco [1.223c], 20
Balada triste [3.574b], 84
Balada triste y equívoca de primavera [1.119], 14
Baladas amarillas (Cuatro poemas de García Lorca) [1.395], 36
Baladas argentinas [1.545], 51
Baladas del querer [1.368], 34
Balança eu [3.1244a], 109
Ballada [3.77], 66
Ballade frivole [3.862], 93
Bambalelê [3.414b], 77
Bamboleia [3.225], 71
Banzo [3.226], 71
Banzo [3.1278e], 110
Barcarola [3.140], 68
Barcarola, op. 92 [3.627], 86
Barco à margem, op. 148, no. 16 [3.1099p], 102
Barquinho esguio, op. 169, no. 1 [3.1130a], 105
Barré [12.25j], 171
Barrio de Córdoba (Tópico nocturno) [1.25b], 7
Basta de ser o outro [3.677], 88
Batuque no. 1 [3.628], 86
Batuque no. 2 [3.629], 86
Beijaste os meus cabelos [3.480a], 80
Beijos mortos [3.678], 88
Beiramar, op. 21 [3.1014], 99
Belgrano nos dio bandera [1.303d], 28
Bella Granada [3.863], 93
Belo, belo [3.42b], 65
Bem pior que a morte [3.1170c], 106
Bem-te-vi [3.2], 63
Bem-te-vi [3.193], 69
Bemteví (Lundu) [3.117a], 67
Bem-vinda [3.45a], 65
Bendita pois seja a água divina [3.208h], 70
Bendito [3.1541e], 122
Benedito pretinho [3.1239a], 109
Benedito pretinho [3.1322a], 112
Benteveo [1.335a], 31
Berceuse [1.4c], 4
Berceuse [3.108], 67
Berceuse [3.227], 72
Berceuse [3.308], 74
Berceuse [3.1066], 101

Berceuse [3.1163], 106
Berceuse [5.14], 136
Berceuse [21.12a], 204
Berceuse, op. 11 [3.630], 86
Berceuse, op. 84 [3.1098], 102
Berceuse à la bien-aimée (Vocalise-étude) [12.41g], 173
Berceuse da onda que leva o pequenino náufrago, op. 57 [3.324], 75
Berimbau [3.919a], 95
Berimbau [3.1262], 110
Berimbau, op. 4 [3.1085], 101
Bestiario [4.5], 129
Between Two Gardens (song cycle) [22.1], 209
Bien amada... [15.79b], 186
¡Bien haya!... [1.456b], 43
Bienvenido y el barroso [6.13], 142
Big-Ben [3.1435], 116
Bilhete àquela que ainda está por nascer [3.679], 88
Billet [12.33], 172
Bito Manué [7.14], 150
Blanca noche [15.41a], 182
Boas festas [3.1441b], 117
Boas vindas [3.1441e], 117
Boca [3.680], 88
Boca de forno [3.1218], 109
Boca de forno, op. 9, no. 3 [3.1027c], 100
Bocas de ira [1.442h], 41
Bohemio [3.260], 72
Boi surubim-Suite Cearense [3.163], 68
Boi-Bumbá [3.580], 84
Boi-ê [3.216a], 71
Bombo [3.283], 73
Bonequinha de seda [3.1275], 110
Bonita rama de sauce [1.302a], 28
Bonsoir, Paris! [3.1462c], 118
Borboleta, op. 10 [3.1356], 114
Borboletas [3.141], 68
Borralheira [3.574c], 84
Borriquito Blanco (Canción de Navidad) [1.102], 13
Bôto [3.581], 84
Botoncito [15.45b], 182
Botoncito (Canción de cuna) [1.165], 16
Bouclé noué [12.25b], 171
Bouclé noué [12.25x], 171
Boyerito lindo [1.260], 25
Brasileirinha [3.429d], 78
Brauna [3.121], 67
Brea [1.20f], 6
Brejeirice [3.303a], 74

Breve serenata [3.1164], 106
Breve serenata [3.1194b], 108
Brinde (Fontoura Xavier) [3.142], 68
Brinquedo [3.446], 79
Brisa que apenas mueve [7.2b], 150
Brisas del lago (Barcarola india) [2.6], 57
Brisas do Sul [3.292], 73
Brisas norteñas (Vals) [6.50], 143
Brizna, pequeño tallo [7.2a], 150
Brunetta [3.814a], 92
Buen día, señor invierno [1.303h], 28
¡Buen viaje! [1.467], 44
Buenas maneras [4.6], 129
Buquê [3.1105d], 103
Buquê de trovas, op. 148 [3.1099], 102
Buquê saudades de Bastos Tigre (I), op. 148 no. 31 [3.1099e], 102
Búsqueda [5.13], 136

Caballito [15.69a], 184
Caballito criollo [1.546], 51
Caballito criollo (Gato) [21.1d], 203
¡Caballito pampa! [1.468], 44
Caballitos [1.438f], 40
Caballo del diablo [15.78f], 186
Cabana de palha [3.261], 72
Cabanavenú [6.82e], 145
Cabeça, op. 148, no. 18 [3.1099r], 102
Cabedelo [3.447], 79
Cabôca de Caxangá (Embolada from the north) [3.1443j], 117
Cabocla malvada [3.582], 85
Caboclo bom [3.1276], 110
Caboclo do rio (Toada) [3.1032], 100
Cabra da peste [3.51], 65
Caçador (Tema do) [3.607a], 85
Cachumba, caracatachún [1.162c], 16
Cada vez mas presente [1.442d], 41
Cadê minha pomba rola [3.448], 79
Cadeirinha [3.52a], 65
Café de la paix [3.23], 64
Cair da tarde [3.1456e], 118
Caixinha de música (Cenas infantis) [3.1277], 110
Caja chayera [1.446], 43
Calla niño, calla [20.3], 199
Cállate, por Dios (Ah! tais-toi, par Dieu) [1.437a], 40
Calle de la pimienta [21.54d], 206
Calor de ayer [2.10e], 57
Caminamos [6.16], 142
Caminando [15.70b], 185
Caminhando (op. 121) [3.1402a], 115

INDEX OF SONG AND SONG CYCLE TITLES

Caminhando, op. 121 [3.1400], 115
Caminito [1.1a], 4
Caminito de Avilés [11.13f], 164
Caminito de la pena [1.120], 14
Caminito de la sierra [1.510], 48
Caminito de mi huerto [6.87], 146
Caminito de sol [1.469], 44
Caminito del maizal (Canción típica) [6.86], 146
Camino arriba [15.54d], 183
Camino de plata [1.400d], 37
Camino de tu capricho (Zamba canción) [1.511], 48
Camino para la sonrisa de una muchacha (Cammino pel sorriso d'una ragazza) [1.501b], 47
Caminos tristes [21.21], 204
Camoniana no. 1 (Sete anos de pastor) [3.1331], 113
Campana [6.79b], 145
Campana mayor [6.68], 144
Campanário de São José [3.788], 91
Campanas [1.309], 29
Campanilla ¿adónde vas? [1.324c], 30
Campanillas [1.543g], 50
Campanita [6.82a], 145
Campo de Buenos Aires [1.470], 44
Caña dulce (Canción popular) [6.90], 146
Canção [3.24], 64
Canção [3.197d], 70
Canção [3.206d], 70
Canção [3.275], 73
Canção [3.403a], 77
Canção [3.449], 79
Canção [3.1067], 101
Canção [3.1077], 101
Canção [3.1167], 106
Canção [3.1168], 106
Canção (1a. versão) [3.864], 93
Canção (2a. versão) [3.865], 93
Canção (I) [3.1165], 106
Canção (II) [3.1166], 106
Canção, op. 30, no. 2 [3.954], 97
Canção à toa [3.177], 69
Canção à toa [3.681], 88
Canção ao luar [3.325], 75
Canção árabe [3.751], 90
Canção árabe [3.1436], 116
Canção bárbara [3.631], 86
Canção da ausência [3.955], 97
Canção da brisa (I) [3.1128b], 104
Canção da brisa (II) [3.1128c], 104
Canção da chuva [3.1134], 105
Canção da despedida [3.78], 66

Canção da esperança, op. 85 [3.1401], 115
Canção da felicidade (Modinha) [3.79], 66
Canção da folha morta [3.1473c], 120
Canção da fonte [3.326], 75
Canção da fuga impossível [3.1169], 106
Canção da garoa [3.658], 87
Canção da garoa [3.910e], 95
Canção da guitarra [3.1326], 113
Canção da indiazinha [3.1484], 120
Canção da Jamaica [3.1386], 114
Canção da liberdade [3.866], 93
Canção da menina triste [3.1485], 120
Canção da ruazinha desconhecida [3.910a], 95
Canção da saudade (Modinha) [3.80], 66
Canção da velhinha [3.309], 74
Canção das águas claras [3.1437], 116
Canção das iaras [3.450], 79
Canção das morenas [3.1100], 103
Canção de amor [3.632], 86
Canção de amor (Liebeslied) [3.956], 97
Canção de berço [3.390], 76
Canção de Carolina [3.1486], 120
Canção de cristal [3.1438], 116
Canção de inverno [3.133], 68
Canção de Lavinia [3.81], 66
Canção de ninar [3.1263], 110
Canção de Romeu [3.143], 68
Canção do amor [3.82], 66
Canção do amor [3.1456a], 118
Canção do amor distante [3.1033], 100
Canção do amor perfeito [3.25], 64
Canção do baú [3.574d], 84
Canção do baú [3.910b], 95
Canção do Beijo [3.109], 67
Canção do berço [3.378], 76
Canção do berço, op. 35 [3.327], 75
Canção do carreiro [3.1473h], 120
Canção do dia inútil [3.682], 88
Canção do embalo [3.228], 72
Canção do exílio [3.683], 88
Canção do mar [3.128], 67
Canção do mar [3.328], 75
Canção do marinheiro [3.1465a], 119
Canção do passado [3.524b], 82
Canção do poeta do século XVIII [3.1439], 116
Canção do rio [3.957], 97
Canção do Siriry (Ciranda) [3.583], 85
Canção do trovador [3.634], 87
Canção do vento [3.893a], 94
Canção do vento e da chuva [3.910c], 95
Canção do violeiro, op. 38 [3.329], 75
Canção dos artistas [3.1440], 117

Canção dos olhos [3.633], 87
Canção dos pescadores [3.1328], 113
Canção dramática [3.382], 76
Canção evocativa [3.1325a], 113
Canção goiana [3.293], 74
Canção ingênua [3.229], 72
Canção ingênua [3.451], 79
Canção nômade [3.584], 85
Canção para uma valsa lenta [3.659c], 87
Canção para uma valsa lenta [3.910d], 95
Canção perdida, op. 148, no. 27 [3.1099a], 102
Canção quase melancólica (Quasi-melancholic song) [3.1343], 113
Canção sentimental, 102
Canção sertaneja [3.83], 66
Canção sertaneja, op. 31 [3.330], 75
Canção simples [3.829], 92
Canção simples, op. 83 (Berceuse) [3.635], 87
Canção tímida [3.403b], 77
Canção tímida [3.524c], 82
Canção triste [3.206e], 70
Canción [1.512], 48
Canción [1.542e], 50
Canción [15.4a], 179
Canción [20.7], 199
Canción (para mi niño) [7.9], 150
Canción, op. 13 [4.24b], 130
Canción a la luna lunanca [1.272b], 26
Canción a la viuda Shin (Escena 7) [6.80a], 145
Canción al árbol del olvido [1.272a], 26
Canción arcaica para niños [15.37a], 181
Canción cantada [1.531a], 49
Canción celeste [1.428c], 39
Canción china en Europa [1.22b], 7
Canción china en Europa [1.531c], 49
Canción costeña [15.36e], 181
Canción de amor [1.557i], 52
Canción de ausencia [1.372], 34
Canción de Cleia (Quasi griega) [7.16], 150
Canción de cuna [1.31], 9
Canción de cuna [1.121], 14
Canción de cuna [1.175b], 17
Canción de cuna [1.515b], 48
Canción de cuna [1.542h], 50
Canción de cuna [4.34c], 132
Canción de cuna [10.2c], 160
Canción de cuna [15.69d], 185
Canción de cuna a Patricia [11.6], 163
Canción de cuna afro-cubana [7.34a], 151
Canción de cuna (Canción a dos voces) [1.417], 38
Canción de cuna (Canción escolar) [1.258], 24

Canción de cuna de la virgen (A dos voces) [1.251b], 24
Canción de cuna incaica [19.2], 195
Canción de cuna india [1.261], 25
Canción de cuna (Nenito mio) [1.543c], 50
Canción de cuna, op. 2 no. 1 [1.407], 37
Canción de cuna para despertar a un negrito [19.14], 196
Canción de cuna para dormir a un negrito [1.162b], 16
Canción de cuna para dormir un negrito [22.4b], 210
Canción de cuna para la tarde [22.18a], 212
Canción de cuna para mi corazón solitario [1.555a], 51
Canción de cuna para un niño ciego [1.396], 36
Canción de cuna vallecaucana [5.43], 137
Canción de estudiante (Canço d'estudiant, serenata) [1.415d], 38
Canción de jinete [1.24f], 7
Canción de jinete (1860) (Andaluzas) [1.24a], 7
Canción de la guagua (Arrorró indio) [1.497a], 46
Canción de la niña gaucha [1.364a], 33
Canción de la primavera (de la comedia infantil "Pedro, Pedrito y Pedrin") [1.181], 17
Canción de la tarde [5.1], 136
Canción de las hadas [5.50], 138
Canción de las hojas [1.557b], 51
Canción de las siete doncellas (Teoría del arco iris) [1.22a], 7
Canción de las tardes tristes (Escena 3) [6.80c], 145
Canción de los caballitos blancos [1.148], 16
Canción de los niños bajo la lluvia [1.543f], 50
Canción de los sembradores [1.499], 47
Canción de Navidad [1.310], 29
Canción de Navidad (no. 2) [1.311], 29
Canción de otoño [7.53], 153
Canción de otoño [22.10g], 210
Canción de Perico [1.374], 34
Canción de pollitos con sueño [1.428b], 39
Canción de primavera [15.39c], 182
Canción de primavera (Romanza) [1.231], 21
Canción de Shen-te ante los dioses [6.80b], 145
Canción de tu dedo meñique [1.225g], 20
Canción de un azul imposible [5.18], 136
Canción de vendimia [1.415f], 38
Canción del agua [6.80d], 145
Canción del ángel sin suerte [4.32a], 131
Canción del árbol [1.11e], 5
Canción del beso robado [1.253], 24

INDEX OF SONG AND SONG CYCLE TITLES

Canción del beso robado [1.270], 26
Canción del carretero [1.382e], 35
Canción del niño pequeñito [1.373], 34
Canción del Pañuelo (Canco del mocador) [1.415b], 38
Canción del peligro [1.292], 27
Canción del regreso [1.63], 10
Canción del trovero Pedro Vidal (from ballet "Cuento de abril") [1.182], 17
Canción gitana [1.399], 37
Canción ingenua [1.541b], 50
Canción integrata, op. 18 [6.10], 141
Canción ligera [1.428a], 39
Canción ligera [5.59], 138
Canción marinera [1.103], 13
Canción mística [5.26], 137
Canción nuestra [15.40e], 182
Canción otoñal [1.560c], 52
Canción para el niño en la cuna [1.447], 43
Canción para la abuela (Canzone per la nonna) [1.500], 47
Canción pasional [1.557c], 51
Canción primaveral [1.557f], 51–52
Canción que es llanto en el mar [15.45c], 182
Canción quichua (El sucho) [1.416g], 38
Canción sin nombre y sin palabras, no.1 [21.52], 206
Canción tonta [1.531b], 49
Canción tonta [15.69b], 185
Canción tonta [20.1], 199
Cancioncilla sevillana [1.22c], 7
Cancioncilla sevillana [1.531d], 49
Cancioneiro [3.144], 68
Cancionero del niño peruano [19.11], 196
Cancionero juvenil dominicano [8.1], 156
Cancionero y romancero de ausencias [1.442], 41
Canciones [6.65], 144
Canciones [19.3], 195
Canciones al estilo de mi tierra [15.36], 181
Canciones antiguas [4.23], 130
Canciones argentinas [1.1], 4
Canciones argentinas [1.369], 34
Canciones argentinas [1.520], 48
Canciones con árboles (Cuaderno 1) [1.19], 6
Canciones con árboles (Cuaderno 2) [1.20], 6
Canciones de Altisidora, op. 35 [1.384], 35
Canciones de amor [1.490], 45
Canciones de arena [22.2], 209
Canciones de la infancia [1.21], 6
Canciones de la noche [6.79], 145
Canciones de la pampa y la sierra, op. 82 [1.557], 51

Canciones de la soledad [4.28], 130
Canciones de mi juventud [22.12], 210
Canciones del alba [1.312], 29
Canciones del mar, op. 29 [4.33], 128, 132
Canciones del ocaso [15.19], 180
Canciones españolas [15.40], 182
Canciones incaicas, op. 45 [1.558], 52
Canciones incásicas (en el estilo popular), op. 57 [1.559], 52
Canciones infantiles [1.11], 4
Canciones infantiles [1.542], 50
Canciones mejicanas para niños [15.52], 183
Canciones modales [15.65], 184
Canciones para niños [1.531], 49
Canciones para soprano y piano [2.11], 58
Canciones pirenaicas [1.385], 35
Canciones populares [22.13], 210
Canciones simbólicas, op. 14 [19.12], 196
Canciones sobre poemas de Armando Soriano Badani [2.10], 57
Cancó [1.385b], 35
Canço del lladre [7.35h], 152
Canções [3.830], 93
Canções brasileiras [3.1278], 110
Canções Brejeiras [3.1325], 113
Canções de Amor (1a. série) [3.1170], 106
Canções de amor (2a. série) [3.1171], 107
Canções de cordialidade, no. 1 [3.1441], 117
Canções de Débora [3.531], 82
Canções de Ofélia [3.573], 84
Canções de Ofélia [3.684], 88
Canções de Sônia Maria [3.571], 84
Canções do vento [3.659], 87
Canções indígenas [3.1442], 117
Canções líricas brasileiras, Album no. 1 [3.429], 78
Canções marinhas [3.585], 85
Canções populares brasileiras, Caderno I [3.413], 77
Canções populares brasileiras, Caderno II [3.414], 77
Canções populares brasileiras, Caderno III [3.415], 77
Canções típicas brasileiras (Chanson brésiliennes) [3.1443], 117
Candela fui [1.245b], 22
Candomblé [3.1155], 106
Candonga (Batuque) [3.1327], 113
Candura [3.958], 97
Canide ioune-sabath-Ave Amarela [3.1476a], 120
Canjerê (Canto do caboclo) [3.1135], 105
Canoeiro, canoerio [3.566e], 84
Canoeiro, op. 18, no. 1 [3.1026a], 99

INDEX OF SONG AND SONG CYCLE TITLES

Canta la morena (Romance) [1.490b], 46
Canta mi corazón (Chante mon coeur) [12.36], 172
Canta tu canto, ruiseñor y vuela ... (Soneto) [1.375], 34
Cantad, pájaros [15.67b], 184
Cantafora I [2.9b], 57
Cántame ... [1.361b], 33
Cantar [1.166], 16
Cantar [3.295b], 74
Cantar [6.84], 146
Cantar (Barrio adentro) [21.54e], 206
Cantar de arriero [1.535], 49
Cantar del campesino [6.85], 146
Cantar galego (Canção trovadoresca no. 2) [3.1393b], 114
Cantar margariteño [22.15g], 211
Cantarcillo [15.75e], 185
Cantarcillo (de Canciones Gallegas) [1.104], 13
Cantarcillo del aire ligero (Callejón del agua) [21.54b], 206
Cantarcillo marinero [20.14c], 200
Cantares [1.370], 34
Cantares [3.941], 96
Cantares criollos [21.16], 204
Cantares de amor [1.149], 16
Cantares de Cuyo [1.440], 41
Cantares de la tierra mía [1.351], 32
Cantares de Pernambuco [3.1034], 100
Cântico das árvores [3.147], 68
Cântico do sol (da Missa de São Francisco) [3.789], 91
Cântico XXV [3.1489a], 120
Cânticos de Obaluaiê [3.867], 93
Cánticos para soñar [1.555], 51
Cânticos serranos no. 1 [3.532], 83
Cânticos serranos no. 2 [3.533], 83
Cânticos serranos no. 3 [3.534], 83
Cânticos serranos no. 4 [3.535], 83
Cantiga [3.197c], 70
Cantiga [3.287a], 73
Cantiga [3.383], 76
Cantiga [3.516b], 81
Cantiga [3.792c], 91
Cantiga [3.919b], 95
Cantiga [3.1202], 108
Cantiga [3.1250c], 110
Cantiga [3.1264], 110
Cantiga [3.1332], 113
Cantiga [3.1548b], 123
Cantiga [4.29a], 131
Cantiga [15.66c], 184

Cantiga (Chanson) [3.84], 66
Cantiga, op. 8, no. 2 [3.685], 88
Cantiga boêmia [3.1068], 101
Cantiga contraditória [3.452], 79
Cantiga da ausência [3.453], 79
Cantiga da porteira [3.454], 79
Cantiga da tua lembrança [3.524d], 82
Cantiga de amor [3.145], 68
Cantiga de leito [3.1279], 111
Cantiga de ninar [3.134], 68
Cantiga de ninar [3.868], 93
Cantiga de ninar escrava [3.688], 88
Cantiga de Nossa Senhora [3.1280], 111
Cantiga de quem te quer [3.455], 79
Cantiga de roda [3.295c], 74
Cantiga de São Francisco [3.659d], 87
Cantiga de viúvo [3.689], 88
Cantiga de viúvo [3.869], 93
Cantiga do ai [3.870], 93
Cantiga do ausente [3.1195c], 108
Cantiga do mar, op. 97 [3.1101], 103
Cantiga do viúvo [3.1473g], 120
Cantiga dos olhos que choram (Canção trovadoresca no. 6) [3.1393f], 115
Cantiga I [3.686], 88
Cantiga II [3.687], 88
Cantiga maritime [3.262], 72
Cantiga noturna [3.456], 79
Cantiga para ninar [3.1219], 109
Cantiga para os olhos fechados [3.363], 76
Cantiga Praiana [3.197a], 70
Cantiga sentimental [3.457], 79
Cantiga triste [3.458], 79
Cantigas [3.1148], 106
Cantigas (A Guitarra) [3.959], 97
Cantigas de amigo [1.491], 46
Cantigas do amor existencial [3.536], 83
Cantigas dos sertanejos cuiabanos [3.1278c], 110
Cantigas praianas [3.164], 68
Cantiguinha [3.574e], 84
Cantilena [1.299b], 27
Cantilena [3.3], 63
Cantilena [3.960], 97
Cantilena [3.1465c], 119
Cantique marin [3.40a], 65
Canto [3.210d], 71
Canto a cañas [6.1], 141
Canto à divina mãe bem-amada [3.752], 90
Canto a la tierra [15.6], 179
Canto chico (Seis canciones sobre temática infantil), Serie II, op. 18 [1.246], 23
Canto da coroação [3.1069], 101

300

INDEX OF SONG AND SONG CYCLE TITLES

Canto da saudade (Adeus à Vila Aida) [3.288], 73
Canto da vida a chegar [3.122], 67
Canto d'amore [3.1357], 114
Canto de amor [1.81], 12
Canto de chingolo (Vidalita) [21.5], 203
Canto de esclavos (Cuba 1870) [7.46], 153
Canto de las Repúblicas Centroamericanas [6.54], 143
Canto de Negros [3.871], 93
Canto de nodriza [1.555b], 51
Canto de Ofélia, op. 14 [3.753], 90
Canto de una muchacha negra [15.68], 184
Canto jovem [3.123], 67
Canto Karabalí [7.23], 151
Canto nupcial [3.961], 97
Canto patriótico [6.73], 144
Canto triste [22.18b], 212
Cantorias Paulistas [3.1203], 108
Cantos da sulamita [3.962], 97
Cantos de España [11.13], 164
Cantos de Kulka [3.661], 88
Cantos de melancolía [1.492], 46
Cantos de melancolía [1.493], 46
Cantos de otoño [4.7], 129
Cantos de soledad, op. 10 [4.34], 128, 132
Cantos infantiles: para los jardines de niños [15.53], 183
Cantos líticos, Primera colección [2.9], 57
Canzón da noite do afiador [15.66b], 184
Capillita de Renca [1.105], 13
Capim di pranta [3.165a], 69
Capricho de la rueda redonda [1.293], 27
Capullito [1.555d], 51
Caracola [5.32], 137
Caras [1.99c], 13
Caravana, op. 116, no. 3 [3.1102], 103
Caravelas [3.574f], 84
Cardo en flor (Canción criolla) [1.391], 36
Carícia [3.459], 79
Caricia [4.2], 129
Carita de cielo (Serenata serrana) [1.82], 12
Carmo [3.235a], 72
Carnaval [3.1282b], 111
Carnaval ... (Las carpas) [1.416h], 38
Carnaval do desamor [3.690], 89
Carnavalito [1.506], 47
Carreiros [3.565a], 83
Carretera costanera (Popular) [6.91], 146
Carreterita (Popular) [6.92], 146
Carretilla de Madera [1.330j], 31
Cartas interdimensionales [10.1], 160
Casa de caboclo [3.1278d], 110

Casa de caboclo (Série regional) [3.1281], 111
Casadita [15.35b], 181
Cascavel [3.1444], 117
Casinha pequenina [3.166], 69
Casita de mis recuerdos (Lied para canto y piano) [1.67], 11
Castelo de sonhos [3.364], 76
Castigo [3.474b], 80
Castigo de amor [3.691], 89
Castilla tiene castillos [4.30j], 131
Casulo [3.1487], 120
Catavento [3.292a], 73
Categiró [3.790], 91
Catita [3.146], 68
Cazador [4.25d], 130
Ceguinha [3.85], 66
Ceibo, ceibo, zuiñandí [1.3241], 30
Cenas coloniais [3.1282], 111
Ceniza, lluvia, vino, ... [10.5c], 160
Cerca de tí [15.55a], 183
Cerca del agua te quiero llevar [1.442m], 42
Cerrar podrá mis ojos [1.98d], 13
Cerro, luna y aire [1.448], 43
C'est jodi moin nan lanmè [12.25e], 171
Céu azul, op. 54, no. 2 [3.773b], 91
Chacarera [1.175c], 17
Chacarera [1.271a], 26
Chacayalera (Serranilla) [1.204c], 19
Chacayaleras [1.204], 19
Chama [3.1105e], 103
Chamaste-me tua vida [3.692b], 89
Chañar [1.20c], 6
Changó [3.379], 76
Changuito (Canción infantil) [1.536], 49
Chanson [3.196a], 70
Chanson à boire [1.23b], 7
Chanson au bord de l'eau [1.16f], 5
Chanson d'amour, op. 24 [3.1358], 114
Chanson d'automne [1.16b], 5
Chanson d'automne [1.432a], 39
Chanson d'automne [21.13], 204
Chanson d'automne, op. 167 [3.1103], 103
Chanson de Barberine [1.16c], 5
Chanson de Barbérine [3.405a], 77
Chanson de bergère [1.16g], 5
Chanson de la liberté [3.1172], 107
Chanson de la mélancholie [3.1173], 107
Chanson druidique [3.196b], 70
Chanson du chat qui dort [1.16h], 5
Chanson du Marron [3.1174], 107
Chanson du troubadour Pons de Capdeuil [3.196c], 70

INDEX OF SONG AND SONG CYCLE TITLES

Chanson galante [1.430], 39
Chanson Jean Brierre [12.22], 170
Chanson pour ton sommeil [3.61], 66
Chanson triste [12.17d], 170
Chansons folkloriques d'Haïti [12.23], 171
Chant arabe [1.26c], 8
Chant de croisés [3.196d], 70
Chant de l'aube [1.26d], 8
Chant hindou [1.26e], 8
Chant spirituel [12.7], 169
Chant vénitien [1.26f], 8
Charada [15.1b], 179
Chariô op. 10 no. 1 [3.1089a], 101
Charrada [11.13c], 164
Chères mains [12.41e], 172
Chi mi ridona [1.4a], 4
Chililin-uth'aja (Campanita de mi pueblo) [19.16d], 196
China del alma [15.61e], 184
Chingolo [1.335g], 31
Chingolo ante las espumas [1.68], 11
Chismecito [1.456a], 43
Chora coração [3.1136], 105
Chora Mané, não chora [3.1333], 113
Chora morena [3.1325b], 113
Chorinho [3.287b], 73
Chorinho [3.586], 85
Choro urbano [3.1488], 120
Choucoune [12.34], 167, 172
Chove-chuva! [3.1283], 111
Chuva com sol [3.1249], 109
Chuva de setembro [3.20a], 64
Chuva fina, matutina, op. 38, no. 2 [3.194], 69
Chuva miúda [3.523b], 82
Chuva miúda [3.537], 83
Ciclo Brecht [3.1175], 107
Ciclo Cecília Meireles [3.1489], 120
Ciclo de canciones [7.17], 150
Ciclo de canciones [22.8], 210
Ciclo de canciones para mezzo-soprano y piano [20.27], 201
Ciclo Rio Quatrocentão [3.52], 65
Cidade [3.1540c], 122
Cidadezinha [3.791], 91
Cidadezinha qualquer [3.812], 92
Cidadezinha qualquer [3.1550a], 123
Cidadezinha qualquer, op. 151, no. 1 [3.1108a], 103
Cielito lindo [11.14], 164
Ciência [3.19a], 64
Cierra el labio [15.74a], 185
Cigarra, op. 112, no. 2 [3.1104b], 103

Cima [4.22], 130
Cinco canciones [1.205], 19
Cinco canciones [1.459], 44
Cinco canciones [4.25], 130
Cinco canciones a la madre muerta [15.24], 180
Cinco canciones al estilo popular [1.376], 34
Cinco canciones al estilo popular rioplatense [21.1], 203
Cinco canciones argentinas [1.175], 17
Cinco canciones de Brecht (La buena mujer de Sezúan) [6.80], 145
Cinco canciones de la cantata "El Tamarit" [1.243], 22
Cinco canciones de niños [15.69], 184
Cinco canciones de verano [6.81], 145
Cinco canciones para niños [6.82], 145
Cinco canciones populares argentinas [1.271], 26
Cinco canciones tradicionales españolas [7.33], 151
Cinco canções [3.792], 91
Cinco canções [3.1250], 109
Cinco canções Franco-suíças [3.195], 70
Cinco canções internacionais [3.391], 76
Cinco canções medievais [3.196], 70
Cinco canções nordestinas do folclore brasileiro [3.165], 68
Cinco canções. op. 124 [3.1540], 122
Cinco fulias sobre melodias folklóricas venezolanas [1.18], 6
Cinco haikais, op. 112 [3.1104], 103
Cinco peças para canto, op. 5 [3.197], 70
Cinco pequeñas canciones judías [1.443], 42
Cinco piezas [1.400], 37
Cinco poemas aztecas [20.25], 200
Cinco poemas de Alice [3.460], 79
Cinco poemas de outono, op. 136 [3.1402], 115
Cinco sonetos [3.392], 76
Cinco trovas [3.692], 89
Cincuenta cánticos sagrados [6.55], 143
Cinq chants funèbres [12.8], 168, 169
Cinq interprétations d'Omar Khayyam [12.9], 168, 169
Cisnes [3.289], 73
Cisnes, op. 9 [3.331], 75
Cita [1.313], 29
Cita [22.8b], 210
Ciúme [3.198], 70
Ciúme [3.461], 79
Claire de lune [12.24], 171
Claire de lune [12.40], 172
Claro rayo de luna [22.15c], 211
Clic-clic (Comadrerã) [3.13], 63
Clytie [3.393], 77

INDEX OF SONG AND SONG CYCLE TITLES

Cobra grande (Canção amazônica) [3.587], 85
Coco de los Santos [11.15], 164
Côco de minha terra (Biá-tá-tá) [3.1284], 111
Côco perenuê [3.588], 85
Cogedme, cogedme [1.442f], 41
Cogiendo café (Dramatizable) [6.55a], 143
Coleção brasileira [3.1445], 117
Collares de perlas [1.206], 19
Colloque sentimental [1.432c], 39
Colonial [3.287c], 73
Colora abril el campo [1.98c], 13
Columnas y círculos [20.8], 199
Comadre Rana [4.1f], 129
Comboio de corda (Modinhas) [3.1105], 103
Comboio de corda (Modinhas) [3.1106], 103
Começo [3.28c], 64
Comendo bola [3.1285], 111
Com'estou d'amor ferida, op. 55 [3.1403], 115
Comme un profil perdu [12.31], 172
Como abejas [6.17], 142
Como el bosque... [1.122c], 14
Como el toro... [1.151b], 16
Como lámpara eterna [15.80d], 187
Como las frutas del monte (Aire de chacarera) [21.1e], 203
Cómo los pájaros [21.50], 206
Como o coração da noite [3.475a], 80
Como sa mu trista [15.40g], 182
Compañero viento [1.32], 9
Comunión de luna [6.18], 142
Con el alba en las manos [1.525], 48
Con una manzana verde (Araucana) [1.387c], 36
Confidência [3.178a], 69
Confidência [3.215g], 71
Confidência [3.1446], 117
Confissão [3.217], 71
Confissão [3.1490], 121
Confissão, op. 34a [3.754], 90
Confissões [3.1491], 121
Confusão [3.533b], 83
Confusão [3.830c], 93
Conseil pour l'homme [3.86], 66
Conselho [3.963], 97
Constância [3.462], 79
Contemplación [1.185b], 18
Contemplo o lago mudo [3.659e], 87
Contigo [3.1137], 105
Contrição [3.693], 89
Copla [1.106], 13
Copla [1.167], 16
Copla [1.184a], 17
Copla [1.366a], 33

Copla criolla [1.377], 35
Copla de la soledad [1.168], 16
Copla triste (Elegy) [11.2], 163
Coplas [1.176], 17
Coplas [1.363], 33
Coplas [1.370a], 34
Coplas [1.389], 36
Coplas a la acequia con luna [1.83], 12
Coplas al Tulumaya [1.513], 48
Coplas de la paloma, op. 45 [1.386], 35
Coplas de soledad [1.245], 22
Coplas jujeñas [1.514], 48
Coplas para el amor que se fue [1.268a], 25
Coplas para la herida reciente [1.268b], 25
Coplas para tu boca [1.268c], 25
Coplas para tus ojos [1.262], 25
Coplas para un bailecito [1.33], 9
Coplas puntanas [1.107], 13
Coplas venezolanas [22.3b], 209
Copo de cristal [3.636], 87
Coqueiro-coqueirá [3.230], 72
Coração cosmopolita [3.523a], 82
Coração indeciso, op. 30, no. 1 [3.964], 97
Coração inquieto [3.332], 75
Coração inquieto [3.1447], 117
Coração triste, op. 18, no. 1 [3.965], 97
Corazón más no llores [1.515a], 48
Corazón mío no llores (Canción criolla) [1.275], 26
Corderito [1.343d], 31
Corderito [4.42c], 132
Cordillera [2.9a], 57
Coro (Do solo calcinado) [3.607b], 85
Corpo da própria cantora [3.4], 63
Corpo de Cristo [3.5], 63
Corpo do povo [3.6], 63
Corre que corre... [3.7], 63
Correría mañanera [1.530c], 49
Cortadera, plumerito... [1.324a], 30
Cortejo (Criolla-Bolero) [7.17g], 150
Costa Rica (Corrido tico) [6.93], 146
Cotidiano [3.945a], 96
Cotón colorado [4.1e], 129
Courana [3.1541n], 122
Courana [3.1542g], 122
Creciente [22.9a], 210
Crepuscular [22.10e], 210
Crepuscular, romanza para canto y piano [5.52], 138
Crepúsculo de abril [3.210b], 71
Crepúsculo de ouro [3.755], 90
Crepúsculo de outono [3.215b], 71

INDEX OF SONG AND SONG CYCLE TITLES

Crespuscular (Cantar indio) [2.1], 57
Cristo en la tarde... (en modo eólico) [15.65e], 184
Cromo (Chromo) [3.310], 74
Cromo no. 1 [3.179], 69
Cromo no. 2 [3.180], 69
Cromo no. 2 [3.1464a], 119
Cromo no. 3 [3.1464c], 119
Cruauté, op. 38 [21.22], 204
Cruel saudade (Modinha) [3.1112d], 104
Cual abeja los pétalos... [6.83c], 145
Cuando acaba de llover... [1.301a], 28
Cuando caigan las hojas [5.6], 136
Cuando el caballo se para [22.16c], 211
Cuando el camino me fatiga [22.15h], 211
Cuando en silencio me veas [1.123b], 14
Cuando haya tomado... [10.3b], 160
Cuando hayamos muerto... [15.791], 186
Cuando la luna... [1.368a], 34
Cuando lejos, muy lejos [5.21], 136
Cuando muere la tarde [1.471], 44
Cuando salgo con mi niño [1.123c], 14
Cuando se te llenen los ojos de lejanía [20.30b], 201
Cuando voy a la aldea [20.4], 199
Cuando voy por la calle [1.386d], 35–36
Cuatro apuntes líricos [4.8], 129
Cuatro baladas del paraná, op. 79 [1.223], 20
Cuatro canciones [1.122], 14
Cuatro canciones [1.437], 40
Cuatro canciones [1.494], 46
Cuatro canciones [1.540], 50
Cuatro canciones [4.26], 130
Cuatro canciones [15.3], 179
Cuatro canciones al estilo popular argentino [1.364], 33
4 Canciones argentinas [1.300], 27
4 Canciones coloniales [1.301], 28
Cuatro canciones de amor [15.77], 185
Cuatro canciones de Federico García Lorca [1.22], 7
Cuatro canciones en el estilo popular argentino [1.34], 9
Cuatro canciones escolares [1.140], 15
Cuatro canciones para canto y piano [15.66], 184
Cuatro canciones para soprano y piano [10.2], 160
Cuatro canciones para soprano y piano [10.3], 160
Cuatro cantos: para voz y piano [15.81], 187
Cuatro coplas [1.123], 14
Cuatro melodías [19.13], 196
Cuatro melodías, op. 26 [1.185], 18
Cuatro milpas [11.16], 164
Cuatro piezas [15.4], 179

Cuatro poemas, op. 9 [4.35], 128, 132
Cuatro recitativos [4.9], 129
Cuatro sonetos de amor, op. 97 [1.98], 12
Cuatro sonetos de Quevedo [1.314], xix, 29
Cuatros poemas de Francisco A. de Icaza (De la vida honda y de la emoción fugitiva) [15.54], 177, 183
Cueca, op. 61 [1.2], 4
Cuerpo de mujer [3.1423a], 116
Cuerpo presente [3.1018b], 99
Cumbia [1.444c], 42
Cumbre [1.84], 12
Cunera [6.82c], 145
Cunita (Arrorró) [1.246d], 23
Curupira [3.598a], 85
Curuzibambo [3.463], 79
Custo, op. 148, no. 2 [3.1099b], 102
Cuyana [1.370d], 34

D. Janaína [3.793], 92
Da fatalidade (Modinha) [3.538], 83
Da música de Maria Ifigènia [3.1489d], 120
Da pinheira nasce a pinha [3.1541g], 122
Daba el reloj las doce... [1.438b], 40
Dale a mi copla, Dios mío [1.538d], 49
Dambala oh [12.251], 171
Dá-me as pétalas de rosa [3.694], 89
Dame la mano.... (Canción escolar) [1.365], 33
Dame pápiro de luna [15.36b], 181
Damisela encantadora [7.24], 151
Dança de caboclo [3.1323a], 112
Dança negra [3.1286], 111
Dansa (Martelo) [3.1434b], 116
Danza de los alcaravanes [5.24], 136
Danza irregular [1.263], 25
Danzas y canciones argentinas (1st Album): 6 Cantos [1.64], 10
Danzas y canciones argentinas (2nd Album): 5 Cantos [1.65], 11
Das Lied von der wolke Nacht [3.1175a], 107
Das Ständchen [1.190c], 18
Dawn [14.2a], 176
De aquellos días [6.19], 142
De Castilla [1.438], 40
De extremadura a Léon (en modo lidio) [15.65c], 184
De la contemplación [1.442a], 41
De la infancia queda todo [1.21c], 6
De la muchacha dorada (Casida) [1.243b], 22
De la rosa (Casida) [1.243c], 22
De la sierra... (Cinco canciones argentinas) [1.35], 9
De las sierras [15.60c], 183

De los ramos (Casida) [1.243e], 22
De mi patria [1.472], 44
De noche [1.459d], 44
De oro [15.54a], 183
De pronto, hay un dolor de cerrajos [1.100b], 13
De puerta en puerta [1.99a], 13
De puerta en puerta, op. 50 [1.99], 13
De qué vale decirlo [22.18c], 212
De todo te acordarás [1.440c], 41
De tu padre... [6.83b], 145
De você [3.471], 79
Debajo de la hoja [7.37c], 152
Debussy [1.532a], 49
Debussy [3.1220], 109
Décima [1.7], 4
Décima de Pavón [1.12], 5
Decires de espanto y amor [4.10], 129
Declaração [3.464], 79
Declaração de Lereno [3.746a], 90
Dedal [1.330b], 31
Dedo mindinho [3.1321b], 112
Dei a você! [3.778], 91
Dei-te os sonhos de minh'alma [3.731d], 90
Deixa estar [3.1035], 100
Déjame dormir, amor... [1.225f], 20
Déjame esta voz [1.315], 29
Déjame que me vaya [1.442p], 42
Déjame soñar tu sueño [15.43], 182
Del amor con cien años (Gacela) [1.243d], 22
Del amor maravilloso (Gacela) [1.243a], 22
Del rosal nace la rosa [1.440a], 41
Delgadina [1.496b], 46
Delírio vão [3.695], 89
Den-Báu [3.465], 79
Dengues da Mulata Desinteressada [3.872], 94
Dengues da Mulata Desinteressada [3.1015], 99
Dentro da noite [3.215f], 71
Dentro da noite [3.333], 75
Dentro da noite [3.919c], 95
Deprisa tierra, deprisa [7.19g], 151
Der Krieg [11.3], 163
Der wunde Ritter, op. 20, no. 1 [3.966], 97
Desafio [3.668], 88
Desafio [3.696], 89
Desafio [3.873], 94
Desalento [3.1492], 121
Desciende, gris, de las olas lentas del aire... [10.5b], 160
Desciendo el valle... [15.60e], 183
Desde lo alto [4.331], 132
Desde que te conocí [1.300a], 27
Desdén [1.400e], 37

Desdichas de mi pasión... (Tonada) [1.382c], 35
Desejo [3.148], 68
Desejo [3.466], 79
Desejo [3.756], 90
Desejo [3.1156], 106
Desejo [3.1221], 109
Desejo [3.1448], 117
Desejo [3.1473j], 120
Desejo, op. 47 [3.637], 87
Desejos de doente [3.697], 89
Desencanto [3.215a], 71
Desencanto [3.831], 93
Desencanto [3.1387], 114
Desencontros [3.832], 93
Deseo [1.327b], 30
Deseo (Canción cubana) [7.47], 153
Desesperança [3.467], 79
Desesperança [3.477a], 80
Desespero [3.477b], 80
Desfolho a vida [3.874], 94
Desiludida [3.167], 69
Desilusão [3.1222], 109
Désirs d'hiver [3.967], 97
Deslumbramento [3.468], 79
Desolación [1.502a], 47
Despedida [1.444a], 42
Despedida [6.2], 141
Despedida (Modinha sertaneja) [3.1287], 111
Despedida, op. 31, no. 2 [3.968], 97
Despedida de Coimbra (Barcarola) [3.1112e], 104
Despedida sentimental [3.469], 79
Despeito [3.470], 79
Desposorio [2.5c], 57
Desterro [3.969], 97
Desterro, op. 31: para canto y piano [15.33], 181
Destornillador [1.330i], 31
Detrás del Monasterio Junto al Camino [10.9c], 161
Deux chansons populaires cubaines [7.34], 151
Deux estampes japonaises [1.526], 48
Deux mélodies [12.4], 169
Devant le couchant [12.12a], 170
Devoção [3.875], 94
Dez caboquinho... (Impressão brasileira) [3.430], 78
Dezesseis melodias do passado com acompanhamento novo, First album [3.1541], 122
Dezesseis melodias do passado com acompanhamento novo, Second Album [3.1542], 122
Dia da Graça, op. 32a [3.1016], 99
Día de diciembre, pasillo [5.60], 138
Día de diciembre (Romanza) [5.33], 137

Día de fiesta [1.545b], 51
Dia e noite, op. 148, no. 22 [3.1099v], 102
Dia seguinte [3.28d], 64
Diafanidad [11.4c], 163
Diálogo [7.19h], 151
Diálogo elegante [3.1036], 100
Dibujos sobre un puerto [15.75], 185
Dice la esperanza... [1.438e], 40
Dicen que andan diciendo... [1.369c], 34
Dicen que el mundo es redondo [4.26d], 130
Dicen que tu cariño... [1.351a], 32
Dichosa historia del amor pensado [1.150], 16
Die goldne Wiege [3.394], 77
Diez canciones, op. 22 & 42 [1.560], 52
Diez epigramas, op. 114 [1.247], 23
Diez Haikais [15.78], 186
Dime desde alla abajo [1.442n], 42
Dime ensueño, dime [6.69], 144
Dime perché [3.1449], 117
Din don [15.38a], 181
Dinga-donga [3.1450], 117
Dióme el cielo dolor [1.98b], 13
Dios te otorgó la gracia [15.66a], 184
Disfraz [21.40a], 205
Disseste... [3.921a], 95
Distâncias [3.1204], 108
Distante álamo [21.40], 205
Divagação [3.779], 91
Dizei, senhora [3.833], 93
Do caçador feliz [3.1489b], 120
Do caçador feliz [3.1493], 121
12 Canciones [22.5], 210
12 Canciones populares [1.302], 28
Doçura de manhãzinha fresca [3.927b], 96
Dodo titit' [12.3], 169
Dois amô [3.876], 94
Dois cantos [3.26], 64
Dois epigramas, op. 36 [3.334], 75
Dois poemas [3.472], 79
Dois poemas de Geir Campos [3.1205], 108
Dolor [4.34a], 132
Dolor serrano (Triste) [1.473], 45
Dolor supremus, op. 21, no. 2 [3.970], 97
Dolores y Consuelo [1.225b], 20
Don pastores de Belén [1.244c], 22
Dona Domitilla [3.1288], 111
Dona Janaína [3.473], 80
Dona Janaína [3.919d], 95
Doña Paula Albarracín [1.303m], 29
¿Donde estás? [6.20], 142
Donde habite el olvido [1.298c], 27
¿Dónde vais zagala? [1.60b], 10

Dones sencillos [1.299c], 27
Donzela (Eu nasci no amor perfeito) [3.607c], 85
Dor [3.1105a], 103
Dor sem consolo, op. 32, no. 2 [3.971], 97
Dorme, dorme coração [3.1149], 106
Dorme... dorme... filhinho [3.62], 66
Dorme sobre o meu seio [3.571a], 84
Dorme-dorme [3.877], 94
Dos bueyes rojos [1.395d], 36
Dos canciones [15.1], 179
Dos canciones [15.7], 179
Dos canciones [15.25], 180
Dos canciones [15.70], 185
Dos canciones de Amado Villar [1.501], 47
Dos canciones de cuna, op. 57 [1.3], 4
2 Canciones infantiles [9.2], 158
Dos canciones, op. 2 [15.46], 182
Dos canciones, op. 3 [1.272], 26
Dos canciones para soprano y piano [15.37], 181
Dos cantares galaico-portugueses del siglos XIII, op. 18 [1.57], 10
Dos cantos gallegos, op. 3 [1.58], 10
Dos coplas para canto y piano [3.813], 92
Dos laúdes [1.433], 40
Dos Lieder [19.10], 196
Dos melodías, op. 31 [1.187], 18
Dos muchachas, op. 13 [3.1543], 122
Dos nanas [15.2], 179
Dos nocturnos para voz y piano [15.41], 182
Dos piezas [1.502], 47
Dos poemas de B. Dávalos [15.55], 183
Dos poesías de Amado Nervo, op. 28 [1.186], 18
Dos sonetos del toro [1.151], 16
Dos sonetos, op. 15: para canto y piano [15.34], 181
Dos tonadas cuyanas [1.515], 48
Douze chansons populaires de Catalogne / Dotze cançons populars de Catalunya [7.35], 151
Doze cantigas sensíveis, op. 99 [3.1107], 103
Doze músicas para canto e piano [3.574], 84
Dream Variations [14.1], 176
Dream variations [14.1e], 176
Drei Liebeslieder [4.36], 132
Drei Lieder--Trois mélodies, op. 19 [1.188], 18
Drömd lycka [3.972], 97
Du bist wie eine Blume [15.8], 180
Du hast Diamanten und Perlen [3.1017a], 99
Duas aves [3.1111b], 104
Duas canções [3.474], 80
Duas canções brasileiras [3.178], 69
Duas canções de Celso Brandt [3.475], 80
Duas canções de Cleómenes Campos [3.476], 80
Duas canções de Drummond [3.1108], 103

INDEX OF SONG AND SONG CYCLE TITLES

Duas canções de Gisele Ganade [3.1109], 103
Duas canções de Menotti del Picchia [3.477], 80
Duas canções de Renata [3.478], 80
Duas canções de Sílvia Celeste de Campos [3.479], 80
Duas canções de Susana de Campos [3.480], 80
Duas canções de Virginia Victorino (Tríptico de Virgínia Victorino), op. 141 [3.1110], 104
Duas canções, op. 17 [3.335], 75
Duas canções praianas [3.1251], 110
Duas cantigas de amor [3.481], 80
Duas cantigas de roda [3.380], 76
Duas coisas, op. 148, no. 4 [3.1099d], 102
Duas elegias místicas [3.757], 90
Duas flautas [3.27], 64
Duas irmãs [3.482], 80
Duas miniaturas [3.483], 80
Duas paisagens (Deux paysages) [3.1451], 117
Duas peças [3.1324], 113
Duas trovas para Luíza, op. 125 [3.1111], 104
Duda [1.449], 43
Due Madrigali [3.814], 92
Duelo de la patria (Marcha fúnebre) [6.44], 143
Duerme muñeca [21.27], 204
Duermen las nubes, op. 26 [21.23], 204
Dulce engaño [1.525b], 48
Dulce río Paraná [1.264], 25
Dunkelheit [5.15], 136
Dúo para pato y canario [15.71], 185
Dúvida [3.823], 92

É a ti flor do céu [3.231], 72
E agora... só me resta a minha voz [3.460a], 79
E agora José? [3.794], 92
É assim que eu faço [3.824], 92
É bem feito, torne a amar [3.746d], 90
Ê boi! [3.539], 83
E fico a pensar [3.484], 80
É Maracatu [3.589], 85
Ê mô kanceô [3.486], 80
E nada mais! [3.1290], 111
E quando o amor chegar [3.540], 83
É uma pena, doce amiga [3.492], 80
É vontade de te ver [3.1038], 100
Ea [1.3b], 4
Ê-bango-bango-ê [3.232], 72
Echa la copla, coplero [1.459e], 44
Edad del asombro [1.316], 29
Efeitos da saudade [3.746f], 90
Ein geistlich' Abendlied [1.188c], 18
Ein Lied..., so schön [1.191c], 18
Einklang [3.973], 97

Eis a vida [3.1452a], 117
Eita Brasil [3.1289], 111
El abanico [1.205d], 19
El abejorro [15.78d], 186
El alacrán [15.38f], 182
El alba [1.274a], 26
El alba [15.75a], 185
El Alba del Alhelí, op. 29 [4.30], 131
El albeador [1.312d], 29
El alma de la rosa [1.13e], 5
El ama y la chinita [1.193], 18
El amor de las flores (Canción) [1.490a], 45
El amor en los pañelos (Zamba para canto y piano) [1.276], 26
El amor melancólico (En estilo de Vidala) [1.490c], 46
El amor pícaro (Gato) [1.490d], 46
El ángel ángel [4.32d], 132
El ángel bueno [4.32c], 132
El ángel ceniciento [4.32e], 132
El ángel de los números [4.32b], 132
El ángel desengañado [7.3], 150
El anillo [2.5], 57
El arco iris [1.383g], 35
El arrepentío [1.445], 42
El arriero invisible [1.355], 33
El arriero serrano (Zamba) [1.474], 45
El arroyo [1.161a], 16
El arroyuelo [1.184c], 17
El ave marina [1.521], 48
El balandro (Balada) [7.17f], 150
El bambú [15.78j], 186
El bambú de la ventana de Li Ts'e Yun [2.11b], 58
El barrilete (Le cerf-volant) [1.85], 12
El barrio misterioso [21.54a], 206
El benteveo [1.205b], 19
El boyero [6.94], 146
El burro'e chilo [6.88], 146
El caballo de mar [1.194], 18
El caimán [15.78g], 186
El canario [1.383f], 35
El canto de las piedras [20.19b], 200
El carpintero [1.564], 53
El castigo [1.351b], 32
El cerro estaba plateado [1.312b], 29
El charquito [1.108], 14
El Chasque (Milonga) [1.195], 18
El chichemito (Guaracha panameña) [17.1], 191
El cielo hasta mi casa [1.386b], 35
El clavel del aire blanco [1.324b], 30
El clavelito en tus lindos cabellos [3.878], 94
El "Cola-blanca" [1.433b], 40

INDEX OF SONG AND SONG CYCLE TITLES

El colibrí [1.36], 9
El coyotillo (Callejera) [6.46], 143
El día inútil [1.37], 9
El embrujao [1.456c], 43
El encuentro [7.51], 153
El espejo de agua [4.11], 130
El faro [15.75f], 185
El farolero y su novia [4.30h], 131
El flechazo (Canción en el estilo popular argentino) [1.450], 43
El forastero (Canción) [1.302i], 28
El galán y la calavera [1.496c], 46
El gato [1.249f], 23
El gnomo silbodo [1.183], 17
El grillo [21.28], 204
El indiecito [1.542c], 50
El indiecito de Pichi-Mahuida [1.540d], 50
El instante [1.494a], 46
El jardín de mi escuela [1.383c], 35
El jardín encantado [1.390], 36
El labrador y el pobre [1.318], 30
El lagarto [15.69e], 185
El lago [1.38], 9
El lago [1.557e], 51
El lucero [1.458b], 43
El mágico jardín [1.240], 21
El mate amargo [1.39], 9
El mediodía [1.274c], 26
El mishito [11.17], 164
El morir de la rosa [6.21], 142
El murciélago [1.547], 51
El negrito de Esquipulas (Parrandero) [6.56], 143
El nido [21.29], 204
El nido ausente, op. 50 [1.1b], 4
El niño azul [15.38e], 182
El niño mudo [2.5a], 57
El ojo de agua [20.19a], 200
El ombú [1.256a], 24
El pajarito del frío [1.303c], 28
El pájaro y el gato (L'oiseau et le chat) [1.86], 12
El palito (Aire nacional) [1.207], 19
El palito (Danza) [1.64f], 11
El paraiso [1.392], 36
El pardal quan s'ajocava [7.35i], 152
El paso de las estrellas [1.312c], 29
El patio [1.383e], 35
El pavo real [15.78a], 186
El payador [1.109], 14
El peregrino [1.414], 37
El pescadito [1.457e], 43
El pescador sin dinero [4.30f], 131
El picaflor [1.457c], 43

El pino que fue monje [1.152], 16
El pino y la palmera [7.48], 153
El pobre alegre [7.36c], 152
El poeta a su amada, op. 8 [19.1], 195
El poncho [1.475], 45
El poncho [21.30], 204
El pozo [22.17f], 211
El pregón [4.30c], 131
El prisionero [1.319], 30
El puente [1.249a], 23
El quetzal [1.40], 9
El ram de la passió [7.35b], 151
El retorno [1.541c], 50
El río de montaña (Zamba) [1.486e], 45
El rosal [1.41], 9
El ruido de las grandes crecientes [1.21g], 6–7
El sampedrino (Canción pampeana) [1.302b], 28
El sauz [15.78c], 186
El señor de la casa del tiempo [10.5], 160
El silencio [22.8i], 210
El sirirí [1.250c], 23
El sol [1.256b], 24
El sol de tu querer (Zamba) [1.476], 45
El sueño [1.99e], 13
El sueño hoy no quiere venir por acá [1.15f], 5
El sueño (Il sogno) [1.141], 15
El tala [21.31], 204
El tecolote [11.18], 164
El tecolote [15.72], 185
El testament d'Amelia [7.35d], 151
El toro sabe [1.151a], 16
El triunfo de la muerte [21.4], 203
El único camino [1.320], 30
El vaso [1.321], 30
El viaje de papel [1.303f], 28
El viejo cacique [1.477], 45
El viento [1.153], 16
El viento [1.418], 38
El vinagrillo morado [1.324d], 30
El vuelo [1.61b], 10
El yaraví [1.42], 9
El zorzal [1.205c], 19
El zorzal [1.256c], 24
El zorzal (Canto tucumano), op. 54 [1.3c], 4
Ela era virgem [3.1223], 109
Elegía [1.346g], 32
Elegia [3.303b], 74
Elegia [3.659f], 87
Elegia [3.795], 92
Elegia [3.1176], 107
Elegía [15.75d], 185
Elegia da manhã [3.336], 75

INDEX OF SONG AND SONG CYCLE TITLES

Elegía de junio [10.4], 160
Elegía frente al mar [15.29c], 181
Elegía para un gorrión [1.317], 30
Élégie [12.17c], 170
Elisabeau [3.195a], 70
Elle est si jolie [1.124], 14
Elle s'avance, elle s'éloigne... [1.23f], 7
Elogio de las rosas [1.13], 5
Elogio del poncho (Canción pampeana) [1.69], 11
Els fadrins de Sant Boi [7.351], 152
Elvira, escuta [3.485], 80
Em algum lugar [3.1171d], 107
Em cantos do Brasil [3.1494], 121
Em louvor do silêncio [3.524e], 82
Em meu coração fycays, op. 45 [3.1404], 115
Em uma frondosa roseira [3.698], 89
Embolada do Brigadeiro [3.879], 94
Empolvado de seda... [10.10a], 161
En casa del tío Vicente [11.13b], 164
En ce gracieux temps d'estè [3.195b], 70
En Cuba [11.19], 164
En el barrio de arriba... (El día de las almas) [1.416b], 38
En el brocal (Romanza) [5.34], 137
En el café de Chinitas [7.33c], 151
En el camino (de Aromas de Leyenda) [22.15f], 211
En el corazón del sueño [15.40d], 182
En el huerto [6.22], 142
En el parque [22.10d], 210
En el pimpollo mas alto [1.322], 30
En el portal de Belén [1.251a], 23
En el templo [1.522], 48
En la alameda de ese jardín [5.68], 138
En la arboleda [1.21f], 6
En la ausencia [1.400a], 37
En la copa de los montes [21.6], 203
En la cuna blanca (Canción escolar) [1.273], 26
En la mañana azul [1.437c], 40
En la playa [5.7], 136
En la punta del aquel cerro [1.363b], 33
En la ribera [1.187a], 18
En la ribera [1.459c], 44
En lo alto de aquel monte [1.395b], 36
En los surcos del amor... [1.300c], 28
En Madrid la bella (Bolero) [1.241], 21
En mai [1.232], 21
En mañanas como ésta [15.29a], 180
En mi escuela hay un naranjo [1.303a], 28
En mi nocturno sueño [15.80a], 186
En mi soledad [1.527], 48
En nia lando [3.149], 68

En paz [1.185c], 18
En Puntarenas (Popular) [6.15], 142
En San Luis no te enamores... [1.107a], 13
En sourdine [1.432d], 39
En su llama mortal [3.1423b], 116
En vano me has de buscar [1.107c], 13
Encantamiento [1.343c], 31
Encanto [1.458a], 43
Encontrei-te, op. 148, no. 6 [3.1099f], 102
Encontro [3.1495], 121
Enemiga le soy madre... [4.23b], 130
Engenho d'água [3.1291], 111
Engenho novo [3.165b], 69
Engenho novo [3.1323c], 112
Enigma [6.23], 142
Enigma de la palabra [1.556], 51
Enjambre [1.560f], 52
Ensueños, romanza para soprano [5.55], 138
Entardecer, op. 44, no. 1 [3.199], 70
Entendimiento [15.29b], 181
Entonces [1.21e], 6
Entracto cantado-Shenta se transforma en Shuita [6.80e], 145
Entre casados de honor (Quasi punto) [7.17c], 150
Entre-estrelas [3.1540a], 122
Entretanto, eu canto [3.590], 85
Entschluss [1.191a], 18
Epigrama [3.366], 76
Epigrama [3.825], 92
Epigrama [3.1452d], 118
Epigrama 1 [1.247a], 23
Epigrama 2 [1.247b], 23
Epigrama 3 [1.247c], 23
Epigrama 4 [1.247d], 23
Epigrama 5 [1.247e], 23
Epigrama 6 [1.247f], 23
Epigrama 7 [1.247g], 23
Epigrama 8 [1.247h], 23
Epigrama 9 [1.247i], 23
Epigrama 10 [1.247j], 23
Epigrama número 9 [3.233], 72
Epigramas irônicos e sentimentais [3.1452], 117
Epílogo [3.477c], 80
Epílogo-"Guitarra sola" [6.79e], 145
Episódio [3.834], 93
Epitafio de una rosa [1.154], 16
Epitafios [7.42], 153
Epitalâmio [3.974], 97
Equando ele voltar [3.365], 76
Era aquilo só [3.1320b], 112
¿Eres tú? [1.125], 14
Eres tu (Bolero) [11.20], 164

INDEX OF SONG AND SONG CYCLE TITLES

Erzulie [12.25s], 171
Erzulie eh [12.25w], 171
Erzulie malade [12.25v], 171
Erzulie oh [12.25h], 171
És a mais bela... [3.487], 80
És a totalmente amada [3.488], 80
Es de noche, te estoy viendo [15.36c], 181
Es la mañana llena de tempestad [3.1423d], 116
És na minha vida [3.489], 80
¡Es Navidad! (Canción a dos voces) [1.419], 38
Es verdad... [1.155], 16
Es verdad [15.5a], 179
Es verdad (Andaluzas) [1.24g], 7
Esa canción [1.461a], 44
Escadas da Penha, op. 118, no. 2 [3.1109b], 103
Escena [2.5b], 57
Escogiendo novia [1.496d], 46
Esconde esses teus olhos [3.1253], 110
Escondido (Estilización) [1.110], 14
Escondumba-a-rê [3.1265], 110
Escoteiro pequenino [3.1292], 111
Escravo [3.19d], 64
Escrito em minha vidraça [3.403f], 77
Escuadra [1.330d], 31
Espelho [3.234], 72
Espelhos [3.1496], 121
Espera [3.490], 80
Espera [15.56], 183
Espera inútil [3.206b], 70
Espinillo [1.19b], 6
Espiral [3.28e], 64
Espiral II [3.28], 64
Espíritu guanacasteco [6.4], 141
Esquecimento [3.367], 76
Essa negra fulô [3.337], 75
Essa negra fulô [3.591], 85
Esse vazio que nada enche [3.491], 80
Esta arte de cortar flores [3.380a], 76
Esta iglesia no tiene... [1.323], 30
Está lloviendo en mi escuela [1.303b], 28
Esta verde hierba... (en modo mixolidio) [15.65d], 184
Estado yo aqui (Az ij bin do) [1.443c], 42
Estampas de Vila Rica [3.235], 72
Éstas lágrimas tan bellas [20.5], 199
Est-ce toi? [1.26h], 8
Este es el viento [1.478], 45
Este galapaguito: nana [7.33d], 151
Este niñito compró un huevito [4.1a], 129
Este pajarito [1.383a], 35
Est-il mort? [5.44], 137
Esto [1.61c], 10

Estos ojos que ahora están mirándo... [10.1c], 160
Estou com medo [3.513b], 81
Estoy continuando al aire que me sigue... [10.8f], 161
Estoy en un verde prado [1.370c], 34
Estrela [3.1138], 105
Estrela azul [3.1037], 100
Estrela do Mar [3.1014a], 99
Estrela do mar op. 10 no. 3 [3.1089c], 101
Estrela é lua nova [3.1443e], 117
Estrela pequenina [3.1293], 111
Estrella [22.10c], 210
Estrella doble [1.557g], 52
Estrella perdida [6.24], 142
Estrellas fijas [15.9], 180
Estrellita [15.57], 177, 183
Estudiante baleado [4.37], 132
Et cette herbe délicieuse [3.890c], 94
Et le desert sera mon paradis [3.890d], 94
Était-il une heure [3.195c], 70
Etéreo, op. 118, no. 1 [3.1109a], 103
Eterna música [3.1497], 121
Eu bem sei [3.1325c], 113
Eu cantador [3.1334], 113
Eu diferente da vida [3.1546b], 123
Eu digo a meu próprio coração [3.479b], 80
Eu gosto de você [3.510d], 81
Eu ia nadá [3.541], 83
Eu não sei [3.1177], 107
Eu queria cair na tua vida [3.927c], 96
Eu quero bem... [3.692c], 89
Eu sinto dentro do peito [3.493], 80
Eu sou como a garça triste [3.1542e], 122
Eu sou flor arremessada [3.400c], 77
Eu te amo [3.1453], 118
Eu te encontrei [3.494], 80
Eu te esperei na hora silenciosa [3.472a], 79
Eu te esperei na hora silenciosa [3.927d], 96
Eu vi uma lagartixa [3.1294], 111
Europa, França e Bahia [3.1544], 122
Evocação [3.1105c], 103
Evocação [3.1465g], 119
Evocação Paulista, 1st Album [3.302], 74
Evocação Paulista, 2nd Album [3.303], 74
Evocação sertaneja [3.304], 74
Evocación a mi tierra [2.7], 57
Evocaciones indias [1.3a], 4
Exágono I [15.17a], 180
Exágono II [15.17b], 180
Exágono III [15.17c], 180
Exaltação [3.391a], 76

INDEX OF SONG AND SONG CYCLE TITLES

Exaltação [3.592], 85
Exercicio de prosódia [3.53], 65
Extase [3.880], 94
Extase [15.10], 180
Extasis [22.10f], 210
Ezili malad [12.30c], 172

Fada azul [3.1308f], 111
Fala [3.532a], 83
Fala o poeta, op. 148, no. 33 [3.1099g], 102
Fantasía (Romanza) [1.177], 17
Fantasma [19.5b], 195
Farândola das horas [3.881], 94
Farei o que tu fizeres [3.699], 89
Fatalità, op. 96 [3.1359], 114
Faz isso comigo não (Toada) [3.1295], 111
Fé [3.368], 76
Featureless [18.1c], 193
Feliciano me adora [15.34b], 181
Felicidade [3.431], 78
Felicidade [3.542], 83
Felicidade [3.700], 89
Felicidade [3.1319b], 112
Felicidade [3.1320a], 112
Felicidade I [3.830d], 93
Felicidade II [3.830e], 93
Feliz aniversário [3.1441a], 117
Feliz Ano Novo [3.1441d], 117
Feliz Natal [3.1441c], 117
Féminité [12.41c], 172
Fenomenologia da certeza [3.835], 93
Ferreira (Tango) [9.4b], 158
Festa [3.1296], 111
Festa na Bahia [3.882], 94
Festa no brejo [3.1550c], 123
Festim pagão [3.1454], 118
Festival (Maracatu) [3.1303c], 111
Fèy ô [12.30b], 172
Fi nan bois [12.15b], 170
Fibra de herói [3.543], 83
Fides [3.762a], 91
Fiesta en Santa Cruz [6.58], 143
Filant [1.87], 12
Filha, se grado edes [1.57b], 10
Filomela (Philomela), op. 18, no. 2 [3.975], 97
Fim de romance [3.925b], 95
Fin de un sueño [10.4a], 160
Fin del mundo [1.56a], 10
Finismundo—A última viagem I [3.836], 93
Fiz da vida uma canção (valsa) [3.593], 85
Fleur fanée, op. 18 [3.1455], 118
Fleur mourante [1.233], 21

Fleurs d'amour (Romance) [1.234], 21
Flor andaluza [3.883], 94
Flor de bronce (Canto indio) [2.2], 57
Flor de cardo [1.17c], 6
Flor de cardón (Vidala), op. 2 no. 3 [1.408], 37
Flor de ceibo [1.226], 21
Flor de ceibo [1.504c], 47
Flor de durazno [1.504b], 47
Flor de ruína [3.403c], 77
Flor de tuna [1.504a], 47
Flor invisible [6.25], 142
Florcita de aire [1.208], 19
Flores [3.976], 97
Flores argentinas [1.324], 30
Flores de almendro [1.196], 18
Flores de cardón [1.43], 9
Flores del monte [21.32], 204
Flower of Hope (Fior di speranza) [1.227], 21
Foi assim o seu amor [3.395], 77
Foi Bôto, sinhá! [3.598b], 85
Foi n'uma noite calmosa [3.414a], 77
Foi numa noite calmosa [3.1239e], 109
Foi o vento . . . foi a vida [3.495], 80
Folhas soltas [3.1224], 109
Folklores harmonisés, op. 7 [12.16], 170
Fonte eterna [3.1498], 121
Food for Thought [3.1462d], 118
Forest of the Amazon/Canções da floresta do Amazonas (Excerpt)/Green Mansion [3.1456], 118
Fragmento [3.28f], 64
Fragmento para um réquiem [3.1196b], 108
Francisca'e Paula Chirimoya [1.18e], 6
Frescas sombras de sauces [1.376c], 34
Frio manto de estrelas bordado [3.1542f], 122
Friquitín [20.17a], 200
Frühlingsfeier [1.191d], 18
Fuensanta [15.26], 180
Fuente [21.54c], 206
Fuga da inspiração [3.54], 65
Fugueta a dos voces [5.11], 136
Fui no livro do destino [3.692d], 89
Funeral coya [1.44], 9
Funeral de ilusões (op. 120) [3.1402b], 115
Funeral de ilusões, op. 120 [3.1405], 115
Funeral d'um rei Nagô (Canto do Alufá) [3.1297], 111
Furinhos, op. 148, no. 15 [3.1099o], 102
Futuro [5.61], 138

Gaita [3.427a], 78
Gaivota [3.1039], 100
Galán, galancillo . . . [1.24i], 7

INDEX OF SONG AND SONG CYCLE TITLES

Gallinita blanca [1.11b], 4
Garça parda leviana [3.1541b], 122
Garlopin [1.330f], 31
Gato [1.175e], 17
Gato [1.271e], 26
Gato [1.472c], 44
Gato preto [3.638], 87
Gauchinha [3.135], 68
Gauchinha [3.284], 73
Gaucho mensajero [1.507], 47
Gavião de penacho [3.150], 68
Gavião Penerô [3.1250d], 110
Gavião penerô (Coco) [3.1252], 110
Gaviotas [4.33j], 132
Gedicht [3.977], 97
Génesis [1.99d], 13
Geografía física [1.346e], 32
Gimiendo por ver el mar... [15.35e], 181
Gisella [3.1308e], 111
Gitana [5.8], 136
Gitana (Tango-canción) [6.95], 146
Glosa [1.244d], 22
Glosa de Beatriz [22.17i], 209, 211
Glosa para hablar mal del amor [22.17e], 211
Goces de la creación, op. 113 [1.248], 23
Gorrión [1.335h], 31
Gosto de estar a teu lado [3.496], 80
Gotas de pranto [3.1106c], 103
Goteira do coração [3.1111a], 104
Gotitas de agua (Canción de cuna) [22.8f], 210
Gozo efímero [20.25e], 200
Granada (Fantasía española) [15.42], 178, 182
Gratidão [3.1406], 115
Gratidão (op. 124) [3.1402e], 115
Green [1.432b], 39
Grietas [7.4], 150
Grito [1.492b], 46
Gros loa moin [12.25r], 171
Guacyra (Baião) [3.1298], 111
Guédé Nibo [12.25t], 171
Guédé Zareigné [12.25u], 171
Guerra insondável [3.780], 91
Güeya [1.178], 17
Guitarra [1.431], 39
Guitarra [22.4a], 209, 210

Há nos teus olhos [3.266], 72
Há o mutismo exaltado dos astros 1929 [3.513c], 81
Há sempre uma palavra [3.1040], 100
Habanera [3.1070], 101
Hace ocho meses [15.61f], 184

Hacia el comienzo [15.47], 183
¡Hacia el mar! himno patriótico [5.53], 138
H'acuchu! (¡Vámonos!) [19.16b], 196
Hai Guetaza [3.1266], 110
Haïti ma jolie... [12.10], 169
Haïtienesques [12.15], 167–68, 170
Hallazgo [1.343a], 31
Hallazgo [4.42b], 132
Hame contado Don Diego [15.74h], 185
Harmonização de Acchile Picchi de canção do Cancioneiro de músicas populares de César das Neves [3.1112], 104
¿Has venido a mí, llena de pena? [1.126], 14
Hasta siempre [7.44], 153
Hat sie sich denn nie geäussert [3.1017b], 99
Hay un instante en el crepúsculo [5.37], 137
Hayno (Al caer la tarde) [1.559c], 52
Hayno (Canción de otoño) [1.559a], 52
Hayno (Las semillas del cardo) [1.559b], 52
He aquí el líquido puro de mi amor [6.63a], 144
He guardado (Callejera) [6.77], 145
He pasado a otros mundos... [10.8g], 161
He tomado los gestos... [10.8d], 161
He vestido con encajes de espuma [20.30c], 201
He vivido horas sin igual (Hesitation waltz) [7.17a], 150
Hei de morrer cantando [3.594], 85
Hei de seguir teus passos: maracatú [3.595], 85
Herbst [3.978], 97
Hermano (Canción del sur) [1.302k], 28
Hermione et les bergers [3.1457e], 118
Hidrófana [3.979], 97
Hijo'el pais (a la manera popular) [1.111], 14
Hilando el copo del viento [22.16d], 211
Himno a la madre [15.53a], 183
Himno agrario [7.50], 153
Himno de la CUT [4.12], 130
Hino a Brasília [3.263], 72
Hino ao governador da cidade [3.432], 78
Hino aos Arcanjos São Miguel e São Gabriel [3.596], 85
Hino do Amazonas [3.1178], 107
História antiga [3.533c], 83
História curta [3.369], 76
Historieta [3.276], 73
Historieta (Pastoral) [3.63], 66
Historietas [3.1457], 118
Ho sognato [1.127], 14
Homenaje a Julián Aguirre [1.112], 14
Homenaje a Masías [19.15], 196
Hormiguita (Canción infantil) [1.378], 35
Hornero [1.335c], 31

INDEX OF SONG AND SONG CYCLE TITLES

Horquilla [1.330e], 31
How Should I Your True Love [3.573a], 84
How Should I Your True Love [3.684b], 88
Hoy... [6.26], 142
Hoy buscarás en vano... [1.438d], 40
Hoy como ayer... [1.494d], 46
Hoy es Nochebuena [1.244b], 22
Hoy no lució la estrella de tus ojos [15.18b], 180
Huainito [1.209], 19
Huainito (Manchay Puito) [1.277], 26
Huaynu [1.204e], 19
Huella [1.128], 15
Huella [21.1b], 203
Huerto de marzo [7.19d], 151
Hueya [1.14], 5
Humaitá [3.1323b], 112
Hymne aux héros [12.37], 172
Hymne du bicentenaire [12.6], 169
Hymno à escola [3.111], 67
Hymno ao estudo [3.87], 66
Hymno ao trabalho [3.112], 67
Hymno dos voluntários [3.113], 67
Hymno escolar [3.88], 67

I, too, sing America [14.1a], 176
Iara [3.1476c], 120
Ich wollte bei dir weilen [1.190d], 18
Ici-bas, op. 46 [3.1360], 114
Ida e volta (op. 118) [3.1402c], 115
Ida e volta, op. 118 [3.1407], 115
Ideti (a menina preta que buscava Deus) [3.236], 72
Idilio [1.113], 14
Idilio [1.461c], 44
Iemanjá oto [3.1014b], 99
Igreja de Arrabalde [3.1139], 105
Il a neigé [12.5], 169
Il était jadis un berger [1.16i], 5
Il était une fois [1.16j], 5
Il flotte dans l'air (La chanson du silence) [3.980], 98
Il ne revient pas! [1.28], 8
Il neo [3.1071], 101
Il nome di Maria [3.1458], 118
Il pleure dans mon coeur [12.17b], 170
Il te versera sa chaleur [12.9d], 169
Ileana [10.9a], 161
Ilusão [3.210a], 71
Ilusión [5.2], 136
Ilusión [22.13a], 210
Imagem [3.206a], 70
Imagem [3.884], 94

Imagem [3.1452g], 118
Imaginária serenata [3.1499], 121
Imaginário serenata [3.1489c], 120
Imillita [19.15a], 196
Impresión (Canción escolar) [1.420], 38
Impresiones boriquenses [20.17], 200
Improviso [3.1194c], 108
Improviso no. 1 [3.885], 94
In der Ferne [1.190b], 18
In der Wüste [3.396], 77
In dono [1.401], 37
In extremis [3.433], 78
In mein gar zu dunkles Leben [3.1017c], 99
In Memoriam Elisa Huezo Paredes: Yo tengo que decir mi palabra [10.6], 161
Incerto nexo, op. 86 [3.1545], 122
Incompatibilidades [3.264], 72
Indio enamorado (Danza típica) [6.47], 143
Indiscrição [3.1244b], 109
Infância, op. 112, no. 1 [3.1104a], 103
Infância brasileira [3.416a], 78
Ingemisco [3.981], 98
Ingratidão [3.830f], 93
Inquietação [3.19e], 64
Insomnio [15.58], 183
Inspiração súbita [3.1113], 104
Instantâneo do adeus [3.237], 72
Instrumento [3.29], 64
Interior [3.200], 70
Intermezzo [3.497], 80
Interpretações [3.416], 78
Interrogação [3.311], 74
Inútil epigrama [3.1452b], 118
Inutil epigramma [15.11], 180
Invierno [1.45], 9
Invierno [1.140b], 15
Invocação (Maracatú) [3.1303a], 111
Invocação à natureza [3.89], 67
Io non ho che l'amor del mio tesor [3.886], 94
Iorando p'adentro (Puneña) [1.402], 37
Iremos a los Astros... [5.45], 137
Irene no céu [3.1225], 109
Ironia [3.19b], 64
Irremediável canção [3.1179], 107
Isla [20.19c], 200
Ismália, op. 46a [3.758], 90
Itabaiana [3.14431], 117

Já hoje que aqui me vistes [3.498], 80
Ja sempr'en coita viverei, op. 38 [3.1408], 115
J'ai cueilli cette fleur... [1.210], 19
J'ai des p'tites fleurs bleues [1.551b], 51

INDEX OF SONG AND SONG CYCLE TITLES

J'ai gardé dans mon coeur [1.26k], 8
J'ai presque peur [12.17e], 170
J'ai soif de ton âme [1.26l], 8
J'ai ta tête sur mon épaule, 173
J'ai voulu, op. 26 [3.136l], 114
Janaína, op. 18, no. 3 [3.1026c], 100
Jangada [3.201], 70
Japonesas [3.1464e], 119
Jardim fanado [3.1459], 118
Jardim noturno [3.1171a], 107
Jardín antiguo [1.327a], 30
Jardín de amores [1.346a], 32
Jardín de ensueño [22.8g], 210
Jardins . . . [1.4], 4
Jazmín del país: ¡qué lindo . . . ! [1.324h], 30
Je ne peux apercevoir le ciel [12.9b], 169
Jesus [3.90], 67
Jicarita [15.27a], 180
João cambuête [3.1466e], 119
Jogo da lua nova [3.1213b], 108
Jogo de Varisto [3.1213c], 108
Jogo do Tantanguê [3.1213a], 108
Jogo negro [3.815], 92
Joropo [11.21], 164
Jous sans retard, car vite s'écoule la vie [3.1457f], 118
Joven divina [15.61c], 183
Juan Ramón Jiménez [1.532b], 49
Juierio [1.88], 12
Juierio [1.129], 15
Jujeña [1.35d], 9
Jujeña [1.382f], 35
Juju, sossego (Acalanto) [3.202], 70
Junto al tempisque (Danza) [6.3], 141
Juntos amamos [3.531a], 82
Juntos amamos [3.536c], 83
Júrame (Tango) [15.32], 181
Júri do coração [3.925c], 95
Juriti [3.397], 77
Juriti (Canção amazônica) [3.597], 85
Jurupanã (Coco) [3.1250b], 110
Juventud [7.25], 151

Kamaló [3.1442c], 117
Kapuri (La hilandera) [2.3], 56, 57
Kessy [3.1227], 109
Kleine Gedichte, op. 90 [3.1017], 99
Kori Killa (Luna de oro) [2.4], 56, 57

La amistad [20.25d], 200
La aurora [15.52c], 183
La barca [1.548], 51

La batalla [15.77b], 186
La belenista (Chacarera catamarqueña) [1.64b], 10–11
La belle aux fleurs [3.78l], 91
La cabrita blanca [1.542a], 50
La calandria [1.457a], 43
La calesita [1.415e], 38
La campana (Ecuatoriana) [1.387b], 36
La campera (Estilo zamba) [1.64a], 10
La campesina [5.22], 136
La caña la están cortando [22.8e], 210
La canción de la moza de los ojos pardos [21.9c], 203
La canción de los ojos amados [1.265], 25
La canción del chingolo [1.171c], 17
La canción del Saldán, op. 2 no. 2 [1.409], 37
La canción desesperada [3.1423g], 116
La canción desolada [1.379], 35
La canción mi vida [1.56c], 10
La casa [15.38b], 182
La casada infiel [1.156], 16
La casada infiel [15.12], 180
La casita [6.42], 143
La casita del hornero [1.383b], 35
La Cenicienta (Canción), op. 6 no. 2 [1.410], 37
La chacarerita doble (Danza) [1.65d], 11
La chanson de Marie-des-Anges [1.385c], 35
La chanson des baisers [1.29], 8
La chileciteña (Zamba) [1.278], 26
La chucara [1.451], 43
La cloche fêlée [3.168], 69
La cogida y la muerte [3.1018c], 99
La comparsa [7.26], 151
La copla es copla si nace . . . [1.538b], 49
La corriente continuaba . . . [10.8c], 161
La cosecha [6.72], 144
La dama d'Aragó [7.35c], 151
La danza de las liebres [1.254], 24
La dernière feuille [1.211], 19–20
La despedida [15.63c], 184
La dulce noche [1.356], 33
Lá em cima daquele morro [3.1267], 110
La ermita [15.37b], 181
La escuela de las flores [1.421], 38
La escuelita nacional [1.543a], 50
La espera [5.29], 137
La euforia nos nace y muere adentro [10.4e], 160
La fe del ciego [4.26a], 130
La fée aux chansons [1.26j], 8
La feuille [3.1363], 114
La filla del marxant [7.35j], 152
La flecha [21.42], 205

INDEX OF SONG AND SONG CYCLE TITLES

La fleur ardente [3.40b], 65
La flor de aguapé [1.324j], 30
La flor del aire [1.46], 9
La flor del Candil [4.30d], 131
La flor en el alma [1.361a], 33
La frontera: Detrás de la pared [1.316i], 30
La frontera: En el sueño de la calle [1.316h], 29
La frontera: Era un día de lluvia [1.316g], 29
La fuente [8.2], 156
La fuente [15.54c], 183
La fuente [19.13b], 196
La fuente abandonada [22.15a], 211
La garza herida [6.55b], 143
La gata i el belitre [7.36d], 152
La gitana [4.30e], 131
La glosa de los ríos [22.17g], 211
La golondrina [11.22], 164
La güeya [21.33], 204
La guitarra de los negros [1.162a], 16
La hija del viejo Pancho [20.10], 199
La hora tranquila [15.77a], 185
La huella gaucha (Huella) [1.486d], 45
La imagen de tu perfil, rondó [5.3], 136
La inicial [1.400b], 37
La lampe dans la nuit [3.40c], 65
La lavandera [1.528], 49
La lluvia [6.74], 144
La lluvia [15.52d], 183
La lluvia lenta [4.35d], 132
La loba, la loba le compró al lobito [1.15b], 5
La Lola, op. 13, no. 1 [3.1543a], 122
Lá longe, no sul [3.513d], 81
La luna [15.52b], 183
La luna es entre las nubes (de Las Pastorales) [22.15e], 211
La luna se llama Lola [1.142], 15
La luna sobre el agua de los lagos [5.46], 137
La lune [1.4g], 4
La madrecita [1.403], 37
La madrugada [1.440h], 41
La madrugada [1.561f], 52
La malagueña [11.23], 164
La mañana [1.274b], 26
La mañana está de fiesta [1.122b], 14
La mano del hombre [1.99b], 13
La mar de Déu [7.35a], 151
La mariposa [15.78h], 186
La mariposa (Canción), op. 6 no. 1 [1.411], 37
La más bella niña [15.40c], 182
La moza que quiere un viejo (Tonada) [1.64d], 11
La muerte sube que sube [1.100a], 13
La muerte ya no es un toro [1.100c], 13

La música [1.303i], 28
La neblina [1.557d], 51
La niña ausente [15.45a], 182
La niña de Guatemala (Guajira romance) [7.34b], 151
La niña de la guitarra [5.62], 138
La noche [1.274e], 26
La noche [4.33i], 132
La noche [10.9b], 161
La noche blanca de luna [21.10a], 203
La Noche Buena (Canción tradicional de Navidad) [6.96], 146
La noche del Llano Abajo [22.16b], 211
La noche murmura [6.79c], 145
La novia [1.346d], 32
La novia [4.30b], 131
La nuit n'est jamais complète [3.1180], 107
La ofrenda del trovado (Estilo) [1.279], 26
La orden de Lázaro, romanza [5.9], 136
La paloma [11.25], 164
La paloma torcaza [1.250b], 23
La palomita [1.299a], 27
La parra quebrada [1.70], 11
La pasionaria [1.47], 9
La Paula i en Jordi [7.35e], 151
La pena [1.560a], 52
La peña [15.61b], 183
La plegaria [1.205e], 19
La plenitud [15.4b], 179
La prière du marchand de sable [3.1181], 107
La primavera [15.52a], 183
La primavera viene (Melodía) [1.259], 24
La primera pregunta (El adolescente muerto) [1.325], 30
La profecía [1.169], 16
La provincianita (Zamba) [1.542d], 50
La razón de mi cariño [1.171b], 17
La rosa [1.479], 45
La rosa de la aurora [1.13a], 5
La rosa del ensueño [1.13d], 5
La rosa enflorece [7.39c], 152
La rosa y el colibrí [1.13c], 5
La rosa y el sauce [1.326], 30
La rose [1.4d], 4
La rose [1.235], 21
La ruina y el viento [1.48], 9
La saca, op. 56 [1.100], 13
La sangre derramada [3.1018d], 99
La sed del agua [20.20a], 200
La señora Luna le pidió al naranjo [1.15e], 5
La shulca [1.549], 51
La Siempre Viva (Canción del litoral) [1.302j], 28

La siesta [1.561e], 52
La signora del fuoco [3.887], 94
La silenciosa [1.236], 21
La sombra [15.54b], 183
La sombra salió del monte [22.16f], 211
La sombra (Yaraví) [1.175d], 17
La Soncoyeña [6.59], 143
La suyuqueña (Chacarera), op. 8 no. 1 [1.412], 37
La tabaquerita [1.204f], 19
La tacuarita [1.457d], 43
La tapera [1.17a], 6
La tapera [1.34c], 9
La tapera [1.364c], 33
La tarde [1.17b], 6
La tarde [1.274d], 26
La tarde [15.75b], 185
La tarde era triste [11.27], 164
La telesita (Estilo) [1.280], 26
La tempranera [1.328], 30
La terruca [20.15], 200
La tierra estaba amarilla [1.395c], 36
La tristeza del güetar [6.98], 146
La última hoja [1.303j], 28
La urna [1.560g], 52
La vaca dorada [1.244a], 22
Lá vai São Francisco [3.1336], 113
La vaquera esquiva [1.357], 33
La vejez de los pueblos [1.442q], 42
La vertiente [1.525a], 48
La vida pasa... [20.25b], 200
La vidalita [21.41], 205
La vieja Inés [15.38c], 182
La viuda que se casa [1.460c], 44
La viudita [1.250a], 23
Là-bas [1.161], 6
L'absence [1.89], 12
Ladainha [3.701], 89
Lagoa [3.837], 93
Lagoa [3.888], 94
Lágrimas (Romanza) [19.4g], 195
Lágrimas brancas [3.782], 91
Lágrimas de cera [3.151], 68
Lais de Leonoreta, op. 53 [3.1409], 115
Lament: Vocalise [11.24], 164
Lamentação da hora perdida [3.702], 89
Lamento [3.838], 93
Lamento [3.1335], 113
Lamento (en la tumba de Manuel de Falla), op. 13 [1.59], 10
Lamento (Mírala como ha venido) [1.380], 35
Lamento dos pinheirais [3.136], 68
Lamento indio (Vidala) [1.452], 43

Lamento lento [19.5a], 195
L'amour naissant, op. 51 [3.1362], 114
Languidece [21.10c], 204
Lapacho [1.19c], 6
Las abejas [15.78b], 186
Las acacias [1.35e], 9
Las achiras coloradas [1.324g], 30
Las calesitas (Les chevaux de bois) [1.90], 12
Las campanas de San Juan [6.82b], 145
Las canciones de Natacha [1.15], 5
Las canciones felices [1.249], 23
Las cinco horas [15.69c], 185
Las erupciones [15.20], 180
Las estrellas binarias... [10.1a], 160
Las flores del macachín [1.324f], 30
Las garzas, op. 44 [5.38], 137
Las horas de una estancia, op. 11 [1.274], 26
Las mañanitas [11.26], 164
Las mañanitas, op. 43 [1.1c], 4
Las mariposas [1.457f], 43
Las mujeres son las moscas [3.889], 94
Las nubes [1.327], xx, 30
Las nubes de mi mente [1.560e], 52
Las palabras [1.556b], 51
Las playas del coco (Vals) [6.97], 146
Las puertas de la mañana... [1.301d], 28
Las rosas de la tarde [1.13b], 5
Las seis cuerdas [15.5b], 179
Las siete notas [1.49], 9
Las toninas [15.78e], 186
Las tres toronjas (Para niños) [1.422], 38
Laudate Dominum, Psalm 16, op. 226 [3.1410], 115
Laude L (Palabras filiales a la Virgen) [1.433a], 40
Lauf der Welt [1.190f], 18
Laura [3.91], 67
Laurel [1.19f], 6
Lavandeirinha [3.1299], 111
L'aveugle á la rose [3.398], 77
Laza oh [12.25k], 171
Le Bohémien [1.551a], 51
Le chevalier amoureux [1.526a], 48
Le ciel est transi [1.4f], 4
Le colibri [15.67e], 184
Le corbillard [12.8a], 169
Le fruit ardent [3.40d], 65
Le jardin [12.41a], 172
Le lac endormi [1.23e], 7
Le livre de la vie, op. 16 [3.1364], 114
Le marché [3.1457g], 118
Le miracle de la sémence [3.982], 98
Le miroir d'or [3.983], 98

INDEX OF SONG AND SONG CYCLE TITLES

Le papillon [1.23c], 7
Le petit peloton de fil [3.1457d], 118
Le plus gai des lieds [1.550], 51
Le Ruisseau [1.16k], 5
Le silence [3.391c], 76
Le sylphe [1.23i], 7
Le tombeau de la négresse [12.8d], 169
L'eche [3.110], 67
Leilão de jardim [3.796], 92
Leilão de jardim [3.1415d], 115
Lejanía [4.33e], 132
Lejos [21.38], 205
Lejos de tí [15.55b], 183
Lembrança boa [3.513e], 81
Lembrança boa, op. 10, no. 3 [3.1025a], 99
Lembrança de amor [3.703], 89
Lembranças do coração I [3.30], 64
Lembranças do coração II [3.31], 64
Lembranças do coração III [3.32], 64
Lembranças do losango cáqui [3.499], 81
Lembrando (op. 114) [3.1402d], 115
Lembrando, op. 114 [3.1411], 115
Lembrar/ esquecer, op. 148, no. 23 [3.1099w], 102
Lembras-te [3.64], 66
Leñatero [1.335j], 31
Lenda brasileira [3.792d], 92
Lendas amazônicas [3.598], 85
L'enfant de Bohème [1.26g], 8
Lenta, descansa [3.1549d], 123
Les anges pleurent [1.26b], 8
Les carmélites [12.8c], 169
Les colonnes infinies [3.40f], 65
Les corbeaux [12.8b], 169
Les grenades [1.23h], 7
Les mères, op. 45 [3.1460], 118
Les peupliers de Kéranroux [15.67d], 184
Les roses de saadi [1.212], 20
Les Rubaiyat [3.890], 94
Les séparés (Romance) [1.213], 20
Les yeux desirés [3.40g], 65
Les yeux élus [3.984], 98
L'esperance de ce monde [3.890b], 94
L'estridencia dels orgues . . . [1.385a], 35
L'étoile [1.26i], 8
Lettres [12.41b], 172
Levavas a madrugada [3.1182], 107
Leyenda [1.542g], 50
L'hermosa Antonia [7.36b], 152
L'heure mystíque [1.551c], 51
L'hostal de la peira [7.35f], 152
Libera-me [3.500], 81

Liebes Lied (with piano and magnetic tape) [3.1183], 107
Lied [1.187b], 18
Lied [1.255], 24
Lied, op. 60 [1.5], 4
Lied ancien [1.26m], 8
Lied de la boca Florida (Chacarera) [1.267h], 25
Lied de la boca florido [1.434d], 40
Lied de la ciencia de amar [1.267j], 25
Lied de la estrella marina [1.267b], 25
Lied de la eterna ventura [1.267l], 25
Lied de la gracia triunfante [1.267i], 25
Lied de las manos amigas [1.267f], 25
Lied de los ojos amados [1.267e], 25
Lied de los ojos amados [1.434f], 40
Lied del amor verdadero [1.267d], 25
Lied del amor verdadero [1.434a], 40
Lied del misterio gentil [1.267k], 25
Lied del misterio gentil [1.434c], 40
Lied del pájaro y la muerte [1.267a], 25
Lied del secreto dichoso [1.267m], 25
Lied del secreto dichoso [1.434b], 40
Lied del tesoro escondido [1.267c], 25
Lied del viento y de la fuente [1.267g], 25
Lied del viento y de la fuente [1.434e], 40
Lied no. 14 de "Rimas y abrojos" [1.214], 20
L'île magique [3.40e], 65
Linda entre mil [3.1541p], 122
Língua Portuguesa [3.759], 91
Linhas de catimbó [3.544], 83
Lira [3.704], 89
Liscano [7.18], 150
Litania [3.1122b], 104
Livro brasileiro no.1 [3.33], 64
Livro brasileiro-II caderno: Três invocações mágicas [3.34], 64
Llama y espina: Tres sonetos para soprano y piano [10.7], 161
Llankirái [1.204b], 19
Llanto por Ignácio Sanchez Mejías, op. 93a [3.1018], 99
Llegó un Jíbaro a San Juan [20.21], 200
Llévame a donde quieras [15.44], 182
Llora el gaucho (Estilo) [1.256d], 24
Llora un niño [10.4c], 160
Lloraba la niña [1.184b], 17
Llorando (Aire de Vidala) [1.497e], 47
Llorando yo en el bosque [1.4b], 4
Lluvia [1.50], 9
Lluvia . . . lluvia [15.81d], 187
Lluvia con sol [1.525c], 48
Lluvia en el campo [1.51], 9

317

INDEX OF SONG AND SONG CYCLE TITLES

Lo que con la boca niego [15.74f], 185
Lo que yo quiero (Lied para canto y piano) [1.71], 11
Loanda [3.1239c], 109
L'oiseau [1.23d], 7
Longe de ti [3.1228], 109
Longe de ti, op. 148, no. 25 [3.1099y], 103
Lord, give ears to my words (V) [4.31a], 131
Lorsque je serai vieux et que tu seras vieille [12.18], 170
Lorsque la coquette Espérance [1.16e], 5
Los álamos bajo la luna [1.294], 27
Los amanezqueros [6.7], 141
Los asombros: El día [1.316a], 29
Los asombros: El sueño [1.316c], 29
Los asombros: La noche [1.316b], 29
Los camalotes (Zamba) [1.480], 45
Los catañecitos [20.14a], 200
Los conejitos [1.542f], 50
Los cuatro muleros [7.37b], 152
Los desencuentros (Canción del litoral) [1.302c], 28
Los días de la voz: cuatro poemas para canto y piano [15.80], 186
Los días perdidos (Soneto) [1.329], 30
Los dos Jinetes [6.57], 143
Los llantos del alba [1.312a], 29
Los mozos de Monleón [7.38a], 152
Los ojos de mi morena [7.38c], 152
Los pobres (Five Songs) [13.2], 174
Los poemas que al verbo se resisten ... [10.1b], 160
Los puñalitos (Copla) [1.382b], 35
Los reseros [1.52], 9
Los Reyes Magos [1.11a], 4
Los ríos de la mano [1.330], 30
Los seres: El amigo [1.316f], 29
Los seres: El árbol [1.316d], 29
Los seres: Los pájaros [1.316e], 29
Los suspiros son aire ... [20.26d], 201
Louco [3.1461], 118
Louco devaneio [3.650a], 87
Louvação [3.1337], 113
Love's apotheosis [14.2b], 176
Lua boa [3.14], 64
Lua branca (Harmonização) [3.1078], 101
Lua cheia [3.1206], 108
Lua cheia, A [3.1300], 111
Luar de meu bem [3.1195a], 108
Luar do rio [3.893b], 94
Luar do Sertão [3.891], 94
Lucero de Alba [20.22], 200

Lugar assombrado [3.399], 77
Lullaby [11.28], 164
Lumen [11.4a], 163
Luna [22.8a], 210
Luna y suspiros (Vals) [1.481], 45
Lunar [22.8d], 210
Lundu da Marquesa de Santos [3.1465b], 119
Lundú dos caboclos [3.607d], 85
Lune d'octobre [3.1457b], 118
Luz [1.249e], 23
Luz [7.43], 153
Luz e névoa [3.985], 98
Luz mala [21.34], 205
Luz mediterrânea—no olvido do tempo [3.839], 93

Ma scovario non potrò [3.897], 94
Machao [1.453], 43
Macumba [3.338], 75
Macumba do Pai Zusé [3.1229], 109
Macumbebê op. 3 no. 2 [3.1088b], 101
Madeleine [1.26n], 8
Mademoiselle Satan [9.3], 158
Madre mía [4.34b], 132
Madre mía, cuando muera [15.25b], 180
Madre vidalitay [1.73], 11
¡Madrecita! (Canción de cuna infantil) [1.72], 11
Madrigal [1.91], 12
Madrigal [1.215], 20
Madrigal [1.461b], 44
Madrigal [1.540b], 50
Madrigal [1.540c], 50
Madrigal [3.215d], 71
Madrigal [3.339], 75
Madrigal [3.760], 91
Madrigal [3.892], 94
Madrigal [3.1230], 109
Madrigal [3.1388], 114
Madrigal [11.29], 164
Madrigal [15.40f], 182
Madrigal [20.28], 201
Madrigal, op. 17, no. 2 [3.986], 98
Madrigal amable [1.130], 15
Madrigal amargo [1.216], 20
Madrigal del peine perdido [4.30g], 131
Madrigal escrito en invierno [19.5c], 195
Madrigal muito fácil, op. 129 [3.1114], 104
Madrugada [3.215c], 71
Madrugada [3.1316b], 112
Madrugada [10.4d], 160
Madrugada [15.36d], 181
Madrugada [20.9c], 199

INDEX OF SONG AND SONG CYCLE TITLES

Madrugada no campo [3.286c], 73
Mãe preta [3.65], 66
Magdala [3.1157], 106
Magdalena [3.1462e], 119
Magdalena: A Musical Adventure [3.1462], 118
Mágoa [3.1106a], 103
Mais cinco canções [3.893], 94
Mais nada [3.571b], 84
Mais uma vez [3.840], 93
Maizales de Buenos Aires [1.538f], 49
Mal secreto [3.1463], 119
Mal secreto, op. 45 [3.1365], 114
Mala (Yaraví) [1.423], 39
Malagueña [1.25a], 7
Malagueña [7.27], 149, 151
Malhaya de los morenos ... (La quinta de los Grañas) [1.416d], 38
Malyaha la suerte mia [1.376e], 34–35
Mamãe Emanjá (Marcha-baião) [3.545], 83
Mamãe-preta (Lullaby) [3.1301], 111
Mamãezinha que estás no céu! ... [3.1318a], 112
Mamãi preta [3.599], 85
Mañana con sol (Tonada) [1.486c], 45
Mañana es domingo [4.1d], 129
Mañana me voy [1.18d], 6
Mandaste a sombra de um beijo [3.705], 89
Mando tiro, tiro lá [3.1466d], 119
Mandu sarará [3.517b], 82
Manglar, agua y cielo [6.27], 142
Manhã molhada [3.45b], 65
Manhã na praia [3.1451a], 117
Manhã-nungára [3.598c], 85
Mãos frias [3.335b], 75
Mãos Frias [3.1302], 111
Máquina do tempo [3.124], 67
Mar [3.277], 73
Mar de luna [21.7], 203
Maracatu [3.169], 69
Maracatu [3.1239d], 109
Maracatu, op. 9, no. 1 [3.1027a], 100
Maracatu do Chico Rei (Ballet) [3.894], 94
Maracatú do Chico Rei Uandala-iê [3.894b], 94
Maracatús: Três fragmentos [3.1303], 111
Marcha nupcial [3.66], 66
Marches funèbres [12.8e], 169
Márcia bela (Modinha) [3.1112f], 104
Marguerite [3.1184], 107
Maria do mar [3.546], 83
María La O [7.28], 151
Maria Rosa (Série regional) [3.1304], 111
Mariagneta [7.35k], 152
Marilia de Dirceu [3.706], 89

Marimorena [1.225a], 20
Marina [1.560j], 52
Marinero, porque no has venido? [3.895], 94
Marinero en tierra, op. 27: para canto y piano [15.35], 181
Mariposas [1.482], 45
Mariz [3.896], 94
Martírio [3.707], 89
Más quiero morir, por veros ... [15.60a], 183
Massacre [3.1549b], 123
Mater dolorosa [3.987], 98
Matinal tristeza (Lied) [7.17e], 150
Matinta Perera [3.181], 69
Matinta-perêra [3.598d], 85
Maxima no.1 [3.137], 68
Me atormentan las voces ... [10.8b], 161
Me deu uma vontade de chorar [3.1320c], 112
Me dice palabras tiernas [1.225d], 20
Me gusta la mitología [1.3031], 28–29
Me gustan las matemáticas [1.303g], 28
Me mataron en la víspera de tu silencio ... [10.10b], 161
¡Me miras mucho! [1.351c], 32
Mea culpa [3.405c], 77
Meciendo [1.343f], 31–32
Meciendo [8.3], 156
Media luna [20.2], 199
Meditação (da Missa de São Paulo) [3.797], 92
Medrosamente ibas [19.10a], 196
Medroso de amor (Moreninha), op. 17, no. 1 [3.988], 98
Meia canha (Canção gaúcha) [3.170], 69
Meia-Noite [3.1110b], 104
Méjico (Himno) [9.4a], 158
Melancolía [1.493c], 46
Melancolía [1.502b], 47
Melancolía [1.540a], 50
Melodia popular d'anadia (Fado) [3.1112g], 104
Melodia sentimental [3.1456b], 118
Melodias e canções [3.400], 77
Mélodies [1.23], 7
Melodies, op. 14 [1.551], 51
Mélodies et chansons [1.16], 5
Mélodies populaires indiennes [9.4], 158
Mendigo! [3.1072], 101
Menina, minha menina [3.708], 89
Menina de fita e renda, op. 169, no. 2 [3.1130b], 105
Menina me dá teu remo (Côco) [3.1268], 110
Menos tu vientre [1.442i], 41–42
Mensaje [1.35a], 9
Mensaje (Romanza) [21.46], 205

INDEX OF SONG AND SONG CYCLE TITLES

Mensajes líricos [1.17], 6
Meprise [3.67], 66
Mes larmes [12.12c], 170
Message [12.17a], 170
Messaggio d'amore [1.483], 45
Mestre Escola [3.1308d], 111
Metamorfosis [10.7a], 161
Meteoros [1.228], 21
Meu amor me disse adeus [3.1185], 107
Meu amor tão bom [3.1278a], 110
Meu barco é veleiro [3.1244c], 109
Meu "boi" vai-se embora [3.600], 85
Meu cavalo pimpão [3.1231], 109
Meu clarim, meu tambor [3.278], 73
Meu coração, op. 41 (Modinha) [3.340], 75
Meu coração sonhador [3.114], 67
Meu destino [3.1186], 107
Meu engenho d'Humaitá [3.1232], 109
Meu Guriaba [3.216c], 71
Meu limão, meu limoeiro [3.1233], 109
Meu pensamento [3.341], 75
Meu povo, meu poema [3.1540d], 122
Meu velho Rio [3.429e], 78
Meu violão [3.370], 76
Meus oito anos [3.129], 67
Meus pecados [3.475b], 80
Mi canción [1.424], 39
Mi corazón ... [6.28], 142
Mi corazón lo tragó el mar [7.19a], 150
Mi corazón se ha perdido (Aire cuyano) [1.65e], 11
Mi Costa Rica (Corrido) [6.76], 144
Mi derrotero [1.560b], 52
Mi garganta ... [1.300d], 28
Mi niña se fue a la mar [1.24d], 7
Mi niña se fue a la mar [4.25c], 130
Mi oración [6.29], 142
Mi padre ... (El brujo) [1.416f], 38
Mi patria (Marcha) [6.99], 146
Mi patria para vivir [1.538e], 49
Mi querer pasaba el río [15.27b], 180
Mi rancho [20.9b], 199
Mi se spezza la testa (Romanza), op. 33 [3.1366], 114
Mi señorita [1.383d], 35
Mi suegra la negra [7.39e], 152
Mi sueño [1.200b], 19
Mi testamento [21.43], 205
Mi vallecito florido (Zamba) [1.484], 45
Mi vida es un erial: ... [20.26e], 201
Mi viña de Chapanay (Cueca) [1.3021], 28
Mi voz [1.492a], 46

Miel [1.179], 17
Miel y canela [1.114], 14
Mientras sean nuestras almas dulce hoguera [1.123d], 14
Migalhas [3.501], 81
Milagre [3.524f], 82
Milagro [1.197], 18
Milonga [1.472b], 44
Milonga calabacera [1.557j], 52
Milonga de dos hermanos [1.331], 31
Milonga del destino [1.537], 49
Milonga para ti [1.561j], 52–53
Minha amada tão longe [3.598e], 85
Minha carta a você [3.709], 89
Minha Estrela [3.1073], 101
Minha mãe [3.710], 89
Minha Maria, op. 1, no. 2 [3.711], 89
Minha saudade [3.1500], 121
Minha terra [3.502], 81
Minha terra [3.601], 85
Minha'lma [3.1329], 113
Miniaturas [3.1464], 119
Minue [1.358], 33
Mios fueron mi corazón [4.23c], 130
Mirando las altas cumbres [15.67c], 184
Miró Celia una rosa ... [15.34a], 181
Mis abuelos [15.29d], 181
Mis caballos suben despacio [4.18], 130
Mis flores [11.30], 164
Mis ojos tienen la culpa (Canción al estilo nativo) [1.281], 26
Mis soldaditos [1.542b], 50
Missa do galo [3.1041], 100
Missiyé Ouèzan [12.25n], 171
Mistério [3.712], 89
Mistol [1.19e], 6
Moda da menina trombuda [3.1415b], 115
Modinha [3.219], 71
Modinha [3.287d], 73
Modinha [3.421], 78
Modinha [3.713], 89
Modinha [3.1389], 114
Modinha [3.1473e], 120
Modinha, op. 15 [3.203], 70
Modinha, op. 23a [3.1019], 99
Modinha, op. 44, no. 3 [3.204], 70
Modinha da moça de antes [3.1501], 121
Modinha no. 1 [3.35], 64
Modinha no. 2 [3.36], 64
Modinha no. 3, Devaneio [3.37], 65
Modinha no. 4, Canção [3.38], 65
Modinha op. 5 [3.1086], 101

INDEX OF SONG AND SONG CYCLE TITLES

Modinhas e canções, Album I [3.1465], 119
Modinhas e canções, Album II [3.1466], 119
Moin tandé youn cannon [12.25d], 171
Moinho [3.714], 89
Moinho, op. 151, no. 2 [3.1108b], 103
Mokocê-cê-maká [3.1443a], 117
Moldura [3.1106b], 103
Moleque de Rugendas [3.52b], 65
Molle [1.20e], 6
Molle, molle (Popular song from Cuzco, Peru) [19.6], 195
Momento (Lied) [1.92], 12
Momento, op. 148, no. 7 [3.1099g], 102
Momentos líricos [3.761], 91
Momentos líricos (Álbum no. 1) [3.762], 91
Mon coeur [1.495], 46
Mon rêve familier [1.432f], 39
Monólogo do tempo, op. 56c [3.1020], 99
Monotony [14.1c], 176
Moqueca (Lundu) [3.1112h], 104
Mor [1.131], 15
Morena (Chula marajoara) [3.602], 85
Morena, morena [3.417], 78
Morena, morena (Harmonization) [3.898], 94
Morena, morena (Modinha) [3.1542b], 122
Morena encanto, op. 148, no. 29 [3.1099c], 102
Morena linda (Callejera) [6.45], 143
Moreninha [3.152], 68
Moreninha [3.171], 69
Mormaço na varanda [3.1042], 100
Morrir vorrei [3.814b], 92
Mors, amor, op. 73 [3.1367], 114
Morta (Trovas do Norte) [3.989], 98
Mosaico [3.238], 72
Mosteiro [3.783], 91
Motivo [3.1489e], 120
Motivo [3.1502], 121
Motivos del son [7.45], 153
Mozart no céu [3.715], 89
Muerta [20.9a], 199
Muerte de Elena [1.496a], 46
Muerte del señor don Gato [1.496e], 46
Muerto en las miesas [1.530b], 49
Mujeres de Costa Rica [6.70], 144
Mulher rendeira [3.1234], 109
Muñeca [1.246c], 23
Muntanyes regalades [7.35g], 152
Murmúrio [3.716], 89
Muros (Vent) [1.443d], 42
Musa que passa [3.925d], 95
Music for Nada [7.10], 150
Música brasileira [3.763], 91

Música e letra de modinha [3.503], 81
Música eterna [3.209a], 71
My Bus and I [3.1462a], 118
My Love Is Like a Red Rose [3.391b], 76

Na beira da praia [3.1541d], 122
Na capela [3.392b], 76
Na capela [3.1368], 114
Na corda da viola [3.1466f], 119
Na curva do caminho [3.893c], 94
Na minha terra tem [3.1278b], 110
Na palma da mão uma estrela [3.1207], 108
Na partida [3.1151], 106
Na paz do outono [3.1473f], 120
Na praia deserta [3.1541j], 122
Na rua do sabão [3.1235], 109
Na sua ausência [3.1504], 121
Na zona da mata [3.513f], 81
Nada [3.138], 68
Nada alumbra [1.122d], 14
Nada tenho [3.1236], 109
Nadie percibe [6.30], 142
Nagô, nagô, nagô [3.547], 83
Náiades (Soneto) [3.1187], 107
Naides [1.552], 51
Nana [1.249d], 23
Nana [15.40a], 182
Nana del niño malo [1.348c], 32
Nana del niño malo [15.4c], 179
Nandayure (Capricho chorotega) [6.100], 146
Nandayureña [6.60], 143
Nandayureña [6.101], 146
Não [3.1079], 101
Não chega bem ao meu ombro [3.731b], 90
Não creias [3.434], 78
Não digas nada [3.571c], 84
Não posso mais esconder que te amo [3.460b], 79
Não sabes? op. 3 [3.1369], 114
Não sei... [3.504], 81
Não sei [3.516c], 81
Não sei, op. 118 [3.1131c], 105
Não sei porque... [3.481a], 80
Não sei porque espírito antigo [3.513g], 81
Não sei porque os tetéus [3.513h], 81
Não sei se estou vivo [3.513i], 81
Não te digo adeus [3.1188], 107
Não viveu quem não ficou [3.1503], 121
Natió [3.1239h], 109
Naufragio [15.76], 185
Navio negreiro [3.1312b], 112
Nebel, op. 119 [3.1412], 115
Neblina, op. 106 [3.1115], 104

INDEX OF SONG AND SONG CYCLE TITLES

Nega em teu ser primário [3.513j], 81
Nêgo bola-sete [3.548], 83
Negra está la noche [22.14], 211
Negro bembón [7.45a], 153
Nell'aria della sera umida e molle, op. 55 [3.1370], 114
Nenina [1.249c], 23
Nesta manhã [3.549], 83
Nesta rua [3.1239f], 109
Nesta rua [3.1466c], 119
Neuf poésies de Paul Verlaine [1.432], 39
Never more, canción [5.10], 136
Nhanderu [3.139], 68
Nhapopé [3.1080], 101
Nhapopé [3.1465f], 119
Nhapopé (toada) [3.422], 78
Niebla en la pampa [1.557a], 51
Nigue-nigue-ninhas [3.165c], 69
Niña, limón, limonero [15.40b], 182
Ninando [3.68], 66
Ninguém faz falta a ninguém [3.1152], 106
Ninguém mais [3.524g], 82
Ninho desfeito [3.893d], 94
Ninon (Romance) [21.47], 205
Nirvana [12.29c], 172
No, no hay carcel para el hombre [1.442r], 42
No. 11 [16.1k], 189
¡No! Canto de esperanza [7.49], 153
No corras [15.81a], 187
No faltes [1.217], 20
No fundo dos teus olhos [3.505], 81
No hay una pena más pena [1.538c], 49
No jardim de Oeira [3.617c], 86
No jardim do mosteiro [3.401], 77
No me censuren ni riñan [5.16], 136
No meio do caminho [3.900], 94
No meio do caminho [3.1550b], 123
No meio fio da rua [3.1189], 107
No nosso tempo de colégio [3.1321c], 112
No ouro sem fim da tarde morta [3.659g], 87
No passar dos anos [3.784], 91
No Pegi de Ochossi [3.1312c], 112
No se puede, no se puede [1.440e], 41
No te asomes a la ventana [1.442e], 41
No te detengas alma sobre el borde [1.397c], 36
Noche [4.28e], 131
Noche azul [7.29], 151
Noche clara y estrellada [3.899], 94
Noche de luna [1.485], 45
Noche en la selva [6.14], 142
Noches de Santa Fé [1.332], 31
Nocturna rosa [15.18c], 180

Nocturno [1.170], 16
Nocturno [1.295], 27
Nocturno [1.393], 36
Nocturno [6.81d], 145
Nocturno [15.75c], 185
Nocturno (de Rafael Solana) [15.39b], 182
Nocturno de la estatua [15.13], 180
Nocturno de las rosas [15.63a], 184
Nocturno en las frondas [1.561d], 52
Nocturno en los muelles [1.394], 36
Nocturno en los muelles [22.4c], 210
Nocturno en que nada se oye [15.14], 180
Nocturno pampeano (Triste) [1.486a], 45
Nocturno sueño [15.15], 180
Noite cheia de estrelas [3.335a], 75
Noite de encantos [3.764], 91
Noite de junho [3.342], 75
Noite de luar [3.1467], 119
Noite de São João [3.603], 85
Noite de São Paulo [3.239], 72
Noite e dia [3.945b], 96
Noite mansa, op. 54, no. 3 [3.773c], 91
Noitinha [3.205], 70
Non posso amarti (Romanza) [21.48], 205
North Carolina blues [15.7b], 179
Nós [3.921b], 95
Nós [3.1237], 109
Nossa amor... [3.566d], 84
Nossa Senhora da Neve [3.901], 94
Nossa velhice [3.990], 98
Nossos olhos [3.531b], 82
Nossos olhos [3.536a], 83
Nostalgia [1.364b], 33
Nostalgia [3.902], 94
Nostalgia [11.13d], 164
Nostalgía [15.3a], 179
Nostalgia indígena (Canción serrana) [1.282], 26
Noturno [3.343], 75
Noturno [3.717], 89
Noturno com palavras [3.639], 87
Noturno no. 1 [3.1194d], 108
Noturno no. 3 [3.640], 87
Noturnos para voz media y piano [3.662], 88
Nova canção do exílio [3.125], 67
Novo amor, op. 65 (Berceuse) [3.641], 87
Nozani-ná [3.1443b], 117
Ñudo [1.266], 25
Nuestro instante [6.31], 142
Nueve canciones [7.19], 150
Nueve canciones [22.10], 210
Nueve canciones de Federico García Lorca [1.24], 7
Nuit [12.11], 170

INDEX OF SONG AND SONG CYCLE TITLES

Num imbaiá [3.240], 72
Numa coluna (Ecrit sur une colonne) [3.115], 67
Numa concha [3.785], 91
Numa concha [3.991], 98
Nunca e sempre [3.295d], 74
Nunca sinto inveja [3.927e], 96
Nupcial [5.39], 137
Ñuritay (Vidala) [1.65a], 11
Nuvens [3.292b], 74
Nymphes et sylvains (Ninfe e silvani) [1.30], 8

O adormecer [3.384], 76
O alcoviteiro [3.718], 89
O amanhecer, op. 16 [3.765], 91
O amante [3.1196c], 108
O amor de agora [3.506], 81
O amor e a morte [3.1158], 106
O anjo da guarda [3.903], 94
O anu [3.400a], 77
O apocalipse: A mulher e o dragão [3.841], 93
O ar [3.241], 72
O atropelado [3.719], 89
O boiadeiro [3.1317a], 112
O canto do mar [3.550], 83
O canto e o choro, op. 148, no. 12 [3.10991], 102
O canto multiplicado, op. 38a [3.1021], 99
O canto multiplicado, op. 38b [3.1022], 99
O carreiro [3.1305], 111
O cavalinho de pau [3.1190], 107
O condenado à morte [3.392a], 76
O coração [3.400b], 77
O coração, op. 136 [3.1116], 104
O cravo brigou com a rosa [3.1191], 107
O Dio del cielo [3.819b], 92
O doce nome de você [3.904], 94
O fogo [3.242], 72
O haikai, op. 112, no. 4 [3.1104d], 103
O ignoto [3.400d], 77
O impossível carinho [3.507], 81
O impossível carinho [3.1238], 109
O ipê e você, op. 127 [3.1117], 104
O jasmineiro [3.312], 74
O jasmineiro [3.1043], 100
O Kinimbá [3.165d], 69
O laço [3.1507], 121
O lago dos haikais, op. 112 no. 5 [3.1104e], 103
O legado [3.1324a], 113
O leilão [3.1282c], 111
O lenço [3.55], 66
O livro de Maria Sylvia, op. 28 [3.206], 70
Ô Lua que estás tão clara [3.567c], 84
O Luandê-Luá [3.45c], 65

O mar, op. 18, no. 2 [3.1026b], 100
O menino atrasado [3.285], 73
O menino doente, 102
O menino doente [3.720], 89
O menino doente [3.798], 92
O menino doente [3.920a], 95
O meu amigo na guarda, op. 56 [3.1413], 115
O meu barco é veleiro [3.1322c], 112
O mort, vieux capitaine [12.26], 171
O mosquito escreve [3.1415e], 115
O mudo falante, op. 184 [3.1414], 115
O novelozinho de linha [3.1457c], 118
O pai do universo [3.842], 93
O passarinho da praça da matriz [3.1508], 121
O passo da ema [3.604], 85
O pastor pequenino, op. 38, no. 1 [3.207], 70
O pato [3.799], 92
O Pipoqueiro (pregão) [3.244], 72
O pobre peregrino [3.1466a], 119
O poder das lágrimas [3.153], 68
O poente [3.314], 74
O preto velho Cambindo [3.1306], 111
O príncipe [3.1308g], 112
O que eu queria dizer ao seu ouvido [3.1307], 111
O que fizeram do Natal [3.905], 95
O que podia ter sido [3.509], 81
O que sou [3.551], 83
O realejo [3.1318c], 112
O Rei [3.1308b], 111
O Rei mandou me chamá [3.423], 78
O relógio [3.721], 89
O relógio [3.801], 92
O sabiá e a mangueira [3.178b], 69
O salutaris hostia [3.997], 98
O salutaris hostia [12.42], 173
O sapo dourado (Suite infantil) [3.1308], 111
O seringueiro [3.605], 85
Ô seu marinheiro [3.1541f], 122
O soldado [3.1192], 107
O soldado de fogo [3.1192e], 107
O soldado do amor [3.1192d], 107
O soldado guardião dos caminhos [3.1192f], 107
O soldado inválido [3.1192h], 107
O soldado menino de ontem [3.1192b], 107
O soldado nu [3.1192i], 107
O soldado obediente [3.1192g], 107
O soldado recruta [3.1192c], 107
O sonho [3.643], 87
O sonho da netinha [3.69], 66
O sono [3.998], 98
O tear [3.385], 76
O tesouro [3.1509], 121

O trem de ferro [3.1240], 109
O trovador [3.843], 93
O trovador do sertão [3.154], 68
O vale, op. 17 [3.766], 91
Ô Vaqueiro [3.552], 83
O Vassalo [3.1308c], 111
O vento é quando? [3.659b], 87
Ô viageiro [3.1541c], 122
Ô vida de minha vida (Modinha) [3.344], 75
O vizir [3.155], 68
O wag es nicht [3.999], 98
Obras para canto y piano [22.15], 211
Ocaso [1.439], 40
Ocaso [3.992], 98
8 Canciones salteñas [1.416], 38
Ocho poemas, op. 33 [1.224], 20
Oda celeste [15.67a], 184
Odas celestes [15.67], 184
Odas de safo, op. 14, no. 2 [1.180], 17
Ode a Cassandre [3.816], 92
Oferenda [3.1505], 121
Oferta [3.478a], 80
Oferta [3.508], 81
Ofertorio: Deus dedit, deus abstulit [1.186a], 18
Offrandes vodouesques (original title: Complaintes haïtiennes) [12.25], 167, 171
Ofrenda [1.553], 51
Ofrenda [4.29e], 131
Ofrenda a Guido Spano [1.53], 9
Ogum de lê [3.1014c], 99
¡Oh, luna!... [15.79k], 186
¡Oh Costa Rica! [6.55c], 143
¡Oh madre mia! (Vidalita) [21.39], 205
Oh querida, eu goto de ti (Cantiga) [3.1112i], 104
Oh sutil invisible [15.80c], 187
Oh! Viens avec le vieux Khayyam [3.890e], 94
Oíd Efebos y atletas [7.17d], 150
Oigo cocherito... (La reis y la leocaria) [1.416e], 38
Oiseau blessé d'une flèche, op. 10 [3.1468], 119
Oito canções populares brasileiras [3.1239], 109
Ojos de tiempo (Zamba) [1.333], 31
Olá [3.1506], 121
Olas [4.33c], 132
Olha-me! [3.993], 98
Olha-me tão somente [3.510e], 81
Olhos azuis [3.313], 74
Olhos tristes [3.92], 67
Olhos tristes, os teus olhos! [3.267], 72
Olhos verdes, op. 155 [3.1118], 104
Olvido [1.132], 15
On the beach [18.1b], 193

Onda [15.63b], 184
Onde estás [3.243], 72
Onde o nosso amor nasceu [3.1443m], 117
Ondulación etérea [1.560d], 52
One life [14.2d], 176
Onimba [12.25o], 171
Ontem, hoje, amanhã [3.1269], 110
Ora dize-me a verdade, op. 12, no. 1 [3.995], 98
Oração [3.757a], 90
Oração (de Missa de São Francisco) [3.800], 92
Oração à esperança [3.642], 87
Oração a Santa Teresinha [3.371], 76
Oração a Tupãssy [3.1338], 113
Oração ao diabo, op. 20, no. 2 [3.994], 98
Oração da Estrela Boieira [3.15], 64
Oração da estrela boieira [3.427b], 78
Oração da pobre [3.93], 67
Oração e dança [3.1303b], 111
Oración [15.75g], 185
Oración de duelo [6.102], 146
Oración de quietud (Poema sinfónico) [15.66d], 184
Oración por las novias tristes [1.437d], 40
Oraison, op. 11 no. 2 [3.996], 98
Orfãzinha [3.94], 67
Ortografia, op. 148, no. 11 [3.1099k], 102
Os amantes sem dinheiro (Penniless lovers) [3.1344], 113
Os nossos olhos [3.372], 76
Os oinho d'ela [3.1309], 112
Os olhos de Maria [3.268], 73
Os olhos do meu benzinho [3.1208], 108
Os pratos na cantareira (Dança) [3.1112j], 104
Os rios [3.1081], 101
Os sinos [3.802], 92
Os teus olhos (Canção) [3.1112k], 104
Os teus olhos, os meus olhos [3.1044], 100
Oscuro fuego [1.556a], 51
Otoño [1.140a], 15
Otoño [22.10b], 210
Otoño, op. 8 [4.24c], 130
Otoño último [15.3c], 179
Ou isto ou aquilo [3.1415f], 116
Ou isto ou aquilo [3.1415g], 116
Ou isto ou aquilo, op. 134 [3.1415], 115
Outono [3.574g], 84
Outra voz, outra paisagem [3.722], 89
Outro improviso [3.906], 95
Ouve o canto da noite [3.279], 73
Ouve o silêncio [3.1170a], 106
Ouvir estrelas, op. 13 [3.1371], 114
Oye mi llanto [1.376d], 34

INDEX OF SONG AND SONG CYCLE TITLES

Pa que me estás mirando (Gato al modo popular) [1.65b], 11
Pacará [1.20b], 6
Padre Nosso [3.1372], 114
Pai do mato [3.416b], 78
Pai do Mato (Native Indian text) [3.1442a], 117
Paining the talus [18.1a], 193
Paisagem [3.373], 76
Paisaje [1.22d], 7
Paisaje [1.334], 31
Paisajes [1.458], 43
Pajarillo del querer [1.198], 18–19
Pajarito carpintero [1.457b], 43
Pajarito Chichiltote [6.48], 143
Pajarito de la nieve [1.107d], 13
Pajaritos criollos, op. 6 [1.250], 23
Pájaro muerto [1.298b], 27
Pájaros [1.335], 31
Pájaros en el alba [22.15d], 211
Palabras sueltas [1.397b], 36
Palavras de anjo [3.659h], 87
Pálida Madona (Modinha antiga) [3.1443h], 117
Palma verde, garza blanca [22.16g], 211
Paloma blanca [15.27c], 180
Paloma de la mañana [1.386a], 35
Paloma del aire (Canción criolla) [1.516], 48
Palomita [15.59], 183
Palomita [15.61a], 183
Palomitay vidala [1.133], 15
Palpar [15.46a], 182
Pampa, sierra y sol (Canciones y danzas de mi tierra) [1.486], 45
Pampa sola (Canción del sur) [1.302h], 28
Pampamapa (Aire de huella) [1.302f], 28
Pampeana (Canción en el estilo popular argentino) [1.454], 43
Pampeanas [1.256], 24
Pañales y sonajas, Lullaby for Elisa [15.48], 183
Panamá viejo (Bolero canción) [17.2], 191
Panis angelicus [6.43], 143
Papa curumiassu (Tema indígena) [3.1310], 112
Papae curumiassu [3.1443c], 117
Papae Curumiassú op. 3 no. 3 [3.1088c], 101
Papagaio azul [3.1510], 121
Papai Noel [3.907], 95
Papai Noel [3.1319c], 112
Papaizinho [3.1311], 112
Para acordar teu coração [3.510], 81
Para mi corazón basta tu pecho [3.1423e], 116
Para ninar [3.70], 66
¿Para que me han parido, mujer? [1.442b], 41
Para sempre [3.1515a], 121

Para ti (Lied) [5.69], 138
Para um mestre de canto [3.294], 74
Para uma cigarra [3.803], 92
Para você, por mim [3.1511], 121
Parabola [1.487], 45
Pardonnez-moi [3.908], 95
Paremia de cavalo [3.126], 67
Parte I. [1.94a], 12
Parte VIII. [1.94h], 12
Partir e ficar (Canção trovadoresca no. 3) [3.1393c], 115
Pasacalle [1.218], 20
Pascalle [4.29c], 131
Pasión (Aire de pasillo guanacasteco) [6.6], 141
Pasó... [1.404], 37
Passarinho da lagoa [3.606], 85
Passarinho está cantando [3.909], 95
Pássaro da terra [3.607], 85
Pássaro da terra [3.607e], 85
Pássaro fugitivo [3.1443k], 117
Pasto puna (Milonga) [1.115], 14
Pastor, pastor, ya viene la luna [21.26], 204
Pater noster [3.1074], 101
Pau-piá [3.245], 72
Paysage [3.182], 69
Paz [3.525c], 82
Pecado [3.374], 76
Peces voladores [15.78i], 186
Pêche d'ombres [12.41i], 173
Pedido [3.460c], 79
Peixes de prata [3.844], 93
Pena [3.511], 81
Pêndulo [3.522a], 82
Pensamiento (Marcha premiada en concurso) [6.103], 146
Pensei em ti com doçura 1951 [3.510b], 81
Penso em você [3.480b], 80
Pequeño oasis [6.32], 142
Perché [3.1000], 98
Perdão [3.246], 72
Perdão, felicidade! [3.95], 67
Perdi minha liberdade, op. 61 [3.1119], 104
Perdidos, op. 148, no. 10 [3.1099j], 102
Peregrinos do Joazeiro [3.1390], 114
Perfume triste, op. 148, no. 8 [3.1099h], 102
Perlas blancas [1.206a], 19
Perlas negras [1.206b], 19
Pero cómo habríamos de permanecer aquí... [10.5a], 160
Persévérance [1.26o], 8
Perversidade [3.1452e], 118
Pescadores [1.74], 11

Pescaria [3.1415a], 115
Petit rondell [1.93], 12
Pianito [1.246e], 23
Picaflor (Zamba), op. 2 no. 4 [1.413], 37
Pièce de circonstance, op. 33 [21.24], 204
Piececitos [1.336], 31
Piececitos [4.35b], 132
Pièces pour chant et piano [12.17], 170
Piedade, Cristo, op. 41 [3.1416], 116
Piedra [2.9c], 57
Pierrot [3.269], 73
Pimpín sarabín [4.1c], 129
Pingo d'água [3.1254], 110
Pinião [3.39], 65
Pinos de costa [4.33h], 132
Pirincho [1.335f], 31
Plancha [1.330a], 30
Plegaria, op. 24 [1.189], 18
Plenilunio [4.33f], 132
Plenilunio [6.33], 142
Plomada [1.330g], 31
Pluguiera a Dios [15.74g], 185
Plus qu'ennuyée [12.12b], 170
Pobre cega [3.1473a], 119
Pobre cego [3.247], 72
Pobre mi negra (Vidala) [1.283], 27
Pobreza [3.20c], 64
Pode entrar saudade [3.644], 87
Poema [3.553], 83
Poema [3.565b], 83
Poema [3.663], 88
Poema [3.1193], 108
Poema [3.1512], 121
Poema, op. 33 [3.1087], 101
Poema da água, op. 35 [3.208], 70
Poema da saudade, op. 30a [3.767], 91
Poema da tua luz [3.1209], 108
Poema das cinco canções [3.910], 95
Poema das duas mãosinhas [3.381], 76
Poema de amor [1.441], 41
Poema de Itabira [3.1469], 119
Poema de la conquista [20.25c], 200
Poema de palavras [3.1471], 119
Poema del sembrador (Poem of the Sower) [1.75], 11
Poema interior [3.512], 81
Poema otoñal [1.94], 12
Poema para Manuel Bandeira [3.911], 95
Poema para una muerta voz [1.367a], 34
Poema tirado de uma notícia de jornal [3.723], 89
Poema V (Raio de luz) op. 94, no.5 [3.1023], 99

Poema XIII (Raio de luz) op. 94, no. 13 [3.1024], 99
Poemas azuis [3.768], 91
Poemas da negra [3.513], 81
Poemas da negra, op. 10 [3.1025], 99
Poemas da vida e da morte, op. 110 [3.1417], 116
Poemas del amor y de la muerte [15.79], 186
Poemas en tiempos de guerra [4.13], 130
Poème de l'enfant et de sa mère [3.1470], 119
Poemeto [3.183], 69
Poemeto erótico [3.724], 89
Poeminha poemeto poemeu poesseu poessua da flor [3.845], 93
Poético [3.1549c], 123
Polquinha [3.1045], 100
Polvo, caldén, espinillo [1.225c], 20
Ponto de Oxalá [3.725], 89
Ponto de terreiro [3.1203a], 108
Por debajo corre el agua [1.18c], 6
Por el caminito [1.122a], 14
Por el campo [1.459a], 44
Por eso [1.200a], 19
Por eso te quiero [7.30], 151
Por estos cuatro caminos [22.16e], 209, 211
Por la senda oscura yo camino ... [6.62b], 144
Por las ramas del laurel [1.157], 16
Por los caminos de Zorca [22.8c], 210
Por los campos de la Patria [1.538a], 49
Por los campos verdes [1.337], 31
Por los campos verdes [1.529], 49
Por los campos verdes de Jerusalém [1.15c], 5
Por piedade, op. 148, no. 28 [3.1099b], 102
¿Por qué? [1.200c], 19
Por quê [3.280], 73
Por que? [3.524h], 82
¿Por qué lloras, morenita? [3.912], 95
Por toda a eternidade [3.525a], 82
Por un beso de tu boca (Bambuco) [11.31], 164
Por una mirada, un mundo; ... [20.26b], 200
Por vos penando (Zamba) [1.64e], 11
Porque? [3.726], 89
Porque estás sempre comigo [3.510c], 81
Porquoi mentir [3.913], 95
Porto seguro [3.514], 81
Portrait de Nadia Boulanger [3.40], 65
Pour endormir la belle au bois [1.23g], 7
Pour ton visage [12.41j], 173
Pour une statue de l'amour [3.402], 77
Pourquoi [12.9e], 169
Pourquoi me fuir? ... [1.359], 33
Pousa a mão na minha testa [3.920b], 95

INDEX OF SONG AND SONG CYCLE TITLES

P'rá sinhozinho drumi [3.1312a], 112
Praia dos encantos [3.1513], 121
Praianas, op. 18 [3.1026], 99
Praias de minha terra [3.1046], 100
Praieira [3.1251a], 110
Praise the Lord (CXLVIII) [4.31e], 131
Prece [3.156], 68
Prece [3.727], 89
Prece, op. 157 [3.1120], 104
Prece de chuva [3.817], 92
Prefiro [3.1514], 121
Pregão [3.914], 95
Pregão da saudade [3.1171b], 107
Pregões [3.52c], 65
Prégon [6.81a], 145
Pregón [22.3d], 209
Pregón submarino [15.77d], 186
Pregunta [20.11], 199
Pregúntale a las estrellas [11.32], 164
Preguntas [10.2d], 160
Pregunto a mi guitarra (Gato) [1.486b], 45
Prelúdio das cinco miniaturas brasileiras [3.1515], 121
Prelúdio no. 2 [3.515], 81
Prendeditos de la mano [1.376a], 34
Prenúncio de outono [3.209d], 71
Prequeté [3.184], 69
Prés la ville de Ioba [1.526b], 48
Presença [3.248], 72
Presencia plural [2.10d], 57
Presente [3.1516], 121
Presentimiento [1.116], 14
Presságios [3.1047], 100
Prestame tu pañuelito... [1.301b], 28
Prière [12.12f], 170
Prière de Madame Elizabeth à sa prison [12.12d], 170
Prière pour tous [3.185], 69
Primavera [1.140c], 15
Primavera (Canción a dos voces) [1.425], 39
Primavera d'alma [3.157], 68
Primavera del campamento (Primavera d'accampamento) [1.501a], 47
Primaveral [1.95], 12
Primeiro motivo da rosa [3.41a], 65
Primer nocturno [15.16], 180
Printemps [21.14], 204
Profecía [10.7c], 161
Projeto de carta [3.281], 73
Prólogo [4.30a], 131
Prólogo (La guitarra) y la noche amiga [6.79a], 145

Promessa [3.460e], 79
Promessa [3.728], 90
Proposição [3.1540e], 122
Protesto [3.1250e], 110
Provérbios no. 1 [3.554], 83
Provérbios no. 2 [3.555], 83
Provérbios no. 3 [3.556], 83
Prudência [3.535a], 83
Psalms, op. 74 [4.31], 131
Pudor [3.1452f], 118
Puebla [3.664], 88
Pueblito, mi pueblo [1.338], 31
Puedo escribir los versos [3.1423f], 116
Puisque le ciel t'envoie [12.27], 171
Punto de luz, suspenso lampo [7.2c], 150
Puntos cubanos [20.9], 199
Puxa o melão sabiá (Desafio) [3.117b], 67

Quadras [3.915], 95
Quadras ao gosto popular [3.804], 92
Quadras no. 2 [3.375], 76
Quadrilha [3.916], 95
Quadrinhas [3.1210], 108
Qual quebra [3.1541o], 122
Qualquer tempo [3.557], 83
Quand je serai mort [12.12e], 170
Quand on vous dira [12.29a], 172
Quando [3.513k], 81
Quando [3.1025b], 99
Quando a saudade voltar [3.931a], 96
Quando amanhecer [3.8], 63
Quando cruzamos no caminho, op. 39 [3.769], 91
Quando embalada [3.521a], 82
Quando entardece, op. 1, no. 1 [3.729], 90
Quando eu morrer [3.1105b], 103
Quando eu morrer [3.1517], 121
Quando eu não conhecia a saudade [3.931b], 96
Quando na roça anoitece [3.917], 95
Quando ouvires o pássaro [3.730], 90
Quando te vi pela primeira vez [3.476a], 80
Quando te vi pela primeira vez [3.818], 92
Quando te vinha buscar [3.1048], 100
Quando uma flor desabrocha (Toada) [3.918], 95
Quarto motivo da rosa [3.41d], 65
Quase seresta [3.1150], 106
Quatre chansons populaires de Catalogne/Cuatro canciones populares de Cataluña [7.36], 152
Quatre chansons populaires de L'Andalousie/Cuatro canciones populares de Andalucía [7.37], 152
Quatre chansons populaires de Salamanque/Cuatro canciones populares de Salamanca [7.38], 152

INDEX OF SONG AND SONG CYCLE TITLES

Quatro canções da madrugada [3.1194], 108
Quatro canções sobre poemas brasileiros para voz aguda e piano [3.1546], 123
Quatro canti Veronesi [3.819], 92
Quatro cantigas [3.516], 81
Quatro líricas [3.919], 95
Quatro líricas [3.920], 95
Quatro líricas brasileiras [3.921], 95
Quatro miniaturas de Adelmar Tavares [3.731], 90
Quatro motivos da rosa [3.41], 65
Quatro peças, op. 39 [3.209], 71
Quatro poemas de Helena Kolody, op. 43 [3.210], 71
Quatro poemas de Macunaíma [3.517], 82
Quatro poemas de Manuel Bandeira [3.42], 65
Que adornada primavera [15.74b], 185
Qué altos los balcones... [15.35a], 181
¿Qué ansías? [1.520b], 48
Que bobagem, meu filho [3.1339], 113
Qué bonito está el altar [1.18b], 6
¿Qué es la poesía? [20.25a], 200
"¿Qué es poesía?" ... [20.26a], 200
¡Qué hermosa te dou dios! [1.158], 16
¡Qué linda la madreselva! [1.324e], 30
¡Qué me has hecho, qué me has hecho! [1.363c], 33
¡Qué mezquino el corazón...! [15.79d], 186
¿Qué pasa? [1.442g], 41
Qué pronto [15.61d], 184
¿Qué quiere el viento de enero...? [1.4421], 42
Que se va a dormir... [15.2b], 179
Que si, que no (Bailecito al modo popular) [1.65c], 11
Que tal? [12.4a], 169
¡Que venga el leñador! (Zol kumen der heker!) [1.443e], 42
Que vos me permitáis [1.98a], 12–13
Quebra o coco, menina [3.521b], 82
Quebracho [1.20d], 6
Queimada pelo sol desvairada [3.927f], 96
Queixa, op. 126 [3.1121], 104
Queixa da moça arrependida [3.732], 90
Queixa da moça arrependida [3.805], 92
Queixas [3.211], 71
Queja [15.39a], 182
Queja Coya (Vidala) [1.486f], 45
Quejas [2.8], 57
Quem me dirá quem sou? [3.659a], 87
Quem sofre [3.249], 72
Quem te viu... op. 169, no. 3 [3.1130c], 105
Quena [1.558a], 52
Quenas [19.12b], 196
Querendona (Motivos serranos) [1.381], 35

Querer bem não é pecado [3.1255], 110
Quero afagar-te o rosto docemente [3.510g], 81
Quero dizer baixinho [3.510a], 81
Quero mana [3.400e], 77
Quero-quero [3.574h], 84
Quibungo tê-rê-rê [3.250], 72
Quién dijo acaso...? (en modo jónico) [15.65f], 184
¡Quién fuera granaderito! [1.303k], 28
Quién no ha amado nunca... [15.79a], 186
Quiere a tu casita... (Canción escolar) [1.426], 39
Quiero hundir la mirada en el vacío... [10.8a], 161
Quietud [4.21], 130
Quijonguito [6.8], 141
Química [1.303e], 28
15 Canciones escolares [1.303], 28
Quinguê-lê [3.251], 72
Quiriri, op. 112, no. 3 [3.1104c], 103
Quise despedirme más... [1.442k], 42
Quisiera ser... [6.62a], 144
Quisiera ser por un rato... (Zamba) [1.302d], 28
¡Quizás ya no venga...! [6.62c], 144
Quizomba [3.894a], 94

Rabicho [3.1330], 113
Raças: sobre a raça africana no Brasil [3.1312], 112
Ramo de rumos, op. 166 [3.1122], 104
Ranas [15.73], 185
Ranchinho desfeito [3.1241], 109
Rancho solo [21.9b], 203
Rapadura [3.558], 83
Rapasgotori [22.17], 208, 211
Rappelle-toi [21.15], 204
Raro dom [3.1211], 108
Razão e amor [3.1001], 98
Realejo [3.14731], 120
Recado [3.1049], 100
Receita para o amor [3.9], 63
Receita para o amor [3.733], 90
Rechtfertigung [1.190a], 18
Reclamo [1.561a], 52
Recolhi no meu coração a tua voz [3.460d], 79
Recomendação [3.1050], 100
Recueillement [3.158], 68
Recuerdo [1.21d], 6
Recuerdo [22.10a], 210
Redondilha [3.1473k], 120
Redondilha, op. 130 [3.1123], 104
Reflejos [4.33k], 132
Reflets d'âme [12.12], 168, 170
Reflexões [3.770], 91

INDEX OF SONG AND SONG CYCLE TITLES

Reflexos n'água [3.16], 64
Refrão do mutum [3.1391], 114
Regarde la rose qui fleurit près de nous [3.890f], 94
Regreso [22.17j], 211
Regresso ao Lar [3.96], 67
Relance [3.734], 90
Relíquia [21.17], 204
Relíquia apócrifa (Canção trovadoresca no. 1) [3.1393a], 114
Relógio, op. 148, no. 24 [3.1099x], 102
Rema tu bote (Quasi spiritual) [7.17b], 150
Remadores seringueiros [3.608], 86
Remansos [1.56b], 10
Remedio [21.35], 205
Remeiro de S. Francisco [3.1465e], 119
Reminiscência [3.1242], 109
Renascença [3.1518], 121
Repose-toi [1.26p], 8
Ressonâncias [3.1140], 105
Resta sim, é remover [3.559], 83
Restituo estas chaves [3.1519], 121
Resume of Life [3.1392], 114
Retazos de poesía [4.14], 130
Retiradas (Cena-nordestina) [3.1256], 110
Retrato [3.735], 90
Retrato [3.942], 96
Retrato, op. 148, no. 9 [3.1099i], 102
Retrato da alma [3.1520], 121
Revelação [3.786], 91
Revelación [1.554], 51
Revelación [10.7b], 161
Reversible [15.46b], 182
Reyerta [4.19], 130
Ricordi? [3.922], 95
Ricordi? (Romanza) [1.350], 32
Rima XVII [1.488a], 45
Rima XVIII [1.488b], 45
Rimas [5.40], 137
Rimas [20.26], 200
Rimas de Becquer [1.229], 21
Rimas de Bécquer [1.488], 45
Río, río [11.33], 164
Rio abaixo [3.1082], 101
Rio de planície [3.209c], 71
Rio de ternura [3.1521], 121
Rio desvelo [3.1159], 106
Río indígena [21.8], 203
Riqueza [1.339], 31
Riqui, Riqui, Riquirrán [11.34], 164
Risos de dor [3.212], 71
Risposta [21.18], 204

Ritornello [3.97], 67
Rocas [4.33a], 132
Rocio [1.343e], 31
Rocío [21.25], 204
Rodopis... [15.79e], 186
Rolinha [3.609], 86
Romance [22.11], 210
Romance, op. 3 [3.647], 87
Romance, op. 6 [3.649], 87
Romance, op. 11 [3.645], 87
Romance, op. 13 [3.646], 87
Romance, op. 56 [3.648], 87
Romance con lejanías [1.503], 47
Romance da inconfidência [3.1141], 105
Romance de José Cubas [1.340], 31
Romance de la Delfina [1.341], 31
Romance de la Luna, Luna [1.159], 16
Romance de la Luna, Luna [4.20], 130
Romance de la Luna, Luna [15.5c], 179
Romance de la muerte temprana [1.367c], 34
Romance de la niña negra [5.36], 137
Romance de la pena negra [1.160], 16
Romance de las tres ranas [1.517], 48
Romance de morenita [1.143], 15
Romancello [3.1142], 105
Romances de la niña negra [1.144], 15
Romancillo [7.19e], 151
Romancillo del beso [6.104], 146
Romancillos de la colonia [1.496], 46
Romanza [1.134], 15
Romanza [3.1075], 101
Romanza (Stecchetti) [3.159], 68
Romanza de los adolescentes [7.54], 153
Romanza gaucha [1.284], 27
Romería Mariana [11.13a], 164
Ronda con sabor a mar [1.518], 48
Ronda del sol [1.455], 43
Rondel [1.246f], 23
Rondel violet [1.219], 20
Ron-ron [15.38d], 182
Rosa de abril (Romanza) [1.237], 21
Rosa do meu sonho [3.771], 91
Rosa en la nieve [6.34], 142
Rosal [22.6], 210
Rosamor [3.43], 65
Rosamor [3.806], 92
Rosas [3.315], 74
Rosas orientales, op. 51 [1.1d], 4
Roseira, op. 63 [3.1124], 104
Rossinyol que vas a França [7.36a], 152
Rotação [3.10], 63
Rotação [3.736], 90

INDEX OF SONG AND SONG CYCLE TITLES

Rotação [3.807], 92
Rua aurora [3.1522], 121
Rua Vilaça [3.302b], 74
Ru-chu-chu (Cantiga das ruas) [3.11121], 104
Rudá, rudá [3.517c], 82
Rudá! Rudá! [3.923], 95
Ruego [1.35c], 9
Rumbo estelar [5.27], 137
Rumores del parque [1.561], 52

Sabelliades a Ruiseñor Rojo [4.15], 130
Sabença [3.737], 90
¿Sabes tú? [1.565], 53
Sabiá [3.1313], 112
Saca ejemplo del río [1.123a], 14
Sacy Pererê (Toada sertaneja) [3.270], 73
Sagesse [1.432i], 39
Sai aruê [3.517d], 82
Salgamos al amor [6.63], 144
¡Salgamos al amor, hermano hombre! [6.63c], 144
Salmo 127 [3.808], 92
Salmo a la tierra animal de tu vientre [6.63b], 144
Salmodia [15.21], 180
Salta, niña, en mi barquilla [3.930b], 96
Salutaris [3.98], 67
Salutaris [3.1373], 114
Salve Miss Brasil [3.99], 67
Samaritana [3.252], 72
Samaritana da floresta [3.345], 75
Samba clássico [3.1472], 119
Samba-lenço [3.1203b], 108
Santo Antonio, op. 148, no. 20 [3.1099t], 102
São Francisco de Assis [3.235b], 72
São João-da-ra-rão [3.165e], 69
São Paulo [3.1523], 121
São Paulo antigo [3.302c], 74
Saphirs [1.242], 21
Sapo [3.17], 64
Sapo [3.1308a], 111
Sapo-cururu [3.1319a], 112
Sarmiento fundaba escuelas [1.303n], 29
Saucecito, palma verde (Popular song from Conchucos-Huari, Peru) [19.7], 195
Saudade [3.116], 67
Saudade [3.213], 71
Saudade [3.525b], 82
Saudade [3.1316c], 112
Saudade [3.1524], 121
Saudade amiga [3.100], 67

Saudade da minha vida [3.1473d], 120
Saudade definitiva [3.478b], 80
Saudade é uma fogueira [3.1243], 109
Saudades de Bastos Tigre (II), op. 148, no. 32 [3.1099f], 102
Scène de Paris [3.1462g], 119
Schäfers Sonntagslied [1.190e], 18
Se casa el boyero [1.364d], 33
Se dice cubano [7.55], 153
Se enojó la luna, se enojó el lucero [1.15a], 5
Se equivocó la paloma [1.342], 31
Se eu fora poeta [3.1541i], 122
Se eu fora poeta [3.1542h], 122
Se eu fosse pé de pau [3.692e], 89
Se eu me sentasse agora [3.1546a], 123
Se eu morresse amanhã [3.101], 67
Se eu morresse amanhã [3.738], 90
Se eu pudesse . . . [3.481b], 80
Se eu sei o que é saudade [3.931c], 96
Se eu tiver que partir . . . op. 90 [3.1418], 116
Se gran maten [12.15d], 170
Se oye tu risa en la tarde [21.10b], 204
Se procurar bem [3.1526], 121
Se te esqueceres de mim [3.1051], 100
Se te llenó la vida lentamente de mar . . . [10.10c], 161
Se tu soubesses [3.924], 95
Se va la barca, pasillo [5.51], 138
Se você compreendesse [3.524i], 82
Sechs Lieder, op. 4 [1.190], 18
Secretos quero descuvrir [7.39f], 152
Segador [15.18a], 180
Segredo [3.943], 96
Segredo, op. 15 [3.1374], 114
Segue-me [3.524j], 82
Seguidillas Sevillanas [7.37d], 152
Segundo ciclo de romanzas y canciones: para contralto y piano [22.3], 209
Segundo motivo da rosa [3.41b], 65
Sehnsucht nach vergessen [3.1003], 98
Seigneur, lorsque viendra [12.28], 171
Seio de Deus [3.772], 91
Seis aires argentinos [1.497], 46
Seis canciones [1.415], 38
Seis canciones [1.457], 43
Seis canciones [1.460], 44
Seis canciones al estilo popular [1.382], 35
Seis canciones arcaicas (Seis poemas arcaicos), op. 35 [15.60], 177, 183
Seis canciones de cuna [1.343], 31
Seis canciones para cantar a los niños [15.38], 181

INDEX OF SONG AND SONG CYCLE TITLES

Seis canciones populares mejicanas, op. 7 [15.61], 183
Seis canciones populares sefardíes [7.39], 152
Seis canciones sobre "El barrio de Santa Cruz" de José María Pemán [21.54], 206
Seis canções de Cléomenes Campos [3.403], 77
Seis canções trovadorescas [3.1393], 114
Seis cantos infantiles [4.1], 129
Seis coplas [1.257], 24
Seis coplas [1.538], 49
Seis Lieder [1.434], 40
Seis líricas para canto e piano [3.925], 95
Seis missivas: Series of six short songs for baritone and piano [3.56], 66
Seis poemas de Helena Kolody [3.295], 74
Selva apacible (Tonada) [1.117], 14
Sem nome [3.1525], 121
Sem título (Untitled) [3.1345], 113
Sem—fim (Modinha) [3.1394], 115
Sempre! op. 32, no. 1 [3.1002], 98
Sem-seu (Candomblé de Ilhéus) [3.617a], 86
Senhora Dona Sancha [3.610], 86
Señor jardinero; déme usted a mí [1.15d], 5
Sentença [3.757b], 90
Sequência [3.1527], 121
Serei... serás [3.186], 69
Sereia do mar [3.1251b], 110
Seremos dois [3.532c], 83
Sérénade [1.432e], 39
Serenata [1.34d], 9
Serenata [3.346], 75
Serenata [3.403e], 77
Serenata [3.1212], 108
Serenata [3.1473m], 120
Serenata [5.23], 136
Serenata (O luar da minha terra) [3.290], 73
Serenata, en la mayor para canto y piano [5.25], 137
Serenata, op. 14 [4.25a], 130
Serenata, op. 33 [6.11], 141
Serenata, op. 75 [3.1375], 114
Serenata campera, op. 42 [1.1e], 4
Serenata de amor, aire de danza [5.54], 138
Serenata del Indio (Danza) [6.49], 143
Serenata di un moro [3.1004], 98
Serenata dotrefoá (Tríptico) [3.18], 64
Serenata española [20.16], 200
Serenata gitana [11.35], 164
Serenata mejicana [15.62], 184
Sérénitié [12.41d], 172
Seresta [3.926], 96
Seresta antiga [3.739], 90

Seresta de amor [3.57], 66
Serestas [3.1473], 119
Serpens [3.404], 77
Serrana [1.35b], 9
Serrana [1.370b], 34
Sertão no estio (Cantico brasileiro) [3.1474], 120
Serventois du trouvère Quenes de Bethune sur la Croisade [3.196e], 70
Sete anos de pastor [3.392c], 76
Sete anos de pastor, op. 108 [3.1376], 114
Sete líricas [3.927], 96
Sete vezes [3.1475], 120
Sette liriche [3.820], 92
Seu olhar [3.1528], 121
Seus olhos, op. 20 [3.1377], 114
Seven Compositions [19.4], 195
Severa Villafañe [1.344], 32
Sevilhana, op. 148, no. 17 [3.1099q], 102
Sfinge (Pagina d'album) [1.523], 48
Shibumú [5.17], 136
Si acaso crees a mi alma [1.440d], 41
Si al mecer... [1.494b], 46
Si alguna vez... [10.3c], 160
Si el silencio fuera mío [22.3a], 209
Si les étoiles pouvaient te dire [1.188a], 18
Si lo hallas [1.376b], 34
Si me está negado el amor [1.135], 15
Si muero... [1.34a], 9
Si quieres comprender [20.12], 199
Si quieres que yo te diga... [1.204a], 19
Si quieres que yo te quiera [3.930c], 96
Si tú... [6.35], 142
Si tu madre quiere un rey [7.33b], 151
Si un niño muere en la guerra [10.2a], 160
Si ves el ciervo herido (en modo dórico) [15.65a], 184
Si ves un mote de espumas [7.40], 152
Si vous saviez [3.928], 96
Siba oh [12.25g], 171
Siboney [7.31], 151
Sie haben heut' abend Gesellschaft [3.1017d], 99
Sie liebten sich beide [3.1017e], 99
Siempre crece un pino [22.17k], 211
Siempre en mi corazón [7.32], 151
Siempre que sueño las playas... [15.35c], 181
Siesta [1.345], 32
Siete canciones [1.346], 32
Siete canciones [10.8], 161
Siete canciones amerindias, op. 165a [6.12], 141
Siete canciones de Amado Villar, op. 45 [1.225], 20
Siete canciones infantiles [1.383], 35

INDEX OF SONG AND SONG CYCLE TITLES

Siete canciones para niños [15.22], 180
Siete canciones venezolanas: Suite para canto y piano [22.16], 207, 211
Siete cantos breves: para soprano y piano [15.50], 183
Siete de abril (Zamba) [1.285], 27
Siete poemínimos, op. 9 [15.30], 181
Signor Sergento [3.819c], 92
Sigue [7.45c], 153
Silencio [1.296], 27
Silencio [6.66], 144
Silencio [20.18a], 200
Silêncios do céu [3.292c], 74
Silenciosamente (Yaraví) [1.220], 20
Silenciosamente... [1.368c], 34
Silenzio ci vuole (Stornello popolare) [1.524], 48
Silueta [1.35f], 9
Silvia [7.56], 153
Simbi [12.25q], 171
Similitude [12.41h], 173
Simpatías amorosas [1.440g], 41
Simplicidade [3.1122c], 104
Sin niño [1.77b], 11
Sin poder con esta lengua [1.363a], 33
Sin tu amor [11.36], 164
Sina de cantador [3.1529], 121
Sinal de terra [3.253], 72
Sinfonía matinal [6.105], 146
Sing a new song (XXXIII) [4.31d], 131
Singela canção de Maria [3.1052], 100
Sinimbu [3.46b], 65
Sino da aldeia [3.1464f], 119
Sinos, 102
Síntese [3.28g], 64
Síntesis [5.19], 136
Sinto e provo [3.560], 83
Sitio Sin Nombre [7.11], 150
Só (ou Canção sozinha) [3.187], 69
Só o amor ficou [3.1530], 121
Só sim [3.1531], 121
Só tu [3.740], 90
Sobre el cielo de las margaritas ando [1.395a], 36
Sobre el gavilán [6.64], 144
Sobre los ángeles [4.32], 131
Sobrevivência [3.210c], 71
Soeur Beatrice, cantique (2nd act) [3.1378], 114
Sofrer, op. 148, no. 21 [3.1099u], 102
Soirs [12.13], 170
Sol, sol, gi, gi... [15.60d], 183
Sol de Maiakovski [3.846], 93
Sol nulo dos dias vãos [3.659i], 87
Solau do desamado [3.920c], 95

Solè oh [12.25f], 171
Soleá [11.13e], 164
Soledad [1.371], 34
Soledad [1.541a], 50
Soledad [6.36], 142
Soledad [15.3d], 179
Soledad [22.8h], 210
Soledad pampeana [1.545c], 51
Soledades, op. 21 [3.1379], 114
Solfeggietto [3.296], 74
Solidão [3.214], 71
Solidão [3.347], 75
Solidão [3.518], 82
Solidão [3.1457a], 118
Solitude... (Romance) [1.238], 21
Solo he sembrado en tu alma [20.30a], 201
Sólo por cantar [6.82d], 145
Sólo por el rocío [7.19c], 150
Sólo por el rocío [7.20], 151
Sólo quisiera [6.37], 142
Sombras (Canción criolla) [21.19], 204
Son [5.63], 138
Son míos, ¡Ay! son míos [1.442j], 42
Sonâmbula [3.1395], 115
Sonatina (en modo frígio) [15.65b], 184
Soñé un canto [1.493a], 46
Soneto [5.64], 138
Soneto, op. 21 no. 3 [3.1005], 98
Soneto a la armonia [1.347], 32
Soneto à lua [3.1143], 105
Soneto da separação [3.571d], 84
Soneto da separação [3.944], 96
Soneto de la guirnalda de rosas [5.65], 138
Soneto del cielo [22.17a], 211
Soneto del infierno [22.17c], 211
Soneto del purgatorio [22.17b], 211
Soneto para un tango [1.397a], 36
Song no. 2 [7.12], 150
Songs of Love and Solitude, op. 12 [4.3], 129
Sonhando [3.762b], 91
Sonhei [3.1542c], 122
Sonhei, op. 19, no. 1 [3.1006], 98
Sonho [3.1464d], 119
Sonho, op. 148, no. 3 [3.1099c], 102
Sonho atrevido [3.71], 66
Sonho de amor [3.58], 66
Sonho de curumim [3.611], 86
Sonho de uma noite de verão [3.665], 88
Sonho de uma noite de verão [3.1452c], 118
Sonho póstumo [3.847], 93
Sonho póstumo [3.929], 96
Sonho póstumo [3.1419], 116

INDEX OF SONG AND SONG CYCLE TITLES

Sonrisas (Canciones infantiles) [1.543], 50
Sorpresa [4.25f], 130
Sorriso interior [3.19], 64
Sos un sueño... [10.3a], 160
Soupir [1.26q], 8
Sous le ciel bleu [12.20], 170
Souvenance [1.26r], 8
Souvenances et souffrances (Méringue) [12.35], 172
Souvenir [3.572], 84
Soy el verano [6.81e], 145
Spes ultima Dea, op. 43 [3.1380], 114
Storia breve, op. 66 [3.1381], 114
Suave [3.561], 83
Sueño del atardecer [1.427], 39
Sueños negros [1.76], 11
Sugestões do crepúsculo [3.848], 93
Suite bucolicas infantiles [20.18], 200
Suite de canciones infantiles no. 1 [7.57], 153
Suite de canciones infantiles no. 2 [7.58], 153
Suite de seis peças [3.650], 87
Suite lírica, op. 25 [3.215], 71
Sum-sum [3.254], 72
Súplica [3.376], 76
Súplica [3.1144], 105
Súplica para ser feliz, op. 158 [3.1420], 116
Suprema angústia [3.102], 67
Sur la terre bariolée [12.9a], 169
Sur nos monts [3.195d], 70
Suray surita [19.16a], 196
Surdina [3.418], 78
Suspeita [3.522b], 82
Suspiro cuando te miro [22.3c], 209
Suspiros [3.565c], 83
Sussuarana [3.1314], 112
Sympathy [14.2e], 176

Tacuarita [1.335d], 31
Tahwa Inka' j Tak'y-nam [19.16], 196
Talvez [3.524k], 82
Talvez, op. 117 [3.1125], 104
Tamanduá [3.46c], 65
Tamba-tajá (Canção amazônica) [3.598f], 85
Tanka II [3.666], 88
Tanta coisa a dizer-te [3.519], 82
Tanta tinta [3.1415c], 115
Tanto amor nunca mais [3.424], 78
Tanto verso que eu sabia [3.567d], 84
Tão simples [3.574i], 84
Tapera [3.348], 75
Tarantela [3.103], 67
Tarco [1.19d], 6

Tarde [1.367b], 34
Tarde [22.15b], 211
Tarde (¿Estaba mi Lucía con los pies en el arroyo?) (Andaluzas) [1.24e], 7
Tarde azul [3.1456c], 118
Tarde de la noche vengo (Popular song from Cuenca, Ecuador) [19.8], 195
Tarde de verano [5.66], 138
Tarde de verano [21.9a], 203
Tarde en el río [1.199], 19
Tarde maravillosa [5.47], 138
Tarde na glória [3.1451b], 117
Tarde triste, op. 148, no. 5 [3.1099e], 102
Tardes [1.21a], 6
Tardes de noviembre (Barcarola) [6.106], 146
Tayêyras [3.413a], 77
Te has ido [5.67], 138
Te he soñado [1.440f], 41
Te quiero más que a mis ojos [1.460e], 44
Te quiero porque te quiero [11.37], 164
Te recuerdo, op. 270 [3.1423h], 116
Te seguiré [19.10b], 196
Te voy a llevar conmigo [1.223b], 20
Teirú [3.1476b], 120
Tem pena da nega (Batuque amazônico) [3.615], 86
Tem piedade de mim [3.669], 88
Tema de Jovino [3.612], 86
Tema de triste [3.613], 86
Tema e variações [3.792e], 92
Tema Severino (Tema teatral) [3.614], 86
Temblando estaba del frío [1.60c], 10
Tempo de Amor (Modinha) [3.562], 83
Tempos atrás [3.1445a], 117
Temps [12.14], 170
Tendido [6.38], 142
Tengo [6.39], 142
Tengo los ojos azules [7.33e], 151
Tenho medo do vento [3.1340], 113
Tenho uma raiva de vancê [3.1321a], 112
Tente liviana [15.74d], 185
Teotônio [3.607f], 86
Terceiro motivo da rosa [3.41c], 65
Teresita [22.13b], 211
Terra natal [3.522c], 82
Terú-terú [1.335i], 31
Tes yeux sont des adieux [12.4b], 169
Testimonio [15.41b], 182
Teu nome [3.42d], 65
Teu nome [3.925e], 96
Teu nome, op. 9, no. 2 [3.1027b], 100
Teu nome, op. 116, no. 1 [3.1126], 104

INDEX OF SONG AND SONG CYCLE TITLES

Teu rosto azul [3.255], 72
Teurer Freund! [3.1017f], 99
Teus olhos... água parada [3.425], 78
Teus olhos... o outono [3.271], 73
Teus olhos [3.563], 83
Teus olhos [3.741], 90
Teus olhos [3.1053], 100
Teus olhos (Balada no. 1) [3.651], 87
Teus olhos são como a noite [3.1054], 100
The earth is the Lord's (XXIV) [4.31b], 131
The Emerald Song [3.1462b], 118
The Island [3.1226], 109
The Negro speaks of rivers [14.1b], 176
The Shadow of Dawn: Five Poems by Paul Laurence Dunbar [14.2], 176
The Singing Tree [3.1462f], 119
Three Poems by Rabindranath Tagore, 177
Three poems/Tres poemas [15.18], 180
Three Songs/Tres canciones con texto de John Thurman [18.1], 193
Ti Zando [12.1], 169
Tiempo [1.297], 27
Tiempo, lugar y ventura [15.74c], 185
Tiempo de noche [6.79d], 145
Tierra [4.28g], 131
Tijera [1.330h], 31
Tijuana [15.29e], 181
Timidez, op. 52 [3.1127], 104
Tionti mañan eu [1.77c], 11
Tiradentes [3.1547], 123
Tite Jeanneton [3.195e], 70
Titilar de estrellas [1.561h], 52
Toada [3.220], 71
Toada [3.426], 78
Toada (Série regional) [3.1315], 112
Toada Baré [3.1153], 106
Toada da Canoa [3.1145], 105
Toada da saudade [3.1055], 100
Toada das horas [3.386], 76
Toada do amor [3.1550d], 123
Toada do Pai do Mato [3.520], 82
Toada no. 1: Brasileira [3.652], 87
Toada no. 2: Morena [3.653], 87
Toada no. 3 [3.1396], 115
Toada no. 3: Não sei viver sem ti [3.654], 87
Toada no. 4: Amor [3.655], 87
Toada no. 5: Quando o amor vem [3.656], 87
Toada p'ra você [3.349], 75
Toadas de Xangô [3.564], 83
Toca a cantá [3.117c], 67
¡Toda una vida! [1.360], 33
Todo [1.61a], 10

Todo [15.7a], 179
Todo el mundo me murmura [4.26b], 130
Todo es ronda [4.27], 130
Todo es un ajedrez... [15.79i], 186
Todo fue así [6.40], 142
Todos creen... [6.41], 143
Todos me piden que cante [1.493b], 46
Toi, op. 23 [3.350], 75
Tomara achar quem me diga [3.566b], 83
To-morrow is Saint Valentine's Day [3.684c], 88
Ton image [1.4e], 4
Tonada [1.8], 4
Tonada [1.96], 12
Tonada [22.10i], 210
Tonadas de Navidad [1.251], 23
Torcacita [1.335b], 31
Tormenta [3.1056], 100
Tormento [6.81c], 145
Toujours!! (Ognor) (Mélodie pour chant) [21.49], 206
Traço profundo, op. 148, no. 30 [3.1099d], 102
Tra-la-la-la [3.1057], 100
Tránsito [7.19f], 151
Tránsito [7.21], 151
Trece Lieder [1.267], 25
30 Canciones para la patria de ayer y mañana, op. 81 [6.9], 141
Trem de Alagoas [3.616], 86
Trem de ferro [3.44], 65
Tres árboles [4.35c], 132
Tres baladas de Liliencron [1.530], 49
Tres cancioncitas del mar [20.14], 200
3 Canciones [1.298], 27
Tres canciones [1.361], 33
Tres canciones [1.397], 36
Tres canciones [1.461], 44
Tres canciones [4.24], 130
Tres canciones [7.7], 150
Tres canciones [15.27], 180
Tres canciones [20.20], 200
Tres canciones [20.30], 201
Tres canciones (also titled Canciones argentinas) [1.366], 33
Tres canciones americanas, op. 15 [1.387], 36
Tres canciones argentinas [1.171], 16
Tres canciones argentinas [1.456], 43
Tres canciones azules [7.5], 150
Tres canciones breves [15.39], 182
Tres canciones chinas [15.49], 183
Tres canciones cordobesas [1.161], 16
Tres canciones de amor [4.38], 132
Tres canciones de Ariel (La Tempestad) [6.83], 145

INDEX OF SONG AND SONG CYCLE TITLES

Tres canciones de cuna de estrella florida [1.428], 39
Tres canciones de soledad [1.200], 19
Tres canciones epigramáticas [10.9], 161
Tres canciones españolas: para canto y piano [15.5], 179
Tres canciones grises [7.6], 150
Tres canciones, op. 1 [1.56], 10
Tres canciones panameñas [1.444], 42
Tres canciones para soprano [6.62], 144
Tres canciones para soprano y piano [10.10], 161
Tres canciones para una bandera [4.16], 130
Tres canciones para voz y piano [15.45], 182
Tres canciones populares [22.18], 212
Tres canciones sobre poemas de Enrique Gonzáles Martínez [11.4], 163
3 Canciones sobre poesías de José Iglesias de la Casa [1.299], 27
Três canções [3.20], 64
Três canções [3.45], 65
Três canções [3.565], 83
Três canções brasileiras [3.521], 82
Três canções brasileiras (3a. série: Das cenas infantis) [3.1318], 112
Três canções brasileiras I [3.1316], 112
Três canções brasileiras II [3.1317], 112
Três canções de Chico Moura [3.1128], 104
Três canções do folclore brasileiro [3.117], 67
Três canções francesas [3.405], 77
Três canções modernas [3.1319], 112
Três canções modernas (1a. série) [3.1320], 112
Três canções modernas (2a. série) [3.1321], 112
Três canções, op. 9 [3.1027], 100
Três canções para canto e piano [3.1244], 109
Três canções populares [3.1195], 108
Três canções simples [3.945], 96
Tres cantos de Navidad, op. 4 [1.60], 10
Três cantos nativos, op. 3 (3.1088), 101
Tres cantos negros [1.162], 16
Três cantos populares espanhóis [3.930], 96
Três ciclos de quatro canções, op. 32, I [3.1548], 123
Três ciclos de quatro canções, op. 32, II [3.1549], 123
Três ciclos de quatro canções, op. 32, III [3.1550], 123
Três côcos (Sobre temas Pernambucanos) [3.1322], 112
Tres coplas [1.268], 25
Tres cuidades [1.25], 7
Três danças sertanejas (Côcos) [3.1323], 112
Tres días hace que Nina dormida en su lecho está [5.48], 138
Três epigramas [3.522], 82

Tres episódios de animais [3.46], 65
Tres exágonos [15.17], 180
Tres hai-kai [3.72], 66
Três lembranças do folclore infantil [3.1213], 108
Tres líricas para canto y piano [1.145], 15
Tres madrigales [19.5], 195
Três manchas gaúchas [3.286], 73
Três manchas para canto e piano [3.287], 73
Tres melodías [1.367], 34
Tres morillas... [15.60f], 183
Tres morillas me enamoran en Jaén [7.33a], 151
Três números de Bumba-meu-boi [3.216], 71
Tres piezas [1.184], 17
Tres poemas [1.541], 50
Três poemas [3.523], 82
Tres poemas [4.39], 132
Três poemas de Augusto Meyer [3.427], 78
Tres poemas de Enrique Gonzáles Martínez [15.63], 177, 184
Tres poemas de Gabriela Mistral, op. 20 [4.42], 132
Tres poemas de José de Diego [20.19], 200
Tres poemas de Lermontow, 177
Tres poemas de Mariano Brull, 177
Tres poemas galegos [1.77], 11
Três poemas indígenas [3.1476], 120
Tres poemas minimos [7.2], 150
Três pontos de santo [3.1089], 101
Três pontos rituais [3.617], 86
Tres recitativos breves [4.17], 130
Tres retratos [1.532], 49
Tres sonetos de Francisco Luis Bernárdez, op. 17 [1.61], 10
Três trovas de Manuel Bandeira, op. 114 [3.1129], 104
Três trovas de Mário de Andrade, op. 169 [3.1130], 105
Três trovas, op. 6 [3.1028], 100
Treva, penumbra e luz [3.316], 74
Treze canções de amor [3.524], 82
Trigo limpio [1.201], 19
Trigueña mía [1.136], 15
Triolet [19.13a], 196
Triolets [3.1058], 100
Tríptico [3.1196], 108
Tríptico [22.9], 210
Tríptico criollo [21.9], 203
Triptico da saudade [3.931], 96
Triptico de amor, op. 54 [3.773], 91
Triptico de Virginia Victorino [3.1131], 105
Triptico de Yeda [3.525], 82
Tríptico floral [1.504], 47
Triptico para os oitenta anos de C. D. A. (An-

INDEX OF SONG AND SONG CYCLE TITLES

drade, Carlos Drummond de), op. 137 [3.1551], 123
Tríptico primaveral [21.10], 203
Tríptico sobre poesía cubana: para canto y piano [22.4], 210
Triste [1.271b], 26
Triste [1.352], 32
Triste [1.400c], 37
Triste [1.472a], 44
Triste [1.520a], 48
Triste (Canción a dos voces) [1.429], 39
Triste (Triste no. 4) [21.36], 202, 205
Triste, muy tristemente [5.4], 136
Triste estoy (Aire de Yaraví) [1.497f], 47
Triste me voy a los campos [1.440b], 41
Tristes guerras [1.442o], 42
Tristesse, (21.51), 206
Tristesse de la lune [3.172], 69
Tristeza [1.533], 49
Tristeza [2.10b], 57
Tristeza [3.118], 67
Tristeza [3.292d], 74
Tristeza [3.523b], 82
Tristeza [3.1445b], 117
Tristeza no céu [3.821], 92
Tristezas (Popular song from Cuenca, Ecuador) [19.9], 196
Trois chansons d'après des textes d'Ida Faubert [12.29], 172
Trois chansons vodouesques [12.30], 172
Trois poèmes/Tres poemas de Gil Vicente [7.41], 152
Trois rondes haïtiennes [12.32], 172
Tropical [15.36a], 181
Tropilla de estrellas [1.369a], 34
Trova [3.1325d], 113
Trova 1, op. 114, no. 1 [3.1129a], 105
Trova 2, op. 114, no. 2 [3.1129b], 105
Trova 3, op. 114, no. 3 [3.1129c], 105
Trova de muito amor para um amado Senhor [3.47b], 65
Trova de muito amor para um amado senhor [3.1214], 108
Trova no. 1 (Lundu) [3.1028a], 100
Trova no. 2 (Modinha) [3.1028b], 100
Trova no. 3 (Final) [3.1028c], 100
Trovas [3.298–3.300], 74
Trovas [3.317], 74
Trovas [3.574j], 84
Trovas [3.932], 96
Trovas [3.1007], 98
Trovas [3.1245], 109
Trovas, op. 29, no. 2 [3.1008], 98

Trovas alagoanas [3.566], 83
Trovas capixabas [3.567], 84
Trovas de amigo [3.742], 90
Trovas de amor [3.351], 75
Trovas de amor [3.526], 82
Trovas de amor [3.933], 96
Trovas de muito amor para um amado senhor [3.47], 65
Trovas e danças no. 1 [3.1112m], 104
Trovas e danças no. 2 [3.1112n], 104
Trozo [1.444b], 42
Tu [3.73], 66
Tu [3.921c], 95
Tu [15.80b], 187
Tu amor de las entrañas me arranqué [1.566], 53
Tu e o vento [3.670], 88
Tu és o sol, op. 14, no. 2 [3.1009], 98
Tu nombre en la distancia [2.10c], 57
Tu passaste por este jardim [3.1443i], 117
Tu pie (Madrigal) [1.221], 20
Tu secreto (Lied en ritmo de tango estilizado) [1.78], 11
Tu vais ao mar [3.1197], 108
Tu veux savoir [1.26s], 8
Tua boca diz que não [3.531c], 83
Tua boca diz que não [3.536b], 83
Tua boca mágica [3.28h], 64
Tua memória, op. 243 [3.1421], 116
Tuas mãos [3.934], 96
Tuas mãos [3.1532], 121
Tudo o mais são penas [3.743], 90
Turqueza, op. 26, no. 1 [3.1010], 98
Tutito hagamos ya [4.1b], 129
TVgrama 1 [3.849], 93

Uai ni-nim [3.256], 72
Ualalocê (Parecis Legend) [3.1442b], 117
Ueremen [3.822], 92
Uirapuru (Canção amazônica-valsinha do Marajóa [3.598g], 85
Uirapuru e o violão [3.1146], 105
Última ilusão [3.534b], 83
Último retrato [3.257], 72
Último sino [3.429f], 78
Último tango [3.272], 73
Um adeus (no. 3) [3.650b], 87
Um beijo [3.352], 75
Um momento qualquer, op. 108 [3.1422], 116
Uma barquinha branca [3.1083], 101
Uma cabocla, dois caboclos e um violão [3.935], 96
Uma canção de amor [3.618], 86

INDEX OF SONG AND SONG CYCLE TITLES

Uma casinha paulista [3.303c], 74
Uma estrela brilhou [3.1533], 122
Uma folha ... outra folha [3.1324b], 113
Uma nota, uma só mão [3.744], 90
Uma saudade [3.104], 67
Uma toada [3.1317b], 112
Un abanico (Un ventall) [1.415c], 38
Un ami, 115
Un ange est venu [1.26t], 8
Un asra [1.97], 12
Un desiderio [3.1382], 114
Un grand sommeil noir [1.16a], 5
Un instante de reposo ... [15.79j], 186
Un organetto suona per la via, op. 56 [3.1383], 114
Un peu de pain! ... Un peu d'eau fraîche [12.9c], 169
Un signo [1.186b], 18
Una copla [1.497d], 47
Una noche de luna [1.353], 32
Una noche tropical (Serenata) [17.3], 191
Una vez clavelina [11.38], 164
Unianguripê op. 3 no. 1 [3.1088a], 101
Única mar [7.19b], 150
Única ventura [3.429g], 78
Único amor, op. 65 (Berceuse) [3.657], 87
Uno ojos dulces [1.459b], 44
Unto Thee I lift my soul (XXV) [4.31c], 131
Utopia [3.568], 84
Uyara, 69

Vá como vai! [3.406], 77
Vadeia caboclinho [3.1239b], 109
Vadeia cabocolinho [3.1322b], 112
Vai, azulão [3.527], 82
Vai meu suspiro [3.1246], 109
Vai torná a vortá (cateretê) [3.569], 84
Valentina [3.380b], 76
Valsa proibida [3.74], 66
Valsa-canção, op. 35b [3.774], 91
Valse presque noble et sentimentale [3.936], 96
Valsinha [3.1128a], 104
Valsinha de roda [3.1534], 122
Vamo saravá (ponto das baianas [3.1059], 100
Vamos a cantar (Zamba) [1.543e], 50
Vamos bebendo (Vamos bebiendo) [1.58b], 10
Vamos dar a despedida [3.516d], 81
Variações sem tema [3.1546d], 123
Ve la conto e ve la canto [3.819d], 92
Vecchio tema [3.160], 68
Veinte canciones escolares en el estilo popular, op. 67 [1.562], 53
20 Mélodies [1.26], 8

Veinte poemas de amor y una canción desesperada, op. 179 B [3.1423], 116
21 Romanzas [16.1], 189
Vela branca [3.1060], 100
Vela morena [3.1147], 105
Vela que passou [3.585a], 85
Velas ao mar [3.258], 72
Veleiro [3.130], 67
Veleiros [3.1456d], 118
Velha canção [3.161], 68
Velha canção [3.173], 69
Velha modinha [3.1341], 113
Velhas árvores [3.392d], 77
Velhice [3.392e], 77
Velhos amigos [3.893e], 94
Vem comigo, op. 54, no. 1 [3.773a], 91
Ven, Sol (Kum, Zun) [1.443b], 42
Vengan vientos [15.1a], 179
Vengo desde mi sombra para verte [21.40c], 205
Vengo otra vez a ti, op. 122 [3.1424], 116
Veni Creator Spiritus, op. 241 [3.1425], 116
Vente con nosotros [1.146], 15
Vento [3.574k], 84
Vento balançava aquela rosa tão de leve [3.937], 96
Vento da manhã [3.938], 96
Vento noturno, op. 12 [3.775], 91
Vento que corropia [3.927g], 96
Vento serrano [3.1535], 122
Verano [1.140d], 15
Verano [1.525d], 48
Verano [15.35d], 181
Verano largo [6.81b], 145
Verdade [3.1452h], 118
Verde que te quiero verde [1.163], 16
Verlaine [1.532c], 49
Vesperal [3.353], 75
Vévélo [12.25p], 171
Viagem infinita [3.295e], 74
Victoria (Canción colombiana) [5.35], 137
Victoria, op. 109 [3.1426], 116
Victoria sobre el tiempo [11.4b], 163
Vida, que és o dia de hoje [3.745], 90
Vida, vidita ... [1.539], 49
Vida, vidita (Canción norteña) [1.66], 11
Vida criolla [20.9d], 199
Vida criolla [20.23], 200
Vida formosa [3.1466b], 119
Vida mía, ya me voy [1.460b], 44
Vidala [1.172], 17
Vidala [1.175a], 17
Vidala [1.366b], 33
Vidala [1.382d], 35

INDEX OF SONG AND SONG CYCLE TITLES

Vidala del regreso [1.286], 27
Vidala del secadal (Vidala) [1.302e], 28
Vidala santiagueña [1.269], 25
Vidalita [1.54], 9
Vidalita [1.239], 21
Vidalita [1.366c], 33
Vidalita [1.405], 37
Vidalita [1.558c], 52
Vidalita [11.39], 164
Vidalita (Canción al estilo popular) [1.382a], 35
Vidalita, op. 36 [1.6], 4
Vidalita del payador [1.561i], 52
Vidalita del querer [21.1c], 203
Vidalita Tucumana [1.137], 15
Vidita [1.55], 9
Vidita [1.171a], 16
Vieja danza: sobre un antiguo tema mexicano [15.28], 180
Vieja palabra [21.40b], 206
Vier Lieder, op. 9 [1.191], 18
Vieste enrolado no perfume dos manacás [3.472b], 80
Vigília [3.1196a], 108
Vigilia [22.10h], 210
Vilancete (canção trovadoresca no. 5) [3.1393e], 115
Villancico [4.29b], 131
Villancico (Argentina) [1.387a], 36
Villancico de la adoración [1.251d], 24
Villancico del rey negro [1.246a], 23
Villancico del sol de las cinco [21.54f], 206
Villancico y bailecito de Noche Buena [1.251c], 24
Villancicos, op. 42 [1.244], 22
Villanela natalicia [1.246b], 23
Vine al mundo ... [15.79g], 186
Viniendo de Chilecito ... [1.300b], 27
Vino (Vain) [1.443a], 42
Viola de Lereno [3.746], 90
Viola do Amor [3.1540b], 122
Viola quebrada [3.1443f], 117
Violão [3.427c], 78
Violão [3.5741], 84
Violão do capadócio [3.939], 96
Violão do capadócio [3.940], 96
Violeiro da estrada [3.619], 86
Violetas [1.298a], 27
Vira [3.1477], 120
Virgens mortas [3.162], 68
Virtus [3.377], 76
Visión [1.406], 37
Visione del Gange (Romanza hindú) [21.3], 203
Visões [3.945c], 96

Vita, op. 8 [3.1384], 114
Vling sou Vling [12.25i], 171
Vocalise [1.555c], 51
Vocalise [3.528], 82
Vocalise [3.1478], 120
Vocalise [3.1536], 122
Vocalise [15.23], 180
Vocalise, op. 47 [3.1132], 105
Vocalise em estilo romântico [3.131], 68
Vocalize [3.297], 74
Você [3.5241], 82
Você [3.747], 90
Você [3.921d], 95
Você [3.1247], 109
Você [3.1537], 122
Você diz que me quer bem [3.221], 71
Você é tão suave [3.5131], 81
Você é tão suave [3.1025c], 99
Você gosta de mim [3.1215], 108
Você não sabe [3.1538], 122
Você nasceu [3.524m], 82
Voces de la tarde (Canción de cuna) [13.1], 174
Voces en la distancia [7.13], 150
Volar y volar [3.1198], 108
Volonté [12.21], 170
Volta [3.1539], 122
Volverán ... [1.494c], 46
Vontade, op. 148, no. 14 [3.1099n], 102
Vôo [3.1473n], 120
Vorrei [1.489], 45
Vorrei baciarti, O fillis, op. 4 [15.31], 181
Vos yeux ont des langueurs [1.138], 15
Vou vivendo a minha vida [3.483b], 80
Vou-me embora [3.521c], 82
Vou-me embora pra Pasárgada [3.570], 84
Vou-me embora, vou-me embora [3.567e], 84
Vous êtes belle [12.2], 169
Voy a medirme el amor [7.19i], 151
Voy caminito [1.362], 33
Voz da noite [3.295f], 74
Voz del güiro [20.13], 200
Vozes da floresta [3.105], 67
Vuelo supremo [6.67], 144

Wanderers Nachtlied [3.1199], 108
W'ay! (¡Ayes!) [19.16c], 196
We wear the mask [14.2c], 176
Werdet nur nicht ungeduldig [3.1017g], 99
Wiege sie sanft, o Schlaf [3.1011], 98

Xácara, op. 20, no. 1 [3.1012], 96
Xangô [3.419], 78

INDEX OF SONG AND SONG CYCLE TITLES

Xangô [3.1443d], 117
Xangô, meu Orixá [3.1061], 101

Y ese lunar que tienes ... (El tapao) [1.416a], 38
Y no me atreví ... [1.361c], 33
Y pensar que pudimos ... [15.77c], 186
¿Y quién eres ... ? [10.5d], 161
Y se muriu el burru [7.38b], 152
Y sé por dónde voy ... [10.8e], 161
Ya llega la aurora [1.543h], 50
Ya llegan las vacaciones [1.303o], 29
Ya me voy a retirar ... [1.301c], 28
Ya salió de la mar [7.39d], 152
Yambambó [7.15], 150
Yaraví [1.204d], 19
Yaraví [1.498], 47
Yaraví [1.558b], 52
Yaraví [9.1], 158
Yaveñita [1.497b], 46
Yayá (Lundu) [3.1112o], 104
Yemanjá [3.1250a], 110
Yo, señora [15.74e], 185
Yo bajé del monte (Tonada) [1.9], 4
Yo boli de foja en foja [7.39a], 152

Yo digo si y es que si [1.147], 15
Yo me quedé triste y mudo [22.16a], 211
Yo no sé [20.29], 201
Yo no tengo soledad [4.42a], 132
Yo ouè bo mio couè [12.25m], 171
Yo pensé enamorarte [1.18a], 6
Yo pienso en tí [11.5], 163
Yo sé cuál el objeto de tus suspiros es; ... [20.26c], 200
Yo soy una flor ... (Los reyes en la montaña) [1.416c], 38
Yo voy soñando caminos [1.438a], 40
Yuchán (Palo borracho) [1.20a], 6

Zagaleja del casar ... [15.60b], 183
Zamba [1.271c], 26
Zamba del quiero [1.348], 32
Zarzamora con el tronco gris [1.24c], 7
Zarzamora con el tronco gris [20.6], 199
Zé Raymundo, op. 1 [3.1090], 101
Zorzal [1.222], 20
Zwei Augen [1.188b], 18
Zwei Lieder [4.40], 132
Zwei Lieder vom Tode [4.41], 132

Index of Tessituras and Voice Types

Catalog numbers are used as locators.

Songs by Tessitura

High—1 (Argentina): 1.2, 1.4a, 1.4d, 1.4e, 1.4f, 1.5, 1.13c, 1.13e, 1.16d, 1.19a, 1.19d, 1.20a, 1.20b, 1.21c, 1.26a, 1.26c, 1.26e, 1.26j, 1.30, 1.33, 1.34d, 1.36, 1.38, 1.39, 1.48, 1.53, 1.54, 1.55, 1.64f, 1.73, 1.79, 1.80, 1.81, 1.83, 1.84, 1.87, 1.89, 1.91, 1.92, 1.93, 1.96, 1.97, 1.108, 1.116, 1.118, 1.122a, 1.122b, 1.122c, 1.122d, 1.123a, 1.123b, 1.123c, 1.128, 1.129, 1.131, 1.132, 1.133, 1.134, 1.139, 1.149, 1.155, 1.158, 1.159, 1.165, 1.168, 1.170, 1.177, 1.180, 1.185a, 1.185c, 1.186, 1.187, 1.188a, 1.188c, 1.189, 1.190f, 1.191d, 1.193, 1.204f, 1.205a, 1.205b, 1.208, 1.222, 1.223d, 1.229, 1.240, 1.241, 1.243a, 1.243d, 1.244a, 1.244d, 1.250a, 1.250c, 1.253, 1.256b, 1.256c, 1.267a, 1.267f, 1.269, 1.271e, 1.272a, 1.281, 1.284, 1.288, 1.291, 1.327b, 1.327c, 1.336, 1.339, 1.358, 1.359, 1.363b, 1.363c, 1.364c, 1.364d, 1.369b, 1.370c, 1.371, 1.395, 1.397b, 1.398, 1.402, 1.404, 1.406, 1.407, 1.411, 1.412, 1.415a, 1.415b, 1.415c, 1.415d, 1.430, 1.437a, 1.437d, 1.440a, 1.445, 1.456c, 1.458c, 1.461a, 1.470, 1.479, 1.482, 1.490a, 1.501b, 1.504, 1.507, 1.513, 1.515b, 1.520, 1.523, 1.525c, 1.525d, 1.541b, 1.548, 1.556, 1.557b, 1.557e, 1.557h, 1.558a, 1.560i, 1.561f, 1.561g, 1.561h, 1.561i

High—2 (Bolivia): 2.1, 2.2, 2.11a, 2.11b

High—3 (Brazil): 3.1165, 3.1167, 3.1175a, 3.1412, 3.1434, 3.1457, 3.1465, 3.1541, 3.1542, 3.1543, 3.1546, 3.1548, 3.1550

High—4 (Chile): 4.2, 4.24c, 4.28e, 4.28f, 4.29, 4.30c, 4.30d, 4.30e, 4.30i, 4.30j, 4.33, 4.34a, 4.34b, 4.35d, 4.42

High—5 (Colombia): 5.1, 5.2, 5.5, 5.6, 5.9, 5.11, 5.22, 5.25, 5.28, 5.30, 5.33, 5.34, 5.35, 5.37, 5.39, 5.40, 5.41, 5.42, 5.43, 5.46, 5.47, 5.48, 5.49, 5.50, 5.51, 5.52, 5.53, 5.54, 5.55, 5.56, 5.58, 5.59, 5.60, 5.62, 5.63, 5.65, 5.67

High—6 (Costa Rica): 6.52, 6.62, 6.64, 6.79a, 6.79e, 6.85

High—7 (Cuba): 7.1, 7.14, 7.17f, 7.17g, 7.22, 7.37, 7.38, 7.39

High—8 (Dominican Republic): 8.2, 8.3

High—10 (El Salvador): 10.1, 10.2, 10.3, 10.5, 10.7a, 10.7c, 10.8a, 10.8c, 10.8f, 10.8g, 10.9, 10.10

High—12 (Haiti): 12.11, 12.26, 12.31, 12.32

High—14 (Jamaica): 14.1b, 14.1e, 14.2a, 14.2b, 14.2c

High—15 (Mexico): 15.8, 15.9, 15.11, 15.13, 15.17, 15.30, 15.35a, 15.35b, 15.35d, 15.35e, 15.36, 15.37a, 15.55, 15.65d, 15.65e, 15.65f, 15.66a, 15.66b, 15.66c, 15.67a, 15.67b, 15.67d, 15.67e, 15.71, 15.72, 15.74, 15.77, 15.78i, 15.80

High—19 (Peru): 19.5b, 19.5c, 19.10a, 19.15b, 19.16

High—20 (Puerto Rico): 20.25a, 20.25b, 20.25c, 20.25d, 20.25e, 20.30c

High—21 (Uruguay): 21.15, 21.17, 21.18, 21.21, 21.22, 21.45, 21.48, 21.52, 21.54c

High—22 (Venezuela): 22.6, 22.12

Medium-high—1 (Argentina): 1.1, 1.3a, 1.3b, 1.4b, 1.4c, 1.4g, 1.6, 1.7, 1.8, 1.9, 1.13a, 1.13b, 1.13d, 1.14, 1.16b, 1.16c, 1.16e, 1.16f, 1.16g, 1.16h, 1.16i, 1.16j, 1.16k, 1.161, 1.17a, 1.17b, 1.17c, 1.18a, 1.18c, 1.18e, 1.19c, 1.19e, 1.19f,

INDEX OF TESSITURAS AND VOICE TYPES

1.20c, 1.20d, 1.20e, 1.20f, 1.21a, 1.21d, 1.21e, 1.21f, 1.22a, 1.22c, 1.23, 1.25a, 1.25b, 1.25c, 1.26b, 1.26f, 1.26g, 1.26h, 1.26m, 1.26n, 1.26o, 1.26q, 1.26r, 1.26s, 1.26t, 1.27, 1.29, 1.32, 1.34, 1.35, 1.37, 1.42, 1.43, 1.44, 1.45, 1.46, 1.47, 1.50, 1.51, 1.56, 1.61b, 1.61c, 1.67, 1.71, 1.76, 1.77a, 1.77b, 1.77c, 1.78, 1.82, 1.88, 1.94a, 1.95, 1.98b, 1.98c, 1.98d, 1.100b, 1.100c, 1.102, 1.103, 1.104, 1.105, 1.107b, 1.107c, 1.107d, 1.109, 1.110, 1.112, 1.113, 1.117, 1.119, 1.120, 1.121, 1.123d, 1.124, 1.125, 1.126, 1.127, 1.130, 1.135, 1.136, 1.137, 1.138, 1.141, 1.143, 1.144, 1.146, 1.147, 1.148, 1.150, 1.152, 1.153, 1.154, 1.156, 1.157, 1.161a, 1.162, 1.163, 1.164, 1.166, 1.167, 1.169, 1.171b, 1.171c, 1.172, 1.173, 1.174, 1.175, 1.175a, 1.175c, 1.175d, 1.175e, 1.176, 1.178, 1.179, 1.181, 1.182, 1.184, 1.185b, 1.188b, 1.190, 1.191, 1.192, 1.194, 1.195, 1.196, 1.197, 1.199, 1.200, 1.202, 1.204, 1.205c, 1.205d, 1.205e, 1.206a, 1.210, 1.212, 1.213, 1.214, 1.215, 1.216, 1.217, 1.218, 1.219, 1.220, 1.221, 1.223a, 1.223b, 1.223c, 1.224d, 1.225a, 1.225c, 1.225d, 1.225e, 1.225f, 1.225g, 1.227, 1.228, 1.230, 1.231, 1.232, 1.233, 1.234, 1.235, 1.236, 1.237, 1.238, 1.239, 1.243b, 1.243c, 1.243e, 1.244b, 1.244c, 1.245a, 1.246c, 1.246e, 1.246f, 1.247a, 1.247b, 1.247c, 1.247d, 1.247f, 1.247g, 1.247h, 1.247i, 1.247j, 1.249a, 1.249c, 1.249e, 1.250b, 1.251c, 1.251d, 1.252, 1.254, 1.255, 1.256a, 1.256d, 1.259, 1.260, 1.261, 1.262, 1.263, 1.264, 1.265, 1.267b, 1.267c, 1.267d, 1.267e, 1.267g, 1.267h, 1.267i, 1.267j, 1.267k, 1.2671, 1.267m, 1.268a, 1.268b, 1.268c, 1.271b, 1.271c, 1.271d, 1.272b, 1.274b, 1.274c, 1.274d, 1.274e, 1.275, 1.277, 1.279, 1.280, 1.282, 1.286, 1.287, 1.289, 1.290, 1.292, 1.293, 1.294, 1.296, 1.297, 1.298a, 1.298b, 1.299, 1.300a, 1.300b, 1.302c, 1.302k, 1.3021, 1.305, 1.315, 1.323, 1.325, 1.327a, 1.329, 1.333, 1.334, 1.337, 1.338, 1.342, 1.343b, 1.345, 1.346b, 1.346c, 1.346g, 1.349, 1.350, 1.351, 1.352, 1.353, 1.355, 1.356, 1.357, 1.360, 1.361, 1.362, 1.363a, 1.364a, 1.364b, 1.365, 1.366a, 1.366c, 1.367, 1.368, 1.369a, 1.369c, 1.370a, 1.370b, 1.370d, 1.375, 1.376a, 1.376c, 1.377, 1.378, 1.379, 1.381, 1.382a, 1.382b, 1.382c, 1.382e, 1.382f, 1.383b, 1.383c, 1.383d, 1.384, 1.386c, 1.387a, 1.387c, 1.388, 1.389, 1.390, 1.391, 1.393, 1.396, 1.397a, 1.397c, 1.400a, 1.400c, 1.400d, 1.400e, 1.405, 1.408, 1.409, 1.410, 1.413, 1.415f, 1.416b, 1.416c, 1.416d, 1.416e, 1.416f, 1.416g, 1.416h, 1.418, 1.423, 1.431, 1.432b, 1.432c, 1.432f, 1.432g, 1.432h, 1.432i, 1.433, 1.434b, 1.434c, 1.434d, 1.434e, 1.434f, 1.435, 1.436, 1.437b, 1.437c, 1.438b, 1.438c, 1.438d, 1.438f, 1.440b, 1.440c, 1.440d, 1.440f, 1.440h, 1.441, 1.4421, 1.443c, 1.444a, 1.446, 1.447, 1.448, 1.449, 1.450, 1.451, 1.452, 1.453, 1.454, 1.455, 1.456a, 1.456b, 1.457a, 1.457b, 1.457f, 1.458a, 1.458b, 1.459a, 1.459b, 1.459c, 1.459d, 1.460b, 1.460d, 1.460e, 1.460f, 1.461c, 1.463, 1.464, 1.465, 1.466, 1.468, 1.469, 1.471, 1.472, 1.473, 1.474, 1.475, 1.476, 1.477, 1.478, 1.483, 1.486a, 1.486b, 1.486c, 1.486d, 1.487, 1.488b, 1.488c, 1.489, 1.490b, 1.490c, 1.490d, 1.492, 1.493a, 1.493c, 1.494c, 1.494d, 1.495, 1.497b, 1.497c, 1.499, 1.500, 1.501a, 1.505, 1.506, 1.508, 1.510, 1.511, 1.512, 1.515a, 1.516, 1.519, 1.521, 1.522, 1.524, 1.525a, 1.525b, 1.526, 1.528, 1.530b, 1.530c, 1.531a, 1.531c, 1.533, 1.534, 1.537, 1.538a, 1.538c, 1.538d, 1.538e, 1.538f, 1.539, 1.540a, 1.540b, 1.540c, 1.541a, 1.541c, 1.545, 1.546, 1.549, 1.550, 1.551, 1.552, 1.553, 1.554, 1.555a, 1.555b, 1.555d, 1.557a, 1.557c, 1.557d, 1.557g, 1.557i, 1.557j, 1.558b, 1.558c, 1.559, 1.560b, 1.560c, 1.560d, 1.560e, 1.560f, 1.560g, 1.560h, 1.560j, 1.561a, 1.561b, 1.561c, 1.561d, 1.561e, 1.563, 1.566

Medium-high—2 (Bolivia): 2.7, 2.8, 2.9b, 2.10a, 2.11c

Medium-high—4 (Chile): 4.24a, 4.24b, 4.25f, 4.26d, 4.28g, 4.30a, 4.30b, 4.30f, 4.30g, 4.30h, 4.31b, 4.31d, 4.31e, 4.33g, 4.33i, 4.35c

Medium-high—5 (Colombia): 5.8, 5.21, 5.57, 5.66, 5.68

Medium-high—6 (Costa Rica): 6.2, 6.3, 6.16, 6.18, 6.19, 6.20, 6.21, 6.22, 6.24, 6.25, 6.27, 6.31, 6.33, 6.34, 6.35, 6.36, 6.37, 6.40, 6.41, 6.59, 6.60, 6.63a, 6.63b, 6.63c, 6.67, 6.71, 6.72, 6.78, 6.79b, 6.79c, 6.79d

Medium-high—7 (Cuba): 7.17b, 7.23, 7.24, 7.25, 7.28, 7.29, 7.31, 7.34b, 7.45

Medium-high—9 (Ecuador): 9.1

Medium-high—10 (El Salvador): 10.4e, 10.6, 10.7b, 10.8b, 10.8d, 10.8e

Medium-high—11 (Guatemala): 11.1, 11.3, 11.5, 11.39

Medium-high—12 (Haiti): 12.15, 12.16, 12.17, 12.18, 12.25, 12.27, 12.28, 12.29, 12.33, 12.35, 12.41

Medium-high—14 (Jamaica): 14.1a, 14.1c, 14.1d, 14.2d, 14.2e

Medium-high—15 (Mexico): 15.3b, 15.3c, 15.4b, 15.4d, 15.5, 15.26, 15.27b, 15.38c, 15.38d,

15.38e, 15.45b, 15.45c, 15.46, 15.60a, 15.60b, 15.62, 15.66d, 15.67c, 15.70b, 15.73, 15.75a, 15.75b, 15.75c, 15.75e, 15.75f, 15.75g, 15.78e

Medium-high—19 (Peru): 19.5a, 19.13b, 19.13d, 19.15a

Medium-high—20 (Puerto Rico): 20.4, 20.9a, 20.9b, 20.9c, 20.9d, 20.18a, 20.19a, 20.19b, 20.19c, 20.20a, 20.23, 20.28

Medium-high—21 (Uruguay): 21.3, 21.7, 21.12a, 21.19, 21.20, 21.40, 21.46, 21.53, 21.54b

Medium-high—22 (Venezuela): 22.4c, 22.10a, 22.10i, 22.14, 22.15a, 22.15b, 22.15c, 22.15e, 22.15g, 22.16g

Medium—1 (Argentina): 1.3c, 1.10, 1.11, 1.11d, 1.11e, 1.12, 1.15, 1.16a, 1.18b, 1.18d, 1.19b, 1.21b, 1.22b, 1.22d, 1.24b, 1.24c, 1.24d, 1.24e, 1.24f, 1.24g, 1.24h, 1.24i, 1.26d, 1.26i, 1.26k, 1.26l, 1.26p, 1.28, 1.31, 1.40, 1.41, 1.49, 1.52, 1.59, 1.60, 1.61a, 1.63, 1.64a, 1.64c, 1.64d, 1.64e, 1.65, 1.66, 1.68, 1.69, 1.70, 1.72, 1.74, 1.75, 1.85, 1.86, 1.90, 1.94h, 1.99, 1.100a, 1.101, 1.106, 1.107a, 1.111, 1.114, 1.115, 1.140, 1.142, 1.151, 1.160, 1.171a, 1.175b, 1.183, 1.185d, 1.201, 1.203, 1.206b, 1.207, 1.209, 1.225b, 1.226, 1.242, 1.245b, 1.246a, 1.246b, 1.246d, 1.247e, 1.249b, 1.249d, 1.249f, 1.251a, 1.251b, 1.258, 1.266, 1.270, 1.271a, 1.273, 1.274a, 1.276, 1.278, 1.283, 1.285, 1.295, 1.298c, 1.300c, 1.300d, 1.301, 1.302a, 1.302b, 1.302d, 1.302e, 1.302f, 1.302g, 1.302h, 1.302i, 1.302j, 1.303a, 1.303b, 1.303c, 1.303d, 1.303e, 1.303f, 1.303g, 1.303h, 1.303i, 1.303j, 1.303k, 1.303m, 1.303n, 1.303o, 1.304, 1.306, 1.307, 1.308, 1.309, 1.311, 1.312, 1.313, 1.316, 1.317, 1.318, 1.320, 1.321, 1.322, 1.324, 1.326, 1.328, 1.330a, 1.330b, 1.330c, 1.330d, 1.330e, 1.330f, 1.330g, 1.330h, 1.330j, 1.331, 1.332, 1.335a, 1.335b, 1.335d, 1.335e, 1.335f, 1.335g, 1.335h, 1.335i, 1.335j, 1.340, 1.341, 1.343a, 1.343c, 1.343d, 1.343e, 1.344, 1.346a, 1.346e, 1.346f, 1.347, 1.348, 1.354, 1.366b, 1.372, 1.373, 1.374, 1.376b, 1.376d, 1.380, 1.382d, 1.383a, 1.383e, 1.383f, 1.383g, 1.385a, 1.385b, 1.385c, 1.386a, 1.386b, 1.387b, 1.392, 1.394, 1.399, 1.400b, 1.401, 1.403, 1.414, 1.415e, 1.416a, 1.417, 1.419, 1.420, 1.422, 1.425, 1.426, 1.428, 1.429, 1.432a, 1.432e, 1.434a, 1.438a, 1.438e, 1.439, 1.440e, 1.440g, 1.442, 1.443a, 1.443b, 1.443d, 1.443e, 1.444b, 1.457c, 1.457d, 1.457e, 1.459e, 1.460a, 1.460c, 1.461b, 1.462, 1.480, 1.481, 1.484, 1.485, 1.486e, 1.486f, 1.488a, 1.493b, 1.494a, 1.494b, 1.496, 1.497a, 1.497d, 1.497e, 1.497f, 1.498, 1.503, 1.509, 1.517, 1.518, 1.527, 1.529, 1.530a, 1.531b, 1.531d, 1.532, 1.535, 1.536, 1.538b, 1.540d, 1.542, 1.543, 1.544, 1.547, 1.555c, 1.560a, 1.562a, 1.564, 1.565

Medium—2 (Bolivia): 2.5b, 2.9a, 2.10b, 2.10d, 2.10e

Medium—3 (Brazil): 3.516, 3.521c, 3.792b, 3.1163, 3.1168, 3.1171e, 3.1172, 3.1174, 3.1176, 3.1177, 3.1178, 3.1183, 3.1189, 3.1192, 3.1196, 3.1198, 3.1199, 3.1401, 3.1430, 3.1442a, 3.1452c, 3.1473, 3.1474, 3.1545

Medium—4 (Chile): 4.1d, 4.1e, 4.23a, 4.23c, 4.25a, 4.25b, 4.25c, 4.25d, 4.25e, 4.26a, 4.26b, 4.26c, 4.27, 4.31a, 4.31c, 4.34c, 4.35a, 4.35b

Medium—5 (Colombia): 5.3, 5.4, 5.10, 5.12, 5.13, 5.14, 5.18, 5.19, 5.20, 5.23, 5.24, 5.26, 5.27, 5.31, 5.32, 5.36, 5.44, 5.45, 5.61, 5.64, 5.69

Medium—6 (Costa Rica): 6.4, 6.7, 6.8, 6.13, 6.17, 6.23, 6.26, 6.28, 6.29, 6.30, 6.32, 6.38, 6.39, 6.43, 6.55b, 6.56, 6.57, 6.58, 6.68, 6.69, 6.74, 6.80a, 6.80b, 6.80c, 6.80d, 6.82a, 6.82c, 6.87, 6.88

Medium—7 (Cuba): 7.16, 7.17a, 7.17c, 7.17e, 7.20, 7.21, 7.26, 7.30, 7.32, 7.34a, 7.35, 7.36, 7.46, 7.47, 7.48, 7.49, 7.50

Medium—9 (Ecuador): 9.2

Medium—10 (El Salvador): 10.4a, 10.4b, 10.4c, 10.4d

Medium—11 (Guatemala): 11.2, 11.4, 11.6, 11.11, 11.13, 11.28, 11.31

Medium—12 (Haiti): 12.1, 12.2, 12.3, 12.4, 12.5, 12.6, 12.7, 12.8, 12.9, 12.10, 12.12, 12.19, 12.20, 12.21, 12.30, 12.36, 12.37, 12.38, 12.39, 12.40

Medium—15 (Mexico): 15.1, 15.3a, 15.3d, 15.4a, 15.4c, 15.7a, 15.7b, 15.10, 15.16, 15.18, 15.25a, 15.25b, 15.27a, 15.27c, 15.32, 15.33, 15.34a, 15.34b, 15.35c, 15.37b, 15.38a, 15.38b, 15.38f, 15.41a, 15.45a, 15.52c, 15.52d, 15.53a, 15.54, 15.56, 15.58, 15.60, 15.60c, 15.61a, 15.61b, 15.61c, 15.65a, 15.65b, 15.65c, 15.69b, 15.69c, 15.78a, 15.78c, 15.78f, 15.78g, 15.78h, 15.78j, 15.79a, 15.79b, 15.79c, 15.79f, 15.79g, 15.81

Medium—17 (Panama): 17.2

Medium—19 (Peru): 19.4g, 19.10b, 19.13a

Medium—20 (Puerto Rico): 20.1, 20.2, 20.5, 20.6, 20.7, 20.10, 20.11, 20.12, 20.13, 20.14, 20.15, 20.16, 20.17a, 20.21, 20.22, 20.24, 20.26, 20.27a, 20.29, 20.30a

Medium—21 (Uruguay): 21.1, 21.2, 21.5, 21.6, 21.8, 21.9, 21.10, 21.13, 21.14, 21.16, 21.23, 21.24, 21.25, 21.28, 21.29, 21.30, 21.31, 21.32,

INDEX OF TESSITURAS AND VOICE TYPES

21.33, 21.34, 21.35, 21.37, 21.38, 21.39, 21.41, 21.42, 21.43, 21.44, 21.47, 21.49, 21.50, 21.54a, 21.54d, 21.54e, 21.54f

Medium—22 (Venezuela): 22.7, 22.10b, 22.10c, 22.10d, 22.10e, 22.10f, 22.10g, 22.10h, 22.11, 22.13a, 22.13b, 22.15d, 22.15f, 22.15h, 22.16

Low-medium, 1.319, 2.5c, 2.6, 2.9c, 3.792a, 3.792c, 3.792d, 3.792e, 3.1170a, 3.1170b, 3.1170d, 3.1170e, 3.1171a, 3.1171b, 3.1190, 3.1549c, 3.1549d, 3.1549, 4.23b, 6.1, 6.5, 6.42, 15.2a, 15.2b, 15.6, 15.12, 15.14, 15.15, 15.41b, 15.52, 15.63, 15.78d, 15.78b, 15.791, 15.79k, 20.30b, 21.26

Low, 1.57, 1.58, 1.62, 1.310, 1.330i, 1.335c, 1.346d, 2.5a, 3.789, 3.800, 3.1170c, 3.1180, 3.1195a, 3.1316c, 3.1316, 4.1a, 4.1b, 4.1c, 4.1f, 4.22, 5.7, 5.29, 6.66, 6.82d, 6.82b, 6.82e, 6.83a, 6.83b, 6.83c, 6.84, 11.29, 15.29a, 15.29b, 15.29c, 15.29d, 15.29e, 15.68, 15.69a, 15.70a, 15.75d, 15.79i, 15.79d, 15.79e, 15.79h, 15.79j, 20.3, 22.3

Songs by Voice Type
(as indicated by composers)

Soprano—2 (Bolivia): 2.10c, 2.11a, 2.11b, 2.11c

Soprano—3 (Brazil): 3.787, 3.791, 3.796, 3.797, 3.801, 3.805, 3.806, 3.1015, 3.1016, 3.1019, 3.1021, 3.1025, 3.1026, 3.1028, 3.1122a, 3.1122c, 3.1414, 3.1415a, 3.1415b, 3.1415c, 3.1415d, 3.1415e, 3.1421, 3.1424, 3.1426, 3.1456e, 3.1459, 3.1508, 3.1540, 3.1544, 3.1546, 3.1548, 3.1550

Soprano—4 (Chile): 4.4, 4.5, 4.7, 4.17, 4.18, 4.20, 4.29, 4.30, 4.33

Soprano—5 (Colombia): 5.1, 5.2, 5.3, 5.12, 5.13, 5.69

Soprano—6 (Costa Rica): 6.11, 6.12

Soprano—7 (Cuba): 7.4, 7.5, 7.9, 7.10, 7.11, 7.12, 7.13

Soprano—8 (Dominican Republic): 8.2, 8.3

Soprano—10 (El Salvador): 10.2, 10.3, 10.5, 10.8, 10.9, 10.10

Soprano—12 (Haiti): 12.11

Soprano—13 (Honduras): 13.2

Soprano—14 (Jamaica): 14.2

Soprano—15 (Mexico): 15.22, 15.45a, 15.45b, 15.74

Soprano—19 (Peru): 19.2

Soprano—20 (Puerto Rico): 20.8

Soprano—21 (Uruguay): 21.45, 21.46

Soprano—22 (Venezuela): 22.1

Mezzo-Soprano, 3.788, 3.790, 3.798, 3.802, 3.1122c, 3.1122b, 3.1160, 3.1166, 3.1173, 3.1185, 3.1197, 3.1400, 3.1402, 3.1405, 3.1406, 3.1407, 3.1410, 3.1411, 3.1417, 3.1423, 4.2, 6.81, 7.8, 7.9, 15.7a, 15.7b, 15.12, 15.19, 15.21, 15.43, 15.44, 15.45c, 15.46, 15.48, 15.49, 19.14, 22.2, 22.9

Contralto (Alto), 2.10c, 3.808, 3.1419, 3.1549c, 3.1549d, 3.1549b, 4.14, 7.3, 7.6, 15.20, 22.3

Tenor, 3.795, 3.799, 3.806, 3.1052, 3.1546, 3.1548, 3.1550, 4.13, 4.15, 4.16, 4.19, 4.38, 4.40, 5.1, 5.2, 14.1, 15.31, 15.74, 18.1, 21.45, 21.46, 22.17

Baritone, 1.65b, 3.788, 3.790, 3.793, 3.802, 3.804, 3.1013, 3.1014, 3.1017, 3.1018, 3.1020, 3.1022, 3.1425, 3.1508, 3.1547, 3.1549b, 3.1549c, 3.1549d, 4.6, 4.11, 4.31, 5.29, 7.40, 9.3, 11.29, 12.4a, 12.4b, 12.5, 15.7a, 15.12, 15.23, 22.9a

Bass, 3.1184, 4.9, 4.10, 15.29

Bass clef, 1.19, 1.20, 7.17b, 7.18, 15.70b, 22.10a

Mezzo-soprano **Maya Hoover** is an active performer, teacher, clinician, music education philosopher, and author. Her accomplishments in the performance and teaching arenas have earned her invitations to appear around the world, and her specialty in the music of the twentieth and twenty-first centuries has led her to collaborations with some of today's leading composers. Hoover serves on the Advisory Board of the Latin American Art Song Alliance, and her publications have appeared in *Classical Singer, The Mentoring Connection,* and the *Philosophy of Music Education Review.* She holds a Doctor of Music degree in voice performance and literature with a minor in music education from Indiana University, and is currently Assistant Professor of Voice at the University of Hawai'i at Mānoa.

www.ingramcontent.com/pod-product-compliance
Lightning Source LLC
Chambersburg PA
CBHW021800220426
43662CB00006B/126